Behavior in Organizations

An Experiential Approach

Ninth Edition

Behavior in Organizations

An Experiential Approach

Ninth Edition

A. B. (RAMI) SHANI, Ph.D.
Professor of Organization Behavior and Management

DAWN CHANDLER, DBA
Assistant Professor of Organization Behavior and Management

JEAN-FRANCOIS COGET, Ph.D.
Assistant Professor of Organization Behavior and Management

JAMES B. LAU, Ph.D.
Professor Emeritus

All of Orfalea College of Business, California Polytechnic State University, San Luis Obispo, California

McGraw-Hill Irwin

Boston   Burr Ridge, IL   Dubuque, IA   New York   San Francisco   St. Louis
Bangkok   Bogotá   Caracas   Kuala Lumpur   Lisbon   London   Madrid   Mexico City
Milan   Montreal   New Delhi   Santiago   Seoul   Singapore   Sydney   Taipei   Toronto

McGraw-Hill
Irwin

BEHAVIOR IN ORGANIZATIONS: AN EXPERIENTIAL APPROACH

Published by McGraw-Hill/Irwin, a business unit of The McGraw-Hill Companies, Inc., 1221 Avenue of the Americas, New York, NY, 10020. Copyright © 2009, 2005, 2000, 1996, 1992, 1988, 1984, 1979, 1975 by The McGraw-Hill Companies, Inc. All rights reserved. No part of this publication may be reproduced or distributed in any form or by any means, or stored in a database or retrieval system, without the prior written consent of The McGraw-Hill Companies, Inc., including, but not limited to, in any network or other electronic storage or transmission, or broadcast for distance learning.

Some ancillaries, including electronic and print components, may not be available to customers outside the United States.

This book is printed on acid-free paper.

1 2 3 4 5 6 7 8 9 0 QPD/QPD 0 9 8

ISBN 978-0-07-340493-6
MHID 0-07-340493-4

Publisher: *Paul Ducham*
Managing developmental editor: *Laura Hurst Spell*
Editorial assistant: *Jane Beck*
Marketing director: *Krista Bettino*
Marketing manager: *Natalie Zook*
Marketing coordinator: *Michael Gedatus*
Senior project manager: *Susanne Riedell*
Senior production supervisor: *Debra R. Sylvester*
Design coordinator: *Joanne Mennemeier*
Typeface: *10/12 Times Roman*
Compositor: *Laserwords Private Limited*
Printer: *Quebecor World Dubuque Inc.*

Library of Congress Cataloging-in-Publication Data

Behavior in organizations : an experiential approach / A. B. (Rami) Shani . . . [et al.]. —9th ed.
    p. cm.
    Updated ed. of: Behavior in organizations : an experiential approach / A. B. (Rami) Shani, James B. Lau. 8th ed.
    Includes index.
    ISBN-13: 978-0-07-340493-6 (alk. paper)
    ISBN-10: 0-07-340493-4 (alk. paper)
    1. Organizational behavior. 2. Group relations training. I. Shani, Abraham B. II. Shani, Abraham B. Behavior in organizations.
HD58.7.S476 2009
302.3'5—dc22

                                                        2008011928

www.mhhe.com

Acknowledgments

Jim Lau embarked on the journey of producing a book to facilitate learning about human behavior at work 35 years ago. The first edition of this book was published in 1975. During the past 35 years our knowledge about organizational behavior has increased many-fold. Yet, the pedagogical orientation of learning-by-doing continues to be at the core of the book throughout all the editions.

The ninth edition of this book is a continuation of our collaborative learning process with colleagues, students, and managers from around the globe. Dawn Chandler and J. F. Coget join the OB group at Calpoly, bringing with them rich and diverse academic backgrounds and practical experiences. Together we share a fascination with the discovery of adult learning in the context of the work organization. We wish to acknowledge the many learners, scholars, and managers who contributed to the development of this text over the past 35 years. We are indebted to all those individuals who granted permission for the use of figures, tables, experiential activities and exercises, cases, and simulations. The rich input from many of the adopters of the book over the years has helped in shaping this product. Your support and encouragements are greatly appreciated.

This edition of the book was shaped significantly by a few colleagues: David Coghlan at Trinity College, Dublin, Ireland; Michael Stebbins, David Peach, Rebecca Ellis, and James Sena at the Orfalea College of Business, Calpoly University; Carol Sexton at Pepperdine University; Flemming Norrgren at Chalmers University of Technology, Goteborg, Sweden; and Mina Westman at Tel Aviv University. They have shared and put into practice a common belief that experiential learning is a synergistic and exhilarating way to discover and learn about organizational behavior and management. Robert Grant at Georgetown University and Bocconi University; Bengt Stymne at the Stockholm School of Economics; Mariano Corso, Gianluca Spina, Roberto Verganti, and Emilio Bartezzaghi at the Politechnico de Milano; Torbjorn Stjernberg at The University of Goteborg; Peter Docherty at IMIT Institute, Chalmers University of Technology; Tobias Fredberg, Susanne Ollila, Maria Backman, and Alexander Styhre at the Chalmers University of Technology; Armand Hatchuel at Ecole des Mines de Paris; Susan Mohrman at the Center for Effective Organization, University of Southern California; Victor Friedman at Emek Isreel College; Yoram Mitki at the Ruppin Institute; David Kolb at Case Western Reserve University; William Pasmore at MercerDelta Consulting and the Center for Creative Leadership; Harvey Kolodny at the University of Toronto; Gervase Bushe at Simon Fraser University; Asya Pazy and Dov Eden at Tel Aviv University; Kenneth Murrell at the University of West Florida; Samuel Culbert, Barbara Lawrence, David Lewin, and Sandy Jacoby at UCLA; Angelo Fanelli, Elie Matta, and Charles-Henri Beyssere-des-Horts at HEC Paris; and Christophe Haag at EM Lyon have exchanged ideas, materials, and views over the years, many of which are reflected in the book.

This edition, as with the previous editions, is a reflection of a continuous collaboration with the learners around the globe who had the courage to join the learning process through experimentation, appreciation, ongoing dialogue, and discoveries. All of us have been involved in developing, testing, and evaluating the learning process and finding out what triggers individual and team discoveries in different universities and programs around the globe. Since you know who you are—we are grateful and thankful!

Finally, our thanks to our families—Elaine, Talia, Liat, Leora, Danielle, Susie, Ryan, Mike, Gerald, Yvette, Xavier, Anne-Noelle, and Arlene—who, have listened, watched, and continuously supported us as we worked to complete this edition of the book.

Rami Shani, Dawn Chandler, J. F. Coget, and Jim Lau

v

Contents in Brief

Contents

List of Activities

List of Cases

List of Additional Activities on the Book's WWW Site

Introduction

The first edition of this book was published 35 years ago. The concept of *sustainable work systems* was not an issue that organizations, managers, or society were concerned with. Today, we hear more and more about the importance of sustainability. Sustainability is a value-based concept. Within the context of this textbook, the most profound step, when promoting sustainability in work systems is to adopt a very specific way of thinking about work and business. Sustainability in working life stands for a value base that recognizes the need to balance the economic aspirations with equal regard for human, social, and ecological outcomes. Sustainability, therefore, makes visible the multiple responsibilities of people at work and work systems as a whole.[1] Recently, a member of the Interface Company described the company's ongoing work toward sustainability:

> *Each time we have a decision to make around here, we have to consider three questions: Is it good for the environment, is it good for people and will it make us money. We are constantly juggling these three questions.*

We define work as an intentional value-creating process. This general definition gains meaning with the specification of the goals and rules, resources, and context for the work process. These parameters are related to the stakeholders in the process—workers, investors, suppliers, customers, and communities. The resources are financial, material, physical, intellectual, and technological. The context is cultural, ecological, economic, historical, and social. Addressing sustainability in a work system means, therefore, addressing all these elements that form it, influence it, and are influenced by it. Understanding the nature of human and organizational behavior at work is critical if the value creation process is to be developed, managed, and sustained.

In the early 1970s very few organizational behavior textbooks were published. Only a handful of educators recognized the need to teach organizational behavior and management experientially. As this edition of the book is completed, the Organizational Behavior Division of the Academy of Management is the largest division, all undergraduate business programs and MBA programs have an organizational behavior course as part of the required business core courses, many journals have incorporated the term *organizational behavior,* the Organizational Behavior Society is growing, and a few hundred textbooks are available on this subject. The original textbook that Jim launched has become a continuing enterprise, the essence of which is to learn about organizational behavior and management issues in the context of work in an experiential way—going beyond summarizing and memorizing the existing and growing body of interdisciplinary knowledge.

An organizational behavior approach is used in the design and facilitation of exploration and learning. The current approach is an attempt to influence behavior and outcomes through the use of design, whether it be architectural, organization, work, or job design. We have designed a template with large degrees of freedom for the instructors to craft their own distinct courses such that they fit the students, learning context, and the instructor's style. The instructors are viewed as *designers, coaches, managers,* and *content experts.*[2] They are the managers of educational design, the learning processes, the classroom, and the learning community, using the OB methods in which they are instructing the students.

This ninth edition of the book, like the previous editions, is designed first and foremost to meet needs that other texts do not satisfy. There are many continuities with the prior editions, but some important changes freshen and update the text. We have revised the overall design to include 16 core modules in the text and 4 advanced modules on the website. Each module is designed as a stand-alone unit such that the instructor can have more freedom to develop the overall structure of the course. The text is organized into four major clusters of modules in the book and a fifth, an advanced cluster, on the website: The Organizational Behavior Context: A Sustainability-Based Perspective; Managing Individual Processes; Managing Interpersonal Processes; Managing Organizational Processes; and Managing Emerging Complex Processes. We strived to improve the balance between theoretical and current scientific knowledge, experiential activities, and cases for each module and cluster of modules. We added three modules in the text, Learning-in-Action, A Psychodynamics Perspective on Human Behavior, and Mentoring. We also added a few new cases and activities.

The major continuity with previous editions is the basic approach, the aims, the emphasis, and the learning process. As before, the text is intended for use in an experiential learning course for undergraduate or graduate business administration students in a required organizational behavior core course. Thus, the text provides basic coverage of essential OB topics. These topics are often taught solely by lectures and readings, a cognitive approach primarily emphasizing content. Content-based learning approaches do not deal adequately with the need for student involvement, nor do they help students acquire behavioral skills. *Behavior in Organizations* emphasizes involvement exercises to help students quickly and effectively enter into the process of thinking about behavior, applying concepts, arriving at new discoveries, and developing their own expertise as reflective practitioners. Integrating the *experiential learning* approach with *appreciative inquiry* sets the stage for higher levels of learning. Lectures and readings are intended to bolster this process orientation. At the graduate level, we usually supplement our book with a book of readings and a few comprehensive cases.

Experiential learning methods (or what is called by some "learning-by-doing" or "learning-in-action") and the appreciative inquiry process provide a stimulus for learning, growth, and change by helping learners focus on their own behaviors and reactions as data to explore. For this very reason, some students may at first be uncomfortable about encountering experiential methods in a required course. To help students deal with this challenge, we begin with more structured and less personal activities and introduce early on the appreciative inquiry orientation.[3] Personal growth and self-understanding activities are introduced later in the text, after students have had enough experience to become more comfortable with the approach and each other as a community of learners.

The *learning-by-doing* orientation was retained in this edition. As such, the text includes adult education methods such as team activities, role playing, case studies, simulations, and team project activities in the communities within and outside the university boundaries. The action-oriented exercises provide a new data set that can be explored by the learner, the team, and the learning community. When integrated with the scientific body of knowledge, the sense-making process of the data leads to new insights, discoveries, and possibly new experimentation. Thus, the combined learning by doing and appreciative inquiry processes establish the context, the climate, and the self-help competencies for lifelong learning.

Human behavior in organizations is both fascinating and critical to understand. It surrounds and concerns us all and affects every aspect of our lives. Moreover, it is the heart of effective management and sustainability orientation.[4] Students respond with great eagerness to organizational behavior concepts in a properly designed course. Their enthusiasm offers the quickest route to the working skills they will find essential in the business world. This text's main aim is to help our students be the best that they can be as tomorrow's socially responsible leaders of organizations.

Notes

1. P. Docherty, M. Kira, and A. B. (Rami) Shani (eds.), *Creating Sustainable Work Systems: Developing Social Sustainability* (London, UK: Routledge, 2008).

2. R. J. Boland, Jr., and F. Collopy, *Managing as Designing* (Stanford, CA: Stanford University Press, 2004).

3. R. Goffee and G. Jones, "Leading Clever People," *Harvard Business Review* 85, no. 3 (2007), pp. 72–79.

4. J. Moon, "The Contribution of Corporate Social Responsibility to Sustainable Development," *Sustainable Development* 15 (2007), pp. 296–306.

Behavior in Organizations

An Experiential Approach

Ninth Edition

Part 1

The Organizational Behavior Context: A Sustainability-Based Perspective

Sustainability as a term or phenomenon has been receiving increased attention all around us. In the broadest sense, sustainability means protecting the richness of the world's resources in a way that their utilization does not destroy them but rather leaves equal opportunities to future generations. This view of sustainability emphasizes protecting the richness of the world's resources through their preservation, regeneration, and development. The sustainability concept entails being aware of the interconnected nature of our world. As such, the sustainability concept has a moral dimension stating that no single generation has the right to devour the world's resources for the satisfaction of its needs. In addition to this future-oriented perspective of sustainability, it has also been argued that the various concurrent needs should receive equal attention: it is evenly wrong to satisfy the needs of some at the expense of the needs of others.[1] For instance, in a work organization, the economic goals of shareholders should not be fulfilled by relying on exploitative labor practices or by destroying natural resources. Sustainability means utilizing the world's resources in a responsible manner such that the needs of the various concurrent stakeholders and even the future generations can be met.

In the context of working life, the concept of sustainability is viewed as a holistic concept that includes environmental, social, and economic resources.[2] It is argued that focusing on any particular type of resource, at the expense of others, is suboptimization. A sustainable organization can therefore be defined as one that is able to sustain dynamically its existence and secure its heritage in the short term, without endangering the possibility of the resources it utilizes being renewed and regenerated in the long term. Sustainability is not a steady state or a plateau in a development curve but entails a continuous process of balancing such factors as resource goals, stakeholder goals, static and dynamic efficiency goals, individual and team development, balancing stability and change, and creation and destruction. A sustainable organization is able to operate in and adapt to its environment, building its operational capability by promoting the various resources engaged in its operations to retain also their operational capability.

Our point of departure is that work is essential for sustainable development due to work's active, creative, and developing nature.[3] Work has always affected and changed humans, their values, goals, and social and environmental orientations.[4,5] The dynamics between people at work result in people experiencing new and continuously changing dimensions of reality and life. This book is about exploring the nature of human behavior in the context of work. We will explore the nature and dynamics of individuals; between individuals and teams; and between teams, organizations, and their environment while utilizing a sustainable development perspective.

The global economy runs on knowledge.[6] In the knowledge economy, the value of individuals is directly related to their knowledge level and their ability to facilitate knowledge creation and transfer among individuals, teams, and organizational units—the essence of organizational operational capacity.

Organizations use teams, cross-functional teams, customer- or product-focused teams, work groups, knowledge teams, and virtual work teams (to name a few organizational forms) to capture and develop knowledge—or what has come to be known as *intellectual capital.* At the core of the knowledge economy are individuals, teams, and organizational behavior processes. As such, knowledge workers are viewed as the engine that drives innovations, designs, markets, and sustainable development.[7] Understanding and influencing behavior in the context of the emerging organization within the context of developing sustainable work systems is the focus of this course.

The pedagogical perspective taken in this book—which is congruent with sustainable development orientation—centers on individual and team learning. As such we are concerned with *how* you learn as well as *what* you learn about human behavior in organizations. The how and the what are closely connected in this course because so much of what you will learn is a process: a different way of looking at your own experience, a deeper way of understanding the power of attitudes or expectations, or a new awareness of how people experience work organizations. Management education strives to provide viewpoints and *learn-by-doing* or what some call *learning-in-action* methods that help participants walk through new learning. We use experience in this way. Your own experiences in this course will be the basic data upon which to build your understanding. The activities of this course are structured to help you understand and influence the behavior of people in organizations.

Design matters for learning and sustainable development.[8,9] By design attitude, we refer to expectations and orientations one brings to a learning space. Management and executive workshops often spend the first hours or days developing a sense of community and deciding how to use experience and the interactions of participants for maximum learning. The workshop becomes a *learning community*—a community in this sense refers to a group of people with common interests, values, and purposes who meet regularly; it suggests supportiveness; it implies exchange of information; it implies self-reflection and appreciative inquiry as primary processes for individual and community discovery, learning, and development. Learning session participants find out about one another and about the faculty, become part of a team, and learn more effective ways of interacting as they inquire into self and others.

The learning community provides the foundation for learning and development in this course. The climate that best promotes learning is one in which participants support one another; are open with one another about their responses; and are willing to confront or compare different responses, insights, and experiences. Learning to learn is a key to sustainable development. We too will spend time learning to learn and creating an appropriate learning climate. A key aspect of this sort of learning environment involves learning how to effectively utilize our own experiences and those of others, how to be reflective, how to engage in appreciative inquiry, and how to take action.

Part 1 of this book is designed to accomplish these ends. Allocating the limited classroom time available for lectures and exercises is a continuous struggle for instructors using the experiential learning or learning-by-doing approach. The assumption in this "workshop model" is that class time will be used primarily for examining more intently a limited number of theories and concepts at the sacrifice of extensive content coverage in lectures and readings. However, many students feel the need for more complete cognitive learning. The modules lay the foundation for content learning. The references and endnotes provide a window into the extensive material available to enhance knowledge and understanding of the topics covered in the organizational behavior area.

PREVIEW OF PART 1

The triple goals for the first part of this book are to frame the context within which organizational behavior evolves, to develop the learning community, and to establish the learning-in-action climate. In Module 1 and Activity 1–1, class members participate in a triad exercise in which each tells of an experience from his or her work situation. A number of participants then relate their experiences to the entire class. From these experiences, the professor constructs the topic areas of organizational behavior for the class to demonstrate that the behavioral study of the course has immediate relevance to everyone. The perspective of sustainable work systems is presented as a point of departure for our exploration of human behavior. Next, the experiential learning orientation in this course, the challenge of rationality and irrationality in managing, the framework for the exploration of effectiveness, and the systems approach at the workplace are followed by a brief historical review of the evolution of the organizational behavior field. Activity 1–2 provides an opportunity for an initial investigation of sustainability and sustainable development, and Activity 1–3W on the book's website provides an opportunity to explore organizational behavior topics while using the World Wide Web.

In Module 2 and Activity 2–1, an open communication dialogue enables participants to examine the assumptions of the students and the professor that are relevant to the course and its learning goals. Content, cognitive, and process learning are discussed, and the first activity is used as an illustration to enhance understanding of process (experiential) learning. The role of the participant as a coach and contributor to the learning of others gets special emphasis. A review of expectations is followed by a discussion of the adult learner; experiential learning; individual, team, and organizational learning; and appreciative inquiry. The values of the learning community model are also discussed. Activity 2–2 provides an opportunity for individuals to diagnose their learning style and a way for teams to explore similarities, differences, and team learning. Activity 2–4 provides an opportunity to begin the development of the cognitive learning process. Optional Activity 2–6W, on the book's website, provides an opportunity for the learner (1) to articulate individual learning objectives, performance goals, potential obstacles, and specific action statements in a contract and (2) to have the contract co-signed with the instructor. The final optional activity, Activity 2–7W, allows the learner the initial exploration of organizational behavior issues with a practicing manager.

Once the classroom learning climate is established, participants are assigned to working teams. Two activities were designed in order to help the teams develop shared expectations about learning outcomes and behavior. Activity 2–3 fosters team dialogue around the development of the team's name and the creation of the team's logo. Activity 2–5 helps the team develop a team contract about team learning objectives and desired team members' behavior. This is an opportunity for team members to begin a dialogue about expectations at the individual and team levels. The next critical contextual dimension in the development of the learning community is the focus on the learning-in-action pedagogical orientation. It is also the focus on the development of reflective practitioner skills.

In Module 3 we start the exploration of the process of human knowing. Our point of departure is that knowing the steps in the process of human knowing and doing provides an essential foundation for both studying and influencing how people behave in organizations—hence, this is a key element in the framing section of the book. Building on the learning content presented in Modules 1 and 2, this module provides additional learning content on the three phases in the process of knowing: the paradigm of inquiry; single-, double-, and triple-loop inquiry; and alternative scientific approaches within the learning-in-action family. Activities 3–1 and 3–2 provide an opportunity to explore learning-in-action skills and to practice using journal writing as a critical tool to acquire reflective practitioner skills. Activities 3–3 and 3–4 at the end of the chapter provide further opportunity to develop reflective practitioner skills using the ORJI methodology and using the course learning team in the development of both individual and team reflective skills.

The establishment of the learning method and climate through interaction exercises and the introduction of the framework of the content areas to be studied should satisfactorily prepare course participants for Part 2, which deals with the core concepts in understanding and managing individual behavior.

Notes

1. P. Docherty, M. Kira, and A. B. (Rami) Shani, *Creating Sustainable Work Systems: Developing Social Sustainability* (New York: Routledge, 2008).

2. W. Sissell, *Ants, Galileo and Gandhi: Designing the Future of Business through Nature, Genius, and Compassion* (Sheffield, UK: Greenleaf Publishing, 2003).

3. Docherty et al., *Creating Sustainable Work Systems.*

4. D. Dunphy, J. Benventiste, A. Griffiths, and P. Sutton, *Corporate Sustainability* (Sydney, Australia: Allen and Unwin, 2000).

5. H. Hvid and H. Lund, "Sustainable Work: Concepts and Element of Practice," *Journal of Transdisciplinary Environmental Studies* 1, no. 2 (2002), pp. 1–20.

6. R. Goffee and G. Jones, "Leading Clever People," *Harvard Business Review* 85, no. 3 (2007), pp. 72–79.

7. T. Davenport, *Thinking for a Living: How to Get Better Performance and Results from Knowledge Workers* (Boston, MA: Harvard Business School Press, 2005).

8. H. Bradbury, "Sustaining Inner and Outer Worlds: A Whole-Systems Approach to Developing Sustainable Business Practices in Management," *Journal of Management Education* 27, no. 2 (2003), pp. 172–87.

9. J. Moon, "The Contribution of Corporate Social Responsibility to Sustainable Development," *Sustainable Development* 15 (2007), pp. 296–306.

Module

1

Organizational Behavior and Sustainable Work Systems

LEARNING OBJECTIVES

After completing this module, you should be able to

1. Describe what is meant by the terms *organization, sustainable work systems,* and *sustainable development.*
2. Define the field of organizational behavior.
3. Summarize the essence of the four evolutionary clusters in the development of the organizational behavior field of study.
4. Briefly describe the systems approach to understanding and effectively managing people in organizations.
5. Explain the relationship between rationality and irrationality in management.

KEY TERMS AND CONCEPTS

Administrative school

Behavioral science schools

Classical era

Communication

Contingency school

Creativity

Dialogue

Effectiveness

Expectations

Human relations school

Innovation

Interpersonal dialoguing

Leadership

Leadership competencies

Management science school

Mental models

Mentoring

Modern era

Motivation

Neoclassical era

Organization

Organizational culture

Perception

Perceptual differences

Personal growth and development

Prescientific era

Rationality

Reflective practitioner skills

Role relationships

Scientific management school

Sociotechnical systems school	Team dynamics
Structuralist school	Team skills
Systems school	Value systems
Systems thinking	Work-design systems

MODULE OUTLINE

PREMODULE PREPARATION

Activity 1–1: Learning from Experience: Defining Organizational Behavior

Objectives:

a. To identify course topic areas from your own work experiences.

b. To introduce involvement learning and appreciative inquiry to begin building the learning environment.

c. To introduce the communication skills of sharing, listening, and paraphrasing.

Task 1:

Your past work experiences often make intriguing case studies and interesting stories to learn from. The worksheet for Activity 1–1 presents three alternatives for selecting your case study. Your professor will assign one of these to the entire class or divide the class into three groups, one for each alternative. Use the worksheet for Activity 1–1 to make notes on your case study. (Time: Individuals have 5 minutes to think about their experiences and jot down notes.)

Task 2:

Participants form triads. Member A tells his or her case study and what it illustrates to member B. Member B listens carefully and paraphrases back to A the story and what it illustrates. Member B must convince member A that B has understood fully what A was trying to communicate. Member C is the observer and remains silent during the process (a role many find difficult). Member B tells an experience to member C while A observes. Member C tells an experience to member A while B observes. (Time: Each person will have 5 minutes to relate a case study and have it paraphrased back by the listener. Do not be judgmental in the process. The goal is to inquire collaboratively into the experience without inserting a value or perceptual judgment into the other's experiences. The instructor will call out the time at the end of each 5-minute interval to allow for equal "airtime" among participants. Total time: 15 minutes.)

Task 3:

Each group selects a member to relate his or her case study to the class. The instructor briefly analyzes for the class how the incident fits in with some topic to be studied in the course, such as motivation or leadership style. Topic areas are listed on the board.

Task 4:

Questions for discussion: What are the general character and tone of the stories you have heard? What are the implications of these findings for managers who have the responsibility for persons similar to those in this class? What was the experience like? What can we learn from using an appreciative inquiry orientation?

Name _____ Date _____

WORKSHEET FOR ACTIVITY 1–1

Make notes below on your case study for the alternative you were assigned for task 1.

Alternative 1: Describe an experience in a past work situation that you think illustrates something about human behavior in organizations. What does it illustrate?

Alternative 2: Describe a difficult problem you encountered while working. What caused the problem? What was done or could have been done to reduce or overcome the problem?

Alternative 3: Describe a work experience that illustrated good management. What happened? Why was it good? How did it affect you?

INTRODUCTION: SUSTAINABILITY-BASED PERSPECTIVE

Sustaining human development and growth is an individual, organizational, and societal necessity. Sustainable development is defined by the World Commission on Environment and Development (WCED) as "development that meets the needs of the present without compromising the ability of future generations to meet their own needs."[1] Sustainable development is a complex phenomenon and a process that can neither be clearly described nor simply applied. In a broad sense, within the context of work organizations and organizational behavior, sustainable development refers to the continuous development of individuals, teams, and organizations. The common denominator of the different definitions and interpretations of sustainable development leads to four distinct features: The *first* indicates that sustainable development occurs at several levels, ranging from global to regional to local to organizational to team and to individual. The *second* suggests that sustainable development is an intergenerational phenomenon: It is a process of transference from one generation to another. In other words, individuals, teams, and organizations are able to transfer learning processes and best practices continuously. The *third* indicates that sustainable development consists of at least three domains: social, economic, and ecological.[2] Although sustainable development can be defined in terms of each of these domains alone, the interrelationship between the three domains is what makes the concept of utmost relevance within the context of human behavior at work. The *fourth* suggests that sustainable development is a complex process, with phases and activities that center on continuous development of human systems.[3]

Understanding and influencing interrelationships require the mastery of critical analytical tools such as **systems thinking, dialogue,** and working with **mental models.** At the same time, leaders in business, industry, and government have identified certain skills and knowledge levels that are critical when addressing the growing needs of the global knowledge economy in the years ahead: conscientiousness, personal responsibility, and dependability; the ability to act in a principled, ethical fashion; skills in oral and written communication; interpersonal and team skills; skill in critical thinking and in solving complex problems; respect for people different from oneself; the ability to adapt to change; and the ability and desire for lifelong learning.[4] The amount of knowledge being created today is enormous in comparison to any other time in history. Some claim that during the past two decades we have experienced a 40 percent yearly increase in new knowledge creation.[5] Knowledge today becomes obsolete relatively quickly. No wonder that when we have dialogues with participants during our opening class sessions to determine how they perceive our course of study, they generally ask two questions: What can I get out of a course in organizational behavior? and Will I learn something that I really can use? These are fair questions—especially in the context of the emerging global knowledge-based economy.

Exploring and developing mental models that guide action is part of the response. This course is an experiential learning-based course, meaning that the interactive exercises focus on developing skills, attitudes, and mental models that will carry into the future. An experiential course in organizational behavior should focus directly on you and the interactions of your behavior with that of others. At the more personal level, you will want to know what you can learn that will help you become more effective in achieving your goals as you confront that exciting, but nevertheless scary, world of accelerating change. This environment means you are looking forward to a career pathway that will wend its way through a number of organizations, most of which are continually reshaping themselves on a dynamic basis. You can see evidence of this trend across industries as many new companies merge or fall out of mergers, are acquired by others, or even disappear in a very short time. Those investing in the stock market of the late 1990s found that the areas for future growth and financial gains were in the high-tech fields; however, investors also found high price variability, and companies ravished one another as creativity produced market changes and opportunities.

Returning to the focus of what you may learn that will help you cope with change, we will discuss what we believe to be some primary areas of concern. We realize that you are already familiar with many aspects of these areas; however, learning better-defined concepts and alternative mental models and developing related behavioral skills is something many executives find sufficiently meaningful to study at university graduate programs. Behavioral skills and understandings require continuous renewal and awareness.

Herbert Simon, Nobel laureate in economics, wrote *The Sciences of the Artificial,* which is one of the finest examples we have of a well-developed theory of the design attitude for managers. Let us start with a viewpoint, or a way to think about organizations based on a design perspective. When you enter the world of Boeing, General Electric, Disney, Microsoft, or Toyota, you are entering a community that by design and evolution meets the primary purposes of the corporation and the people involved. The community is set upon a blueprint, a hardwired substructure of interrelated roles that ensure the desired outputs of the corporation. The manner in which each organizational community has evolved and emerged is unique and distinct, and the character of the total complex of interactions is referred to as an **organizational culture.** (Sometimes we hear that two recently merged corporations had such a culture clash that they had to break up again.) Because a corporation is a community, rather than just an organization of people carrying out their functional roles, managers wear many hats. In a sense they may be mayors concerned for the welfare and needs of the workers and charged with supporting the value system of "what this company stands for." Or managers may be seen as educators attending to the learning needs and professional and skills development of employees. Or they may be seen as designers, coaches, or mentors. So when you report to the world of IBM, Procter & Gamble, or Firm X, you have an obligation to yourself and your company to learn the design orientation, the culture, and the practice—that is, the behavioral **expectations,** the **value systems,** and the **role relationships.**

Once under way in this venture, probably the most useful analytical concept is **perception:** people perceive the world differently, depending in part on where they are standing on the landscape. The Microsofts, the Procter & Gambles, the BMWs, the Blue Cross Blue Shields, and the Dells may perceive the world very differently—obviously because of their dissimilar products, services, markets, cultural contexts, and so on, but you will also find many other factors at play. And within each organization, people in different departments (for example, sales, engineering, marketing, production) will perceive the same topic of discussion very differently. Carrying this right down to **interpersonal dialoguing,** two people often perceive the same activities differently. Now this does not sound profound. What is profound is that every day in every way, these differences in perception cause breakdowns, misunderstandings, inefficiencies, and ineffectiveness—and the parties involved do not even realize that they are not perceiving the topic of discussion in the same way. **Perceptual differences** can be incredible barriers to communication. Corporations often have professionals who accelerate relationships or overcome conflicts between departments and groups by first working out differences in perceptions between the parties. Participants in this course have indicated that the interpersonal dialoguing exercises and units are among the most rewarding learning areas—which brings us to the subject of communication.

Surveys have consistently shown that when managers are asked what additional areas of education and training universities should provide to better prepare students for employment in their organizations, the most frequent reply is that greater **communication, team skills, leadership competencies,** and **reflective practitioner skills** are needed. In this course, having recognized perceptual differences as a major deterrent to organizational and interpersonal effectiveness, we focus on communication as a means through which barriers can be avoided and overcome. Communications means not only the transmission of hard data needed to perform tasks but the softer-ware of viewpoints, attitudes, emotions, and feelings. The greater your awareness of how communication can occur effectively in the organization, between groups, within groups, and in interpersonal interactions, the more able you will be. For instance, if you carry away from this course nothing more than the skills and understanding of the value of interpersonal dialoguing, you will find lifelong application for your learning, not only in your work but also in your personal life.

You will learn that perception and communication are basic, interrelated aspects of behavior in organizations, but even more basic are the third and fourth concepts that hold them together: **motivation** and **leadership.** Much of what is perceived depends on the underlying motivation of the parties involved; for example, their goals, or what they want to achieve, will largely determine how they perceive the activity about which they are communicating. The human organization of a corporation can be regarded as a reservoir of energy arising from what people bring to work, their motivational needs, and what the work situation, in addition, creates and shapes. Managers who design and lead organizations and units shoulder the responsibility of developing and sustaining individual, team, and organizational success. Understanding the motivation to work, and how organizational processes such as **work-design** systems and **mentoring** can shape it, is important. Equally important to understand is the concept of frustration. Managerial practices or work systems that set up barriers to achieving goals or that do not permit needed **creativity** and **innovation** can have dire consequences such as inefficiencies and anti-organizational activities. Knowing what "turns people off" is as important as knowing what "turns people on."

Moving down from the total organization to work groups, the area of team skills presents one of the best arenas for individual learning. If you improve your understanding of how you function in a team, learn how others in your team perceive your skills, and find roles with which you are most comfortable in groups, the results will be impressive, for instance, understanding that people play many informal roles in groups and that it is important to be able to play a number of these yourself. If you are not the group leader and desire to facilitate progress, you may move the group forward by performing roles such as "definer of goals," "summarizer," or "clarifier." In addition, becoming sensitive to small-group dynamics is an asset. Knowing that whenever two or more people come together to perform a task, the web of **team dynamics** begins to spin. Knowing that shared expectations or norms, roles, and subgrouping into dyads and triads spontaneously occur not only provides you with the advantage of understanding what is going on but also presents an opportunity to influence or shape the development of that group.

Finally, we see as the most important area of learning for you as you wind your way through one or many careers in this kaleidoscopic period of change to be that of **personal growth and development.** Every professional needs not only improved, updated skills to stay current but also—and above everything else—the attitudes and viewpoints to cope with change. And the most basic of these attitudes is this: If I don't achieve what I want, it is my own fault. With this attitude goes the practice of setting goals, coping with barriers, regrouping and cutting losses when failure occurs, and moving on to redefined goals. Wasting energy on or blaming others or the system does not move us on to new challenges. Taking responsibility for your own career—directing your energy into renewed plans—is personal learning at its most basic level.

The preceding concepts are selected from the following three areas of emphasis in this course:

- Cognitive skills development, or the body of knowledge, theory, concepts, and research of organizational behavior.
- Behavioral skills development, or the basic process skills to understand and enhance human performance.
- Organizational behavior processes, or the means by which managers and behavioral specialists can design and change organizations and work systems to achieve sustainable human and organizational effectiveness.

Obviously, all the areas of learning described in this introduction are overwhelming for one humble course. But this is what the course is about. You can take away a good deal or maybe just one idea or a different analytical road map to explore the nature of behavior dynamics in the workplace. *Your personal choice of how much you invest in the course will have a direct effect on what you will take from this learning opportunity.*

ORGANIZATIONAL BEHAVIOR: TOWARD A DEFINITION

Building on the preceding discussion, organizational behavior can be defined as the utilization of theory and methods of multiple academic disciplines—such as anthropology, biology, economics, political science, social psychology, and psychology—for the purpose of understanding, influencing, and predicting the behavior of people in organizations. Definitions of organizational behavior vary widely because the field has evolved with parallel developments in the social sciences, behavioral sciences, biological sciences, and management and human relations courses in schools of business. One large frame of reference focuses on the differences between organizations without people and people without organizations. The former, the realm of organizational sociology, relates to organizations as systems interacting with their environment; the latter, the realm of psychology, relates to human relations in work situations. More recent approaches have emphasized the need for integrating these two realms to account for the great variability among people, tasks, and environment. Another point of focus is the macro–micro perspective. The *macro view* emphasizes the big picture, such as the entire organization and its relationships to the environment. The *micro view* considers smaller units, such as the individual, work groups, or work systems. This text works with the micro initially and moves on to the macro as the course progresses.

As such, organizational behavior is viewed as an interdisciplinary field of study that includes four levels of behavior—individual, team, interteam, and organizational—for the purpose of improving both effectiveness and sustainability of individual, team, and organizational development. The origin of the field is not a new invention, although it continues to be rediscovered by new generations of managers and researchers who bring fresh perspectives to the practice. In our view, organizational behavior research dates back at least to the time and motion studies of Frederick Taylor shortly after the turn of the last century. Others might mark the true beginning of efforts to understand human behavior in the workplace with the famous Hawthorne studies conducted by Harvard researchers in collaboration with AT&T in the 1930s. Still later, researchers from the Tavistock Institute in London explored ways to enhance the productivity of British coal mines, Lewin and his colleagues undertook their classic studies on groups, and Blake and Mouton worked with companies in the United States to develop the concepts behind the managerial grid. Thereafter, the field of organizational behavior research exploded, with intensified interaction between companies and scholars examining issues ranging from the effects of expectation, personality, motivation, perception, communication, learning, leadership, mentoring, creativity, conflict on human dynamics, and performance; to group dynamics, problem solving, and decision making on team performance; to the causes of turnover and stress; to the optimal design of jobs and organizations; to designing learning mechanisms that can enhance creativity; to creating a workplace culture that enhances sustainable individual, team, and organizational development.

A SYSTEMS VIEW OF AN ORGANIZATION

What Is an Organization?

The work experiences described by participants in Activity 1–1 illustrate numerous topics to be discussed in this book. They include behavior of bosses, relationships with fellow workers, what makes people want to and not want to perform well, and communication problems. We can organize these subjects into a conceptual framework that will make organizational behavior easier to study in a systematic way by using the idea of effectiveness. **Effectiveness,** as we will use it, means the ability to achieve goals.

At the most basic level, an **organization** is viewed as a social entity created for the basic purpose of accomplishing tasks that individuals cannot accomplish alone.[6] As such, an organization relies on coordinated activities and systems to achieve a common goal or set of goals. Thus, an organization is a response to and a means of creating value that satisfies human needs. Organizations require agreements among people. The nature of the agreements, the process used to arrive at shared agreements, and the need to continuously revisit the agreements are critical for the survival and success of the entity. (See our discussion on dialogue and expectation clarification in Module 2.) If agreements are good—meaning that individuals are fully committed to helping the organization succeed, are able to work together effectively, and have the proper tools and resources—the organization is more likely to adapt to its changing environmental context, survive, and achieve a sustainable success. On the other hand, if agreements are poor, individuals sometimes feel compelled to protect their own interests instead of being concerned with the success of the organization as a whole. Poor agreement might mean that products and services fail to meet market needs.[7] Thus, organizations and all groupings of people within them perform tasks to achieve goals. Organizational behavior provides guidelines for defining goals and methods for augmenting the process of attaining them. To organize the learning process, we use a systems approach to understanding, predicting, and managing people in organizations. Later we devote a complete module (Module 13) to the development of the systems view of work and the exploration of alternative ways to design sustainable organizations. For this stage, however, we define a system as a purposefully designed arrangement of two or more interrelated parts that provides an added value in the form of a product or a service within an environmental context.

Initial Framework of System Effectiveness and Sustainability

As an initial framework we use the systems approach to study the collection of people making up an organization. The total unit is a system, and the interacting groupings and individuals within are subsystems. We can create a systems approach to effectiveness and sustainability as follows:

1. *Total organizational effectiveness.* This includes a definition of the overall purposes and goals of the organization. Thus, business organizations must continuously determine whether they are in the right business to avoid becoming obsolete in a changing environment. They also must evaluate the extent to which the system meets the needs of the present without compromising the ability of future communities to meet their own needs. Small-town newspapers, for example, after finding they could not survive solely as a press, have redefined their role to be that of distributor of advertising brochures. Management practices to divide up the responsibilities of all subunits may include managing by output. Practices that focus on the development of learning mechanisms that foster continuous improvements of products and services as well as human development are discussed in terms of total system development and effectiveness (Module 16). Integrating people of diverse professions, skills, and cultural backgrounds into a harmoniously operating company may require leadership skills similar to those of a symphony conductor. Climate building provides a supportive environment for workers. Designing procedures for use of technology as well as providing education and training, particularly for managers, are other examples.

2. *Intergroup effectiveness.* Groups coordinating their processes to achieve company objectives must have well-developed methods and routines that allow for continuous improvement and are sustainable over time, for example, the establishment of communication methods and channels that are continuously improved and the development of procedures and processes for conflict prevention and resolution that are understood and practiced by interacting subsystems.

3. *Team effectiveness.* Small-group skills related to teamwork design, goal setting, problem solving and creativity, communication, decision making, and conflict resolution must be used. Self-managed teams, virtual teams, and cross-functional teams are currently emerging as specific, organized forms. Regardless of the specific team format, team skills require continuous education, practice, and development investment by both leaders and members.

4. *Individual effectiveness.* At the core of individual effectiveness are the learning skills that the individual has acquired. Sustaining human development is dependent on the individual's ability to continuously learn and improve. The ability to perform well is the obvious focus for individual employees. But to go beyond that we must be concerned with the personal growth and development of all personnel. Skills in goal setting and interpersonal communication as well as attitudes toward failure and success are of prime relevance for the individual who must ever face a turbulent workplace that is always undergoing restructuring. Motivation to work is the driving force around which all other aspects of individual effectiveness can be viewed. Models of leadership and leadership styles are an important ingredient of managerial education and practice in acquiring the skills of coaching and development of others.

Understanding behavior in organizations can start with the total system and delve down into the subsystems or with the individual and work out into groups on up to the whole. The specific order of the learning journey itself can vary from individual to individual and from situation to situation.

Rationality in Managing

As we attempt to define our area of study, a special comment should be made about rationality. Typically, managers look at employee behavior from the viewpoint of how people *ought* to behave. People should make sense, they should do what they are supposed to do, and they should do what is good for the organization. After all, the basic definition of an organization is a rational model: people gathered together to achieve a purpose. Only logic, rationality, and objectivity (that is, common sense) can achieve that purpose. Specialty areas of business management, such as finance, engineering, marketing, accounting, and law, are based on rational, logical models. Thus, **rationality** is a process that is based on logic and reason. When executives and managers participate in workshops and when students come to courses in organizational behavior, someone almost always makes the comment that understanding behavior is just a matter of common sense. If rationality were our only concern in this field, there would be no reason to study behavior. Managers would simply plan, organize, direct, and control. But as shown in Figure 1–1, rationality is just the tip of the iceberg. Below the water line are forces

**Figure 1–1
Rational Behavior Is Only
the Tip of the Iceberg**

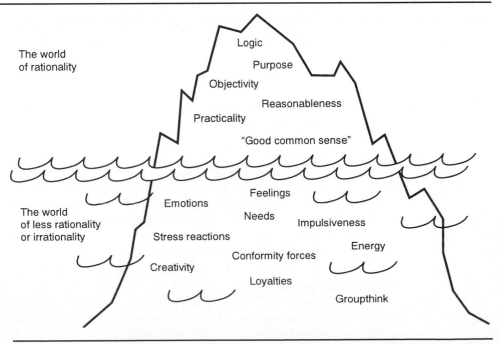

The study of organizational behavior focuses heavily on the less rational aspects of human action and interactions to understand why people do not always behave according to the rational model of organizations.

that are potent generators of behavior: emotions, feelings, needs, stress reactions, impulsiveness, energy, creativity, conformity forces, loyalties, and groupthink, just to mention a few. We will explore some of these forces throughout the course but will begin the systematic discovery process with the modules in this section (that is, Modules 2 and 3). Are we saying that managers do not know what is below that water level? Not at all. The problem is that managers are so involved in the rational model they often fail to take into account, or understand, the less rational forces. They are so involved with tasks, purposes, goals, deadlines, and balance sheets that they can become blinded to the realities below the surface until some eruption occurs.

It is fascinating to watch students in these courses switch perceptions from employee to management viewpoints and in the process completely forget or ignore what is below the water line. When students are engaged in task 1 from Activity 1–1 on defining human behavior in business, more than 90 percent of their examples are negative experiences that illustrate how little concern managers have for the factors below the water line. Yet by the time they assume the role of managers taking remedial action at a later stage in the course, they most always design solutions that take only the rational factors into consideration; they assume workers should respond rationally to management direction.

Our hope, an improbable one, is that managers will develop viewpoints that (1) maximize the human assets of employees for purposes of economic gain, (2) humanistically focus on quality, and (3) sustain the development of human potential and economic success of organizations without compromising future development. This presumes a more integrated awareness of the rational and irrational forces within a complex context. In turn, we hope that employees develop more trust and understanding of the rational model, which is essential to help our industries become sustainable productive and competitive entities.

ORGANIZATIONAL BEHAVIOR: HISTORICAL PERSPECTIVE

Although discussions about management, administration, organization, and organizing can be traced to ancient Greek, Egyptian, and biblical times, the study of management and organizational behavior as a distinct and separate field has largely been confined to the beginning of the 20th century. Today's theories are an integral part of the logical and natural evolution in management thought and practice. The systematic theorizing of the field has been clustered in many ways. For our purpose we follow the sociology of knowledge perspective that proposed four clusters: prescientific (pre-1880s), classical (1880s–1930s), neoclassical (1930s–1960s), and modern (1960s–present).[8] Figure 1–2 captures the essence of each era.

The Prescientific Era (pre-1880s)

The **prescientific era** is characterized by little systematic theorizing about management and organizations. Yet we find Jethro's advice to Moses to delegate authority over the tribes of Israel along hierarchical lines around 1491 B.C. Sun Tzu's *The Art of War* (written in 500 B.C.) recognizes the need for hierarchical organizations, interorganizational communications, and staff planning. Socrates' work, around 344 B.C., argues for the universality of management as an art unto itself. Aristotle, around 360 B.C., asserts that the nature and power of executive functions must reflect a specific cultural environment. Xenophon, around 370 B.C., records and describes the Greek shoe factory focus on the advantages of the division of labor. Machiavelli's *The Discourses* (1513) and *The Prince* (1532) focus on both the principles of unity of command and how to succeed as a leader. Adam Smith's *The Wealth of Nations* (1776) describes the optimal organization of a pin factory and focuses on the economic rationale for the division of labor and the factory system.[9] The ruling class in the preindustrial societies perceived work, trade, and commerce as being beneath its dignity, something to be accomplished by slaves and "low-level" classes.[10] The sources of authority were based on long-standing institutions and procedures that citizens of these societies perceived as legitimate. Most individuals obeyed the ruling elite in accordance with traditional customs.[11]

Figure 1–2   **Historical Evolution of Management Thought: A Brief Road Map**

	Period			
	Prescientific pre-1880s	**Classical 1880–1930s**	**Neoclassical 1930–1960s**	**Modern 1960–present**

Emerging schools of thought		• Scientific management
		• Administrative school
		• Structuralist school
			• Human relations school
			• Behavior schools:
			  -Group dynamics
			  -Leadership
			  -Decision making
				• Systems school
				• Sociotechnical system school
				• Management science school
				• Contingency school

Focus/emphasis	• Basic principles for nature and society • The position of authority and order in society • Economic rationale • Division of labor (early development)	• Basic principles of organizing and managing the most effective firm • The basic functions of managers • Characteristics of "the ideal type of an organization"	• Organizations are cooperative systems • Informal roles and norms influence individual performance • Work group dynamics influence individual and group performance • Leadership styles affect individual and group behavior • Decision making styles influence performance	• Organization is a system composed of subsystems • Organization as an open system composed of social, technological, and environmental subsystems • Use of quantitative methods to solve organization and managing issues • Exploration of alternative organization design configurations and managerial actions for changing situations
Representative scholars	• Jethro (Moses' father-in-law) • Sun Tzu • Socrates, Aristotle • Xenophon • Machiavelli • Adam Smith	• Taylor • Fayol • Gulick • Weber	• Barnard • Roethlisberger • Lewin • McGregor • Maslow	• Bertalanffy • Katz and Kahn • Emery and Trist • Thompson • Lorsch and Lawrence • Galbraith

The Classical Era (1880s–1930s)

The **classical era** of management thought evolved between the end of the 19th century and into the beginning of the 20th. The transition from agrarian to industrial society coupled with the changing economic, social, and technological environment established the condition to begin the systematic study of management and organizations. The focus of the early studies centered on the search for alternative ways to organize and structure the industrial organization; the way to organize, delegate, and coordinate work; and the ways to motivate people who work within the emerging organizational structures. Three dominant schools can be identified in this era:

1. The **scientific management school,** led by Frederick Taylor, focused on the measurement of work. It followed four basic principles of organization and management with the aim of creating the most effective way to carry out work tasks. The four basic principles included (a) finding the one best way to do each job, (b) the scientific selection of individuals for the position, (c) the development of financial incentives to ensure that the work is carried out as required, and (d) the establishment of functional foremanship.[12]

2. The **administrative school,** led by Henry Fayol, focused on the functions of management. Five basic functions of management were identified: planning, organizing, commanding, coordinating, and controlling.[13]

3. The **structuralist school,** led by Max Weber, focused on the basic tenets of the ideal type of organization, the bureaucratic model, as the most effective way to organize and manage organizations. The model emphasized order via a system of rules and procedures, rational–legal authority, division of labor based on functional specialization, a well-defined hierarchy, differentiation between organizational functions, rationality, uniformity, and administrative consistency.

The Neoclassical Era (1930s–1960s)

The **neoclassical era** is characterized by direct challenges to the classical schools, their assumptions, and their implications. The neoclassical theories focused on the dimension of human interaction, which the classical schools neglected. During this era, behavioral science theories were introduced and integrated with management thought. The theories are anchored in two major sources: (1) social psychologists and sociologists who focused on human interactions and human relations within groups (the human relations or the group dynamics schools) and (2) psychologists who focused on individual behavior in different settings (the behavioral science school).

The **human relations school** argued that organizations are cooperative systems and not the product of mechanical engineering.[14] The first large-scale empirical studies that focused on the relations between productivity and social interaction were conducted at the Hawthorne plant of the Western Electric Company. They illustrated the importance of workers' attitudes and feelings and argued that informal roles and norms influence individual performance.[15]

The **behavioral science schools** include three clusters of theories that were an outgrowth of the human relations school and focused on individual behavior within work groups:

- *Group dynamics* focused on the effect of work group dynamics on individual and group performance.

- *Leadership* stressed the importance of groups having both task and social leaders, differentiated between Theory X and Theory Y management, and identified different theories of leadership and leadership styles.

- *Decision making* focused on the degree of individual involvement in decision making and its influence on performance. The contributions of these schools to our understanding of human behavior are discussed in depth in the appropriate modules throughout this book.

The Modern Era (1960s–Present)

The **modern era**—or what some call the contemporary management and organization era—is characterized by an increased emphasis on integration of some key elements of the classical and neoclassical eras. The underlying assumption is that organizations are systems composed of interrelated and interdependent components that function within an environmental context. Throughout this course we explore in depth many key elements of the modern era schools of thoughts. Four clusters of schools can be delineated:

1. The **systems school** is anchored in general systems theory. The organization is viewed as a system composed of subsystems or subunits that are mutually dependent on one another and that continuously interact. General systems theory concepts such as holism, equifinality, equilibrium, input, transformation, output, and feedback provide the foundation for this school of thought (to be discussed in a later module).[16]

2. The **sociotechnical systems school** at the most basic level believes that every organization is made up of a social subsystem (the people) using tools, techniques, and knowledge (the technical subsystem) to produce a product or a service valued by the environmental subsystem. This school further argues that the degree to which the technical subsystem and the social subsystem are designed with respect to each other and the environmental subsystem determines how successful and competitive the organization will be.[17]

3. The orientation of the **management science school** and operational research school is to apply quantitative techniques, methods, and technologies to organization and management issues. The emphasis of this problem-solving approach is relatively narrow; it centers on merging strategic concern for planning and forecasting with the administrative concern for organizational objectives and goal accomplishment. Recently, the field of management science expanded its focus to include advanced technologies such as computer-integrated manufacturing, flexible manufacturing systems, and new manufacturing and integrated orientations such as just-in-time, total quality management, and reengineering.[18]

4. The **contingency school** seeks to (a) understand the relationships within and among subsystems as well as between the organization and its environment and (b) define

patterns of relationships or configurations of variables. The essence of this orientation is that there is "no one best way" and that there is a middle ground between "universal principles" and "it all depends." Furthermore, the emphasis is on the degree of fit between organizational processes and characteristics of the situation. Contingency views are ultimately directed toward suggesting organizational designs and managerial actions most appropriate for specific situations.[19]

OBJECTIVES OF THE COURSE

Our aims for the course are high. To the extent possible in a one-quarter or one-semester experience, we would like you to achieve the following:

- Scientific-based interdisciplinary knowledge, methods, and techniques that are helpful in developing sustainable effectiveness in individuals, teams, and organizations.
- Appreciation of diversity; its dynamics; and its impact on individual, team, and organizational effectiveness.
- Understanding of how perceptual distortion affects communication, motivation, and human dynamics in organizations.
- Understanding the dynamics of leadership and mentoring at work.
- Understanding of the potential cause-and-effect relationships among motivation; perception; communication; and the management processes of work design, creativity and innovation, organizational culture, organization development, and change.
- Ability to effectively use team skills, such as group problem solving and decision making.
- Ability to analyze diverse management situations and your own experience while utilizing course concepts.
- Improved skills in personal goal setting and interpersonal communications.
- Improved reflective practitioner skills—learning-in-action skills.
- Better awareness of your own behavior in different work settings.
- Understanding of the process of change and the management of change in organizations.
- Appreciation of a sustainable work system perspective within the context of individual and organizational behavior, development, and performance.

Our overall intent is to emphasize skills development, understanding, and cognitive knowledge acquisition that you can use.

SUMMARY

We started our textbook with the focus on the sustainability and sustaining humans in the workplace. We introduced the course by examining your own experience with human behavior in organizations. We suggested that the diversity of people's experiences in organizations typically includes many problems that affect individual, group, and organizational performance and the sense of satisfaction or dissatisfaction felt. Both task and human dimensions are important for understanding organizational effectiveness. Such topics as fair treatment, good supervision, effective communication, and motivation are closely interwoven. This situation implies that an effective theoretical framework must deal with both task and human dimensions of effectiveness and must include all four levels of behavior: individual, group, intergroup, and organizational. Objectives of the course are drawn from this theoretical approach but emphasize improving effectiveness in real organizations, not just academic knowledge. In addition, we stressed that our studies will include the "irrational" as well as the rational factors in behavior (see Figure 1–1), the latter being the perceptual window through which management typically views employee conduct.

Organizational behavior is an interdisciplinary field of study. While the study of organizational behavior is relatively young, issues of human behavior in the context of work, organization, and management can be traced to ancient Greek, Egyptian, and biblical thought. We provided a brief review of the historical evolution of management thought. Following the sociology of knowledge perspective, we identified four clusters of thoughts: the prescientific, classical, neoclassical, and modern eras. In each era we briefly discussed the major schools of organization and management thought with their focus and emphases.

Because our approach to learning stresses involvement, learning-in-action, and appreciative inquiry, the first activity helped integrate your experience with organizational behavior ideas. Your experience, perceptions, and reactions will continue to be a key part of this course. In Activity 1–1 we saw that individuals' experiences offer important data that we can draw upon to increase our understanding. We saw that many common experiences and perceptions were widely shared among participants and that, even so, effective communication can be difficult. The communication skills of listening, paraphrasing, and sharing were explicitly related to participants' attitudes and responses to one another. We saw that differences can be either useful or troublesome, depending on how they are handled. We saw that by being appreciative of the experience through appreciative inquiry we can gain more insights. Finally, we began the process of applying organizational behavior knowledge directly to your own experience. We will build on these experiences throughout the course.

Study Questions

1. What is meant by the term *sustainable development?*

2. What is meant by the term *organization?* Illustrate your understanding by applying it to an organization that you know.

3. What is a "learning community"? In what way did Activity 1–1 (Defining Organizational Behavior) contribute to the development of the classroom learning community?

4. What is the "systems approach" to studying organizational behavior?

5. Why do we emphasize "irrational" as well as rational aspects of behavior?

6. Review the historical evolution of organizational behavior. Select any two schools of thought that you feel influenced our understanding of individual behavior the most. Provide the reasoning for your choice.

7. Review the goals of the course. Select the two that you feel have the greatest potential for improving your learning at this time. Name the two and give the reasons.

Endnotes

1. World Commission on Environment and Development (chairman: Gro Harlem Brundtland), *Our Common Future* (Oxford, UK: Oxford University Press, 1987), p. 8.

2. P. Martens, "Sustainability: Science or Fiction," *Sustainability: Science, Practice, and Policy* 2, no. 1 (2006), pp. 36–41.

3. P. Docherty, M. Kira, and A. B. (Rami) Shani, *Sustainable Work Systems* (New York: Routledge, 2008).

4. L. F. Gardiner, "Redesigning Higher Education: Producing Drastic Gains in Student Learning," *ASHE-ERIC Higher Education Report* 23, no. 7 (2001).

5. M. Dierkes, A. Berthoin Antal, J. Child, and I. Nonaka, *Handbook of Organizational Learning and Knowledge* (Oxford, UK: Oxford Press, 2001).

6. C. Barnard, *The Function of the Executive* (Cambridge, MA: Harvard University Press, 1938).

7. W. A. Pasmore, *Designing Effective Organizations: Sociotechnical System Perspective* (New York: Wiley, 1988).

8. Many scholars examined the evolution of management thought in the context of the evolution of the society. Among them we find R. Miles, *Theories of Management* (New York: McGraw-Hill,

1975); D. A. Nadler and M. L. Tushman, *Competing by Design* (New York: Oxford University Press, 1997); T. Parsons and N. Smelser, *Economy & Society* (London: Routledge & Kegan, 1956); C. Perrow, "The Short & Glorious History of Organizational Theory," *Organizational Dynamics* (Summer 1973), pp. 2–15; M. Weber, *The Theory of Social & Economic Organization* (New York: Free Press, 1947); and D. Wern, *The Evolution of Management Thought* (New York: Wiley, 1979).

9. A nice summary of the chronology of organization theory is found in J. M. Shafritz and J. S. Ott, *Classics of Organization Theory* (Chicago: Dorsey, 1987).

10. See, for example, Parsons and Smelser, *Economy & Society.*

11. See, for example, J. Bowditch and A. Buono, *A Primer on Organizational Behavior* (New York: Wiley, 1998).

12. F. Taylor, *The Principles of Scientific Management* (New York: Harper & Brothers, 1911).

13. H. Fayol, *General and Industrial Management* (London: Pitman, 1916).

14. C. I. Barnard, *The Function of the Executive* (Cambridge, MA: Harvard Press, 1938).

15. F. J. Roethlisberger and W. Dickson, *Management and the Worker* (Cambridge, MA: Harvard Press, 1938).

16. L. Bertalanffy, *General Systems Theory: Foundations, Development, and Applications* (New York: Braziller, 1967).

17. For a full description of the sociotechnical systems school of thought, see F. E. Emery, *Some Characteristics of Sociotechnical Systems* (London: Tavistock, 1959); Pasmore, *Designing Effective Organizations;* J. C. Taylor and D. F. Felton, *Performance by Design: Sociotechnical Systems in North America* (Reading, MA: Addison-Wesley, 1994); A. Majchrzak, "What to Do When You Can't Have It All: Toward a Theory of Sociotechnical Dependencies," *Human Relations* 50, no. 5 (1997), pp. 535–65; E. L. Trist, "Sociotechnical System Perspective," in *Perspectives on Organization Design & Behavior,* A. H. Van de Ven and W. F. Joyce (eds.) (New York: Wiley, 1982), pp. 19–75; F. Eijnatten, A. B. (Rami) Shani, and M. Leary, "Socio-Technical Systems: Designing and Managing Sustainable Organizations," in T. Cumming (ed.), *Handbook of Organization Development and Change* (Thousand Oaks, CA: SAGE, 2008).

18. See, for example, C. W. Churchman, R. L. Ackoff, and E. L. Arnoff, *Introduction to Operations Research* (New York: Wiley, 1961); and N. Slack, *The Manufacturing Advantage* (Oxfordshire, UK: Management Books 2000 Ltd., 1998).

19. See, for example, J. R. Galbraith, *Designing Organizations* (San Francisco: Jossey-Bass, 1995); D. Nadler and M. Tushman, *Competing by Design* (New York: Oxford University Press, 1997); P. Bate, "Bringing the Design Sciences to Organization Development and Change Management," *Journal of Applied Behavioral Sciences* 43, no. 1 (2007), pp. 6–8.

Activity 1–2: Initial Exploration of Sustainability and Sustainable Work Systems

Objectives:

a. To identify the meaning of sustainable development within the context of work.

b. To explore issues associated with sustainable work systems.

Task 1:

In this chapter, it was argued that sustainable development refers to the *continuous development* of individuals, teams, and organizations. Drawing from your cumulative experiences, identify and briefly describe a few features that you would like to see as an integral part of any workplace that you would like to work for in the future that would nurture sustainable development.

Task 2:

Each participant shares these thoughts with a small group. After each has done so, discuss what common elements seem to emerge. Have a spokesperson make a list.

Task 3:

The spokesperson reports findings to the class.

Module 2

Appreciative Inquiry, Expectations, and Learning

LEARNING OBJECTIVES

After completing this module, you should be able to

1. Appreciate the process and the importance of developing a "psychological contract."

2. Explain the importance of managing expectations, dialoguing, and appreciative inquiry.

3. Describe the role of expectations, expectations discrepancies, and self-fulfilling prophecies in organizational settings.

4. Explain the basic assumptions about the adult as learner.

5. Describe the similarities and differences among cognitive learning, content learning, and process learning.

6. Appreciate the meaning of a learning community and the roles of the participant and the instructor in an experiential learning-based course.

KEY TERMS AND CONCEPTS

Adults as learners	Learning-in-action
Appreciative inquiry	Organization learning
Cognitive development hierarchy	Process learning
Communication dialoguing	Psychological contract
Content learning	Reflection
Expectations	Self-fulfilling prophecy (Pygmalion)
Experiential learning	Self-learning competency
Individual learning	Social contract
Learning	Team learning
Learning community	

MODULE OUTLINE

PREMODULE PREPARATION

Activity 2–1: Organizational Dialoguing about Learning, Expectations, and Teams

Objectives:

a. To help you understand the learning goals and methods of the course, the instructor's viewpoints about the course, and other participants' learning needs and attitudes in several areas.

b. To help the instructor understand your viewpoints, attitudes, and needs.

c. To build the classroom learning climate by involvement learning, appreciative inquiry, and dialoguing.

Task 1:

Individuals, while reflecting on their learning goals and this specific course, should write a few notes in response to the following five questions:

a. What things would you like to learn, study, or have emphasized in this course on human behavior in organizations?

b. What doubts or concerns do you have about this course? What are some things you would not like to study or have happen in the course?

c. What are your viewpoints toward college life, college education, or your major course of study that might influence your attitudes toward this course?

d. What was your best group learning experience? What was great about it?

e. What was your worst group learning experience? What made it that way?

In general, these questions should bring out any factors that may account for your expectations, hopes, or doubts for the course. These may be directly related to the subject of study, but they may also be related to the life you are experiencing on campus or in the larger environment. Feel free to express any views. Your representative does not have to identify who said what. (Time: 15 to 20 minutes)

Task 2 (To Be Completed in Class):

Participants will form work groups of five to seven members (no larger). Individuals are to share their responses to the five questions in task 1. Each group will elect a representative and keep notes of the discussion. Each group is to prepare its answer to the five questions. (Time: 15 to 20 minutes)

Task 3:

Representatives from the groups will meet in a fishbowl circle in the center of the room to report and discuss their groups' viewpoints. The instructor will raise issues for clarity and understanding after they have completed their discussion but will not respond at this point. (Time: 10 to 15 minutes)

Task 4:

Work groups will choose a second representative for this task. Groups will prepare a list of questions you would like to have the instructor answer to help you understand his or her expectations and attitudes about the course (such as learning approach, education, background, satisfactions or frustrations gained from teaching, or what the instructor hopes to see participants gain from the course). Any questions that will help you get to know the instructor or understand the course and how it is to be conducted are appropriate. The instructor's expectations of students should be probed here. Try to prepare confrontational questions such as those a good television interviewer would use. (Time: 10 minutes)

Task 5:

Put the instructor on the hot seat. Representatives will meet in a circle with the instructor. Each poses one question at a time until all have been answered. (Time: 15 to 20 minutes)

INTRODUCTION

In most organizations the nature of the **social contract** between the individual and the organization seems to have a long-lasting effect on performance and behavior. At the most basic level, "a social contract refers to the assumptions, values, and norms about appropriate behavior within a social entity."[1] What further complicates the human dynamics is the increasing diversity of the workforce. Individuals see situations, issues, or goals differently, depending on their particular perspectives, experiences, educational and cultural backgrounds, personality traits, competencies and skills, and biases—yet everyone typically assumes that everyone else sees things as they do. We fail to take into account that what seems "obvious" and "common sense" to us may appear bizarre and inexplicable to others. Or, lacking some key piece of information to interpret the situation, someone may come to a resoundingly different conclusion about data that others agree upon. Neither the problem nor its recognition is new. One study showed relatively low agreement between bosses and subordinates on what subordinates' job duties were and very low agreement on what obstacles were faced in accomplishing these duties.[2] In another study, 80 percent of supervisors said they "very often" praised good performance, but only 14 percent of their employees agreed.[3] Similar results are found widely both in formal research and in studies of contemporary organizations by consultants.

Diversity and Expectations

The difficulties just described seem typical of human interactions and interpersonal relations at work, at school, in social settings, and even in the family. Yet we seldom discuss the assumptions, values, and beliefs on which we base our behavior, so it is often difficult to identify the causes of the failures, let alone to deal effectively with them. But whether they are discussed or ignored, underlying assumptions and beliefs have a powerful effect on our behavior. Two people with contradictory expectations of one another are probably doomed to ongoing conflict. Such conflict can result in low productivity, alienation, absenteeism, dissatisfaction with work in the organization, or even divorce in marriage.

As the workforce becomes more diverse, are there some things that have to be done differently to more fully utilize human potential? We think yes. Are we trapped in our own assumptions and beliefs, forever separated from others? We think not. Methods exist to improve understanding and communication within a diverse workforce by creating shared assumptions, thus enabling common interpretations. **Communication dialoguing** and **appreciative inquiry** are two ways to overcome diversity and contradictory expectations by bringing similarities and differences in perspective out into the open. They can then be discussed, modified by other data or new interpretations, and shared. The premodule activity uses a form of dialoguing to develop an effective learning climate in the classroom. Figure 2–1 diagrams this dialoguing process as it might exist between a boss and employees or between a professor and students. Somewhat different methods might be used in business, but the shared exchange of perspectives and expectations would be visible there as well. For instance, an employee might explicitly inquire about the boss's expectations for a project or report, about the extent of his or her discretion, or the flexibility possible in time schedules. Such exchange is the foundation for understanding, trust, and, thus, effective working relations. Successful managers and employees use this exchange frequently.

The Psychological Contract

A specific form of the social contract is the psychological contract.[4] As an individual becomes a member of an organization, she or he establishes an unwritten, implicit or explicit psychological contract with the organization. The **psychological contract** consists

---

Figure 2–1
Dialoguing to Overcome Differences in Expectations in Business or the Classroom

In Business

- My expectations of what subordinates should, ought, and must do.
- My managerial philosophy.
- What I hope subordinates will get from the workplace.
- What I want from the workplace.

- Our expectations of what bosses and organizations should, ought, and must do.
- Our attitudes toward work, the workplace, bosses, and peers.
- Our goals—what we want out of our work, jobs, and the organization.

In the Classroom

- My expectations of what students should, ought, and must do.
- My educational philosophy.
- What I hope students will get out of this course.
- What I want from the course.

- Our expectations of what instructors should, ought, and must do.
- Our attitudes toward education, professors, and college life.
- What we want out of college.

of the mutual understanding of the expectations the individual and the employer have of each other. According to Edgar Schein, the notion of a psychological contract implies that the individuals have a variety of expectations of the organization and that the organization has a variety of expectations of the individuals. These expectations not only cover how much work is to be performed for how much pay but also involve the whole pattern of rights, privileges, and obligations between worker and organization.[5] The clearer these expectations are to both sides, the more coordination and cooperation are possible. The dynamic nature of the human interaction facilitates the creation of individual perceptions about the nature of work; the expectations around effort, performance, and pay; and the importance of a specific behavioral code.[6] Even though such expectations may never formally be stated, they do exist and have an impact on both the relationship between employees and employers and on employees' performance. When the psychological contract is violated, or perceived to be violated, intense emotional reactions such as shock, resentment, outrage, or anger result. Furthermore, the disillusionment over broken psychological contracts affects employee satisfaction, productivity, employee commitment, and desire to stay with the organization.[7]

The psychological contract is viewed as a dynamic, living process in that it needs to be revisited periodically, beyond its initial formation, due to ongoing activities and experiences. Activity 2–6W attempts to facilitate the beginning of the process of making expectations explicit "right from the start." As such, it initiates a set of understandings between you and the instructor on (1) the educational program for this course and (2) the conduct and attitudes of those who will take part in it. In a sense it is a psychological contract we hope to follow. Activity 2–6W (Personal Learning Statement), which can be found on the book's website, will make the learning contract more explicit. The model in Activity 2–1 makes a continuous flow of communication between instructor and participants possible. This means that a value system that includes some degree of openness and trust must exist as part of the organizational culture. We might say that organizations need a fair conditioning system, a continuous and open flow of communication in which fairness—fair treatment—is an essential ingredient. Activity 2–6W in this module was created both as a learning tool and as an experiential mechanism to help you develop a psychological contract between you and your instructor.

EXPECTATIONS AND SELF-FULFILLING PROPHECY

Psychological contracts compose expectations of an exchange agreement between employers and employees.[8] Recent research indicates that many organizational problems can be traced to **expectations** discrepancies. Interpersonal dialoguing is seen as a managerial tool to bridge the discrepancy gap. Raising managerial expectations about employees' abilities and performances can improve performance and boost productivity. Hence productivity as a self-fulfilling prophecy presents a variety of unique possibilities for crafting desired behavior and outcomes in the workplace. Based on the experience of working with several organizations, Livingston concluded that (1) what a manager expects of his subordinates and the way he treats them largely determine their performances and career progress; (2) a unique characteristic of superior managers is their ability to create high-performance expectations that subordinates fulfill; (3) less effective managers fail to develop similar expectations and, as a consequence, the productivity of their subordinates suffers; and (4) subordinates, more often than not, appear to do what they believe they are expected to do.[9]

The **self-fulfilling prophecy (Pygmalion)** has been attracting growing interest in the past decade. Self-fulfilling prophecy (SFP) is described as a three-stage process beginning with a person's belief that a certain event will occur. In the second stage this expectation or "prophecy" leads to some new behavior that the person would not have performed were it not for the expectation. In the third stage the expected event occurs and the prophecy is fulfilled.[10] The phenomenon of self-fulfilling prophecies has become widely recognized in the behavioral, social, educational, and organizational sciences.

Recent empirical studies shed light on the multiple dimensions of the phenomenon and its important role in the context of work. For example, a set of studies carried out by Dov Eden and his colleagues demonstrated empirically that high expectations resulted in improved performance, raised self-expectancy, increased overall satisfaction, and improved leadership, which, in turn, augmented subordinates' productivity. Furthermore, Eden envisions managers as prophets. He argues that managers as prophets expect certain things to happen and then act in ways to fulfill their expectations.[11] The relationship between expectancy and learning, leadership, group behavior, motivation, perception, and performance is addressed in later modules.

At this point we will continue to clarify expectations and build the psychological contract by discussing our view about learning, the adult learner, learning competencies, team learning, the learning community, and appreciative inquiry. Your awareness of these is important not only for understanding the course but also for learning techniques and competencies that you can acquire and apply later when you are supervising people.

LEARNING AND EXPECTATIONS

Why explore learning? Why do we devote part of this module, most of the next module (Module 3), and part of the last module (Module 16) in this book to learning? These are good questions. If you have no question about the quality of your learning or the quality of learning in your team or your organization and if you are sure that it's the best it can be, perhaps you should not. However, if you have any question about learning, you should consider seriously exploring learning. Learning is an essential process for attaining individual and organizational success.[12] Sustaining the learning process requires the development of learning mechanisms.[13] A recent set of studies argued that the ability to learn faster than one's competitors may be the only sustainable competitive advantage.[14] Rapid and continuing changes of the workplace foster the preoccupation of most human beings with learning and the need to learn—just to survive. The expectations that individuals must be willing to learn are increasing. **Learning** is defined as the process whereby new skills, knowledge, ability, and attitudes are created through the transformation of experience.[15] At the most basic level, organizations expect individuals to learn productive work behaviors. Furthermore, individuals and organizations alike must learn to adapt to the new rules of the game and the ever-changing and increasingly diverse global business environment. The major challenge that organizations face has to do with providing learning experiences in an environment that will promote employee behaviors desired by the organization.

Learning within an organization context can be explored at three levels: individual, team, and organization. **Individual learning** refers to the change of skills, insights, knowledge, attitudes, and values acquired by a person through self-study, technology-based instruction, insight, and observation. Group or **team learning** alludes to the increase in knowledge, skills, and competencies that is accomplished by and within groups.[16] **Organization learning** refers to the principles, mechanisms (processes and structures), and activities that enable the organization to create, acquire, and transfer knowledge to continuously improve products, services, practices, processes, and financial results.[17] (The areas of team learning and organization learning receive focused attention later in the book.)

Learning and Self-Learning Competency

The most critical skill that an individual must acquire is self-learning competency. **Self-learning competency** enables a person to learn actively in a variety of situations. This means, for example, that a person has the skills to apply knowledge gained in one situation to other situations. This competency makes a person aware of, and open to, learning opportunities in their day-to-day experiences. A workforce possessing this competency sees learning as an everyday natural occurrence. This kind of workforce is able to exploit learning opportunities that arise "on the job," as well as make effective use of formal structured learning experiences, open learning, and multimedia delivery systems.[18]

Self refers to the fact that the learner must take primary responsibility for his or her own learning and that learning is an inner activity. A *competency* is viewed as "an inter-related set of abilities, behaviors, attitudes, and knowledge needed by an individual to be effective in a professional life and/or managerial role." *Competency* is meant to focus on the development of independent self-learners as a goal of training as distinct from the narrower use of the term *self-learning,* which refers to "individualized delivery systems," often using computer-based packages. As we can see, self-learning is related to self-motivation, self-awareness, and self-control. It presupposes that the learners are interested in learning. Further, knowing yourself and having the ability for planning and a sense of commitment seem critical.

Skills that the adult learner must master to develop self-learning competency include the ability to engage in divergent thinking and the ability to be in touch with curiosities; the ability to perceive yourself objectively and accept feedback about your performance nondefensively; the ability to diagnose your learning needs in the light of models of competencies required for performing life roles; the ability to formulate learning objectives in terms that describe performance outcomes; the ability to identify human, material, and experiential resources for accomplishing various kinds of learning objectives; the ability to design a plan of strategies and carry out the plan systematically while utilizing the appropriate learning resources effectively; and the ability to collect evidence of the accomplishment of learning objectives and have it validated through performance.[19]

The Role of Questions in Learning

At this point it is important to raise the question: If the development of self-learning competencies are necessary skills for lifelong learners, then how are these learning skills developed? To answer that question, we must first explore the thinking processes involved in learning. Good questions are at the root of thinking and learning. In fact, the development of every area of scientific thought centers around answering new questions in that field of study. For example, in Module 1 we explored the evolution of management thought throughout history. Beneath this progression of management science lies the dominant questions posed by researchers and practitioners during different eras. Although answers are important to the health of a science, its continued existence is determined by the development of new questions to guide future thinking, learning, and exploration.[20] Therefore, the purpose of every branch of science is to provide answers *and* questions for society. This learning process is also true for education as a whole. The relationship between questions and answers is so important that true learning cannot exist if the two are separated.

Indeed, so buried are questions in established instruction that the fact that all assertions—all statements that this or that is so—are implicit answers to questions is virtually never recognized. For example, the statement that water boils at 100 degrees centigrade is an answer to the question, At what temperature centigrade does water boil? Hence, every textbook could be rewritten in the interrogative mode by translating every statement into a question. That this has not been done is testimony to the privileged status of answers over questions in instruction and the continued misunderstanding of the significance of questions in the learning process.[21] In short, questions serve as guides for our minds to think in new and better ways. Consequently, the value of the learning experience is significantly affected by the quality of the question that piqued our interest and motivated our thinking. For this reason, an integral component in developing self-learning competency is the ability to pose questions that will facilitate continued learning—or what some call the development of cognitive ability.

Cognitive Development—Bloom's Taxonomy

In 1956 Benjamin Bloom and a team of educators developed a map of educational goals for cognitive development that has guided learning and teaching methodologies at all levels of education for the past half century. Bloom's Taxonomy of Educational Objectives organizes the critical thinking skills of individuals into a **cognitive development hierarchy** of six levels: knowledge, comprehension, application, analysis, synthesis, and

**Figure 2–2
Cognitive Development—
Bloom's Taxonomy**

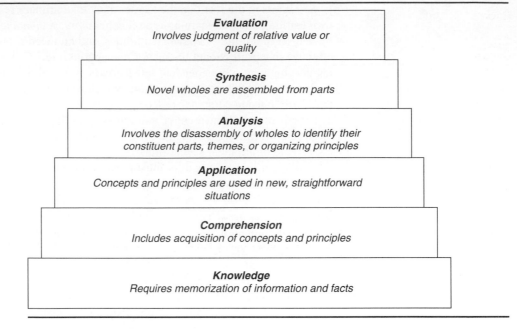

Evaluation
*Involves judgment of relative value or
quality*

Synthesis
Novel wholes are assembled from parts

Analysis
*Involves the disassembly of wholes to identify their
constituent parts, themes, or organizing principles*

Application
*Concepts and principles are used in new, straightforward
situations*

Comprehension
Includes acquisition of concepts and principles

Knowledge
Requires memorization of information and facts

evaluation[22] (see Figure 2–2). Beginning with knowledge as the foundational ability, the critical thinking skills required for reasoning at each level of the taxonomy build upon the previous and become progressively more difficult. Through this process, the cognitive development of individuals can be evaluated according to their ability to perform tasks and answer questions at each level of learning. The top three levels of Bloom's Taxonomy constitute the higher-order intellectual processes that are needed for complex problem solving and divergent thinking.[23]

The value of Bloom's Taxonomy is that it provides a framework for educators and practitioners to organize thinking processes and to provide a pathway for critical thinking development.[24] Specifically, it can be used as a guide in developing a series of sequential questions that induce progressively higher levels of thinking. For example, one elementary school teacher created an activity that leads students through all six stages of thinking using the Pledge of Allegiance as the topic of focus. After each question is sufficiently answered, the teacher then poses a new question designed to facilitate the students' thinking at the next level (see Figure 2–3). This type of instruction is an effective learning tool because questions present our mind with an implicit set of thinking tasks. These tasks are often embedded in "cues" found in words at the beginning of the question. Column two of Figure 2–3 lists some common words that cue the mind to think at specific levels. By being aware of how these "question cues" facilitate both thinking and learning, we can expand our ability to pose powerful questions that develop our knowledge *and* critical thinking skills. This type of learning process is useful for learners in every context—whether business or academia—as it facilitates knowledge *retention, application,* and *creation.*[25]

Throughout your learning experience in this course you will have the opportunity to develop thinking skills at all six levels of Bloom's Taxonomy. You will be required to

1. Remember facts, theories, and concepts.

2. Understand their purpose and usefulness to organizational and group dynamics.

3. Apply concepts and theories to case studies and your own experiences (both past and present).

4. Analyze your experiences and case studies while using course concepts.

5. Synthesize experiences and key learning points throughout the course to help you learn how to learn better in new contexts.

6. Evaluate the quality and value of the knowledge you have gained according to your future application of it in the real world.

Figure 2–3   Application of Bloom's Taxonomy: An Illustration

Bloom's Taxonomy	Question Cues[a]	Facilitator's Question
Knowledge	List, define, tell, say, describe, identify, show, label, collect, examine, quote, name, who, when, where, etc.	*Say* the Pledge of Allegiance
Comprehension	Summarize, explain, interpret, contrast, predict, associate, distinguish, estimate, differentiate, discuss, extend	*Explain* what indivisible, liberty, and justice *mean*
Application	Apply, demonstrate, calculate, complete, illustrate, show, solve, examine, modify, relate, change, create, classify, experiment, discover	*Create* your own pledge to something you believe in
Analysis	Analyze, separate, order, connect, arrange, divide, compare, contrast, select, infer	*Discuss* the meaning of "and to the Republic for which it stands" *in terms of* its importance to the pledge
Synthesis	Combine, integrate, modify, rearrange, substitute, plan, create, design, invent, what if, compose, formulate, prepare, rewrite, generalize	*Write* a contract between yourself and a friend that includes an allegiance to a symbol that stands for something you both believe in
Evaluation	Assess, decide, rank, grade, test, measure, recommend, convince, select, judge, discriminate, support, conclude, compare, summarize	Describe the *purpose* of the Pledge and *assess* how *well it achieves that purpose.* Suggest *improvements.*

[a]An adaptation of B. S. Bloom, et al., *Taxonomy of Educational Objectives, Handbook I: Cognitive Domain* (David McKay Company, Inc., 1956), cited in *Learning Skills Program: Bloom's Taxonomy (www.coun.uvic.ca/learn/program/hndouts/bloom.html).*

Just as importantly, as you seek to practice what you are learning, you will be given the opportunity to formulate new questions that will identify areas of future learning beyond the scope and duration of this class. In the context of this course, Bloom's Taxonomy is a tool to help frame individual and team learning and a guide for the collaborative appreciative inquiry process. Through action and reflection, individuals and teams seek answers and pose new questions that will shape the development of their learning community. The next module, Module 3, is devoted to the topic of learning-in-action that maps up a process for acquiring these managerial skills.

THE ADULT LEARNER AND EXPERIENTIAL LEARNING

This book, and the learning that it attempts to foster, is based on a few assumptions about **adults as learners:**[26]

1. Adults have a need to be self-directed in establishing and implementing their learning goals.

2. Adults desire to integrate their past experiences with new learning.

3. Adults have a dominant and a preferred learning style.

4. Adults can modify their learning processes to suit changing needs and conditions.

5. Learning is a continuous, lifelong process that is grounded in experience.

Experiential Learning Process

As can be seen from the preceding set of assumptions, the guiding approach to this book is **experiential learning.** That is,

> learning, growth, and change are facilitated by an integrated process that begins with a here-and-now experience followed by collection of data and observation about the experience. These observations are assimilated with previous knowledge into a "theory" from which new implications for actions can be deduced. These implications then serve as guides in acting to create new experiences.[27]

A few variations of experiential learning theories and models can be found in the literature. One school of thought argues that learning occurs not only through thinking and cognition but also through experience and affect or feeling.[28] Furthermore, two dimensions of learning were identified: for David Kolb the dimensions are *concrete to abstract* and *reflective observation to active experimentation,* and for Kenneth Murrell the dimensions are *abstract to concrete* and *affective to cognitive.* The two sets of dimensions create a matrix upon which we can plot our personal style via the response to a pencil-and-paper instrument. Activity 2–2 at the end of this module provides an opportunity to map your learning style, using Murrell's instrument and matrix. The other school of thought focuses on work-based learning.[29] The two dimensions advanced by Joseph Raelin are knowledge (from explicit to tacit) and learning (from theory to practice). These two dimensions create a somewhat different matrix. Despite their differences, all experiential learning schools of thought strongly advocate the importance of the learner's active involvement in the learning process.

Rationale for Learning by Involvement

So far the course has been developed almost entirely by interaction exercises. Involvement methods (developed widely in business and government workshops for training managers, supervisors, and executives) are designed for adult education. It is essential for you to understand that in this course, the basis for learning is not simply the instructor or a textbook. Instead, the course is built around using the participants' own experiences, both before and during the course. Participants are involved in sharing with one another what they have learned in the process of working with others. Exercises or experiences allow participants to apply the insights of theory in practice, try alternative methods, and experience first-hand the situations and issues they are studying. In essence, the participants use their own experiences as a laboratory for exploring how people behave in organizations. Team interactions examine different perspectives; solutions naturally arise out of diverse backgrounds and experiences. Even more important, teams provide a rich resource for participants to draw upon; team members learn from one another just as they learn from the instructor and text. This approach to learning is participant-centered rather than instructor-centered. The instructor's role is that of facilitator of learning as well as specialist or expert.

Most large companies—such as IBM, Ford, Intel, Digital Equipment, Boeing, General Motors, Procter & Gamble, and General Electric—regularly use these workshop methods for management education and training. So do federal government agencies such as the Internal Revenue Service, National Park Service, Forest Service, Central Intelligence Agency, and Office of Personnel Management. The methods are widely used by consultants and management institutes that specialize in the education of executives and managers. We have used all of the activities in this book (or variants of them) with various levels of management in business and government as well as with undergraduate, MBA, and executive MBA students.

After completing Activity 2–1, participants often express their hopes that the course will provide them with understanding and skills that will be useful in the real world of work and, more important, in their personal and university life at present. The fact that managers and executives testify that they get practical, useful learning from workshops conducted within their corporations indicates that the involvement method is on target.

Process Learning Methods

Process learning, or **learning-in-action** (the focus of Module 3), is the central approach in this course. It places primary emphasis on the process of interaction and thinking, rather than on rote memorization of factual content of the area being studied. In contrast, **content learning** is learning based on knowledge, facts, and theory only, which serve as the database for analysis and reasoning. Application of ideas, experience in the subject, and attention to participants' responses are crucial in process learning. We chose this approach because we believe it is more effective for three reasons: (1) Content or subject matter is proliferating so rapidly that knowledge soon becomes outdated. Keeping current will be a lifelong process for any manager; (2) Changes in attitudes and behavior (that is, real learning) come about by doing and understanding, not just by knowing intellectually; (3) The most effective learning is learning in which the student participates knowledgeably.

Because the effective manager will have to continue to learn in a self-directed manner, learning how to learn from his or her own experience acquires a special importance. For each of these issues, process learning has proven superior to content-oriented approaches.

Your experience is important because ultimately *you* must apply and interpret whatever you learn. So we start here. There is no substitute for experience in this as in other matters. You cannot really understand what honey tastes like until you have tasted it, and you cannot comprehend group problem solving until you have been involved and seen it work. You may read a book on skiing or tennis that is very helpful, but you will not really develop skill in your sport until you have practiced it. The same thing could be said about sex—no amount of intellectualizing or theoretical knowledge will substitute for actual experience. So it is with the knowledge of people and interactions that are our subjects. Some differences between process learning and content learning are shown in Figure 2–4.

In an involvement learning course, "students" are participants as well. This condition implies a dual role—that of learning from others and that of contributing to the learning of others. Your views, your reflections, your interactions, your reactions to others, and your ideas are the essential database from which others gain knowledge and develop skills and viewpoints. We assume the classroom activities are where the primary learning takes place, and the textbook only reinforces that process. Therefore, if you are reflecting, interacting, and sharing your views with others, you are providing them with an opportunity to learn. In a sense you are a coach for your fellow participants, just as you will coach your employees in your future role as a manager.

An important component of lifelong learning is the ability to be reflective. The experiential learning approach and theoretical foundations presented earlier in this chapter identified reflection as a critical dimension of learning and experiential learning. In this context, **reflection** is viewed as the mental discipline of distancing yourself from the immediate situation/experience and focusing on understanding the meaning of ideas and situations. Through this process, the mind makes *meaningful connections* between existing knowledge and new experiences and knowledge. These "connections" are the essence of the learning experience: They enable us to *organize* what we know and *interpret* new experiences and knowledge that we encounter. Active reflection is carried out through carefully observing what took place, impartially describing the experience/situation, and exploring the possible implications. As part of the activities in this course, you will have the opportunity to further develop your reflective skills. Module 3 further develops the learning-in-action process.

Figure 2–4
Some Differences between Types of Learning and Methods Used in Process and Content Courses

Process Learning	Content Learning
Ways of thinking	Theories and concepts
Inductive reasoning	Knowledge
Deductive reasoning	Facts
Viewpoints (for example, change as a way of life)	Database for reasoning
Models	
Application of theories and concepts	
Skills	
Interaction	
Communications	
Working with feelings and emotions	
Learning-to-learn skills	
Methods of instruction	*Methods of instruction*
Involvement exercises	Reading
Group exercises	Lecturing
Application case studies	Discussion
Role playing	
Discussion	

APPRECIATIVE INQUIRY AND DEVELOPMENT OF THE LEARNING COMMUNITY

Appreciative Inquiry

The experiential learning approach is anchored in a systematic collaborative inquiry process into a person's own experience. During the last 20 years, *appreciative inquiry* has been developed and advanced as a theory and method for system's learning and development.[30] So, what is appreciative inquiry?

> *Ap-pre' ci-ate, v.,* 1. Valuing; the act of recognizing the best in people or the world around us; affirming past and present strengths, successes, and potentials; to perceive those things that give life (health, vitality, excellence) to living systems. 2. To increase in value; for example, the economy has appreciated in value. Synonyms: valuing, prizing, esteeming, and honoring.
> *In-quire', v.,* 1. The act of exploration and discovery. 2. To ask questions; to be open to seeing new potentials and possibilities. Synonyms: discovery, search, systematic exploration, and study.[31]

At the foundation of appreciative inquiry is the co-inquiry between two or more individuals for the best in people, their organizations, and the relevant world around them. "In its broadest sense, it involves systematic discovery of what gives life to a living system when it is most alive, most effective, and most constructively capable in economic, ecological, and human terms."[32] As such, an integral part of experiential learning is the spirit of appreciative inquiry. We would like individuals to begin to explore the thinking behind their views, the deeper assumptions they may hold, and the evidence they have that leads them to these views with the utmost respect to individual differences. So it will be fair to begin to ask other questions such as, What leads you to say or believe this? or What makes you ask about this?

In his attempt to clarify further, David Cooperrider differentiates between problem solving and appreciative inquiry. Problem solving includes identification of the problem, analysis of the causes, analysis and possible solutions, and action planning; appreciative inquiry includes appreciating and valuing the best of what is, envisioning what might be, and dialoguing on what should be. Appreciative inquiry can be viewed as a cycle composed of four basic elements: *discovery* (what gives life), or the best of what is—appreciating; *dream* (what might be), or what the world is calling for—envisioning results; *design* (what should be, the ideal)—co-constructing; and *destiny* (how to empower, learn, and adjust/improvise)—sustaining. Figure 2–5 illustrates the appreciative inquiry cycle.

Developing a Learning Community

Our approach views the classroom as a dynamic learning social system/**learning community**/organization that is guided by appreciative inquiry. We strive to develop a learning organization. As we saw earlier, a learning system is characterized by a

**Figure 2–5
Appreciative Inquiry
4-D Cycle**

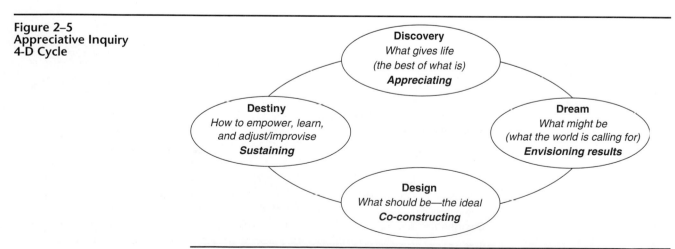

Source: Adapted from D. I. Cooperrider and D. Whitney, "A Positive Revolution in Change: Appreciative Inquiry," 1998.

particular culture, climate, managerial/instructional style, and capacity that enable the entity to improve itself systematically. As such, the system is guided by a set of principles, activities, processes, and structures that enable it to realize the potential inherent in its human capital's knowledge and experience. In the first two activities of this course, our efforts were aimed at developing the interaction and communication atmosphere conducive to learning and the establishment of the foundations for a climate conducive to appreciative inquiry. Some special requirements for the learning organization include:

1. Willingness to immerse oneself in the learning situation/experience.
2. Mutual respect.
3. Appreciation of individual differences and uniqueness.
4. Two-way communication and influence.
5. Openness in expressing views, feelings, and emotions. Tell it like it is, but do so with a respect for others, whose views may differ.
6. Supportiveness. When you are in agreement with others, give them your support. But also learn to express differences without offending. Often two people in conflict are 90 percent in agreement but focus only on their differences. Acknowledging areas of agreement can help provide the basis for a satisfactory resolution, making each person more inclined to consider the validity of the other's view.
7. Recognition that conflict can be creative when differences are expressed appropriately. Differences can lead to new and better perspectives and new bases for acceptable solutions.
8. Effective confrontation:
   a. Do you have the courage to express your own convictions?
   b. Can you take feedback as well as give it usefully?
   c. Are you overly concerned about disagreement or disapproval?
   d. Are you willing to risk learning and change?
   e. Are you using your share of the air time, not too much nor too little?
9. Tolerance for ambiguity, the willingness to explore uncertain issues (which includes most important issues), rather than leaping to what H. L. Mencken called the simple, obvious, and wrong solution that typically presents itself for every complex problem.
10. Active reflection. Support others in developing reflection skills by being patient, impartial, considerate, and thoughtful.

Caution: How much openness is desirable? How much confrontation? How can you effectively protect yourself and others from undue intrusion?

SUMMARY

Differences in perception and expectations among individuals, groups, or levels of the hierarchy of an organization can be sources of conflict and frustration for all concerned. Organizational dialoguing and appreciative inquiry are methods used to explore differences and similarities in expectations in these interface situations and to develop a "psychological contract." In Activity 2–1 dialoguing focuses on instructor–participant expectations relevant to the goals and methods of the course, an additional purpose being to develop the classroom climate/learning community and interaction patterns that will facilitate learning. Activity 2–6W takes the psychological contract one step further: Individuals refine and articulate their learning objectives, goals, potential roadblocks, and desired outcome. The instructor reviews and co-signs the student learning contract. Activity 2–2 provides you with the opportunity to diagnose your learning style, begin the appreciative inquiry process, and appreciate individual differences in your team as they pertain to the individual learning styles. Activity 2–3 takes expectations from the individual level to the team level. Each team is asked to create a name and logo that capture its essence. This activity sets in motion the formation of team identity. Activity 2–4 provides an opportunity to begin the appreciation of challenges that we face when we focus on cognitive development/learning through appreciative inquiry. Activity 2–5 provides an opportunity to sign a team contract around expectations, learning goals, and desired behavior. Activity 2–7W provides an opportunity to explore expectations that managers have about behavior, learning, and performance at work. Overall, the first nine possible activities of the course illustrate the advantage of appreciative inquiry for attitudinal, behavioral, and cognitive learning, with primary emphasis on the process of interaction and thinking rather than on the pure factual content of the area being studied.

Study Questions

1. What is a "psychological contract"? What is the relationship between "psychological contract" and Activities 2–1, 2–3, 2–4, 2–5, or 2–6W?

2. How did Activities 2–1 and 2–3 contribute to the development of the learning community?

3. Describe the roles of expectations, expectations discrepancies, and self-fulfilling prophecy in organizational settings.

4. Explain the relationship among expectation, self-efficacy, learning, experiential learning, and self-learning competency.

5. Discuss the relationship between appreciative inquiry and experiential learning.

6. Identify the differences and similarities among cognitive learning, content learning, and process learning.

7. Explain the basic assumptions about the adult as learner.

8. What are the roles of participants and instructors in an appreciative inquiry–based course?

Endnotes

1. Z. Aycan and H. Kabasakal, "Social Contract and Perceived Justice of Workplace Practices to Cope with Financial Crisis," *Group and Organization Management* 31, no. 4 (2006), pp. 469–502.

2. A. S. Tannenbaum, *Social Psychology of the Work Organization* (Belmont, CA: Wadsworth, 1966), p. 47.

3. R. Likert, *New Patterns of Management* (New York: McGraw-Hill, 1961), p. 91.

4. L. Uchitelle, "Employer-Employee Social Contracts: Fashioning a New Contract for Workers," *The Academy of Management Perspectives* 21, no. 2 (2007), pp. 5–15.

5. E. H. Schein, *Organizational Psychology* (Englewood Cliffs, NJ: Prentice-Hall, 1970), p. 12.

6. D. M. Rousseau, *Psychological Contract in Organizations: Understanding Written and Unwritten Agreements* (Newbury Park, CA: Sage, 1995).

7. S. L. Robinson and D. M. Rousseau, "Violating the Psychological Contract: Not the Exception but the Norm," *Journal of Organizational Behavior* 15 (1994), pp. 245–59; and R. A. Guzzo, K. A. Noonan, and E. Elron, "Expatriate Managers and the Psychological Contract," *Journal of Applied Psychology* 79, no. 4 (1994), pp. 617–26.

8. P. Bosch-Sijtsema, "The Impact of Individual Expectations and Expectation Conflicts on Virtual Teams," *Group and Organization Management* 32, no. 3 (2007), pp. 358–88.

9. J. S. Livingston, "Pygmalion in Management," *Harvard Business Review* 47, no. 4 (1969), pp. 81–89; and J. S. Livingston, "Retrospective Commentary," *Harvard Business Review* (September–October 1988), p. 125.

10. The original scientific work on SFP was conducted by Robert K. Merton and reported in R. K. Merton, "The Self-Fulfilling Prophecy," *Antioch Review* 8 (1948), pp. 193–210. Dov Eden's research provides a holistic understanding of the phenomenon, part of which is published in D. Eden, *Pygmalion in Management* (Lexington, MA: Lexington Books, 1990). A recent study demonstrated the effect of self-fulfilling prophecy on seasickness and performance. See D. Eden and Y. Zuk, "Seasickness as a Self-Fulfilling Prophecy: A Field Experiment on Self-Efficacy and Performance at Sea," *Journal of Applied Psychology* 80 (1995), pp. 628–35. For a comprehensive study that examined the impact of Pygmalion leadership training on leadership effectiveness, see D. Eden et al., "Implanting Pygmalion Leadership Style through Training: Seven Field Experiments," *Leadership Quarterly* 11, no. 2 (2000), pp. 171–210. For a comparative investigation of self-fulfilling prophecy on women leaders, see O. Davidson and D. Eden, "Remedial Self-Fulfilling Prophecy: Two Field Experiments to Prevent Golem Effects among Disadvantaged Women," *Journal of Applied Psychology* 85, no. 3 (2000), pp. 386–98.

11. See, for example, D. Eden and G. Ravid, "Pygmalion vs. Self-Expectancy: Effects of Instructor- and Self-Expectancy on Trainee Performance," *Organizational Behavior and Human Performance* 30 (1982), pp. 351–64; and D. Eden and A. B. Shani, "Pygmalion Goes to Boot Camp: Expectancy, Leadership, and Trainee Performance," *Journal of Applied Psychology* 67 (1982), pp. 194–99.

12. J. Hayes and C. W. Allinson, "Cognitive Style and the Theory and Practice of Individual and Collective Learning in Organizations," *Human Relations* 51, no. 7 (1998), pp. 847–71.

13. A. B. (Rami) Shani and P. Docherty, *Learning by Design: Building Sustainable Organizations* (London, UK: Blackwell Publishing, 2003).

14. A. De Geus, "Planning as Learning," *Harvard Business Review* (March–April 1998), pp. 71–80; and B. Guns, *The Faster Learning Organization* (San Francisco: Jossey-Bass, 1997).

15. While many definitions of learning can be found in the literature, for our purpose we have modified Kolb's definition that can be found in D. A. Kolb, *Experiential Learning* (Englewood Cliffs, NJ: Prentice-Hall, 1984), p. 38.

16. M. J. Marquardt, *Building the Learning Organization* (New York: McGraw Hill, 1996).

17. A. B. (Rami) Shani and Y. Mitki, "Creating the Learning Organization: Beyond Mechanisms," in B. Golembiewski (ed.), *Handbook of Organizational Consultation,* 2nd ed., (New York: Marcel Dekker, 1999).

18. B. Nahan, *Developing People's Ability to Learn* (Brussels: European Interuniversity Press, 1991), p. 16.

19. Adapted from Knowles, *The Adult Learner: A Neglected Species.* See also M. Knowles, E. Holton III, and R. Swanson, *The Adult Learner: The Definitive Classic in Adult Education and Human Resource Development,* 6th ed. (New York: Elsevier, 2005).

20. Adapted from the Critical Thinking Institute, "The Role of Questions in Thinking, Teaching and Learning" (www.criticalthinking.org/university/univclass/roleofquest.html).

21. Ibid.

22. B. S. Bloom et al., *Taxonomy of Educational Objectives, Handbook 1: Cognitive Domain,* (David McKay Company, 1956), pp. 201–207.

23. Ibid.

24. Ibid, p. 41.

25. C. Wiederhold, *The Q-Matrix/Cooperative Learning and Higher-Level Thinking* (San Clemente, CA: Kagan Cooperative Learning, 1997). Adapted from Center for Studies in Higher Order Literacy, "Higher-Order Thinking Strategies for the Classroom" (www.members.aol.com/CSHOLUMK/home.htm). See also E. Blakey, "Developing Metacognition," *ERIC Identifier: ED327218* (New York: ERIC Digest, Clearinghouse on Information Resources, 1990), p. 1.

26. For an in-depth discussion on adults as learners, see M. Knowles, *Self-Directed Learning: A Guide for Learners and Teachers* (Chicago: Association Press, 1975); and M. Knowles, *The Modern Practice of Adult Education: From Pedagogy to Andragogy* (Chicago: Association Press, 1980).

27. The theoretical foundation for experiential learning theory can be found in the works of K. Lewin, *Field Theory in Social Science* (New York: Harper & Row, 1951); J. Dewey, *Experience and Education* (New York: G. P. Putnam Books, 1938); J. Piaget, *Play, Dreams and Imitation in Childhood* (New York: W. W. Norton, 1951); C. Argyris and D. Schon, *Organizational Learning: A Theory of Action* (Reading, MA: Addison-Wesley, 1978); and Kolb, *Experiential Learning*.

28. Ibid; C. Mainemelis, R. Boyatzis, and D. Kolb, "Learning Styles and Adaptive Flexibility: Testing Experiential Learning Theory," *Management Learning* 33, no. 1 (2002), pp. 5–34; and K. L. Murrell, *The Learning-Model Instrument: An Instrument Based on the Learning Model for Managers* (Chicago: Metrex, 1998).

29. J. A. Raelin, "A Model of Work-Based Learning," *Organization Science* 8, no. 6 (1997), pp. 563–78.

30. More than 20 years ago D. L. Cooperrider began to develop the theory and vision for appreciative inquiry and organizational life. Since then, many reports have discussed the utilization of appreciative inquiry in different organizations, systems, and countries. See, for example, D. L. Cooperrider and S. Srivastva, "Appreciative Inquiry and Organizational Life," in W. A. Pasmore and W. Woodman (eds.), *Research in Organization Change and Development*, vol. 1 (Greenwich, CT: JAI Press, 1987), pp. 129–69; G. R. Bushe, "Advances in Appreciative Inquiry as a Team Development Intervention," *Organization Development Journal* 13, no. 3 (1995), pp. 2–22; F. J. Barrett, "Creating Appreciative Learning Cultures," *Organizational Dynamics* 24, no. 1 (1995), pp. 36–49; and D. L. Cooperrider and D. Whitney, "A Positive Revolution in Change: Appreciative Inquiry," *Weatherhead School of Management* (Case Western Reserve University, Cleveland, OH, 1998). For a comprehensive and systematic review of the literature, see R. T. Golembiewski, "Appreciating Appreciative Inquiry," in R. Woodman and W. Pasmore (eds.), *Research in Organization Change and Development*, vol. 11 (Greenwich, CT: JAI Press, 1999), pp. 1–45. A Meta-Case analysis was conducted by Bushe and Kassman in which 20 detailed cases were analyzed; see G. R. Bushe and A. F. Kassam, "When Is Appreciative Inquiry Transformational? A Meta-Case Analysis," *The Journal of Applied Behavioral Science* 41, no. 2 (2005), pp. 161–81.

31. Cooperrider and Srivastva, Ibid.

32. D. Cooperrider and D. Whitney, *Appreciative Inquiry* (San Francisco, CA: Berrett-Koehler, 1999); S. Annis Hammond, *The Thin Book of Appreciative Inquiry* (Plano, TX: Thin Books, 2002); R. Fry, F. Barrett, J. Seiling, and D. Whitney (eds.), *Appreciative Inquiry and Organizational Transformation: Reports from the Field* (Westport, CT: Quorum Books, 2002).

Activity 2–2: Individual Learning Style: Diagnosis and Appreciation of Individual Differences

Objectives:

a. To allow you to examine your own learning style.

b. To provide you and your team an opportunity to get to know each other via the appreciative inquiry learning process.

c. To continue with the development of team and community learning environments.

Name _____   Date _____

THE LEARNING MODEL INSTRUMENT*

Task 1 (Individual Activity):

Step 1: For each statement choose the response that is more true for you. Place an X on the blank that corresponds to that response.

1. When meeting people, I prefer

   ____ *a.* to think and speculate on what they are like.

   ____ *b.* to interact directly and to ask them questions.

2. When presented with a problem, I prefer

   ____ *a.* to jump right in and work on a solution.

   ____ *b.* to think through and evaluate possible ways to solve the problem.

3. I enjoy sports more when

   ____ *a.* I am watching a good game.

   ____ *b.* I am actively participating.

4. Before taking a vacation, I prefer

   ____ *a.* to rush at the last minute and give little thought beforehand to what I will do while on vacation.

   ____ *b.* to plan early and daydream about how I will spend my vacation.

5. When enrolled in courses, I prefer

   ____ *a.* to plan how to do my homework before actually attacking the assignment.

   ____ *b.* to immediately become involved in doing the assignment.

6. When I receive information that requires action, I prefer

   ____ *a.* to take action immediately.

   ____ *b.* to organize the information and determine what type of action would be most appropriate.

7. When presented with a number of alternatives for action, I prefer

   ____ *a.* to determine how the alternatives relate to one another and analyze the consequences of each.

   ____ *b.* to select the one that looks best and implement it.

8. When I awake every morning, I prefer

   ____ *a.* to expect to accomplish some worthwhile work without considering what the individual tasks may entail.

   ____ *b.* to plan a schedule for the tasks I expect to do that day.

9. After a full day's work, I prefer

   ____ *a.* to reflect back on what I accomplished and think of how to make time the next day for unfinished tasks.

   ____ *b.* to relax with some type of recreation and not think about my job.

10. After choosing the above response, I

    ____ *a.* prefer to continue and complete this instrument.

    ____ *b.* am curious about how my responses will be interpreted and would prefer some feedback before continuing with the instrument.

11. When I learn something, I am usually

    ____ *a.* thinking about it.

    ____ *b.* right in the middle of doing it.

12. I learn best when

    ____ *a.* I am dealing with messy real-world issues.

    ____ *b.* concepts are clear and well organized.

13. In order to retain something I have learned, I must

    ____ *a.* periodically review it in my mind.

    ____ *b.* practice it or try to apply the information.

14. In teaching others how to do something, I first

    ____ *a.* demonstrate the task.

    ____ *b.* explain the task.

*Copyright by Kenneth L. Murrell. All rights reserved, and no reproduction should be made without the expressed approval of Professor Murrell, University of West Florida. We appreciate Professor Murrell's permission to include this activity in this textbook.

15. My favorite way to learn to do something is

____   *a.* reading a book of instructions or enrolling in a class.

____   *b.* trying to do it *and learning* from my mistakes.

16. When I become emotionally involved with something, I usually

____   *a.* let my feelings take the lead and then decide what to do.

____   *b.* control my feelings and try to analyze the situation.

17. If I were meeting jointly with several experts on a subject, I would prefer

____   *a.* to ask each of them for his or her opinion.

____   *b.* to interact with them and share our ideas and feelings.

18. When I am asked to relate information to a group of people, I prefer

____   *a.* not to have an outline, but to interact with them and become involved in an extemporaneous conversation.

____   *b.* to prepare notes and know exactly what I am going to say.

19. Experience is

____   *a.* a guide for building theories.

____   *b.* the best teacher.

20. People learn easier when they are

____   *a.* doing work on the job.

____   *b.* in a class taught by an expert.

Name _____ Date _____

THE LEARNING MODEL INSTRUMENT SCORING SHEET

Step 2: Transfer your responses by writing either *a* or *b* in the blank that corresponds to each item in the Learning Model Instrument.

	Abstract/Concrete		Cognitive/Affective	
	Column 1	Column 2	Column 3	Column 4
	1. _____	2. _____	11. _____	12. _____
	3. _____	4. _____	13. _____	14. _____
	5. _____	6. _____	15. _____	16. _____
	7. _____	8. _____	17. _____	18. _____
	9. _____	10. _____	19. _____	20. _____
Total circles	_____	_____	_____	_____
Grand totals	_____		_____	

Step 3: Now circle every *a* in column 1 and in column 4. Then circle every *b* in column 2 and column 3. Next total the circles in each of the four columns. Then add the totals of columns 1 and 2; plot this grand total on the vertical axis of the Learning Model for Managers and draw a horizontal line through the point. Now add the totals of columns 3 and 4; plot that grand total on the horizontal axis of the model and draw a vertical line through the point. The intersection of these two lines indicates the domain of your preferred learning style.

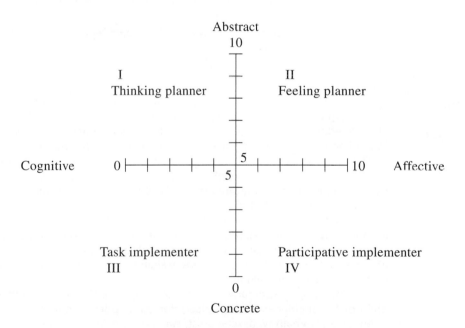

The Learning Model for Managers

Because each individual has a unique learning style, teams will be composed of a variety of learning strengths. This diversity can be an advantage for a well-integrated team, assuming there is built-in mutual respect for the inherent differences. In planning and decision making, the range of learning styles can greatly add value to the process. Organizations like teams can take advantage of different learning styles to organize around particular strengths. Operating decisions and strategic thinking both can be enriched if the organization makes a special effort to value the learning differences of its members. Ideally in these fast changing times, both individuals and organizations will learn to learn better together by understanding and using different learning styles shown here.

Task 2 (Team Activity):

Individuals are to meet in their teams, share scores, and explore their meaning. The following is a suggestion on how to conduct the sharing and begin the appreciative inquiry process.

- Each person, in turn, should share with the group his or her thoughts on the following three topics:
    a. How do you characterize the way in which you learn? Do your learning profile scores seem valid to you? Why?
    b. What are some of your greatest strengths as a learner?
    c. What might be a learning strength (competence or skill) that you would want to develop?
    d. How could the team and/or learning community help you acquire that desired learning strength?
- Other team members may ask clarifying questions as each individual speaks. However, the team should budget its time carefully to provide each team member with the airtime to share his or her insights.
- A spokesperson for each team will provide a brief report to the total class on the main points of the team's discussion.

The Learning Model Instrument Interpretation Sheet	The cognitive-affective axis or continuum represents the range of ways in which people learn. Cognitive learning includes learning that is structured around either rote storing of knowledge, intellectual abilities and skills, or both. Affective learning includes learning from experience, from feelings about the experience, and from one's own emotions.

The concrete-abstract axis or continuum represents the range of ways in which people experience life. When people experience life abstractly, they detach themselves from the immediacy of the situation and theorize about it. If they experience life concretely, they respond to the situation directly with little subsequent contemplation.

The two axes divide the model into four parts or domains. Most people experience life and learn from it in all four domains but have a preference for a particular domain. Liberal arts education has typically concentrated on abstract learning (domains I and II), whereas vocational and on-the-job training usually takes place in the lower quadrants, particularly domain III.

Occupations representative of the four styles include the following: domain I, philosopher or chief executive officer; domain II, poet or journalist; domain III, architect or engineer, domain IV, psychologist, supervisor, or team leader.

Managerial jobs require an ability to learn in all four domains, and a manager's development depends on his or her ability to learn both cognitively and affectively. Thus management education and development demand the opportunity for the participants to learn how to learn in each domain.

Activity 2–3: Group Dialoguing: The Development of a Team Name and Logo

Objective:

To help the newly formed teams begin to develop a distinct identity.

Task 1:

The newly assigned team is to get together and brainstorm about a name for itself. The name that the group agrees on is going to be the team's name throughout the course. You might want to choose a name that reflects who you are, that you can be proud of, and that reflects what you would like to become as a team.

Task 2:

Working together as a group, your assignment is to create a team logo, on a regular size page, that captures creatively who you are. Your team logo is due at the beginning of the next class session.

Task 3:

A group spokesperson will be asked to share with the rest of the learning community your team's name, its logo, and how they were developed or created.

Activity 2–4: Developing a Questioning Mind*

Objectives:

a. To help you understand Bloom's Taxonomy and its relationship to the cognitive development of individuals.
b. To facilitate the development of your critical thinking skills through the process of asking questions.

Task 1 (Individual Homework Activity):

Step 1: Review the reading on "Rationality in Managing" in Module 1.
Step 2: Compose a list of 10 questions that you think would facilitate a significant learning experience on the topic of "rationality in managing" for a group of your peers.
Step 3: Select the best three questions to share with your group.

Task 2 (In-Class Team Activity):

- Each person should share with the group his or her three questions and discuss the intended learning outcome of each question.
- Select the three most thought-provoking questions from the group discussion to share with the class. Be prepared to discuss the intended learning outcome of each question and their value in creating a meaningful learning experience.

Task 3:

Each team will present its questions and the intended learning outcomes to the total learning community.

Task 4: (Team Activity)

- Categorize your questions according to their ability to facilitate thinking at the six levels of Bloom's Taxonomy.
- Develop a question that will facilitate thinking at each level of Bloom's Taxonomy that is missing from your list of questions.

*Developed and contributed by our colleague Cory Willson. We are grateful to Cory.

Activity 2–5: Developing a Team Contract*

Objectives:

To help you develop a team contract that outlines expectations, goals, and rules of interactions.

Team Instructions: You will develop a "team contract" outlining (1) team expectations, (2) team goals, (3) team member strengths and chosen area for skill development (each person will pick one skill area of interest from the "Questionnaire on Group Skills Development") and a member who will act as his or her coach, (4) policies for rules and interactions, and (5) at least two established meetings for this quarter. In the following, you will find subheadings related to each of the listed contract elements. *If you finish the five requirements and have time remaining, brainstorm a team name.*

Finishing all five of the contract elements is likely unrealistic for this class period. Your instructor will not grade the assignment (although he or she will read the contracts closely). The class today is designed to stimulate your team's thinking around the preceding issues. Thus, to the extent that your team converses about some, but not all of the elements, the exercise will be a productive one.

At the end of the class period, give the contract to your instructor.

*Developed and contributed by our colleague Dawn Chandler. We are grateful to Dawn.

Team Name _____   Date _____

TEAM CONTRACT

1. *Team expectations.* Write out at least *three* team expectations related to issues such as attendance (to class or outside meetings), level of participation, communication, and productivity (e.g., work quality). For example, you might determine that you expect all team members to check their e-mail once a day as a means to effectively communicate.

2. *Team goals.* List two or more team goals (write out goals in full sentences). Attempt to develop measurable goals (for example, "Our team will demonstrate high-quality work by achieving a B+ or better on all assignments").

3. *Team members' strengths and areas for development.* For each team member, write down a perceived strength and an area identified for development (the latter is based on "Questionnaire on Group Skills Development"). Examples of strengths are attentiveness to detail, excellent or good writing skills, presentation skills, and PowerPoint proficiency. With respect to each person's chosen area for development, identify a peer coach who will aid that person's growth throughout the quarter.

Team Member Name:

a. Strength

b. Areas for development

c. Name of peer coach (individual who will help the team member's development)

4. *Team Policies/Rules.* To ensure that the team's expectations are met, state several policies or rules that will guide members' behavior.

5. *First two class meetings*

Scheduled (or likely) meeting time: _____

Scheduled (or likely) meeting time: _____

Member Signatures (Write in names of team members.)

1. _____
2. _____
3. _____
4. _____
5. _____

Module 3

Learning-in-Action*

LEARNING OBJECTIVES

After completing this module, you should be able to

1. Know how to engage in learning-in-action so as to engage with the material of organizational behavior.
2. Explain the many terms that describe the various approaches to learning-in-action: action inquiry, action research, action learning, reflective practice, work-based learning, action science, collaborative inquiry.
3. Describe the four phases in journaling.
4. Begin the development of the reflective practitioner skill.
5. Gain insights into how to reflect on-action *and* in-action.
6. Acquire the skills of comprehensive journal writing.
7. Know how to test assumptions and inferences.

KEY TERMS AND CONCEPTS

Action inquiry

Action learning

Action research

Action science

Collaborative inquiry

Experiential learning

Journal keeping

Process consultation

Reflective practice

Reflective practitioner

Work-based learning

MODULE OUTLINE

Premodule Preparation

    Activity 3–1: Learning-in-Action Skills

    Activity 3–2: Capturing the Team's Experience: Practicing Journal Writing

* This module was developed by Dr. David Coghlan of Trinity College Dublin's (Ireland) School of Business. We are grateful to Dr. Coghlan.

PREMODULE PREPARATION

Activity 3–1: Learning-in-Action Skills

Objective:

To help individuals develop skills in attending to their own inner cognitive processes and to outer events.

Task 1:

Select a term paper that you have written recently. Review the rough notes you wrote from the beginning in the original plan; work through the different revisions, additions, and subtractions to the final product. Note the blind alleys that you explored, the insights when things fitted together, the frustration of not finding your way out of the confusion, and the sense of satisfaction when it was completed and handed in.

Task 2:

Open a double page of your notebook and on the left-hand page write down the progress of a conversation you have (or have had) with another person with whom you are working (or have worked) on a project. Write down what you said and what the other person said and what you said in response and so on. Then on the opposite page write down what you have been thinking privately about what is being said in the conversation and what you have *not* said. Notice then what differences there are, especially where you are forming judgments about the other person's attitude and motivations, and how you tried to counter them without being up-front about what you were thinking because you were trying to be sensitive to the other person's feelings. (See Table 3–3 on page 55 for an example.)

Activity 3–2: Capturing the Team's Experience: Practicing Journal Writing

Objective:

To help individuals begin to develop reflective practitioner skills by utilizing journal writing methodology.

Task 1:

Select the most recent team activity in which your team had to work on a task and deliver an outcome. Using the four phases of journaling listed subsequently, write your journal entry. According to Coghlan and Brannick (2005) there are four phases at the center of a manager's reflective practitioner skills: experiencing, reflecting, interpreting, and taking action.[1] As such, you are being asked to organize your journal entry following these four phases.

- *Experiencing.* As we go through life we experience a great deal. Some of our experiences are planned; others are unplanned. Some are what others do to us. Some experiences are cognitive; they occur through the intellectual processes of thinking and understanding. Some occur in feelings and emotions. At times we feel angry, frustrated, sad, lonely, and so on. Others may be experienced in the body: excited energy, embarrassed blushing, tightness in the stomach, lump in the throat, ulcers, headaches, and so on. Experiencing occurs in these three areas—cognitive, feelings, and body awareness—and we can learn by attending to them.[2]

- *Reflecting.* Attending to experience is the first step in learning. The second step is to stand back from these experiences and ask questions about them (inquire into them). Reflection is the process of stepping back from experiences to inquire what they mean so that we may understand them. By reflecting we move beyond raw experience to make explicit to ourselves what we have experienced.

- *Interpreting.* Interpreting is where we find answers to the questions posed in the reflection. We can draw on theory and constructs to help us make sense of the experiences.

- *Taking action.* Taking action is the process of acting as a consequence of experiencing, reflecting, and interpreting.

For example, as you participate in a team project, you may notice yourself feeling flushed and tense (experience). On reflection you realize that you are getting annoyed at one of your team members whose behavior in the team is antagonizing you. As you interpret your annoyance, ask yourself whether it is coming from your expectations or whether it is behavior in the group. Your interpretation now needs to distinguish between whether your perceptions and expectations (Module 6) are the issue and your intolerance or short fuse is what needs examination or whether it is a particular team member performing a particular team role that, while it antagonizes you, is valuable for the team (Modules 11 and 12). In this way, theory is helping you understand what is happening. Now you have to decide what you are going to do and how you are going to behave at the next team meeting.

Task 2:

After completing Task 1, take 10 minutes and try to capture some insights about areas of strengths and weaknesses that you have in the practice of journaling. Identify ways in which you can improve your journaling.

INTRODUCTION

Do you practice learning in action? Most people understand what "learning" and "action" mean when they are used in sentences by themselves. Put together, as "learning-in-action," new and potent ways to performance and learning emerge.[3] As we have discussed in Module 2, learning is an act or process by which behavioral change, knowledge, skills, and attitudes are acquired. What differentiates us humans from other forms of living organisms is our ability to be self-aware, that is, to be conscious of ourselves as we ask questions, hold opinions, weigh options and make decisions, and take actions. This self-awareness is central to learning and to learning-in-action because it means that we can be aware of our experience, ask questions about it, come to judgments about it, and make decisions and take action.[4] Following our initial exploration of learning, experiential learning, self-learning competency, appreciative inquiry and cognitive learning, content learning, and process learning and basic assumptions about the adult as learner in the previous module, the focus in this module is on the development of the reflective practitioner skills that are embedded in a learning-in-action orientation. The module begins with the topic of knowing and argues that knowing the steps in the process of human knowing and doing provides an essential foundation for both studying and engaging in how people behave in organizations.

THE PROCESS OF HUMAN KNOWING

What are we doing when we know something? We begin, not with a theory but by attending to what it is that we are doing when we know and by developing confidence in our own knowing.

Experience

Knowing begins with experience. Experience is an interaction of inner and outer events. Inner events are your own thoughts, feelings, imagining, remembering, and so on, and outer events are what your five senses see, hear, taste, feel, smell, or touch. But seeing something is not knowing it; imagining something is not knowing it. Otherwise you would have to hold that people who have difficulties with seeing or hearing or who have no sense of smell could not know anything. Or you would not be able to distinguish between what you imagine and what is real. If you hear a noise, it is not the sound that tells you what the noise is. Rather it is the experience of the noise that leads to the question that you ask: What was that? Right now you are reading these words on this page. If you stay at the level of experience, all you are doing is seeing dots on sheets of paper.

Understanding

You go beyond experience by asking questions. What was that noise I heard? What do these dots on the page mean? So you get an insight into what the noise that you heard was. Was it someone crying for help? Was it coming from the TV downstairs or from out in the street? Insight is an act of understanding that provides an intelligible answer to the question you have from experience. This act of understanding grasps a pattern in data. So you say, that cry for help is from the TV; it didn't sound like a person in the street. Your act of understanding can happen quickly or more slowly. It was easy for you to understand that the voice was from the TV. You are reading this module right now. In order to go beyond the mere sense experience of seeing the dots on the page, you are engaging in understanding by relating these words and ideas to what you already think and know. Do you get it? Do you get what I'm at in these pages? Maybe so far, you don't get it. "Getting it" occurs all the time and in all sorts of situations. This might take more time than figuring out where the cry for help is coming from.

The search for understanding is intelligent, focusing on the question or problem. While you don't know yet if your search is intelligent, you anticipate intelligent answers. It is one thing to have an insight and quite another to state clearly just what it is you have understood. Insights reoccur and accumulate, and so the habit of understanding develops. You are continuously transforming yourself from being questioner to being an "understander" and coming to understand the activity of understanding. This is a process of learning.

You may also get insights that there is no intelligibility, that there is no sense to something, like when you are asked the old joke, "How would you know if there was an elephant in your fridge?"

Judgment

We get lots of insights every day. They are not always accurate or true. The question then is, Is the insight accurate? This opens up a question for reflection. Is it so? Yes or no? The shift in attention turns to accuracy, sureness, and certainty of understanding. Was it a voice in the street or a voice on the TV? You decide that the evidence is such that you can affirm that the cry for help was not from a real person in trouble in the street outside but a voice on the TV. Or if you are not sure, then you check. You might look out the window, and then you have to understand what you see or don't see outside. Or you check what's on TV downstairs and if it's a police drama that might confirm your insight, as you remember that people often scream and cry for help in police dramas. Now you have moved to a new level of the cognitional process, where you have marshaled and weighed evidence and assessed its sufficiency. Now as you read this chapter, you have to decide whether your insight into what I'm getting at in these pages is accurate or not.

Deciding and Doing

We need to distinguish judgments of fact and judgments of value. A judgment of fact affirms that something is true or false or is correct or not. A judgment of value affirms that something is good/bad, valuable/valueless, and so on. Making decisions and taking action follow judgments that have some value attached to them. You can make judgment of fact; it is the noise I heard. If you have judged that it is a voice on TV, then you can choose to ignore it and continue what you were doing. If you judge that it is a person crying for help out in the street, you can make a judgment of value that it is terrible that someone is being attacked in the street. Maybe you say to yourself, "I need to do something about it, so I'll phone the police or I'll go out and intervene." Or you may say to yourself, "I'm not getting involved. Let someone else sort that out." Then you have made a judgment of value that places more value on your own safety or convenience than the other person's safety. What you decide is good or bad leads to a decision to do something or not. This opens up questions of value, morality, and ethics.

In summary, human knowing is a three-step process: experience, understanding, and judgment. Human knowing is not any of these three activities by themselves. Experience is not knowing. So taking a look at something does not constitute knowing it. The "aha" of insight is not knowing until it is verified by judgment. Knowing is the result of the complex operations of experiencing, understanding, and judging. Knowing can be accompanied by making decisions and taking action, when the judgment is a judgment of value. A judgment of value, as contrasted with a judgment of fact, leads to consideration of whether to do something or not and what to do.

Learning is the process that describes changes in knowing and doing. When you learn, you know something new or know it differently and you behave differently. In this module you are seeking to engage in learning-in-action; you learn how to learn as you go or "with your boots on" as John Wayne might have put it. There are many frameworks that describe adult experiential learning, and this module presents some of them. You'll notice that while these frameworks may use different terminology and have different emphases, they all boil down to the core process experience, understanding, judgment, and decision/action. (See Table 3–1 below.)

Table 3–1 The Operations of Human Knowing		
	Experience	Seeing, hearing, smelling, tasting, touching, remembering, imagining, feeling
	Understanding	Inquiring, understanding, formulating what is being understood
	Judgment	Marshaling evidence, testing, judging
	Decision/action	Deliberating, valuing, deciding, choosing, taking action, behaving

TAKING AN ATTITUDE OF INQUIRY

Having an attitude of inquiry is integral to being human, as you saw in Module 2. Questioning is at the core of adult learning. As you experience processes in organizations, you see things and you hear things. How do you understand them? And then what judgments do you make about them? So you need to learn to be attentive to what is happening and to ask yourself relevant questions, questions based on wanting to find out what is going on. Keep an open mind as to what events might mean until you have verified by judgment. Inquiring attentiveness to organizational processes that occur around you is a core skill for you to learn. You can learn to observe yourself being an observer and learn to understand yourself as a questioner. As you engage with the material in this textbook and begin to apply it to your experiences in the workplace, whether in part-time jobs you might be doing in conjunction with your studies or in group projects you do as part of this and other courses and in future employment, you are developing an attentiveness to what goes on and a spirit of inquiry. If you are attentive and inquiring while these events are happening, you are engaging in learning-in-action.

The world of organizational behavior is complex and messy because human beings are wonderful, unique, and unpredictable. We can be enthusiastic one day and be stressed another. We can be skilled at working in groups and be unfocused in planning. We can be inconsistent. We change our minds. As the chapters in this textbook aptly discuss, behavior in organizations is a world of adventure as we try to understand people and work with them across a variety of organizational settings, structures, and tasks.

Accordingly, we need to understand our ways of knowing in settings that shift and change. For example, the weekly team meeting is not totally predictable. Some weeks people may feel that the meeting went well; on other occasions people may complain about that "awful meeting." Yet it is the same people meeting to discuss the same issues. In these shifting settings, knowing cannot be constant in the way that one knows that a scientific formula will always provide the same answer. Organizational behavior varies from place to place and from situation to situation. What is familiar in one place may be unfamiliar in another. No two situations are identical. Time has passed. The place has changed. We remember differently. So in each of these situations we attend to experience, seek insights, and make judgments in order to know how to act. You can say one thing in one setting but not in another; something will work in one setting but not in another. This is why we reason, reflect, and judge in order to move from one setting to another, grasping what we can understand in a given situation in order to know what to say and do.

In sum, the world of organizational behavior is different from the world of engineering and science. Revans makes a useful distinction between "puzzles," which are those difficulties for which there is a single solution and are amenable to expert advice, and "problems," which are those difficulties where there is no single solution because people advocate different solutions, depending on their values, past experience, and intended outcomes.[5] In a not dissimilar vein, Schon contrasts how researchers can view practice from the high ground, where they can study issues from a distance, for example, because they are not organizational members or because their data are based on preconstructed surveys or interviews.[6] Or they can be immersed in "swampy lowlands" where problems are messy and confusing and incapable of a technical solution, because they are either organizational members whose actions influence the reality they see or are outsiders who are contracted to influence what they see. He concludes that unimportant issues may be studied from the high ground according to predetermined standards and rigor, while the critically important ones, such as how to generate whatever changes in practice we wish to see, can only be confronted by being immersed in the swampy lowlands. This module is adopting the perspective of engaging in organizational behavior as "problems" in Revans' sense and as Schon's "swampy lowlands."

"Inquiry from the inside" and "inquiry from the outside" are two modes of inquiry presented by Evered and Louis.[7] They juxtapose the two approaches. Inquiry from the outside refers to traditional science where the researchers' relationship to the setting is detached and neutral. The basis for validity is measurement and logic. Typically researchers act as onlookers, and they apply a priori categories to create universal,

Table 3–2 Issues and Roles of Engagement in Puzzles and Problems		Puzzles	Problems
	Issues	Technical issues have a single solution and are amenable to expert advice.	Problems are messy, with no single solution and are not amenable to expert advice. People propose different solutions out of their own perspectives and values.
	Roles of engagement	Detached observers and experts who can analyze, assess, and make recommendations based on their expertise	Actors who are close to the action and who engage in experience, understanding, judgment, and decision/action and collaborate with others to solve problems

context-free knowledge. In contrast, inquiry from the inside involves researchers as actors, immersed in local situations generating contextually embedded knowledge that emerges from experience. Learning-in-action is about engaging in the everyday actions of the organization as an active participant, as an insider, attending to what goes on around you in a spirit of inquiry (What's going on? Why is that happening?), having insights, making judgments, and, where appropriate, taking action.[8]

To learn from your experience of behavior in organizations, you need to attend to how you are experiencing, understanding, and judging these events. You bring the quality of your knowing process to your judgments about organizational situations, and by attending to experience, understanding, and judgment you can develop some clarity about the judgments you make about these situations. So as you make judgments about organizational processes you can articulate how you have made these judgments. In this way you can learn to distinguish between what you actually know and what you infer. Distinguishing between what you actually know, what you think you know (but haven't verified), and what you know that you don't know is critical. The minefield is where you don't know that you don't know and where you act unwittingly.

REFLECTION

Reflection is the process of stepping back from experience to process what the experience means, where you search for insight into an experience with a view to understanding it and to moving on to planning and taking further action. It is the critical link between the concrete experience, the interpretation, and taking new action. It is the key to learning as it enables you to develop an ability to uncover and make explicit to yourself what you have planned, discovered, and achieved in practice. So you reflect on your thoughts (How was I thinking about this situation?), your feelings (How did I feel in that situation?), and the process (What was going on in that situation?). It is useful to share your reflections so that your privately held taken for granted assumptions may be exposed and tested, which helps you to see how your knowledge is constructed.

Reflection takes us to different areas of our experience. There are four areas of experience.[9]

- *Intentionality.* This is the area of purpose, goals, aims, and vision.
- *Planning.* This is the area of plans, strategy, tactics, ploys, and schemes.
- *Action.* This is the area of action, behavior, implementation, skills, and performance.
- *Outcomes.* This is the area of results, outcomes, consequences, and effects.

The parallel equivalent for organizations is visioning, strategizing, performing, and assessing. The central process of learning-in-action is to develop our awareness, understanding, and skills in each of these areas. Inquiry helps us to understand our intentions, develop our capacity to plan, develop strategies that reflect our aspirations, reflect on the skills of our implementation, and see the impact of our actions. Inquiry can also take us through how each of the areas is linked. Refer to Figure 3–1. A first or

**Figure 3–1
Single-, Double-, and Triple-Loop Inquiry**

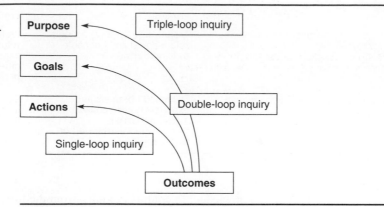

Adapted from D. Fisher, D. Rooke, and W. Torbert, *Personal and Organizational Transformation through Action Inquiry* (Boston: Edge\Work Press, 2000).

single-loop inquiry can begin from outcomes and inquire into how we acted to produce those outcomes. A second or double-loop inquiry can take us from outcomes to action to what we intended or planned. A third or triple-loop inquiry can take us from outcomes, through action, and through strategy to ask questions about our intention, aspirations, and values.

A good deal of our reflection is reflection *on* action; that is, it is a retrospective look at what has happened. The U.S. military has developed a sophisticated approach, called *After Action Review* (AAR), whereby postmortems on events can move from being a review of the past to a living practice that anticipates issues and generates emergent learning *in* action.[10] The skill to learn is the skill to move from reflection-on-action to reflection-in-action. (See Figure 3–2 for some useful techniques to help reflection.)

Experience and understanding are grounded in directly observable behavior, that is, things that we see and what we hear, about which there is no dispute. If we had a video running, we would all see what people did and hear what they said. The problem arises when we move beyond what we see and hear and begin to infer meanings and attribute motives: "She did that because she wants attention." The *ladder of inference* plots how meanings and assumptions are attributed to selected observable data and experiences, and conclusions and beliefs are adopted on which actions are based.[11] For example, at a team meeting you make a proposal for action. One of your colleagues, Joe, doesn't say anything. You think he looks as if he is sulking and conclude that he is sulking because his proposal has not been considered. Accordingly, you decide that Joe won't be on your

**Figure 3–2
Ladder of Inference**

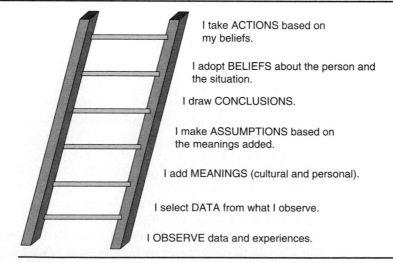

I take ACTIONS based on my beliefs.

I adopt BELIEFS about the person and the situation.

I draw CONCLUSIONS.

I make ASSUMPTIONS based on the meanings added.

I add MEANINGS (cultural and personal).

I select DATA from what I observe.

I OBSERVE data and experiences.

Table 3–3   **Right-Hand–Left-Hand Column Technique**

Conversation	Private Thoughts Not Said
Me: How are you progressing on your part of the assignment? When will you have it done so that we can meet to put our parts together? **Other:** I've not got it completed yet; I'm really only at the start as I've been working out what is being asked of us.	I suspect that he has not done anything on our assignment, but I had better go easy as he's likely to get upset and become impossible to work with and we have to produce the assignment jointly.
Me: What is confusing you as to what is being required of us in the assignment? **Other:** Well it's everything really. I just don't get the assignment.	As I suspected; he has done nothing. He's playing dumb and is waiting for me to do the work. Let me put him on the spot in a gentle way. You mean you haven't even read the readings on which the assignment is based.
Me: Why don't you ask the professor? She'll help you clarify what the assignment is about. If we don't hand in our assignment on time we'll have marks deducted. **Other:** I'm in enough trouble with that professor from a previous course so I couldn't ask her.	You're one lazy person and I'm stuck with you for the remainder of the course. We won't be able to work together. This is a disaster for me and the end of any hope of a decent grade.

side and that you cannot rely on him for support and subsequently you do not inform him of meetings as the project progresses. What has happened here is that you observed an event, that is, colleagues responding to your proposal (directly observable behavior). You selected part of that event (Joe not speaking) and added your own interpretations and meaning, which you did share or test (inference and attribution), and then your own subsequent actions of excluding Joe from further meetings were based on the beliefs and assumptions deduced from your private interpretation. In terms of the image of a ladder, you have ascended the steps of inference, from the bottom rung of what is directly observable behavior to upper rungs of acting on privately held, untested inferences. The ladder of inference helps us retrace our steps from what we have seen and heard (directly observable behavior) to the conclusions we draw (inferences and attributions). The challenge is how to inquire into other people's thoughts so that you're not jumping to conclusions.

Table 3–3 provides a scenario by which you can see the ladder of inference in action by means of the *right-hand–left-hand column* technique. Notice how Me in the case is making inferences about why Other has not done the work and attributes laziness to him and then easily moves to writing off a good grade for the course.

The right-hand–left-hand column technique, which was introduced in Task 2 of Activity 3–1, can help you learn how to censor your conversations and uncover your own privately held inferences and attributions. By this method you can learn to identify how you filter information and make inferences and attributions privately in your own head out of what is rather hazy evidence (what you think others' motivations are) and how you act on them by what you say in response.

DEVELOPING REFLECTIVE SKILLS THROUGH JOURNALING

Journal keeping is a significant mechanism for developing reflective skills. You note your observations and experiences in a journal and over time learn to differentiate between different experiences and ways of dealing with them. Journal keeping helps you reflect on experiences, see how you think about them, and anticipate future experiences before you undertake them. It enables you to integrate information and experiences which, when understood, help you understand your reasoning processes and consequent behavior and so anticipate experiences before embarking on them. Keeping a journal regularly imposes a discipline and captures your experience of key events close to when they happen and before the passage of time changes your perception of them.

Journals may be set to a particular structure. Schein's observation, reaction, judgment, intervention (ORJI) model is a useful one and complements the other frameworks in this module.[12] The ORJI model focuses on what goes on inside your head and how it affects your covert behavior. You observe (O); react emotionally to what you have observed (R); analyze, process, and make judgments based on the observations and feelings (J); and intervene in order to make something happen (I). Schein pays particular attention to the movement from observation to judgment, because he believes that frequently the individual does not pay attention to the reaction stage. In his view, the individual typically denies feelings, short circuits them, and moves straight to judgment and action. You may react to an event by saying to yourself, "That's stupid"—a judgment. What you have probably done is to miss an emotional reaction of feeling threatened by the event. You may not have recognized or acknowledged that feeling of being threatened, yet it is present and is governing your judgment. By learning to identify and attend to feelings as initial reactions and as influencing judgments, you may learn to deal with them and choose whether or not to act on them. Denial of feelings frequently means acting on them without adverting to the fact that you are acting on them. Acknowledgment of feelings to yourself and the subsequent judgment as to the origins and validity of those feelings are critical to learning and change. Activity 3–3 provides an opportunity to practice the ORJI method.

Learning-in-action is not only about you as an individual. Organizational behavior comprises not only behavior at the individual, team, interdepartmental group, and organization level but also across these levels.[13] When working in groups, you'll be inquiring into what the experience of the group is, what insights individual members of the group have, what judgments they make, and how they take action. If you're working at the interdepartmental group level, then you'll be inquiring into what experience the different participating groups have, what insights they have, and so on. At the organization level, experience, understanding through insight, judgment, and decision refer to complex engagement with the external environment and with multiple stakeholders, both inside and outside the organization, and to how the organization engages with the strategic process. When you study business strategy and policy, you will learn to understand the experience and insights at industry and global levels. You will also notice how these levels are interrelated, for example, how the work of an individual can affect the work of the team (for better or for worse) or how the work of one team can impact on the work of another team. So what you are learning becomes increasingly more complex.

HELPING OTHERS TO LEARN-IN-ACTION

There are many ways in which to help other people learn. We're familiar with the teaching approach, where an instructor gives theory input in a lecture and structures application by means of setting and giving feedback on assignments. We give advice to one another all the time. However, helping people learn themselves requires skill. It involves adopting an appreciative stance (Module 2) and being able to listen and to intervene in such a manner that the other person is able to engage in their own reflection on experience, have their own insights, make their own judgments, and develop their own action strategies. Professor Edgar Schein calls this approach **process consultation**.[14]

He describes several types of inquiry. His first category is what he calls *pure inquiry.* This is where you prompt the elicitation of the story of what is taking place and listen carefully and neutrally. You ask, "What is going on? Tell me what happened." The second type of inquiry is what Schein calls *exploratory diagnostic inquiry,* in which you begin to manage the process of how the other person can have insights into his or her experience by exploring reasoning, emotional processes, and actions. So you may ask,

**Table 3–4
Helping Others
Learning-in-Action**

	Intervention	Examples
Uncovering experience	*Pure inquiry*	What is going on? What happened? Tell me the story. What did you do?
Probing for insight	*Exploratory–diagnostic inquiry*	Why do you think that happened? What do you think is going on? How do you feel about that? What are you going to do?
Aiming for judgment and decision/action	*Confrontive*	Have you considered . . . ? If you read . . . , you might find an explanation.

"Why do you think this happened? What did you do? How do you feel about this? What are you going to do?" and so on. The third type of inquiry is what Schein calls *confrontive inquiry*. This is where you, by sharing your own ideas, challenge the other to think from a new perspective. These ideas may refer to process and content. Examples of *confrontive* questions would be, Have you thought about doing this . . . ? Have you considered that . . . might be a solution? Activity 3–4 provides a structure for you to practice these intervention skills. (See Table 3–4 above.)

APPROACHES TO LEARNING-IN-ACTION

There are a number of approaches to learning-in-action that are well-established and widely used in different contexts. While you may not be using them explicitly in this course, they are important to know, both for the field of organizational behavior and for how they inform the theory and practice of learning-in-action. Appreciative inquiry would be included in this section, but it is covered in Module 2.

Experiential Learning

In Module 2, we presented two slightly different approaches to **experiential learning,** the one by Kolb and the one by Murrell. Experiential learning is a term used in training and development and is often associated with the work of David Kolb.[15] He describes adult learning in terms of four activities: experiencing, reflection, conceptualization, and experimentation. Attending to experience is the first step to learning. The second step is to stand back from these experiences and inquire into them. Then you conceptualize what the reflection means and draw on theories and constructs to help you make sense of your experience. Then you attempt to behave differently, which sets up a new experience, and so the cycle continues. Learning becomes a continuous cycle through life. Learning is not any one of these four activities on its own but each of them together. You need to develop skills at each activity: be able to experience directly; be able to stand back and ask questions; be able to conceptualize answers to your questions; and be able to take risks and experiment in similar or new situations. This approach was introduced in Module 2.

Action Research

Action research in its traditional sense comes from the work of Kurt Lewin and involves a collaborative change management or problem-solving relationship between an organization development (OD) consultant and client aimed at both solving a problem and generating new knowledge.[16] The researcher and client engage in collaborative cycles of planning, taking action, and evaluating. Action research is central to the theory and practice of organization development.[17]

Action Learning

Action learning comes from the work of Reg Revans. Marquardt presents six distinct interactive components of action learning: a problem, a group that engages in a questioning and reflective process and trying to solve the problem, a commitment to taking action about the problem, a commitment to learning from the process, and a learning coach to help the learning process.[18]

Action Science

Action science is associated with the work of Chris Argyris.[19] In action science, you focus on how your actions tend to produce defensiveness and undesired outcomes, the opposite of what you intend. This happens because you hold assumptions that govern your behavior, and you make private inferences and attributions about the motives and thought processes of others that you do not test. Accordingly, the core of the action science is learning how to identify the assumptions that govern behavior and develop skills at testing assumptions and inferences, while at the same time exposing your own privately held theories to public testing. Argyris places an emphasis on the cognitive processes of individuals' "theories-in-use," which he describes in terms of Model I (strategies of control, self-protection, defensiveness, and covering-up embarrassment) and Model II (strategies eliciting valid information, free choice, and commitment). Attention to how individuals' theories-in-use create organizational defensiveness is an important approach to organizational learning. The ladder of inference and the double-page techniques come from this approach.

Action Inquiry

Action inquiry is associated with the work of Bill Torbert.[20] He defines action inquiry as "a kind of scientific inquiry that is conducted in everyday life . . . that deals primarily with 'primary' data encountered 'on-line' in the midst of perception and action." While Torbert draws extensively on Argyris, he develops the inquiry process by linking the ability to engage in the rigor of action inquiry with the stages of ego development. In his view, it is in the latter stages of ego development that an individual can engage in **collaborative inquiry,** whereby as the individual reflects on her behavior-in-action, her behavior toward others is such that it invites them to do likewise.

Reflective Practice

Reflective practice refers to how individuals engage in critical reflection on their own action. It is associated with the work of Schon, who presents four ways that you might engage in reflective practice and learn to become a **reflective practitioner.**[21]

- *Frame analysis.* When you become aware of how you tend to understand situations (your "frames") and you consider alternatives.
- *Repertoire building research.* Where you accumulate and describe examples of reflection in action.
- *Research on fundamental methods of inquiry and overarching theories.* When you examine episodes of practice in an action science.
- *Research on the process of reflection in action.* Studying processes whereby you learn to reflect in action.

Work-Based Learning

Work-based learning is a hybrid of action research, action learning, and action science, and reflective practice presents learning-in-action as an approach to management development.[22]

Collaborative Research

Collaborative research, as the term suggests, is an emerging action research approach to conducting inquiry in organizations, with the aim of " . . . generating new insights that can simultaneously serve both action and the creation of new theoretical development."[23] At the most basic level, collaborative research attempts to refine the relationship between academic researchers and organizational actors from research "on" or "for" to research "with." In doing so, it attempts to integrate knowledge creation with problem solving and "inquiry from the inside" with "inquiry from the outside."

SUMMARY

Learning-in-action begins with knowing about knowing itself, and particularly knowing what you do when you know something. Knowing comprises a series of interrelated operations: experiencing, understanding through insight, judging if that insight is correct, and consequently making decisions and taking action, when the judgment is a judgment of value. By attending to these operations, you can notice what you are doing and catch yourself in the process of knowing and in this way learn how you know.

In the context of this course you are developing your learning-in-action skills with respect to the field of organizational behavior. You can, of course, be developing these skills for all aspects of your life. Within this course your main avenue for learning is through the material in this textbook. As this module features at the beginning of the book, we can only anticipate the learning-in-action of later modules. What is key is that you keep an attitude of inquiry. For instance, in Modules 11 and 12, when you engage in group and team activities to learn how groups and teams work and how they solve problems and make decisions, you'll learn-in-action by attending to:

- Your experience as you engage with others.
- The insights you get about what is going on.
- The judgments you make about whether what is going on is good for the group's task.
- What you decide you are going to say and do.

Ladder of inference, right-hand–left-hand column, and ORJI are techniques to help you do this. Throughout the course, keep a journal for yourself of your experiences in the course and the insights you get about yourself and about the field of organizational behavior.

Attending to your own learning-in-action, both in terms of the process of attending to experience, understanding, judgment, and decision/action and to your own preferred style in doing this (Module 2), is central to the skills of becoming a reflective practitioner. Being a reflective practitioner involves getting to know yourself and how you think and how you learn. You develop a learning competency that sustains you through life, a "personal mastery," which is the basis of how you learn to work with others and become an effective member of teams, organizations, and communities.[24,25] Enjoy the learning adventure.

Study Questions

1. Why philosophy?
   a. Why did we start with the philosophy of knowing?
   b. Have you an insight into why we did this?
   c. How might it apply to the field of organizational behavior?
2. How is the study of organizational behavior different from the study of engineering?
   a. From your experience of organizations, what might be examples of puzzles?
   b. What might be examples of problems?
   c. Describe how you might apply Schon's notion of "swampy lowlands" to organizational behavior.
3. Discuss the relationship between appreciative inquiry, experiential learning, and the reflective practitioner skills.
4. Discuss the unique features of learning-in-action while utilizing any two of the various approaches described in the chapter (that is, action research, action inquiry, action learning, action science, collaborative inquiry, reflective practice, work-based learning).
5. Identify the differences and similarities among cognitive learning, content learning, and learning-in-action.

Endnotes

1. D. Coghlan, and T. Brannick, *Doing Action Research in Your Own Organization,* 2nd ed. (London: Sage, 2005).

2. D. Coghlan, "Learning from Emotions through Journaling," *Journal of Management Education* 17, no. 1 (1993), pp. 90–94

3. B. Torbert, *Action Inquiry: The Secret Timely and Transforming Leadership* (San Francisco: Berrett-Koehler Publishers, Inc.).

4. B. Lonergan, "Insight: An Essay in Human Understanding," F. Crowe and R. Doran (eds.), *The Collected Works of Bernard Lonergan* vol. 3 (Toronto: Toronto University Press, 1992); J. Flanagan, *Quest for Self-Knowledge* (Toronto: Toronto University Press, 1997).

5. R. W. Revans, *ABC of Action Learning* (London: Lemos and Crane, 1998).

6. D. A. Schon, "Knowing-in-Action: The New Scholarship Requires a New Epistemology," in vol. III of B. Cooke and J. Wolfram-Cox (eds.), *Fundamentals of Action Research* (London: Sage, 2004), pp. 377–94.

7. R. Evered and M. R. Louis, "Alternative Perspectives in the Organizational Sciences: 'Inquiry from the Inside' and 'Inquiry from the Outside,'" *Academy of Management Review* 6 (1981), pp. 385–95.

8. D. Coghlan and T. Brannick, *Doing Action Research in Your Own Organization,* 2nd ed. (London: Sage, 2005).

9. D. Fisher, D. Rooke, and W. Torbert, *Personal and Organizational Transformation through Action Inquiry* (Boston: Edge\Work Press, 2000).

10. M. Darling, and C. Parry, *From Post-Mortem to Living Practice: An In-depth Study of the Evolution of the After Action Review* (Boston: Signet, 2000).

11. R. Ross, "The Ladder of Inference," in P. Senge, C. Roberts, R. Ross, B. Smith, and A. Kleiner (eds.), *The Fifth Discipline Fieldbook* (New York: Doubleday, 1994), pp. 242–6.

12. E. H. Schein, *Process Consultation Revisited* (Reading, MA: Addison-Wesley, 1999).

13. D. Coghlan and N. S. Rashford, *Organizational Change and Strategy: An Interlevel Dynamics Approach* (London: Routledge, 2006).

14. E. H. Schein, *Process Consultation Revisited* (Reading, MA: Addison-Wesley, 1999).

15. D. A. Kolb, *Experiential Learning* (Englewood Cliffs, NJ: Prentice-Hall, 1984).

16. D. Greenwood, and M. Levin, *Introduction to Action Research,* 2nd ed. (Thousand Oaks, CA: Sage, 2007).

17. W. French and C. Bell, *Organization Development,* 6th ed. (Englewood Cliffs, NJ: Prentice-Hall, 1999).

18. M. Marquardt, *Optimizing the Power of Action Learning* (Palo-Alto, CA: Davies-Black, 2004).

19. C. Argyris, *Reasons and Rationalization* (New York: Oxford University Press, 2004); C. Argyris, and D. A. Schon, *Organizational Learning II* (Reading, MA: Addison-Wesley, 1996).

20. B. Torbert, *Action Inquiry: The Secret Timely and Transforming Leadership* (San Francisco: Berrett-Koehler Publishers, Inc.).

21. D. A. Schon, *The Reflective Practitioner* (New York: Basic Books, 1983).

22. J. A. Raelin, *Work-Based Learning* 2nd ed. (Upper Saddle River, NJ: Prentice-Hall, 2008).

23. N. Adler, A. B. (Rami) Shani, and A. Styhre, *Collaborative Research in Organizations* (Thousand Oaks, CA: Sage, 2004); A. B. (Rami) Shani, S. Mohrman, W. Pasmore, B. Stymne, and N. Adler, *The Handbook of Collaborative Management Research* (Thousand Oaks, CA: Sage, 2008).

24. P. Senge, *The Fifth Discipline,* revised edition (New York: Doubleday, 2006); A. B. (Rami) Shani and P. Docherty, *Learning by Design: Building Sustainable Organizations* (London, UK: Blackwell Publishing, 2003).

25. O. C. Scharmer, *Theory U* (Cambridge, MA: Society of Organizational Learning, 2007).

Activity 3–3:
Using the ORJI Methodology to Develop the Reflective Practitioner Skills

Objective:

To help you develop the journaling skill while applying Schein's ORJI (observation, reaction, judgment, intervention) model.

Task 1:

Identify a situation or event where your own behavior resulted in an unpredicted outcome. Capture in writing the essence of what took place.

Task 2:

Following the four stages that were identified by Schein (observation, reaction, judgment, intervention) create the four subheadings and write a paragraph under each; that is, reconstruct the observation you made prior to your intervention, the emotional reaction you had, and the judgment you made.

Task 3:

Read your reconstruction of the event, and identify whether the emotional reaction, judgment, or intervention may have contributed to the unpredicted outcome.

Activity 3–4:
The Reflective Practitioner Skills— Learning with Others

Objective:

To help you further develop your reflective practitioner skills while working with your team mates.

Task 1:

Coaching one another is helpful for learning at many levels. In your learning group or with colleagues, form a triad and adopt roles A, B, and C.

- A presents an issue that she is dealing with currently.
- B inquires into the issue, using Schein's intervention typology.
- C observes and then facilitates reflection on the process using Schein's intervention typology.
- Change roles and repeat.
- Change roles and repeat.

Task 2:

Reflecting on the experience, what are some of your own takeaways? Feel free to focus on insights related to both process and content (cognitive) learning.

Part 2 | Managing Individual Processes

An integrated perspective on organizational behavior is designed to improve human, ecological, and economic sustainability. We take human sustainability to mean the development and fulfillment of human needs. Understanding and managing individuals requires a comprehensive holistic orientation that is embedded in continuous learning. An integral part of learning is creating the space and time for reflection. We argued in Module 2 that reflection is the mental discipline of distancing oneself from the situation, experience, or content and focusing on meaning, ideas, and linkages. Module 3 provided a framework to guide our learning-in-action and learning-on-action. As a part of the learning process, as we advance through the course, we need to stop periodically to reflect on our progress. Thus far, we have explored the context within which individuals and groups function in organizational settings. Part 1 helped establish the boundaries and process of the course: The field of study was defined; the learning community was established, expectations were clarified, and individual learning goals were set; the role and skills to be an effective learner via the learning-in-action perspective were examined and discussed.

Part 1 had two distinct purposes: (1) to create the content and process boundaries for the course and (2) to establish the learning community. Five key elements of the learning community were advanced:

1. *Content.* In defining organizational behavior, the topic areas were identified. The course objectives were given.

2. *Process (technology).* Experiential learning methods (that is, involvement learning through interaction activities) were used and contrasted with cognitive learning methods. We have introduced appreciative inquiry and learning-in-action as key pedagogical orientations in the learning process. The crucial role of the manager as a reflective practitioner was presented as one of the key learning objectives for the course.

3. *Roles.* The instructor's role was defined as that of a facilitator, coach, and resource person. The participant's role was defined as that of a learner and coach who is responsible for the learning of fellow participants.

4. *Climate.* Values of openness, sharing, full participation, and appreciative inquiry were discussed as critical elements of a learning community.

5. *Structure.* Teams were established as a key learning engine for the course under the guidance of the facilitator.

All of these factors and more are of the utmost relevance when you are building the learning community at any organization; they apply to any level from basic supervision up to top management.

Part 2 concentrates on the understanding and managing of individual behavior in organizations. The four core components of psychodynamics of human behavior, motivation, perception, and communication as the foundations of individual behavior are explored.

PREVIEW OF PART 2

We start the second part of the book with a focus on the psychodynamics of human behavior. An integral part of Module 4 is the development of an appreciation for individual differences. We review how unconscious and psychodynamic mechanisms influence individual behavior. We review the nature of individual diversity, explore some basic notions of emotions at work, present three theories of personality, discuss their implications in the workplace, and propose a path for personal growth and development. Motivation theory is considered in Module 5. We review some of the theories of motivation and examine their implications for human behavior. The module discusses applications in the workplace, managerial approaches, and organizational policies and practices that might affect motivation. The role of perception and perceptual differences among individuals is addressed in Module 6. This module also deals with perceptual differences between different organizational levels. Module 7 addresses communications at the interpersonal level, at the small-group level, and between groups. The module integrates the four core concepts by examining some of the barriers and inducements to interpersonal communication. Personal effectiveness in communication is one of the key skills of a manager. Exercises here help to develop active listening skills and techniques of paraphrasing, feedback, and influencing. A road map that can aid in understanding the relationship between the psychodynamics view of human behavior, perception, communication, motivation, and individual effectiveness is presented in the following diagram. The psychodynamics nature of human behavior plays a major role in shaping perception, communication, and motivation. All four core concepts are essential to understanding and managing individual behavior.

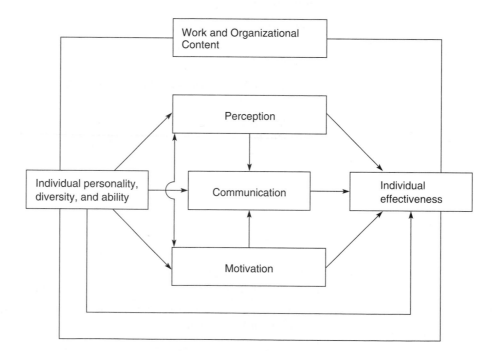

Module 4

A Psychodynamics Perspective on Human Behavior

LEARNING OBJECTIVES

After completing this module, you should be able to

1. Appreciate the nature and foundation of individual differences.
2. Understand and describe how unconscious and psychodynamic mechanisms influence individual behavior.
3. Understand, appreciate, and engage individual differences.
4. Develop an appreciation for a psychological growth and development perspective.
5. Develop a cursory understanding of how psychopathologies undermine interpersonal effectiveness.
6. Define personality and the basic dimensions of personality differences.
7. Explain the relationship between personal growth and individual effectiveness.

KEY TERMS AND CONCEPTS

Anima	Emotional intelligence
Animus	Espoused theories
Archetypes	Four preferences
Big Five personality theory	Free associations
Collective unconscious	Id
Conventional	Individual differences
Defense mechanisms	Neurosis
Defensiveness	Persona
Developmental psychology	Personal development
Double-loop versus single-loop learning	Personal growth
Dream analysis	Personality
Ego	Personality types

Postconventional	Theories-in-use
Preconventional	Traits
Psychosis	Transference
Shadow	Unconscious
Superego	Worldview

MODULE OUTLINE

Premodule Preparation:

    Activity 4–1: Exploring Individual Biases and Diversity

Introduction

A Psychodynamic View of Personality

    The Freudian Unconscious

    Defense Mechanisms and Psychological Growth

    The Jungian Unconscious

Human Development and Growth

Exploring the Unconscious: Techniques and Processes for Growth

    Freudian Psychoanalysis

    Jungian Analysis

An Overview of the Psychodynamic View of Personality

Personality and Emotional Intelligence

    The Myers–Briggs Model

    The Big Five Personality Theory

    Emotional Intelligence

Emotions in Organizations

Summary and Managerial Applications

Study Questions

Endnotes

    Activity 4–2: Exploring Individual Personality Profile: The Big Five Locator Questionnaire

Optional Activities on the WWW

    Activity 4–3W: Learning about Self and Others: Personal Reflection via "Collage"

    Activity 4–4W: Transactional Analysis in the Work Situation

    Activity 4–5W: Exploring Individual Personality Profile: The Keirsey Temperament Sorter

    Activity 4–6W: Assessing Your Emotional Intelligence

    Activity 4–7W: Assessing How Personality Types Affect Your Goal-Setting Skills

PREMODULE PREPARATION

**Activity 4–1:
Exploring Individual
Biases and Diversity**

Objectives:

a. Explore individual biases and their origins.

b. Appreciate individual differences in the mapping of rational and irrational forces.

c. Identify ways to circumvent problems that biases may cause.

Task 1:

Using the worksheet for Activity 4–1, list a bias you hold about certain categories of people. This bias could, but need not, be extreme. Examples of categories of people you could include are:

- Race.
- Nationality.
- Gender.
- Age.
- Tidiness or untidiness.
- People who are organized or disorganized.
- People who are emotionally expressive or not.
- Athletes or people who never exercise.
- Members of sororities and/or fraternities.
- Authority figures.
- People who like cream cheese.

Most people feel defensive when asked if they are biased and are eager to show they are not. Being biased does not mean that you are prejudiced. Everybody has biases. It is a necessity caused by the way we function psychologically, as will be shown in this Module 6. You must therefore do your best to find a realistic bias.

Task 2:

Once you have identified a bias you hold, try to identify its origin in your past experiences. You may for instance assume that every authority figure will lose their patience when you make a mistake because your elementary school teacher did. Your elementary school teacher is therefore the experience at the origin of your bias toward authority figures.

The past experiences that gave rise to a bias may include parents, siblings, friends, teachers, classmates, books and articles, movies or TV programs, and events.

Use the worksheet for Activity 4–1.

Task 3:

Identify the feelings, thoughts, and action tendencies you experience when you are exposed to members of the category toward which you hold a bias. Then, try to assess what are the negative (or positive) consequences of these feelings, thoughts, and action tendencies.

Use the worksheet for Activity 4–1.

Task 4:

Try to find counterexamples of members of the biased category who did not conform to your bias. Finally, try to identify strategies that you could use to have a different experience than the one you last had when exposed with a member of the biased category.

Task 5:

Start again with a second and then a third bias.

Name _____   Date _____

WORKSHEET FOR ACTIVITY 4–1

Bias 1

1. I have the following bias _____
   against the following category of people: _____

2. This bias arose as a result of my being exposed to the following experience(s):

   _____
   _____
   _____
   _____
   _____

3. When exposed to a member of this category of people, I usually feel _____
   _____, think _____
   _____, and do _____
   _____

4. When I feel, think, and do the above mentioned, it (sometimes/often) results in the following (negative) consequences:

   _____
   _____
   _____
   _____
   _____

5. I met one member of the category to which I hold a bias that did not fit the bias: _____
   _____

   This bias may be unwarranted in the following case(s): _____

   _____
   _____
   _____

6. I could prevent the above-mentioned negative consequence (or extend the above-mentioned positive consequences) by engaging in the following strategies: _____

   _____
   _____
   _____
   _____

Bias 2

1. I have the following bias _____
   against the following category of people: _____

2. This bias arose as a result of my being exposed to the following experience(s): _____

   _____
   _____
   _____
   _____

3. When exposed to a member of this category of people, I usually feel _____
   _____, think _____
   _____, and do _____
   _____

4. When I feel, think, and do the above mentioned, it (sometimes/often) results in the following (negative) consequences:

_____

_____

_____

_____

5. I met one member of the category to which I hold a bias that did not fit the bias: _____

_____

This bias may be unwarranted in the following case(s): _____

_____

_____

_____

6. I could prevent the above-mentioned negative consequence (or extend the above-mentioned positive consequences) by engaging in the following strategies: _____

_____

_____

_____

_____

Bias 3

1. I have the following bias _____
against the following category of people: _____

2. This bias arose as a result of my being exposed to the following experience(s):

_____

_____

_____

_____

_____

3. When exposed to a member of this category of people, I usually feel _____
_____, think _____
_____, and do _____

_____

4. When I feel, think, and do the above mentioned, it (sometimes/often) results in the following (negative) consequences:

_____

_____

_____

_____

5. I met one member of the category to which I hold a bias that did not fit the bias: _____

_____

This bias may be unwarranted in the following case(s): _____

_____

_____

_____

6. I could prevent the above-mentioned negative consequence (or extend the above-mentioned positive consequences) by engaging in the following strategies: _____

_____

_____

_____

_____

INTRODUCTION

One of the pillars in organizational behavior is the individual. Understanding and managing human behavior is critical in the context of work. In this section of the book, we focus on investigating the nature and dynamics of individual behavior. Our objective in this course is to provide you with perspectives that can allow you to interact more effectively with other people at work. To most of you, this goal may seem a bit odd. You may be telling yourself, "I already know how to interact with people! I do it every day! Why do I need a course to teach me that?" In a sense, you are right. All of us are lay psychologists. We all have implicit theories about how to handle people in different situations based on our past experience. Unlike engineering or finance, where it is easier for students to recognize their lack of knowledge, one of the challenges in organizational behavior is to convince students that there are certain aspects of human behavior that they do not fully understand. Even though their existing knowledge allows them to get by, it certainly does not always lead to effective interactions. Consider the following real-life interaction, reported by Coget,[1] that happened between Elizabeth, a film director, and Helena, one of her actresses:

> Elizabeth, a film director, was shooting a film about the difficult relationship between a second generation Chinese-American young woman and her Chinese-born grandmother. In the script, the grandmother did not speak English while the granddaughter did not speak Chinese, which exacerbated their misunderstandings. This theme was inspired by Elizabeth's own experience as a young Chinese–American teenager with her judgmental Chinese grandmother.
>
> As Elizabeth started shooting the scene in which the grandmother arrives from China to meet her granddaughter for the first time, Elizabeth noticed that Helena, the actress playing the grandmother, seemed bothered. As she inquired about the issue, Helena started complaining that the scene perpetuated the Western stereotype that Chinese women are stupid because it emphasized that she did not speak English rather than that her granddaughter did not speak Chinese.
>
> Elizabeth, who had also written the script, explained the scene from a narrative point of view: since the granddaughter is the main character, the film's audience experiences the scene from her perspective. The grandmother is just a supporting character. However, as Elizabeth further tried to explain rationally her directorial choices, Helena grew increasingly resistant and even aggressive toward Elizabeth. The two of them went over the same arguments several times until Helena abruptly broke the conversation off. Elizabeth had lost one hour talking with her, which is extremely damaging on a movie shoot, where time is of the essence. As the day went on, Helena continued to be increasingly difficult to direct, leaving Elizabeth frustrated, puzzled, and fearing for the quality of her movie.
>
> What had happened? Helena had read the script beforehand and had never voiced any problem about it. As Elizabeth pondered over the situation, she gathered all the information she had about Helena. Helena was a highly educated Chinese woman, with a Ph.D. in anthropology. Her research aimed at raising awareness on the difficult condition of women in China, and the admirable role they played in their society. She had actually made several documentaries on the subject. Also, Helena was not a professional actress but had been cast in a few other films.
>
> Elizabeth had concluded that two possible issues were causing the problem: first, she hypothesized that Helena might be trying to make a political statement about the stereotyping of Chinese women in the US, because of what she knew about her research involvement. The problem was that Elizabeth's film was not at all about that. She thus was having an intellectual disagreement with Helena and a power struggle about it. Second, since Helena was not a professional actress, Elizabeth wondered whether Helena was having difficulty differentiating herself from her character who was uneducated and did not speak English.
>
> A surprising resolution to this problem happened the next morning, after Elizabeth had spent a sleepless night worrying about Helena. As Elizabeth arrived on set, she asked Helena how she was doing. As she did so, Helena burst into tears. Elizabeth could not recognize the Helena of the day before, who had been fierce, aggressive, and authoritarian. She was one more time puzzled, but she embraced Helena and comforted her. After a while, Helena explained the situation, which she had just figured out: when she was a child in China, her mother never allowed her to talk. She was always to remain silent, which terribly frustrated her exuberant nature and aggravated the lack of connectedness she felt toward her mother. In the scene she had to play, she unknowingly started to feel the same way as she did as a child because she had to remain silent since her character did not speak English. As she had done in her childhood, she acted out by criticizing the authority figure, which she had associated with her mother. Helena needed her

director's attention, but she only managed to do so by aggravating her. The rational discussions they had did not solve the problem. Only when emotions poured out, in the form of tears for Helena and in the forms of a motherly concern and comforting behavior, for Elizabeth, did the real underlying issues surface and the problem find its resolution.

This story illustrates a few of the points that will be made in this chapter. First, it serves as a cautionary tale about the illusion of rationality, which pervades modern life, especially the workplace. In our efforts to be rational, we ignore deeper dynamics that influence our perceptions, our emotions, and even our thinking (see Module 1). These "unconscious" dynamics often find their roots in previous experiences we had, the most powerful of which often happen in childhood.

One of the unconscious dynamics that the story illustrates is "transference." It was first documented by Freud,[2] the founder of psychoanalysis. Elizabeth and Helena thought that they were having an intellectual disagreement about the portrayal of the grandmother to the American public. This disagreement was in fact a pretext for Helena to attempt to find a resolution to a deeper and less acceptable conflict: her problematic relationship with her mother. In effect, she transposed the relationship she had as a child with her mother to the relationship she had with Elizabeth, the authority figure. She also transposed the feelings that she had toward her mother as a child to Elizabeth. **Transference** is thus the tendency that people have to transpose past situations to the present to try to solve unresolved issues, usually with their parents, siblings, or other intimate relationships they have had. Authority figures are often the target of transference, but so are any of the intimate or close relationships people have. It often proves self-defeating for the target of transference to try to react "rationally" to solve emotional issues that have little to do with the present situation. Solving a problem caused by transference requires acute psychological awareness and skills.

Another unconscious dynamic that the story illustrates is a defense mechanism called "intellectualization." **Defense mechanisms,** also documented by Freud and refined by his daughter,[3] are unconscious resources that help reduce the anxiety caused by conflict between different parts of the psyche, the id, and the superego. The notions of ego, id, superego, and defense mechanisms will be expanded upon later in the chapter. In the preceding example, Helena intellectualized her feelings of abandonment and rage toward her mother. Because these feelings were too threatening for her to face, she unconsciously attributed her discomfort to the issue of stereotyping. She thus was able to have what appeared to be an intellectual discussion with Elizabeth. Nonetheless, she still expressed aggressive feelings that were out of proportion with the topic at hand, which surprised Elizabeth and seemed irrational.

Most of us believe that we are entirely rational and that we understand ourselves. Freud and his successors, who established the field of psychodynamics, have shown that this is not the case. They have shown that a large set of unconscious dynamics offer logical explanations to what appears to be aberrant behavior from a rational standpoint. Activity 4–1 was designed to help you trace some of the past events or situations that have shaped your current psychology and have led you to be biased toward certain categories of people and experience feelings toward them that may not be warranted given the lack of knowledge you have about these categories.

As a future employee, colleague, or manager, but also as a friend, significant other, family member, and member of different communities, it is essential that you understand the psychological mechanisms that cause people to behave the way they do. Doing so will allow you to prevent communication breakdowns and correctly diagnose the real issues that people face, instead of losing time trying to solve the wrong problem, like Elizabeth and Helena did at first. It will also allow you to better influence and motivate people around you. Finally, it will allow you to enhance your **personal growth** and that of people around you, and find a productive way to discuss moral and political issues that transcend logic and reason alone.

In order to understand what causes people to behave the way they do, you need to understand how they perceive things, what motivates them, and how to communicate with them. All of these themes are treated in detail in Modules 5 to 7. This chapter, however, will provide you with an overarching theory that puts these topics together and shows their interrelationships. This chapter will also provide you with a perspective about what psychological growth is, how it happens, and how it relates to personal meaning in one's life. It will provide you with a means to understand, appreciate, and engage individual differences. This chapter will also present two popular theories of personality, and recent research on emotional intelligence. Finally, it will provide you with a cursory understanding of the different psychological pathologies that undermine interpersonal effectiveness.

A PSYCHODYNAMIC VIEW OF PERSONALITY

Freud considered that his psychoanalytical theory cast the third great blow to the human ego in the history of Western thought.[4] The first one was cast by Galileo, who demonstrated that the Earth was not the center of the universe. The second blow was cast by Darwin, whose theory of evolution undermined the notion that humans have a special place in the animal world: according to his theory, they simply evolved from other species. Freud cast the third blow to the Cartesian image that men have of themselves: we are not even in control of our own mind. The conscious mind, with which we usually most identify, is at the mercy of psychodynamic processes which we not only fail to understand, but which we are also unconscious of.

The idea of an unconscious makes sense from an evolutionary perspective and from the perspective of cognitive limitations. Neurobiologists have found evidence that the human brain is composed of three superimposed brains: the reptilian brain, or the brainstem, which controls vital unconscious processes, such as breathing; the mammalian brain, or the limbic system, which is at the origin of emotions among other things; and the truly human brain, the neocortex, which controls higher-order thinking skills, reason, and speech.[5] The two lower-level brains constitute biological evidence of the unconscious because they control processes that are for the most part unconscious.

Cognitive psychologists have also found evidence that supports the notion of an unconscious. Reality is frighteningly complex, and people have limited mental capacities. Research suggests that we can only keep track of seven (plus or minus two) mental objects at any given moment.[6,7] In order for us to function, we need to filter reality so as to perceive only the few elements that are the most relevant to our survival and disregard the rest. The **unconscious** is what allows us to do so.

But what exactly is the unconscious? Various theories have been developed about it. We begin with the first one, that of the founder of psychoanalysis, Sigmund Freud.

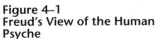

The Freudian Unconscious

According to Freud[8] the human psyche is composed of three parts: the **id,** the **ego,** and the **superego** (see Figure 4–1).

The id, which is the primary source of the unconscious, can be viewed as the repository of repressed instincts. When they are newly born, infants are primarily under the

Figure 4–1
Freud's View of the Human Psyche

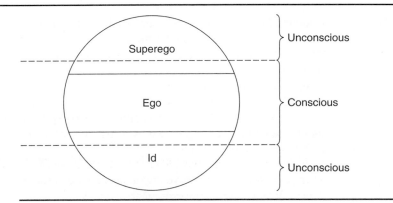

influence of the id, which demands immediate gratification without regard for social norms or the needs of others. When newborns are hungry, tired, or under the influence of another basic need, they cry without restraint until their caretakers take care of their needs. The id is also the source of a person's libido, or sexual desires. Freud regarded the sex drive as the most potent of the desires that shape the human psyche.

As infants grow up, they become aware of their surroundings. They realize that there is an external world independent of them that does not always conform itself to their desires or needs. Not only is this world composed of objects that need to be manipulated correctly in order for infants to satisfy their needs, but it is also composed of other people who have their own needs and agendas. From this evolution in the human psyche, the ego is born. The Freudian ego has nothing to do with the popular term *ego,* which refers to a person's aggrandized sense of self. In the Freudian model of the psyche, the ego comes closest to our everyday sense of self, to our conscious and rational mind. When asked who they are, adults primarily identify with their ego.

As the ego develops and infants become aware of their environment, they also begin their education. Their parents teach them how to become "good children" by respecting social and moral norms of cleanliness, social interaction, restraint, and so forth. From education, the superego is born. It is the part of the psyche in which social and moral norms become internalized.

Freud developed his theory of the unconscious by observing and treating mental patients. His theories thus put special emphasis on problems that arise within the psyche: psychopathology. According to Freud, the psyche is the seat of a continual struggle between the id and the superego. This struggle is mediated by the ego, which arbiters between them. In the course of becoming civilized, humans need to curb the sometimes inappropriate demands of the id. It is their superego that alerts them that some of their impulses may be harmful to others. For instance, when attending a cocktail party, our id may direct us to rush to the table and gorge on canapés, but the sense of etiquette that has been carved by our mother in our superego will intimate us to restrain ourselves and behave. A healthy ego is one that maintains an adequate balance between the id and the superego.

Some individuals have an incompletely developed superego, which leaves their id freer to seek immediate gratification. Freud called this particular type of psychopathology **psychosis.** At the extreme, psychopaths have no capacity to empathize with others and are capable of committing horrendous crimes that satisfy their unleashed id. A less severe form of psychosis will lead individuals to be socially maladapted, prone to inappropriate, possibly criminal social behavior. Psychoses are considered to be the most serious forms of psychopathology.

At the other extreme, some individuals have an overly developed superego that smothers their id. This class of psychopathology is called **neurosis.** At the extreme, obsessive-compulsive disorder leads individuals who suffer from it to repetitively engage in thought or behavioral rituals in order to neutralize their obsessions. A less extreme form of neurosis will lead individuals to depression because they do not allow enough of their basic needs or desires to be gratified. Freud considered that most socially adapted people suffered from at least a mild form of neurosis.

Defense Mechanisms and Psychological Growth

Sigmund Freud's daughter, Ana Freud, developed a classification of the resources that the ego musters in order to alleviate the anxiety that arises when a person experiences conflicts between the id and the superego or between conflicting impulses from the id.[9] An illustration of how defense mechanisms work may help understanding. Imagine that an employee is angry at his boss because she has given him negative feedback about his attitude during the last meeting. However, the employee's superego prevents him from becoming fully aware of his anger because it is inappropriate to express anger to an authority figure. The employee may solve the problem by using some of the following defense mechanisms:

- *Denial.* The employee completely rejects the thought or feeling: "I'm not angry with her!"
- *Suppression.* The employee is vaguely aware of the thought or feeling, but tries to hide it: "We just had a conversation about work, as usual."

- *Reaction formation.* The employee turns the feeling into its opposite: "I think she's a great boss!"

- *Projection.* The employee assigns his feeling to someone else: "I know Larry hates her guts."

- *Displacement.* The employee redirects his feelings to another target: "I really hate my desk."

- *Rationalization.* The employee comes up with a rational explanation to justify the situation, while denying his feelings: "I know that she takes a special interest in my success as an employee: that's why she gives me a lot of feedback, sometimes a bit harsh."

- *Intellectualization.* A more intellectualized form of rationalization: "This situation is very interesting: it is reminiscent of the dialectic of the master and the slave, developed by Hegel."

- *Undoing.* The employee tries to reverse or undo his feeling by doing something that indicates the opposite feeling: "I think I'll show her how good of a boss she is at our next meeting by bringing her donuts."

- *Isolation of affect.* The employee "thinks" the feeling but does not really feel it: "I think I'm angry with her, in a detached sort of way."

- *Regression.* The employee reverts to an old, usually immature behavior to vent his feeling: "I'm going to spill ink onto her files!"

- *Sublimation.* The employee redirects the feeling into a socially productive activity: "I'm going to play my guitar tonight, and write a song about the woes of work."

While defense mechanisms are healthy in the sense that they protect us from anxiety, they can also prevent us from facing the unconscious dynamics that impede our growth. In the example we gave in the introduction, Helena's intellectualization of her feelings prevented her from realizing that she was replaying her childhood dynamics with Elizabeth. Only once she realized what was happening was she able to take corrective action and repair her relationship with Elizabeth, and possibly other authority figures that would elicit the same type of reaction in the future.

In the context of work, Argyris has shown how **defensiveness** prevents smart employees from learning.[10] He applied the insights of psychoanalysis to the workplace and asked managers to describe their guiding philosophy about how to interact with their subordinates, which he called their **espoused theories.** He then observed them in action and noticed that their behavior strayed significantly from their espoused theories. He named the principles that guided their actions their **theories-in-use.** A theory-in-use is akin to the set of unconscious processes that influence a manager's actions, and it is very different from what the manager's conscious mind believes it is doing. According to Argyris, and consistent with psychoanalysis, the gap between espoused theories and theories-in-use cannot be attributed to malicious intents but rather to the fact that managers are unaware of what their theories-in-use are. In order for managers to progress in their ability to manage other people, Argyris advocates a **double-loop versus single-loop learning** (see Modules 2 and 3). Single-loop learning occurs when a manager adjusts her behavior to avert a problem she has faced in the past, but does not think about how her own thinking may have contributed to the problem. Double-loop learning, however, involves reflecting upon how her own thinking may have contributed to the problem, which involves an exploration of her unconscious patterns. For instance, the CEO of a large airline company learns that her board of directors has rejected her planned merger with a major competitor once again. She may start to consider which alliances she could build with key board members to win her case the next time around. Or she may call her financial analysts to identify another more suitable candidate for a merger. These would be examples of single-loop learning. If, however, she starts to wonder whether the way she thinks about mergers with competitors needs revisiting, she is now engaging in double-loop learning. The main obstacle that Argyris identified to double-loop learning is defensiveness: when faced with mistakes, high-level managers often become defensive in order to avert negative retributions and to protect their ego because engaging in double-loop learning means acknowledging responsibility for one's mistakes. Managers thus often become closed-minded to examining their theories-in-use at a moment that would be most propitious for learning. As teachers, we have to admit that we have witnessed students behave similarly in many instances.

According to Freud, the role of psychoanalysis is to promote psychological growth by facilitating the process by which a patient overcomes his defenses and becomes aware of dysfunctional unconscious processes that prevent his optimal functioning. Psychoanalysis has been successful in curing mild psychopathologies, such as neurosis and depression, but its track record is more questionable in the treatment of serious pathologies, such as psychosis.

In the context of work, self-awareness is also a necessary skill to possess in order to understand how we interact with others and can change some of our counterproductive patterns. One of the most pressing duties of an effective manager or leader is to protect her subordinates from her own unconscious.

The Jungian Unconscious

Another prominent figure in psychoanalysis is Carl Jung, who was a student of Freud. Although Jung was once considered to be the intellectual heir of Freud, he eventually distanced himself from the man.

His two main disagreements with Freud were over the topics of sexuality and religion. Freud's theory of psychology put a strong emphasis on the sex drive, the libido. In most of his analysis of patients, Freud identified unconscious sexual desires as important unresolved issues. Prominent in his theory was the Oedipus complex (or its female equivalent, the Electra complex) in which male (or female) infants harbor sexual desires toward their mother (or father) and death wishes toward their father (or mother) whom they see as a competitor in love. While Jung, and later other psychoanalysts, recognized the importance of sexuality, they disagreed with the overemphasis that Freud placed on it. Jung, in particular, believed that the deepest desire of humankind was not sexual gratification, but rather, the search for meaning.[11] It is noteworthy to remember that Freud wrote at the height of the Victorian era, when sexuality was far more repressed than today, which may have led him to overemphasize its importance.

Another area of disagreement between the two men was religion. While Freud was an atheist and called religion "a collective neurosis," Jung was a spiritual man who was interested in religions and myths from all over the world. One of his lasting contributions to psychoanalysis is indeed the idea that the world myths, including religions, are representations of some of the deepest collective aspirations of humankind toward meaning. Jung believed that in addition to a personal unconscious, which is similar to Freud's unconscious, we also have a **collective unconscious,** in which **archetypes** are stored.[12] In Jung's theory, archetypes are innate, universal prototypes for ideas that have evolved throughout human history in our struggle for meaning, and which we inherit, like a psychological DNA.

Figure 4–2 represents Jung's view of the psyche. At the center lies the **persona,** which represents the social image that people show to the world, the mask that they wear for the outside world. The persona is conscious and the shallowest part of the psyche. Deeper in the psyche, but still in the conscious arena, is the ego. Jung's ego approximates Freud's ego. It is the conscious part of the psyche that most people identify with; the seat of rational thought. It is deeper than the persona because it includes elements of the psyche that a person is aware of but might not want to share with the world. Past these two initial circles of the psyche, we enter into the unconscious. The **shadow** is akin to the Freudian unconscious; it is the area in which people store information about themselves that is threatening to their ego. The shadow contains parts of one's self-concept that the individual has not accepted and usually judges as evil. In the shadow may lurk sexual desires that are judged inappropriate, as Freud emphasized; violent impulses; or even simple qualities that a person has not accepted she possesses, at least in potential, like beauty or vulnerability, because she has constructed her whole self-concept with the idea that she does not possess them. Past the shadow, in the

Figure 4–2
Jung's View of the Psyche

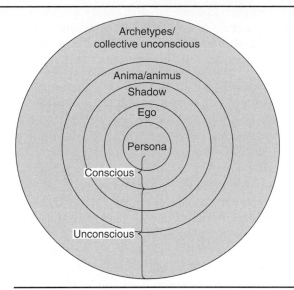

ever-widening and deepening circles of the psyche, we find the **anima** and **animus,** which represent, respectively, the female qualities that men have not accepted in themselves and the male qualities that women have repressed. The anima and animus are already partially part of the collective unconscious, but also partially part of the personal unconscious, which is mainly represented by the shadow. Jung and his followers spent a lot of time studying the anima. The anima is the eternal, idealized feminine that men project onto women in order to reconcile themselves with it. Hence, they tend to idolize the anima. Representations of the anima abound throughout history, from Greek and Roman goddesses to modern movie stars and pop icons. These icons do not possess the qualities of actual women, but rather the idealized qualities of the female representation within the male psyche, the anima. Finally, at the deepest level of the psyche lies the collective unconscious; the repository of motifs that humans have been creating and re-creating throughout history in their struggles toward meaning. All myths from around the world are testimonies of the collective unconscious, as Joseph Campbell, a student of mythology and an adept of Jung, has shown.[13] According to Jung, and Campbell, mythology, like dreams, is not just stories invented out of thin air. Nor do we do justice to them if we discard them as untrue because they do not conform to our religious beliefs or modern scientific theories. The key to understanding mythology is to analyze it as a metaphor of psychological transformation. In his book *The Hero with a Thousand Faces,* Campbell shows that all myths have the same structure: A hero living in the realm of normality enters an otherworldly realm that represents the unconscious.[14] In this realm, the hero undergoes trials that reveal his true character. He can then return to normality with a new understanding.

According to Jung, the goal of psychoanalysis, and indeed of life, is to extend and deepen one's awareness by exploring one's unconscious. This is what heroes of all time have done, reaching higher levels of consciousness and passing them on to others in the form of stories, which we call myths. Jung called the process of finding oneself "individuation," which is reminiscent of Nietzsche's injunction to "Become the one who you are," or Maslow's "self-actualization."

HUMAN DEVELOPMENT AND GROWTH

Both Freud and Jung agreed that the conscious mind emerged from the unconscious mind. Our conscious understanding of the world, the theories we use to make sense of it, rationality itself and its rules, all emerged from the unconscious, which forms their footing. This hypothesis is supported by McLean's theory of three superimposed brains[15] and Freud's observation of the development of children. What this means is that throughout the history of our development as a species, as well as through our **personal development,** from infants, to adolescents, to grown men and women, our psyche changes and develops. In fact, a whole subset of psychology, **developmental psychology,** is devoted to the study of human development. Various prominent psychologists have studied human development: Freud and Piaget focused on infants and children[16,17] and Maslow and Wilber focused on adult development.[18,19] What they all agree upon is that development happens in stages, rather than incrementally, and that these stages are hierarchically organized, with only a subset of the population reaching the highest stages. Switching from one stage to another, such as moving from childhood to adolescence, is not easy. It is a cataclysmic event in which one's worldview is shattered to pieces, so that a new worldview may emerge. By **worldview,** we mean the sum total of a person's experience and theories about reality that allow that person to orient herself to the world. While it could be argued that there are as many worldviews as there are people on earth, Wilber's[20] review of research in domains as various as moral development,[21,22] values development,[23] needs,[24] and cognitive development[25] tends to show that people mature through three to eight hierarchically organized stages of development. For instance, Kohlberg[26] found that people tend to go through three stages of moral development: preconventional, conventional, and postconventional. Until about 9 years of age, most children adopt a **preconventional** view of morality, where they judge an act to be moral if they can get away with it. Their goal is primarily to avoid punishment and obtain rewards. From about 9 to 20, adolescents and young adults usually have adopted a **conventional** approach to morality, where they judge an act to be moral if most people would perform it. They are primarily trying to gain approval from others and avoid feelings of guilt. Finally, from around 20, adults may switch to a **postconventional** view of morality, although some adults never reach that stage. At the postconventional stage, an act is judged to be moral if it does not violate agreed-upon rights or personal values of the individual. Maslow,[27] whose theory of motivation will be exposed in more detail in Module 5, also developed a hierarchically organized model of motivation. In this model, people are first and foremost motivated to fulfill their physiological needs, such as hunger or thirst. Only once these needs are taken care of can they be motivated by the next level of needs, security needs. The following levels are social acceptance/love, self-esteem, and finally self-actualization, which Maslow defines as "becoming everything that one is capable of becoming."

   Two important lessons can be derived from this research. First, it constitutes strong evidence that psychological growth is possible and that it requires one to go through successive stages of growth to reach the highest stages. Expanding one's consciousness is not an empty exercise. It leads to higher levels of growth. Second, this research shows that when two individuals are at different levels of growth within a given category, such as moral development or cognitive development, they will see the world in a radically different fashion. Since a worldview is the total meaning system with which an individual orients himself to the world, it does not appear as a mere theory or opinion to the individual. Rather, it becomes the world. Conflicting worldviews can therefore lead to major conflict between two individuals or groups of people. Module 10 provides theories that can help you better understand conflict and ways to resolve it.

EXPLORING THE UNCONSCIOUS: TECHNIQUES AND PROCESSES FOR GROWTH

Given that exploring one's unconscious is so important to achieving continuous psychological growth and avoid psychopathologies, how does one go about it? All psychoanalysts agree that **dream analysis,** which Freud[28] pioneered, is the royal route to the unconscious.

Freudian Psychoanalysis

What Freud calls the "manifest" content of a dream is all the parts of the dream that we remember. A dream may incorporate elements from the recent past, such as events that happened the day before the dream; distant events and characters that one has not interacted with in a long time; strong feelings; and bizarre situations, objects, and creatures that seem to have nothing to do with one's life. In order to make sense of the dream and use it as a tool to explore the unconscious, the patient and the psychoanalyst need to get at the "latent" content of the dream. In Freudian psychoanalysis, this is done primarily through the process of free association. Feelings are particularly important in dreams. When interpreting a dream, it can be very fruitful to wonder when one felt the same feelings as those felt in the dream. This may lead the dreamer to remember important emotional episodes of her life and reconsider how they have impacted *her* unconscious and her worldview.

Jungian Analysis

Jung's method, which he called "analysis" to distinguish it from Freudian "psychoanalysis" also relies on **free associations,** but it also makes use of symbols and myths as keys to the interpretation of a dream. Jung believed that the collective unconscious manifests itself in our lives as we go through the same universal struggles that our ancestors faced. When elements of a dream are reminiscent of known symbols or myths, these symbols and myths can clarify the particular struggle that the dreamer is facing in his or her life. For instance, if a young man dreams of killing dragons, the myth of Siegfried and the dragon may be brought upon to clarify the dream. Through free associations, the dragon will be identified as a symbol for something that is impeding the dreamer's growth. It may be the dreamer's overly authoritarian father, fear of leaving one's home to go to college, fear of failure, the impending divorce of his parents, and so forth. The myth of Siegfried is a coming-of-age story. Siegfried has to face one of his biggest fears, slay it, and incorporate it in his life, to move on to his next level of existence. While none of us literally slay dragons in our daily lives, we do slay metaphorical dragons to come to terms with life and grow.

For Jung, dreams, like myths, were not to be taken literally. However, he believed that their language, symbols, was the language of the psyche, of the soul, that we needed to master in order to maintain a healthy dialogue between our conscious and our unconscious. Anybody who has undergone a serious analysis usually comes out of it liberated, exuberant, with a stronger and truer sense of self, and a revived vitality. Dream analysis can help a person understand what makes her feel vital, for the conscious mind does not know the meaning of life. It is just a tool that can be used to help the unconscious lead a person toward individuation.

AN OVERVIEW OF THE PSYCHODYNAMIC VIEW OF PERSONALITY

Psychodynamic theories, in spite of their diversity, provide us with an integrative model of human psychology (see Figure 4–3), which can help connect several of the modules of this textbook, such as Modules 5 to 7 and 15 to 17.

Our personal experience, together with our collective history and culture, shape our unconscious, which determines our worldview. Our worldview, in turn, allows us to interpret reality and therefore shapes what we perceive, what we feel, and our motivation to act. All of these psychological functions, in turn, influence our behavior directly, when we act intuitively or impulsively, and indirectly, through the medium of our thoughts. Metacognition, a particular type of thoughts in which we reflect upon our worldview, our experience, and our unconscious, allows us to keep growing psychologically and update our worldview, occasionally revising it so dramatically that we grow to a higher level of psychological development.

Figure 4–3   **An Integrative View of Human Behavior**

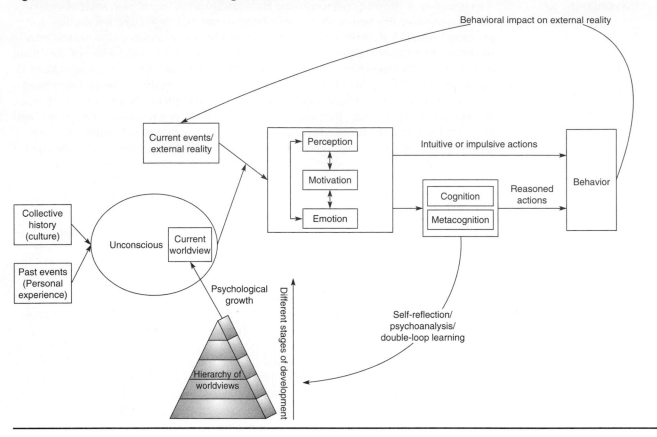

PERSONALITY AND EMOTIONAL INTELLIGENCE

Although some modern psychologists, in particular, the behaviorists,[29] have criticized psychodynamics for studying phenomena that cannot be observed directly, others have tried to evolve it into a more systematic and measurable theory: personality theory. **Personality** is defined as "a relatively stable set of characteristics, tendencies, and temperaments that have been significantly formed by inheritance and by social, cultural, and environmental factors. This set of variables determines the commonalities and differences in the behavior of individuals (thoughts, feelings, and actions) that have continuity over time and that may not be easily understood as the sole result of the social and biological pressures of the moment."[30] Those stable characteristics are often referred to as **traits,** which can be measured with psychometric tests.

In the context of organizational studies, many relevant personality characteristics were identified. In recent years, a few conceptual frameworks for understanding **individual differences** have become very popular among organizational behavior educators, students, and managers. Two frameworks—the Myers–Briggs model,[31] rooted in Carl Jung's work, and the Big Five personality theory[32]—have been translated into sets of concepts and tools that have practical applications. More recently still, a particular trait, emotional intelligence, has received particular attention. These three theories are developed next.

The Myers–Briggs Model

Carl Jung first coined the terms *introversion* and *extroversion,* which provided the impetus for Briggs and Myers[33] to formalize one of the first *type indicators.*

Jung believed that we have an inborn preference for how we function just as we have a preference for using one hand over the other. The preference for how we function is a characteristic, so we may be "typed" by these preferences. Although various researchers have contributed to Jung's work by refining and reorganizing the preferences in various combinations, 16 basic **personality types** have been identified from his model. The result of this scholarly work is an understandable model of human personality that can be verified by simple observation of friends and family. By reading descriptions of each type, people can identify and predict both the strengths and weaknesses of themselves and others, thereby appreciating individual differences and avoiding the expectation that others should behave like they do.

Four basic preferences in the way we approach life can be identified (see Figure 4–4). The term *preference* means that we have an inborn tendency to behave a certain way. This does not mean that a preferred way of behaving will be the *only* way we function; it is just the most comfortably favored way. It is the same as being born with a tendency to use either our right or left hand, which results in our developing one over the other. We can only use the nondominant hand in an awkward way, while the dominant hand is used without thinking. Some personality functions and behaviors become second nature to us and define our personality type.

1. *Introversion or extroversion.* The first preference is demonstrated when an individual is extroverted and attends more to the outer world of things and people or else is introverted and attends more to the inner world of the experience (a private world of ideas, principles, values, and feeling). As in all the personality preferences, one does not exclude the other—a person will attend to both the outer and inner worlds but will be most at home in one as opposed to the other. Extroverts will use more energy when attending primarily to outside events, while introverts will use more energy in pondering their own thoughts or feelings. Extroverts get their batteries charged by being sociable and the "life of the party," while introverts seem to draw their energies from more solitary activities shared with few or no other people. There are three times as many extroverts as there are introverts, which may explain the tendency for pop psychology books to sell extroversion as the "healthy" preference. This conclusion, of course, is false.

2. *Intuition or sensing.* There are two ways to perceive information about the inner and outer worlds: through one's senses or through one's intuition. A preference to perceive with the senses (touch, smell, sight, hearing, and taste) is especially useful for gathering the facts of a situation. Intuition on the other hand shows meanings, relationships, and possibilities that are beyond the reach of the senses. Intuition is especially useful for perceiving what one might do about a situation. People tend to operate and become expert at one over the other.

3. *Thinking or feeling.* People not only take in information but also make decisions based on how they think and feel about the issues and people involved. Decisions based on thinking utilize judgments that predict the logical results of any particular action in an impersonal and analytical way. Feeling-based decisions do not require logic; only personal values and the impact on others are primarily important. Those who put more confidence in decisions based on feeling typically become sympathetic and skillful in dealing with people as opposed to that part of the world that requires cold-hearted, matter-of-fact decisions.

4. *Judging or perceiving.* As maturation takes place, one of the perceptive preferences (intuition or sensing) will become further developed, and information will be received more confidentially in one of these two ways. Judgments based on this information will also be made by one of two ways (feeling or thinking), and more trust will be put in one over the other.

Figure 4–4
The Four Pairs of Preferences Based on the Myers–Briggs Type Indicator (MBTI)

Ways of gaining energy	}	Introversion	←——→	Extroversion
Ways of taking in information	}	Intuition	←——→	Sensing
Ways of making decisions	}	Thinking	←——→	Feeling
Ways of living in the world	}	Judging	←——→	Perceiving

Not only will an individual favor one of two ways within each of these preferences, but he or she will also rely on one type of preference to deal with the world. Some people will use the taking in of information (perceptive) more often than making decisions (judging). One type will be more comfortable in making judgments (thinking or feeling) before all the information about a situation is completely perceived. This type lives in a planned, decisive, orderly way of life. Others rely mainly on the perceptive process (intuition or sensing) and live in a flexible, spontaneous, reactive way.

The **four preferences** or tendencies form the basis of the 16 personality categories. If you are interested, most advisement and counseling centers in universities have access to the Myers–Briggs and/or Keirsey instruments. Use of the instruments is controlled through professionally trained people who can administer, score, and interpret the data with you.

A variation of the Myers–Briggs test can be found on the Web at www.keirsey.com/cgi-bin/keirsey/newkts.cgi. This variation—the Keirsey Temperament Sorter II—is based on the development and research carried out by Dr. David Keirsey and his associates. The site provides additional information about references and sources of interest. (Activity 4–1W provides an opportunity for you to assess your individual personality profile, based on Keirsey's conceptual framework.)

The Big Five Personality Theory

The past decade witnessed a resurgence of usage and support for a trait theory of personality—the Five Factor Model (FFM).[34] The FFM has received increased attention because it can withstand every kind of statistical analysis. The FFM—popularly referred to as the **Big Five personality theory**—is founded on the discovery that people describe themselves and others in terms of five fundamental dimensions of individual differences.[35] Although some differences in the specific labeling of the Big Five are debated in the literature, there is agreement about the Big Five factor structure.[36] The Big Five factors (and prototypical characteristics for each factor) are extroversion (sociable, talkative, assertive, ambitious, and active); agreeableness (good-natured, cooperative, and trusting); conscientiousness (responsible, dependable, able to plan, organized, persistent, and achievement oriented); adjustment/emotional stability (calm, secure, and not nervous); and openness to experience (imaginative, sensitive, and intellectual). Figure 4–5 captures the five dimensions and some of the prototypical characteristics at the end of the continuum of each factor.

In addition to providing a framework to explore personality dimensions, research on the Big Five has also found important relationships between these personality dimensions and job performance. For example, a study that looked at a broad spectrum of occupations found that conscientiousness predicts job performance for all the occupational groups studied. "The preponderance of evidence shows that individuals who are dependable, reliable, careful, thorough, able to plan, organized, hardworking, persistent, and achievement oriented tend to have higher job performance in most if not all occupations."[37] For the other personality dimensions, predictability depends on both the occupational group and the performance criteria. This study is one reason that the area of personality testing and employee selection seems to be regaining credibility and increased

Figure 4–5
The Five-Factor Model of Personality—The Big Five

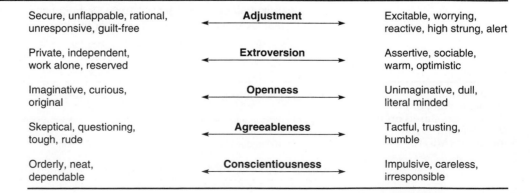

	Adjustment	
Secure, unflappable, rational, unresponsive, guilt-free	← Adjustment →	Excitable, worrying, reactive, high strung, alert
Private, independent, work alone, reserved	← Extroversion →	Assertive, sociable, warm, optimistic
Imaginative, curious, original	← Openness →	Unimaginative, dull, literal minded
Skeptical, questioning, tough, rude	← Agreeableness →	Tactful, trusting, humble
Orderly, neat, dependable	← Conscientiousness →	Impulsive, careless, irresponsible

utilization. Activity 4–2, at the end of the module, enables you to use the Big Five model of personality to explore your individual profile.

Emotional Intelligence

Alongside the four bipolar types of the Myer-Briggs and the five traits of the Big Five, a new trait (or ability) has recently emerged as important in the academic literature: **emotional intelligence** (EI), as distinct from the intelligence quotient (IQ). EI is defined as the ability of an individual to know one's emotions, manage them, motivate one's self, recognize emotions in others, and manage relationships with others.[38,39] EI has now been associated with numerous positive outcomes in the workplace.[40,41] It is important to recognize and manage one's emotions because they are fundamental links between our past experience and the current situation. Emotions sometimes lead us to reproduce past stories inappropriately, like Helena did in the example at the beginning of the chapter, or to rapidly mobilize our past experience appropriately to react to crisis situations. Recognizing other people's emotions and managing them, in turn, can greatly improve communication because it allows them to perceive the subtext of an apparently rational conversation. It is therefore a key skill for managers to possess, since so many of the managerial problems that occur in organizations are due to communication issues as we will see in Module 7 (on communication). It also allows leaders to formulate compelling visions and motivate their followers to a great extent, as we will see in Module 8 (on leadership).

Emotional intelligence can be developed by engaging in activities that are similar to psychoanalysis. To truly understand your own emotional intelligence, you have to be open to feedback about your behavior and be willing to suspend your overreliance on rationality or your perspective on the world. Tools such as videotaping role plays, assessment center activities (for example, Activities 4–2 and 4–5W), and feedback from coaches and multirater feedback instruments are highly beneficial. Activity 4–6W provides you with an opportunity to assess your EI. Activity 4–7W can provide some insight into how your personality affects your goal-setting skills.

EMOTIONS IN ORGANIZATIONS

Weber's work on bureaucratic authority based on formal rules that were exercised objectively without emotion and without regard to persons has been the foundation of much of our understanding of organizational processes. Weber presented organizations as formal hierarchies with defined roles, rules, and procedures, and populated by people viewed as a collection of functions and skills and who were devoid of emotion, gender identity, and sexuality. Organizations, for Weber, were rational and asexual. The more dehumanized the bureaucracy was the better it succeeded.

There is a growing interest in organizations as emotional arenas.[42] The notion of emotional labor is now an accepted construct in organizational behavior.[43] By *emotional labor* it is meant that the expression of feeling is imposed on particular role functions, irrespective of the particular feelings that an individual may have at the time. There is a requirement that frontline employees of Disney and McDonalds constantly portray a happy disposition and display a positive attitude. Debt collectors may be under an obligation to portray a stern if not a nasty disposition. The popular notion of "good cop, bad cop" is an artificial construction that forces both to play a role that may be other than how they may be actually feeling about the situation at hand. Contemporary organizations increasingly demand outward expression of loyalty, commitment, and dedicated performance. In effect they are asking employees to be someone different.

Bento explores how organizations have difficulty in coping with grief.[44] She notes that while organizations allow people a few days to deal with the death of loved ones, according to a sliding scale of love—so many days for a partner, a child, a parent, a friend—after that period with an awkward pat on the back, the bereaved worker is expected to "get over it." Any subsequent expression of grief is deemed inappropriate. Yet we cannot turn expressions of grief on and off. While we may be embarrassed to find a colleague in tears at his or her desk, it is harder when we see the person keeping an impassive demeanor and acting out grief indirectly through moodiness, making mistakes, being late and so on.

Frost portrays a chilling view of the management of pain in organizations, which he refers to as "toxicity."[45] He found that when companies cause emotional pain through nasty bosses, layoffs, and change, a certain breed of "healing" manager steps in to listen to those in pain. These managers, whom he calls "toxic handlers," act as shock absorbers and listen to people's anger and frustration and deflect the pressure from higher management. These managers listen empathically, suggest solutions, work behind the scenes to prevent pain, carry the confidence of others, and act as translators of difficult messages. These toxic handlers receive no acknowledgment of this emotional work. Unlike professional helpers, such as counselors, therapists, and medical personnel, they have no training, and so they tend to internalize the pain of others and that tends to lead to a deterioration of their own health. What is chilling in Frost's portrayal is that he himself acknowledges that the origin of this work lay in his time as associate dean where he had to deal with difficult and painful issues for his staff and out of which he developed melanoma cancer. From his portrayal of this role, he sought to get companies to support these individuals and to prevent them from carrying a lot of stress and from burning out.

SUMMARY AND MANAGERIAL APPLICATIONS

Individual behavior in the context of work varies. Any attempt to learn why people behave as they do in work settings requires some basic understanding of the factors that influence action. The scientific field that provides the most insight into human behavior is psychodynamics. Yet, some students may wonder what the relevance of psychodynamic theories is to organizational behavior and management. This is an important question. The answer is at least threefold.

First, psychodynamic theories provide a path that students as future managers and employees can follow to understand themselves better. It can allow them to identify problematic areas of their psyche that routinely impede their interpersonal effectiveness. The story given at the beginning of the chapter illustrates how Helena's past relationship with her mother influenced her attitude toward Elizabeth. Once she understood what was happening, she was able to rectify her behavior. But the story was in fact even more complicated than described earlier. Elizabeth's past was also coming to bear with the way she dealt with the situation. Simply said, she was reliving her past difficult interaction with her grandmother. When Helena started criticizing her, she became defensive, and removed herself from her feelings, which prevented her from attending to Helena's needs. Furthermore, her Chinese education, which emphasized a strong respect of elders, prevented her from confronting Helena more directly about her irrational attitude. The denouement of the story allowed Elizabeth to realize that she could have a different sort of relationship with older Chinese women from the mainland than the one she had with her grandmother. Activity 4–1 allowed you to start to identify the origin of some of your biases, which may create similar problems for you as the one Helena faced.

Elizabeth learned a second lesson, which brings us to the second main managerial learning point of this chapter. Elizabeth realized that as a director, even though she was much younger than her actress, she needed to adopt a motherly role. She learned how to cope with transference. Every manager eventually has to cope with transference from her employees, and how to cope with employees' different worldviews. Different worldviews lead people to have different motivations and needs, to perceive the same situation differently, and thus behave differently. Culbert engages managers to gain consciousness of the different mindsets of their employees, in order to be effective at influencing them and developing them.[46] Managers who understand how their unconscious influences them will eventually become better equipped at understanding how their employees' unconscious influences them, or for that matter, that of their peers, bosses, or clients. Problems of miscommunication, which plague work life, as will be seen in more details in Modules 7 and 10, often cannot be resolved by having a rational conversation alone. A manager who understands and accepts that his or her employees cannot be fully rational, because their cognition stems from their unconscious, has an edge in building bridges of mutual understanding and trust. The Myers–Briggs and the Big Five can provide managers with models with which they can better understand how their subordinates are different from them. Indeed, many companies now routinely use one of these models to train their managers to better adapt to their subordinates and to recruit their personnel. Developing EI can also help managers to better understand their employees by allowing them to read their employees' emotional subtext and correctly diagnose emotional issues even when subordinates pretend to be having an intellectual problem.

Finally, psychodynamic theories can help us better understand charismatic and transformational leadership, which will be developed in Module 8, and change processes, which will be developed in Module 16. A big part of being a charismatic or transformational leader or of engaging a successful change process is to articulate a compelling vision that elevates and federates followers. A compelling vision is more than a strategically correct plan. It must be a story that moves followers viscerally. In order to articulate such a story, transformational leaders need to be in touch with their unconscious, their worldview, and also with the collective worldviews of their followers. Engaging in dream analysis and intimate interpersonal communication with their followers can help them do so more than reasoning by themselves or having a rational conversation with others.

In the end, understanding emotions and managing emotions at work takes a significant human effort. Successful managers and leaders have to be good psychologists because the heart of their work is to engage people, and it is impossible to do so effectively if one assumes that people are merely rational. Another critical element to the engagement of others can be found in the field of motivation—addressed in Module 5.

Study Questions

1. What are the three great blows in the history of Western thought?

2. Can you cite evidence that supports the notion of an unconscious?

3. Compare and contrast Freud's and Jung's models of the human psyche.

4. Can you find examples in which friends, families, acquaintances, or even you yourself have unconsciously used a defense mechanism? Which one was it? Can you identify the threatening feelings or realizations that this defense mechanism was protecting your ego from?

5. According to Argyris, how does defensiveness reduce effectiveness at work, and how can this be prevented?

6. How does human development happen? Describe two theories that illustrate it.

7. Can you analyze a dream you have had by making associations and identifying mythical symbols or themes?

8. How do past experiences influence our present?

9. What are the differences between an extrovert and an introvert? Is it always better to be an extrovert?

10. What are the five dimensions of the Big Five?

11. What is emotional intelligence?

Endnotes

1. JF. Coget, *Leadership in Motion: An Investigation into the Psychological Processes That Drive Behavior When Leaders Respond to "Real-Time" Operational Challenges, in Anderson School of Management—Human Resources and Organizational Behavior Area* (UCLA: Los Angeles, 2004), p. 232.

2. S. Freud, *The Standard Edition of the Complete Psychological Works of Sigmund Freud* (Hogarth: London, 1953), p. 74.

3. A. Freud, *The Ego and the Mechanisms of Defence* (New York: International Universities Press, 1946).

4. S. Freud, "A Difficulty in the Path of Psychoanalysis," in *Complete Psychological Works of Sigmund Freud* (Hogarth Press: London, 1955), pp. 135–44.

5. P. S. MacLean, *The Triune Brain, Emotion and Scientific Basis,* in F. O. Schitt (ed.), *The Neurosciences: Second Study Program* (Rockefeller University Press: New York, 1970).

6. R. M. Shiffrin and R. M. Nosofsky, "Seven Plus or Minus Two: A Commentary on Capacity Limitations," centennial issue of the *Psychological Review* 101, no. 2 (1994), pp. 357–61.

7. G. A. Miller, "The Magical Number Seven, Plus or Minus Two: Some Limits on Our Capacity for Processing Information," *Psychological Review* 101, no. 2 (1994), pp. 343–52.

8. S. Freud and J. Riviere, *A General Introduction to Psycho-Analysis.* Authorized English translation of the revised edition by J. Riviere (ed.); with a preface by E. Jones and G. Stanley Hall. (eds.), A Clarion book (New York: Simon and Schuster, 1969).

9. A. Freud, *The Ego and the Mechanisms of Defence.*

10. C. Argyris, "Teaching Smart People How to Learn," *Harvard Business Review* (May–June 1991), pp. 99–109.

11. C. G. Jung, *The Collected Works of C. G. Jung,* 2nd ed., Bollingen series 20, (Princeton, NJ: Princeton University Press, 1966).

12. Ibid.

13. J. Campbell, *The Hero with a Thousand Faces* (New York: Meridian Books, 1967).

14. Ibid.

15. MacLean, *The Triune Brain, Emotion and Scientific Basis.*

16. S. Freud, *The Standard Edition of the Complete Psychological Works of Sigmund Freud.*

17. J. Piaget, *Six Psychological Studies* (Brighton: Harvester Press, 1980), p. 169.

18. A. H. Maslow, *Motivation and Personality* (New York: Harper, 1954), p. 411.

19. K. Wilber, *A Brief History of Everything* (Boston: Shambhala, 1996), p. 339.

20. Ibid.

21. C. Gilligan, *In a Different Voice* (Cambridge, MA: Harvard University Press, 1982).

22. L. Kohlberg, "Essays on Moral Development," vol. 1, *The Philosophy of Moral Development* (San Francisco: Harper, 1981).

23. C. Graves, "Levels of Existence: An Open System Theory of Values," *Journal of Humanistic Psychology* 10, no. 2 (1970), pp. 131–54.

24. Maslow, *Motivation and Personality.*

25. Piaget, *Six Psychological Studies.*

26. Kohlberg, "Essays on Moral Development."

27. Maslow, *Motivation and Personality.*

28. S. Freud, *The Interpretation of Dreams* (New York: Gramercy Books, 1996), p. 438.

29. B. F. Skinner, *About Behaviorism,* (New York: Vintage Book, 1976), p. 291.

30. S. F. Maddi, *Theories: A Comparative Analysis* (Burr Ridge, IL: Dorsey, 1980).

31. I. Briggs-Myers and P. Myers, *Gifts Differing* (Consulting Psychologists Press, 1980).

32. J. M. Digman, "Higher-Order Factor of the Big Five," *Journal of Personality and Social Psychology* 73, no. 6 (1997), pp. 1246–56.

33. Briggs-Myers and Myers, *Gifts Differing.*

34. Digman, "Higher-Order Factor of the Big Five."

35. L. R. Goldberg, "The Structure of Phenotypic Personality Traits," *American Psychologist,* 48, no. 1 (1993), pp. 26–34.

36. Ibid.

37. M. R. Marrick and M. K. Mount, "The Big Five Personality Dimensions and Job Performance: A Meta Analysis," *Personnel Psychology* 44 (1991), pp. 1–26.

38. D. Goleman, *Emotional Intelligence* (New York: Bantam Books, 1995).

39. P. Salovey and J. D. Mayer, *Emotional Intelligence. Imagination, Cognition and Personality* 9, no. 3 (1990), pp. 185–211.

40. C.-S. Wong, and K. S. Law, "The Effect Of Leader and Follower Emotional Intelligence on Performance and Attitude: An Exploratory Study," *The Leadership Quaterly* 13 (2002), pp. 243–74.

41. Q. N. Huy, "Emotional Capability, Emotional Intelligence, and Radical Change. Academy of Management," *The Academy of Management Review* 24, no. 2 (1991), p. 325.

42. S. Fineman, *Emotion in Organizations* (London: Sage, 2000); N. Ashkenazy, C. Hartel, and W. Zerbe, *Emotions in the Workplace: Research, Theory and Practice,* (Westport, CT: Quorum, 2000).

43. A. Rafaeli and R. Sutton, "Expression of Emotion as Part of the Work Role," *Academy of Management Review* 12, no. 1 (1987), pp. 23–37.

44. R. Bento, "When the Show Must Go On: Disenfranchised Grief in Organizations," *Journal of Managerial Psychology* 9, no. 6 (1994), pp. 35–44.

45. P. J. Frost, *Toxic Emotions at Work* (Boston: Harvard Business School Press, 2003).

46. S .A. Culbert, *Mind-Set Management: The Heart of Leadership* (New York: Oxford University Press, 1996), p. 340.

Activity 4–2: Exploring Individual Personality Profile: The Big Five Locator Questionnaire*

Objectives:

a. To investigate a trait model of personality.

b. To enable students to begin to examine their personality profile.

Task 1:

a. Complete the Big Five Locator Questionnaire. On each numerical scale, indicate which point is generally more descriptive of you. If the two terms are equally descriptive, mark the midpoint.

b. Complete the scoring sheet, following the instructions.

Place your scores on the Big Five Locator Interpretation Sheet.

*The Big Five Locator Questionnaire is a quick assessment tool to be used with an instructor and willing learners. Care should be taken to follow up this profile with a more reliable personality assessment instrument. This instrument was developed by P. J. Howard, P. L. Medina, and J. M. Howard, "The Big Five Locator: A Quick Assessment Tool for Consultants and Trainers," in J. W. Pfeiffer (ed.), *The 1996 Annual,* vol. 1, *Training* (San Diego: Pfeiffer & Company, 1996), pp. 119–22. Reprinted with permission. Copyright by Jossey-Bass Inc., Publishers. All rights reserved.

Name _____ Date _____

THE BIG FIVE LOCATOR QUESTIONNAIRE

Instructions: On each numerical scale that follows, indicate which point is generally more descriptive of you. If the two terms are equally descriptive, mark the midpoint.

1.		Eager	5	4	3	2	1	Calm
2.	Prefer Being with Other People		5	4	3	2	1	Prefer Being Alone
3.		A Dreamer	5	4	3	2	1	No Nonsense
4.		Courteous	5	4	3	2	1	Abrupt
5.		Neat	5	4	3	2	1	Messy
6.		Cautious	5	4	3	2	1	Confident
7.		Optimistic	5	4	3	2	1	Pessimistic
8.		Theoretical	5	4	3	2	1	Practical
9.		Generous	5	4	3	2	1	Selfish
10.		Decisive	5	4	3	2	1	Open Ended
11.		Discouraged	5	4	3	2	1	Upbeat
12.		Exhibitionist	5	4	3	2	1	Private
13.		Follow Imagination	5	4	3	2	1	Follow Authority
14.		Warm	5	4	3	2	1	Cold
15.		Stay Focused	5	4	3	2	1	Easily Distracted
16.		Easily Embarrassed	5	4	3	2	1	Don't Give a Darn
17.		Outgoing	5	4	3	2	1	Cool
18.		Seek Novelty	5	4	3	2	1	Seek Routine
19.		Team Player	5	4	3	2	1	Independent
20.		A Preference for Order	5	4	3	2	1	Comfortable with Chaos
21.		Distractible	5	4	3	2	1	Unflappable
22.		Conversational	5	4	3	2	1	Thoughtful
23.	Comfortable with Ambiguity		5	4	3	2	1	Prefer Things Clear-Cut
24.		Trusting	5	4	3	2	1	Skeptical
25.		On Time	5	4	3	2	1	Procrastinate

SCORING THE BIG FIVE QUESTIONNAIRE

Instructions:

1. Find the sum of the circled numbers on the *first* row of each of the five-line groupings (Row 1 + Row 6 + Row 11 + Row 16 + Row 21 = _____). This is your raw score for "adjustment." Circle the number in the Adjustment column of the Score Conversion Sheet that corresponds to this raw score.

2. Find the sum of the circled numbers on the *second* row of each of the five-line groupings (Row 2 + Row 7 + Row 12 + Row 17 + Row 22 = _____). This is your raw score for "sociability." Circle the number in the Sociability column of the Score Conversion Sheet that corresponds to this raw score.

3. Find the sum of the circled numbers on the *third* row of each of the five-line groupings (Row 3 + Row 8 + Row 13 + Row 18 + Row 23 = _____). This is your raw score for "openness." Circle the number in the Openness column of the Score Conversion Sheet that corresponds to this raw score.

4. Find the sum of the circled numbers on the *fourth* row of each of the five-line groupings (Row 4 + Row 9 + Row 14 + Row 19 + Row 24 = _____). This is your raw score for "agreeableness." Circle the number in the Agreeableness column of the Score Conversion Sheet that corresponds to this raw score.

5. Find the sum of the circled numbers on the *fifth* row of each of the five-line groupings (Row 5 + Row 10 + Row 15 + Row 20 + Row 25 = _____). This is your raw score for "conscientiousness." Circle the number in the Conscientiousness column of the Score Conversion Sheet that corresponds to this raw score.

6. Find the number in the far right or far left column that is parallel to your circled raw score. Enter this norm score in the box at the bottom of the appropriate column.

7. Transfer your norm score to the appropriate scale on the Big Five Locator Interpretation Sheet.

Big Five Locator Score Conversion Sheet

Norm Score	Adjustment	Sociability	Openness	Agreeableness	Conscientiousness	Norm Score
80						80
79			25			79
78						78
77	22					77
76			24			76
75						75
74						74
73	21		23			73
72		25				72
71				25		71
70	20	24	22			70
69					25	69
68				24		68
67		23	21		24	67
66	19					66
65		22		23	23	65
64			20			64
63					22	63
62	18	21	19	22		62
61					21	61
60		20				60
59	17		18	21	20	59
58						58
57		19				57
56			17			56
55	16	18		20	19	55
54		16		19		54
53						53
52		17			18	52
51	15					51
50		16	15	18	17	50
49						49
48	14	15			16	48
47			14	17		47
46		14			15	46
45			13			45
44	13			16	14	44
43		13				43
42			12			42
41				15	13	41
40	12	12	11			40
39						39
38				14	12	38
37		11	10			37
36	11					36
35		10		13	11	35
34			9			34
33	10	9			10	33
32				12		32
31			8			31
30		8			9	30
29	9			11		29
28		7	7		8	28
27				10		27
26		6			7	26
25	8		6			25
24				9	6	24
23						23
22			5		22	22
21	7	5				21
20				8		20

Enter Norm Scores Here: Adj =   S =   O =   A =   C =

(Norms based on a sample of 161 forms completed in 1993–94.)

Name _____   Date _____

BIG FIVE LOCATOR INTERPRETATION SHEET

Scores:

Adjustment   _____

Sociability   _____

Openness   _____

Agreeableness   _____

Conscientiousness   _____

Strong Adjustment: secure, unflappable, rational, unresponsive, guilt-free	Resilient 35	45	Responsive	55	Reactive 65		**Weak Adjustment:** excitable, worrying, reactive, high strung, alert
Low Sociability: private, independent, works alone, reserved, hard to read	Introvert 35	45	Ambivert	55	Extrovert 65		**High Sociability:** assertive, sociable, warm, optimistic, talkative
Low Openness: practical, conservative, depth of knowledge, efficient, expert	Preserver 35	45	Moderate	55	Explorer 65		**High Openness:** broad interests, curious, liberal, impractical, likes novelty
Low Agreeableness: skeptical, questioning, tough, aggressive, self-interest	Challenger 35	45	Negotiator	55	Adapter 65		**High Agreeableness:** trusting, humble, altruistic, team player, conflict averse, frank
Low Conscientiousness: private, independent, works alone, reserved, hard to read	Flexible 35	45	Balanced	55	Focused 65		**High Conscientiousness:** dependable, organized, disciplined, cautious, stubborn

Note: The Big Five Locator is intended for use only as a quick assessment for teaching purposes.

Module 5

Motivation

LEARNING OBJECTIVES

After completing this module, you should be able to

1. Appreciate the complex nature of motivation at work.
2. Gain insight into some managerial viewpoints of motivation.
3. Explain and apply basic theories of motivation.
4. Gain insights into your own motivation patterns.
5. Identify some basic managerial and organizational actions that can foster individual motivation.

KEY TERMS AND CONCEPTS

Alienation

Behavior modification

Dissatisfiers

Demotivation

Employee stock ownership plan (ESOP)

Equity theory

Expectancy theory

Goal-setting theory

Hierarchy of needs

Hygiene factors

Management by objectives and results (MBO&R)

Motivation

Motivation theory

Motivators

n achievement

n power

P–L (Porter–Lawler) model

Process theories of motivation

Profit-sharing plans

Pygmalion effect

Self-efficacy

Skill-based pay

Team motivation

Work motivation

MODULE OUTLINE

Premodule Preparation

Activity 5–1: Motivation to Work

Introduction

Managerial Viewpoints on Motivation

Traditional Viewpoint

Human Relations Viewpoint

Human Resources Viewpoint

Theoretical Viewpoints on Motivation

The Role of Needs in Motivation

Maslow's Hierarchy of Needs

McClelland's *n* Achievement, *n* Power, and *n* affiliation

Herzberg's Motivation–Hygiene Needs Theory

The Role of Equity in Motivation

The Role of Goals and Expectations in Motivation

Goal-Setting Theory

Expectancy Theory

The Role of Work Context in Motivation

The Role of Rewards in Motivation

Porter–Lawler Model

Linking Theory and Managerial Practice

Alienation at Work

The Process of Demotivation

Management by Objectives

Profit-Sharing Plans

Skill-Based Pay

Pygmalion and Motivation

Behavior Modification

Motivation in Work Teams

International Viewpoint on Motivation

Summary

Study Questions

Endnotes

Activity 5–2: The Slade Plating Department Case

Activity 5–3: Alternative Courses of Managerial Action in the Slade Plating Department

Activity 5–4: Motivational Analysis of Organizations-Behavior (MAO-B)

Optional Activities on the WWW

Activity 5–5W: Motivation through Goal Setting

Activity 5–6W: Reinforcement Theory

PREMODULE PREPARATION

Activity 5–1:
Motivation to Work

Objectives:

a. To determine your views of what has made you most and least productive in past work situations.

b. To compare your results with some current motivational studies and theories.

Task 1:

Each individual, working alone, is to use the accompanying worksheet for answers to the following:

a. Think back on your work experience to a time when you were performing at your very best. What were the factors that accounted for your high performance? List them on the accompanying worksheet. (Time: 5 minutes)

b. Think back on your work experience to a time when you were performing less than your best or poorly. What were the factors that accounted for this performance? List them on the accompanying worksheet. (Time: 5 minutes)

Task 2:

Each team should select a spokesperson.

a. List the important factors agreed upon by the group for the two areas of "best" performance and "less than best." Be prepared to give an example from one member's experience for each factor on the list. (Time: 15 minutes)

b. The instructor will call upon spokespersons, one at a time, to give one factor from the group's "best" list to be written on the board. Examples should be given for clarification. This exercise will continue until all the best factors from the groups have been presented.

c. Repeat this procedure for "less than best."

The instructor will give a short lecture.

Name _____   Date _____

WORKSHEET FOR ACTIVITY 5–1

a. Think back on your work experience to a time when you were performing at your very best. What factors accounted for your high performance? List them. (Time: 3 minutes)

b. Think back on your work experience to a time when you were performing at less than your best or poorly. What factors accounted for this performance? List them. (Time: 3 minutes)

INTRODUCTION

Motivation, at the most basic level, refers to the inner urges that cause people to behave in certain ways. In the workplace, while some explore the issue of what motivates or demotivates individuals, we argue that a more accurate focus should be on understanding what motivates people in a specific direction. Since the firm's success, profitability, and sustainability are directly linked to individual performance and productivity, a central theme for managers is how to ensure that employees are performing at the highest possible level.[1] A more careful examination of the issue reveals that the answer to this critical question rests in the understanding of the mix of psychological, personal, and contextual forces. We begin our discussion of the subject by first providing a short case study; second, providing some philosophical viewpoints that can help managers approach motivation challenges such as productivity, satisfaction, absenteeism, and turnover; third, using a few activities, self-assessment tools, and cases; and fourth, presenting some of the most dominant motivation theories, some of which are universal and some of which are culture bound.

We open with a short case study reported by one of our students who had worked in two car washes as a teenager. The car washes were in a small city and operated by different owners. In the first, the dripping vehicle would come off the rinse line, where four teenagers waited with towels to wipe it dry. When the wipers were finished, they signaled the car owner by leaving the car door standing open. The car owner would generally walk past a pot placed in his or her path with a sign that read "Tips, Thank You," climb into the car, and drive away with the windows still wet and water streaming from some parts of the car. Occasionally, one of the wipers dropped a wet towel on the ground, only to pick it up and continue wiping. One customer complained to the manager that the wet towel could pick up sand from the pavement and scratch the car. Only a few small coins got into the pot. Turnover of wipers was high, and they expressed hostile attitudes toward management.

The second car wash was opened by a vigorous, enthusiastic young owner. A system was established whereby each customer paid for the service when entering the wash. A ticket was handed to the customer (a practice not followed at the first car wash), which was to be given to the final wiper when the car was dry. The car coming off the rinse line was received by four teenage wipers, three of whom would go on to another car after doing the initial work, while the fourth did the final wiping. This individual did everything possible to please because the customer was not inclined to give the ticket to the wiper until the work was done to her or his satisfaction. The customers usually stood beside the wiper pointing out places where more drying was needed. While doing this, the customer generally took change out of his or her pocket or purse and waited for the wiper to ask for the ticket. Tips were generous, and customers drove away in well-dried cars. The manager often got the entire work crew together for pep talks that ran something like this:

> We're the best car wash on the coast. We do the best work, have the most satisfied customers, have the happiest workers, and hopefully make the most money of any car wash of equal size. Your tips will be good if you do a perfect job. I've set up 10 customer chairs alongside the wiping area. This is your audience. Show them how well you can do. When you finish, give your customer a guided tour of the car and ask if everything is all right. With this treatment, your customer standing there waiting to give you the ticket will develop the expectation that you should have a good tip. The "audience" on the sideline will see you get tipped. The audience will also tell other people what a great job we do here.

The owner's practices also included job rotation so workers did all jobs (all got a share of the wiper jobs so they would get tipped), flexibility in choosing work hours, and (on weekends) bonuses if a certain volume was reached. The car wash prospered. This simple case illustrates many of the basic concepts and approaches to motivation that we discuss in this module. We shall refer to this case during the discussion.

MANAGERIAL VIEWPOINTS ON MOTIVATION

Global competition, productivity, quality, and *product safety (as of late)* have become buzzwords of this decade. *Productivity* and *quality* have many definitions. Most are related to motivation—whether it is the "zero defect" ratio in manufacturing, individual production averaged over a number of people, hours of work and dollar cost of labor, or individual effort and performance, the implied, ever-present question is, How do you get the individual to accomplish more, achieve better quality, all at a lesser cost?

Because this is a management course, we will start with some ways of thinking about **motivation** that can be helpful in guiding your specific managerial activities. Ask executives and managers attending workshops what the primary problems of motivation are, and they will place blame on people: Workers are not committed; they don't care if they do a good job; they are poorly trained in the school systems; parents don't bring up kids like they used to. Sometimes there is the complaint that you cannot find good first-line supervisors who will accept full responsibility. Our answer to this complaint is the same as for problems of personal growth and effectiveness: If you aren't achieving what you want, it's not the fault of your family, teachers, ethnic background, girlfriend, boyfriend, and so on. The only way you're going to achieve goals is to assume full responsibility for your own progress and stop blaming others.

And so it is with management. There is little to be gained by blaming the workers and much to be gained by planning, stimulating, and influencing motivation. A helpful way of focusing on the motivation challenge is to assume there are no "bad" people, just bad management practices—that is, management is causing the problem; working conditions are poor; or the architectural, organizational, or work designs are faulty.

Following this logic, three general patterns of managerial approaches to motivation were identified: the traditional model, the human relations model, and the human resources model.[2] The basic assumptions made by managers that follow the specific approach guide them in setting up policies, which in turn communicate a set of managerial expectations to their subordinates. Table 5–1 summarizes the managerial approaches and their assumptions, policies, and expectations.

Traditional Viewpoint

The *traditional model* (labeled by McGregor as *theory X*) assumes that for the average worker work is inherently distasteful; that what the individual does is less important than what he or she earns for doing it; that the individual by nature is self-centered, is inclined to be lazy, and prefers to be led rather than take responsibility; and that few individuals want or can handle work that requires creativity, self-direction, or self-control. Therefore, the manager's basic task is to closely supervise and control subordinates. He or she must break down tasks into simple, repetitive, easily learned operations; he or she must establish detailed work routines and resources and must enforce these firmly but fairly through rewards and punishments.

Human Relations Viewpoint

The *human relations model* (labeled by McGregor as *theory Y*) assumes that people want to feel useful and important, that people desire to belong and to be recognized as individuals, and that these needs are more important than money in motivating people to work. Therefore, the manager's basic task is to arrange organizational conditions so that people can achieve their goals by directing their efforts toward organizational objectives. He or she should make each worker feel useful and important, should keep subordinates informed and listen to their feedback, and should allow subordinates to exercise some self-direction and self-control on routine matters.

Human Resources Viewpoint

Having made our assumption about people, let us amend it. From the human resource development viewpoint, it is assumed that work is not inherently distasteful, that people want to contribute to meaningful goals that they have helped establish, and that most people can exercise far more creative, responsible self-direction and self-control

**Table 5–1
General Patterns
of Managerial
Approaches to
Motivation**

	Traditional Model	Human Relations Model	Human Resources Model
		Assumptions	
	Work is inherently distasteful to most people.	People want to feel useful and important.	Work is not inherently distasteful. People want to contribute to meaningful goals that they have helped to establish.
	What they do is less important than what they earn for doing it.	People desire to belong and to be recognized as individuals.	
	Few want or can handle work that requires creativity, self-direction, or self-control.	These needs are more important than money in motivating people to work.	Most people can exercise far more creative, responsible self-direction and self-control than their present jobs demand.
		Policies	
	The manager's basic task is to closely supervise and control subordinates.	The manager's basic task is to make each worker feel useful and important.	The manager's basic task is to make use of "untapped" human resources.
	Managers must break down tasks into simple, repetitive, easily learned operations.	Managers should keep subordinates informed and listen to their objections to managers' plans.	Managers must create an environment in which all members may contribute to the limits of their ability.
	Managers must establish detailed work routines and procedures and enforce these firmly but fairly.	Managers should allow subordinates to exercise some self-direction and self-control on routine matters.	Managers must encourage full participation on important matters, continually broadening subordinate self-direction and control.
		Expectations	
	People can tolerate work if the pay is decent and the boss is fair.	Sharing information with subordinates and involving them in routine decisions will satisfy their basic needs to belong and to feel important.	Expanding subordinate influence, self-direction, and self-control will lead to direct improvements in operating efficiency.
	If tasks are simple enough and people are closely controlled, they will produce up to standard.	Satisfying these needs will improve morale and reduce resistance to formal authority—subordinates will "willingly cooperate."	Work satisfaction may improve as a by-product of subordinates making full use of their resources.

Source: Adapted from R. M. Steers, L. W. Porter, and G. A. Bigley, *Motivation and Learning at Work* (New York: McGraw-Hill, 1996).

than their present jobs demand. There may be no "bad" people, but there are those who are unsuitable or less suitable, which brings us to another assumption: People will work well if they have the abilities, aptitudes, interests, attitudes, and temperament that make them most suitable to perform the job—that is, people must be matched with jobs. Therefore, the manager's basic task is to make use of "untapped" human resources. He or she should create an environment in which all members can contribute to the limits of their ability, and he or she should encourage full participation on important matters, continually broadening subordinates' self-direction and self-control.

THEORETICAL VIEWPOINTS ON MOTIVATION

The scientific literature includes a wide variety of theories and models on what motivation at work is all about and on how to motivate employees. Since the formal inception of the field of work motivation during the 1930s, many theoretical models have been developed to help explain and predict human motivational behavior in work settings. Although no clear consensus exists as to the definition, **work motivation** can be generally defined as "a set of energetic forces that originates both within as well as beyond an individual's being, to initiate work-related behavior, and to determine its form, direction, intensity and duration."[3] The sustainability perspective would suggest emphasis on duration, that is, what would sustain motivated behavior in the long term.

The literature indicates a wide range of theories and models that are varied in terms of focus and emphasis.[4] Several attempts have been made to cluster the many theories:

- Content theories of motivation (emphasizing reasons for motivated behavior or the specific factors that cause it) versus process theories of motivation (focusing on how behavioral change occurs) versus reinforcement theories of motivation (focusing on the elements that will increase the likelihood that described behavior will be repeated).

- Intrinsic theories (emphasizing the drive to perform that results from a person's internalized values and beliefs that the task is rewarding in and of itself) versus extrinsic theories (focusing on the drive to perform that results from a person's expectations that a specific action will result in a desired outcome such as a pay increase).

- Endogenous theories (focusing on the dynamics of the motivational process) versus exogenous theories (focusing on motivationally related elements that can be changed by external agents).

- Organizational-centered versus individual-centered frameworks.

- The role of needs, equity, rewards, goals and expectations, and delegation in motivation.[5]

In this module, we are using the broad classification schema of the role perspectives. We will briefly describe the basic theories within each role set. We believe that this typology not only can help you sort out the many different theories and models of motivation but also can boost understanding of the conditions and practices affecting work motivation.

The Role of Needs in Motivation

The "need perspective" in motivation is based on the idea that individuals have certain needs and their behaviors are designed to help them fulfill these needs. As such we strive to understand and explain the individual needs that arouse, start, initiate, or energize individual behavior. For example, if we examine the car wash case at the beginning of the chapter from a content theory point of view, the focus would be on what might have motivated the workers to behave the way they did. One can argue that in the more successful car wash, the individuals' needs for money, status, and achievement were more satisfied and served as motivators for their behavior. Representative theories in this cluster include Maslow's hierarchy of needs, Herzberg's two-factor theory, and McClelland's achievement/power theory.

Maslow's Hierarchy of Needs

Perhaps the best known of the need perspective theories is Maslow's **hierarchy of needs.** Under his concept, a need for achievement describes goals the individual is striving to attain in areas such as education, career, and work.[6] Because his theory is so well-known, we will focus on the basic assumptions and present only the aspect that will help you use the hierarchy as a tool for analyzing motivation in our case studies.

Underlying the hierarchy of needs are the following basic assumptions:

- The hierarchy of needs progresses from the most basic needs at the bottom of the hierarchy (that is, physiological and security) to the highest-level needs at the top (that is, esteem and self-actualization).

- If a need is not satisfied, it generates tension and a drive to act. Once a need has been satisfied, it does not motivate. Yet, when that occurs, another need gradually emerges to take its place.

- The needs move from concrete to abstract.

- At any point in time, several needs seem to affect individual behavior.

- The needs and the needs hierarchy are culturally and nationally contingent.

Our adoption of the five levels of the need hierarchy is depicted in Figure 5–1. Maslow assumed that the lower level had to be adequately satisfied before the next higher level became an important motivating force; that is, if the individual was highly concerned about physical needs, the other needs were not going to be the active basis for goal pursuance.

Figure 5–1
Maslow's Hierarchy of
Needs Requiring Fulfillment
in a Work Environment

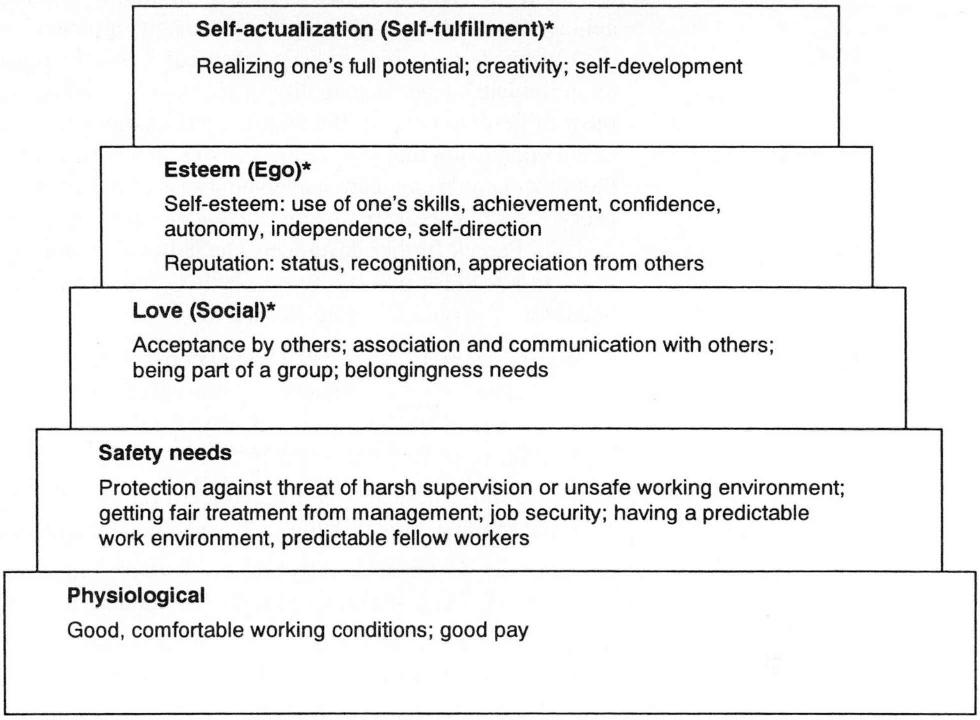

Self-actualization (Self-fulfillment)*

Realizing one's full potential; creativity; self-development

Esteem (Ego)*

Self-esteem: use of one's skills, achievement, confidence, autonomy, independence, self-direction

Reputation: status, recognition, appreciation from others

Love (Social)*

Acceptance by others; association and communication with others; being part of a group; belongingness needs

Safety needs

Protection against threat of harsh supervision or unsafe working environment; getting fair treatment from management; job security; having a predictable work environment, predictable fellow workers

Physiological

Good, comfortable working conditions; good pay

*Terms in parentheses are Douglas McGregor's, which are in common use.

Maslow believed that without having the first three needs met, an individual will fail to develop into a healthy person, both physically and psychologically. The next two needs—the higher-order needs—are known as growth needs, and their gratification is said to help individuals grow and develop to their potential.

McClelland's n Achievement, n Power, and n Affiliation

David C. McClelland focused on the needs for achievement, power, and affiliation. He found that salespersons and small-business entrepreneurs tended to be high in ***n achievement*** (*n* standing for need), and he concluded they need freedom in the working environment to exercise their strong self-direction tendencies.[7] However, *n* achievement is "a one-man game and need never involve other people." In contrast, managers are not necessarily high in *n* achievement but tend to be high in ***n power.*** The desire to influence, guide, and control others is an important aspect of a manager's motivation. D. G. Winter found, in a limited sample, that business and journalism students were significantly higher in *n* power than those from other occupational categories.[8]

McClelland distinguishes between *p* power (personalized) and *s* power (socialized) and speculates that the former precedes the latter in the development of the individual. The extreme of *p* power is raw control over others expressed in an interpersonal way, whereas *s* power is altruistic and is exercised for the benefit of others. Power fascinates executives; the topics of manipulation, win–lose situations, and Machiavellianism are of top interest when introduced into business workshops.

The concept of *n* power enhances the understanding of Maslow's hierarchy of needs. Persons having power can be assumed to have financial resources for their personal (physiological) needs; control over their environment (safety); considerable interaction with others (social); leeway for self-direction, status, and respect from their position (esteem); and opportunities to excel (self-actualization). Power thus can add considerably to the satisfaction of the person's need pattern and also is a strong reinforcer of managerial role behaviors.

In an extensive review of the research on the relationship between organization structural variables and need and job satisfaction, L. L. Cummings and C. J. Berger found excellent support for the conclusion that satisfaction increases as one moves up the organizational ladder.[9] This conclusion appears to support our analysis of *n* power. An important aspect of McClelland's work is success in training small-business people in India in *n* achievement behaviors. He reports that many of them changed dramatically after only five days of exposure to his workshop methods.[10] Psychologists have traditionally believed that an individual's basic personality structure is formed during the first 5 years of life and is most difficult to change. But McClelland's experience over years of work brings him more to the conclusion that leaders are not so much born as made. The emphasis in this book is that most people can learn leadership types of behaviors; however, we are not saying that everyone will necessarily become a leader—for one thing, *n* power is needed.

Udai Pareek further developed McClelland's work by extending the need for achievement and need for power into six needs or motives that are relevant for understanding the behavior of people in organizations:

1. *Achievement.* Characterized by concern for excellence, competition with the standards of excellence set by others or by oneself, the setting of challenging goals for oneself, awareness of the hurdles in the way of achieving those goals, and persistence in trying alternative paths to one's goals.

2. *Affiliation.* Characterized by a concern for establishing and maintaining close, personal relationships, a value on friendship, and a tendency to express one's emotions.

3. *Influence.* Characterized by concern with making an impact on others, a desire to make people do what one thinks is right, and an urge to change matters and develop people.

4. *Control.* Characterized by a concern for orderliness, a desire to be and stay informed, and an urge to monitor and take corrective action when needed.

5. *Extension.* Characterized by concern for others, interest in superordinate goals, and an urge to be relevant and useful to larger groups, including society.

6. *Dependence.* Characterized by a desire for the help of others in one's own self-development, checking with significant others (those who are more knowledgeable or have higher status, experts, close associates, and so on), submitting ideas or proposals for approval, and having an urge to maintain an "approval" relationship.[11]

Activity 5–4 provides an opportunity to diagnose individual motivation and provide the individual with a motivational profile.

Herzberg's Motivation–Hygiene Needs Theory

According to Frederick Herzberg, people have two major kinds of needs: The first of these Herzberg called "hygiene needs," which are influenced by the physical and psychological conditions in which people work. The second set of needs was called "motivator needs," which are described by Herzberg as being very similar to the higher-order needs in Maslow's need hierarchy perspective. Herzberg further claimed that these two types of needs were satisfied by different types of outcomes or rewards. Hygiene needs were said to be satisfied by the level of certain conditions hygiene factors or dissatisfiers.[12] The **dissatisfiers** include company policy and administration, supervision, relationships with supervisors, working conditions, salary, relationships with peers, personal life, relationships with subordinates, status, and security. These are potential dissatisfiers because employees expect and hope that they will all be good. If they are not good, the employees will be unhappy; if they are good, they only measure up to what the employees expect. The fact that all of these factors are favorable, however, does not make an individual happy or productive. It simply means that the individual is not unhappy. An analogy would be from garbage collection: If the garbage is collected from your home every week, you are almost unaware of it because this is what you expect. You are not unhappy, because conditions are as they should be. If the garbage collector fails to pick it up, you are very much aware of your dissatisfaction and the unhygienic consequences. If all the dissatisfier factors are good in your work life, everything is hygienic.

What really makes you want to work are the **motivators.** These include achievement, recognition, the nature of the work itself, responsibility, and opportunities for advancement and growth. For college students, the skills and abilities they learn are part of their self-esteem; the opportunity to use these in their first job and to do good work will be a primary motivator. Using their experience and skills remains a primary force throughout their careers.

Figure 5–2 presents results of a study by Herzberg and his colleagues that shows that factors such as achievement, recognition, and the work itself are most frequently mentioned in connection with satisfying work experiences. Dissatisfying work experiences were reported most frequently as arising from company policy and administration, supervision, and other **hygiene factors.** Thus we see more than 40 percent of the workers indicated achievement as a source of satisfaction, while more than 30 percent found company policy and administration were reasons for dissatisfaction.

Figure 5–2 also can be used to discuss Herzberg's assumption that motivation can be thought of as two entirely separate factors. Thus, people may be satisfied and dissatisfied at the same time. They can, for example, appreciate the opportunity the job offers for achievement and still be most unhappy about company policy, pay, or working conditions. Figure 5–3 illustrates this concept by showing that the motivators can start at zero (or neutral) and increase to highly satisfied as opportunities for achievement or responsibility improve. The hygiene factors can start at zero and increase to highly dissatisfied as conditions such as bad policy or salary get worse; being at zero on the hygiene scale does not mean you are satisfied. It only means that you are not dissatisfied—the garbage was picked up today, so everything is hygienic.

Figure 5–2
Comparison of Satisfiers (Motivators) and Dissatisfiers

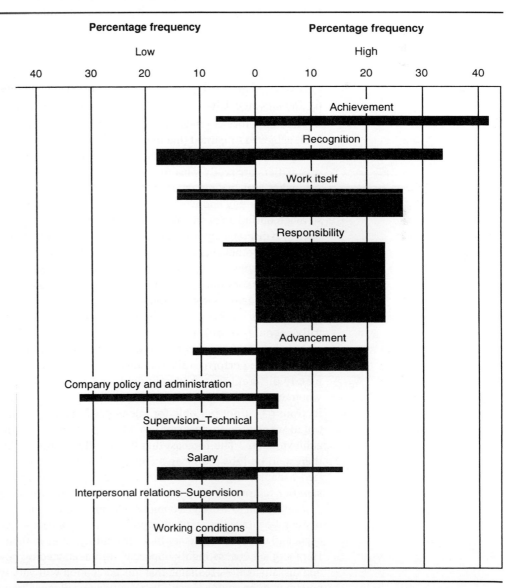

Source: Adapted from F. Herzberg, B. Mausner, and B. Snyderman, *The Motivation to Work,* 2nd ed. Copyright © 1959 by John Wiley & Sons. Reprinted by permission.

Figure 5–3
Two-Factor Continua

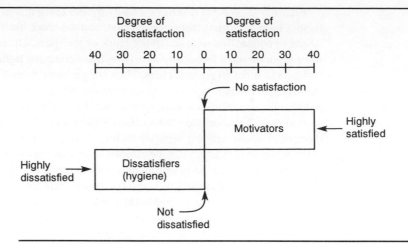

The results college students register in Activity 5–1 generally are similar to Herzberg's findings, which adds a certain amount of apparent validity to his theory. However, some factors Herzberg lists as dissatisfiers are seen by students as motivators. For instance, students enjoy working hard for a boss they like, and they like working hard with peers who are also working hard, even if the job is not exciting (possibly reflecting conformity to the social norms of the group). One reason for the basic agreement between Herzberg's findings and students' results may be that the data were selected by a similar method, asking people to recall past experience. This method is subject to criticism, however, because people unconsciously recall unpleasantness as due to things that are not under their control and therefore not their fault (the dissatisfiers). Pride in what they remember as having been achieved or earned (the motivators) can easily be unconsciously attributed to their own good efforts. Because of these psychological factors of recall, we cannot say that the dissatisfiers are really what turn people off; they are only what people *think* turn them off. And what turns people on or off under one set of circumstances may not do so under another; poor pay and working conditions may turn people off during prosperity but not so much during an economic depression when nothing else is available. There is also frequently a discrepancy between what young people say they want and the way they behave. Most will say they want challenge and self-direction, but many find difficulty in performing without considerable guidance and structure. The high turnover rate of young insurance salespersons during their first year provides an example of how the self-direction requirement can be overwhelming.

There has not been sufficient research to show that dissatisfiers and motivators truly account for differences in work performance.[13] Thus, it cannot be said that the motivation–hygiene theory has yet provided the evidence that the motivators are what make people perform well. Whether dissatisfaction and satisfaction are two completely different factors also has not been validated. The question might be raised whether the motivators themselves are not potentially the greatest source of dissatisfaction.[14] Is it not possible for talented, educated individuals to be completely frustrated when the job does not provide opportunities for the use of their abilities and achievements? The forecast that there will be more college-educated people than there will be jobs requiring a college education means many people may be dissatisfied because they cannot experience enough of the motivators even though all the dissatisfier factors offering a good life and pleasant working environment are present.

Motivation to work is a complex phenomenon. Some can claim that any specific theory can be viewed as an oversimplification. Managers should be aware of the various concepts and determine whether they have utility value in their own working situations. Herzberg's theory is highly important for understanding how people perceive satisfaction and dissatisfaction, realizing that this perception will vary with specific individuals. One person may be saying, I can't work without challenge; by comparison, another may be saying, just let me do the routine work so I can think about what I will be doing after work. Most important is Herzberg's position that (1) it is the nature of the work itself that turns on the self-directing generators for accomplishment and (2) emphasis on human relations alone will not result in high productivity or job satisfaction. Herzberg's use of the terms *satisfaction* and *dissatisfaction* in regard to work performance suggests there is a positive relationship between satisfaction and productivity.

The Role of Equity in Motivation

The basic premise of **equity theory** is that individuals want their efforts and performance to be judged fairly relative to others and that individuals engage in a process of evaluating their social relations much like they evaluate economic transactions in the marketplace. Thus, equity theory relies heavily both on the assessment of individual inputs and outputs and on social comparison. Figure 5–4 presents a general model of equity theory.

Four key elements are used to explain motivation dynamics in equity theory: input, outcomes, comparative analysis, and action. *Inputs* are what the person brings to the exchange—for example, education, past experience, skills, and knowledge—and these are perceived by the person and/or by others. *Outcomes* are what the individual receives from the exchange (for example, recognition, pay, fringe benefits, promotion, and status). *Comparative analysis* is the comparison of the weights ratio attached by individuals to the perceived inputs and outcomes for themselves versus relevant others who are in the same situation. The comparison to relevant others helps individuals determine the extent to which they feel that they have been treated equitably. Inequity causes tension both within the individual and between individuals. *Action* refers to the specific steps or behaviors that the individual undertakes to reduce the tension that results from the feeling of inequity. The energy source for the individual's motivation is restoring equity. Equity theory further states that an individual is motivated in proportion to the perceived fairness of the rewards received for a certain amount of effort, as compared to the rewards received by relevant others.[15] Perception plays a critical role in the equity theory point of view. We explore the phenomenon of perception in Module 6.

The Role of Goals and Expectations in Motivation

There is an increasing scientific body of knowledge that provides evidence that goals and expectations help people establish clearer focus, channel energies, and increase performance. Below we explore both goal-setting and expectancy theories.

Goal-Setting Theory

At the most basic level, **goal-setting theory** is concerned with the effect of goals on individual performance. The emphasis is on the intended outcomes and the motivational process that the establishment of the intended outcomes has on the behavior of

Figure 5–4
Equity Theory of Motivation

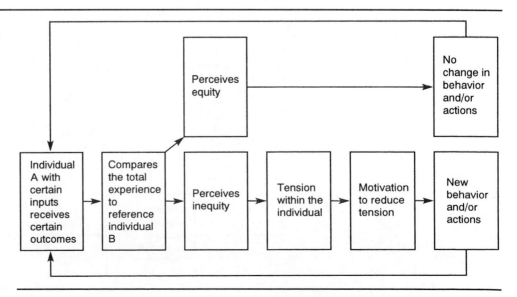

the individual. Goal-setting theory suggests that goals are associated with enhanced performance because they mobilize effort, direct attention, and encourage persistence and strategy development.

Locke and Latham developed a theory of individual goal setting and performance.[16] They claim that an assigned goal influences a person's beliefs about being able to perform that task—labeled **self-efficacy**—and encourages the acceptance of those goals as personal goals. Both factors in turn influence performance. Goals can be implicit or explicit, vague or clearly defined, and self-imposed or externally imposed. Many studies have shown that relative to general do-your-best goals, job performance is enhanced by the setting of specific goals.[17] Some studies suggest that people will accept and work hard to attain difficult goals until they reach the limits of their capabilities. However, as goals become difficult, they may be rejected, and performance will suffer.[18] Activity 5–5W provides an opportunity to experience some powerful notions of goal-setting theory as a motivational mechanism.

Expectancy Theory
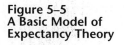

Expectancy-valence motivation theory is perhaps the most researched theory of work motivation. **Expectancy theory** suggests that individuals consider alternatives, weigh costs and benefits, and choose a course of action of maximum utility. Individuals make decisions among alternatives based on their perceptions of the degree to which a behavior can satisfy a desired want or need. At the most basic level, the expectancy that a specific level of effort will lead to a certain level of performance and the expectancy that a certain level of performance will result in a specific outcome are what facilitate an individual's motivation. Motivation is a function of expectancy, valence, and instrumentality.[19] Figure 5–5 presents a general model of expectancy theory.

The level and the amount of effort that the individual will exert in a given situation is a result of a cumulative effect of (1) the person's perceived probability that the level of the effort will lead to a desired level of performance *(expectancy)*, (2) the person's perceived probability that the level of performance will lead to a desired level of outcomes *(instrumentality)*, and (3) the person's perceived value of the projected outcomes *(valence)*. Although expectancy theory has dominated research in motivation since the early 1970s, because it identifies three useful elements to managers, its complexity has

**Figure 5–5
A Basic Model of
Expectancy Theory**

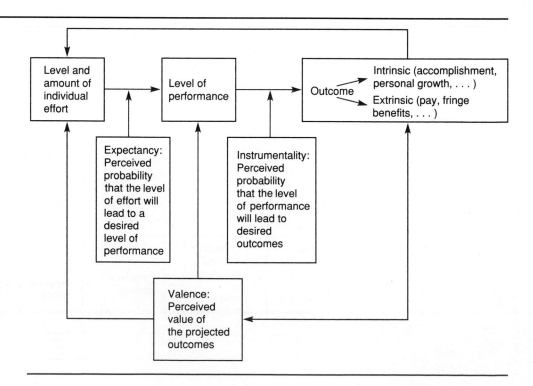

resulted in mixed empirical support.[20] Critics of the theory state that the model is too complex to measure and that the key elements are problematic in terms of definition and operationalization.[21] The comprehensiveness of the theory makes it a useful conceptual guide for understanding and fostering motivation at work.

The Role of Work Context in Motivation

One of the emerging assumptions about human behavior is that work context, such as degree of involvement, participation, empowerment, and delegation are important elements of work motivation and performance.[22] As managers get their subordinates more involved in decision making that is relevant to their work, as they provide them with more work autonomy, and as they delegate more responsibilities to them, employees are likely to put forth more effort and their job performance will improve. Among other effects of this set of scientific discoveries, we have seen the development of alternative theories about job, work, and organization design.

We will explore work and organization design in Part 4. For the purpose of this module, we focus briefly on job characteristic theory, which starts with the claim that the core characteristics of a job create critical psychological states that impact work motivation, job satisfaction, and work effectiveness. The psychological states—labeled the experience of meaningfulness of the work, the experience of responsibility for outcomes of the work, and the knowledge of the actual results of the work activities—are affected by the nature of the job and five core job dimensions: skill variety, task identity, task significance, autonomy, and feedback. In turn, the critical psychological states impact personal and work outcomes such as internal work motivation, quality of work performance, satisfaction with the work, as well as impact absenteeism and turnover.[23]

Delegation and participation are viewed as important positive aspects of effective management. The act of delegating responsibilities to employees and providing them with the authority necessary to carry out the delegated responsibility are viewed as powerful forces in motivating employees. This view is embedded in the assumptions that employees want to have responsibility, they appreciate the implicit trust in their skills and abilities, delegation is an effective tool to develop employees, and employees want to participate in decision making that affects their working life experience. As intriguing as the preceding set of assumptions is, the universal effectiveness of them is questionable. As we will see later in this module, many societies do not have a tradition of delegation, participation, and involvement.[24]

The Role of Rewards in Motivation

The role of equity that we explore earlier in this module also advocates the notions that rewards are means to motivate employees assuming that the rewards are distributed fairly. Rewards seem to be a part of many different perspectives in motivation. Porter and Lawler's motivation perspective provides a comprehensive and integrative view.

Porter–Lawler Model

This model relates a number of different factors to performance and satisfaction, and it highlights how these factors interact. In simplest terms, the **P–L model** relates rewards to effort to performance. Various factors affect effort, and others affect performance. The outcome or consequences of performance are also affected by individual factors.

In Figure 5–6, we can see that (1) *reward valence,* the value an individual places on a reward, together with (2) *expectancy,* a person's estimate of how probable an outcome is, affect (3) *effort.* An individual simply may not value the awards the organization is offering or may value other outcomes more. The employee who values social relationships with the work group more than potential rewards for outstanding performance will be unlikely to respond to incentives for increased production where group norms restrict performance. A person who believes that no reasonable amount of effort will produce the desired result is unlikely to try to perform. However, a challenging but possible goal is likely to be quite motivating.[25]

Expectancy is the individual's estimate of whether effort will lead to a desired reward (7a or 7b in Figure 5–6). There are several expectancy linkages. First, the individual may not believe that effort (3) will lead to performance (6). Where the job standard appears

**Figure 5–6
The Porter–Lawler
Motivation Model**

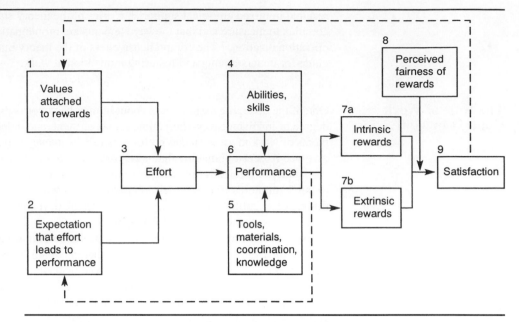

Source: Adapted from L. W. Porter and E. E. Lawler III, *Managerial Attitudes and Performance* (Burr Ridge, IL: Richard D. Irwin, 1968).

impossible to achieve, workers typically do not put in increasing effort—whether or not management shares workers' impression that the job is impossible. Similarly, if an individual believes the job is impossible, then even if others can do it, that person is unlikely to put forth the effort.

Another sort of expectancy concerns performance and outcomes. If I do, in fact, perform, will the desired reward actually come to me? From the manager's perspective, this sort of expectancy concerns the organization's reward system. Where rewards are closely tied to performance and administered fairly, people should have high expectancy that performance will result in the specified reward. Where no such linkage exists or where people believe the system does not operate accurately, people will have very different expectancies. Individuals' self-esteem, their past experiences in similar situations, the present situation, and communications from others (including group norms) will affect both the value they place on rewards (the reward valence) and their expectancies.[26]

In addition to people's values and expectancies, several other factors clearly affect the linkage between effort and performance. A person's abilities (4) clearly affect whether effort leads to performance; so too do the tools, material, and knowledge of when and where to apply effort (5). These factors are of special interest to managers because they seem particularly amenable to managerial change. Employees' skills can be improved by training, and their knowledge of when and where to apply effort can be improved by explicit role descriptions or directions.

The rewards actually received from performance affect both satisfaction and subsequent performance. Two sorts of outcomes can flow from performance: intrinsic rewards (7a) and extrinsic rewards (7b). (Of course, "rewards" can be negative as well as positive. Physical abuse from fellow employees attempting to restrict production or a chewing out from a supervisor constitute negative rewards.) Rewards that others provide (whether positive or negative) include money, praise or recognition, censure, and promotions. These rewards from external sources (outside the individual and the work itself) are *extrinsic rewards;* they depend on others' perceptions and assessments of performance. These rewards are like Herzberg's hygiene factors. These are the sorts of rewards most managers think of and most organizations at least partly control. Some of them, most notably those coming from work group members, may be not only outside management's control but also outside the manager's knowledge. But they are no less real or important.

Intrinsic rewards are those that individuals get from the work itself or give to themselves. Herzberg's motivators are intrinsic. A sense of accomplishment, self-esteem, pleasure at a job well done, and the feelings of growth, triumph, and success that may come from a difficult task are all examples of intrinsic rewards. These rewards are profoundly connected both to individual needs and preferences, on the one hand, and to the design of the work, on the other. Thus, challenging work creates the potential for this sort of intrinsic reward. But people looking for easy jobs that allow them simply to do the job and go home to really live will not find additional challenge rewarding. Similarly, for many college students, autonomy and self-direction are important values in general—but a part-time job that permits concentration of energies on schoolwork may be preferable.

Equity (8), the perception that rewards are fair or just, is also a factor. It is important to note that we are speaking of perception here and not necessarily fact. A reward system can be perfectly fair in actuality and still be *perceived* as biased (for instance, if employees are not told the basis for decisions about promotion). Where workers believe favoritism or unfairness is the rule, there will be dissatisfaction, especially with extrinsic rewards. (People may also be dissatisfied if they perceive someone was unfairly given a job that's high in intrinsic rewards, while they are left to contend with a less rewarding job.) Another aspect of equity is the balance between effort and reward. Either too little or too much reward will be perceived as inequitable and will be resented. Comparisons of the rewards that others receive for what appears to be equal effort are also a part of equity.

Satisfaction (9) is depicted as the outcome of valences, expectancies, effort, performance, reward, and perceived equity. Of course, this means degree of satisfaction, because individuals might very well be dissatisfied. The feedback loop between satisfaction and earlier factors in the model indicates that motivation is a dynamic, ongoing process. People learn from their experiences and adjust their values, attitudes, and expectations accordingly. Managers must be aware of the feedback loops for two reasons. First, individuals come to the workplace with a prior history or experience (in life if not at work). This past experience colors and affects people's values and expectations no less than their skills do. Managers must deal with people as they are (at least to begin with). Second, people's new experiences in the work setting and with their manager also affect their values and expectations. Therefore, managers will have to live with the results of their behaviors toward individuals and with the results of the organizational script for those individuals.

LINKING THEORY AND MANAGERIAL PRACTICE

Alienation at Work

An integral part of understanding and impacting motivation at work is the ability to counter the feeling of **alienation.** The phenomenon of alienation at work is a topic long discussed in organizational sociology. Marx's analysis was that the distance that workers experienced from their product led to estrangement. Weber developed the notion of the alienated worker to a more general situation that is part of the process of bureaucratization. Blauner described alienation in four ways: powerlessness (modes of freedom and control), meaninglessness (purpose and function of manual work), social alienation (integration and membership in industrial communities), and self-estrangement (alienation from inner self in the activity of work).[27] Argyris contrasted the psychology of individual development with the impact formal bureaucratic organizations have on their individual members.[28] He put forward a number of propositions that illustrated how the formal organization, in its attempts to optimize its own efforts, actually negates the developmental thrust of individuals. Individuals tend to develop from a state of passivity as infants to a state of increasing activity as adults. They move from dependence on others to relative independence and interdependence. They move from having a few ways of behaving to being capable of behaving in many different ways. They move from having a short-term perspective to a much longer time perspective. They develop a sense of self-awareness and self-reflection. They develop an ability to set personal goals and have values. Bureaucratic organizations by adopting a short-term perspective, foster dependency and expect their employees to adopt a passive, dependent, and subordinate stance. Individuals are given minimal control over their work. They are expected to utilize a few skin-surface skills. The effect, in Argyris's view, is that bureaucratic organizations keep their employees immature.

The Process of Demotivation

We can safely assume that people generally come to a job already motivated and that they are set on the road to **demotivation** by thoughtlessness and neglect. Meyer describes six stages of demotivation.[29] Stage 1 is the *Confusion* stage, where productivity drops slightly and the employee is wondering whether it is the boss or himself who is at fault. Stage 2 is the *Anger* stage where the employee's attitude becomes less positive and more angry as he tries to get the boss to notice that he is angry so that the boss will do something. Stage 3 is the *Subconscious Hope* stage where there is no longer any doubt as to who is at fault and the employee tends to avoid the boss and withholds information. Stage 4 is the *Disillusionment* stage where the employee gives up taking any initiative and only does the basic job. Stage 5 is the *Uncooperative* stage where the employee refuses to do anything that is not clearly part of his job, and Stage 6 is the *Final* stage where the employee either leaves the job or accepts it as a plodding 8 hours to be filled.

The options for any individual who finds herself at stage 6 of Meyer's six stages of demotivation are to leave the organization, sit on the fence, work the system, grumble persistently, find a niche, withdraw inwardly, or create a neurotic mechanism.[30] Leaving may not be a viable option, particularly in an economic recession, so the disillusioned employee may opt to work the system, which is to stay in the organization and exploit it as best as possible for her own self-interest—securing all the benefits available, avoiding all volunteering and extra work, and managing to spend as little time as possible doing anything significant. Persistent grumbling is where the individual always complains and grumbles about conditions and how things are in the organization. Some individuals manage to find a niche for themselves in which they create their own private enclave and reduce interdependence with others.

Ashforth and Lee describe defensive behavior as avoiding action by overconforming, passing the buck, playing dumb, depersonalizing and stalling, and avoiding blame by playing it safe, justifying, and scapegoating.[31] The final option is to collaborate with others who feel the same as they do in creating a collective delusion, which in Merry and Brown's view becomes a neurotic mechanism. So there is blaming, hostility, aggression, anger, feelings of frustration, and dysfunctional organizational behavior that bind people into a collective delusion and serve to relieve the organization of responsibility of confronting and dealing with its problems.

Motivation theory thus, is a complex core concept in the understanding of human behavior. As such it is linked to many aspects of work behavior.[32] The purpose of what follows is to discuss some of the linkages and explore managerial practices that are built on the various motivational theories that we reviewed earlier in the module. We explore the relationship between goal-setting theory and management by objectives, motivation and profit-sharing or stock-ownership programs, motivation and skill-based pay programs, Pygmalion and motivation programs, and motivation programs based on behavior modification.

Management by Objectives

Management by objectives and results (MBO&R) is a system that serves both as a planning tool and a motivational philosophy. This approach reflects synthesis of three areas: goal setting, participative decision making, and feedback. MBO&R is viewed as a participative process whereby managers and employees together set goals for work performance, personal development, and periodic reviews to assess progress. The process allows managers to integrate individual, team, unit/department, and organizational goals.

The process involves four key components: goal setting, mutual involvement of supervisor and employee, implementation, and performance appraisal and feedback. As such, in an MBO&R program, the supervisor and subordinate attempt to reach consensus on the following: the goals the subordinate will strive to accomplish during a specific time period, the means that the subordinate will utilize to reach the goals, and how and when the progress toward the goal accomplishment will be measured and evaluated.

Developed in the 1950s by Peter Drucker,[33] this managerial application has gone through many transformations.[34] While many organizations are using MBO&R successfully, critics have attacked the approach, particularly with respect to the ways in which some organizations apply it. Some critics argue that MBO&R places too much emphasis on rewards and punishments, generates an excessive amount of paperwork, places too much emphasis on individual goals versus team goals, and fosters game playing between managers and subordinates.[35]

Profit-Sharing Plans

Employee participation in work-planning programs, or **profit-sharing plans,** is frequently reported as a method to link employee compensation with organization profits. It is an old idea that has attracted new interest as a means of increasing productivity and quality. The Scanlon Plan, which goes back to the 1930s, is a program in which employees are involved in making and integrating suggestions into the company's operating processes. A formula is used to distribute a percentage of the resulting cost savings and profits to employees. The plan has been used for many years by the Lincoln Electric Company of Cleveland and has benefited both the company and the employees. A unique and relatively recent development of profit-sharing plans is the **employee stock ownership plan (ESOP).**

ESOP activities have been spreading at an increasing rate over the past decade. It is estimated that 10 million workers, or nearly 10 percent of the private-sector workforce, are participating in ESOPs with assets of about $20 billion in 7,500 companies, about 1,500 of which are majority or fully employee owned.[36] There are three main types of ESOPs:

1. *The nonleveraged ESOP.* The company contributes stock or cash to buy stock in a trust that buys workers' shares, which workers receive upon retirement or leaving the company.

2. *The leveraged ESOP.* Workers' ownership is established with money the company borrows to invest in company stock for the workers. The company guarantees that it will make periodic payments to the worker-ownership trust to amortize the loan.

3. *The tax-credit ESOP.* The company gets dollar-for-dollar tax credit for stock purchased for workers.

Research indicates that ESOP companies showed an average annual productivity increase, improved employee motivation,[37] and increased growth rate of two to four times that of companies where employees did not own stock.[38]

Skill-Based Pay

Skill-based pay (at times called competency-based pay) has emerged as an alternative to job-based pay. Rather than having an individual's job title define his or her pay category, skill-based pay determines pay levels by the number of skills the individual has mastered.[39] Skill-based pay programs motivate employees to learn, expand their skills, and grow. A recent study of *Fortune* 1000 companies found that companies that pay employees for learning skills reported higher job satisfaction, improved product quality, and increased productivity. Furthermore, 75 percent of those companies reported lower operating costs and turnover.[40]

Skill-based pay programs are consistent with many of the process and content motivational theories. For example, acquiring new skills is congruent with McClelland's *n* achievement needs theory because it provides more freedom and flexibility in the work environment and, for high achievers, offers new skills that help them deal successfully with more challenging jobs. Another example that "fits" is equity theory. Individuals are likely to perceive the equity in the program. The more one learns, the more one gets paid. At the same time, tension within the individual might motivate him or her to learn more skills.

From an organization and management perspective, skill-based pay provides clear advantages: It is a way to continually upgrade employees' skills, provide managerial flexibility in terms of grouping people based on changing customer needs and demands, improve communications and understanding across units boundaries, and stay competitive with a dynamic workforce that is current in its knowledge and competencies.

Pygmalion and Motivation

As we saw in Module 2 on expectations and learning, the self-fulfilling prophecy (SFP) or **Pygmalion effect** is a major social phenomenon with far-reaching implications. In a recent study, a unique and practical model that pulls together leadership, expectation, motivation, and performance at work was proposed[41] (see Figure 5–7).

The model encompasses five interrelated variables: manager expectations, leadership, subordinate self-expectations, effort, and achievement. The manager's performance expectations for a subordinate influence the leadership dynamics between the manager and the subordinate. As a result, the subordinate raises his or her expectations, which increases the motivation to exert a greater deal of effort on the job, the outcome of which is improved performance and better achievement. Dov Eden's research demonstrated that the combination of raising self-expectations, self-efficacy, and setting specific, hard goals increases performance. Furthermore, this line of research and its findings provided additional support for the combined effect of Pygmalion and goal setting on motivation. This combined effect appears especially promising in increasing motivation and performance.[42]

Behavior Modification

A very different kind of practical technique that has been attracting much managerial attention is behavior modification. Based especially on the work of B. F. Skinner, **behavior modification** insists that internal states of mind (such as needs) are misleading, scientifically immeasurable, and, in any case, hypothetical. Instead, what managers and behavioral scientists need to pay attention to is behavior—the observable outcomes of situations and choices, or what people actually do. This approach to behavior rests on two underlying assumptions: (1) Human behavior is determined by the environment; and (2) human behavior is subject to observable laws (such as the laws of physics or chemistry) and thus can be predicted and changed. Behavior is changed by rewarding it, ignoring it, or punishing people for using it. The behavior modification view says that behavior is a response to a combination of specific stimuli and other environmental factors (such as time and previous experiences).

Figure 5–7
A Model of Self-Fulfilling Prophecy at Work

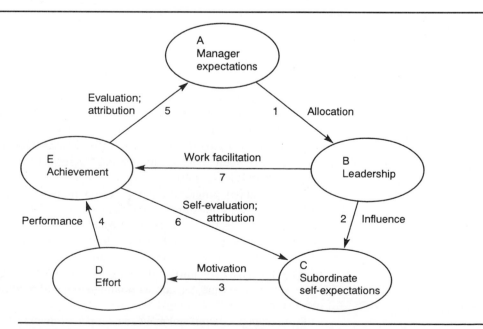

Source: Reprinted by permission of the publisher, from D. Eden, *Pygmalion in Management* (Lexington, MA: Lexington Books, D. C. Heath and Company, copyright 1990 Lexington Books).

Continuous reinforcement rewards every occurrence of the desired behavior. (You give your dog a biscuit every time it sits up.) This is the quickest way to get a person to act in the desired way. *Extinction* rewards no behavior; you ignore the behavior (a 2-year-old child's tantrum or your dog's chasing its tail instead of sitting up). Behavior receiving no external reward will be less frequent than behavior that is rewarded. *Intermittent reinforcement* rewards some responses but not others according to a preset schedule (rewarding the dog only after five successful sits). Intermittent reinforcement establishes the desired behavior more slowly than continuous reinforcement but has longer-term effects. Moreover, intermittently reinforced behavior is less easily extinguished than continuously reinforced behavior.

In behavior modification (or *operant conditioning,* to use its more formal name), consequences are arranged for some voluntary behavior that is desired. For instance, workers are praised for properly doing their jobs. The most effective reinforcements seem to be specific, detailed, and concrete praise about how and what the employee has done, closely and directly related to the desired behavior. Thus, rather than saying, "Good job, Jones!" the supervisor says something like, "Jones, your use of the new package format has really increased—the record says you're making over 90 percent use on your shipments, and as I watch, I can see you've got a good system."

Behavior modification has had some notable successes. At Emery Air Freight, to use a classic case, managers thought workers were not using containers to combine small package shipments as often as they could. A study showed that containers were deployed in less than half of the cases when they could be used. A behavior modification program resulted in significant improvements in container use that saved the company some $650,000 annually, and the improved behavior persisted over several years. Other companies are also using varied forms of behavior modification, among them General Electric, B. F. Goodrich, and Michigan Bell. Of course, many good managers and supervisors (and parents) have used it for years without the fancy name. There are some concerns about *why* it works, however.

While Skinner's reinforcement suggests that the consequences themselves govern behavior, a close look at Emery Air Freight suggests that feedback and goal setting played as much a part of the success story as reinforcement. A high, explicit goal was set, and workers were given training on how to attain it. Employees were provided with timely, accurate reports on their performance, which they monitored themselves. Hence, they reinforced themselves by direct access to performance information and always knew where they stood relative to their performance goals.

Most behavior modification programs to date have been applied at operating levels—to clerical help, production workers, or mechanics, for instance. Behavior modification is most easily applied to relatively simple jobs, where critical behaviors can be easily identified and specific performance goals can be readily set. For managerial jobs, these key factors may be more difficult to apply. Further, it is not clear that supervisor praise, recognition, and feedback are enough. After some years, Emery had to introduce new reinforcers, such as special luncheons, because the old ones had become routine.

Criticisms of behavior modification include the charge that it is essentially bribery and that workers are already paid for performance. Because it disregards people's attitudes and beliefs, behavior modification has been called misleading and manipulative. Particularly where money is involved, one critic has noted that there is little difference between behavior modification and "some key elements of scientific management presented more than 60 years ago by Taylor."[43] Another criticism is that behavior modification does not take into consideration group norms, which can have an antiorganization character, such as group norms to restrict production. Indeed, behavior modification improperly used can generate much group resistance.

Why does it matter whether behavior modification works because of reinforcement or because of goals? Because you, as a manager, will need to know the essentials for getting the performance you want—whether those essentials are praise or self-administered feedback. Moreover, Emery was careful to avoid setting groups or individuals in competition with one another. Instead, people were encouraged to compete with their own previous records. You, as a manager, should know about this important factor.

Successful behavior modification requires the following:

1. A careful analysis of the job to identify specific key behaviors for targeting.

2. Careful, explicit communication to employees of what is wanted, including both behaviors and concrete, measurable goals.

3. "Reinforcers" to attach consequences to desired behaviors. Most often used are praise and recognition. (Union agreements may make other reinforcers—such as money or promotions—unavailable.)

4. Concrete, continuous feedback or feedback soon after performance that workers can use to check on themselves.

The evidence suggests that behavior modification and goal setting, creatively applied, do seem to improve *some* performance at *some* levels. The thoughtful manager will be wary of any simple solutions and instead pay close attention to the weaknesses and problems of many approaches. He or she may even combine approaches for their strengths. Activity 5–6W provides an opportunity for you to examine and reflect on your reinforcement orientation.

Motivation in Work Teams

As we have experienced thus far in this course, motivation can be an issue that faces most work teams. As the primary work in organizations is shifting from individuals to teams, team leaders face additional challenges. Earlier in this module, we defined motivation as "a set of energetic forces that originates both within as well as beyond an individual's being, to initiate work-related behavior, and to determine its form, direction, intensity, and duration." Moving to the team level, we view **team motivation** as a set of energetic forces that originate both within as well as beyond a team's being, to initiate work-related team behavior and to determine its form, direction, intensity, and duration.[44]

In Modules 11 and 12 we will explore different dimensions of teams and present a framework that focuses on the different factors that affect team development and performance. Using the same skeleton, we argue that a similar cluster of factors will influence team motivation and performance, namely, team processes (formation, coordination, communication, decision making, problem solving, cooperation, conflict resolution), leadership (leadership style, emotional intelligence), team structure and stage of development (size, norms, role differentiation, subgrouping), team composition (individual attributes, demographic characteristics, needs), purpose (goals and objectives, task and project characteristics) and context (the nature of external environment, organization culture).

For a large group of researchers, one of the most important determinants of the motivational potential of work teams is the task contents. Thus, the design of tasks for teams is critical because it influences work team motivation. Later in this book (in Module 13), we devote a major portion to the exploration of alternative task designs for teams.

The motivation of individuals in teams fosters dilemmas—dilemmas between levels, dilemmas between stages of team development, and dilemmas between types of outcomes. As you have experienced in your own learning team in this course, like any dilemmas, there exists no solution that optimizes on all dimensions. To address a team motivational issue, the team needs first to recognize that the issue exists. Next the team can consider alternative solutions or courses of action, just like solving any problem as a team. The problem-solving cycle presented in Module 11 can be used as a guiding roadmap. As experience indicates, any action chosen by the team will represent trade-offs. Working through the dilemmas as a team is likely to enhance team motivation and performance.[45]

INTERNATIONAL VIEWPOINT ON MOTIVATION

Most theories of motivation in use today were developed in the United States by Americans and about Americans. Of those that were not, most were influenced by American theories.[46] Studying theories of motivation can lead us to assume that we are dealing with "human nature"—the way people really are regardless of what part of the world they live in. This assumption would be inaccurate. Motivation, like any other behavioral phenomenon, is culture bound. As Geete Hofstede has shown in his comparative study of 40 modern nations, people carry "mental programs" that are rooted in the family and reinforced throughout the educational system. These mental programs contain a component of national culture that usually is most clearly expressed in the different values that predominate among people of different nations.[47]

This becomes very relevant when we hear that some managers and companies attempt to apply management practices that were developed in other cultures, assuming that because they worked well in another culture they will work well in their own. Furthermore, industries need to expand the awareness they already have of the cultural differences in motivation that exist between different regions of the world as well as between regions within any nation. For example, within the U.S. context, this is shown in the relocation from the industrial Northeast, where union practices and attitudes affect productivity, to the Sunbelt states, where past economic conditions have left the population more compliant to rigorous work standards.

The United States is an achievement-oriented society that has historically encouraged and honored individual accomplishment and the attainment of material prosperity.[48] The American dream tells people that with hard work and perseverance, one can attain anything. Individualism, independence, self-confidence, and speaking out against injustice and threat are important elements of American culture. Materialism and the concomitant rewards of living well are basic goal systems in the motivation patterns.

For example, does Maslow's motivation theory, which was developed in the U.S. context, work for employees outside America? Hofstede[49] and Trompenaars[50] have shown that it does not. More specifically, in countries higher on uncertainty avoidance (such as Greece and Japan) as compared with those lower on uncertainty avoidance (such as the United States), security motivates employees more strongly than does self-actualization.[51] In contrast to American motivation characteristics, Howard et al. found the Japanese motivation and values to be quite different, with obvious implications for management practices.[52] Their research showed that Americans put greater value on individuality, while Japanese place greater value on socially oriented qualities. The social orientation of the Japanese may be traced to Confucianism, which stresses a rigid hierarchy in a collective society, where members are expected to maintain absolute loyalty and obedience to authority. The stress on dependency and security are part of the Japanese upbringing, whereas autonomy and early independence are typically American. In their corporate lives, Japanese show great dependency and are highly conforming and obedient in return. Japanese management recognizes the inhibiting effects this character has on creativity and innovation; at present, they are emphasizing the need to integrate programs into their schools that will free up and develop the creativity and ingenuity they envy in America.

As of late, work motivation in mainland China seems to be an issue of concern. The problem of low work motivation that was identified by foreign researchers and practitioners was a forbidden topic of investigation for Chinese researchers until the end of the Cultural Revolution.[53] Factors that have been postulated as responsible for low motivation and productivity include lack of an effective reward–punishment system, "unscientific" work quotas, the problematic promotion–wage system, lifetime employment, and an ineffective "political work-system."[54]

We discussed McClelland's work on achievement in this module. Adler reviewed the cross-cultural research on achievement and found it relatively robust across cultures.[55] For example, managers in New Zealand appear to follow the pattern developed in the United States. However, the literature would show that the word *achievement* itself is hardly translatable into any language other than English. However, countries characterized by a high need for achievement also have a high need to produce and a strong willingness to accept risk. Anglo-American countries such as the United States, Canada, and Great Britain follow the high-achievement motivation pattern, while countries such as Chile and Portugal follow the low-achievement motivation pattern. (Admittedly, these broad generalizations are based on very limited research data.)

Implications for managerial style, practices, and motivational planning for U.S. firms operating branches in foreign countries or for foreign-based companies that would want to operate in the U.S. context are apparent. The social character, the values, and the cultural practices of each country must be taken into consideration when planning and operating the human organization. Corporations operating outside of their country of origin have long known this but have often not taken it sufficiently into account. Yet as the economic infrastructure and the social fabric of the societies in different parts of the globe change, we need to pay attention to the actual changes and their nature. The transformations that we have seen during the last decade in the Pacific Rim countries, South American countries, the Middle East, and Eastern Europe are challenging the managers of international companies to stay away from making assumptions about human behavior based on the recent past. The indications are that some changes might be occurring in the value base, yet we cannot substantiate this view empirically. At the same time, human expectations and goals in different parts of the globe seem to be shifting and as such so should our motivational programs and practices. Effective managers who operate in a different national culture (to their origin) will be sensitive to the cultural context and to the cultural transformation that has occurred and try a variety of approaches to motivate their employees while carefully examining their impact.

SUMMARY

The fields of psychology, sociology, and economics share a common desire to understand human motivation. Attempts to develop an integrated theory that focuses on the fundamental features of motivation are yet to be successful.[56] Some understanding of motivation can be gained by examining your own work experience and that of your classmates and then sorting out factors accounting for "best" and "less than best" performance. For this purpose, Activity 5–1 yields results similar to Herzberg's dissatisfiers (those factors that make workers unhappy when they are not present) and motivators (those factors that provide opportunities for self-direction and challenge). Motivation is commonly thought of as being inherent in the individual: One either has it or not. When defined as psychological energy directed toward goals, all behavior is motivated; goals are the direction for achievement of wants or avoidance of threats. All "nonproductive" behavior can be viewed as an attempt to avoid or counteract threats or alienation.

Motivation was viewed from managerial, theoretical, and international perspectives. The theories of motivation can be classified in a variety of ways, and in this module we have used the schema and clustered them by role: the role of needs, the role of equity, the role of goals and expectations, the role of context, and the role of rewards. Within each cluster we briefly discussed the basic theories.

This module focused on understanding motivation dynamics at work; therefore, the last sections explored both the notion that motivation is both culture bound and to some degree universal and the specific managerial implications and programs. We argued that at times, the business context triggers demotivation and alienation at work. Those can be combated by carefully thought out programs such as management by objectives, profit-sharing plans, employee stock ownership plans, skill-based pay, employee involvement programs, behavior modification, and team work motivation. Finally, motivation in the global context of work was discussed.

Study Questions

1. When this book's authors created the classroom workshop model, which of the following viewpoints did they use: traditional, human relations, or human resources? Give reasons and illustrations to support your answer.

2. Compare and contrast Maslow's hierarchy of needs, McClelland's perspective, and Herzberg's perspective.

3. Your manager tells you Herzberg's theory applies to himself and other managers he knows, so his advice is to forget about other fancy theories of motivation. If he is the type of manager you can talk to, how would you respond?

4. Explain the unique added perspective of each one of the role's perspectives (that is, needs, equity, goals and expectations, context, and rewards) to understanding the challenge of employee demotivation at work.

5. Compare and contrast one theory from each one of the role clusters.

6. What is the basic management issue when you manage people according to their individual needs, abilities, and experiences? What actions can supervisors take to manage according to individual differences while trying to avoid the problems inherent in such an approach?

7. If you were the human resources manager of a large corporation and the executive office told you to prepare a report on installing an employee profit-sharing program, what major topics would your report include?

8. Explain the phrase "Motivation is culture bound."

Endnotes

1. G. P. Latham and C. C. Pinder, "Work Motivation Theory and Research at the Dawn of the 21st Century," *Annual Review of Psychology* 54 (2005), pp. 495–516; R. M. Steers, R. T. Mowday, and D. L Shapiro, "The Future of Work Motivation Theory," *Academy of Management Review* 29 (2004), pp. 379–87.

2. R. M. Steers, L. W. Porter, and G. A. Bigley, *Motivation and Leadership at Work* (New York: McGraw-Hill, 1996).

3. E. A. Locke, and G. P. Latham, "What Should We Do about Motivation Theory? Six Recommendations for the 21st Century," *Academy of Management Review* 29 (2004), pp. 388–403; J. Donovan, "Work Motivation," in N. Anderson, D. Ones, H. Sinangil, and C. Viswesvaran (eds.), *Handbook of Industrial and Organizational Psychology* (Thousand Oaks, CA: Sage, 2001), p. 53.

4. T. S. Pittman, "Motivation," in D. T. Gilbert, S. T. Fiske, and G. Lindzey (eds.), *The Handbook of Social Psychology* (New York: McGraw-Hill, 1998), pp. 549–90; and F. J. Landy and W. S. Becker, "Motivation Theory Reconsidered," in L. L. Cummings and B. M. Staw (eds.), *Research in Organizational Behavior,* vol. 9 (Greenwich, CT: JAI Press, 1987), pp. 1–38.

5. The role-based perspective was initially advanced by Punnet. See B. J. Punnett, *International Perspective on Organizational Behavior* (Armonl, NY: M.E. Sharpe, Inc., 2004).

6. A. H. Maslow, "A Theory of Human Motivation," *Psychological Review* 50 (1943), pp. 370–96.

7. D. C. McClelland, "Power Motivation and Organizational Leadership," *Power: The Inner Experience* (New York: Livington Publishers, 1975), pp. 252–71.

8. D. G. Winter, *The Power Motive* (New York: Free Press, 1973), pp. 108–9.

9. L. L. Cummings and C. J. Berger, "Organization Structure: How Does It Influence Attitudes and Performance?" *Organizational Dynamics* 5 (Autumn 1976), pp. 34–49.

10. McClelland, "Power Motivation and Organizational Leadership," p. 269. See also D. C. McClelland and R. S. Steele, *Motivation Workshops* (New York: General Learning Press, 1972), for the type of training program used.

11. U. Pareek, "Motivational Analysis of Organizational-Behavior (MAO-B)," *The 1986 Annual Developing Human Resources* (1986), pp. 121–28.

12. For the best discussion of this theory, see F. Herzberg, "One More Time: How Do You Motivate Employees?" *Harvard Business Review* 46 (January–February 1968), pp. 53–62.

13. For a critique of Herzberg's work, see E. E. Lawler III, *Motivation in Work Organizations* (Monterey, CA: Brooks/Cole, 1973), pp. 69–72.

14. The ERG theory discusses frustration of the growth needs. See C. P. Alderfer, *Existence, Relatedness, and Growth* (New York: Free Press, 1972) and C. P. Schneider and C. P. Alderfer,

"Three Studies of Measures of Need Satisfaction in Organizations," *Administrative Science Quarterly* (December 1973), pp. 489–505.

15. J. S. Adams, "Toward an Understanding of Inequity," *Journal of Abnormal and Social Psychology* 67 (1963), pp. 422–36; J. Brockner, J. Greenberg, A. Brockner, J. Bortz, J. Davy, and C. Carter, "Equity Theory and Work Performance: Further Evidence of the Impact of Survivor Guilt," *Academy of Management Journal* 29 (1986), pp. 373–84; R. C. Huseman, J. D. Hatfield, and E. W. Miles, "A New Perspective on Equity Theory: The Equity Sensitivity Construct," *Academy of Management Review* 12 (1987), pp. 222–34; and J. Greenberg, "Cognitive Reevaluation of Outcomes in Response to Underpayment Inequity," *Academy of Management Journal* 32, no. 1 (1989), pp. 174–84.

16. E. A. Locke and G. P. Latham, *A Theory of Goal Setting and Task Performance* (Englewood Cliffs, NJ: Prentice-Hall, 1990); and E. A. Locke, "Self-Set Goals and Self-Efficacy as Mediators of Incentive and Personality," in M. Erez, U. Kleinbeck, and H. Thierry (eds.), *Work Motivation in the Context of a Globalizing Economy* (Mahwah, NJ: LEA, 2001), pp. 13–26.

17. See, for example, G. P. Latham, and T. W. Lee, "Goal Setting," in E. A. Locke (ed.), *Generalized from Laboratory to Field Settings* (Lexington, MA: Lexington Books, 1986), pp. 100–17.

18. See, for example, D. E. Terpstra and E. J. Rozell, "The Relationship of Goal Setting to Organizational Profitability," *Group & Organization Management* 19, no. 3 (1994), pp. 285–94.

19. V. H. Vroom, *Work and Motivation* (New York: John Wiley & Sons, 1964).

20. M. J. Stahl and D. W. Grisby, "A Comparison of Unit, Subjectivity and Regression Measures of Second Level Valences in Expectancy Theory," *Decision Sciences* 18 (1987), pp. 62–72; H. J. Klein, "An Integrated Control Theory Model of Work Behavior," *Academy of Management Review* 14, no. 2 (1989), pp. 150–72; M. E. Tubbs, D. M. Boehne, and J. G. Gahl, "Expectancy, Valence, and Motivational Force Functions in Goal Setting Research: An Empirical Test," *Journal of Applied Psychology* 78, no. 3 (1993), pp. 361–73.

21. R. J. House, H. J. Shapiro, and M. A. Wahba, "Expectancy as a Predictor of Work Behavior and Attitudes: A Reevaluation of Empirical Evidence," *Decision Sciences* 5 (1974), pp. 481–506; and S. T. Connolly, "Some Conceptual and Methodological Issues in Expectancy Theory Models of Work Performance," *Academy of Management Review* 1 (1976), pp. 37–47.

22. A. M. Grant, "Relational Job Design and the Motivation to Make a Prosocial Difference," *Academy of Management Review,* 32, no. 2 (2007), pp. 393–417; M. Gagne and E. L. Deci, "Self-Determination Theory and Work Motivation," *Journal of Organizational Behavior* 26 (2005), pp. 331–62.

23. J. Hackman and G. Oldham, *Work Design* (Reading, MA: Addison Wesley, 1980).

24. N. J. Adler, *International Dimensions of Organizational Behavior* (Cincinnati, OH: South-Western, 2005); B. J. Punnett, *International Perspective on Organizational Behavior* (Armonl, NY: M.E. Sharpe, Inc., 2004).

25. L. W. Porter and E. E. Lawler III, *Managerial Attitudes and Performance* (Burr Ridge, IL: Richard D. Irwin, 1968); and L. W. Porter and G. A. Bigley, "Motivation and Transformational Leadership" in Erez, Kleinbeck, and Thierry (eds.), *Work Motivation in the Context of a Globalizing Economy,* pp. 279–92.

26. For an extensive discussion of the impact of groups on individuals in organizations, see J. R. Hackman, "Group Influences on Individuals," in M. D. Dunnette (ed.), *Handbook of Industrial and Organizational Psychology* (Skokie, IL: Rand McNally, 1976), pp. 1455–1525. Hackman pays special attention to the effect of group norms and influences on member performance effectiveness.

27. R. Blauner, *Alienation and Freedom* (Chicago: University of Chicago Press, 1964).

28. C. Argyris, *Understanding Organization Behaviour* (Homewood IL: Dorsey Press, 1960).

29. M. C. Meyer, *Six Stages of Demotivation. International Management* (April 1977), pp. 14–17.

30. U. Merry and G. Brown, *The Neurotic Behavior of Organizations* (Cleveland, OH: Gestalt Institute of Cleveland Press, 1987).

31. B. Ashforth and R. Lee, "Defensive Behavior in Organizations: A Preliminary Model," *Human Relations* 43, no. 7 (1990), pp. 621–48.

32. Erez, Kleinbeck, and Thierry (eds.), *Work Motivation in the Context of a Globalizing Economy;* N. J. Adler, *International Dimensions of Organizational Behavior* (Cincinnati, OH: South-Western, 2005); B. J. Punnett, *International Perspective on Organizational Behavior* (Armonl, NY: M.E. Sharpe, Inc., 2004).

33. R. G. Greenwood, "Management by Objectives," *Academy of Management Review* 6 (1981), pp. 225–30.

34. See, for example, G. S. Obiorne, *Management by Objectives* (New York: Pitman Publishing Company, 1965); J. N. Kondrasuk, "Studies in MOB Effectiveness," *Academy of Management Review* 6, no. 3 (1981), pp. 426–31; and G. P. Latham, *Increasing Productivity through Performance Appraisal* (Reading, MA: Addison-Wesley, 1992).

35. C. D. Pringle and J. G. Longnecker, "The Ethics of MBO," *The Academy of Management Review* 7, no. 2 (1982), pp. 177–86; Latham, *Increase of Productivity through Performance Appraisal;* and T. H. Poister and G. Streib, "MBO in Municipal Government: Variations on Traditional Management," *Public Administration Review* (January–February 1995), pp. 48–56.

36. Two thoughtful and comprehensive books on the subject have been written by J. R. Blasi, *Employee Ownership: Revolution or Ripoff* (Cambridge, MA: Ballinger, 1988); and *The New Owners* (New York: Harper Business, 1993).

37. T. R. Marsh and D. E. McAllister, "ESOP Table: A Survey of Companies with Employee Ownership Plans," *Journal of Corporation Law* 6, no. 3 (1981), pp. 552–623.

38. *ESOP Survey: 1990* (Washington, DC: ESOP Association of America, 1990), and M. Trachman, *Employee Ownership and Corporate Growth in High Technology Companies* (Oakland, CA: National Center for Employee Ownership Publications, 1985).

39. For a good review, see E. E. Lawler III, G. E. Ledford, Jr., and L. Chang, "Who Uses Skill-Based Pay, and Why," *Compensations & Benefits Review* (March–April 1993), pp. 22–38; and G. E. Ledford, Jr., "Paying for Skills, Knowledge, and Competencies of Knowledge Workers," *Compensations & Benefits Review* (July–August 1995), pp. 55–62.

40. E. E. Lawler III, S. A. Mohrman, and G. E. Ledford, Jr., *Creating High-Performance Organizations: Practice Results in the Fortune 1000* (San Francisco: Jossey-Bass, 1995).

41. D. Eden, "Self-Fulfilling Prophecies in Organizations," in J. Greenberg (ed.), *Organizational Behavior: The State of the Science* (Mahwah, NJ: Lawrence Erlbaum, 2003), pp. 91–122; D. Eden, *Pygmalion in Management: Productivity as Self-Fulfilling Prophecy* (Lexington, MA: Lexington Books, 1990), p. 70.

42. D. Eden, "Means Efficacy: External Sources of General and Specific Subjective Efficacy," in Erez, Kleinbeck, and Thierry (eds.), *Work Motivation in the Context of a Globalizing Economy,* pp. 73–85; D. Eden, "Pygmalion, Goal Setting, and Expectancy: Compatible Ways to Boost Productivity," *Academy of Management Review* 13, no. 4 (1988), pp. 639–52; D. Eden, "Self-Fulfilling Prophecy as a Management Tool: Harnessing Pygmalion," *Academy of Management Review* 6 (1984), pp. 64–73; and D. Eden and A. B. Shani, "Pygmalion Goes to Boot Camp: Expectancy, Leadership, and Trainee Performance," *Journal of Applied Psychology* 67 (1982), pp. 194–99.

43. E. A. Locke, "The Myth of Behavior Mod in Organizations," *Academy of Management Review* (October 1977).

44. A. M. O'Leary-Kelly, J. J. Martocchio, and D. D. Frink, "A Review of the Influence of Group Goals on Group Performance," *Academy of Management Journal* 37, no. 5 (1994), pp. 1285–1301; D. Ilgen and L. Sheppard, "Motivation in Work Teams," in Erez, Kleinbeck, and Thierry (eds.), *Work Motivation in the Context of a Globalizing Economy,* pp. 169–79.

45. Locke, "The Myth of Behavior Mod in Organizations."

46. N. J. Adler, *International Dimensions of Organizational Behavior* (Cincinnati, OH: South-Western, 2005); B. J. Punnett, *International Perspective on Organizational Behavior* (Armonl, NY: M.E. Sharpe, Inc., 2004).

47. G. Hofstede, *Culture's Consequences: International Differences in Work-Related Values* (Beverly Hills, CA: Sage Publications, 1990).

48. J. T. Spence, "Achievement American Style, The Rewards and Costs of Individualism," *American Psychologist* (December 1985), pp. 1285–94.

49. G. Hofstede, "Motivation, Leadership and Organization: Do American Theories Apply Aborad?" *Organizational Dynamics* 9, no. 1 (1980), pp. 42–63.

50. F. Trompenaars, *Riding the Wave of Culture* (London, UK: The Economics Books, 1993).

51. N. Adler, *International Dimensions of Organizational Behavior* (Mason, OH: South-Western, 2002).

52. A. Howard, K. Shudo, and M. Umeshima, "Motivation and Values among Japanese and American Managers," *Personnel Psychology* 36 (1983), pp. 883–98.

53. See, for example, O. Shenkar and S. Ronen, "Structure and Importance of Work Goals among Managers in the People's Republic of China," *Academy of Management Journal* 30 (1987), pp. 564–76; and M. M. Yang, "Between State and Society: The Construction of Cooperativeness in a Chinese Socialist Factory," *The Australian Journal of Chinese Affairs* 22 (1989), pp. 36–60.

54. See, for example, P. Jin, "Work Motivation and Productivity in Voluntarily Formed Work Teams: A Field Study in China," *Organizational Behavior & Human Decision Processes* 54 (1993), pp. 133–55.

55. N. J. Adler, *International Dimensions of Organizational Behavior* (Cincinnati, OH: South-Western, 2005); B. J. Punnett, *International Perspective on Organizational Behavior* (Armonl, NY: M.E. Sharpe, Inc., 2004).

56. P. Steel and C. J. Konig, "Integrating Theories of Motivation," *The Academy of Management Review* 31, no. 4 (2006), pp. 889–913.

Activity 5–2: The Slade Plating Department Case

Objectives:

a. To allow you to examine motivational processes.

b. To provide you and your team an opportunity to investigate motivational issues from different theoretical perspectives.

c. To provide you with the opportunity to integrate many of the content areas covered thus far in the course via the analysis of the case.

Task 1 (Individual Activity):

Read the following case carefully and answer these questions:

a. What background factors are important in understanding the emergent role system that developed in the plating room?

b. Exhibit 6 shows the various subgroups that developed in the plating room. The Sarto and Clark subgroups are the two most important. What are some of the factors or characteristics that probably account for group membership in each subgroup?

c. Make a complete list of the norms of the emergent role system that developed in this case.

d. What are some of the major problems at the Slade Plating Department?

Task 2 (Class Discussion):

The instructor will lead a class discussion to capture the basic facts in the case.

Task 3 (Team Activity):

Teams will examine the case from a specific theoretical perspective assigned by the instructor. Each team is to focus on the following:

- Capture the essence of the assigned theoretical perspective.
- Identify the major facts in the case as viewed by the assigned perspective.
- Conduct the analysis of the facts from the assigned perspective.
- Identify potential problems in the case.
- Identify the most critical problem.
- Provide some alternative solutions.

Task 4:

Each team will present its analysis and findings to the total learning community.

The Slade Plating Department

Ralph Porter, production manager of the Slade Company, was concerned by reports of dishonesty among some employees in the Plating Department. From reliable sources, he learned that a few were punching the time-cards of a number of their co-workers who were leaving early. Porter had only recently joined the Slade organization. From conversations with the previous production manager and other fellow managers, he judged that they were pleased, in general, with the overall performance of the Plating Department.

The Slade Company was a small but prosperous manufacturer of metal products designed for industrial application. Its manufacturing plant, located in central Michigan, employed 500 workers who were engaged in producing a large variety of clamps, inserts, knobs, and similar items. Orders for these products were usually large and came in on a recurrent basis. The volume of orders fluctuated in response to business conditions in the primary industries that the company served. At the time of this case, sales volume had been high for over a year. The bases on which the Slade Company secured orders, in rank of importance, were quality, delivery, and reasonable price.

The organization of manufacturing operations at the Slade plant is shown in Exhibit 1. The departments listed there, from left to right, are approximately in the order in which material flowed through the plant. The die making and set up operations required the greatest degree of skill, which was supplied by highly paid, long-service crafts-people. The finishing departments, divided operationally and geographically between plating and painting, attracted less highly trained but relatively skilled workers, some of whom had been employed by the company for many years. The remaining operations required largely unskilled labor and contained positions characterized by relatively low pay and high turnover of personnel.

This case was prepared as the basis for class discussion rather than to illustrate either effective or ineffective handling of an administrative situation.

Exhibit 1   **Manufacturing Organization**

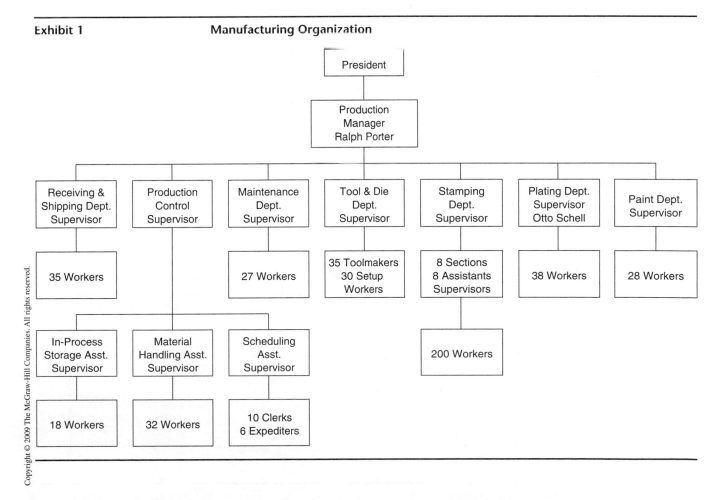

The plating room covered the entire top floor of the plant. Exhibit 2 shows the floor plan, the disposition of workers, and the flow of work throughout this department. Thirty-eight people worked in the department, plating or oxidizing the metal parts or preparing parts for the application of paint at another location in the plant. The department's work occurred in response to orders communicated by production schedules that were revised daily. Schedule revisions, caused by last-minute order increases or rush requests from customers, resulted in short-term volume fluctuations—particularly in the plating, painting, and shipping departments. Exhibit 3 outlines the activities of the various jobs, their interrelationships, and the type of work in which each specialized. Exhibit 4 rates the various types of jobs in terms of the technical skill, physical effort, discomfort, and training time associated with their performance.

The activities that took place in the plating room were of three main types:

1. Acid dipping, where parts were etched by being placed in baskets that were manually immersed and agitated in an acid solution.

2. Barrel tumbling, where parts were roughened or smoothed by being loaded into machine-powered revolving drums containing abrasive, caustic, or corrosive solutions.

3. Plating, either manual, where parts were loaded on racks and were immersed by hand through the plating sequence; or automatic, where racks or baskets were manually loaded with parts that were then carried by a conveyor system through the plating sequence.

Within these main divisions of work, there were a number of variables, such as cycle times, chemical formulas, abrasive mixtures, and so forth, that distinguished particular jobs as in Exhibit 3.

Exhibit 2
Plating Room Layout

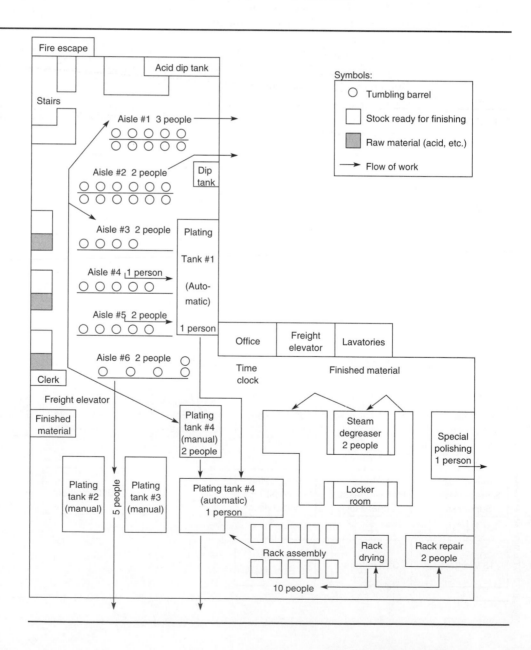

Exhibit 3
Outline of Work Flow, Plating Room

Aisle 1: Worked closely with Aisle 3 in preparation of parts by barrel tumbling and acid dipping for high-quality* plating in Tanks 4 and 5. Also did a considerable quantity of highly specialized, high-quality acid-etching work not requiring further processing.

Aisle 2: Tumbled items of regular quality and design in preparation for painting. Less frequently, did oxidation dipping work of regular quality, but sometimes of special design, not requiring further processing.

Aisle 3: Worked closely with Aisle 1 on high-quality tumbling work for Tanks 4 and 5.

Aisles 4 and 5: Produced regular tumbling work for Tank 1.

Aisle 6: Did high-quality tumbling work for special products plated in Tanks 2 and 3.

Tank 1: Worked on standard, automated plating of regular quality not further processed in plating room, and regular work further processed in Tank 5.

Tanks 2 and 3: Produced special, high-quality plating work not requiring further processing.

Tank 4: Did special, high-quality plating work further plated in Tank 5.

Tank 5: Automated production of high- and regular-quality, special- and regular-design plated parts sent directly to shipping.

Rack Assembly: Placed parts to be plated in Tank 5 on racks.

Rack Repair: Performed routine replacement and repair of racks used in Tank 5.

Polishing: Processed, by manual or semimanual methods, odd-lot special orders which were sent directly to shipping. Also, sorted and reclaimed parts rejected by inspectors in the shipping department.

Degreasing: Took incoming raw stock, processed it through caustic solution, and placed clean stock in storage ready for processing elsewhere in the plating room.

*High or regular quality: The quality of finishes could broadly be distinguished by the thickness of plate and/or care in preparation. Regular or special work. The complexity of work depended on the routine or special character of design and finish specifications.

Exhibit 4
Skill Indices by Job Group

Job	Technical Skill Required	Physical Effort Required	Degree of Discomfort Involved	Degree of Training Required*
Aisle 1	10	10	10	10
Tanks 2 to 4	8	9	10	9
Aisles 2 to 6	6	10	10	6
Tank 5	10	8	4	9
Tank 1	3	6	6	4
Degreasing	2	8	4	1
Polishing	5	2	2	4
Rack assembly and repair	1	1	1	1

Note: Rated on scales of 1 (the least) to 10 (the greatest) in each category.

*The amount of experience required to assume complete responsibility for the job.

The work of the plating room was received in batch lots averaging 1,000 pieces each. The clerk moved each batch, which was accompanied by a routing slip, to its first operation. This routing slip indicated the operations to be performed and also when each major operation on the batch was scheduled to be completed, so that the finished product could be shipped on time. From the accumulation of orders presented, each worker organized his or her own work schedule so as to make optimal use of equipment, materials, and time. Upon completion of an order, each worker moved the lot to its next work position or to the finished material location near the freight elevator.

The plating room was under the direction of its supervisor, Otto Schell, who worked a regular 8:00 A.M. to 5:00 P.M. day, five days a week. The supervisor spent a good deal of working time attending to maintenance and repair of equipment, procuring supplies, handling late schedule changes, and seeing to it that people were at their proper work locations.

Working conditions in the plating room varied considerably. That part of the department containing the tumbling barrels and the plating machines was constantly awash, alternately with cold water, steaming acid, or a caustic soda. Workers in this part of the room wore knee boots, long rubber aprons, and high-gauntlet rubber gloves. This uniform, consistent with the general atmosphere of the wet part of the room, was hot in the summer, cold in winter. In contrast, the remainder of the room was dry, relatively odorless, and provided reasonably stable temperature and humidity conditions for those who worked there.

The men and women employed in the plating room are listed in Exhibit 5. This exhibit provides certain personal data on each department member, including a productivity

Exhibit 5   **Plating Room Personnel**

Location	Name	Age	Marital Status	Company Seniority (yrs.)	Department Seniority (yrs.)	Education (yrs.)	Familial Relationships	Productivity Skill Rating[a]
Aisle 1	Tony Sarto	30	M	13	13	12	Pete Facelli, cousin Louis Patrici, uncle	10
	Pete Facelli	26	M	8	8	12	Tony Sarto, cousin	9
	Joe Iambi	31	M	5	5	10		9
Aisle 2	Herman Schell	48	S	26	26	8	Otto Schell, brother	3
	Philip Kirk	23	M	1	1	16		NA[b]
Aisle 3	Dom Pantaleoni	31	M	10	10	9		9
	Sal Maletta	32	M	12	12	11		8
Aisle 4	Bob Pearson	22	S	4	4	12	Father in tool & die dept.	10
Aisle 5	Charlie Malone	44	M	22	8	8		4
	John Lacey	41	S	9	5	9	Brother in paint dept.	4
Aisle 6	Joyce Martin	27	S	7	7	12		7
	Bill Mensch	41	M	6	2	8		7
Tank 1	Henry LaForte	38	M	14	6	12		5
Tanks 2 & 3	Ralph Parker	25	S	7	7	12		7
	Angela Harding	27	S	8	8	12	Brother in tool & die dept.	7
	George Flood	22	S	5	5	12		6
	Harry Clark	29	M	8	8	12		8
	Tom Bond	25	S	6	6	12		7
Tank 4	Frank Bonzani	27	M	9	9	12		9
	Alice Bartolo	24	M	6	6	12		8
Tank 5	Louis Patrici	47	S	14	14	14	Tony Sarto, nephew Pete Facelli, nephew	10
Rack Assembly	10 women	30–40	9M, 1S	10 (av.)	10 (av.)	8 (av.)	6 with husbands in Co.	7 (av.)
Rack Maintenance	Will Partridge	57	M	14	2	8		4
	Lloyd Swan	62	M	3	3	8		4
Degreasing	Dave Susi	45	S	1	1	12		6
	Mike Maher	41	M	4	4	8		5
Polishing	Russ Perkins	49	M	12	2	12		7
Supervisor	Otto Schell	56	M	35	35	12	Herman Schell, brother	8
Clerk	Bill Pierce	32	M	10	4	12		7
Technician	Frank Rutlage	24	S	2	2	14		5

[a]On a potential scale of 1 (bottom) to 10 (top), as evaluated by the workers in the department.
[b]Kirk was the source of data for this case, and as such, he was in a biased position to report accurately perceptions about himself.

skill rating (based on subjective and objective appraisals of potential performance), as reported by the members of the department.

Pay in the department was low for the central Michigan area. Employees typically started at a few dollars over minimum wage, with small increases given over time based on seniority and skill. However, working hours for the plating room were long. To keep employee training and benefit costs down, the company practice was to increase overtime rather than hire new employees. The typical Monday-through-Friday workweek in the department was 60 hours (except for the rack assembly area, which worked a standard 40-hour week). The first 40 hours were paid for on a straight-time rate basis while the next 20 hours were paid on a time-and-one-half basis. All weekend work was paid on a double-time rate basis.

As Exhibit 5 indicates, Philip Kirk, a worker in aisle 2, provided the data for this case. After he had been a

member of the department for several months, Kirk noted that certain members of the department tended to seek each other out during free time on and off the job. He then observed that these informal associations were enduring, built upon common activities and shared ideas about what was and what was not legitimate behavior in the department. His description of the pattern of these associations is diagrammed in Exhibit 6.

The Sarto group, named after Tony Sarto who was its most respected member and the arbiter between the other members, was the largest group in the department. Except for Louis Patrici, Alice Bartolo, and Frank Bonzani (who relieved each other during break periods), the group invariably ate lunch together on the fire escape near aisle 1. On those Saturdays and Sundays when overtime work was required, the Sarto group operated as a team, regardless of weekday work assignments, to get overtime work completed as quickly as possible. (Few department members

Exhibit 6
Informal Groupings
in the Plating Room

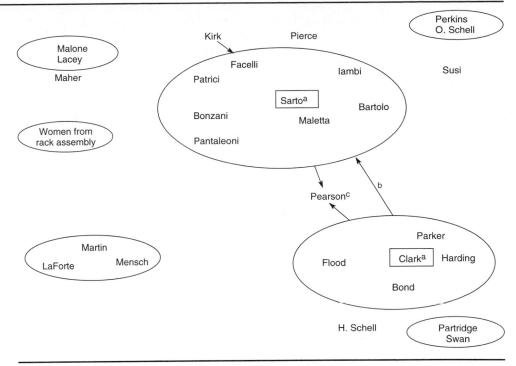

[a]The boxes indicate those individuals who clearly demonstrated leadership behavior (most closely personified the values shared by their groups, were most often sought for help and arbitration, and so forth).

[b]While the two- and three-person groupings had little informal contact outside their own boundaries, the five-man Clark group did seek to join the largest group in social affairs outside the plant, these were relatively infrequent.

[c]Though not an active member of any group, Bob Pearson was regarded with affection by the two large groups.

not affiliated with either the Sarto or the Clark groups worked on weekends.) Off the job, Sarto group members often joined in parties or weekend trips, with Sarto's summer house being a frequent rendezvous.

Sarto's group was the most cohesive one in the department in terms of its organized punch-in and punch-out system. Since the group's members were regularly scheduled to work from 7:00 A.M. to 7:00 P.M. weekdays, and since all supervisors left at 5:00 P.M., it was possible almost every day to finish a "day's work" by 5:30 P.M. and leave the plant. Moreover, if one of the group's members stayed until 7:00 P.M., he or she could punch the time cards of a number of others and help gain them free time without pay loss. (This system operated on weekends also, at which time supervisors were only present for short periods, if at all.) In Sarto's group the duty of staying late rotated, so that no one did so more than once a week. In addition, the group would punch in a member if he or she were unavoidably delayed. Such a practice never occurred without prior notice from the person who expected to be late and never if the tardiness was expected to last beyond 8:00 A.M., the start of the day for the supervisor.

Sarto explained the logic behind the system to Kirk:

You know that our hourly pay rate is quite low, compared to other companies. What makes this the best place to work is the feeling of security you get. No one ever gets laid off in this department. With all the hours in the workweek, all the

company ever has to do is shorten the workweek when orders fall off. We have to tighten our belts, but we can all get along. When things are going well, as they are now, the company is only interested in getting out the work. It doesn't help to get it out faster than it's really needed—so we go home a little early whenever we can. Of course, some people abuse this sort of thing—like Herman—but others work even harder, and it averages out.

Whenever an extra order has to be pushed through, naturally I work until 7:00 P.M. So do a lot of others. I believe that if I stay until my work is caught up and my equipment is in good shape, that's all the company wants of me. They leave us alone and expect us to produce—and we do.

When Kirk asked Sarto if he would rather not work shorter hours at higher pay in a union shop (Slade employees were not organized), he just laughed and said: "It wouldn't come close to an even trade."

The members of Sarto's group were explicit about what constituted a fair day's work. Customarily, they cited Herman Schell, Kirk's work partner and the supervisor's brother, as a man who consistently produced below level. Kirk received an informal orientation from Herman during his first days on the job. As Herman put it:

I've worked at this job for a good many years, and I expect to stay here a good many more. You're just starting out, and you don't know which end is up yet. We spend a lot of time in here; and no matter how hard we work, the pile of work never goes down. There's always more to take its place. And I think you've found out by now that this isn't light work. You can wear yourself out fast if you're not smart. Look at Pearson up in aisle 4. There's a kid who's just going to burn himself out. He won't last long. If he thinks he's going to get somewhere working like that, he's nuts. They'll give him all the work he can take. He makes it tough on everybody else and on himself, too.

Kirk reported on his observations of the department:

As nearly as I could tell, two things seemed to determine whether or not Sarto's group or any others came in for weekend work on Saturday or Sunday. It seemed usually to be caused by rush orders that were received late in the week, although I suspect it was sometimes caused by the fact that people spent insufficient time on the job during the previous week.

Tony and his group couldn't understand Herman. While Herman arrived late, Tony was always half an hour early. If there was a push to get out an extra amount of work, almost everyone but Herman would work that much harder. Herman never worked overtime on weekends, while Tony's group and the people on the manual tanks almost always did. When the first exploratory time study of the department was made, no one on the aisles slowed down, except Herman, with the possible exception, to a lesser degree, of Charlie Malone. I did hear that the people in the dry end of the room slowed down so much you could hardly see them move; but we had little to do with them, anyway. While the people I knew best seemed to find a rather full life in their work, Herman never really got involved. No wonder they couldn't understand each other.

There was quite a different feeling about Bobby Pearson. Without the slightest doubt, Bob worked harder than anyone else in the room. Because of the tremendous variety of work produced, it was hard to make output comparisons, but I'm sure I wouldn't be far wrong in saying that Bob put out twice as much as Herman and 50% more than almost anyone else in the aisles. No one but Herman and a few old-timers at the dry end ever criticized Bob for his efforts. Tony and his group seemed to feel a distant affection for Bob, but the only contact they or anyone else had with him consisted of brief greetings.

To the people in Tony's group the most severe penalty that could be inflicted was exclusion. This they did to both Pearson and Herman. Pearson, however, was tolerated; Herman was not. Evidently, Herman felt his exclusion keenly, though he answered it with derision and aggression. Herman kept up a steady stream of stories concerning his attempts to gain acceptance outside the company. He wrote country western music that was always rejected by producers. He attempted to join several social and athletic clubs, mostly without success. His favorite pastime was fishing. He told me that fishermen were friendly, and he enjoyed meeting new people whenever he went fishing. But he was particularly quick to explain that he preferred to keep his distance from the people in the department.

Tony's group emphasized more than just quantity in judging a person's work. The group stressed high standards of both quality and inventiveness. A confidence had grown among them that they could master and even improve upon any known finishing technique. Tony himself symbolized this skill. Before him, Tony's father had operated aisle 1 and had trained Tony to take his place. Tony, in turn, was training his cousin Pete. When a new finishing problem arose from a change in customer specifications, the supervisor, the department technician, the plant process engineer or any of the people directly involved would come to Tony for help, and Tony would give it willingly. For example, when a part with a special plastic embossing was designed, Tony was the only one who could discover how to treat the metal without damaging the plastic. To a lesser degree, the other members of the group were also inventive about solving the problems that arose in their own sections.

Herman, for his part, talked incessantly about his feats in design and finish creations. As far as I could tell during the year I worked in the department, the objects of these stories were obsolete or of minor importance. What's more, I never saw any department member seek Herman's help.

Willingness to be of help was a trait Sarto's group prized. The most valued help of all was of a personal kind, though work help was also important. The members of Sarto's group were constantly lending and borrowing money, cars, clothing, and tools among themselves and, less frequently, with other members of the department. Their daily lunch bag procedure typified the "common property" feeling among them. Everyone's lunch was opened and added to a common pile, from which each member of the group chose his or her meal.

On the other hand, Herman refused to help others in any way. He never left his aisle to aid those near him who were in the middle of a rush of work or a machine failure, though this was customary throughout most of the department. I can distinctly recall the picture of Herman leaning on the hot and cold water faucets that were located directly above each tumbling barrel. He would stand gazing into the tumbling pieces for hours. To the passing, casual visitor, he looked busy; and as he told me, that's just what he wanted. He, of course, expected me to act this same way, and it was this enforced boredom that I found virtually intolerable.

More than this, Herman took no responsibility for breaking in his assigned helpers as they first entered the department or thereafter. He had had four helpers in the space of little more than a year. Each had asked for a transfer to another department, publicly citing the work as cause, privately blaming Herman. Tony was the one who taught me the ropes when I first entered the department.

The people who congregated around Harry Clark tended to talk like and imitate the behavior of the Sarto group, although they never approached the degree of inventive skill or the amount of helping activities that Tony's group did. They sought outside social contact with the Sarto group; and several times a year, the two groups went out on the town together. Clark's group did maintain a high level of performance in the volume of work it turned out.

The remainder of the people in the department stayed pretty much to themselves or associated in pairs or threesomes. None of these people were as inventive, as helpful, or as productive as Sarto's or Clark's groups, but most of them gave verbal support to the same values as those groups held.

The distinction between the two organized groups and the rest of the department was clearest in the punching-out routine. The women in rack assembly were not involved. Malone and Lacey, Partridge and Swan, and Martin, La Forte, and Mensch arranged within their small groups for punch outs, or they remained beyond 5:00 P.M. and slept or read when they finished their work. Perkins and Pierce went home when the supervisor did. Herman Schell, Susi, and Maher had no punch-out organization to rely on. Susi and Maher invariably stayed in the department until 7:00 P.M. Herman was reported to have established an arrangement with Partridge whereby the latter punched Herman out for a fee. Such a practice was unthinkable from the point of view of Sarto's group. Evidently, it did not occur often because Herman usually went to sleep behind piles of work when his brother left, or particularly during the fishing season, punched himself out early. He constantly railed against the dishonesty of other people in the department, yet urged me to punch him out on several "emergency occasions."

Just before I left the Slade Company to return to school after 14 months on the job, I had a casual conversation with Mr. Porter, the production manager, and he asked me how I had enjoyed my experience with the organization. During the conversation, I learned that he knew of the punch-out system in the Plating Department. What's more, he told me, he was wondering if he ought to "blow the lid off the whole mess."

Activity 5–3: Alternative Courses of Managerial Action in the Slade Plating Department

Objectives:

a. To use the individual-first, team-second decision-making model to synergistically develop alternative courses of managerial action for the situation described in the Slade case.

b. To use course concepts to make the analysis.

c. To evaluate the consequences of alternative proposals.

Task 1 (Individuals Working Alone)
Alternative 1 (for one-half of the teams in the class):

Working alone, complete the Slade case assignment immediately preceding this exercise.
   Assume you are Mr. Porter, the production manager, and have become fully knowledgeable of all the data given in the case study. You are trying to decide on alternative courses of action. Complete the accompanying worksheet for Alternative 1.

Alternative 2 (for the other half of the teams in the class):

Working alone, complete the Slade case assignment immediately preceding this exercise.
   Assume you are Tony Sarto and his work group. You have heard that Mr. Porter, the production manager, has become fully knowledgeable of all the data given in the case study. You and your group have an informal meeting outside work to discuss the problem. What actions do you think management might take? How would you respond to these? How do you think management should handle this situation? Complete the accompanying Alternative 2 worksheet for the Sarto group.

Task 2 (Team Activity):

Teams are to meet outside class to analyze the questions on the worksheet for the alternative they have been assigned. At the next class session, turn in to the instructor a one-page typed summary of your analysis. (*Note:* Use a brief outline form in your paper.)

Task 3 (Classroom Activity):

A spokesperson for each team will outline its conclusions on the blackboard and present a rationale to the class. Mr. Porter's teams will all report first, followed by the Sarto teams. Discussion follows.

Name _____   Date _____

WORKSHEET FOR ACTIVITY 5–3

Alternative 1: Worksheet for Mr. Porter, Production Manager

What are all the possible alternative actions? List them below.	What are the possible consequences that would be expected to be:	
	Favorable	Unfavorable

Which of the above alternatives would you choose? Why?

Name _____   Date _____

WORKSHEET FOR ACTIVITY 5–3

Alternative 2: Worksheet for Tony Sarto's Work Group

List alternative actions management might take.	List Sarto work group's response to each alternative.

How would Sarto's work group think management should handle this situation? Why?

Activity 5–4:
Motivational Analysis of
Organizations-Behavior
(MAO-B)

Objectives:

a. To examine a behavioral model of motivation.

b. To provide students with the opportunity to diagnose and analyze their own motivation.

c. To compute individuals' operating effectiveness.

Task 1:

Individuals working alone should complete and score the survey.

Task 2:

Individuals in a small group are to share their scores and interpret the results. Each group is to complete the following tasks

a. Identify common themes.

b. Discuss the implications of individuals' motivation to team performance.

c. Develop an action plan to overcome the motivational issues.

Name _____ Date _____

MOTIVATIONAL ANALYSIS OF ORGANIZATIONS-BEHAVIOR (MAO-B) INVENTORY

Instructions: This inventory can help you to understand how different motivations can affect your behavior and your performance at work. There are no "right" or "wrong" responses; the inventory will reflect your own perceptions of how you act at work, so you will gain the most value from it if you answer honestly. Do not spend too much time on any one item; generally, your first reaction is the most accurate.

Read each statement below and decide which of the numbered columns to the right best describes how often you engage in the behavior or have the feeling. Circle the appropriate number next to each statement to indicate your response.

	Rarely/ Never	Sometimes/ Occasionally	Often/ Freqently	Usually/ Always
1. I enjoy working on moderately difficult (challenging) tasks and goals.	1	2	3	4
2. I am overly emotional.	1	2	3	4
3. I am forceful in my arguments.	1	2	3	4
4. I refer matters to my superiors.	1	2	3	4
5. I keep close track of things (monitor action).	1	2	3	4
6. I make contributions to charity and help those in need.	1	2	3	4
7. I set easy goals and achieve them.	1	2	3	4
8. I relate very well to people.	1	2	3	4
9. I am preoccupied with my own ideas and am a poor listener.	1	2	3	4
10. I follow my ideals.	1	2	3	4
11. I demand conformity from the people who work for or with me.	1	2	3	4
12. I take steps to develop the people who work for me.	1	2	3	4
13. I strive to exceed performance/targets.	1	2	3	4
14. I ascribe more importance to personal relationships than to organizational matters.	1	2	3	4
15. I build on the ideas of my subordinates or others.	1	2	3	4
16. I seek the approval of my superiors.	1	2	3	4
17. I ensure that things are done according to plan.	1	2	3	4
18. I consider the difficulties of others even at the expense of the task.	1	2	3	4
19. I am afraid of making mistakes.	1	2	3	4
20. I share my feelings with others.	1	2	3	4
21. I enjoy arguing and winning arguments.	1	2	3	4
22. I have genuine respect for experienced persons.	1	2	3	4
23. I admonish people for not completing tasks.	1	2	3	4
24. I go out of my way to help the people who work for me.	1	2	3	4
25. I search for new ways to overcome difficulties.	1	2	3	4
26. I have difficulty in expressing negative feelings to others.	1	2	3	4
27. I set myself as an example and model for others.	1	2	3	4
28. I hesitate to make hard decisions.	1	2	3	4
29. I define roles and procedures for the people who work for me.	1	2	3	4
30. I undergo personal inconvenience for the sake of others.	1	2	3	4
31. I am more conscious of my limitations or weaknesses than of my strengths.	1	2	3	4
32. I take interest in matters of personal concern to the people who work for me.	1	2	3	4
33. I am *laissez-faire* in my leadership style (do not care how things happen).	1	2	3	4
34. I learn from those who are senior to me.	1	2	3	4
35. I centralize most tasks to ensure that things are done properly.	1	2	3	4
36. I have empathy and understanding for the people who work for me.	1	2	3	4
37. I want to know how well I have been doing, and I use feedback to improve myself.	1	2	3	4

	Rarely/ Never	Sometimes/ Occasionally	Often/ Freqently	Usually/ Always
38. I avoid conflict in the interest of group feelings.	1	2	3	4
39. I provide new suggestions and ideas.	1	2	3	4
40. I try to please others.	1	2	3	4
41. I explain systems and procedures clearly to the people who work for me.	1	2	3	4
42. I tend to take responsibility for others' work in order to help them.	1	2	3	4
43. I show low self-confidence.	1	2	3	4
44. I recognize and respond to the feelings of others.	1	2	3	4
45. I receive credit for work done in a team.	1	2	3	4
46. I seek help from those who know the subject.	1	2	3	4
47. In case of difficulties, I rush to correct things.	1	2	3	4
48. I develop teamwork among the people who work for me.	1	2	3	4
49. I work effectively under pressure of deadlines.	1	2	3	4
50. I am uneasy and less productive when working alone.	1	2	3	4
51. I give credit and recognition to others.	1	2	3	4
52. I look for support for my actions and proposals.	1	2	3	4
53. I enjoy positions of authority.	1	2	3	4
54. I hesitate to take strong actions because of human considerations.	1	2	3	4
55. I complain about difficulties and problems.	1	2	3	4
56. I take the initiative in making friends with my colleagues.	1	2	3	4
57. I am quite conscious of status symbols such as furniture and size of office.	1	2	3	4
58. I like to solicit ideas from others.	1	2	3	4
59. I tend to form small groups to influence decisions.	1	2	3	4
60. I like to accept responsibility in the group's work.	1	2	3	4

Name _____   Date _____

SCORING THE MAO-B INVENTORY

Instructions: Transfer your responses from the MAO-B inventory to the appropriate spaces on this sheet. If you circled the number 2 to the right of item 1, enter a 2 in the space after the number 1 below; if you circled a 4 as your response to item 13, enter a 4 in the space to the right of the number 13 below, and so on until you have entered all your responses in the space below.

A	B	C	D	E	F
1. _____	3. _____	5. _____	10. _____	12. _____	8. _____
13. _____	15. _____	17. _____	22. _____	24. _____	20. _____
25. _____	27. _____	29. _____	34. _____	36. _____	32. _____
37. _____	39. _____	41. _____	46. _____	48. _____	44. _____
49. _____	51. _____	53. _____	58. _____	60. _____	56. _____
A total _____	B total _____	C total _____	D total _____	E total _____	F total _____

a	b	c	d	e	f
7. _____	9. _____	11. _____	4. _____	6. _____	2. _____
19. _____	21. _____	23. _____	16. _____	18. _____	14. _____
31. _____	33. _____	35. _____	28. _____	30. _____	26. _____
43. _____	45. _____	47. _____	40. _____	42. _____	38. _____
55. _____	57. _____	59. _____	52. _____	54. _____	50. _____
a total _____	b total _____	c total _____	d total _____	e total _____	f total _____

Now add the numbers that you entered in each vertical column and enter the totals in the spaces provided. Now add the numbers that you entered in each vertical column horizontally and enter the totals in the spaces provided next to "OEQ". These totals are your scores for the approach–avoidance dimensions of each of the six primary motivators of people's behavior on the job. Transfer those totals to the appropriate spaces in the two middle columns below.

Achievement	A (approach) _____	a (avoidance) _____	OEQ _____
Influence	B (approach) _____	b (avoidance) _____	OEQ _____
Control	C (approach) _____	c (avoidance) _____	OEQ _____
Dependence	D (approach) _____	d (avoidance) _____	OEQ _____
Extension	E (approach) _____	e (avoidance) _____	OEQ _____
Affiliation	F (approach) _____	f (avoidance) _____	OEQ _____

To compute your operating effectiveness quotient (OEQ) for each motivator, find the value for your approach (capital letter) score for the motivator along the top row of the table that follows and then find your avoidance (lowercase letter) score for that motivator in the left column. The number in the cell that intersects the column and row is your OEQ score for the motivator. Transfer that score to the tally marked OEQ at the bottom of the preceding page. Do this for each motivator.

Avoidance Scores	Approach Scores															
	5	6	7	8	9	10	11	12	13	14	15	16	17	18	19	20
5	0	100	100	100	100	100	100	100	100	100	100	100	100	100	100	100
6	0	50	67	75	80	83	85	87	89	90	91	92	92	93	93	97
7	0	33	50	60	67	71	75	78	80	82	83	85	86	87	87	88
8	0	25	40	50	57	62	67	70	73	75	77	78	80	81	82	83
9	0	20	33	43	50	55	60	64	67	69	71	73	75	76	78	79
10	0	17	28	37	44	50	54	58	61	64	67	69	70	72	74	75
11	0	14	25	33	40	45	50	54	59	60	62	65	67	68	70	71
12	0	12	22	30	36	42	46	50	53	56	59	61	63	65	67	68
13	0	11	20	27	33	38	43	47	50	53	55	58	60	62	64	65
14	0	10	18	25	31	36	40	44	47	50	53	55	57	59	61	62
15	0	9	17	23	28	33	37	41	44	47	50	52	54	56	58	60
16	0	8	15	21	27	31	35	39	42	45	48	50	52	54	56	58
17	0	8	14	20	25	29	33	37	40	43	45	48	50	52	54	56
18	0	7	13	19	23	28	32	35	38	41	43	46	48	50	52	54
19	0	7	12	18	22	26	30	33	36	39	42	44	46	48	50	52
20	0	6	12	17	21	25	29	32	35	37	40	42	44	46	48	50

OPERATING EFFECTIVENESS QUOTIENTS

When you have completed this process for all of your scores, you will have a numerical picture of what typically motivates your behavior at work, whether you respond positively (approach) or negatively (avoidance) to each of the six typical motivators, and how your responses to each motivator influence your operating effectiveness.

Source: This questionnaire was designed by Dr. Udai Parcek. The survey is reprinted here with permission of University Associates, San Diego, CA 92121. All rights reserved.

Module

6

Perception, Attribution, and Values

LEARNING OBJECTIVES

After completing this module, you should be able to

1. Appreciate the role of work-related values and belief systems in shaping individual behavior.
2. Define and describe the perceptual process.
3. Understand your own perceptual process and barriers to accurate perception.
4. Describe how the attribution process influences perception and individual behavior.
5. Identify the basic managerial actions that can help create accurate perception.

KEY TERMS AND CONCEPTS

Age stereotype

Attribution process

Attribution theory

Belief systems

Defense mechanisms

Denial

Distortion

Motivation

Perception

Perceptual process

Premature closure

Projection

Pygmalion effect

Race stereotype

Self-fulfilling prophecy

Sex-role stereotype

Stereotypes

Stereotype threat

Values

MODULE OUTLINE

PREMODULE PREPARATION

Activity 6–1:
Values in Business

Objectives:

a. To increase awareness of the importance of values as determinants of organizational behavior.

b. To increase awareness of the differences in team members' perception of values.

c. To experience some of the issues associated with group decision making and group dynamics.

Introduction:

This activity was designed to help your team evaluate the relative importance of certain values with which business organizations must be concerned. Values can be thought of as existing in a hierarchy in our thought processes, some being given higher importance or priority than others. The whole pattern of values in an organization represents the core of its operating philosophy and its organizational culture. Thus, they are major determinants of behavior of management and employees.

Values are defined as things, ideas, beliefs, and acts that are regarded as good or bad, right or wrong, desirable or undesirable, beautiful or ugly, contributing to or detrimental to human welfare, and so on. Societies, organizations, and individuals all have values with priorities of importance. For example, individuals may differ greatly in the values associated with religious beliefs, but a higher-order value that they all presumably would accept is freedom of religious beliefs.

General Exercise:

Assume you are a member of a top-management team of a large corporation. During a team-development retreat, the facilitator–consultant informs the group that she has observed from individual interviews with team members that differences in perception exist as to the values by which they operate. Yet each person seems to be assuming that his or her values are shared by the other team members. As a basis for developing awareness and better consensus in values, the following tasks are undertaken.

Task 1 (Individual Rankings):

Listed in alphabetical order on the accompanying worksheet are 10 values that are among those often discussed in regard to business functioning. Your job is to rank these according to the priority you would assign each in terms of importance for conducting business. Do this by writing in the first column next to the value a 1 for the value of highest importance, a 2 for the next, on down to a 10 for the value of lowest importance. In the second column, briefly note the reason for your ranking. Be sure to do this without consulting others; also, be sure your rankings are not observable to team members while completing this task. (*Note:* There are no right or wrong answers and no definite solution to this exercise. The rankings should be based on your own values and belief system.)

Task 2 (Team Rankings):

Teams meet outside of class. Members compare their rankings of the values and come to a consensus as to how the team would rank the items from 1 to 10. This ranking should reflect what the team believes, not your estimate of how businesspeople would rank the values. (*Note:* Consensus does not necessarily mean that all agree with the final ranking of the team; it does mean that everyone's views were expressed and understood and that agreement was reached on how the values were to be ranked. In a real situation your personal values may differ from your colleagues', but you may decide to support the team's viewpoint for reasons such as hoping eventually to persuade your co-workers to adopt your views or wanting to be open-minded to see whether you could be wrong. If your values are too different, you may find, after a reasonable period, that you do not fit into the team. The main point of the exercise at this time is to increase your awareness of values and belief systems.)

Task 3 (Classroom):

Teams list on the board the rank ordering of their values. Discuss similarities and differences.

Name _____   Date _____

WORKSHEET FOR ACTIVITY 6–1

Values	Your Ranking	Reason	Your Team's Ranking	Reason
Career growth and development of personnel				
Concern for personnel as people				
Efficiency				
Ethics (morality)				
Managerial and organizational effectiveness				
Servicing clients' needs (for example, equipment, orders)				
Profits				
Providing products or services for society				
Quality of goods or services				
Social responsibility				

Activity 6–2: Exploring Perceptual Issues via Dan Dunwoodie's Challenge

Objective:

To have small groups identify and define the problem in a case study so that the process can be studied through the analysis of contrasting results presented by the groups.

Task 1:

Participants are to read the case study, Dan Dunwoodie's Challenge, which follows. Each team is to answer the following three questions on the case study:

a. What is the problem?
b. What is the principal cause?
c. What action should Dan Dunwoodie take?

(Time: 15 minutes)

Task 2:

Each team first presents its results on problem definition, which the instructor lists on the board. Then the same procedure is followed for causes. After these have been listed, the action recommendations are given and listed. During the process of listing the contrasting results from the various teams, team members are not to challenge or discuss the solutions. Questions may be asked for clarification. When the data are all out, there should be open challenges and discussion of differing points of view and of the feasibility of the suggested actions.

The class should develop at least one criterion for deciding upon the problem; a decision should be reached as to what would be the best solution from the standpoint of the criteria developed.
(Time: 30 minutes)

Case Study: Dan Dunwoodie's Challenge

Up to this point I have been doing very well. At 27 years of age, I am chief of an economic analysis branch in the United Automobile Manufacturing Company. I was hired personally by John Roman, my division chief, who interviewed me at the university where I was completing my MBA. John had expressed interest in several of my qualifications: BA in economics from an outstanding university, four years of work experience as an analyst in industry, and a specialty in Information Systems while working on my MBA.

When I came on duty three months ago, John gave me guidance as follows:

Economic analysis functions and processing at United need updating. Analysts are substantive experts and do not comprehend the importance of management or the possible application of information systems to managerial decision making. They keep insisting that judgmental processes cannot be automated; they resist suggestions that they can augment their activities by using computers. After you have had three to six months to learn your job, you are to come up with recommendations for organizational and procedural changes in your branch. You are to keep in close touch with your peers, the other branch chiefs in the division, all of whom have been with the company for five or more years.

(Their responsibilities were almost identical to mine except each branch had different economic specialties.)

I assumed my responsibilities with great energy and soon saw many possibilities for developing the effectiveness of my branch. I worked evenings and weekends on a new plan. As I developed ideas, I would try them out on each of the other branch chiefs. They were helpful and responsive. One objection did arise from Carl Carlson, chief of Branch B, who criticized some of the information systems suggestions. (Carl was regarded in the division as the next man in line for John's job. See Exhibit 1.)

Exhibit 1

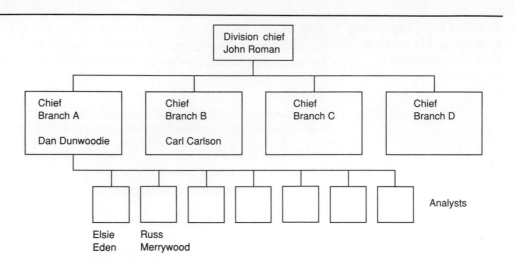

At the end of three months with United, I presented my plan to my entire branch in a briefing session, complete with a statement of objectives, charts, and expected results. In response to my request for their reactions, two people spoke up. One was Elsie Eden, who was a contemporary of John and the branch chiefs. (I had heard she would have had my job if she had been willing to take an extensive computer training program.) The other was Russ Merrywood, also an old-timer, who had been passed over for advancement. (I had also heard that Russ had money and was not too committed to his job, although I find that his work is excellent.) My plan was well thought out, and further clarification of various details appeared to satisfy all questions raised.

On a Wednesday afternoon I gave the same oral briefing to John (division chief), who showed enthusiasm and pleasure. He promised me an early decision and asked for a copy of my written report for further study. On Thursday afternoon I received the report back with the notation, "Sounds great. Proceed soonest with entire plan with the exception of paragraph 6, which I wish to study further." (Paragraph 6 contained an information system suggestion concerning which Carl had expressed disapproval to Dan.)

I spent Friday in meetings with my branch making initial plans for implementing the new program. Over the weekend I continued on my own to make final plans.

Early Monday morning I was asked to come to the division chief's office. I then learned that John had reversed his decision, and no changes were to be put into effect at this time. John appeared rather brusk and said he did not have time to discuss the decision. Later that day, I learned that John had attended a dinner party at Russ's house over the weekend.

INTRODUCTION

Perception, attribution, and values, the third of the major cluster of core concepts for understanding behavior in organizations (the first two being psychodynamic and motivation), provide a framework and a useful tool for understanding effectiveness at the individual, group, intergroup, and organizational levels. The subject has been dealt with indirectly up to this point. Underlying the dialogue process of Module 2 was the question of what differences existed in the way the participants and the professor were perceiving important contextual aspects of the subject to be studied. In Module 3, we explored the role of value judgment in the process of knowing. Module 4 explored the nature of rationality, irrationality, emotions, and psychodynamics in organizations. As Activities 6–1 and 6–2 illustrated, values and work-related belief systems play a critical role in shaping individual perception, attribution, and individual and team behavior. In this module we explore work-related belief systems, the nature of values at work, perception, and attribution.

WORK-RELATED BELIEF SYSTEM AND VALUES

The nature of work and work dynamics is such that it triggers complex, strong, and diverse individual attitudes. At the same time, attitude toward work is also shaped by strongly held values and beliefs. Values are groups of beliefs about a particular object or process. Every human being has certain implicit and explicit values that are a cumulative result of upbringing, community dynamics, and educational experience. Some of the values are materialistic in nature, while others are more of a spiritual nature. Values serve as criteria or a framework against which individual experience is examined. In Module 3, which focused on learning-in-action, we argued that knowing is the result of the complex operations of experiencing, understanding, and judging. Knowing can be accompanied by making decisions and taking action, when the judgment is a judgment of value. A judgment of value, as contrasted with a judgment of fact, leads to consideration of whether to do something or not and what to do.

Values and **belief systems** are partially responsible for people's choice of what company to work for or what product or service to use. Many individuals chose to work for a company that they perceive fits their values. For example, if the individual is ecologically minded and protecting the environment is held as an altruistic value, the likelihood that the individual would choose to work for a company that is known to create significant waste that might cause environmental damage is small. Alternatively, an individual may have a gender belief system around the issues of discrimination against women, biological differences between the sexes, and attitudes toward homosexuals and lesbians that guide their actions. Some individuals choose to leave a company or take on the role of a "whistle-blower" against the company that they just left when they see actions that conflict with their own value set or belief system. Some choose to take the same action and/or role while they are working.[1] Thus, values and belief systems are related to specific individual attitudes, perception, human dynamics, and outcomes within the context of work. In the next few sections we further examine values and belief systems.

Work-Related Belief Systems

Exploring the meaning of beliefs or belief systems seems to have attracted researchers in different academic disciplines. Researchers focused on societal belief systems such as the general belief about work, beliefs in a just world, belief systems of authoritarianism and conservatism, beliefs about internal versus external control, the Protestant work ethic, and workaholism. For the purpose of this chapter, we will focus here on work-related belief systems and review one comprehensive framework.

One of the most comprehensive published accounts of "beliefs about work" was generated by Buchholz who identified and examined five indices, namely, the work ethic, the organization belief system, Marxist-related beliefs, the humanistic belief system, and the leisure ethic.[2] He described the five work-related belief system indices as follows:

- *Work ethic.* The belief that work is good in itself, it offers dignity to a person, and success is a result of personal effort.
- *Organization belief system.* The view that work takes on meaning only as it affects the organization and contributes to one's position at work.
- *Marxist-related beliefs.* The opinion that work is fundamental to human fulfillment, but as currently organized represents exploitation of the worker and consequent alienation.
- *Humanistic belief system.* The view that individual growth and development in the job is more important than the output.
- *Leisure ethic.* The view that regards work as a means to personal fulfillment, through its provision of the means to pursue leisure activities.

Research indicates that the work-related belief systems seem to be fairly predictive of the behaviors and performance of both employees and managers. For example, Furnham found that personal satisfaction and productivity were related to a positive work ethic belief system.[3] Last, cultural background seems to play a differentiating role in the shaping up of a work-related belief system. For example, when comparing three working groups in Scotland and the United States, the researchers found that the Marxist-related and leisure belief systems most differentiated the workers from the two cultures.[4]

Social Values at Work

Furnham argues that "A value is the enduring belief that a specific instrumental mode of conduct and/or a terminal end state is preferable. Once a value is internalized, it consciously or unconsciously becomes a standard criterion for guiding action, for developing and maintaining attitude towards relevant objects and situations, for justifying one's own and others' actions and attitudes, for morally judging self and others, and for comparing oneself with others."[5] The nature of personal values can be linked to many factors such as culture of origin, religion, political persuasion, educational background, personality, age, sex, and generations within a family.

Personal values influence values at work and as such will have an impact on human behavior at work. Values at work can be categorized into a few facets: values that are associated with work ethics, such as achievement and hard working; values that are associated with the outcomes of work, such as recognition, pay, status, and job security; values associated with the context of work such as working conditions and company reputation; values associated with the work process itself such as equity, equality, fairness, and excitement of work; and values associated with interpersonal relationships such as respect, harmony with self and others, and harmony of social groups.

Just like individuals, over time organizations develop a pattern of values and belief systems that represent the organization's core operating philosophy and its culture. The whole pattern of the organizational values and belief system are major determinants of behavior of management and employees. As we saw in Activity 6–1, individuals seem to differ on their perception of the relative importance of business values. The intent of the activity was to help the team evaluate the relative importance of certain values with which business organizations must be concerned and at the same time develop a deeper level of appreciation to the fact that one can not assume that his or her values are shared by others. Yet, from an organization perspective, if all the members of the team would have worked for the same organization, it would be of the utmost importance that individuals' perceptions of the relative importance of the business values would have been more of a similar nature.

PERCEPTION AND PERCEPTUAL DIFFERENCES IN DAILY LIFE

Fundamental values and belief systems influence the work behavior of organizational members and trigger differences in people's perceptions. Perception is a fascinating subject that is being studied in many areas of daily life. Politicians are concerned about how they are perceived by the public and how their images can be improved and maintained; U.S. diplomats want to know how representatives of other nations with whom they will negotiate perceive this country; advertisers must determine how ads and products will be seen by consumers. Students in many law schools are required to take courses in psychology and psychiatry to improve their self-awareness. As one law school dean said, "When you go into the courtroom, you are part of the problem; the better you know what part of it you are, the better you can control and influence the situation." In the mental health arena, the therapist attempts to help the patient build a favorable self-concept and change his or her self-image so that it is more consistent with the way the person is perceived by others, thus reducing misunderstandings in interpersonal relations. Intelligence officers must know how their agents perceive themselves in relation to the operation in which they are engaged and how they see the intelligence officer and his or her country in order to understand, predict, and control the agent's activities.

Everyone is aware that we all see things somewhat differently, but in this complicated and difficult area, few people are aware of the full extent of the differences. Blind spots

Figure 6–1   **The Perceptual Process: An Overview)**

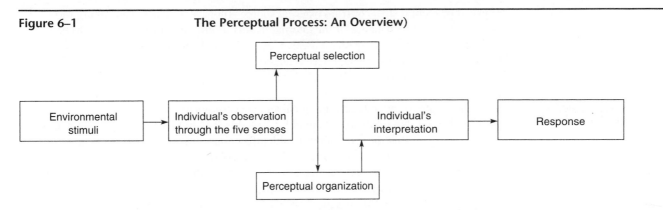

develop to obscure specific happenings. Police surrounded a hotel and conducted a shootout with snipers firing from the hotel roof; some police officers were killed. Only one body was found on the roof after the firing stopped; the other suspects presumably escaped during the battle. It was not until some weeks later that the official investigation revealed that only one assailant was ever on that roof. The police and the television reporters, under the pressure of excitement, "saw" several assailants firing. Were police officers actually killed by the ricocheting bullets of other police in this setting, which maximized perceptual distortion?

Often managers, their subordinates, or co-workers perceive the same situation differently. The way individuals perceive their own competencies, skills, and knowledge; the way they perceive their peers and supervisors; the way they perceive their tasks; and the way their peers and their supervisors perceive them affect their behavior and performance. As such, perceptual differences that are likely to occur in the complex web of relationships and perceptions are likely to have an impact on individuals and their performance.[6] From a management point of view, understanding the perceptual process and the potential barriers for accurate perception is critical.

The Perceptual Process

Perception is an active process by which individuals screen, select, organize, and interpret stimuli. Figure 6–1 captures the key elements of the **perceptual process.** The way an individual perceives a situation is based on what the individual is experiencing at a given moment, which is based on several factors. These include data being received from the five senses (sight, smell, taste, touch, and hearing), data in the memory system, emotions, feelings, needs, wants, and goals. It is important to realize that what individuals experience at any given moment is based primarily upon what goes on inside them (the internal factors affecting perception) rather than what is happening outside them in the external world (physical objects and social interactions).[7]

The degree of influence on the individual of internal and external factors is illustrated in Figure 6–2. It can be assumed that the more pressure the individual is under from

**Figure 6–2
Relationship between
Factors Determining
Perception That Are
Internal to the Individual
and Those That Are in the
External World**

Internal factors	External factors
Physiological	Physical objects
Past experience	People
Psychological	Social interactions
Motivation	
Defense mechanisms	

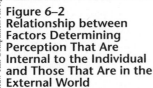

High percentage of influence	Low percentage of influence

physical or mental stress or from external sources (noises, violence, and so on), the greater will be the influence of the internal factors. Figure 6–2 is not intended to be exhaustive; it presents only broad areas relevant to the determinants of perception. The following sections discuss the internal factors listed in the figure.

Physiological Factors

It is impossible to separate physiological and psychological factors because they are so closely blended. No real purpose could be served by trying to make precise distinctions. We are all aware that the state of our health affects our outlook, abilities, and emotions. The effects of drugs on perception have been widely researched and publicized.

An example of a physiological cause of perceptual differences is color blindness. One student reported his experience of undergoing an army physical examination during induction. Standing in line at a medical station, he could hear those ahead of him calling out "49" as they looked at a printed chart of different-colored circles of various sizes. When his turn came, he looked at the patterns formed among the color spots and called out the number he saw, which was 36. He was pulled out of the line for further testing and learned that he was partially color blind and was not perceiving shades of green and red, although he could identify the vivid basic colors. Thinking back on past experiences, he recalled that he had at times not seen certain aspects of distant scenes reported by others, but he had not thought too much of it. Once the test proved his disability, he became aware that he often was not experiencing what others were experiencing in this regard. Many subtle differences between people exist and influence how they see things, but there may be no awareness of the physiological factors that account for the differences.

Past Experience

It is widely hypothesized that everything experienced by the human being from birth on (some say from in the womb on) is stored in the memory system and is available for recall under certain conditions. Our knowledge in the area of memory and recall is most limited, and we do not know the extent to which, or whether, all experience is recorded in the brain. But it is safe to assume from research that the memory traces are vastly greater than any individual is conscious of, and these traces do affect perceptions and actions even though the individual may not be aware of them.

One mechanistic analogy would be to liken the mind to a computer system in which there is a large memory storage bank. To use the data, a program must give directions to the computer. Instead of programs, the mind has coding systems that organize the memory data into units; these are usable in the perceptual processes when the brain gives the directions for their use.

Codes of Past Experience

"Society" is a meaningfully organized element in the mental context; a complex system of expectations exists in each person's brain of how people should, ought, and must behave under both general and specific circumstances. It does not exist out there in the real world but only in the expectation system of all members as to how they are to interact with one another. This includes expectations organized around social roles, norms, customs, symbols, and so on. Life around us is automatically meaningful because of this major aspect of the memory system. Among other important blocks of codes are knowledge, facts, theories, beliefs, attitudes, and language. These codes are widely shared by people in the same society or in subgroupings of that society. There are also many codes of past experience that are unique to the individual and shared with only a few or with no one. The overlap between the coding systems of people with similar experiences is a fundamental requirement of communication. (This concept is explored in Module 7 on communication.)

Psychological Factors

Motivation

Feelings and Emotions: All experience is accompanied by emotions and feelings, which are integral components of the learning process. The individual is not aware of this most of the time. As you read this text, feelings you have had in the past toward education, classrooms, teachers, or your parents' attitudes toward learning are all present and influence what you are reading. Codes of past experience also have a feeling component.

A good classroom demonstration to alert students to this can be done with a dollar bill borrowed from one of the class members. The instructor holds the bill before the group and asks if anyone has any feelings about it. The response is low. He then proceeds to tear the dollar through the center. There are gasps: "You simply don't do that. It's against the law." All of the emotion learned in past experiences with money is brought forth, even though a moment earlier no one felt he or she had any feelings about the dollar.

Of the many psychological factors that could be discussed, we will focus on only two: **motivation** and **defense mechanisms.** Abilities, skills, intelligence, and the cognitive processes are among others that could be included here.

The attachment of feelings to words becomes evident in learning a foreign language. In English the phrase *I am hot* is a socially acceptable way to express the feeling that the atmospheric temperature is too high. In German, the identical phrase, *Ich bin heiss,* means that the person is sexually aroused. An American trying to express the former condition would find the Germans reacting in unexpected ways. (In German, the way to comment on high atmospheric temperature would be *Es ist mir warm,* or "It is warm to me.")

As tourists in a foreign country, people frequently find they can spend the local currency like play money; they have not developed the feelings about it that they have about their own currency. American children going to live abroad will learn easily all the dirty words of the new country and shout them about in public, an activity they would not do with opprobrious language in English. When cautioned on this, their reaction could be that it is a fun language; they have not learned the "no-no" feelings they had with such words in their own language.

The point to stress here is that feelings and emotions affect your perceptions all the time, even though you might not be aware of it.

Goals, Needs, and Wants: What your goals and needs are at a specific time are major determinants in perception. The principle that *perception is selective* means that the individual is not experiencing all of the external world to which he or she is exposed at a given moment; the person experiences only those aspects of it (cues) that are being selected out by the internal determinants. Needs demonstrate this nicely. Three people standing on the same street corner perceive the identical street scene selectively. The sailor on shore leave sees only the woman in the miniskirt walking away from him. The businessman, late for an appointment, sees only the clock on a sign above the woman. The third man sees only the restaurant sign above the clock; it is noon, and he is hungry.[8]

Defense Mechanisms

Objects, events, or social interactions that arouse fears or concerns in an individual are often dealt with psychologically in a manner of which the person is unaware. These are defense mechanisms the brain develops to cope with fear or concern.

Denial: One of the most frequent defensive responses is **denial.** Here, things that individuals would like to do but that are socially unacceptable are dealt with by the brain processes so that people eventually believe they do not want to do those things. The individual is also opposed to anyone else doing them. This is evident in all the "no-no" areas, such as sex, aggression toward others, envy, and desire for power. A woman may hate a man she loves because she unconsciously realizes she cannot have him, but she really is convinced of the hate. An individual with strong status needs may claim he does not really want any recognition for his deeds. Not being able to make much money may lead to expressions of delight with simple living. The *psychology of opposites* is an apt phrase for denial, which can indeed affect how an individual perceives certain behaviors of self and others.

Projection: We illustrate projection in terms of a well-known story. A young man visited a psychiatrist, who asked him why he had come for treatment. The man indicated that he did not know, that his parents had sent him because they thought he was acting strangely, but he did not think there was anything wrong. The doctor said maybe he could determine whether there was a problem by asking a few questions. He then took out a piece of chalk and went to a small blackboard in the office and drew a straight vertical line about 10 inches long. He asked, "Tell me, what do you see here that I have drawn?" The young man replied, "It's a naked woman." The doctor said, "Very good. Now what is this?" He then drew an identical vertical line about six inches to the right of the first. The man replied, "It's a naked man." "And now what do you see?" asked the psychiatrist, as he drew a horizontal line between the two lines, forming an H shape. "It is a naked man and a naked woman and they are in bed together making love." The psychiatrist then gave his diagnosis. "I can see you are very sick. You really have some serious sex problems." The young man was upset and said, "Doc, what do you mean, me having all the sex problems? You're the one drawing all those dirty pictures!"

This story illustrates denial, but the main point is that the patient was projecting his own needs onto some external object. **Projection** means interpreting the world and the actions of others in terms of your own wants, needs, goals, desires, impulses, fears, and so on. If you are feeling aggressive and hostile, you may feel that it is those people out there who are hostile and causing all the trouble. If you are in love, you may believe most young couples you see walking on the street are in love. If you are a fearful person, you may perceive everything that happens in negative terms. If you think everyone is unfriendly, chances are you are really unfriendly and are attributing it to others. Of course, you may be unaware of this and immediately deny it if it is brought to your attention. Projecting one's own tendencies onto others and not being aware of it is a natural brain process that operates most strongly when the individual is feeling defensive. Thus, projection distorts the perceptual processes in terms of the internal determinants interfering with the reception of what is really out there—the external factors.

A number of other defense mechanisms are useful to know about. You may wish to pursue this topic in your outside reading.

Stereotypes

The term **stereotypes** implies modular (constructed as units) perceptions in which visual, factual, emotional, and feeling elements are all integrated into a fixed pattern of viewing persons, problems, activities, or objects. Within a social cognition framework, stereotypes function to reduce information-processing demands, to define group membership, and to predict behavior based on group membership.[9] The term has a negative connotation in that it implies a closed system in which no new information is taken into the modular unit; it is perceived as a source or excuse for social injustice; it is based on little information; it rarely accurately applies to specific individuals.[10] Also, the strongest stereotypes (such as racial stereotypes) are aggressively biased against a group. Even a positive stereotype (for university graduates), such as a company policy that only university graduates are promotable, shuts out information and reduces objectivity. However, stereotyping is not a negative process; rather, it is a neutral, subconscious cognitive process that increases the efficiency of interpreting environmental information that can lead to inaccuracies and/or negative consequences.[11] Stereotyping, prejudice, and discrimination appear to be enduring human traits.[12] The literature identifies three major types of stereotypes: sex role, age, and race.

Sex-role stereotype is the belief that differing traits and abilities make men and women particularly well suited to different roles. Managers may believe that women and men cannot hold the same jobs or that women should be soft spoken and demure and men aggressive and outspoken. Several recent research projects of women managers examined this issue. For example, a survey of 461 female executives in *Fortune* 1000 companies found that 52 percent saw male stereotyping of women's preconceptions about women as the biggest barrier to women's advancement.[13] A recent study compared sex-role stereotypes held by men and women from China, Japan, Germany, the United Kingdom, and the United States. Males in all five countries perceived that successful managers possessed characteristics and traits more commonly ascribed to men in general than to women in general. Among females the same pattern of managerial sex typing was found in all countries except the United States. The U.S. females perceived that males and females were equally likely to possess traits necessary for managerial success.[14] Activities 6–2 and 6–4W provide opportunities to explore this issue a little further.

Age stereotype is the belief that differing traits and abilities make a certain age group more or less suited to different roles or display different behavior toward work. A careful review of empirical research provides inconclusive results about the overall relationship among age, performance, and attitudes. While some studies found age and job performance unrelated, others found that the relationship between age and performance changes as people grow older.[15] A recent review examined 185 different studies of stereotypes. The project revealed that as age increases so do employee job satisfaction, job involvement, internal work motivation, and organizational commitment. Moreover, older workers were not more accident prone than their younger colleagues.[16] The relationship between age and turnover and absenteeism provides some interesting insights. Although one study revealed that the three are not related, another study found that age was inversely related to both voluntary and involuntary absenteeism. Furthermore, the study found that older workers are ready and able to meet their job requirements.

Race stereotype influences how some people might treat others in a variety of work situations. As Module 4 showed, three interrelated forms of racism can be identified: individual, cultural, and institutional. For example, to the extent that an individual holds values, feelings, and/or attitudes and/or engages in behavior that promotes the person's own racial group as superior, the accuracy of the perceptual process will be diminished. A study that examined the relationship of race to employee attitudes across 814 African-American and 814 white managers, demonstrated that African-Americans, when compared with whites, felt less accepted by their peers, perceived lower managerial discretion on their job, reached career plateaus more frequently, noted lower levels of career satisfaction, and received lower performance ratings.[17]

Another study uncovered a same-race bias for Hispanics and African-Americans. The Hispanic and African-American interviewers evaluated applicants of their own race more favorably than they evaluated applicants of other races.[18]

Recently, a cognitive model of stereotyping in the workplace has been proposed by Loren Falkenberg.[19] (See Figure 6–3.)

The classification of individuals and their status assignments provide the background for delineating the processes underlying the maintenance and revision of stereotypes. Inaccurate stereotypes are maintained through interpreting behaviors of minority-status individuals in the workplace that most often lead to actions and behavior expectations that result in enhanced stereotypes. Three processes stimulate the development of more accurate stereotypes: (1) storing distinct or unexpected information in memory; (2) storing personal information on an individual with increased personal interactions; and (3) increasing recognition of individuals working in various occupational roles. Stereotypes can have a **self-fulfilling prophecy,** such as everyone believing an employee has great potential and the beliefs come true. Recently, the Pygmalion effect has been popular in management as a concept to help managers shape the destiny of employees or to help individuals shape their own personal growth.

Stereotype threat is the fear of being judged according to a negative stereotype. Recently, stereotype threat was described as the psychological experience of a person who, while engaged in a task, is aware of a stereotype about his or her identity group suggesting that he or she will not perform well on that task.[20] The increasing diversity of organizational members seems to trigger complex human dynamics in which individual experience is labeled and grouped by others. Furthermore, since every job involves being evaluated and assessed by other people, being evaluated can raise apprehension. Anxieties can be heightened for those employees who are members of a negatively stereotyped group.[21] Table 6–1 captures the essence of a set of experiments conducted in the past 15 years in which researchers compared the performance of two groups—one which is negatively stereotyped, the other which is not—in two tasks conditions: one condition presents the task as stereotype-relevant; the other does not. As can be seen from the Table 6–1, the negatively stereotyped group underperforms when the stereotype is seen as relevant to the task. These findings are related to the Pygmalion effect, which we explore next.

Figure 6–3
Information-Processing Strategies Leading to Maintenance and Revision of Stereotypes

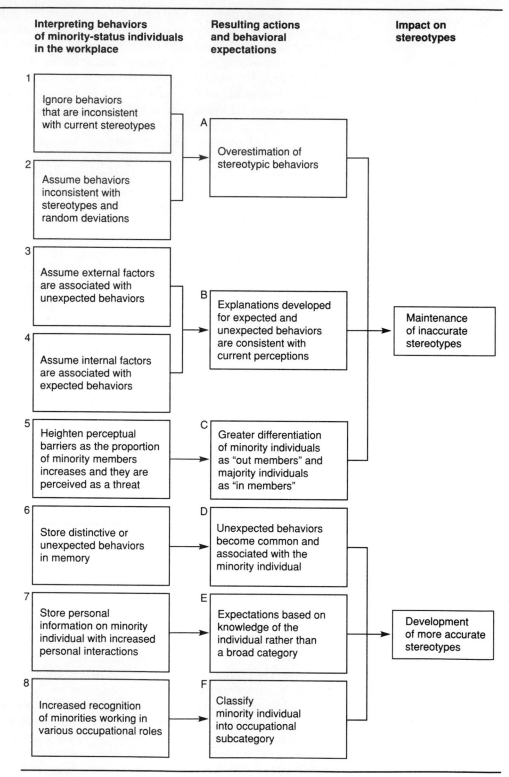

Interpreting behaviors of minority-status individuals in the workplace

1. Ignore behaviors that are inconsistent with current stereotypes

2. Assume behaviors inconsistent with stereotypes and random deviations

3. Assume external factors are associated with unexpected behaviors

4. Assume internal factors are associated with expected behaviors

5. Heighten perceptual barriers as the proportion of minority members increases and they are perceived as a threat

6. Store distinctive or unexpected behaviors in memory

7. Store personal information on minority individual with increased personal interactions

8. Increased recognition of minorities working in various occupational roles

Resulting actions and behavioral expectations

A. Overestimation of stereotypic behaviors

B. Explanations developed for expected and unexpected behaviors are consistent with current perceptions

C. Greater differentiation of minority individuals as "out members" and majority individuals as "in members"

D. Unexpected behaviors become common and associated with the minority individual

E. Expectations based on knowledge of the individual rather than a broad category

F. Classify minority individual into occupational subcategory

Impact on stereotypes

Maintenance of inaccurate stereotypes

Development of more accurate stereotypes

Source: Adopted from L. Falkenberg, "Improving the Accuracy of Stereotypes within the Workplace," *Journal of Management* 16, no. 1 (1990), pp. 107–18.

Table 6–1   **Examples of Stereotype Threats**[22]

Who Was Affected?	How Did the Researchers Create Stereotype Threat?	What Stereotype Was Activated?	What Happened?
Black students	Told the students that they were about to take a very difficult test that was a "genuine test of your verbal abilities and limitations."	"Blacks lack intellectual ability."	The students performed less well on the test.
Latino students	Told the students that they were about to take a very difficult mathematical and spatial ability test that would provide a "genuine test of your actual abilities and limitations."	"Latinos lack intellectual ability."	The students performed less well on the test.
Low socioeconomic status (SES) students	Asked the students to provide background information including their parents' occupation and education; then told them they were about to take a difficult test that would "assess your intellectual ability for solving verbal problems."	"Low SES students lack intellectual ability."	The students attempted to solve fewer problems and had fewer correct answers on the test.
Women	Reminded the women that "previous research has sometimes shown gender differences" in math ability; then asked them to take a test that "had shown gender differences in the past."	"Women have weak math ability."	The women performed more poorly on the math test.
Older individuals (60 years and older)	Gave the older people a series of memory tests and presented them with a list of "senile" behaviors ("can't recall birthdate") too quickly for conscious awareness. Then researchers gave the older people the memory tests a second time.	"Older people have bad memory."	The older people had a significant decline in memory performance from pretest to posttest.
Gay and bisexual men	Asked the men to indicate their sexual orientation on a demographic survey; then videotaped the participants while they engaged in a "free play" activity with children.	"Gay men are dangerous to young children."	Judges rated the men as more anxious and less suitable for a job at a daycare center.
People with a head injury history	Told participants that a "growing number" of neuropsychological studies find that individuals with head injuries "show cognitive deficits on neuro-psychological tests"; then gave participants a series of tests assessing memory and attention.	"Persons with a head injury history experience a loss of cognitive performance."	The participants performed worse on tests of general intellect, immediate memory, and delayed memory.
Whites	Told participants that a "high proportion of Whites show a preference for White people" before asking them to complete the IAT (implicit attitude test) that would measure their "unconscious racial attitudes toward Blacks and Whites."	"Whites are racist."	The participants had a larger IAT effect (the difference in response time between incompatible and compatible trials), suggesting a preference for White faces.
White students	Gave the students a packet of newspaper articles emphasizing a "growing gap in academic performance between Asian and White students" before asking them to take a very challenging math test.	"White students have less mathematical ability than Asian students."	The students solved fewer problems on the math test.
Men	Reminded participants that "it is a well-known fact that men are not as apt as women to deal with affect . . . and to process affective information as effectively"; then asked them to indicate whether a series of words were "affective" or not.	"Men are less capable than women in dealing with affective (emotional) information."	The men made more errors on the task.
White men	Told the men that they would be engaged in a golf task that measured their "natural athletic ability." The men completed a demographic survey that included a question about their racial identity, and then took the test.	"White men have less athletic prowess than Black men."	The men made more strokes (performed worse) on the golf task.

Source: Adopted from L. Roberson and C. Kulik, "Stereotype Threat at Work," *Academy of Management Perspective* 21, no. 2 (2007), pp. 28–29. We are grateful to Professors Roberson and Kulik.

THE PYGMALION EFFECT

The Pygmalion effect dramatically demonstrates the influence of perception and expectation on the potential of people to grow, or not to grow, depending on the labels accorded them.[23] Rosenthal and his associates conducted experiments in an elementary school in which all students were given a nonverbal IQ test.[24] The teachers, who were not informed of the experimenter's true purpose, were told the IQ tests identified a number of children who were "intellectual bloomers." Each teacher was given the names of 20 percent of the students in each of their classes who fell into this classification for high intellectual growth. In reality, the 20 percent named were randomly selected and were in the average IQ range for their classes. The general results were that the intellectual bloomer groups did show a significant gain in IQ over the rest of the class. The difference in the students existed only in the minds of the teachers, who assumed they were working with brighter students.

The experimenters explained the **Pygmalion effect,** based on their observations, to be due to four factors: The teachers (1) created a warm, supportive learning climate for their special students, (2) gave them more feedback on their performances, (3) gave them more material and more difficult work, and (4) gave them more opportunity to ask questions and respond. This experiment showed that student growth was stimulated by raising the expectations of the teacher that the child could achieve—the expectations were beyond what would have been expected if the teacher had seen these students as average. The point raised earlier that social attitudes and stereotypes generate expectations that are a deterrent to change was also demonstrated by another aspect of the Rosenthal experiments in which there was some tendency for low-income children with high IQs to be viewed negatively by their teachers. When these children surpassed the expectations of their teachers, they were somewhat resented.

Although Rosenthal's experiments have been evaluated as controversial by reviewers (one reason being that the results have not always been easy to replicate), they will strike a note of truth for many managers who have seen employees sponsored and labeled in order to influence them to move into management positions. To have a high executive label a young professional as a real "comer" can start a career. In Washington, D.C., an Ivy League degree can move one up the ladder of some agencies.

Since the early 1980s, an increasing number of studies attempted to replicate the Pygmalion paradigm with adults.[25] As we have seen in Modules 2 and 8, Dov Eden has led the research frontier on the Pygmalion phenomenon with adults. Some of the best studies on the Pygmalion effect among adults have been conducted in military organizations. In one of the studies, military trainees were randomly assigned to three groups and were described to their instructors as possessing high, regular, or unknown "command potential." Data indicated that trainees who had been labeled as having high potential significantly outperformed trainees in each of the other groups on objective measures.[26] In a different study, the same effects were obtained by raising supervisors' expectations toward their subordinates as a group.[27]

At a personnel review board meeting in one company, the executive conducting the meeting described one young professional employee as having outstanding potential and dismissed the individual's mistakes the record showed with the comment, "He needs an opportunity to grow by falling on his face a few times." At a later point, he commented on the mistakes of another subject as "goofing more than you would expect." The record of the second individual actually was stronger in terms of background preparation and achievement in the company, but the comment of the chairperson went unchallenged.

Managers generally pride themselves on their ability and objectivity when judging people. But consider the implications of employee appraisal systems, particularly in large organizations. Some type of a scale is typically used to rate people in their performance, and it is highly probable over a period of time that a manager's employees become typed as outstanding, average, below average, and so on. If we apply what we learned of the Pygmalion effect—as articulated and summarized by Eden—in his book, *Pygmalion in Management: Productivity as a Self-Fulfilling Prophecy,*[28] and in his review article, "Leadership and Expectations"[29]—the chances are rather low that the employees labeled as average or below average will ever be perceived as outstanding, even if their performance improves.

The Pygmalion effect has been dramatically described in another form by Maxwell Maltz, whose theory has gained widespread popularity in management growth workshops.[30] Maltz, a plastic surgeon, noted that some of his patients who underwent a surgical transformation from an ugly face to a beautiful face showed a marked change in their lives; they developed more self-esteem and confidence. However, others continued to experience feelings of inadequacy and inferiority just as if they were still "ugly." From his studies, he concluded that those who had grown through the facial change had also undergone an inner change; they had developed a new self-image to correspond to the new beautiful face. Their expectations of change resulted in new behaviors that "worked" and brought them an increase in satisfaction.

ATTRIBUTION THEORY

One way to understand the relationship between perception and individual behavior is attribution theory. **Attribution theory** focuses on the process by which individuals interpret events around them as being caused by a relatively stable portion of their environment.[31] The underlying assumption is that individuals are motivated to understand the causes of particular events in their environment. According to attribution theory, it is the perceived causes of events, not the actual events, that influence individuals' behavior.

The **attribution process** includes four phases: (1) A particular behavioral event triggers a cognitive analysis that (2) focuses on what causes the event, (3) followed by a modification or reinforcement of previous assumptions of causality that (4) leads to behavioral choices regarding future behavioral events. For example, an individual who received a bonus will attempt to attribute the bonus to some underlying cause. If the employee perceives the explanation for the bonus to be the fact that he is a hard worker and consequently concludes that working hard leads to rewards in this organization, he will decide to continue to work hard in the future. Another employee may attribute her bonus to the fact that she is a "team player" and decide that it makes sense to continue to be a team player for that reason. In both cases, individuals have made decisions affecting their future behavior based on their attributions.

The attribution process provides insights into the understanding of the behavior of other people. A central question in the attribution process concerns *how* perceivers determine whether the behavior of another person stems from internal causes (such as personality traits, motives, and emotions) or external causes (such as the situation or other people). In making attributions, people focus on three factors:

Consensus. The extent to which others, faced with the same situation, behave in a manner similar to the person perceived.

Consistency. The extent to which the person perceived behaviors in the same manner on other occasions when faced with the same situation.

Distinctiveness. The extent to which the person perceived acts in the same manner in different situations.

In the context of managing work and managing others, managers cannot assume that their attributions will be the same as their employees' attributions. The managerial challenge is to understand both the attributions that employees make and the ones that the manager makes of a specific event. This knowledge will enhance the manager's ability to work effectively with others.

PERCEPTUAL CHALLENGES IN MANAGEMENT

Management research has found large perceptual differences among individuals at different levels of the managerial hierarchy. In a study by N. R. F. Maier et al., 58 manager and subordinate pairs were asked questions concerning the job duties of the subordinate.[32] Only 46 percent of the pairs agreed on more than half of the topics. More striking was the difference for the obstacles standing in the way of the subordinates' performance; in this category only 8 percent of the pairs were in agreement on more than half of the topics discussed. It would appear that either the subordinates were not fully aware of what their superiors expected of them or the superiors did not know what work the subordinates were required to perform. In either case, the question can be raised as to how much communication occurred between the levels to provide understanding of the job requirements.

Part of the difficulty arises from authority and status differences, which inhibit individuals from communicating freely with their superiors about important job matters. Thus, the different perceptions of subordinates and superiors are likely to remain different. Furthermore, there is some tendency at all levels of the hierarchy for supervisors and managers to see themselves as better communicators than their superiors. We have demonstrated this trend in many management workshops, using the following exercise. Participants complete a questionnaire indicating on a 10-point scale (from poor to outstanding) a number of their abilities as a manager, such as administrator, problem solver, and communicator. These rating sheets are picked up; the next day participants are given an identical sheet and asked to rate their bosses on the same abilities. Both questionnaires are completed anonymously to increase the validity of the ratings and protect the individual respondent. Sheets are identified for matching purposes by a code number the individual selects.

The results from one such study of middle managers in the federal government are shown in Table 6–2. The upper part of the table shows that in topics dealing with task completion (problem solver and administrator) the respondents tended to see their bosses as either as good as or better than themselves. In areas of communication (ability to communicate with subordinates, willingness to stand up for subordinates, and candidness), this situation is true to a lesser degree—as many as 46 percent of respondents indicated that they believe they are better than the boss in these attributes.

The degree of intensity of feelings on these factors is shown in the lower part of Table 6–2, which gives the total number of scale points, for the total sample, by which respondents felt they exceeded the boss or were exceeded by the boss. The results were quite pronounced. When individuals think their bosses are better than them on a certain ability, they do not see their bosses as much better. But when they see themselves as better, they tend to see themselves as considerably better. This is most apparent on the item "stand up for subordinates," where the 29 percent of the respondents who considered their bosses better gave the bosses a total of 16 points, whereas the 40 percent who considered themselves better allotted themselves 62 points. It is least true in the more task-oriented area of problem solver. The communicate and administer factors all involve more interpersonal relations, which may account for the degree to which individuals felt more intensely why they were better.

The principal point to be made about perceptual differences is that no one perceives with complete objectivity. The determinants of perception are in operation all the time. A positive aspect of this process is that the world can be made immediately meaningful for the individual by his or her codes of past experience. Coding is a normal function of the brain processes, as are the defense mechanisms that protect the individual against being overwhelmed with fears and anxieties.

Table 6–2	**Midcareerists' Self-Boss Perceptions of Managerial Abilities (N = 48)**				
	Solve Problems	Administer	Communicate with Subordinates	Stand Up for Subordinates	Candidness
Percentage saying					
My boss is better.....................................	40%	29%	35%	29%	31%
No difference...	29	38	19	31	23
I am better..	31	33	46	40	46
	100%	100%	100%	100%	100%
Total number of scale points by which respondent said					
Boss is better	34	26	27	16	38
I am better	37	44	57	62	50

The disadvantages of perceptual differences are related to the fact that most people rely on the meanings coming from their codes without realizing that the perceptions are primarily from internal determinants rather than from the external world. Stereotyping people, for instance, can shut out new data required to understand others; stereotypes lead to **premature closure,** that is, drawing conclusions too quickly. Identifying someone as a hippie, jock, nerd, frat boy, or minority member provides the already packaged data of what such people are like without bothering to understand the person further.

Stereotypes related to management, employees, unions, and other categories of people serve a similar function in the work world. Stereotypes fulfill the needs of people (particularly when they are frustrated for ready answers) and create major communication problems in organizational life.

REDUCING PERCEPTUAL DIFFERENCES AND DISTORTION

The major thrust of this presentation on perceptual differences has been to emphasize the need for people to be more aware of the ever-present **distortion** and differences in everyone's perceptions. Recognition of the condition is the first step in reducing these differences and the most difficult to learn. Alertness to the differences is required for improvement of effectiveness. It could be said that the theory, concepts, and social technology of this text are generally directed toward helping participants with problems related to this area. For example, a recent study—see Table 6–3—that focused on reducing sex stereotyping identified

**Table 6–3
Student Perceptions of How Men and Women Can Promote Equal Ways of Relating at Work**

What women do/can do to promote equal relationships between the sexes:
- Be assertive and confident; take selves seriously.
- Be knowledgeable and well organized.
- Support each other more.
- Network with men; mentor men.
- Push for day care, pay equity, parental leaves (flexibility in workplace).
- Do not ignore or promote sexist behavior at work; don't let it go by.
- Don't negate or undermine selves. (For example, don't play dumb.)
- Aspire to higher positions.
- Break traditional home roles (equality in personal relationship).
- Don't perpetuate stereotypes (male or female)—break the mold.
- Be patient and understanding with men (but challenge them to change).

What men do/can do to promote equal relationships between the sexes:
- Ask women their opinions; take them seriously.
- Don't just look at women as "girls," but see them as partners and team members.
- Involve women in decision making; don't patronize them.
- Delegate responsibility to women; trust them.
- Acknowledge and respect women's talent and ability.
- Compliment women on their work and performance.
- Approach women for advice and input.
- Compete with women like they are "one of the gang."
- Listen better; don't interrupt women.
- Share power more readily; mentor women.
- Don't stereotype women.
- Share in child rearing and housework.
- Give more support to women (networks, mentoring); be an ally.
- Accept interdependence in marriage.
- Acknowledge to the organization that family issues are men's issues too.
- Support other men in working through personal change; be patient.
- Don't ignore sexist behavior by male colleagues—"challenge to change."
- Don't "obsess" on work/career success—be willing to let go a little.
- Let go of masculine stereotypes.

Source: M. Maier, "The Gender Prism," *Journal of Managerial Education* 17, no. 3 (1993), p. 306. Used with permission.

students' perceptions of how men and women can promote equal ways of relating at work.[33] The second step is to help individuals gain better competencies in gathering factual data in the areas of performance, behavior, and attitudes; reviewing their decision-making assumptions and outcomes; and verifying them for validity and accuracy. A third step is the development of organizational mechanisms that will nurture dialoguing and appreciative inquiry (as discussed in Module 2). As we have seen in this module, overcoming barriers to accurate perception is a major undertaking. Yet if we are to fully utilize human potential, meeting this challenge is a must. Because workplace diversity is becoming the increasing reality for most organizations, managers are charged with finding ways to reduce distortions such that the potential of the human asset can be realized. Communications theory and techniques are most relevant in this process; these are explored in Module 7.

SUMMARY

Organizational members bring to their work pre-established values, belief systems, and attitudes that their organization might reinforce or attempt to change. Many of these values and belief systems are both good predictors of work-related behavior but also influence the perceptual process. Perceptual differences between people and groups are a major problem area for many fields of study, including foreign affairs, politics, advertising, mental health, and interpersonal relations. In management, perceptual problems are pervasive. Recognition of their existence is of major importance in understanding organizational behavior. The problems are inherent in the nature of the perceptual process.

The determinants of perception are primarily internal to the individual, rather than arising from observed external objects or social interaction. Internal factors can be divided into physiological, past experience, and psychological categories. Codes of past experience and the motivational and defensive processes can filter and greatly distort what the individual perceives.

Perceptual differences are normal functions of the brain processes that help make life immediately meaningful. However, they do shut out data that are needed for more objective meaning. Awareness of these processes and particularly of one's own blind spots is seen as a primary need for understanding organizational life and improving all four levels of managerial effectiveness. Approaches to overcoming problems of perceptions and perceptual differences are explored throughout the book via a variety of experiential activities.

Study Questions

1. Describe the role that work-related values and belief systems play in shaping the behavior of individuals. Provide examples from your experience.

2. Identify and describe the key elements in the perceptual process.

3. "Perception influences team performance." Illustrate your understanding of the phrase by using some examples from your team experiences to date.

4. Explain the phrase "expectations determine perception." If you are a manager of a number of employees, half of whom have a college education and the other half only a high school background, how can this concept provide you some guidance for supervision?

5. Why are defense mechanisms studied in the field of perception?

6. N. R. F. Maier's findings on differences in perception between bosses and subordinates are so pervasive in organizational surveys that all managers need to understand them. What can be done about these differences?

7. Stereotype threat seems to influence both individual behavior and performance. Provide examples that illustrate this effect. What would you do if you were the manager to overcome stereotype threat?

8. What perceptual errors by managers foster special problems in the assessment of worker performance?

9. Some argue that perception plays a critical role in the problems that women and minorities in management experience at the workplace. State your position, and provide your reasons while incorporating what you have learned about perception.

Endnotes

1. A. Furnham and J. Taylor, *The Dark Side of Behavior at Work* (London: Palegrave Macmillan, 2004).

2. R. Buchholz, "Measurement of Beliefs," *Human Relations* 29 (1976), pp. 1177–88; R. Buchholz, "An Empirical Study of Contemporary Beliefs about Work in American Society," *Journal of Applied Psychology* 63 (1978), pp. 219–21.

3. A. Furnham, *The Protestant Work Ethics* (New York: Routledge, 1990).

4. J. Dickson and R. Buchholz, "Management and Belief about Work in Scotland and the USA," *Journal of Management Studies* 14 (1977), pp. 80–101.

5. M. Furnham, *The Psychology of Behavior at Work* (New York: Routledge, 2005), pp. 257–58.

6. B. I. Bertenthal, "Origins and Early Development of Perception, Action, and Representation," *Annual Review of Psychology* 47 (1996), pp. 431–59; and D. L. Hamilton and S. J. Sherman, "Perceiving Persons and Groups," *Psychological Review* 193 (1996), pp. 336–55.

7. R. Goldstone, "Perceptual Learning," *Annual Review of Psychology* 49 (1998), pp. 585–612.

8. D. Fabun, *Communication* (Beverly Hills, CA: Glencoe Press, 1968); J. C. Cutting, "Perception and Information," *Annual Review of Psychology* 38 (1987), pp. 61–90; B. M. DePaulo, D. A. Kenny, C. W. Hoover, W. Webb, and P. V. Oliver, "Accuracy of Person Perception: Do People Know What Kinds of Impressions They Convey?" *Journal of Personality and Social Psychology* 52 (1987), pp. 303–15; and J. Henderson, and A. Hollingworth, "High Level Scene Perception," *Annual Review of Psychology* 50 (1999), pp. 243–71.

9. R. D. Ashmore and F. K. Del Boca, "Sex Stereotypes and Implicit Personality Theory: Toward a Cognitive-Social Psychological Conceptualization," *Sex Roles* 5 (1979), pp. 219–48; D. Christensen and R. Rosenthal, "Gender and Nonverbal Skill as Determinants of Interpersonal Expectancy Effects," 42 (1982), pp. 75–87; K. Deaux and M. E. Kite, "Gender Stereotypes: Some Thoughts on the Cognitive Organization of Gender-Related Information," *American Psychology Bulletin* 7 (1985), pp. 123–44; A. H. Eagly and V. J. Steffen, "Gender Stereotypes Stem from the Distribution of Women and Men into Social Roles," *Journal of Personality and Social Psychology* 46 (1984), pp. 735–54; M. E. Heilman, M. C. Simon, and D. P. Repper, "Intentionally Favored, Unintentionally Harmed? Impact of Sex-Based Preferential Selection on Self-Perceptions and Self-Evaluations," *Journal of Applied Psychology* 72 (1987), pp. 62–68; and J. L. D. Castella and M. McClunrey, "Sexual Stereotype and Perceptions of Competence and Qualifications," *Psychological Reports* (April 1997), pp. 419–28.

10. B. E. McCauley, C. L. Still, and M. Segal, "Stereotyping: From Prejudice to Prediction," *Psychological Bulletin* 87 (1980), pp. 195–208; G. V. Bodenhausen and R. S. Wyer, "Effects of Stereotypes on Decision Making and Information-Processing Strategies," *Journal of Personality and Social Psychology* 48 (1985), pp. 267–82; J. P. Fernandez, *The Diversity Advantage* (New York: Lexington Books, 1993); L. Gardenswartz and A. Rowe, *Managing Diversity* (Burr Ridge, IL: Richard D. Irwin, 1993); U. Hentschel, G. Smith, and J. G. Draguns (eds.), *The Roots of Perception* (Amsterdam: North-Holland, 1986); E. T. Higgins and J. A. Bargh, "A Social Cognition and Social Perception," *Annual Review of Psychology* 38 (1987), pp. 369–425; E. S. Jackson, *Diversity in the Workplace* (New York: Guilford Press, 1994); G. N. Powell, *Gender and Diversity in the Workplace* (Thousand Oaks, CA: Sage, 1994); and Castella and McClunrey, "Sexual Stereotype and Perceptions of Competence and Qualifications."

11. L. Falkenberg, "Improving the Accuracy of Stereotypes within the Workplace," *Journal of Management* 16, no. 1 (1990), pp. 107–18.

12. S. T. Fiske, "Stereotyping, Prejudice, and Discrimination," in D. T. Gilbert, S. T. Fiske, and G. Lindzey (eds.), *The Handbook of Social Psychology* (New York: Irwin McGraw-Hill, 1998).

13. E. Davis, "Women at the Top," *HR Focus* 73 (May 1996).

14. V. E. Schein, R. Mueller, T. Lituchy, and J. Liu, "Think Manager—Think Male: A Global Comparison," *Journal of Organizational Behavior* (January 1996), pp. 33–41.

15. For a good review of the empirical literature on the topic, see D. A. Waldman, and B. J. Avolio, "Aging and Work Performance in Perspective: Contextual and Developmental Considerations," in G. R. Ferris (ed.), *Research in Personnel and Human Resources Management* 11 (Greenwich, CT: JAI Press, 1993), pp. 133–62.

16. S. R. Rhodes, "Age-Related Differences in Work Attitudes and Behavior: A Review and Conceptual Analysis," *Psychological Bulletin* (March 1993), pp. 338–67.

17. J. H. Greenhaus, S. Parasuraman, and W. M. Wormley, "Effects of Race on Organizational Experience, Job Performance and Evaluation, and Career Outcomes," *Academy of Management Journal* (March 1990), pp. 64–86.

18. T.-R. L. Lin, G. H. Dobbins, and J.-L. Farh, "A Field Study of Race and Age Similarity Effects on Interview Ratings in Conventional and Situational Interviews," *Journal of Applied Psychology* (June 1992), pp. 361–71.

19. Ibid., p. 110.

20. L. Roberson and C. Kulik, "Stereotype Threat at Work," *Academy of Management Perspective* 21, no. 2 (2007), pp. 24–40.

21. F. K. Cocchiara and J. C. Quick, "The Negative Effects of Positive Stereotype: Ethnicity-Related Stressors and Implications on Organizational Health," *Journal of Organizational Behavior* 25 (2004), pp. 781–85.

22. This table was compiled by L. Roberson and C. Kulik and was published in their article "Stereotype Threat at Work," *Academy of Management Perspective* 21, no. 2 (2007), pp. 28–29. The research summarized in this table includes the following articles: C. M. Steele and J. Aronson, "Stereotype Threat and the Intellectual Test Performance of African Americans," *Journal of Personality and Social Psychology* 69 (1995), pp. 797–811; P. M. Gonzales, H. Blanton, and K. J. Williams, "The Effects of Stereotype Threat and Double-Minority Status on the Test Performance of Latino Women," *Personality and Social Psychology Bulletin* 28 (2002), pp. 659–70; J. Croize and T. Claire, "Extending the Concept of Stereotype Threat to Social Class: The Intellectual Underperformance of Students from Low Socioeconomic Backgrounds," *Personality and Social Psychology Bulletin* 24 (1998), pp. 588–94; S. J. Spencer, C. M. Steele, and D. M. Quinn, "Stereotype Threat and Women's Math Performance," *Journal of Experimental Social Psychology* 35 (1999), pp. 4–28; J. K. Bosson, E. L. Haymovitz, and E. C. Pinel, "When Saying and Doing Diverge: The Effects of Stereotype Threat and Self-Reported versus Nonverbal Ability," *Journal of Experimental Social Psychology* 40 (2004), pp. 247–55; J. A. Suhy and J. Gunstad, "'Diagnosis Threat': The Effect of Negative Expectations on Cognitive Performance in Head Injury," *Journal of Clinical and Experimental Neuropsychology* 24 (2002), pp. 448–57; C. M. Frantz, A. J. C. Cuddy, M. Burnett, H. Ray, and A. Hart, "A Threat in the Computer: The Race Implicit Association Test as a Stereotype Threat Experience," *Personality and Social Psychology Bulletin* 30 (2004), pp. 1611–24; J. Aronson, M. J. Lustina, C. Good, K. Keough, C. M. Steele, and J. Brown, "When White Men Can't Do Math: Necessary and Sufficient Factors in Stereotype Threat," *Journal of Experimental Social Psychology* 35 (1999), pp. 29–46; J. Leyens, M. Desert, J. Croizet, and C. Darcis, "Stereotype Threat: Are Lower Status and History of Stigmatization Preconditions of Stereotype Threat?" *Personality and Social Psychology Bulletin* 26 (2002), pp. 1189–99; J. Stone, C. I. Lynch, M. Sjomeling, and J. M. Darley, "Stereotype Threat Effects on Black and White Athletic Performance," *Journal of Personality and Social Psychology* 77 (1999), pp. 1213–27.

23. According to Greek legend, Pygmalion, a king of Cyprus, created an ivory statue of a maiden known as Galatia. He fell in love with the statue, and at his prayer Aphrodite gave it life. In George Bernard Shaw's *Pygmalion,* a professor polishes the language and manners of a cockney flower girl until he is able to pass her off as a princess, only to fall in love with her. *My Fair Lady* is the musical version of Shaw's play.

24. R. Rosenthal, "The Pygmalion Effect," *Psychology Today* (September 1973), pp. 56–63.

25. Dov Eden's research provides a holistic understanding of the phenomenon, part of which is published in D. Eden, "Self Fulfilling Prophecies in Organizations," in J. Greenberg (ed.), *Organizational Behavior: The State of the Science,* 2nd ed. (Mahwah, NJ: Lawrence Erlbaum 2003), pp. 91–122. See also D. Eden, *Pygmalion in Management* (Lexington, MA: Lexington Books, 1990). A recent study demonstrated the effect of self-fulfilling prophecy on seasickness and performance. See D. Eden and Y. Zuk, "Seasickness as a Self-Fulfilling Prophecy: A Field Experiment on Self-Efficacy and Performance at Sea," *Journal of Applied Psychology* 80

(1995), pp. 628–35. A comprehensive study that examined the impact of Pygmalion leadership training on leadership effectiveness is found in D. Eden et al., "Implanting Pygmalion Leadership Style through Training: Seven Field Experiments," *Leadership Quarterly* 11, no. 2 (2000), pp. 171–210. A comparative investigation of self-fulfilling prophecy on women is found in O. Davidson and D. Eden, "Remedial Self-Fulfilling Prophecy: Two Field Experiments to Prevent Golem Effects among Disadvantaged Women," *Journal of Applied Psychology* 85, no. 3 (2000), pp. 386–98.

26. D. Eden and A. B. Shani, "Pygmalion Goes to Boot Camp: Expectancy, Leadership, and Trainee Performance," *Journal of Applied Psychology* 67 (1982), pp. 194–99.

27. D. Eden, "Pygmalion without Interpersonal Contrast Effects: Whole Groups Gain from Raising Manager Expectations," *Journal of Applied Psychology* 75 (1990), pp. 394–98.

28. D. Eden, *Pygmalion in Management.*

29. D. Eden, "Leadership and Expectations: Pygmalion Effects and Other Self-Fulfilling Prophecies in Organizations," *Leadership Quarterly* 3 (1992), pp. 271–305; see also, D. Eden "Implanting Pygmalion Leadership Style through Training," presented at the *13th Annual Meeting of the Society for Industrial and Organizational Psychology,* Dallas (April 24–26, 1998).

30. M. Maltz, *Psycho-Cybernetics* (New York: Pocket Books, 1966).

31. H. H. Kelley, "The Process of Causal Attributions," *American Psychologist* 28 (1973), pp. 107–118; and F. Fosterling, "Attributional Retraining: A Review," *Psychological Bulletin* (November 1985), pp. 495–512.

32. N. R. F. Maier, L. R. Hoffman, J. J. Hooven, and W. H. Read, *Supervisor–Subordinate Communications in Management* (New York: American Management Association, 1961).

33. M. Maier, "The Gender Prism: Pedagogical Foundation for Reducing Sex Stereotyping and Promoting Egalitarian Male–Female Relationships in Management," *Journal of Management Education* 17, no. 3 (1993), pp. 285–314; A. McKee and S. Schor, "Confronting Prejudice and Stereotypes: A Teaching Model," *Journal of Management Education* 18, no. 4 (1994), pp. 447–67; and E. L. Perry, A. Davis-Black, and C. T. Kulik: "Explaining Gender-Based Selection Decisions: Synthesis of Contextual and Cognitive Approaches," *The Academy of Management Journal* 19, no. 4 (1994), pp. 786–820.

Activity 6–3: Mirroring Gender: Perceptual Exploration

Objectives:

a. To heighten students' awareness of their perception of themselves, their perceptions of members of the opposite sex, and the perceptions of themselves by the opposite sex.

b. To elicit data for improved working relationships between the sexes.

Task 1:

Students are to be divided into same-sex groups of not more than seven students in a group. (Ideal size is five students to a group.) Each group is to respond to two questions:

a. How do you see yourselves as women (or men)? Generate a list on a flip chart, using words or short phrases that describe your characteristics or traits individually as a woman (or man) or as a group of women (or men). For example, I see women as being intuitive, good listeners.

b. Make a second list that describes how you think members of the opposite sex see you as a group or as a member of your sex. For example, I think men see us—as women—as nurturing, chatty, always wanting to shop, and so forth.

In the development of these lists, students should use a brainstorming process that eliminates the need for agreement or consensus, includes each individual's contributions, and does not involve any judgment or evaluation on anyone's part. (Time: 15 minutes)

Task 2 (Class Sharing):

The lists should be taped to the walls of the room for all to see. Each group reads its list aloud to the entire class. The only discussion at this stage should be questions of clarification or explication. (Time: 10 minutes)

Task 3:

a. The students should look at their lists and silently reflect on what is there. The students are to try to identify and write down some notes about the tone (negative and positive), intensity, patterns, and themes.

b. Individuals are to share their reflections in the groups.

c. The groups are to address the following question: What would be the ideal working relationship with the opposite sex?

(Time: 10 minutes)

Task 4:

a. Spokespersons will report to the class.

b. The instructor will facilitate further discussion related to the work, content, and process of some of the issues that were raised.

(Time: 10 minutes or longer if time is available)

Source: This activity was contributed by Dr. Judith White, California State University, Monterey, Management Department, Monterey, California. All rights are reserved and no reproduction should be made without the expressed approval of Dr. White. We are grateful to Dr. White.

Activity 6–4: Prejudices and Stereotyping

Objectives:

a. To heighten learners' awareness of their own prejudices and stereotypes.

b. To develop awareness of the effects of one's own prejudices and stereotypes on one's behavior.

Task 1:

The instructor will facilitate 10 minutes of class brainstorming to generate names of groups and persons the students know to have been targets of some form of prejudice, discrimination, or stereotyping.

Task 2:

The instructor will facilitate 5 to 10 minutes of brainstorming that focuses on the specific characteristics or traits they know to be associated with these groups that contribute to the stereotyping or prejudiced attitude and behavior.

Task 3:

a. Students are to find a group on the board that they can associate themselves with and gather in small similar groups. The students might cluster themselves into a group of African-Americans, Latinos, white males, physically disabled, and so on.

b. Each group selects a reporter who may take notes and who will summarize the discussion and report it to the class. Each group should

1. Identify (following a few minutes of reflection) a specific time when you experienced some form of discrimination or prejudice because of your identity as a member of this particular stereotyped group.

2. Describe what occurred, who was there, what you did, and what you felt at the time.

3. Talk about what you feel now and what you think had happened. What has influenced your feelings and thinking since that particular incident?

Task 4:

In the larger class, individuals are asked to share some of their experiences. The instructor will facilitate class discussion around common themes and issues, emphasizing the common and painful experience of suffering from discrimination, prejudice, and stereotyping.

Task 5:

Go back to the same small groups. Each individual will

a. Think of a time when you consciously or unconsciously discriminated against someone, perpetuated a stereotype, or supported some prejudiced attitudes or behaviors.
b. Describe what occurred, who was there, what you did, what you felt and thought at the time, and your current thoughts and feelings.

Task 6:

a. In the larger class individuals are asked to share some of their experiences. The instructor will facilitate class discussion around common themes and issues, emphasizing the importance of awareness as the first step toward understanding and perhaps changing behaviors and the need to be patient and forgiving as change occurs.
b. The instructor will facilitate a discussion about the application to the workplace.

Source: The basic ideas in this activity are adopted from the work by Dr. Anne McKee of the Wharton School, The University of Pennsylvania, and Dr. Susan Schor of Pace University. The activity in its present form was developed by Dr. Judith White, California State University, Monterey, California. All rights are reserved and no reproduction should be made without the expressed approval of Drs. McKee, Schor, and White. We are grateful to Drs. McKee, Schor, and White.

Module 7

Communication

LEARNING OBJECTIVES

After completing this module, you should be able to

1. Explain the basic communication process and its key elements.
2. Appreciate the relationship between personality, perception, motivation, and communication.
3. Understand the different levels of communication and media richness.
4. State the internal and external determinants of interpersonal communication.
5. Identify the potential barriers in the communication episode.
6. Understand your own barriers in the communication process and some of the actions that you can take to overcome them.
7. Identify some managerial actions that can help overcome the barriers for communication in organizational settings.

KEY TERMS AND CONCEPTS

Active listening	Interpersonal communication
Coaching	Kinesic behavior
Communication	Language
Communication media	Media richness
Communication networks	Message
Computer networks	Miscommunication
Conflicting assumptions	Noise
Cross-cultural communication	Nonverbal communication
Decoding	Paralanguage
Encoding	Paraphrasing
Ethnocentrism	Proxemics
Gossip	Rumor
Grapevine	Semantics

MODULE OUTLINE

PREMODULE PREPARATION

Activity 7–1: Reflections on Communication Episodes

Objective:

To determine your views of what made a communication episode most meaningful and least meaningful in past work situations.

Task 1:

Each individual, working alone, is to answer the following:

a. Think back on your work experience to a time that you felt great about communicating with others. Describe the communication episode. Who were the receivers? What was the communication message? What communication media was used? Which factors accounted for the great feeling you had about that communication episode?

b. Think back on your work experience to a time that you felt very bad about communicating with others. Describe the communication episode. Who were the receivers? What was the communication message? What communication media was used? Which factors accounted for the bad feeling you had about that communication episode? How could you have handled the situation differently?

Task 2:

Each team should select a spokesperson. After sharing the experiences, each group is to list the important factors agreed upon by the group for the two areas of "best" and "less than best" experiences.

The instructor will call upon spokespersons, one at a time, to give one factor from the group's "best" and "less than best" lists. The instructor will facilitate a class discussion based on the lists that were generated on the board.

INTRODUCTION

Communication is a multifaceted phenomenon in organizational life. It is a part of everything that takes place at the workplace and seems to influence any organizational process and outcome. Communication emerged as a stand-alone academic discipline with a distinct research agenda, educational programs, and practice. In this course, our focus is on exploring the basic nature of interpersonal communication within the context of work.

As a part of a study that focused on identifying and exploring indicators of new product development teams, few teams that met the criteria of "high-performance team" were investigated. A very proud team member in a response to an interview question shared the following: "When I send an email message to my team leader, whose work space is about 30 feet away from mine, the icon on my computer flashes when he opens my email. The second that I see that he has opened my message, I walk into his office and say, Barry, I wanted to talk with you a bit about an issue that I just e-mailed you." When asked to explain his behavior, the employee claimed that since his boss is so busy, he discovered that the only way for him to be able to spend a few minutes with his boss and to discuss an issue or a challenge that he faced and get his full attention is when he actually reads his e-mails. Another team member from the same team proudly shared with us the fact that he spends only one day a week at the office and the rest of the time he works from home. He stays in constant communication via the Internet with his team mates or others in the company, as needed. The team also had three team members that were based in a different continent. The team leader attributes the continuous high performance of his team to a few facts: They all met face-to-face and spent three days together when the team was formed; the team developed communication channels and procedures that met the needs and style of each team member; the team uses a groupware software that allows the team to work collaboratively as needed; and the team has a weekly phone conference meeting to review progress, identify and discuss challenges, and preview goals for the next week.[1]

In another study a software design engineer reported that for the last three years he had spent about 35 percent of his time with customers in their companies rather than actually designing software and applications. As we learned later, this engineer's talent was on the design side, but his communication skills were limited.[2] In all spheres, the pressure of competition is forcing organizations and vendors to get closer to the customer. Positioning products and/or services closer to the customer is a way to develop long-term relationships as well as to develop an appreciation for the changing needs and interests of the customers. At the core of most business-related activities within organizations and between organizations, their customers, and suppliers is the fundamental process of communication.[3] The complexity of the global business environment and the explosion in information technology have created work environments that use a variety of supplemental communication systems, such as electronic boards, teleconferencing, shared files, group screens, and e-mail. But before we proceed any further, we need to explore the basic nature of communication in the work setting.

Organizational surveys continuously identify communication as a major challenge by managers. The advancement in information technology, the increasing diversity of the workforce in many parts of the United States, coupled with the increasingly global business environment, seems to have increased the communication challenges to managers. For example, a recent study of high-tech manufacturing companies in California's Silicon

Valley found that 16 different languages were spoken on the production floor.[4] Further-more, a survey of managers in three countries found that 74 percent of the responding companies in the United States, 63 percent in Great Britain, and 85 percent in Japan ranked communication as a key barrier to organizational effectiveness. Another recent study of leading companies concluded that effective managers strategically use communi-cation to manage tough organizational changes.[5] Communicating effectively seems to be an area of increasing concern for most managers.[6]

Communication technologies have made it increasingly feasible for employees to work on the same project while being located in a different location or geographical area. Clearly, these technologies have facilitated telecommuting where workers perform some or all of their work outside of a traditional office setting. Furthermore it allows employees to stay connected to work when not in the office. Yet, a set of studies that examine the impact of communication technologies after hours found that the use of communication technologies after hours was associated with work-to-life conflicts for employees and an increase in negative work-related attitudes.[7]

In the context of information technology and the changing nature of communication sys-tems, four types of work environments were recently identified: same time and same place, same time and different places, different times and same place, and different times and dif-ferent places.[8] Figure 7–1 captures the nature of the four general types of work environ-ments, the kinds of meetings that they create, and the information technology media that can be used to foster communication within each type. Module 20, on our website, explores further some of the issues associated with the emerging nature of information technology communication media, media richness, and the complex human dynamics that they foster.

Communication is the primary area of focus for understanding human interactions and for learning methods of changing one's own behavior and influencing that of others. It is an area in which individuals can make great strides in improving their own effectiveness. Communication is also the point of major conflicts and misunderstandings between two people, between members of a team, between groups, and within the total organization as a system. Communication workshops are probably more widespread than any other type. Communication skills training deals with helping people communicate better. Family counseling sessions and group therapy center on overcoming communication challenges. Management workshops deal with communication much as we do in this course.

Communication theory seems to parallel organization theory. We can find a variety of theoretical approaches: The *mechanistic perspective* views communication as a transmis-sion process by which a message physically travels across space through a channel, from one person to another; the *Tayloristic perspective* views communication as vertical (top-down), formal, and hierarchical; the *psychological perspective* views the receiver as the focus, with the assumption that individuals suffer information overload; the *interactive-symbolic perspective* emphasizes the creation of shared meaning as a result of the quality of human interaction and relationship; the *system perspective* focuses on people's external actions and sees communication as a whole being greater than the sum of the parts, and the *integrated organizational perspective* suggests that communication is influenced by

Figure 7–1
Examples of Communication Media and General Types of Work Environments

	Same Time	Different Times
Same Place	*Face-to-face* Meeting rooms PC projectors Copyboards	*Administration/ data management* Shared files Shift work
Different Places	*Remote meetings* Conference calls Data sharing Video/teleconferencing	*Reliance on coordination* E-mail Voice mail

Source: Adapted from R. Johansen, *Leading Business Team: How Teams Can Use Technology and Group Process Tools to Enhance Performance* (Reading, MA: Addison-Wesley, 1992).

the nature of the organization and its culture, technology, and situation.[9] In this book, we approach communication from an integrated perspective.

In this module we continue to build on previously presented theories of psychodynamics of human behavior, motivation, and perception. We begin with a review of the relationship between personality, motivation, perception, and communication. An examination of the basic components of the communication process is followed by a review of the different levels of communication. Next we focus on interpersonal communication, the group's effects on the communication process, and the cross-cultural context of communication. An examination of the many barriers for accurate communication is followed by a discussion of possible managerial actions to overcome the challenges.

PSYCHODYNAMICS, MOTIVATION, PERCEPTION, AND COMMUNICATION

Communication is an interpersonal process. As such, the nature of the personalities involved, the perceptual process, and motivation deeply affect communication. What two people communicate about is determined by who they are and by how they perceive themselves and the other person in the situation. How they perceive depends on their motivation (goals, needs, defenses) at the given moment. This relationship is illustrated in Figure 7–2.

The communicated **message** is so closely related to the personality, perceptions, and motivations of both the sender and the receiver that misunderstandings are built into the nature of the process. In addition, the method (or medium) of communication—face-to-face, telephone, electronically via computer network or via voicemail technology, meetings, formal reports, and memorandums—is likely to influence the nature of the communication episode. Overcoming the natural barriers to communication is a major objective in communicating meaning. Before we begin to examine some of the barriers to accurate communication, we review briefly the communication process.

THE COMMUNICATION PROCESS

At the most basic level, **communication** is the transfer of information from one person to another. As such, the communication episode entails the transfer of information from one person (the sender) to another (the receiver) by some chosen method (the channel). Yet communication is complex and problematic, as we shall see. The process involves five elements: the sender, the message, the medium, the receiver, and feedback. The sender–receiver link (the channel) can be a telephone wire or computer signal, sound waves (the voice), or a written message, to name a few. One key difficulty is **noise** or interference in the channel, which distorts the message. Noise can be literally that, as when you try to hold a conversation in the same room with a band or a loud engine. Any other signal in the channel of communication besides the desired message can be thought of as noise. A beautiful symphony that prevents you from hearing a customer's request,

Figure 7–2
Linkage among Motivation, Perception, and Communication

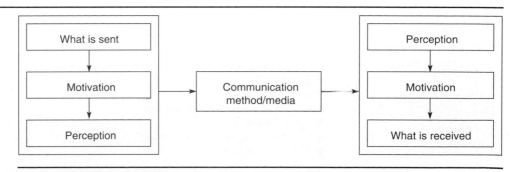

static that disturbs a computer signal, or the poor quality of a photocopy that prevents you from reading a memo—all these are noise. However, other sorts of noise originate within the sender and receiver. Communications are heavily interactive with perceptions, attitudes, and interpretations, being both dependent on them and an important factor affecting them. Figure 7–2 outlines some of these connections.

Still another factor affecting communications is the process of encoding and decoding. Any message to be sent must first be encoded. We formulate our meanings in words, for instance, to hold a conversation; in special circumstances, we use special codes. (The signals of the quarterback on the football field; the special language of surgeons during an operation; the slang with which we communicate with our buddies; the specially ordered, cryptic conversation of air traffic controllers and pilots or dispatchers and police units all offer examples.) If the sender and receiver are not using the same code, accurate communication will not take place even if there is no noise in the channel.

Language is one obvious sort of code, and words and their meaning are a significant source of potential miscommunication where sender and receiver understand different meanings for the same word.

Levels of Communication

A variety of classifications of communication levels can be found in the literature. Some make the distinction between verbal and nonverbal communication, some make the distinction between verbal and electronic communication, some make the distinction between different electronic communication media, and some make the distinction among various other types of communication: intraindividual (for example, a message is sent from sensory organ to the brain), interpersonal (for example, a message is sent between two individuals or more within the same group), intraorganizational (for example, a message is sent between two groups or subsystems within the same organization), and interorganizational (for example, a message is sent between two organizations). In this module, we focus on communications at the interpersonal levels.

Interpersonal Communication

As we have seen, at the most basic level communication is a process that occurs when an individual sends and receives messages through a chosen method of communication in an effort to create meaning in his or her mind or in the mind of others. Figure 7–2 illustrates the multiple elements that participate in the **interpersonal communication** episode. Each element not only plays a critical role in the communication process but also serves as a source of potential barriers for accurate communications.

BARRIERS TO ACCURATE COMMUNICATION

There are many barriers to accurate communication. We have clustered the barriers into nine categories: conflicting assumptions; inadequate information; semantics and language; emotional blocks; nonverbal communication barriers; the nature of the grapevine, rumor and gossip; communication network; the nature of communication methods and technology; and cultural barriers (see Figure 7–3). Four of the barriers that

Figure 7–3
Barriers to Accurate Communication: A Partial List

- Perceptual and attributional biases
- Conflicting assumptions
- Inadequate information
- Semantics
- Emotional blocks
- Nonverbal communication barriers
- Cultural barriers
- Inadequate communication media
- Technological barriers

will be presented here have a basis in the factors included in the discussion of perception in Module 6. The barriers become apparent by asking what two people need to have in common to communicate. By way of helping answer this question, we might ask, If you were an explorer in a jungle area and encountered a native who had never had any contact with the world outside of his own isolated tribe, what could you communicate with him about? The answer is that you could exchange meaning—through sign language—about those things with which both of you had had past experience: food, shelter, temperature, elimination, birth, death, facts about the environment such as where the sun rises and sets, and so on. Both parties must share the codes of past experience before meaning can be exchanged.

Conflicting Assumptions

When one individual sends a communication to another, he or she assumes that the receiver will use the same codes of past experience in interpreting the message that were used in sending it. The receiver, in turn, assumes that the codes he or she uses to give meaning to the message are the same as those used by the sender. This is probably best illustrated by humorous stories that set up a person with one set of assumptions and codes and then switch to an entirely different set in the punch line.

Unfortunately, daily communication between people is frequently distorted because they each use slightly different assumptions and codes but make the assumption that the other is using the same system; there is no punch line to help them out. This *assumed overlap of codes* is incorrect a large percentage of the time, but it is not realized by the participants and the misunderstanding goes undetected.

Organizational life, with its hierarchy of superiors and subordinates, is an ideal culture for nurturing the problems of conflicting assumptions. Employees and bosses perceive many aspects of the subordinate's job duties and the obstacles to performance of them differently as we discussed in Module 6. The boss may well not be the communicator he or she believes, as indicated in Table 6–1. The organizational climate usually generates an atmosphere in which subordinates fear they might appear to be stupid if they ask too many questions; often they assume they understand what is being passed down, but they really do not. Thus, conflicting assumptions are apt to abound between levels of the hierarchy, between sections, and between people in the organization.

Figure 7–4 illustrates the problem of **conflicting assumptions,** or assumed overlap, in the codes of past experience that are active in communication. Each individual's codes of past experience are unique, but to an extent they overlap with those of other individuals in general (as between the explorer and the native) and with those of country, town, social class, family, and so on. The major problem in communications, then, is that each individual is inclined to assume that people with whom he or she interacts are using the same coding systems. That this is not the case often goes undetected.

Inadequate Information

Managers do not always provide enough information for those receiving assignments to do the jobs adequately. The increased complexity of organizational life seems to influence the level of detail that is communicated. Individuals make choices about the amount of information that is required to be transmitted in order to get the job done. When not enough information is shared, or if bits and pieces of the information are provided, individuals are forced to make assumptions about the missing data and act on what they understand the information to be.

Semantics and Language

Semantics (word usage) and **language** (meaning of word) are major sources of communication failure. Most words in the dictionary have multiple meanings. An illustration is the word *charge:*

You *charge* someone a fee for doing a service.

You *charge* something you purchase when you want to pay later.

You *charge* a battery when you want it to provide electricity.

Figure 7–4
Transfer of Meaning

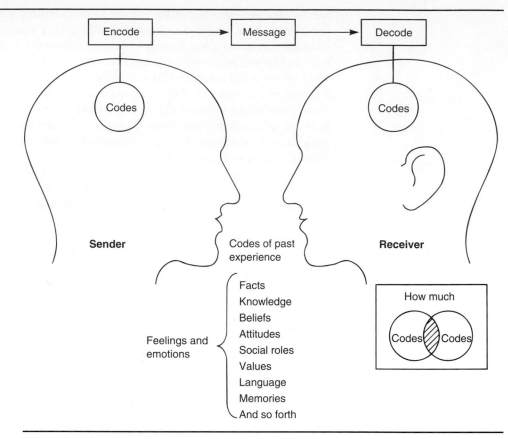

Communication between two persons involves transfer of meaning, which assumes that both individuals use the same coding system. Since each individual's codes are unique, there is never the degree of agreement (overlap) between the two coding systems that either party assumes. Thus conflicting assumptions are primary barriers to communications.

You *charge* an official with duties to perform.

You *charge* a horse into battle against an enemy.

You get a *charge* out of something funny.

You place a *charge* of powder into a cannon.

You *charge* a criminal for crimes committed.

You *charge* a rifle when you level it at the enemy.

A favorite word for discussion in management courses is *fast,* which can have meanings that are directly opposite: A color is fast when it won't run, whereas a horse is fast when it runs well. When two individuals are using different meanings of the same word and do not realize it, a barrier to meaning exists that may go undetected. The phrase "meanings are in people, not words" is commonly used in management workshops. You cannot assume the meaning you give a word will be the one the receiver uses in decoding the message.

In the growing global context, the issue of language and meaning increases the complexity of communication. Two individuals may speak the same language but speak it quite differently. For example, people from the United States and United Kingdom both speak English, but one cannot assume the same meaning. For example, when people from England "table" an issue in a meeting, they act on it immediately, but when Americans "table" an issue, they expect to deal with it at a later stage; the storage compartment of a car for Americans is called a "trunk," but in English, it is called a "boot."

The challenge increases in a situation in which two natives who speak two different languages try to communicate. They might be able to speak a language that the other can understand, use a third language, or use an interpreter. Complicating matters, concepts and words in one language may not have equivalents in another language. For example, the concept "achievement" is almost impossible to translate into languages other than English. Key terms have special meaning in different cultures. Words and terms are socially constructed and thus not easily translatable nor transferable within organizational units, between organizations or cultures.

Emotional Blocks

All experiences and all learning have an emotional and feeling component. The recall of past experiences includes not only the event and content but also the feelings that accompanied them at the time they occurred. In Module 4 we discussed the role of emotions in shaping individual behavior and performance. Figure 7–4 also represents this in the codes of past experience, all of which are learned with a feeling component. The significance of this for communications is that any time the codes of past experience are used, the feelings and emotions are present to influence both sender and receiver at the time the message is exchanged. Most of the time neither is aware of this factor, although the feelings are intense and are a part of the content. Sometimes, however, the content does not indicate the feelings, but the individual is transmitting nonverbal signals of which he or she is not aware though they are being received by others.[10]

Nonverbal Communication Barriers

By *nonverbal* we mean simply "not words." Thus, vocal cues such as voice tones and inflections are nonverbal to the extent that they are not words, as are such dynamic messages as facial expression, gaze, interpersonal spacing, touch, and gesture.[11] Activity 7–2 focuses on the critical role that **nonverbal communication** plays in the communication episode that many times serves as a confusing or reinforcement element. Learning to be aware of nonverbal communication can help in understanding the communication episode as well as in setting the stage and deriving a holistic and more accurate meaning of the communication message. Here are a few basic types of nonverbal communication:

Body motion or **kinesic behavior.** Gestures, facial expressions, eye behavior, touching, and any other movement of the limbs and body.

Physical characteristics. Body shape, physique, posture, height, weight, hair, and skin color.

Paralanguage. Voice quality, volume, speech rate, pitch, nonfluencies (for example, *yaa, um, ah),* laughing.

Proxemics. Ways people use and perceive space (for example, seating arrangements and conversational distance).

Environment. Building and room design, furniture and interior decorating, light, noise, and cleanliness.

Time. Being late or early, keeping others waiting, and other relationships between time and status.

The Grapevine, Rumor, and Gossip as Communication Barriers*

There are also informal communication channels in organizations through which employees pass on information through networks of colleagues and friends. This is typically referred to as the "grapevine," in which the information passed may be true or false, factual or speculative. In these instances we are referring to rumor and gossip.

Rumor and Gossip

Rumor and **gossip** are both important vehicles for informal communication and barriers to accurate communication. What is interesting about rumor and gossip is that they are indirect communication, characterized by something like "I can't remember who told me, but have you heard?"[12] The source or origin of the information is not easily identifiable, and we might wonder why this information is being spread around. The commonly accepted understanding of rumor is that it is talk that is unsubstantiated by authority or evidence as to its authenticity or truth.[13] It is often regarded as synonymous with hearsay.

*Contributed by our colleague David Coghlan. We are grateful to professor Coghlan.

Popularly regarded as idle talk or trivial chatter, gossip ordinarily carries with it the presumption of having some basis in fact. Sometimes rumor is distinguished from gossip, and other times they may not be distinguished. Gossip and rumor are seen to be distinct. The basis of rumor is information that is unsubstantiated; gossip may or may not be a known fact.[14] This distinction is more a matter of degree than substance, and the issue becomes problematic in the context of celebrity or political gossip. In such cases it may be hard to pin down the "facts" or "truth." It is also conceivable that the initiation of a rumor may be underpinned by some element of truth, no matter how obscure or circumstantial the evidence. The extent of the truth or fact is difficult to determine, and we can never know if something is a white lie or a half-truth. Sometimes it is impossible to separate rumor from gossip. When, according to unattributed hearsay, a female executive is alleged to have "slept her way to the top," is this rumor or gossip?[15]

For some rumor and gossip share many similarities although rumor "is a more public and widely disseminated phenomenon than gossip."[16] Conversely, gossip typically occurs in a context of privacy and intimacy and only through friends and acquaintances, and only with friends and acquaintances. Gossip deals with issues or events of interest to an individual or small group, while the parameters of rumor extend beyond a few individuals since its message is of more universal interest. For this reason, some treat gossip as a subset of rumor. However, the claim that gossip is a more private or "secretive" process than rumor ignores the mode of information transmission. Gossip can emerge in the public domain if it is placed on electronic bulletin boards. In such cases, the information is made widely available. Largely as a result of the difficulty of locating the source of the message and, consequently, an ability to either evaluate or confirm it, both rumor and gossip have an additional characteristic in common—suspension of disbelief. A certain level of secrecy accompanies the gossip process since it excludes formal methods of communication such as memos, newsletters, and bulletin boards. It also presumes that the information conveyed is intended to have some impact on the recipients of gossip. Innocuous information is therefore discarded and does not qualify as gossip. Information, no matter how scandalous it might be, isn't gossip unless the participants know enough about the people involved to experience the thrill of revelation.

The functions served by both rumor and gossip (for example, information, influence, and entertainment) appear to be identical. However, their motivations are different: rumors are underpinned by a desire for meaning or clarification to cope with the uncertainties of life; gossip is primarily stimulated by personal ego and status needs in a social context.

The purposes or functions served by rumor or gossip are numerous and wide-ranging.[17] Broadly, these are depicted as information, influence, and entertainment. The first of these represents an attempt by individuals to better understand their social environment. The second function builds on the first by addressing the utilization of information to the individual's benefit. Some contend, for instance, that gossip within organizations may provide a "survival mechanism" in that it could be one means of humanizing bureaucratic structures. One tangible outcome of this may be related to alleviating excessive levels of employee stress. Finally, rumor or gossip may have entertainment value for its own sake. It has been argued that engaging in gossip is an act that can generate pleasure or satisfaction for those involved.

To support the different functions there are a number of rumor types.[18]

1. *Pipe dream or wish fulfillment.* Such rumors largely express the hopes of those who circulate them. One example might be expressing a possible solution to a work problem that the employee wants to change.

2. *Bogey or anxiety rumor.* These rumors are primarily driven by fear and, consequently, create unease among its recipients. An example of this might be a rumor about a company takeover and the prospect of redundancies in the not-too-distant future.

3. *Anticipatory rumor.* These are often precipitated by situations of ambiguity. An illustration of this might be whether or not a new general manager will come from within the organization or be appointed from elsewhere.

4. *Aggressive rumor.* Here, women may face a disadvantage since they are more likely to be the subject of sexual gossip.[19] Sometimes, this may stem from a perception that female employees are romantically involved with other organizational members for the primary purpose of advancing their careers.

A rumor will tend to dissipate if it becomes irrelevant. Once an event has occurred and the facts have been established, the rumor becomes superfluous. In addition, rumors may lose interest among their recipients due to boredom, frustration, or simply because they fail to generate sufficient interest. Rumor and gossip have also been linked to power.[20]

The Grapevine

The informal mechanism through which rumor and gossip move through an organization is the **grapevine.** "The grapevine is an informal and unsanctioned information network."[21] It demonstrates a healthy expression of the human need to communicate because it reflects that employees are interested in their work.[22] The grapevine is unstructured and not under management's control. It moves in all directions—upward, downward, and sideways across and between chains of command. It is dynamic and varied and even fickle. It goes on all day and continues outside of working hours and works faster than the formal organizational communication channels. It performs a useful task in supplementing the formal communication channels by allowing people to think and talk about what they fear will happen and how they might react. In this manner, the grapevine acts as an early warning system. Management may use it to test how a new idea will be received. A carefully planned leak from the senior management group provides an opportunity for management to test the water on a potentially explosive plan.

Davis describes four types of grapevine structures.[23]

1. *The single strand chain.* A tells B who tells C who tells D and so on. The longer the strand, the more distorted the information may become.

2. *The gossip chain.* A tells everyone he or she meets.

3. *The probability chain.* A makes random contact with F and C, and they make random contact with others. In this system some hear the information and others don't.

4. *The cluster chain.* A tells B who may work with A, and they tell other persons with whom they have close contact.

Since the grapevine—rumor and gossip seem to be an integral part of any social system—cannot be held responsible for errors and misinformation, and it cannot be silenced or suppressed, organization and management are challenged to recognize its existence and continuously communicate while utilizing a wide variety of communication channels and communication methods.

Communication Networks

The nature of the communication network that the individual is a part of might create an additional barrier. Communication can be examined by focusing on how and what individuals communicate as well as by focusing on the communication relationships among individuals. **Communication networks** involve oral, written, and nonverbal signals between two or more individuals. For example, the pattern of signals will flow between a manager of a produce department in a large food store and the other managers, while another pattern of signals is flowing between the manager and his or her immediate subordinates and all the other individuals with whom the manager interacts. A manager's network extends laterally (with other managers at the same level) and vertically (with a direct superior or direct subordinates). From this point of view, communication networks can be quite complex, and they have the potential to create barriers to understanding.

Communication Methods and Technology

The method or the tool chosen to transfer the message from the sender to the receiver plays a key role in the communication episode. With the advancement of technology, we are capable of assembling and electronically storing, transmitting, processing, and retrieving words, numbers, and sounds around the globe. **Computer networks** enhance our communication accuracy not only within the small unit or between two individuals but also between large units located in different geographical areas. Yet limiting the communication episode to the computer's screen—which allows for the use of two of the senses only—can be a major barrier in the communication episode.

Communication, as an exchange of meaning, is bounded by culture. As Figure 7–4 shows, **encoding** describes the producing of a symbol into a message, and **decoding** describes the receiving of a message from a symbol.

Cultural Barriers

Any message sender must encode his or her meaning into a form that the receiver will recognize. Translating meaning into words and behaviors (that is, into symbols) and translating the words and behaviors back again into meaning is based on a person's cultural background, which is not the same for every person.[24] Because cross-cultural communication occurs between two individuals from different cultures, it can lead to much miscommunication. Recent research indicates that the greater the differences between the sender's and the receiver's cultures, the greater the chance for miscommunication.[25]

Miscommunication in this context is the result of misperception, misinterpretation, and misevaluation. The following example was provided by Nancy Adler:

> Since in Cantonese the word for "eight" sounds like "faat," which means prosperity, a Hong Kong textile manufacturer Mr. Lau Ting-pong paid $5 million in 1988 for car registration number 8. A year later, a European millionaire paid $4.8 million at Hong Kong's Lunar New Year auction for vehicle registration number 7, a decision that mystified the Chinese, since the number 7 has little significance in the Chinese calculation of fortune.[26]

Cross-cultural communication occurs when a person from one culture communicates with a person from another culture. Miscommunication in the cross-cultural context occurs when the receiving person (from the "other" culture) does not receive the sender's intended message. Coupling individual diversity with cross-cultural differences dictates that one must assume significant differences between the sender and receiver. Furthermore, cross-cultural perceptions seem to play a role in the cross-cultural communication episode. People from diverse cultures tend to view the world differently while at the same time they stereotype individuals from other cultures. As we have seen in the previous module, perceptual patterns are neither innate nor absolute. They are selective, learned, culturally determined, consistent, and inaccurate.[27] Managing the cross-cultural communication episodes presents a set of challenges for organizations and managers of the multinational corporation. Yet some of the skills that are explored in the next section provide the necessary foundation.

Emerging Challenges

The communication episode is a complex process that involves many different dimensions. New forms of communications have emerged over the past decade. Although face-to-face communication is vital to individual, group, and organizational effectiveness, the major technological leap has introduced alternative advanced communication technology that helps overcome some limitations of interpersonal interaction. The transformation of communication-driven technology has been accelerated as a result of increased global competition and the emerging of the global markets. E-mail, communication networks (such as local area networks and wide area networks), electronic bulletin boards, real-time videoconferencing, and groupware software all allow individuals and teams located in different places to work together on a problem and are likely to become the norms in communication.

While globalization and technological development are driving the emerging new forms of communication, the challenge of understanding the impacts of the new communication technologies and attempting to manage them increases. For example, think of yourself as a part of a team where each member is in a different geographical location. You are linked via a local area network and a groupwide software program. The team is trying to solve a problem but is not able to see each other or talk to each other orally. However, you are able to send messages back and forth, and every person on the team is able to take part in the exchange via the computer screen.

Figure 7–5
What Do I Do If They Do
Not Speak My Language?

Verbal behavior

- *Clear, slow speech.* Enunciate each word. Do not use colloquial expressions.
- *Repetition.* Repeat each important idea using different words to explain the same concept.
- *Simple sentences.* Avoid compound, long sentences.
- *Active verbs.* Avoid passive verbs.

Nonverbal behavior

- *Visual restatements.* Use as many visual restatements as possible, such as pictures, graphs, tables, and slides.
- *Gestures.* Use more facial and hand gestures to emphasize the meaning of words.
- *Demonstration.* Act out as many themes as possible.
- *Pauses.* Pause more frequently.
- *Summaries.* Hand out written summaries of your verbal presentation.

Attribution

- *Silence.* When there is a silence, wait. Do not jump in to fill the silence. The other person is probably just thinking more slowly in the nonnative language or translating.
- *Intelligence.* Do not equate poor grammar and mispronunciation with lack of intelligence; it is usually a sign of second-language use.
- *Differences.* If unsure, assume difference, not similarity.

Comprehension

- *Understanding.* Do not just assume that they understand; assume that they do not understand.
- *Checking comprehension.* Have colleagues repeat their understanding of the material to you. Do not simply ask whether they understand or not. Let them explain what they understand to you.

Design

- *Breaks.* Take more frequent breaks. Second-language comprehension is exhausting.
- *Small modules.* Divide the material into smaller modules.
- *Longer time frame.* Allocate more time for each module than usual in a monolingual program.

Motivation

- *Encouragement.* Verbally and nonverbally encourage and reinforce speaking by nonnative language participants.
- *Drawing out.* Explicitly draw out marginal and passive participants.
- *Reinforcement.* Do not embarrass novice speakers.

Source: Adopted from N. J. Adler, *International Dimensions of Organizational Behavior* (Boston: PWS-Kent, 1996), p. 89. Used with permission.

Based on what we have covered in this module, what are some of the barriers for accurate communication that your team is likely to experience? What will be the effect of this barrier on your team? The scientific community is only beginning to investigate the new advanced communication technology and its impact on the behavior and effectiveness of individuals and teams. In Module 20 on the management of technology and information, we explore further some of these issues.

Communication is also faced with the increased challenge of diversity at the workplace and globalization. As we have seen, diversity and cultural differences can play a major role in creating barriers to accurate communication. **Ethnocentrism**—the tendency to consider the values, norms, and customs of one's own country to be superior to those of other countries—has been shown to hinder the communication process.[28] Figure 7–5 presents Nancy Adler's suggestions for overcoming cross-cultural barriers to communication.

MANAGERS' ROLE IN MANAGING COMMUNICATION: OVERCOMING THE BARRIERS

Managers' role in fostering the communication process is critical. Beyond a self-assessment about their own communication style, methods, and competencies, managers can ensure a work environment in which employees feel that they can communicate openly at all times. A recent study found that two-way communication is a critical element in fostering continuous improvement and organizational learning.[29]

Practicing Communication Skills: Each manager must practice communication skills until they become second nature. **Paraphrasing,** for example, is one of the more useful skills practiced in numerous professions. Diplomats spend considerable (sometimes endless) time making sure they understand views of the representatives of other countries. Television journalists frequently pause in their interviews to feed back what they think they have heard. Supervisors giving instructions to employees find it useful to say, "Now, tell me what you are going to do so we will be sure we are in agreement." One top executive we observed had called six other executives together for a preliminary discussion of a problem area. He asked each person to use five minutes to present his initial views on the matter. As each individual finished, he would summarize what he had heard, ask whether he understood correctly, and then ask questions if he had any. After all six had spoken, the executive summarized and integrated their views and then led a discussion concerning what steps should be taken to study the problem.

A middle-level manager informed us that paraphrasing was one of the most meaningful ways to handle a complaint at the initial stage:

> Give the person the time needed to fully express the problem. When the person is through, summarize what you have heard and see if there is agreement on the complaint. Then say you will look into the matter and discuss it further at a later date. This has the advantage of not feeling pressured to make an uninformed decision on the spot, of letting the individual know he or she has been heard, and of giving the individual time to cool off.

Paraphrasing is a useful tool when a disagreement arises. One exercise frequently used in communication workshops is to have a group of people sit in a circle and carry on a discussion on a controversial topic such as the Arab–Israeli conflict in the Middle East or arms limitations. After one person has expressed her view, the next person to respond must paraphrase to the last speaker's satisfaction what has just been said before he expresses his own views. This is continued for the entire discussion. Individuals usually find they are so preoccupied with what they are about to say that they forget to listen to what is being said. (Your class might want to try this as an additional exercise if there is time.)

Active Listening: Listening has been identified by executives as one of the key factors in their success as managers. A variety of filters act as barriers to effective listening, namely, values, biases, attitudes, previous experiences, organizational roles, organizational culture, and language to mention a few. The effect of the filters is minimized if the listening is an **active listening.** Moving away from passive listening and getting engaged via paraphrasing, for example, will ensure that the message sent is accurately received. If any distortions have occurred, they get uncovered and clarified before an action is taken. Yet, the active listening skills are not easy to acquire but can be developed. This section suggests behaviors that can facilitate the development of active listening skills, namely, awareness and understanding, paraphrasing, being nonevaluative, creating a supportive climate, self-awareness, providing constructive feedback, and being reflective.

Awareness and Understanding: Learning that communications problems do exist and studying some of the theory and concepts that might account for them is an initial step. This means learning not only at the content level but also at the dynamic level of what goes on between you and other people when you communicate. It is difficult for some people just to understand that others are not perceiving the world as they do.

Social Technology: Knowledge of the techniques and methods available to help administrators in overcoming communications problems is a major objective of this text. Managers must learn what technology is available and how to use it for all four levels of effectiveness. Practice is necessary in dialoguing, listening, paraphrasing, perceptual checking, and so on.

Creating a Supportive Organizational Climate: The organizational atmosphere is all-important. If it is threatening and suppresses expression of individuals' feelings, there will be serious breakdowns in communications at all levels of the hierarchy. Modern management theory recognizes that a manager's skills must include the handling of feelings and emotions of employees as much as how to work with logic and rationality. The consequences of not developing these skills are that employees' emotional blocks will divert energy into nonproductive or antiorganizational channels. Supportiveness and two-way communication, as basic values of the organizational culture, can reduce employees' feelings of defensiveness.

Managing the Grapevine, Rumor, and Gossip: Since the grapevine cannot be held responsible for errors and misinformation, and it cannot be silenced or suppressed, management needs to provide a sufficient amount and level of information through formal systems of communication so as to minimize any damage done by the grapevine. Rumors can escalate, and so management may need to provide hard facts and as complete information as is possible in order to allay fears and reduce anxiety. Four steps are suggested: Seek to keep employees informed of what is going on and spend less time on worrying about overcommunicating, heed rumors, act promptly, and conduct a training program on the nature of rumors.[30]

Self-Awareness: It is assumed that the more managers are aware of their own needs, goals, feelings, and defenses, the better they will be able to cope with their own growth and behavior. This means being able to communicate with yourself. It means knowing what your strengths are in interaction situations and what part of the problem you represent.

Giving and Receiving Feedback: The effect one person has on another can be a major barrier to communication. Managers need to have some idea of the effect they are having if they are to influence others effectively. Producing an organizational atmosphere in which there is two-way feedback between superior and subordinates is one area of development. Some organizations are having employees fill out anonymous evaluation forms concerning their supervisors and managers. The data become the subject of general discussion between the superior and subordinates as to how the superior's behavior is affecting the progress of the work. Training workshops dealing with communications, leadership, and self-awareness can be helpful in attaining insight into the effect one is having on others; learning how to give others feedback without offending them and learning how to receive feedback without being offended are currently stressed.

Working with the Motivation of Others: In Frederick Herzberg's theory, helping individuals use their own internal dynamos—the motivators—can increase both productivity and satisfaction. A manager can work at the level of trying to produce the conditions in the work situation that augment this result, but he or she also needs to make efforts to understand what motivates each individual. This can be explored in goal setting, in daily conversations when this appears appropriate, and in watching the behavior of the individual. Activity 7–1 focuses on this subject.

Coaching and Goal Setting: Goal setting as an organization-wide practice can help overcome communication barriers. When a boss and a subordinate sit down periodically to define the subordinate's goals, which are part of the organization's goals, many of their perceptual distortions will be greatly reduced. At the same time, the individual's personal goals, what he or she would like to attain careerwise from the present situation, and in the coming years, can be an integral part of the process. Discussion of progress and feedback from the supervisor as to how well the individual is doing should be accomplished as the need arises, based on events as they occur. Saving these discussions for yearly review produces barriers to communications; not only does the subordinate lack the information and guidance needed, but unexpressed feelings can build up and interfere with performance. Milestone points for specific review and revision of the goals should be part of the procedure to ensure that nothing is overlooked.

Coaching: **Coaching** is a very broad topic, and in this book we have designated a complete chapter to this emerging phenomenon. In this section, only two limited aspects of it are considered here. The first concerns developing the manager's attitudes about the employee as a human resource who brings assets to the work situation that need to be nurtured if the employee is to grow and be productive. The manager as a coach needs to know how employees think of themselves in terms of their strengths and what goals they perceive as being meaningful in order to develop and use these strengths. When a manager finds that she and an employee don't agree on these matters, important data for coaching the employee in his or her performance and career become available.

A second aspect of coaching is developing listening skills, which can help the manager determine accurately what the employee is saying about himself. Paraphrasing, as a listening skill, is one way to try to get objective data from others without imposing one's own preconceptions onto what is being said. Asking nonleading questions for clarification is another: "I'm not sure what you are telling me. Could you give me that again more slowly?" does not lead the individual from his or her own trend of thoughts. As an example of a leading question, consider the response to a mother who expressed concern about her teenage son, who had always been a good student, good to his parents, and helpful around the house, but who, during the past six months, had shown all the opposite behaviors. The person who was supposed to have been the listener asked, "Do you suppose he might be on drugs?" Even if the mother did not have a problem when she came, she did when she left.

Media Richness and Communication Effectiveness: Managers can use a variety of media for transmitting messages. Research indicates that media choice has a direct effect on communication effectiveness. Three clusters of media options were identified: written, oral, and electronic.[31] Table 7–1 summarizes the variety of media choices in each of the clusters, their general availability, cost, speed, immediate interactions, impact, and attention.

Media also vary in richness. Recently, **media richness** has received considerable attention in organizational communication. Media richness theory ranks **communication media** along a continuum in terms of their "richness." In this context *richness* denotes the capacity of the medium to (1) carry a large volume of data and (2) convey meaning.[32] More specifically, media richness refers to the ability of a medium to change human understanding, overcome different conceptual frames of reference, or clarify ambiguous issues in a timely manner. Thus, where the mode of communication provides new substantial understanding, it is considered "rich"; otherwise, it is "lean." As tasks become more ambiguous, managers should increase the richness of the media they use. For example,

Table 7–1 Managers Can Use a Variety of Media for Transmitting Messages	Generally Available	Relatively Low Cost	High Speed	Immediate Interaction	High Impact and Attention
Written					
Letters	x	x			
Memos and reports			x		x
Telegrams			x		x
Newspapers and magazines	x				
Handbooks and manuals	x	x			
Bulletins and posters	x	x			
Inserts and enclosures	x	x			x
Oral					
Telephone	x	x	x	x	x
Intercom and paging	x		x		x
Conferences and meetings	x			x	
Speeches	x			x	
Electronic					
Fax			x	x	x
Electronic mail			x	x	
Voice messaging			x		x
Computer conferencing			x		x
Audio conferencing				x	x
Videoconferencing				x	x
Groupware				x	

Source: Adapted with permission from D. A. Level, Jr. and W. P. Galle, Jr., *Business Communications: Theory and Practice* (Burr Ridge, IL: Business Publications, Inc./Richard D. Irwin, Inc., 1998), pp. 91, 93.

simple nonroutine tasks can benefit from a communication medium that is lean, such as a memo, whereas complex nonroutine tasks can benefit from a face-to-face or videoconferencing communication medium that is rich.

SUMMARY

Communication is often ranked as a key problem of organizational life. Communication is closely interrelated with the other core concepts of personality, diversity, perception, and motivation previously reviewed. Messages to be communicated are formulated from the sender's motivation (intent) and perception of the relevant context. The meaning of the message to the receiver is filtered through the receiver's perceptual frame of reference and own needs and defenses.

Nine barriers to communication are conflicting assumptions between sender and receiver, cultural differences, nonverbal communication barriers, limited communication methods and technology, inadequate information, semantics, inadequate communication networks, the nature of the grapevine, rumor and gossip, and emotional blocks. The latter area is complicated by the tendency of the receiver to evaluate and judge the message rather than understand the meaning. Listening for logic and rationality, while ignoring the emotional and feeling content, also interferes with the transmission of meaning. Ways to overcome these barriers and improve communications include developing awareness and understanding, active listening, social technology applications, a supportive organizational climate, and self-awareness.

A variety of activities were developed to enhance improved communication skills. Activities 7–1 and 7–3W and 7–4W provide the experiential base for understanding the communication process and the development of the basic skills of coaching and goal setting. Activity 7–2 provides the opportunity to explore the dynamics of nonverbal communication. Finally, Activity 7–4W provides an opportunity to develop the skill to match between the situation and the best choice of communication medium.

Communication is a complex phenomenon and a multilevel concept that can have an effect on behavior at the individual, group, and organizational levels. In this module, communication was examined and studied at the interpersonal and intragroup levels. In the advanced modules, we discuss how communication influences key organizational processes such as creativity, innovation, work design, and the management of organization development and change. Improving the communication process is an ongoing managerial challenge that requires continuous effort.

Study Questions

1. "The way communication occurs in organizations has changed dramatically in the past 20 years." Describe the nature of the change, what seems to have triggered the changes, and how the changes influenced performance.

2. "In the communication process, meaning is in the mind of the sender and the receiver." Explain this statement. Provide examples from your team experience.

3. Of the barriers to communication given, which is the most basic? Why?

4. Several methods are given for overcoming barriers to communication. Give examples from your own experience of how these methods worked. Give examples of other methods that have worked for you or others you know.

5. Discuss the relationship between communication and perception.

6. "Managing the grapevine, rumor, and gossip are critical to management success." Explain this statement. Do you agree or disagree with the statement? Provide an example from your own experience, and use it to provide the rationale for your position.

7. We discussed a few ways for overcoming barriers to communication. Provide an example from your group's experience that illustrates how you overcame communication barriers.

8. What are some of the similarities and differences between interpersonal and intergroup communications?

9. What does goal setting have to do with communication at both the interpersonal and intergroup levels?

10. Discuss the relationship between "media richness" and communication effectiveness.

Endnotes

1. J. Sena and A. B. (Rami) Shani, "Sociotechnical System Theory and Utilizing Technology," in P. Docherty, M. Kira, and A.B. (Rami) Shani (eds.), *Creating Sustainable Work Systems: Developing Social Sustainability* (London: Routledge, 2008).

2. A. B. (Rami) Shani and J. Sena, "Knowledge Management Processes and Learning," in A. B. Shani and P. Docherty (eds.), *Learning by Design: Building Sustainable Organizations* (Oxford, UK: Blackwell Publishing, 2003), pp. 127–44.

3. See, for example, J. Langan-Fox, "Communication in Organization," in N. Anderson, D. Ones, H. Sinangil, and C. Viswesvaran (eds.), *Handbook of Industrial, Work and Organizational Psychology* (Thousand Oaks, CA: Sage, 2001), pp. 188–205; R. D'Aprix, *Communicating for Change: Connecting the Workplace with the Marketplace* (San Francisco: Jossey-Bass, 1996); and E. Marlow and P. O. Wilson, *The Breakdown of Hierarchy: Communicating in the Evolving Workplace* (Boston: Butterworth-Heineman, 1997).

4. A. B. Shani and Y. Mitki, "Creating the Learning Organization," in R. G. Golembiewski (ed.), *Handbook of Organizational Consultation* (New York: Marcel Dekker, 1999).

5. See, for example, W. A. Gudykunst, *Bridging Differences* (Thousand Oaks, CA: Sage, 1994); and L. L. Chu, "Mass Communication Theory: The Chinese Perspective," *Media Asia* 131 (1986), pp. 14–19.

6. See, for example, M. Young and J. E. Post, "Managing to Communicate, Communicating to Manage: How Leading Companies Communicate with Employees," *Organizational Dynamics* 22, no. 1 (1993), pp. 31–43; D. K. Berlo, *The Process of Communication: An Introduction to Theory and Practice* (New York: Holt, Rinehart & Winston, 1960); P. Burger and B. M. Bass, *Assessment of Managers: An International Comparison* (New York: Free Press, 1979); G. Cheney, "The Rhetoric of Identification and the Study of Organizational Communication," *Quarterly Journal of Speech* 69 (1983), pp. 143–58; D. Fabun, *Communications* (Beverly Hills, CA: Glencoe Press, 1968); L. Gibson, J. M. Ivancevich, and J. H. Donnelly, Jr., "The Communication Process," in *Organizations: Behavior, Structure, Processes*, rev. ed. (Dallas: Business Publications, 1976), pp. 161–85; G. Goldhaber, M.Yales, D. Porter, and R. Lesniak, "Organizational Communication," *Human Communication Research* 6 (1978), pp. 76–96; and W. V. Haney, *Communication and Organizational Behavior* (Burr Ridge, IL: Richard D. Irwin, 1973).

7. See for example, W. Roswell and J. Olson-Buchana, "The Use of Communication Technologies after Hours: The Role of Work Attitudes and Work-Life Conflicts," *Journal of Management* 33, no. 4 (2007), pp. 592–610.

8. R. Johansen, *Leading Business Teams: How Teams Can Use Technology and Group Process Tools to Enhance Performance* (Reading, MA: Addison-Wesley, 1992).

9. Langan-Fox, "Communication in Organization."

10. See Carl Rogers's concept of congruence in communication in C. Rogers, *On Becoming a Person* (Boston: Houghton Mifflin, 1961), pp. 338–46.

11. B. DePaulo and H. Friedman, "Nonverbal Communication," in D. Gilbert, S. Fiske, and G. Lindzey (eds.), *The Handbook of Social Psychology* (Boston: McGraw-Hill, 1998), pp. 3–40.

12. J. M. Suls, "Gossip as Social Comparison," *Journal of Communication* 27, no. 1, (1977), pp. 164–68.

13. G. Michelson and S. Mouly, "Rumour and Gossip in Organisations: A Conceptual Study," *Management Decision* 38, no. 5 (2000), pp. 339–46.

14. R. L. Rosnow, and G. A. Fine, *Rumor and Gossip: The Social Psychology of Hearsay* (New York: Elsevier, 1976).

15. R. L. Rosnow, "Gossip and Marketplace Psychology," *Journal of Communication* 27, no. 1, (1977), pp. 158–63.

16. M. Tebbutt, and M. Marchington, "Look Before You Speak: Gossip and the Insecure Workplace," *Work, Employment and Society* 11, no. 4 (1997), pp. 713–35.

17. Michelson and Mouly, "Rumour and Gossip in Organisations: A Conceptual Study."

18. Ibid.

19. J. Mishra, "Managing the Grapevine," *Public Personnel Management* 19, no. 2 (1990), pp. 213–28.

20. N. B. Kurland and L. H. Pelled, "Passing the Word: Toward a Model of Gossip and Power in the Workplace," *Academy of Management Review* 25, no. 2, (2000), pp. 428–39.

21. Mishra, "Managing the Grapevine," p. 213.

22. K. Davis, "Grapevine Communication along Lower and Middle Managers," *Personnel Journal* (April 1969).

23. Ibid.

24. N. J. Adler, *International Dimensions of Organizational Behavior* (Boston: PWS–Kent, 2002); and R. L. Kohls, *Survival Kit for Overseas Living* (Yarmouth, ME: Intercultural Press, 1979), pp. 30–31.

25. B. J. Reilly and J. A. DiAngelo, "Communication: A Cultural System of Meaning and Values," *Human Relations* 43, no. 2 (1990), pp. 129–40; T. Prekel, "Multi-Cultural Communication: A Challenge to Managers," paper delivered at the *International Convention of the American Business Communication Association,* New York (1983).

26. Adler, *International Dimensions of Organizational Behavior,* p. 65.

27. Ibid, p. 68.

28. See, for example, Adler, *International Dimensions of Organizational Behavior.*

29. Young and Post, "Managing to Communicate"; J. M. Putti, S. Aryee, and J. Phua, "Communication Relationship Satisfaction and Organizational Commitment," *Group and Organization Studies* 15, no. 1 (1990), pp. 44–52.

30. Mishra, "Managing the Grapevine."

31. D. A. Level, Jr., and W. P. Galle, Jr., *Business Communications: Theory and Practice* (Burr Ridge, IL: Irwin, 1988), pp. 91, 93.

32. See R. L. Daft and R. H. Lengel, "Information Richness," in L. L. Cummings and B. M. Staw (eds.), *Research in Organization Behavior,* vol. 6 (Greenwich, CT: JAI Press, 1984), pp. 191–233.

Activity 7–2: Nonverbal Communication

Objectives:

a. To complete small-group tasks without any verbal communication.

b. To explore individual and group reactions when verbal communication is cut off and only nonverbal communication can be used. To test your tolerance for ambiguity.

c. To demonstrate that shared expectations (group norms and roles) are spontaneously generated.

d. To provide behavioral data for a theoretical discussion of communications in this module.

Task 1 (A Structured Task):

Participants are to put their books aside and are not to refer to them again until this exercise and the discussion following it have been completed.

All chairs and tables are moved to the sides of the room. Members of a team or group (five to seven people) stand in a close circle facing one another. The instructor will ask participants to become completely silent before giving instructions and will ask them not to speak until this exercise in nonverbal communication is completed. The instructor will present a poster for all to see upon which the "Shoe Store" problem (included in the

Instructor's Manual) is written. Teams are to reach a consensus on the correct answer. Only nonverbal (no written or spoken) communication is to be used. (Time: 5 minutes)

When the instructor indicates the time is up, each team is to report its solution to the class. Three minutes are then allowed for discussion of the results among team members, after which the instructor will provide the correct solution.

Task 2 (An Unstructured Task):

Participants are to remain completely silent until this exercise is completed. Each group is to carry on, as a team, any activities or conversational topic of its own choosing for seven minutes. No spoken or written communication, only nonverbal communication, is to be used. You might want to start by expressing to each other your feelings about this class and then move on to other activities as a team. Use the space in this room in any way you wish. (Time: 7 minutes)

Task 3:

The instructor will stop all the activity, asking everyone to remain silent until the next instruction has been given.

Take one minute to try to get in touch with your feelings. How are you feeling now, and how were you feeling during the exercise, about the interaction in which you just took part? When the instructor indicates the time is up, you are to speak. Each participant should be given an opportunity to share feelings with the group. (Time: 1 minute of silence and 3 to 5 minutes for sharing)

Individuals are called on to share how they felt about the experience. (Time: 10 to 15 minutes)

Task 4:

Each group is to discuss the following:

a. What shared expectations developed in the group as to what was to be done and how members should or could behave? These may be thought of as group norms.

b. What roles developed among the members?

c. Did any subgrouping take place? (Time: 5 minutes)

Each group is to report its findings. The instructor will add observations of what norms and roles he or she saw evolving in each group.

Part 3

Managing Interpersonal Processes

REVIEW

The first part of the course explored the context within which individuals function in organizational settings. We have established the boundaries and process of the course: The field of study was defined, the learning community was established, expectations were shared and examined, the learning community was established, and the nature of learning-in-action explored. The second part of the book focused on understanding and managing individuals and examined four core elements: psychodynamics of human behavior, motivation, perception, and communication. The nature of the psychodynamics of human behavior within the context of work was explored. Examination of motivation was followed by an exploration of the role of perception and perceptual differences among individuals. The last module in the section addressed communications at the interpersonal level, at the small-group level, and between groups. Parts 1 and 2 provide the foundation for the exploration of interpersonal process—the focus of the next section—Part 3 of the book.

PREVIEW OF PART 3

Understanding and managing interpersonal processes are the focus of the third part of the book. Five core processes are the focus of the section: leadership, mentoring, negotiations and conflict management, team work and effectiveness, and team dynamics and performance. The first module in the section—Module 8—starts with the exploration of leaders and the leadership process. Three broad perspectives that emphasize a different aspect of the phenomenon—the leader-centric perspective, the follower-centric perspective, and the interactional perspective—are presented. The *leader-centric perspective* assumes that leadership flows from characteristics of the leader. The *follower-centric perspective* assumes that leadership is attributed to leaders by their followers, but has nothing to do with the leader's traits or actions. Finally, the *interactional perspective* assumes that leadership is a process that results from the effective interaction of the leader with the situation and his or her followers. This module activities—Exploring the Meaning of Leadership (Activity 8–1), Diagnosing Leadership Behavior (Activity 8–2), Donny Is My Leader (Activity 8–3), Creating a Dialogue with a Leader (Activity 8–4W), Least Preferred Co-Worker (LPC) Scale (Activity 8–5W), and Exercising Your Leadership Skills (Activity 8–6W)—provide an opportunity to develop an understanding of your leadership style, diagnose the complex nature of leadership dynamics, and provide an opportunity to develop your leadership skills.

Next, in Module 9, we focus on the development and management of the mentoring relationship. The mentoring relationship can have powerful, positive effects on the mentor, the protégé, and the employing organization. This module's activities—Exploring the Meaning of Mentoring and Other Developmental Relationships (Activity 9–1), Mentoring Interview (Activity 9–2), A Tale of a Protégé in Two a Mentoring Program (Activity 9–3), A Role Play Involving a Student Mentoring Program (Activity 9–4), and Creating a Game Plan to Use Your Developmental Network to Aid Your Career (Activity 9–5)—provide an opportunity to develop the abilities for and manage interpersonal mentoring processes.

Negotiations and conflict management—the focus of Module 10—are key interpersonal processes that follow. The module presents conflict as a complex phenomenon and a multilevel concept that can have an effect on behavior at the individual, group, and organizational levels. In this module we focus on conflict at the individual, team, and intergroup levels within the organizational context. A framework that can guide the examination of the dynamics between two or more work teams is reviewed. Intergroup communication processes and the dynamics of conflict are focal points for the module. A significant portion of the module is devoted to understanding the context and process that triggers conflict and alternative orientations and processes for handling conflict. Five strategic intentions are presented for handling conflict in a variety of situations. We argue that in situations where there is both conflict and interdependence, the process used to deal with conflict is negotiation. Two basic types of negotiation, distributed and integrative, are discussed. Finally, strategies and structures for negotiations are described. This module's activities—Exploring Conflict and Negotiation Dynamics (Activity 10–1), The Prisoners' Dilemma (Activity 10–2), The SLO Corporation Dilemma (Activity 10–3), The Ugli Orange Case (Activity 10–4), and Discovering How You Typically Handle Conflict (Activity 10–5)—provide an opportunity to develop the ability to diagnose, handle individual and intergroup conflict, and develop and practice negotiation strategies.

Teams are a major focus of study throughout this course because teams and work groups are the basic units of emerging, contemporary enterprises. Interestingly, teamwork is an old idea that is experiencing renewal as a mechanism to carry out complex tasks and integrate work, people, and organizations. As of late, the view of organizations as "teams of teams," or *team-based organizations,* seems to be taking hold. Two modules are devoted to the understanding of managing team processes.

Module 11, Work Teams and Effectiveness, starts by providing an overview of teams, the historical, cultural and global context for the emergence of teams at work and types of teams. Next the module focuses on team decision making and problem-solving processes. A discussion about the application of teams at work is followed by a brief examination of the impact of information technology on team behavior and performance and the review of some of the major challenges that have emerged for teams at work. A wide variety of activities was created for this module. The module's activities include—Team Skills (Activity 11–1), Mountain Survival (Activity 11–2), Who Gets the Overtime (Activity 11–3), Team Development Assessment (Activity 11–4), Important Days Task (Activity 11–5W), Task 21 (Activity 11–6W), Three Essential Process Tools for Team Development (Activity 11–7W), and Decision Making—Japanese Style (Activity 11–8W). These activities should help you understand: (1) the difference between a group and a team; (2) why teams are so often used in organizations; (3) the role of the manager in facilitating group decision making and problem solving; (4) ways in which creativity in problem solving can be enhanced; (5) specific ways in which organizations use teams; (6) team problem solving and decision-making process and skills; (7) the diagnosis of team progress, skill level, and development, and; (8) ways to gauge team progress and utilize process tools for team development. Together, the activities provide an opportunity to diagnose and develop team skills and team leadership skills.

The last module in this part of the book—Module 12—focuses on group dynamics and performance. It is important to note that group development is something that not all groups achieve over time but instead should be viewed as "a journey towards optimal functioning only some groups attained." As such, the module begins with two activities, Tower Building (Activity 12–1) and An Initial Inventory of Group Dynamics (Activity 12–2), designed to help you work as a team on a creative task and reflect on some of the dynamics that emerged in your team. The module explores in detail the factors that affect group development and performance, including leadership, group structure, and member composition. The dynamic nature of group development, the phases that groups progress through, and two models of group development are presented and discussed. The phenomena of social loafing and cohesion are also explored. The module ends with two activities to help you develop further appreciation for individual differences and team development, The Plabaf Company Case (Activity 12–3) and Values in Business (Activity 12–4). The Web provides three additional activities for group development—A Card Game Called *Norms* (Activity 12–5W), Individual Role Assessment (Activity 12–6W), and Status on the Campus (Activity 12–7W)—designed to help you focus on some of the dynamics at work in your classroom group. These activities should help you to enhance the understanding, conceptual implications, and skills discussed in the module as well as the ability to influence the developmental process and phases in the development of teams.

Module

8

Leaders and Leadership

LEARNING OBJECTIVES

After completing this module, you should be able to

1. Understand and explain leadership.
2. Explain the different leadership schools of thought and identify their complementary contribution to our understanding of leaders, leadership, and leadership dynamics.
3. Gain insights into your own leadership potential, its effect on others, and its effectiveness.
4. Prepare an intentional leadership development plan based on your own professional and life goals.

KEY TERMS AND CONCEPTS

Achievement-oriented leadership

Attribution theory of leadership

Authentic leadership development

Charismatic leadership

Consideration

Contingency theory

Democratic versus autocratic leadership

Directive leadership

Emotional intelligence

Follower-centric perspective

Initiating structure

Interactional perspective

Leader-centric perspective

Leadership

Leadership behavior

Leadership ladder

Leadership Practices Inventory

Leadership style

Leadership traits

Management

Participative leadership

Participative versus directive leadership

Path–goal theory

Relationship behavior

Relationship-motivated leader	Task-motivated leader
Situational leadership	Trait theory of leadership
Supportive leadership	Transformational leadership
Task- and people-oriented behaviors	Vision
Task behavior	360-degree leadership feedback

MODULE OUTLINE

PREMODULE PREPARATION

Activity 8–1:
Exploring the Meaning
of Leadership

Objective:

To help you explore your mental model of leadership and its meaning based on your own experience.

Task 1:

Pick either your favorite fictional hero (from a book, movie, or TV show), real-life leader, or boss/coach/teacher.

Task 2:

Write down the following:

a. Why did you select this person?

b. What about this person's style, personality, and behavior makes this person a leader?

c. In which situation(s) did this person demonstrate leadership? Is this person always a good leader?

d. What is your definition of leadership?

e. Use images or metaphors about this person if you feel it will help you.

Task 3:

Each participant will share one of his or her chosen leaders with the team. As a team, discuss your choices and answers. Capture the common elements that emerge, pick one of the leaders you discussed who exemplifies best your insights about leadership, and have a spokesperson ready to share your ideas with the class.

Task 4:

Spokespersons will report findings to the class, and the instructor will lead a class discussion about the meaning of leadership and its key features.

INTRODUCTION

Most individuals carry around mental models of leadership and management. As we saw in Activity 8–1, by bringing to the surface individual's mental models it is possible to imagine or even picture a "leader" and to list the qualities that make him or her a leader. This module provides you with an opportunity to develop and refine your mental model of leadership by helping you examine your mental model in the context of a variety of theoretical models and theories.

Leadership and management are very much on everyone's mind today. Institutions and organizations are struggling as they face increasingly turbulent times, such as war and terrorism, globalization, the intensification of competition, dwindling natural resources, the acceleration of innovation, the emergence of the era of digital information, and changing demographics. Leading and managing occur at the federal government level in Washington, D.C.; at the corporate level as foreign competition increases; and in religious institutions, schools, courts, museums, hospitals, manufacturing facilities, and other institutions that all seem to be in the midst of change and an uncertain future. As the challenges of managing and leading increase, so does our need to understand the unique features of leaders, and the leadership process in organizations. Leadership provides an answer to one of the key questions in organizational behavior: How can a group of diverse people work together toward a common goal?[1]

The phenomenon of leadership spans all three levels of analysis commonly used in organizational behavior: the individual, the group, and the organization. At the individual level of analysis, leadership is understood as the qualities that influential people have and the behaviors they engage in to motivate their followers to work toward common goals. At the group and organizational levels of analysis, leadership can be viewed as a process through which both the leader and his or her followers deeply influence each other in the development of a common mission. Effective leadership can therefore enhance individual, group, and organizational effectiveness. Thus, at the core, leadership is about the management of interpersonal processes.

LEADERSHIP: AN OVERVIEW

Leadership Defined

People have been interested in the phenomenon of **leadership** since antiquity.[2] Yet the systematic scholarly study of leadership and management did not begin until the 1920s.[3] Group discussions of leadership are fascinating, whether the participants are business executives, politicians, college students, or academics. Many executives believe strongly that when it comes to leadership, "you've either got it or you haven't." But when it comes to defining what it is that you've got or haven't got, they can't agree. In contrast, academic views of leadership range from the benign "we don't really know what it is" to rigorous definitions based on very narrow research. In 1974 Stogdill concluded that "there are almost as many definitions of leadership as there are persons who have attempted to define the concept."[4] However, four massive reviews by Bass,[5] Yukl,[6-7] and Hughes et al.[8] have provided excellent surveys of the leadership literature and helped develop a sharper understanding of the phenomenon. Yukl notes that while conceptual disagreements are deep, most definitions emphasize leadership as an *influence process*. Thus, at the most basic level, "Leadership is a process whereby an individual influences a group of individuals to achieve a common goal."[9] This definition contains four important aspects: (a) leadership is a process, (b) leadership involves influence, (c) leadership occurs within a group, and (d) leadership involves goal attainments.

Leadership versus Management

Yet not all employees and managers exercise leadership. Bernard Bass, a leadership scholar, captures the essence of the debate: "Leaders manage and managers lead, but the two activities are not synonymous."[10] Some scholars argue that although management and leadership overlap, each entails a unique set of activities or functions. Certainly, if a leader is loosely defined as a person who influences others in any manner, then the person can be a leader without being a manager. Also, a person can be manager but can fail to lead. **Management** refers to the numerous roles and activities that "managers" must carry out, and leadership activities relate only to a subset of the larger managerial functions and activities.[11] These distinctions are well accepted and have not been part of the debate. The controversy concerns the notion that leading and managing are qualitatively different or mutually exclusive.

The first scholar to take a hard line on this issue was Abraham Zaleznik, when his landmark article was published in *Harvard Business Review* in 1977.[12] Zaleznik argues that managers carry out responsibilities, exercise authority, and worry about how things get done, whereas leaders are concerned with understanding people's beliefs and gaining their commitment. Managers and leaders differ in what they attend to and in how they think, work, and interact. Zaleznik believes that these differences stem from unequal developmental paths, from childhood to adulthood. Essentially, leaders have encountered major hardships or events in stark contrast to the orderly upbringing of the typical manager. Leaders have achieved separateness, or the ability to be bold and controversial without fearing social disapproval, which enables them to dream up ideas and to stimulate others to work hard to bring these dreams into reality. In contrast, managers are process oriented and believe that good systems and processes produce good results.[13] In a related argument, Kotter states that leadership is about coping with change, whereas management is about coping with complexity.[14] Consistently, Warren Bennis believes that the difference between leaders and managers is the ability to master the context rather than surrender to it: "Managers do things right, while leaders do the right thing."[15] Figure 8–1 summarizes the unique features of both management and leadership.

The response to the writers who claimed a distinction between leadership and management was immediate and strong. Many executives and academicians see considerable overlap between leadership and management activities and preoccupations, and they believe it is wrong to assume that a person cannot be good at both. Certainly, there is little or no research to support the notion that selected people can be classified as leaders rather than as managers or that managers cannot adopt visionary behaviors when they are required for success. We maintain that it is important for all managers and supervisors to establish themselves as leaders. Further, team-based organization designs are extending leadership functions to work groups and cross-department teams in most modern organizations. There is opportunity for more innovation and critical thinking at all levels of the organization.

We will not argue that leadership and management are mutually exclusive, but they are distinct. We draw from Clark and Clark[16] when we say that choosing to lead is an intentional act—not everyone is willing to fully accept the responsibilities and burdens of leadership or perceive him- or herself as a leader. Leadership skills can be developed and enhanced at any developmental stage of one's career—the earlier this decision is made, the more likely that those skills will develop to their potential. The decision to lead can have a more dynamic impact on future outcomes based on an early intentional decision. The process of leading involves a progression from low- to high-stake adventures or trials that generate rich feedback with which to self-monitor behavior and its impact. The later in life the decision to lead is made, the higher the risk of failure both in terms of what is at stake and the degree to which the world around us will tolerate our experimentation. The argument that maturational readiness presents itself in the late teens and diminishes dramatically by the late 20s has an intuitive logic. The discussion of the challenge and opportunity of leadership is very timely among college students and needs the same care and deliberate engagement as the earlier proverbial discussion of the "birds and bees."

Many people choose not to lead, but to "boss"; they view their group members as inferior, undisciplined, untrainable, and requiring "management." We surmise that there may be as much tyranny today as the world has ever seen. However, it is widely condoned as the necessary tyranny of the foreman getting the job done, the enforcement of rules by the bureaucrat preventing disorder, the control of thugs by the police protecting the populace, or the right of the "big people" dominating "little people." Our comics and cartoonists find this form of tyranny a dependable source for plying their trade.[17]

Figure 8–1
A Comparative Summary of Leadership and Management Features

Management
Carrying out traditional management functions:
    Planning, budgeting, organizing, staffing, problem solving, and control.
Assuming roles as required:*
    Interpersonal roles of symbolic figurehead, liaison with key people, supervisor of employees.
    Informational roles of information monitor, information disseminator, and spokesperson.
    Decision-making roles of innovator within the unit, disturbance handler, resource allocator, and negotiator.

Leadership
Challenging the status quo.
Developing visions and setting direction.
Developing strategies for producing changes toward the new vision.
Communicating the new direction and getting people involved.
Motivating and inspiring others.

*From H. Mintzberg, "The Manager's Job; Folklore and Fact," *Harvard Business Review*, July–August (1975).

Leadership: Multiple Views

The study of leadership in the behavioral sciences now covers more than six decades and has resulted in more than 7,500 books and articles. What becomes apparent from examining the literature is that no one universal theory of leadership seems to be accepted by all. Instead, several theories have been formulated over time. Overall, these theories can be classified into three broad perspectives that emphasize a different aspect of the phenomenon: the leader-centric perspective, the follower-centric perspective, and the interactional perspective. The **leader-centric perspective** assumes that leadership flows from characteristics of the leader. The **follower-centric perspective** assumes that leadership is attributed to leaders by their followers but has nothing to do with the leader's traits or actions. Finally, the **interactional perspective** assumes that leadership is a process that results from the effective interaction of the leader with the situation and his or her followers. In the next few sections we review the most important leadership theories within the three perspectives.

THE LEADER-CENTRIC PERSPECTIVE ON LEADERSHIP

At the beginning of the 20th century, when scholars first tried to theorize leadership, they naturally focused on leaders themselves. The word *leadership* is based on the word *leader,* which implies that this phenomenon flows from the personality and actions of exceptional people: leaders. Max Weber, for instance, one of the founding fathers of sociology, identified charisma as the key characteristic of leaders, and defined it as "the quality of people touched by the grace of God."[18] Other social scientists, however, not content to have to rely on the notion of God to define a sociological concept, further attempted to unlock the secret of leadership by identifying and mapping the key characteristics of recognized leaders. First, under the influence of personality theory they focused on leaders' traits and personality, which gave birth to the **trait theory of leadership.** Second, under the influence of behaviorism they focused on leaders' behavior and style, which gave birth to the **style theory of leadership.**

The Trait Theory of Leadership

Between 1920 and 1950 researchers hoped to discover how individual traits are connected to leadership effectiveness. Traits can be defined as a person's enduring characteristics or dispositions which give rise to their behaviors or behavior patterns. The "natural born leader" concept seemed a logical basis for investigation. According to this leadership theory, leaders naturally possess traits that set them apart from other people. For example, height, appearance, personality, intelligence, race, sex, and other traits could make it more likely that a given individual will become a leader. Reviews by Kirkpatrick and Locke[19] and Bass[20] have identified the following major **leadership traits:**

1. Drive: achievement, ambition, energy, tenacity, and initiative.
2. Leadership motivation (personalized versus socialized).
3. Participation: activity, sociability, cooperation, adaptability, humor.
4. Honesty and integrity.
5. Self-confidence (including emotional stability).
6. Personal abilities: intelligence, vitality, verbal agility, originality, critical abilities.
7. Expertise (knowledge of the business or the situation).
8. Proven achievements: academic, general culture, athletic.
9. Status: social, popularity.

Alongside these nine traits, Hogan et al.[21] also find that the Big Five dimensions of personality, which we saw in Module 4, predict leadership. The Big Five dimensions of personality are surgency, emotional stability, conscientiousness, agreeableness, and intelligence. Each of these dimensions forms a continuum from positive to negative:

- "Surgency measures the degree to which an individual is sociable, gregarious, assertive, and leader-like versus quiet, reserved, mannerly, and withdrawn."

- Emotional stability is concerned with "the extent to which individuals are calm, steady, cool, and self-confident versus anxious, insecure, worried, and emotional."

- Conscientiousness "differentiates individuals who are hard working, persevering, organized, and responsible from those who are impulsive, irresponsible, undependable, and lazy."

- "Agreeableness measures the degree to which individuals are sympathetic, cooperative, good-natured, and warm versus grumpy, unpleasant, disagreeable, and cold."

- Intelligence "concerns the extent to which an individual is imaginative, cultured, broadminded, and curious versus concrete minded, practical, and has narrow interests."[22]

Hogan et al.[23] find that the closer an individual's personality is to the positive ends of these five dimensions, the more effective that individual's team leadership is, and the more managerial advancement and positive observer ratings that individual gets.

However, the Trait approach to leadership produced mixed results. As researchers kept expanding the list of relevant traits, it became so long that it failed to distinguish between leaders and nonleaders. Furthermore, famous counterexamples could be found for many of the traits identified. For example, while height was identified as a possible leadership trait, Napoleon, who was notoriously short, does not fit the trend. Eventually, at the end of the 1940s, after a thorough review of the research literature, influential leadership scholar Ralph Stogdill concluded, "A person does not become a leader by virtues of the possession of some combination of traits,"[24] thus dealing a significant blow to the Trait theory of leadership. This opened the avenue for a new leadership theory: Leadership style.

Leadership Style

As a reaction to the relative failure of the early studies on the trait approach, three influential independent groups of researchers—at Harvard University, Ohio State University, and the University of Michigan—began studying the behavior of leaders by asking individuals in field settings to describe the behavior of individuals in positions of authority and relating the responses to different criteria of leader effectiveness. This movement was consistent with behaviorism, a school of thought started by B. F. Skinner[25] in psychology that asserts that internal psychological phenomena, such as cognition or emotion, cannot be studied scientifically because they cannot be measured objectively. Behaviorists thus advocate the study of behavior as the only measurable phenomenon in psychology.

The Ohio State Leadership Studies collected 1,800 samples of **leadership behavior** which were classified into 150 leadership functions.[26,27] These 150 leadership functions were further summarized as falling within one of two **leadership styles:** consideration and initiating structure.

Consideration covers a wide variety of behaviors related to the treatment of people, including showing concern for subordinates, looking out for their welfare, and acting in a friendly supportive manner. Finding time to listen to subordinates' problems and consulting with subordinates on important issues before making decisions are good examples of consideration.

Initiating structure is a task-related dimension. It also covers a wide variety of behaviors, including defining roles and guiding subordinates toward attainment of work-group goals. Assignment of work, attention to standards of performance, and an emphasis on deadlines are examples of initiating structure.

In roughly the same time period (the 1950s), a second major program was launched at the University of Michigan. The research methods of that program included interviews and questionnaires; its objective was to determine whether leaders of high-production units behaved differently from leaders of low-production units. The essence of the findings was that effective leaders performed different work than their subordinates, concentrating on planning and scheduling of work, coordinating projects, and offering various types of support. Effective supervisors were also found to be relationship-oriented, showing trust and confidence, trying to understand subordinates' problems and helping to develop their potential.[28] The early Michigan studies identified **task- and people-oriented behaviors** that were surprisingly similar to those found in the Ohio State studies. They also concluded that successful leaders emphasize participation in decision making and rely on group discussions in place of one-on-one supervision.

Further research yielded similar pairs of leadership styles, such as **participative versus directive leadership**[29] or **democratic versus autocratic leadership.**[30] One of the important questions that emerged from this research was whether one of the styles was more effective than the other. In the wake of the Second World War, where democracies, such as the United States, opposed dictatorial regimes such as Nazi Germany, American psychologists, led by Kurt Lewin, the founder of social psychology and a Jewish German refugee in the United States, were motivated to find support for the idea that a democratic style of leadership was more effective than an autocratic style.[31] The findings however, were mixed. Some studies found that a democratic style is associated with higher productivity; others found an autocratic style to be associated with higher productivity, while still others find no difference.[32,33] Nevertheless, available evidence seems to be leaning toward democratic leadership being more effective, as confirmed by the meta-analysis conducted by Gastil,[34] which found a democratic leadership style to be associated with a higher group productivity when the task is complex, while democratic and autocratic styles do not differ in their effectiveness when the task is simple. These weak findings motivated Fiedler to formulate a new leadership theory: the **contingency theory** of leadership,[35] which will be expanded upon in the section on interactional perspectives on leadership. Nonetheless, the two main styles of leadership remain important fixtures of leadership research. We now turn to the follower-centric perspective on leadership.

THE FOLLOWER-CENTRIC PERSPECTIVE ON LEADERSHIP

In the 1970s, Jeffrey Pfeffer articulated a provocative reversal of perspective on leadership:[36] what if the phenomenon of leadership had more to do with leaders' followers than with leaders themselves? The follower-centric perspective on leadership was born. Pfeffer's review of the leadership literature painted a dire picture of the field: not only is there a large amount of ambiguity surrounding the definition of leadership, as we discussed in the introduction, but research has failed to demonstrate that leaders have a real impact on their organizations.[37,38] This lead Pfeffer to put the whole concept of leadership in doubt, and assert that it may be an illusion. For him, leadership, as a phenomenon, has nothing to do with the exceptional qualities of gifted individuals, but rather with the gullibility of their followers. Pfeffer's argument is based on attribution theory, a well-researched psychological theory that has shown that people tend to simplify reality when they make causal inferences.[39] This theory will be discussed in more detail in Module 10. According to attribution theory, people have a tendency to analyze the world and make causal inferences, which seem to trigger effects around them. They do so in order to make predictions in the future, which gives them a measure of control over their environment. The problem is that reality is frighteningly complex, and people have limited cognitive abilities. They thus need to simplify the world when they make attribution judgments. One way in which they do so is to look for salient objects, circumstances, or people in their environment. A person or object is salient when she stands out in contrast to the background. For example, in a group of all-white people, a dark-skinned person stands out. Research on attribution theory has shown that people mistakenly tend to attribute more causal power to salient objects.[40] This led Pfeffer to conclude that because leaders are highly visible, their followers attribute special power to them, assuming that they are the cause of organizational performance, when they have in fact a very modest influence on it. Leadership is this mystification, which is caused by followers rather than leaders.

Pfeffer nonetheless nuances his initial assertion, and recognizes that leaders have an important role to play in the leadership process, although it is not the one that was thought earlier. They have to be good actors. Leadership actions are symbolic rather than real.[41] Effective leaders are those who successfully associate themselves with positive organizational outcomes, pretending they caused them more than they actually did, and divest themselves from negative outcomes, blaming them on the system, or someone else.

While Pfeffer's theory productively stirred the debate on leadership, his assertion that leadership has no real impact on organization was found to be exaggerated.[42] Nonetheless, Pfeffer's **attribution theory of leadership** enforced the notion that (1) leadership does not just reside with the leader, but also involves followers, and (2) that leadership is as much about real action as it is about symbolic action. We now turn to the most complex and complete perspective on leadership: the interactional perspective.

THE INTERACTIONAL PERSPECTIVE ON LEADERSHIP

The relative failure of the leader-centric and follower-centric perspectives on leadership to fully explain the phenomenon gave rise to a third perspective: the interactional perspective. This perspective assumes that effective leadership results from the effective interaction of a leader with the situation and his or her followers. However, as the reader may now have come to expect, different theories disagree about what dimensions of the situation matter most or which types of interactions are most effective. We now review these different theories.

Fiedler's Contingency Theory

Given the failure of the style theories of leadership to identify one best style that was effective across all situations, Fred Fiedler articulated contingency theory,[43] which determines the situational conditions under which a given style is most effective. Contingency theory hypothesizes that leaders have a preferred style: they are either relationship-motivated, which is roughly equivalent to the democratic style referred to earlier, or task-motivated, which is roughly equivalent to the autocratic style. An individual's managerial style is defined with reference to his or her score on the least preferred co-worker (LPC) scale (which can be found in Activity 8–5W, on the book's website), an exercise consisting of 18 pairs of bipolar adjectives. Fiedler's *contingency model theory* provides some insight into certain aspects of directive and nondirective styles of leadership. The focus is on designing the managerial position to match the motivational and personality characteristics of the manager. Fiedler's work is meaningful for two reasons: interesting managerial implications can be drawn from the theory, and it provides an opportunity to examine important critical leadership challenges.

Fiedler posits that **task-motivated** (low-LPC) leaders perform best in situations in which they have either a great deal or very little situational control; while **relationship-motivated** (high-LPC) leaders perform best in situations of moderate situational control. Situational control is higher when (1) leader–member relations (the support and loyalty obtained from the work group) are good, (2) task structure (the clarity with which critical task components, such as goals, methods, and standards of performance are defined) is high, and (3) position power (the degree of power bestowed by the organization to reward and punish subordinates) is high.

In leader–match training, the individual's leadership style and situational control are identified, and the individual is offered strategies for changing critical components of the situation rather than suggestions for modifying his or her personality. The contingency model assumes that the manager's behaviors and personal characteristics are more difficult to change than is the work situation.[44] As the reader may have come to expect, the results of further research on contingency theory were mixed. Doubt was cast on whether the LPC scale actually measured leadership style,[45] and the contingency hypotheses were complicated and difficult to interpret.[46]

Hersey and Blanchard's Situational Leadership

In response to the unwieldiness of Fiedler's contingency model, Hersey and Blanchard developed the *situational leadership mode*.[47] Like contingency theory, this theory incorporates leadership styles similar to initiating structure (task behavior) and consideration (relationship behavior). "**Task behavior** is defined as the extent to which the leader engages in spelling out duties and responsibilities of an individual or group."[48] "**Relationship behavior** is defined as the extent to which the leader engages in two-way or multiway communication." The behaviors include listening, facilitating, and supportive behaviors.[49] However, in contrast with contingency theory, **situational leadership** theory assumes that leaders can adopt different leadership styles to adapt to differing situations (instead of restructuring or avoiding the situation, like was argued by Fiedler). For this reason, this theory has had wide appeal for managers because it gives them a higher sense of control. It has been widely used in corporate training in corporations "such as Bank of America, Caterpillar, IBM, Mobil Oil, Union 76, and Xerox,"[50] the military, and other government agencies in the United States. Furthermore, Hersey and Blanchard assert that styles are not mutually exclusive, in other words that a leader can be both highly task focused, and highly relationship focused, or both low on these dimensions. Hersey and Blanchard propose four types of situation that require a modulation of the leader's style:

S1: When followers are unable to perform a task and unwilling or insecure about it, leaders should adopt a high-task and low-relationship style.

S2: When followers are unable to perform a task but willing or confident about it, leaders should adopt a high-task and high-relationship style.

S3: When followers are able to perform a task but unwilling or insecure about it, leaders should adopt a high-relationship and low-task style.

S4: Finally, when followers are able to perform a task and are willing or confident about it, leaders should adopt a low-relationship and low-task style.

Figure 8–2 represents the range of leader behavior in response to follower readiness.

Despite its popular appeal with managers, Situational leadership theory has failed to receive significant empirical support.[51]

Path–Goal Theory

A third situational approach that has generated considerable interest is path–goal theory.[52] This approach is unique because it combines leadership with motivation theory (see Module 5). **Path–goal theory** suggests that leaders motivate subordinates to achieve high performance by showing them the path to reach valued goals or results. When the tasks along the way have been performed and the goals reached, rewards follow. The leader's role is to show a clear path and to help eliminate barriers to achievement of the goals.

Leadership style was defined earlier in this module as a pattern of philosophy, beliefs, and assumptions about leadership that affects the individual's behavior when managing people. Path–goal theory includes four leadership styles: **directive leadership,** which is similar to the Ohio State concept of initiating structure; **supportive leadership,** which is similar to the concept of consideration; **participative leadership,** which emphasizes consultation with subordinates before decisions are made; and **achievement-oriented leadership,** where the leader is preoccupied with setting challenging goals for the work group. Leader style and behavior interact with several contingency factors to determine the employee's job performance and satisfaction. Figure 8–3 summarizes the contingency and outcome factors involved.

Path–goal theory involves a number of contingency factors. Three subordinate characteristics are covered by the model, including ability, attitude toward authoritarianism, and preference for self-control or internal control (in contrast to control by others). These characteristics influence how subordinates perceive the leader's behavior. For example, people who have an internal locus of control prefer participative leaders; those who are high in authoritarianism react positively to directive leadership. Background factors such as the nature of the task and rewards also come into play. If subordinates know how to do the job and the task is routine, then the path to the goal is clear and the best style may be supportive. When tasks are uncertain, a more directive style of leadership may be welcomed by subordinates. The leader's task is to reduce uncertainty by

Figure 8–2   **Hersey and Blanchard's Situational Leadership Model**

Task behavior

The extent to which the leader engages defining roles—that is, telling what, how, when, where, and, if more than one person, who is to do what in:

- Goal setting
- Organizing
- Establishing time lines
- Directing
- Controlling

Relationship behavior

The extent to which a leader engages in two-way (multiway) communication, listening, facilitating behaviors, and socioemotional support:

- Giving support
- Communicating
- Facilitating interactions
- Active listening
- Providing feedback

Decision styles

1
Leader-made decision

2
Leader-made decision with dialogue and/or explanation

3
Leader/follower-made decision or follower-made decision with encouragement from leader

4
Follower-made decision

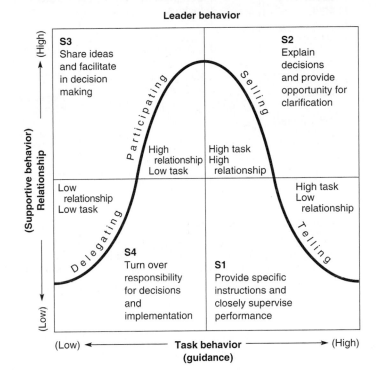

Ability: has the necessary knowledge, experience, and skill

Willingness: has the necessary confidence, commitment, motivation

When a leader behavior is used appropriately with its corresponding level of readiness, it is termed a *high-probability match*. The following are descriptors that can be useful for situational leadership for specific applications:

S1	S2	S3	S4
Telling	Selling	Participating	Delegating
Guiding	Explaining	Encouraging	Observing
Directing	Clarifying	Collaborating	Monitoring
Establishing	Persuading	Committing	Fulfilling

Source: P. Hersey and K. Blanchard, *Management of Organizational Behavior: Utilizing Human Behavior,* 6th ed. (Escondido, CA: Center for Leadership Studies, 1988), p. 207. Reprinted with permission. All rights reserved.

clarifying either the desired results or the tasks to accomplish them. Also, the leader must remove barriers to performance and attempt to influence attitudes about tasks, goals, and rewards.

Because of the nature of path–goal theory, most researchers have focused only on a few aspects of the complete theory.[53] The principal contributions of this approach have been an expanded search for relevant contingency factors and clarification of ways that managers can influence employee motivation and performance. It suggests that managers can determine the best mix of behavior to apply in guiding subordinates toward improved effort, performance, and satisfaction. Like Hersey and Blanchard's situational leadership, and unlike Fiedler's contingency theory, path–goal theory considers that a leader's style is flexible and can be adapted to varying situations.

Figure 8–3
Path–Goal View of
Dynamics

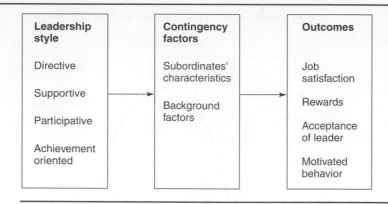

Leadership Style and Culture

A further source of contingency for the effectiveness of given leadership styles has been found in culture. A leader's style must depend on his or her attitudes and beliefs because expectations and assumptions about people are based on belief systems. What leaders actually do is based on what they believe or assume should be done when acting out their roles in a particular set of circumstances. Their style must be rooted in their worldview: their philosophy, beliefs, attitudes, feelings, and assumptions about people and the world. This will become clearer with some examples. If you believe that people are basically "no damned good" and that they will do as little as possible if you let them get away with it, then as a supervisor you will seek to control people closely. You may have the image of yourself as "the boss," who spends a great deal of time checking up on what people are doing. A contrary set of assumptions holds that people are responsible, if given the opportunity for self-direction, and that they work as naturally as they play. If you hold these beliefs, your image of yourself as a supervisor may emphasize helping or coordinating people's efforts—you may concentrate on planning so that employees can act autonomously within the guidelines you set down.

A person's worldview is largely influenced by the general culture (the term *culture* here is used to refer to "culture" in a regional or nationalistic sense) in which they occur. (We will explore culture and organizational culture in Module 15). The autocratic style, with its highly directive involvement by management and a strongly conforming involvement by employees, is apparently more acceptable in societies more structured than the United States. Generally, family style also can be fitted into the models used here. For instance, parents can take the disciplinary role of the autocratic style with their children, or they can place major emphasis on conforming to the community, which parallels the emphasis on system in the corporate style. They can overindulge their young as the permissive style does employees; they can neglect them and assume little responsibility, like the retired-on-the-job type; or they can produce a supportive, problem-solving environment so the offspring can assume the responsibility for their own self-direction as they gain competence, as in the professional-transformational manager style.

Project Globe, which began in 1993, collected data from 17,000 middle managers from 92 different cultures using paired researchers from the United States and the country under study. The project identified 22 specific attributes and behaviors that are viewed as being universal across all cultures that contribute to leadership effectiveness. The study also identified 8 attributes or behaviors that are viewed as impediments to leadership effectiveness and another 35 that are culturally dependent:[54]

Universally positive leadership attributes and behaviors: trustworthy, just, honest, foresighted, plans ahead, encouraging, informed, excellence oriented, positive, dynamic, motive arouser, confidence builder, motivational, dependable, coordinator, intelligent, decisive, effective bargainer, win–win problem solver, administratively skilled, communicative, and team builder.

Universally negative attributes and behaviors: loner, asocial, noncooperative, irritable, nonexplicit, egocentric, ruthless, and doctorial.

Some culturally contingent behaviors and attributes: ambitious, cautious, compassionate, domineering, independent, individualistic, logical, orderly, sincere, worldly, formal, and sensitive.

Most managers believe that they must adapt their style of leadership to the culture of the employees; that is, they believe that leadership is culturally contingent.[55] The interrelationship between lifestyles and the culture or subcultures of a country is also similar to the interrelationship between leadership style and organizational style. They tend to be consistent with and reinforce one another. The study of leadership and its unique dynamics have attracted scholars from a variety of disciplines. Each school of thought contributed insight into this complex phenomenon.

Charismatic and Transformational Leadership

At the end of the 1970s, leadership scholars were dissatisfied with the progress accomplished in the field of leadership. Too many theories seemed to be fighting for the limelight, and these theories had received insufficient empirical support. The field of leadership was ripe for a serious facelift. This happened in the form of two new theories, which became and remain the most influential leadership theories today: charismatic and transformational leadership. The end of the 1970s and the beginning of the 1980s brought revolutionary change to many American businesses. An increase focus that was accelerated emphasized the need for senior leaders to transform their organizations and society at large. Leadership researchers thus started to investigate what came to be termed **transformational leadership.** While distinct, the theories of charismatic and transformational leadership can be considered near "identical twins."[56] **Charismatic leadership** is one of the most exemplary forms of transformational leadership.[57] The term "transformational" leadership was chosen in contrast to a more "transactional" form of leadership, in which followers exchange their services for rewards distributed by the leader.[58] This distinction is reminiscent of the distinction made earlier between management and leadership and discussed at the beginning of the chapter. Charismatic and transformational leaders seem to add something to the social exchange process that takes place with their followers: the end result of the interaction far exceeds a simple transactional zero-sum exchange. Charismatic and transformational leadership theories integrate the leader-centric, the follower-centric, and the interactional perspectives on leadership. How do they characterize the phenomenon of leadership?

Shamir et al.[59] hypothesize that charismatic leaders influence their followers by motivating them to an extraordinary extent. Charismatic leaders do so through at least four mechanisms: (1) they change their followers' perceptions of the nature of work itself; (2) they offer an appealing future vision; (3) they develop a deep collective identity among followers, and; (4) they heighten both individual and collective self-efficacy (the belief that one has the capabilities to perform in a certain manner or attain certain goals).

Bass[60] hypothesizes that transformational leaders (1) heighten their followers' awareness about the importance and value of designated goals and the means to achieve them, (2) induce followers to transcend their self-interests for the good of the collective and its goals, and (3) stimulate and meet their followers' higher-order needs through the leadership process and the mission.

In a recent study of transformational leadership, James Kouzes and Barry Posner asked more than 500 managers first to reflect on all of their leadership experiences and next to focus on one extraordinary experience. Managers were asked to get a clear mental picture of the experience (that is, to see, hear, and feel it again as intensely as possible). They were then asked to respond to a long list of open-ended questions about the situation, the project, their involvement, the leadership actions, and the outcomes. Responses to this "personal bests" study helped the authors to build a new instrument, the **Leadership Practices Inventory.**

The Leadership Practices Inventory is a transformational leadership instrument; it specifically measures the conceptual framework developed in the case studies of managers' personal-best experiences as leaders. The context was the accomplishment of extraordinary things. The original interviews and questionnaire focused on five factors:

1. Challenging the process (search for opportunities, experiment, take risks).
2. Inspiring a shared vision (envision the future, enlist others).
3. Enabling others to act (foster collaboration, strengthen others).
4. Modeling the way (set the example, plan small wins).
5. Encouraging the heart (recognize contributions, celebrate accomplishments).

Both theories emphasize the notion that transformational and charismatic leaders transform and elevate the consciousness of their followers, thereby building a meaningful cohesive identity. As they do so, their own awareness is also transformed and elevated. One of the most important instruments through which charismatic and transformational leadership happen is **vision.** Visions can be understood to be fundamental mythic-like stories that create meaning out of chaos. By articulating a vision, charismatic and transformational leaders' reformulate both their own worldview and their followers' worldviews (see Module 4) so that a new meaning and a new collective mission emerge. Charismatic and transformational leaders have to be very good storytellers and communicators, with high verbal abilities, because the stories they tell must be convincing.[61] They also need to have an intimate knowledge of their followers and their culture (organizational and national) so that the vision they articulate is compatible with them, yet more meaningful and motivating.

This perspective is consistent with the follower-centric perspective on leadership, which emphasizes the need for leaders to be good actors and engage in symbolic actions. Nonetheless, it differs from it because it assumes that symbolic actions have a real and powerful effect on followers, and through them on the bottom line. It is consistent with the leader-centric perspective because certain traits, such as high emotional intelligence, authenticity, and dramaturgical and verbal abilities, help leaders be charismatic and transformational. Yet, it does not assume that leadership resides in these traits, but rather in a process. Finally, this perspective is consistent with the interactional perspective on leadership because it considers that the effect of a vision is dependent upon the worldview of followers. Nonetheless, the charismatic and transformational leadership theories are reminiscent of the early theories of leadership that sought to identify a one best way to lead regardless of the situation. Curiously, these theories have not incorporated the body of research on leadership style, maybe because this body of research referred more to management than leadership.[62]

Summary of Leadership Schools of Thought

Thus far, this section has focused on the unique insights provided by scholars who have investigated leadership and its dynamics from different perspectives. While some perspectives contradict others, they each provide a useful lens through which to make sense of leadership. The leader-centric perspective emphasizes the personal qualities, traits, and behaviors that are most commonly found in leaders. The follower-centric perspective injects a needed dose of suspicion with regards to leaders who exaggerate their power, and recognizes the fact that leadership often equates to acting. The situational perspective provides a more nuanced approach by recognizing the moderating effect of the situation and followers on the phenomenon of leadership. Within this perspective, the theories of charismatic and transformational leadership provide perhaps the most complex and complete picture of leadership as it differs from management.

RECENT THEMES

Emotional Intelligence and Primal Leadership

If you are an astute observer of human behavior, you will probably notice the degree to which subordinates "psych-out" the moods of their bosses. When they have bad news, want a raise, or have a major problem to be solved, they will be paying attention to the boss's current psychological state. The more moody or psychologically distant the boss's personality, the more likely subordinates will try to create "work-a-rounds" and/or avoid letting the boss know altogether (frequently referred to as "blindsiding"). The question arises as to the role of emotionality in leadership and what part if any emotions play in the quality and effectiveness of leaders.

There is currently a body of research that has emerged as a result of a model of **emotional intelligence** (EI) as distinct from intelligence quotient (IQ), first proposed by Peter Salovey and John Mayer.[63] EI is defined as the ability of individuals to be aware of their own feelings and the feelings of others. Salovey and Mayer expand these abilities to five domains: knowing one's emotions, managing one's emotions, motivating oneself, recognizing emotions in others, and managing relationships with others.[64] Daniel Goleman popularized EI in 1995 and defined it as the ability of an individual to know one's emotions, manage them, motivate one's self, recognize emotions in others, and manage relationships with others.[65,66] (See Module 4.)

Goleman's basic argument is that "primal leadership" operates at its best through emotionally intelligent leaders who create resonance. "Quite simply, in any group the leader has maximal power to sway everyone's emotions. If people's emotions are pushed toward the range of enthusiasm, performance can soar; if people are driven toward rancor and anxiety, they will be thrown off stride."[67] John Kotter states, "When you start to think in terms of networks and dependence and leadership, not just hierarchy and formal authority and management, all sorts of interesting implications follow."[68] Traditional, role-based formal authority is less a part of today's organization reality. With its matrixed organizations, organizational imperatives to work across boundaries, and a more egalitarian work setting, today's leaders need to pay attention to their EI.

The emerging school of thought that centers on emotional intelligence argues that EI is a core variable that affects the performance of leaders. A recent study demonstrated empirically that the EI of leaders affected the quality of the interaction between leaders and followers as well as the performance and attitudes of the followers.[69] Emotional intelligence can be learned, but not by just reading a book. To truly understand one's own emotional intelligence, you have to be open to feedback about your behavior. Depending on your awareness of your "gut sense" of how others are perceiving you on an affective level, some major work on understanding your emotions and how they play out is basic. Tools such as videotaping role plays, assessment center activities, and feedback from coaches and multirater feedback instruments are highly beneficial. Courses such as this one provide the opportunity to observe small-group interaction and to validate your perceptions against the perceptions of others.

Leadership Development

If leaders are not born but rather are a product of their development with some assistance from nature, then what can be done to develop our future leaders? The *Personnel Journal* reported on a 1991 survey conducted by the American Society for Training and Development (ASTD) that 60 percent of all major companies offer leadership training. Of the companies offering leadership training, 93 percent offer it to middle management, 66 percent to top management, 48 percent to executives, 79 percent to supervisors, and 33 percent to nonsupervisors.[70] While the cost of such training is not available, the data suggest that leadership training represents a growing proportion of the more than $45.5 billion spent annually on training in the United States. In addition to numerous in-house programs offered by corporations, *Fortune* magazine reports that more than 600 firms are competing to provide leadership training to individuals and corporations.[71] Jay Conger asserts that leadership can be taught. "But to be successful, training must be designed to (1) develop and refine certain of the teachable skills; (2) improve the conceptual abilities of managers; (3) tap individuals' personal needs, interests, and self-esteem; and (4) help managers see and move beyond their interpersonal blocks."[72] Conger identifies four categories of leadership training: personal growth, conceptual understanding, feedback, and skill building:

Personal growth experiences tap the needs and interests of the participant to build self-esteem and are linked to the leader's own motivation to lead and formulate a vision.

Examples of personal growth experiences include Outward Bound, ropes courses, National Training Labs—Management Workshop, EST, and Lifespring. We address the area of personal growth in more depth in a later module.

Conceptual understanding consists of theory and research designed to give the potential leader a framework for cognitive development. Examples include the Tom Peters Group Leadership Challenge; Covey Leadership Principle-Centered Power and Leadership Seminars; and executive leadership programs at graduate business schools such as Harvard, Wharton, Stanford, and INSEAD.

Feedback approaches focus on a variety of data generated by psychometrics such as Myers–Briggs Type Indicator, Fundamental Interpersonal Relationship Orientation (Firo-B), Leadership Style Indicator (a 360-degree feedback instrument), and the California Psychological Inventory. These approaches also use exercises designed to elicit behavior for videotaping and feedback by skilled observers. The Center for Creative Leadership's Leader Lab and National Training Labs's Leadership Excellence programs are examples of feedback-driven leadership development programs.

Skill-building program designers identify key leadership skills that they believe can be taught. An example is the Forum Company's program, which includes interpreting the environment, shaping a vision, and mobilizing employees to reach that vision.

As more corporations are investing in leadership training programs, the need to scientifically assess their effectiveness is growing. Some skepticism is echoed by Conger, who made the following statement: "I believe that radical changes will ultimately have to occur in both content and the process of leadership training if corporations of the future are to ensure an adequate supply of leaders for themselves."[73] The question for students contemplating their own leadership development, if leadership is a choice and leadership skills can be learned—"What can and must I do to develop my potential?"

Learning Leadership from Experience and Authentic Leadership Development

Recently, Bruce Avolio, recognizing that leadership research had provided very little insight into leadership development, articulated a new theory: authentic leadership development (ALD).[74] This theory argues that managers can become leaders by becoming more authentic. They argue that by being authentic, leaders further their followers' authenticity, which has a host of positive organizational outcomes. Authenticity is the quality of a person whose actions and declarations are congruent with his or her inner thoughts and feelings. For leaders to become more authentic, they need to deepen their self-awareness by exploring their autobiography, returning to their roots, avoiding their comfort zones, and getting honest feedback.[75]

But above all, authenticity develops in certain individuals, as they overcome adversity and mature. Warren Bennis, in his book *On Becoming a Leader,* describes a journey toward self-discovery and understanding that comes through experience and not the classroom or workshop. Bennis's work is based on the following premise: "Leaders are people who are able to express themselves fully. They know who they are, what their strengths and weaknesses are, and how to fully deploy their strengths and compensate for their weaknesses."[76] While Bennis arrives at his position through interviews with leaders and observation, research conducted by the Center for Creative Leadership gives strong empirical evidence to support Bennis's position. In research conducted since 1981 and through continuous refinement of that research, the Center has examined key elements in the development of leaders and those factors that have led to the failure (or derailment) of similarly capable managers.[77-79] Results of that research appear in Figure 8–4. Note that the most significant developmental experience for both men and women came from job assignments.

The research findings raise the following questions for those seeking to be leaders: How do we learn the right things from experience, and how do we get the right experiences? The research community has provided a whole new generation of psychometrics to measure on-the-job development called **360-degree leadership feedback.**

Figure 8–4
Key Events in Executive Development

		Men	Women
I.	Challenging assignments	48%	32%
	a. Line to staff	2.1	1
	b. Projects/task forces	12.4	7
	c. Scope	17	9
	d. Fix-it	11	6
	e. Scratch	5.6	6
II.	Significant other people	17	23
	a. Values playing out	9.7	14
	b. Role models	7.4	9
III.	Hardships	18	28
	a. Failures and mistakes	4	9
	b. Demotions, missed promotions, lousy job	5	5
	c. Breaking a rut	4	4
	d. Personal trauma	2	3
	e. Employee problems	4	7
IV.	Other events	17	16
	a. Course work	6	1
	b. First supervision	4.9	6
	c. Early work	3.3	7
	d. Purely personal	2.6	2

Sources: E. H. Lindsey, V. Homes, and M. W. McCall, Jr., *Key Events in Executives' Lives* (Greensboro, NC: Center for Creative Leadership, 1987); M. W. McCall, Jr., M. M. Lombardo, and A. M. Morrison, *The Lessons of Experience: How Successful Executives Develop on the Job* (New York: Lexington Books, 1988); and A. M. Morrison, R. P. White, and E. Van Velsor, *Breaking the Glass Ceiling: Can Women Reach the Top of America's Largest Corporations?* (Menlo Park, CA: Addison-Wesley, 1992).

These instruments invite the individual, his or her bosses, peers, and subordinates to rate leadership skills based on a specific theory (Hersey and Blanchard's LBO-II), a model of leadership (Carlson Learning Corporation's Dimensions of Leadership Profile), or research findings (the Center for Creative Leadership's Benchmarks). All of these approaches seek to accentuate leadership strengths; some seek to mitigate potential weakness leading to derailment. The trend is to bring the work of assessment centers to the job. Current research now begins to focus on how to discover the developmental opportunities in your current job and stake out learning opportunities without ever having to leave the work site.[80] The answer to Conger's plea for further development of leadership training may be unfolding in what is euphemistically referred to as the *school of hard knocks.*

The work of the Center for Creative Leadership has focused on those factors that positively or adversely affect leadership in the work setting. These factors do not rely on innate traits but rather on factors that can be learned from experience. These skills and perspectives really matter in a career. The Center's review of 360-degree feedback instruments revealed that almost all of these psychometrics measure observable workplace behaviors. The factors described in the Benchmark section of the publication *Feedback to Managers* are the basis for developmental leadership continuums.[81]

The Leadership Ladder

When we look back on what has been presented so far about leadership development, we need to look at one other dimension of the journey of development for the emerging leader.

The climb from individual contributor to supervisor on to manager and finally to senior executive does not build in a linear fashion. We need to understand the leadership challenges of each step in the progression. Personnel Decisions International (PDI), in their family of Profiler 360-Degree Feedback Instruments, asserts that there are some core role behaviors or competencies at each step of the promotional **leadership ladder.** It is the degree of complexity and how they deploy that separates each step.[82]

In today's organizations, the *individual contributor* is valued because of his or her content knowledge and skills (for example, engineer or accountant); because of teams in matrix and project organizations, leadership must emerge from the individual contributor, and this leadership is more about the ability to laterally influence others than about positional power. Completing a task requires individuals to stretch beyond traditional roles and show real initiative. In many organizations, this is the first audition for future leadership assignments and requires the development of political savvy, something that few business schools teach. The role of a mentor or internal coach cannot be underestimated in the successful adaptation to these changing circumstances.

The job of *supervisor* is something that usually comes as a reward to the highly skilled and productive individual contributor. The new supervisor usually continues many of the tasks of the individual contributor while becoming accountable for the performance of their reports (that is, subordinates). As a peer, the behavior of others at the same level may have been amusing, entertaining, or, at worst, a minor source of annoyance. In the role of supervisor, these behaviors become a challenge to productivity, quality, and supervisory achievement. In addition, power is still limited; weapons, such as employee discipline or transfer, have a human resources entourage attached to them and restrictions akin to deadly force. Leadership becomes a means of rallying effort, aligning resources, and ensuring the quality that delivers bottom-line results. "Oh-by-the-way," supervisors also have to complete their own work. This course is the one tool that graduates of business schools start to remember in the midst of this crucible of development.

The promotion to *manager* brings prestige, compensation, and responsibilities; for many, this position becomes the pinnacle of their career and they plateau at this level. The manager usually leads many others whose skills, knowledge, and abilities are an unknown to him or her. Individual technical competence on the part of the manager has long since become obsolete. Plus, there are now many more areas of expertise than one individual can master. The good news is that the manager has the guidance of policy and strategy developed by the executive group to create a context for leadership. The skills developed as a supervisor and team member become the source for motivating, challenging, supporting, and growing his or her people. Results can be typically measured against organizational benchmarks, and, for many managers, the results of their collective efforts are usually visible in the shipping department. Technical skills in finance, accounting, human resources, production management, marketing, communications, and organizational behavior become more compelling than the skill set that started his or her career.

Most new *executives* reached this role based on past performance. With the exception of leadership skills, though, such past performance may not be relevant for anything more than "credibility with the troops." The new assignment requires that the executive lead by creating a vision of the future and by establishing the context of that vision for those beneath them on the ladder. This vision and its supporting context must be so compelling as to not be diluted through organizational ranks and must also be powerful enough to foster alignment and execution. Tenures of senior executives appear to be on the decline. One 2002 report states that CEO life spans are down from three years in 1999 to two years in 2002.[83] The role of mutual fund and pension fund analysts and the public outrage over executive conduct at Enron and WorldCom make financial performance, ethics, and accountability today's watchwords and the grist of executive nightmares.

As a student of organizational behavior, the relevance of this course—not as a lexicon of answers, but as a tool for ongoing learning and analysis—becomes painfully apparent. Each new role requires a fresh perspective furnished from the demands of the assignment and the current state of the art in leadership. The rate of learning in most mature industries is exponential; as technology becomes more mature, the growth of human capital and knowledge creation becomes the primary competitive advantage.

LEADERSHIP AND THE DEVELOPMENT OF YOUR CLASS TEAM

If you are assigned to a permanent class team, you have an excellent opportunity to practice leadership skills. You are presumably working in a "leaderless" group, since the instructor has not designated a formal leader. Leadership functions are still needed if the group is to carry out meaningful problem solving and perform various tasks. It may prove worthwhile to scan the list of roles typically assumed by members during the life of a small group. The module on small-group dynamics covers these roles, indicating the task- and relationship-oriented behaviors needed for successful performance. Take time in your next group meeting to discuss these roles and the value of having a facilitator, recorder, and spokesperson. Some groups find it valuable to rotate these responsibilities so that all members can practice different leadership behaviors. Other groups recognize leadership skills in certain members, and the leadership positions are informally assumed early in the course.

SUMMARY

Is leadership a trait or characteristic of a person? Is it an illusion born from the need for people to simplify reality? Is it an interpersonal process between leaders and their followers? As we saw in this module, the answer to these questions is YES! Leadership appears to be a multiperspective phenomenon.[84] A review of these multiple perspectives revealed that although they are very different and sometimes contradictory, taken together they contribute to our holistic understanding of leaders and leadership dynamics. The leader-centric perspective focused our attention on the specific individual skills that are likely to predict leadership effectiveness. The follower-centric perspective emphasized the notion that leaders are actors who influence followers to believe that they have more power than they actually do. The interactional perspective focused on the contextual elements that can influence the leader's performance. Within this perspective, the charismatic and transformational theories of leadership have emphasized the process of leadership, and the importance of leadership visions. Recent research on leadership training and the value of work experience on shaping or derailing leaders were explored. Finally, the challenges of the "corporate ladder" support the need for continuous development and learning as an emerging leader.

Study Questions

1. Describe your own mental model of leadership.
2. What is the difference between leadership and management? Would you apply this characteristic to all levels of management? Give reasons for your answer.
3. Are managers born or made? The argument around this question has raged for many years. Many executives will say, "You've either got it or you haven't." What are the arguments on both sides? What do you believe?
4. In what way can leadership be regarded as a process? How does this apply to your team activities?
5. Compare and contrast the leader-centric, follower-centric, and interactional perspectives on leadership.
6. How do charismatic and transformational leaders influence their followers?
7. How does emotional intelligence help leaders be more effective?
8. How can leaders become more authentic?

9. Why is there a disconnect between executive and midlevel management development?

10. Describe the leadership dynamics within your team. How would you characterize the team? How effective is it? What can you experiment with to improve your team performance?

Endnotes

1. H. Mintzberg, *Mintzberg on Management: Inside Our Strange World of Organizations* (New York: Free Press, 1989).

2. B. M. Bass, *Bass and Stogdill's Handbook of Leadership: A Survey of Theory and Research* (New York: Free Press, 1990).

3. R. J. House, and R. N. Adiya, "The Social Scientific Study of Leadership: Quo Vadis?" *Journal of Management* 23, no. 3 (1997), pp. 409–73.

4. R. M. Stogdill, *Handbook of Leadership: A Survey of the Literature* (New York: Free Press, 1974).

5. Bass, *Bass and Stogdill's Handbook of Leadership*.

6. G. Yukl, "Managerial Leadership: A Review of Theory and Research," *Journal of Management* 15, no. 2 (1989), pp. 251–89.

7. G. A. Yukl, *Leadership in Organizations* 4 (Englewood Cliffs, NJ: Prentice Hall, 2001).

8. R. L. Hughes, R. C. Ginnette, and G. J. Curphy, *Leadership Enhancing the Lessons of Leadership* (Boston: McGraw-Hill, 2002).

9. P. G. Northouse, *Leadership: Theory and Practice* (Thousand Oaks, CA: Sage Publications, 1997).

10. B. M. Bass, *Transforming Leadership* (New York: Lea Publishers, 1998).

11. H. Mintzberg, "The Manager's Job—Folklore and Fact," *Harvard Business Review* 53, no. 4 (1975), p. 49.

12. A. Zaleznik, "Managers and Leaders: Are They Different?" *Harvard Business Review* 55 (1977), pp. 67–78.

13. A. Zaleznik, "The Leadership Gap," *Academy of Management Review* 4, no. 1 (1990).

14. J. P. Kotter, *The Leadership Factor* (New York: Free Press, 1987).

15. W. G. Bennis, *On Becoming a Leader* (Menlo Park, CA: Addison-Wesley, 1998).

16. K. E. Clark and M. B. Clark, *Choosing to Lead* (Greensboro, NC: Center for Creative Leadership, 1996).

17. Ibid.

18. M. Weber, *On Charisma and Institution Building: Selected Papers* (Chicago: University of Chicago Press, 1968).

19. S. A. Kirkpatrick and E. A. Locke, "Leadership: Do Traits Matter?" *Academy of Management Executive* 5, no. 2 (1991), pp. 48–60.

20. Bass, *Bass and Stogdill's Handbook of Leadership*.

21. R. Hogan, G. J. Curphy, and J. Hogan, "What We Know about Leadership," *American Psychologist* 49, no. 6 (1994), pp. 493–504.

22. Ibid.

23. Ibid.

24. R. M. Stogdill, "Personal Factors Associated with Leadership: A Survey of the Literature," *Journal of Psychology* 25 (1948), pp. 35–71.

25. B. F. Skinner, *About Behaviorism* (New York: Vintage Books, 1976), p. 291.

26. J. A. Conger and R. N. Kanungo, "Training Charismatic Leadership: A Risky and Critical Task," in *Charismatic Leadership: The Elusive Factor in Organizational Effectiveness* (Jossey Bass: San Francisco, 1988), pp. 309–23.

27. J. A. Conger and R. N. Kanungo, "Behavioral Dimensions of Charismatic Leadership," in *Charismatic Leadership: The Elusive Factor in Organizational Effectiveness* (Jossey Bass: San Francisco, 1998), pp. 78–97.

28. E. A. Fleishman, "The Description of Supervisory Behavior," *Journal of Applied Psychology* 37, no. 1 (1953), pp. 1–6.

29. R. Tannenbaum and W. H. Schmidt, *How to Choose a Leadership Pattern* 12 (Boston: Harvard Business Review, 1973).

30. K. Lewin and R. Lippitt, "An Experimental Approach to the Study of Autocracy and Democracy: A Preliminary Note," *Sociometry* 1 (1938).

31. K. Lewin, R. Lippitt, and R. K. White, "Patterns of Aggressive Behavior in Experimentally Created 'Social Climates,'" *Journal of Social Psychology* 10 (1939).

32. Bass, *Bass and Stogdill's Handbook of Leadership.*

33. J. Gastil, "A Definition and Illustration of Democratic Leadership," *Human Relations* 47, no. 8 (1994).

34. J. Gastil, "A Meta-Analytic Review of the Productivity and Satisfaction of Democratic and Autocratic Leadership," *Small Group Research* 25, no. 3 (1994).

35. F. E. Fiedler, *A Theory of Leadership Effectiveness* (New York: McGraw-Hill, 1967), viii, p. 310.

36. J. Pfeffer, "The Ambiguity of Leadership," *Academy of Management Review* (January 1977).

37. R. H. Hall, *Organizations: Structure and Process* (Prentice-Hall, 1974).

38. S. Lieberson and J. F. O'Connor, "Leadership and Organizational Performance: A Study of Large Corporations," *American Sociological Review* 37, no. 2 (1972), pp. 117–30.

39. H. H. Kelley, *Attribution in Social Interaction* (Morristown, NJ: General Learning Press, 1971).

40. S. E. Taylor and S. T. Fiske, "Salience, Attention, and Attribution: Top of the Head Phenomena," *Advances in Experimental Social Psychology* 11 (1978), pp. 249–88.

41. J. Pfeffer, "Management as Symbolic Action," *Research in Organizational Behavior* 3, no. S1, (1981), p. 52.

42. A. B. Thomas, "Does Leadership Make a Difference to Organizational Performance?" *Administrative Science Quarterly* 33, no. 3 (1988), pp. 388–400.

43. F. E. Fiedler, "Engineering the Job to Fit the Manager," *Harvard Business Review* 43, no. 5 (1965), pp. 115–22.

44. P. Hersey, K. H. Blanchard, and D. E. Johnson, *Management of Organizational Behavior: Utilizing Human Resources,* 7th ed. (Upper Saddle River, NJ: Prentice Hall, 1996), xxv, p. 627.

45. R. Singh, "Leadership Style and Reward Allocation: Does Least Preferred Co-Worker Scale Measure Task and Relation Orientation?" *Organizational Behavior and Human Performance* 32, no. 2 (1983), pp. 178–97.

46. C. A. Schriesheim, B. J. Tepper, and L. A. Tetrault, "Least Preferred Co-Worker Score, Situational Control, and Leadership Effectiveness: A Meta-Analysis of Contingency Model Performance Predictions," *Journal of Applied Psychology* 79, no. 4 (1994), p. 561–73.

47. Hersey, Blanchard, and Johnson, *Management of Organizational Behavior.*

48. Ibid.

49. Ibid.

50. Ibid.

51. J. M. Phillips, "Leadership Since 1975: Advancement or Inertia?" *The Journal of Leadership Studies,* 2 (1995), pp. 58–80.

52. R. J. House, "A Path-Goal Theory of Leader Effectiveness," *Administrative Science Quarterly* 16 (1971), pp. 321–28.

53. J. Indvik, "Path-Goal Theory of Leadership: A Meta-Analysis," *Proceedings of the Academy of Management Meeting* (1986), pp. 189–92.

54. R. J. House et al., "Cultural Influences on Leadership and Organizations: Project GLOBE," *Advances in Global Leadership* 1 (1999), pp. 171–233.

55. N. J. Adler, *International Dimensions of Organizational Behavior* (Belmont, CA: Wadsworth, 2002).

56. J. A. Conger, "Charismatic and Transformational Leadership in Organizations: An Insider's Perspective on these Developing Perspectives," *Leadership Quarterly* 10, no. 2, (1999), pp. 145–79.

57. J. A. Conger and R. N. Kanungo, "Toward a Behavioral Theory of Charismatic Leadership in Organizational Settings," *The Academy of Management Review* 12, no. 4, (1987), p. 637.

58. J. M. Burns, *Leadership* (New York: Harper & Row, 1978).

59. B. Shamir, R. J. House, and M. B. Arthur, "The Motivational Effects of Charisma: A Self-Concept Based Theory," *Organizational Science* 4 (1993), pp. 577–94.

60. B. M. Bass, *Leadership and Performance Beyond Expectations* (New York: The Free Press, 1985).

61. W. L. Gardner and B. J. Avolio, "The Charismatic Relationship: A Dramaturgical Perspective," *The Academy of Management Review* 23, no. 1 (1998), pp. 32–58.

62. Conger, "Charismatic and Transformational Leadership in Organizations."

63. P. Salovey and J. D. Mayer, "Emotional Intelligence," *Imagination, Cognition and Personality* 9, no. 3 (1990), pp. 185–211.

64. Ibid.

65. Ibid.

66. D. Goleman, *Emotional Intelligence* (New York: Bantam Books, 1995).

67. D. Goleman, R. E. Boyatzis, and A. McKee, *Primal Leadership: Realizing the Power of Emotional Intelligence* (Boston: Harvard Business School Press, 2002), xvii, p. 306.

68. J. P. Kotter, *What Leaders Really Do* (Boston: Harvard Business School Press, 1980).

69. C.-S. Wong and K. S. Law, "The Effect of Leader and Follower Emotional Intelligence on Performance and Attitude: An Exploratory Study," *The Leadership Quarterly* 13 (2002), pp. 243–74.

70. D. Gunsch, "For Your Information—Learning Leadership," *Personnel Journal* 78 (1991), p. 8.

71. J. Huey, "The Leadership Industry," *Fortune* 21 (1994), pp. 54–6.

72. J. A. Conger, *Learning to Lead: The Art of Transforming Managers into Leaders* (San Francisco: Jossey-Bass, 1992).

73. Ibid.

74. B. J. Avolio and W. L. Gardner, "Authentic Leadership Development: Getting to the Root of Positive Forms of Leadership," *Leadership Quarterly* 16, no. 3 (2005), pp. 315–38.

75. R. Goffee and G. Jones, "Managing Authenticity: The Paradox of Great Leadership," *Harvard Business Review* 83, no. 12 (2005), pp. 86–94.

76. Bennis, *On Becoming a Leader.*

77. E. H. Lindsey, V. Homes, and M. W. McCall, *Key Events in Executives' Lives* (Greensboro: Center for Creative Leadership, 1987).

78. M. W. McCall, M. M. Lombardo, and A. M. Morrison, *The Lessons of Experience: How Successful Executives Develop on the Job?* (New York: Lexington Books, 1988).

79. A. M. Morrison, R. P. White, and E. Van Velsor, *Breaking the Glass Ceiling: Can Women Reach the Top of America's Largest Corporations?* (Menlo Park, CA: Addison-Wesley, 1992).

80. C. D. McCauley et al., "Assessing the Developmental Components of Managerial Jobs," *Journal of Applied Psychology* 79, no. 4 (1994), pp. 544–60.

81. E. Van Velsor and J. B. Leslie, *Feedback to Managers,* vols. 1 and 2: *A Review and Comparison of Sixteen Multi-Rater Feedback Instruments* (Greensboro, NC: Center for Creative Leadership, 1991).

82. B. L. Davis et al., *Successful Manager's Handbook—Development Suggestions for Today's Managers* (MN: Personnel Decisions, 2000).

83. S. Critchley, *CEO Turnover and Job Security: A Special Report* (Drake Beam Morrin, 2000).

84. F. J. Yammarino, F. Dansereau, and C. J. Kennedy, "A Multiple-Level Multidimensional Approach to Leadership: Viewing Leadership through an Elephant's Eye," *Organizational Dynamics* 29, no. 3 (2001), pp. 149–63.

**Activity 8–2:
Diagnosing Leadership
Behavior**

Objectives:

a. To examine a behavioral model of leadership.

b. To provide students with an opportunity to evaluate a past boss's leadership behavior.

c. To demonstrate that sound leadership behavior varies with the organizational situation.

Task 1 (Homework):

a. As a homework assignment, complete the Leadership Questionnaire by rating the behavior of a past immediate supervisor.

b. Use the scoring key below to determine high, moderate, and low ratings on each of the five University of Michigan dimensions. Be prepared to discuss the scores and their meaning to the class team.

Enter information and scores below:

Boss rated _____

Type of business _____

Description of the work situation _____

_____

_____

_____   a. *Leadership support.* Behavior that enhances employee feelings of self-worth and importance.

_____   b. *Team facilitation.* Behavior that encourages members of the group to develop close, mutually satisfying relationships.

_____   c. *Work facilitation.* Activities that help achieve goal attainment by doing things such as scheduling; coordinating; planning; and providing resources such as tools, material, and technical advice and knowledge.

_____   d. *Goal emphasis.* Behavior that stimulates an enthusiasm for meeting the group's goals, helps establish priorities, and promotes achievement of excellent performance.

_____   e. *Upward influence.* Behaviors that advance the status of the work group and individuals (for example, acquiring resources needed by the group, securing rewards for group members, and eliminating barriers raised by other organizational units).

Task 2:

a. Meet with your class team. Let each team member describe the work situation and his or her ratings of the leader, without interruption except for clarifying questions. Move around the group until everyone has participated. (Time: 20 minutes)

b. Discuss the following questions:

 * Do the dimensions cover all the behaviors that you believe are important for a leader in your situation?

 * What dimensions would you add that would more fully describe the leader's actions?

 * Which of the dimensions seem to be most relevant? Least relevant? Why?

 * What features of the situation caused the leader to behave the way she or he did?

 * Does job success require the leader to behave in this fashion?

 * How would you use such an instrument in your own organization? What steps would you follow?
   (Time: 10 minutes)

Name _____ Date _____

LEADERSHIP QUESTIONNAIRE*

Instructions:

This short questionnaire on leadership behaviors is based on the University of Michigan model. Identify a current or past manager who was your immediate supervisor. Circle the best choice from the options provided.

1. My supervisor is eager to recognize and reward good performance.

   a. strongly disagree   *d.* agree

   b. disagree   *e.* strongly agree

   c. not sure

2. To what extent does your supervisor encourage you to think and act for yourself?

   a. not at all   *d.* to a great extent

   b. to a small extent   e. to a very great extent

   c. to some extent

3. Generally, decisions are arrived at by my immediate supervisor with no input from people at lower levels.

   a. strongly agree   *d.* disagree

   b. agree   *e.* strongly disagree

   c. not sure

4. My immediate supervisor is usually successful in dealing with higher levels of authority.

   a. strongly agree   *d.* disagree

   b. agree   *e.* strongly disagree

   c. not sure

5. To what extent does your supervisor stress the importance of work goals?

   a. not at all   *d.* to a great extent

   b. to a small extent   *e.* to a very great extent

   c. to some extent

6. My supervisor is friendly and easy to talk to.

   a. strongly agree   *d.* disagree

   b. agree   *e.* strongly disagree

   c. not sure

7. To what extent does your supervisor offer new ideas for job-related problems?

   a. not at all   *d.* to a great extent

   b. to a small extent   *e.* to a very great extent

   c. to some extent

8. How often does your supervisor hold group meetings for his or her employees?

   a. never   *d.* rather often

   b. rarely   *e.* nearly all the time

   c. sometimes

9. My immediate supervisor is very successful in getting management to recognize the success of the employees he or she supervises.

   a. strongly disagree   *d.* agree

   b. disagree   *e.* strongly agree

   c. not sure

*This instrument is a major modification of a survey initially developed at the Institute of Social Research, University of Michigan, Ann Arbor, Michigan, which was discussed in D. G. Bowers and S. Seashore, "Predicting Organizational Effectiveness with a Four-Factor Theory of Leadership," *Administrative Science Quarterly* 11, (1966), pp. 238–63.

10. My supervisor encourages people to give their best efforts.

   a. strongly disagree   *d.* agree

   b. disagree   *e.* strongly agree

   c. not sure

11. To what extent is your supervisor attentive to what you say?

   a. not at all   *d.* to a great extent

   b. to a small extent   *e.* to a very great extent

   c. to some extent

12. To what extent does your supervisor provide the help you need to schedule your work ahead of time?

   a. not at all   *d.* to a great extent

   b. to a small extent   *e.* to a very great extent

   c. to some extent

13. To what extent does your supervisor encourage employees to exchange ideas and opinions?

   a. not at all   *d.* to a great extent

   b. to a small extent   *e.* to a very great extent

   c. to some extent

14. To what extent is your immediate supervisor successful in getting the best possible rewards for his or her employees (for example, merit raises, promotions, challenging work assignments)?

   a. to a very great extent   *d.* to a small extent

   b. to a great extent   *e.* not at all

   c. to some extent

15. To what extent does your supervisor emphasize high standards of performance?

   a. to a very great extent   *d.* to a small extent

   b. to a great extent   *e.* not at all

   c. to some extent

16. To what extent is your supervisor willing to listen to your problems?

   a. not at all   *d.* to a great extent

   b. to a small extent   *e.* to a very great extent

   c. to some extent

17. How would you describe the amount of responsibility delegated by your supervisor?

   a. none   *d.* a considerable amount

   b. a minimum amount   *e.* a maximum amount

   c. a moderate amount

18. To what extent does your supervisor encourage employees to work as a team?

   a. not at all   *d.* to a great extent

   b. to a small extent   *e.* to a very great extent

   c. to some extent

19. How often does your supervisor work with you to set specific goals?

   a. never   *d.* rather often

   b. rarely   *e.* nearly all the time

   c. sometimes

Use the score sheet on the next page to rate the five leadership behavioral dimensions.

SCORE SHEET FOR THE MICHIGAN-BASED LEADERSHIP QUESTIONNAIRE

Score Sheet

Scoring: Enter your answers for each item by circling the alphabetic choice in the scoring grid. Then enter the corresponding numeric score in the right-hand column.

Item #	1	2	3	4	5	
Leadership Support						
1	a	b	c	d	e	_____
6	e	d	c	b	a	_____
11	a	b	c	d	e	_____
16	a	b	c	d	e	_____
				A Total		
				A ÷ 4 =		
Team Facilitation						
3	a	b	c	d	e	_____
8	a	b	c	d	e	_____
13	a	b	c	d	e	_____
18	a	b	c	d	e	_____
				B Total		
				B ÷ 4 =		
Work Facilitation						
2	e	d	c	b	a	_____
7	a	b	c	d	e	_____
12	a	b	c	d	e	_____
17	a	b	c	d	e	_____
				C Total		
				C ÷ 4 =		
Goal Emphasis						
5	a	b	c	d	e	_____
10	a	b	c	d	e	_____
15	e	d	c	b	a	_____
19	a	b	c	d	e	_____
				D Total		
				D ÷ 4 =		
Upward Influence						
4	e	d	c	b	a	_____
9	a	b	c	d	e	_____
14	e	d	c	b	a	_____
				E Total		
				E ÷ 3 =		

Explanation: Total raw scores for each dimension are calculated by summing up scores for individual items. The scoring grid is required because several items are negatively worded. Simply total the raw scores from the right-hand column; then divide by the number of items (4 except for "upward influence") to produce summary scores for each leadership dimension.

Summary Scores

A   Leadership Support   _____

B   Team Facilitation   _____

C   Work Facilitation   _____

D   Goal Emphasis   _____

E   Upward Influence   _____

Your instructor will provide definitions and discuss the "upward influence" dimension.

Activity 8–3: Donny Is My Leader

Objectives:

a. To allow you to examine the leadership process.

b. To provide you and your team with an opportunity to investigate the leadership episode from different theoretical perspectives.

Task 1 (Individual Task):

Read the following case carefully and answer these questions:

a. Which characteristics describe Donny's leadership philosophy and style?

b. What are some of Donny's strengths and weaknesses as a leader? As a manager?

c. What are the likely consequences of Donny's leadership style? What effects does he have on the performance of individual team members (Choc, Herb, Harvey, Harry, Larry, David, Bruce, John, and Bradley)? What effects does he have on the overall performance of the team?

d. How did Donny's absence affect team dynamics?

e. If you were Donny, how would you lead the team? Why?

Task 2 (Class Discussion):

The instructor will lead a class discussion to capture the basic facts in the case.

Task 3 (Team Task):

Teams will examine the case from a specific theoretical perspective assigned by the instructor. Each team is to

■ Capture the essence of the assigned theoretical perspective.

■ Identify the major facts in the case as viewed by the assigned perspective.

■ Conduct the analysis of the facts from the assigned perspective.

■ Identify potential problems in the case.

■ Identify the most critical problem.

■ Provide some alternative solutions.

Task 4:

Each team will present its analysis and findings to the total learning community.

Donny Is My Leader*

The first day I joined the team, Donny asked me how far I was going to run. The team had a goal of running 2 miles every Monday, Wednesday, and Friday morning at a fairly fast pace—about 8 minutes a mile. That speed is not fast by any track club's standard, but it's fairly fast for 35- to 45-year-old occasional jocks. I said I'd try for a mile and a half, a distance I had occasionally managed to complete over the past several months of jogging by myself. I ran at the tail end of the team and did, in fact, run the mile and a half. We run on a small inside track at the Y, which has 18 laps to a mile. At the end of 27 laps, a mile and a half, Donny turned and shouted back to me from his place at the front of the group, "OK, Harvey, that's enough!" And I stopped.

When the others finished (some did the 2 miles, others dropped out at different distances—as little as a mile), Donny came over and congratulated me. He told me I'd run well. He suggested I try adding 3 more laps next

*This case was prepared by Professors Harvey F. Kolodny and Robert J. House of the faculty of management studies at the University of Toronto. All rights are reserved by the authors. We are grateful to Professors Kolodny and House for their permission to include the case in this textbook.

time, staying at that level for a while, and then add another 3 until I reached the team's 36-lap or 2-mile objective.

The "team" is a very informal collection of people with no formally appointed leader. Donny, however, is referred to as "the coach." The team has existed for a while with a small, hard core and with others who come and go. The regulars comprise Donny, who always runs on the right side of the pacer, who is almost always Choc, and Herb, who runs about fourth and takes over as a leader when Donny is away. Barrie generally runs third and sometimes sets the pace but is sort of an irregular regular, since he occasionally forsakes the groups for a squash game or gets in late after a hard night. Harry and Larry are two recent regulars. Larry always runs last, and Harry runs just ahead of me. Three or four others occasionally join us. On some mornings we are as few as four running. On other mornings there are nine running.

			Rail			
						Choc
Larry	Harvey	Harry		Herb	Barrie	Donny
			Wall			

My second day was a beautiful, warm morning, and we ran outside. I quit after a mile and a quarter. Harry quit after a mile. No one said anything to us—good or bad—about the running. My third day was my big mistake! I vowed to myself to run 1 mile and 12 laps, 3 better than my previous inside run. At the end of the 11th lap of the 2nd mile, I still had a little left in me, so I sprinted the last lap, passing everyone. I'd noticed that all the finishers usually sprinted for the last one or two laps. However, when he was done, Donny came over and severely castigated me. How could I possibly have sprinted? If I could sprint, I must have had some strength left in me and therefore I could have gone for several more laps; in fact, I might even have been able to finish the 2 miles. He verbally lashed out at me several times, both on the track and back down in the locker room. The others joined in, though in a more teasing mode. They said that the next time not only was I going to run the 2 miles but also would set the pace.

Soon after this occurrence Harry became the culprit—and the victim of Donny's wrath. We did each lap in about 28 seconds. Donny was the timekeeper. He shouted out the time for the first lap, and for the 1st mile he counted out every second lap each time we passed the starting point (where a wall clock was mounted). Donny constantly encouraged us to keep going. Herb and Larry did so, too. They called out milestones: "Three-quarters done!" or "Two-thirds done!" or "Five laps to go!" Near the end of the run, they kept up a steady stream of comments to urge those of us who were struggling to keep going and to try to finish the distance. On this particular day, at the end of the first lap Harry said, "Hey, we're going too fast! We did it in 20 seconds." It was a bad day. Quite a few of us didn't finish. Donny was angry. He took it out on Harry repeatedly. He said that Harry's statement was incorrect and, furthermore, had discouraged several of the team members, making them, including me, quit. He carried on all the way down to the locker room, in the showers, and even into the next running day.

An incident somewhat similar to my own experience occurred about 2 years after I joined the team. By this time we were all up to 3 miles a day. A fellow named David joined us on the track. He ran 2 miles at first, while we ran 3, but he soon got up to 2 1/2 miles. Then one day it looked as if he might be able to make the 3 miles, so Donny slowed down and ran with David for the remaining distance. At first Donny harangued David very loudly—you could hear Donny all around the track—for threatening to quit. Then as David came closer to completing the distance, Donny became gentle and encouraging until David made it. David was very excited, and we all congratulated him on his success.

The next time out David was having a hard time repeating the 3-mile distance, so Donny slowed down to urge him on and asked us all to encourage him. We all did, mostly by running slowly with him and talking it up, and David successfully completed the 3 miles that day.

However, on our next run it looked certain that David wouldn't make it. It was hot, and we were all dragging. Donny dropped back to help David along for the last 1/2 mile while the better runners sprinted ahead to complete the distance. I stayed back, running behind David. Donny told me to go ahead, that it was OK because he would take care of David. But I was exhausted and said that I would just continue running along behind him, slowly, because I just couldn't go any faster. We all finished together, and then David, to everyone's surprise, kept going and ran for several more laps. I was walking slowly with Donny, to settle down after the run, and he was livid. "What does David think he's doing?" Donny exclaimed. "I've got to teach that boy something!"

As David passed us on the track, Donny shouted out at him several times along the lines of "What do you think you're doing?" Then, when David stopped, Donny walked over and chewed off David's ear. "We are all here to run 3 miles," Donny said, "and if you have enough in you to go farther, then you should try and sprint with the others at the end. The goal is to make 3 miles with the rest of us if you can. Don't you understand? I dropped back and ran with you to help you through, and then you just kept running on. Next time, if you have something left in you, just sprint a little harder a little earlier." David apologized.

The Training of Troy

One morning Donny showed up with Troy, a rather corpulent young man. Troy was not a very good runner.

Donny said he would spend his time with Troy and not run alongside Choc, the pacer. The first morning, amid a lot of puffing, panting, and perspiring, Troy ran about six laps. Donny ran with him. After six laps he told Troy to stop running and just walk for a bit. Then Donny ran up alongside the rest of us, eventually taking his regular place at the head of the team.

Donny followed this routine for many mornings thereafter. Each morning he set increasingly difficult targets for Troy and mixed them up a bit, for example, "This morning you'll walk five laps after you've run, and then you'll run with us for four more." Then Donny would run ahead to join us after running alongside Troy at a slightly slower pace for the first few laps. After a while we got used to the idea of Donny being all over the track: sometimes behind us, encouraging Troy; sometimes ahead of us, pacing alongside of Choc. Within a month Troy was up to a mile and was running with the rest of us.

Weigh-In

Once a month Donny had us weigh in. At that time we set our objectives for how much weight we would lose by the next weigh-in. The successful ones were not pressed.

The next running day after the weigh-in, there was a great ceremony. Herb received a jersey on which was printed "Doctor D's Track Team." Choc had had them made up and kept them in his locker, waiting for the appropriate occasion to hand one out. Herb was the only recipient. He not only had consistently run the distance but also had made his weight target. Donny let us all know that he wasn't going to be generous about giving out the other jerseys—even though they were all ready and printed. Only consistent demonstrations of performance across several fronts would merit a Doctor D's Track Team jersey.

The Breaking of Bruce

Bruce was a bit younger than most of us, in his late 20s. He had been running with us and had been mocking Donny a bit about how slow he ran. One morning Bruce set out in the first lap, passed Donny and Choc and the others, and finished well ahead of everyone. Donny castigated Bruce for setting so severe a pace that he could not possibly maintain it consistently, even if he had done so on that particular day. Well, that was the beginning of quite a situation. Next time out Donny, Bruce, and John (who joined us occasionally) were all running well ahead of the rest of us and lapping us once or twice in the process. John runs well and quickly. Donny had set the pattern for his running by telling him before we started how to pace him, how often to lap us, and so on. Donny stayed with John most of the way, but not all the way all the time. Bruce ran ahead, too. However, he appeared to listen less to Donny's advice, in fact, not to take it at all. At first Bruce was going great guns. He would lap us two and even three times, finishing the 2 miles in as little as

14 1/2 minutes. However, Bruce was running without Donny's help; John, in contrast, was getting better but under Donny's tutelage. Soon John was outperforming Bruce, and Bruce was, in fact, slowing down. He was soon back to running with the team. Donny challenged him almost every day about his pace and pattern of running. Soon he was running regularly with the whole team and then even a little behind the team. I know, because he would run just ahead of me, and I was one of the slower runners.

Donny would harass Bruce quite a bit in the locker room by telling him that he wouldn't last and by telling some of Bruce's buddies, who were also there in the morning but didn't run with us, that they would have to do something about the poor boy because he was getting beyond himself. The criticism appeared to have a significant effect on Bruce, because he kept slowing down, and then one very hot, muggy day near the end of June, when many in the group ran poorly and quit after a mile, Bruce pulled up short of a mile. Donny was sort of gloating in the locker room afterwards. He told everyone, particularly Bruce's buddies, quietly of course, what happened. He told them they would have to get the poor boy's morale up again. He said to me, coming out of the showers, "Well, we broke him, psychologically. Now we'll have to build him up again."

About a year later I asked Donny why he had broken Bruce. He didn't respond immediately, but later, while we were running, he shouted back to me, "I have an answer to your question." And he answered with a question: "Why does a parent discipline a child?"

Emergent Leadership

On a Friday not too long after I joined the team, Donny was absent. Herb took over as leader that day. He asked us each how far we planned to run and assured us that we would run slow enough for everyone to finish. He stressed this goal repeatedly. And we all made it, including two members, and I was one of them, who had never been able to do 2 miles before. Everyone felt great, and we made some joking remarks about how we had to make Herb our new leader.

Herb left for a short holiday that weekend, and Donny reappeared to lead us on the next running day, a Monday. It was a tough run. Several of us quit early, and Donny castigated everyone who quit, particularly Harry. Harry mentioned that he preferred running under Herb. The rest of the week was average, no great performances. Herb returned on the following Monday, and Donny, for the first time in years, failed to show up because he had slept in. Herb took charge, and we all ran the 2 miles again. I looked forward with anxious anticipation to Wednesday, when both Donny and Herb would be there together.

Wednesday turned out to be a strange running day. It happened this way: Donny took the right lead position beside Choc, and Herb was two positions back. After less than a mile, Choc faltered badly and began to slow down. Barrie, running behind, took over as pacer. But as Choc fell back, Herb fell back and kept pace with Choc. Harry, Larry, and I stayed behind. Meanwhile Donny and three others in front moved ahead, and as they continued a normal pace and we kept slowing down, the gap between us widened. We were now two separate groups. Those of us behind Choc and Herb, who were still running side by side, didn't know what to make of it. We muttered about getting farther behind but made no specific effort to pass Choc and Herb and catch up to the front group. Donny kept turning and shouting over his shoulder at all of us to move up, gesturing constantly with his arm and looking very worried about what was happening. In the meantime the gap grew wider.

Then Donny did something unusual. Leaving the front group to fend for itself, he dropped all the way back to our subgroup and urged us to keep running ahead. He commenced with Herb, getting him to leave Choc's side and run ahead. Choc was slowing down more and more. Donny urged us all ahead of Choc, and soon we were all running, not as we normally do in a tight group, but spread out and scattered all along the track.

Then Donny took another assertive action. He dropped all the way back behind everyone to take up a position, his usual one, alongside Choc, who was lagging very far behind now. And though we were all ahead of him, and it was clear he wasn't going to complete the 2 miles in any kind of time, Donny stayed alongside Choc all the way, urging him on in a constant and very audible voice. We all kept going, and we all finished. Donny stayed with Choc, and with Donny's help, Choc finished, although the pace was much slower than normal. After that incident, most of us ran the 2 miles almost every time out, under the original coach's direction.

Challenging the Leader

Larry usually ran in last place with the team. One summer he broke his ankle playing baseball and didn't run with us for most of the year. Then he started running again, sometimes joining us for short periods, sometimes running before or after us, sometimes faster for short spurts, though usually slower. He was slowly getting back into shape.

Then one day he took his usual position at the rear as we were starting. After the first few laps, Donny had not

called out the number of laps, and Larry chose to call them out, loudly. Someone kibitzed and said that wasn't his job. I chipped in jokingly and said that I liked it when Larry called the laps. It was like old times again, having Larry back. Larry kept calling the laps out as we completed them, and Donny, up front, said nothing.

Then Larry lost count somewhere around the eighth or ninth lap. I shouted to Donny to tell us where we were, but he wouldn't answer. I feel kind of lost when I don't know what I've run, so I asked a few more times. "Would someone please say where we are?" Donny didn't answer. Finally, in a loud voice, he said, "Strictly for Harvey, that was 1 mile we just passed." The next mile, he gave us two counts, one at the half mile and one at the end of the 2nd mile. Normally he would count out every two laps, that is, nine times in a mile. In the 3rd mile he gave us three counts.

At the end of the run he muttered something about "teaching you guys respect the hard way." I was away one week when a new fellow, Bradley, joined the group and ran 2 miles with the team. He showed up on the morning I returned, complaining about his leg. He said the tight corners on the track had bothered him, particularly because we always ran in the same direction.

Choc was on vacation, so Herb took up the pacer position, and Donny ran alongside him. After several laps Donny looked back at Bradley and could see why he was hurting. He was doing something wrong. Donny dropped back to run with Bradley and talk to him for quite a while.

Then Donny made some kidding remarks from his position near the back of the group about how Herb was burning up the track and would never have the stamina to keep it up. Someone else made an aside about how leaders shouldn't undermine their subordinates. Donny was running beside me at that point and muttered, "Yeah, but if you don't undermine a subordinate who challenges the leader, you become an ex-leader."

Then he turned to me and said, "That reminds me of the time I was in the office of a chief executive I know. His company normally placed its insurance through my agency, but someone in the organization had placed it with a competitor that year. I found out and went to see him. I was furious; I shouted and yelled at him. And he said, "Don't you think you are overreacting?" I said, "The cemeteries are filled with insurance agents who underreacted."

Module

9

Mentoring*

LEARNING OBJECTIVES

After completing this module, you should be able to

1. Define the concepts *mentoring, developmental relationship, developmental network, diversified mentoring relationship,* and *relational savvy.*
2. Identify the two key mentoring functions.
3. Describe mentoring phases.
4. Name mentoring benefits for the protégé, the mentor, and an organization.
5. Explain symptoms of dysfunctional developmental relationships.
6. Describe challenges and outcomes associated with diversified relationships.
7. Provide an overview of newer areas of interest around mentoring.

KEY TERMS AND CONCEPTS

Career-related functional support

Cultivation phase

Developmental network

Developmental relationship

Diversified mentoring relationships

Dysfunctional mentoring
  relationships

Formal mentoring programs

Initiation phase

Mentoring

Psychosocial functions

Redefinition phase

Relational savvy

Separation phase

MODULE OUTLINE

Premodule Preparation

Activity 9–1: Exploring the Meaning of Developmental Relationships and Mentoring

Introduction

Mentoring and Careers

What Is Mentoring?

What Does Mentoring Look Like in Practice?

PREMODULE PREPARATION

**Activity 9–1:
Exploring the Meaning
of Developmental
Relationships and
Mentoring**

Objective:

To help you explore your mental model of developmental relationships and mentoring on the basis of your own experience.

Task 1:

Reflect upon and write down responses to the following questions:

a. Have you ever had a mentor? If so, how did you know this person (e.g., family member, coach)?

b. Think of one or more individuals whom you perceive as having furthered your personal growth and/or advanced your career. This person (or people) does not have to be someone with whom you have worked; rather, he or she can be a friend, coach, teacher, parent, or other family member.

c. How did the person (or people) identified in parts (a) and (b) help you? Be specific.

d. Was your relationship with this person (or people) always positive? If not, describe an experience that you perceive was negative. How did that experience influence you, the other person, and the relationship overall?

e. If you wanted to have a mentor, what steps would you take to find one and start a relationship with him or her? What personal characteristics would you look for in a mentor?

f. From your perspective, is there value to having a mentor? If so, what are the benefits?

Task 2:

Get into pairs or learning teams and discuss your answers to these questions. Capture common and diverging elements of the discussion on a piece of paper.

Task 3:

The instructor will facilitate class discussion about the emerging common elements and provide a mini-lecture on the topic.

INTRODUCTION

Consistent with this book's examination of the context of organizational life using a sustainable development orientation, one key factor contributing to continuous human development is mentoring. Indeed, much evidence supports the notion that having a mentor benefits a focal person's career in numerous ways. People with mentors experience myriad benefits, including greater personal learning, career and job satisfaction, promotion rates, and compensation.[1]

The first part of this book laid the foundation for viewing the process of student learning and an appropriate classroom climate; the second part examined individual processes that influence the way people think, feel, and behave in organizations, all of which are crucial to understanding how to manage others.

As we saw in Module 8, at the essence of leadership is the ability to develop and manage relationships. Mentoring, the second of the core concepts for this part of the book—Managing Interpersonal Processes—highlights the value of relationships in furthering human development and aiding individual and managerial effectiveness in organizations. As a mentoring relationship involves two individuals—a senior mentor and junior protégé—mentoring can be viewed as an *interpersonal process* that enables personal growth and career advancement and promotes organizational *human capital.*

This chapter overviews the nature of mentoring and its impact on individuals' careers and on the organizations in which they work. Implicit in the discussion will be the assertion that effective management involves recognition of how mentoring benefits employee development, motivation, and the organization. When an organization and, more specifically, managers establish **formal mentoring programs** or encourage the formation of informal mentoring and other developmental relationships within and outside an organization, then that organization is moving toward employee resource optimization, one characteristic of sustainability.

MENTORING AND CAREERS

What Is Mentoring?

Mentoring is considered to have roots dating back to ancient Greece when Mentor, loyal adviser of Odysseus, was chosen to educate and care for Odysseus's son, Telemachus.[2] Although numerous definitions of mentoring have been asserted in the contemporary management literature, traditional definitions center on the **developmental relationship** between the senior, more experienced mentor who provides guidance and support to the relatively junior, less experienced protégé.[3]

More generally, mentoring is a key vehicle to human development and an important organizational process.[4] As an organizational tool, for example, mentoring aids employee socialization, management development, and succession planning.[5] As a concept, mentoring has been distinguished from leadership on the basis of being oriented toward long-term development, while the latter is aimed at short-term performance.[6]

A mentoring relationship can be cultivated as the result of a formal mentoring program—in which mentors and protégés are assigned to each other on the basis of an organization's chosen criteria—or informally as the result of interpersonal liking between the participants.

What Does Mentoring Look Like in Practice?

Mentors provide two general types of support, labeled formally as "functions," to their protégés: *career* (or vocational) and *psychosocial* support. Career functions include providing challenging work assignments, protection, exposure/visibility, sponsorship, and coaching. **Psychosocial functions** include friendship, counseling, acceptance, confirmation, and role modeling and are more generally aimed at helping a protégé to develop a sense of professional identity and competence.[7]

Mentoring relationships are generally considered to last between three to five years and involve four *phases,* although more research examining how they unfold over time is needed.[8] In the **initiation phase,** which lasts between 6 to 12 months, the mentor and protégé become acquainted with each other and establish expectations around their interactions. As shown in Module 2, it is important for mentors and protégés to have an explicit discussion around how often they will meet, what the protégé wants to learn, whether an agenda should be set prior to each meeting and by whom, and other issues to ensure that the mentor and protégé are "on the same page." Research shows that when people report that their expectations are met, they also report having received more mentoring support, suggesting that establishing expectations up front facilitates maximally effective relationships.[9]

The **cultivation phase,** the longest in duration, typically lasts between two and five years and is the period during which mentors provide the greatest amount of career and psychosocial support. During the **separation phase** the protégé begins to seek out more autonomy, having advanced his or her skills during the cultivation phase. This phase is often marked by distress and/or feelings of loss by both relationship participants. Some relationships do not reach the **redefinition phase;** a lack of reconnection can result if the participants do not maintain contact during and/or after the separation phase. If participants do maintain contact after separation, the relationship is often redefined as the two parties begin to view each other as peers.

Benefits of Mentoring: Protégé, Mentor, and Organizational

As shown in Table 9–1, myriad benefits of mentoring exist not only for protégés, but also for mentors and organizations. When most people think of mentoring benefits, they think about how it benefits a *protégé*. Indeed, protégés benefit in a number of ways beyond immediate skill development and knowledge acquisition, including heightened employee motivation, improved job and career satisfaction, enhanced socialization into the employing organization, increased visibility to influential employees, and greater promotions and income.[10]

Mentors benefit from having protégés as well. Early examination of mentoring relationships showed that mentors are often individuals who, having reached midcareer and achieved a certain degree of career success, desire to help others achieve success. Fostering a close relationship with a protégé who achieves success over time creates feelings of

**Table 9–1
Mentoring Benefits:
Protégé, Mentor, and
Organizational***

Protégé Benefits
More promotions
Higher incomes
Greater job satisfaction
Greater career satisfaction
Enhanced career mobility
Heightened career commitment
Accelerated organizational socialization
Alleviated job turnover
Greater access to influential employees and influence on organizational policy
Alleviated role stress and burnout
Clarity of professional identity

Mentor Benefits and Outcomes
Heightened personal satisfaction
Development of base of support within the organization
Higher compensation
Faster promotion rates
Stronger perceptions of career success
Greater intentions to mentor in the future
Enhanced job satisfaction
Greater organizational commitment

Organizational Benefits
Enhanced organizational retention
Stronger organizational culture fostered
Heightened organizational communication
More effective employee "onboarding"
Employee integration
Improved leadership development and succession planning

*This chart is not all-inclusive of the benefits and outcomes for protégés, mentors, and organizations.

personal satisfaction and, at times, of leaving a legacy.[11] A mentor can also experience self-rejuvenation from a relationship with a youthful, energetic protégé. It has been noted that effective leaders often point to having had mentors throughout their careers.

Along this line of reasoning, it has been asserted that sustained leadership excellence results, in part, from coaching or mentoring others. Helping others achieve their dreams creates psychological and physiological benefits to leaders in terms of their ability to manage stress and anxiety. Therefore, leaders should proactively help others, in essence, helping themselves as well.[12] The foregoing suggests that mentoring enhances an individual's sustainability, consistent with this book's overarching framework.

Like protégés, mentors can experience heightened job satisfaction, as well as greater promotions and higher incomes. Protégés also enable mentors to connect with others with whom they would normally interact (for example, individuals at lower hierarchical levels in the organization), thus enhancing their base of support within the organization. Protégés can provide mentors with technical information and psychological support as well. Another benefit of mentoring others is that mentors can receive recognition for having developed organizational talent.

Organizations benefit in a number of ways from implementing formal mentoring programs and encouraging informal mentoring relationships. Mentoring expedites organizational socialization as mentors can show newly hired protégés "the ropes," in essence teaching them about the organization's culture, policies, and procedures, introducing them to people and helping them to understand their role within an organization. The foregoing enables organizational "onboarding," which can be time-consuming and costly because employees are not fully productive as they learn the ropes.

Organizations spend considerable time and effort developing and implementing leadership development and succession programs to ensure that there is an available pool of talent to fill key positions. Mentoring, because it is a relationship dedicated to learning and development, can aid both organizational practices. Other organizational benefits include enhanced managerial succession, employee integration and productivity, and reduced turnover.[13] The foregoing benefits of mentoring are inducements for organizations to invest in implementing formal mentoring programs and fostering an organizational culture that values informal relationships.

Developmental Relationships

Mentoring relationships are one type of developmental relationship, which Kram defined as one "that contributes to personal growth and career development."[14] The notion of a developmental relationship is broader than that of a mentoring relationship, the latter which is characterized by the provision of high levels of career functional support and high levels of psychosocial functional support and involves participants of senior and junior status or rank.[15] Other developmental relationships can provide varying levels and types of functional support. For example, *sponsors* provide high levels of career support and low levels of psychosocial support.[16] They can also vary in terms of the protégé skills they develop (e.g., broad career skills that apply across organizational settings versus organization- and job-specific skills) and various levels within the organization.

It is important to note that developmental relationships can reside inside or outside an employing organization and need not be an individual's supervisor. For example, researchers have distinguished between a senior mentor and a supervisory mentor in that a senior mentor may be two or more hierarchical levels above the protégé or generally have more experience within a position or industry; by comparison, a supervisory mentor, consistent with the name, formally supervises the protégé.

Lateral developmental relationships involve peers that are at comparable levels in the hierarchy and of relatively equal status. Three types of *co-worker mentoring* relationships have been identified: informational peer, collegial, and special peer.[17] Informational peers primarily share job-related or career-strategy information and provide each other with feedback. Collegial peers provide confirmation, emotional support, friendship, assistance, and feedback with personal problems. Special peers fulfill the functions provided by both informational and collegial peers, providing both career and psychosocial support.

Peer (and traditional mentoring) *survivor* developmental relationships help employees adjust to and reduce stress associated with a merger and to cope with having survived a corporate downsizing or restructuring.[18] For example, downsizing can require that people who have survived learn new skills needed to successfully complete a newly designed job (as would be the case if a person's job were designed to incorporate responsibilities formerly designated to a downsized colleague). Peer mentors can aid in securing information, clarifying new rules and procedures, helping prioritize tasks, and assisting with understanding one's role.

Peer mentoring can also help manage the stress and uncertainty associated with domestic or international relocation. Individuals with whom one has a developmental relationship can provide an understanding of an unfamiliar national culture, guidance related to employment for one's spouse and information related to local schools, and job- and task-related feedback.[19]

Intrateam mentoring, another type of development relationship, relates to work teams that can influence knowledge acquisition and skill development as team members work toward completing assigned or mutually-developed tasks, training teammates, and providing performance-related feedback.[20] Furthermore, teams can meet members' social needs for affiliation, identity, and inclusion, the latter of which has been asserted to mirror the friendship and mutuality involved in peer mentoring relationships.[21] Individuals can also have developmental relationships with individuals from other teams (*interteam mentoring*), thus allowing for the development of skills that would not be attained within their team and also aiding the team by providing diverse ideas and information gained beyond team boundaries.[22]

Other types of developmental relationships include community affiliations, networking groups, and mentoring circles.[23]

Dysfunctional Mentoring Relationships

Despite the overwhelming evidence that mentoring leads to positive benefits for protégés, mentors, and organizations, it is important for potential and existing protégés and mentors to be aware of potential pitfalls associated with some relationships. The following are seven types of possible problems that create **dysfunctional mentoring relationships:**[24]

1. *Negative relations.* Mentors who are exploitative and/or egocentric might attempt to bully the protégé. Depending upon how the protégé responds, the two individuals might become enemies or the relationship could become abusive.

2. *Sabotage.* In some cases, one of the parties might attempt to ignore the other person or take revenge for a perceived wrongdoing. Such would be the case, for example, if a protégé were to bad-mouth the mentor to others for having not recommended him or her for a promotion.

3. *Difficulty.* This dysfunction can occur when relationship parties have difficulty communicating with each other. For example, a male mentor who suggests to his female protégé that she not have children to ensure her upward climb in the organization has placed her in a situation where she may feel she must choose between work and family.

4. *Spoiling.* When either the protégé or mentor resents an action of the other, a positive relationship may be "spoiled." Also, spoiling can occur when a protégé is assigned to a person who is not on the fast track or lacks respect in the organization to the extent that it damages his or her reputation if, for example, the protégé emulates the mediocre mentor's behaviors.

5. *Harassment.* This dysfunction can include sexual harassment or race or gender discrimination and results, in part, from power differentials between the two parties. Compounding power differentials between mentor and protégé, cross-race and cross-gender mentoring relationships can become dysfunctional if the mentor uses the power differential to dominate the protégé.

6. *Submissiveness.* If a protégé is overly dependent upon a mentor or submits to a tyrannical mentor, then submissiveness occurs.

7. *Deception.* Mentors and protégés may actively attempt to deceive each other for various reasons, such as would be the case if a protégé were to publicly agree with a mentor's opinion publicly even is he or she actually disagreed on a personal level. Such behaviors as manipulating the truth to gain favor with the other are dysfunctional in that they represent relationship difficulties.

In addition to negative mentoring experiences, it is also the case that being a mentor can come with certain costs. One such cost is a relationship's time and energy consumption in that the mentor must invest in the relationship and the protégé's development in addition to his or her own current responsibilities. Second, it is possible that while the mentor is investing in developing a protégé, other individuals in his or her position are unconstrained in pursing their responsibilities. The foregoing could lead to a situation in which the mentor is passed over for a desired position if the organization does not value mentoring. Mentors also risk having their protégés become so successful that they are viewed as more desirable than their mentors for sought-after positions. Another cost involves the potential of a poorly performing protégé to damage a mentor's reputation.[25]

DEVELOPMENTAL NETWORKS

The Evolution of Mentoring toward the Notion of a Developmental Network

As noted earlier in the chapter, over time and in particular around the end of the millennium, more attention has been paid to the nature and value of developmental relationships beyond the traditional mentoring relationship, including peers, friends, and training groups. It has been posited that studies on relationships beyond the "traditional" mentoring relationships actually reflect the reality that individuals have always drawn on more than one source of developmental support.

Today, people are likely to draw upon a "portfolio of advisors" for developmental and personal growth. This group of advisors has been named a **developmental network,** which is "a set of people a protégé names as taking an active interest in and action to advance the protégé's career by providing developmental assistance."[26] The individuals comprising the network can be considered "developers" who provide varying amounts and types (psychosocial and career) of functional support. Developers can reside inside or outside an employing organization and can be from any number of "social spheres," including from one's family, friends, community, or professional affiliations or at various levels within one's employing organization.

It is important to recognize that a developmental network is one that is a subset of a focal individual's (protégé's) larger social network, which includes everyone with whom an individual interacts or knows. A developmental network includes only those individuals—developers—who provide developmental assistance and consciously take action to further the focal individual's career.

The Story of One Man's Mentoring Experiences

To aid an understanding of mentoring in practice, the following is an example of successful formal and informal mentoring. The example incorporates some mentoring functions and phases, developmental network relationships, mentoring benefits, and negative mentoring experiences throughout the discussion.

John Richards, a technology consultant with ZYX Corporation, who had recently been promoted to a managerial role, sat in his office pondering what factors had led to his early-career successes. He had graduated four years earlier from a top technology university with a degree in computer science. He had received five job offers and ultimately accepted a position as a consultant with ZYX, which had identified him as its most valuable recruit in the New England region.

Although his educational background had certainly furthered his career, John was acutely aware of how his developmental network, and, specifically, the relationships that comprised it, had aided his learning and personal growth. He could identify three individuals who acted as his developers: one of his supervisors, a ZYX peer, and his mother.

Initially, John was unsure of how his relationship with his supervisor would unfold. Michael Bronson, a competent consulting engagement manager and John's boss, tended to give John a significant degree of autonomy yet very little guidance as to how to succeed. John wanted more guidance, yet was unsure how to ask for it. However, to his credit, John was very observant of Michael's behavior in meetings, and initially, Michael served as a *role model* for John in terms of how to communicate with clients, troubleshoot, and give presentations to senior management.

During lengthy meetings with clients, John noticed that Michael took brief notes that later he had difficulty deciphering, and he at times could not recall the meeting's less important details. As someone who could type over 100 words per minute, John offered to take copious, unobtrusive notes during their meetings. Michael was extremely grateful for John's initiative and henceforth made substantial efforts to help John learn whenever possible. In effect, John's attempts to help Michael served to blossom a developmental relationship in lieu of one that was strictly supervisory in nature. Michael *coached* John through a number of challenging technical issues and gave him feedback on his presentation style and client interactions. In spite of his relative junior status with the company, Michael sponsored him for a challenging consulting assignment for which John received a companywide award the following year. Over four years, Michael provided a significant amount of career-related functional support for John's career.

John and Janice were peers who were recruited to ZYX at the same time. While John was technically superior, Janice was the savvier of the two in terms of understanding the political and cultural dynamics of ZYX; Janice *coached* John to maneuver through a few politically challenging situations that he would not have successfully navigated without her insight. They became fast *friends* and confided in each other about issues they would feel uncomfortable sharing with others in the organization. Very importantly, Janice was quick to compliment John's performance, bolstering his confidence. He and Janice provided each other with career and psychosocial support. Unfortunately, for several months, rumors abounded whether the married John and single Janice were having an affair. The rumors ended when Janice announced her engagement to her boyfriend.

John's mother had been an executive for an information technology (IT) based company prior to retiring a few years before John took the position at ZYX. His initial interest in becoming an IT professional had been based on his admiration for his mother's accomplishments. She was the sounding board for John when he was having any job-related challenges. Likewise, John's mother, having been a senior executive, had always been someone with whom John could discuss his longer-term career aspirations. She identified skills he would need to develop at various points in his career and offered ideas as to how to develop them. Also, John attended several invited guest lectures his mother had given at nearby universities, which further endeared her as a key role model.

John found that his developmental network had provided a rich blend of career and psychosocial support since he began his career. More recently, Michael had purposefully introduced John to senior consultants and engagement managers as a means to provide John with visibility. Ultimately, the introductions led to consideration of John for the promotion he had recently received.

DIVERSITY AND MENTORING

Formal mentoring programs arose in part as a response to the recognition during earlier decades—roughly from the 50s to the 80s—that women and other minorities were "plateauing" much earlier than their Caucasian, male counterparts.[27] Part of the logic at the time was that mentoring programs could provide partnerships with senior executives that could redress the inequities experienced by disadvantaged groups.

Since that time, much research has been dedicated to understanding the effects of diversity and mentoring. Most of the research to date has explored how women and African American employees experience mentoring relationships. More recently, age has garnered more attention, in particular because of the salience of the baby boomer generation in the United States and the aging populations of other countries.

Gender and Mentoring

Having a mentor helps women succeed professionally in numerous ways, including developing a professional style, securing favored developmental assignments, and learning how to thrive in masculine organizational cultures.[28]

Although research suggests that women are equally likely as men to be protégés, women perceive more barriers than their male counterparts to securing a mentor. Underlying this perception is the possibility that senior women, while having made strides in "breaking the glass ceiling," are still underrepresented relative to men at midlevel and senior-level positions. Men typically favor mentoring other men (similarly, women feel more comfortable mentoring women) and women may feel uncomfortable initiating with men relative to women. Therefore, given that traditional mentoring relationships are those characterized by a senior mentor and junior protégé pairing, women suffer from having relatively fewer potential mentors.

Men and women have been found to be equally likely to be mentors, although women may experience more potential costs of being one. In particular, should a protégé fail to succeed under a woman's tutelage, the female mentor's reputation could be tarnished, a risk that some might perceive not worth taking given the effort needed to rise in the corporate hierarchy. Also, women may find it more difficult to justify mentoring others as they are so conscientiously furthering their own careers.

Research to date is inconclusive on whether, by comparison to white males, women are as likely to initiate mentoring relationships and receive equal amounts of functional support. However, it is clear that women are equally as likely as men to experience heightened compensation, greater promotions, and career satisfaction from having a mentor.

A key issue around women and mentoring is the disproportionate number of cross-gender mentoring pairings, meaning that the number of women mentored by men outnumbers the number of women mentored by women. Cross-gender relationships are one type of **diversified mentoring relationship**—cross-race relationships being another type—that involves individuals who differ on the basis of belonging to one or more group memberships. More specifically, a diversified relationship is one ". . . comprising mentors and protégés who differ on the basis of race, ethnicity, gender, sexual orientation, class, religion, disability, or other group memberships associated with power in organizations."[29]

While there are definitely benefits for women who have male mentors (e.g., higher compensation relative to women with female mentors), cross-gender relationships face particular challenges, including the possibility of sexual innuendos by others in the organization as well as potential sexual tension.[30] Given the paucity of women relative to men in senior positions, there are fewer male protégés with female mentors relative to the other gender composition possibilities (e.g., same gender or male mentor and female protégé). In spite of the complexities facing women in search of or in existing relationships, research clearly conveys the value of having a mentor for women's careers.

To provide an example of gender and mentoring in action, consider Janice, John's peer at ZYX organization. When reflecting upon her developmental network, she found that she had only one female developer, a friend outside of the company. Few women had been able to break into the senior ranks at ZYX, so, while Janice could identify four developers within the organization, they were all men. Nonetheless, Janice's male developers sponsored her for a number of challenging assignments and, like John, gave her visibility in the organization by discussing her growth and value within the company.

Race and Mentoring

As the world becomes increasingly connected and organizational demography shifts toward a more diverse workforce, race will continue to be a critical mentoring issue. Individuals with dissimilar backgrounds will engage in cross-race mentoring relationships and, more generally, individuals will need to transcend differences in history and cultural background to work together effectively.[31]

Most, but not all, of the mentoring research on race has focused on how African American men and women experience mentoring.[32] Like women, African Americans are disproportionately in cross-race mentoring relationships, resulting largely from underrepresentation of African Americans in senior positions. Some studies suggest that African Americans lack access to mentors relative to Caucasians, while others show equal access between the two groups.

A key challenge facing ethnic minorities is the negative influence of stereotyping. For example, historical relations between blacks and whites sometimes serve as hindrances to the development of close relationships. If either party in a cross-race relationship fails to test assumptions about the other party, then the potential for emotional connectedness is undermined.[33]

As an example of how African Americans experience mentoring, consider Randy Williams, an African American ZYX senior executive, who identified himself as having two developmental networks, one of which included a number of ZYX Caucasian senior executives and another whose members stemmed from an association of African American professionals with whom Randy was affiliated. Randy's network is similar to that of other African Americans, who take advantage of dual mentoring relationships, largely because in order to find a same-race mentor, it is necessary to go beyond one's immediate supervisor, department, and often even one's organization. Randy's ZYX network provided career-related functional benefits, such as access to information and networks, and his relationships with other African Americans provided psychosocial support such as friendship.[34]

It is unclear whether African American protégés experience equally positive objective and subjective career outcomes relative to Caucasians. However, it does seem to be the case that having a white male as a mentor has a positive impact on career outcomes.[35] African American mentors have reported receiving numerous benefits from having a protégé, including enhanced networking capabilities and supervisory skills and a renewed commitment to their chosen career field.[36]

In "Unfinished Business: The Impact of Race and Understanding Mentoring Relationships," Blake-Beard et al. stated, "While Dubois stated that the problem of the 20th century is the color line, we see the opportunity in the 21st century is to show how mentoring helps to create access and inclusion that goes beyond the color line."[37]

Age and Mentoring

Given the aging populations in the United States and other countries such as Canada and New Zealand, it will be important for older employees to have access to mentors. Today's worker transitions between organizations and positions with greater frequency, one implication being that older employees will face climbing learning curves in spite of their relative seniority in organizations. Although older workers appear equally as likely as younger employees to initiate a relationship, they may receive less career-related mentoring functional benefits.

Take, for example, Bob Johnson, a 65-year-old human resources professional at ZYX, who opted not to retire so as to continue his learning and professional development. He had recently accepted the human resources position after having been in IT and manufacturing roles in various organizations throughout his career. Bob, like many other professionals in today's career context, transitions between roles with greater frequency than in earlier decades.[38] Since he had only been with human resources for a brief period when he turned 65 and decided to stay with ZYX, he was a relative novice in the department. Thus, he opted to initiate developmental relationships with two of his peers and his supervisor as a means to climb the learning curve.

FORMAL MENTORING PROGRAMS

As suggested, in earlier decades, formal mentoring programs were most often aimed at select groups of employees, including high-potential employees being groomed for senior positions and women and other minorities. Over time, however, the implementation of a formal mentoring program has increasingly become a human resource strategy to enhance employee talent throughout an organization. The long list of organizations that use formal mentoring programs includes Charles Schwab, IBM, Bank of America, AT&T, Honeywell, Apple Computers, the Internal Revenue Service, and Marriott International.

Formal mentoring programs are, in part, a response to the observation that informal mentoring relationships greatly enhanced the careers of individuals in leadership and senior organizational positions. Implicit in the creation of formal programs is the goal to nurture formal relationships that mirror informal relationships that are based on an initial attraction between participants.

The following factors are influential in determining whether mentoring programs will be successfully implemented.[39]

1. *A clear set of objectives aligned with human resources and business strategy.* Given the resources and time needed to implement an effective formal mentoring program, it is critical to have identified and be committed to a set of objectives. The objectives should be aligned with the needs of the organization and participants to ensure that the right skills are being taught and appropriate knowledge is imparted. As an example, an organization whose success lies in having a particular set of skills at senior levels should create a program with objectives that relate to the development of those skills.

2. *Sponsorship by senior leaders.* Without the sponsorship of the most senior individual in an organization or a number of key leaders, a formal mentoring program will likely not have the momentum or needed resources to be effective.

3. *Communications and training.* Mentors and protégés need information about the program if they are to understand its goals and their interactions. Requisite mentoring skills such as active listening and counseling can be taught through proper training sessions with mentors.

237

4. *Choosing appropriate mentors and matching of mentors and protégés.* Identifying individuals who have the characteristics of outstanding mentors is critical to a program's success. Included among able mentoring characteristics are experience, self-awareness, and interpersonal skills. First, mentors must have achieved mastery of their position and in-depth knowledge of the field. Second, mentors should possess an awareness of their leadership role in the relationship and have established a solid identity and sense of self. Third, in order to provide the numerous mentoring functions, in particular psychosocial functions, mentors must possess attributes such as empathy and listening skills.

The matching process should consider three elements: similarity of participants, input into the matching decision, and voluntary participation in the program. First, successful mentoring pairs are often matched on the basis of similarity in values, attitudes, or interests. Second, input as to whom one will be partnered with instills a sense of control and responsibility for the relationship's success and subsequent outcomes.[40] Third, more generally, voluntary participation by participants is associated with greater motivation and satisfaction.

5. *Evaluation and review of the program.* It is important to periodically reevaluate a program against its stated objectives. The program coordinator should secure feedback from program participants to gauge relationship effectiveness and to assess whether the appropriate skills are being taught and knowledge is gained. Exit interviews—those that occur after the duration of the program—should be conducted as well to aid future programs.

6. *A skilled program coordinator.* A skilled coordinator is critical to managing activities and processes as well as garnering and/or maintaining support for the mentoring program.

Organizations embarking upon the implementation of a formal mentoring program should be aware of the potential pitfalls. For example, it is important to educate both parties to communicate their expectations early in the relationship so as not to undermine trust and rapport later if miscommunication were to occur. Also, the matching process is critical in influencing the quality of the relationship, which will largely dictate the amount of mentoring received and the degree of positive outcomes for both parties. Another potential pitfall is locating mentors who can commit to the time investment necessary to make a relationship function well.

NEWER AREAS OF MENTORING INTEREST

While much examination remains necessary to fully understand the traditional mentoring and other developmental relationships, developmental networks, and formal mentoring programs, the following are three areas that are receiving greater attention.

First, given that organizations are increasingly sending employees abroad, it is important to understand how developmental relationships at home and abroad can aid an expatriate. In spite of best intentions on the part of the organization and the employee, some estimates suggest that expatriate failures are as high as 40 percent.[41] Expatriates have various needs during the three international assignment phases—predeparture, on-site, and repatriation—that can be filled by home- and host-country developers. For example, prior to departing for an international assignment, expatriates need information related to the role, the host country's culture, and the host organization's culture. In addition to the formal training an expatriate receives, home peer and supervisory mentors can meet the expatriate's foregoing needs. Consistent with the notion of a developmental network, the expatriate's needs can only sufficiently be met by multiple mentors in various locations (at home and abroad).

Second, advancements in technology allow mentoring to occur between individuals at distant locations and via various media such as e-mail, chat rooms, blogs, and teleconferencing.[42] E-mentoring has been defined as "a mutually beneficial relationship between a mentor and a protégé, which provides new learning, as well as career and emotional support, primarily through email and other electronic means (e.g., instant messaging, chat rooms, social networking spaces, etc.)."[43] E-mentoring can occur informally or as part of a formal program. Three types of e-mentoring have been identified: CMC-primary, CMC-supplemental, and CMC-only. Computer-mediated communication (CMC) primarily relates to relationships that predominantly involve interactions virtually. CMC-supplemental involves relationships that primarily interact face-to-face but can be supplemented by computer-mediated means. CMC-only relationships are those that never involve face-to-face interactions; parties communicate virtually. Advantages of e-mentoring include heightened access to a mentor throughout the day (mentors could technically be available 24 hours a day and located in various locations and time zones), decreased costs of administering a formal program, and diminished potential for stereotyping or the effects of harmful stigmas given the parties do not meet face to face.

Third, in the face of a complex career environment, individuals need to fashion a developmental network that is responsive to their developmental needs. Although much is known about how protégés benefit from mentoring and other developmental relationships, much less is known about what actions protégés take to initiate relationships and maintain them over time. **Relational savvy,** defined as protégé adeptness with developmental relationships, is a factor that influences an individual's relative ability to build an appropriate network. Highly relationally savvy individuals, relative to lesser savvy individuals, are more proactive in initiating and nurturing relationships, better prepared for meetings with developers, more likely to disclose personal information as a means to build trust and rapport, have superior interpersonal skills, and hold enabling attitudes toward asking for assistance from others (attitudes such as "I believe that people want to help me" versus "I believe that people do not want to help me"). Highly savvy individuals typically have more developmental relationships than their less savvy counterparts.[44]

SUMMARY

Many successful careers have been built, in part, upon the presence of a mentor, which is considered to be the dyadic relationship between a senior mentor and a junior protégé. The mentor aids the protégé's career and personal development by providing career- and psychosocial functions. Most mentoring relationships last between two to five years in length. The mentoring relationship can have powerful, positive effects on the mentor, the protégé, and the employing organization. In spite of the benefits of mentoring, it is important to be knowledgeable of potential negative or dysfunctional dynamics that can undermine a relationship. Although the mentoring relationship is a key vehicle to personal learning and career advancement, over time, other developmental relationships that also provide support for a protégé's career have been identified. Furthermore, in part due to environmental forces such as globalization and technological advancements, mentoring is partially undergoing a shift in conceptualization toward a developmental network, which reflects the notion that people draw upon multiple, simultaneously held "developers" for support. A developmental network's structure is based on its strength of ties and its diversity.

Mentoring can help women and ethnic minorities "break through the glass ceiling," yet the two groups also experience unique challenges such as stereotyping and sexual tension that must be managed if relationships are to be successfully formed and maintained over time. Formal mentoring programs have become increasingly pervasive as a means to stimulate high-quality relationships within an organization and develop talent at various levels. Among the factors that influence the relative effectiveness of formal mentoring programs, clear objectives must be established, senior sponsorship must be gained, and a capable program coordinator must be in place. Newer mentoring themes include an emphasis on international mentoring, e-mentoring, and relational savvy as a necessary ingredient of protégé success.

Study Questions

1. What is a mentoring relationship? A developmental relationship? A developmental network?

2. What are the main functions provided by a mentor?

3. Through what phases do mentoring relationships typically progress?

4. What are the benefits of having a mentor? A protégé?

5. Describe features of a successful formal mentoring program.

6. What are some newer areas of mentoring interest?

Endnotes

1. G. T. Chao, P. M. Walz, and P. D. Gardner, "Formal and Informal Work: Test of a Theory," *Organizational Behavior and Human Performance* 35 (1992), pp. 250–79; G. F. Dreher and R. A. Ash, "A Comparative Study of Mentoring among Men and Women in Managerial, Professional, and Technical Positions," *Journal of Applied Psychology* 75 (1990), pp. 539–46; E. A. Fagenson, "The Mentor Advantage: Perceived Career/Job Experiences of Protégés versus Non-Protégés," *Journal of Organizational Behavior* 10 (1989), pp. 309–20; K. E. Kram, *Mentoring at Work: Developmental Relationships in Organizational Life* (Glenview, IL: Scott Foresman, 1985); W. Whitely, T. W. Dougherty, and G. F. Dreher, "Relationship of Career Mentoring and Socioeconomic Origin to Managers' and Professionals' Early Career Progress," *Academy of Management Journal* 34 (1991), pp. 331–51.

2. A. Roberts, "The Origins of the Term Mentor," *History of Education Society Bulletin,* no. 64 (November 1999), pp. 313–29.

3. K. E. Kram, *Mentoring at Work: Developmental Relationships in Organizational Life* (Glenview, IL: Scott Foresman, 1985).

4. K. E. Kram and D. T. Hall, "Mentoring In a Context of Diversity and Turbulence," in Kossek and S. Lobel (eds.), *Management Diversity: Human Resource Strategies for Transforming Organizations* (Blackwell Publishers, 1996), pp. 108–36.

5. G. T. Chao, "Mentoring and Organizational Socialization: Networks for Work Adjustment," in B. R. Ragins and K. E. Kram (eds.), *Handbook of Mentoring: Theory, Research, and Practice* (Thousand Oaks, CA: Sage).

6. R. J. Burke, C. S. McKenna, and C. A. McKeen, "How Do Mentorships Differ from Typical Supervisory Relationships?" *Psychological Reports* 68 (1991), pp. 459–66; T. A. Scandura and C. A. Schriesheim, "Leader/Member Exchange and Supervisor Career Mentoring as Complementary Constructs in Leadership Research," *Academy of Management Journal* 37 (1994), pp. 1588–1602.

7. Kram, *Mentoring at Work.*

8. K. E. Kram, "Phases of the Mentor Relationship," *Academy of Management Journal* 26 (1983), pp. 608–25.

9. A. M. Young and P. L. Perrewe, "The Role of Expectations in the Mentoring Exchange: An Analysis of Mentor and Protégé Expectations in Relation to Perceived Support," *Journal of Managerial Issues* 16, no. 1 (2004), pp. 103–26.

10. Mentoring researchers have asserted that longitudinal studies are needed in order to better support that mentoring causes particular benefits rather than being associated with them. For example, one could charge that rather than mentoring leading to higher income and greater promotions, individuals who are more capable are those who likely become protégés and are therefore individuals who will likely experience the foregoing outcomes regardless of having a mentor. G. T. Chao, P. M. Walz, and P. D. Gardner, "Formal and Informal Work: Test of a Theory," *Organizational Behavior and Human Performance* 35 (1992), pp. 250–79; G. F. Dreher and R. A. Ash, "A Comparative Study of Mentoring among Men and Women in Managerial, Professional, and Technical Positions," *Journal of Applied Psychology* 75 (1990), pp. 539–46; E. A. Fagenson, "The Mentor Advantage: Perceived Career/Job Experiences of Protégés versus Non-Protégés," *Journal of Organizational Behavior* 10 (1989), pp. 309–20; Kram, *Mentoring at Work;* W. Whitely, T. W. Dougherty, and G. F. Dreher, "Relationship of Career Mentoring and

Socioeconomic Origin to Managers' and Professionals' Early Career Progress," *Academy of Management Journal* 34 (1991), pp. 331–51; T. D. Allen, S. E. McManus, and J. E. A. Russell, "Newcomer Socialization and Stress: Formal Peer Relationships as a Source of Support." *Journal of Vocational Behavior* 54 (1999), pp. 453–70; S. Aryee and Y. W. Chay, "An Examination of the Impact of Career-Oriented Mentoring on Work Commitment Attitudes and Career Satisfaction among Professional and Managerial Employees," *British Journal of Management* 5 (1994), pp. 241–49; S. Aryee, T. Wyatt, and R. Stone, "Early Career Outcomes of Graduate Employees: The Effect of Mentoring and Ingratiation," *Journal of Management Studies* 33 (1996), pp. 95–118; C. Orpen, "The Effects of Formal Mentoring on Employee Work Motivation, Organizational Commitment and Job Performance," *The Learning Organization* 4, no. 2 (1997), pp. 53–60.

11. Kram, *Mentoring At Work.*

12. R. E. Boyatzis, M. L. Smith, and N. Blaize, "Developing Sustainable Leaders through Coaching and Compassion," *Academy of Management Learning and Education* 5, no. 1 (2006), pp. 8–24.

13. M. Zey, *The Mentor Connection* (Homewood, IL: Dow-Jones-Irwin, 1984).

14. K. E. Kram, *Mentoring at Work.*

15. D. A. Thomas and K. E. Kram, "Promoting Career-Enhancing Relationships in Organizations: The Role of the Human Resource Professional," in M. London and E. Mone (eds), *The Human Resource Professional and Employee Career Development* (New York: Greenwood, 1988), pp. 49–66.

16. Ibid.

17. K. E. Kram and L. A. Isabella, "Mentoring Alternatives: The Role of Peer Relationships in Career Development," *Academy of Management Journal* 28 (1986), pp. 110–32.

18. K. E. Kram and D. T. Hall, "Mentoring as an Antidote to Stress during Corporate Trauma," *Human Resource Management* 24 (1989), pp. 493–510.

19. L. T. Eby, "Alternative Forms of Mentoring in Changing Organizational Environments: A Conceptual Extension of the Mentoring Literature,"*Journal of Vocational Behavior* 51 (1997), pp. 125–44; D. C. Feldman and J. M. Brett, "Coping with New Jobs: A Comparative Study of New Hires and Job Changers," *Academy of Management Journal* 26 (1983), pp. 258–72; J. M. Mezias and T. A. Scandura, "A Needs-Driven Approach to Expatriate Adjustment and Career Development: A Multiple Mentoring Perspective," *Journal of International Business Studies* 36 (2005), pp. 519–38.

20. Sundstrom, DeMeuse, and Futrell, (1990); L. T. Eby, "Alternative Forms of Mentoring in Changing Organizational Environments: A Conceptual Extension of the Mentoring Literature,"*Journal of Vocational Behavior* 51 (1997), pp. 125–44.

21. B. Shamir, "Calculations, Values, and Identities: The Sources of Collectivistic Work Motivation," *Human Relations* 43 (1990), pp. 313–32; Eby, "Alternative Forms of Mentoring in Changing Organizational Environments."

22. D. G. Ancona and D. F. Caldwell, "Bridging the Boundary: External Activity and Performance in Organizational Teams," *Administrative Science Quarterly* 37 (1992), pp. 634–65.

23. D. T. Hall and W. A. Kahn, "Developmental Relationships at Work: A Learning Perspective," in C. Cooper and R. J. Burke (eds.), *The New World of Work* (London: Blackwell, 2001), pp. 49–74.

24. I have drawn heavily on Scandura's seminal research on the dysfunctional mentoring relationships in this section. T. A. Scandura, "Dysfunctional Mentoring Relationships and Outcomes,"*Journal of Management* 24 (1998), pp. 449–67.

25. Kram, *Mentoring at Work;* B. R. Ragins and T. A. Scandura, "Burden or Blessing? Expected Costs and Benefits of Being a Mentor," *Journal of Organizational Behavior* 20, no. 4 (1999), pp. 493–509; B. R. Ragins, "Diversified Mentoring Relationships: A Power Perspective," *Academy of Management Review* 22 (1997), pp. 482–521.

26. M. C. Higgins and K. E. Kram, "Reconceptualizing Mentoring at Work: A Developmental Network Perspective," *Academy of Management Review* 26, no. 2 (2001), pp. 264–88.

27. D. E. Chandler and K. E. Kram, "Mentoring and Developmental Networks in the New Career Context," in H. P. Gunz and M. A. Peiperl, *Handbook of Career Studies* (Sage Publications, 2007).

28. C. A. McKeen and M. L. Bujaki, "Gender and Mentoring: Issues, Effects and Opportunities," in B. R. Ragins and K.E. Kram (eds.), *Handbook on Mentoring* (Sage Publications, 2007).

29. B. R. Ragins, "Diversified Mentoring Relationships in Organizations: A Power Perspective," *Academy of Management Review* 22, no. 2 (1997), pp. 482–521.

30. J. G. Clawson and K. E. Kram, "Managing Cross-Gender Mentoring," *Business Horizons* 27, no. 3 (1984), pp. 22–32; A. E. Hurley and E. A. Fagenson-Eland, "Challenges in Cross-Gender Mentoring Relationships: Psychological Intimacy, Myths, Rumours, Innuendoes and Sexual Harassment," *Leadership & Organization Development Journal* 17, no. 3 (1996), pp. 42–49.

31. S. Blake, "At the Crossroads of Race and Gender: Lessons from the Mentoring Experiences of Professional Black Women," in A. J. Murrell, F. J. Crosby, and R. J. Ely (eds.), *Mentoring Dilemmas: Developmental Relationships within Multicultural Organizations* (Mahwah, NJ: Lawrence Erlbaum Associates, 1999), pp. 83–104; K. E. Kram and D. T. Hall, "Mentoring in a Context of Diversity and Turbulence," in E. E. Kossek and S. A. Lobel (eds.), *Managing Diversity: Human Resource Strategies for Transforming the Workplace* (Cambridge, MA: Blackwell Business, 1996), pp. 108–36.

32. S. Blake, "At the Crossroads of Race and Gender: Lessons from the Mentoring Experiences of Professional Black Women," in Murrell, Crosby, and Ely (eds.), *Mentoring Dilemmas;* C. R. Bridges and V. S. Perotti, "Characteristics of Career Achievement: Perceptions of African-American Corporate Executives," *Mid-American Journal of Business* 8 (1993), pp. 61–64.

33. D. A. Thomas and J. J. Gabarro, *Breaking Through: The Making of Minority Executives in Corporate America* (Boston, MA: Harvard Business School Press, 1999).

34. D. A. Thomas, "The Impact of Race on Managers' Experiences of Developmental Relationships (Mentoring and Sponsorship): An Intra-Organizational Study," *Journal of Organizational Behavior* 11, no. 6 (1990), pp. 479–92.

35. G. F. Dreher and T. H. Cox, Jr., "Race, Gender and Opportunity: A Study of Compensation Attainment and the Establishment of Mentoring Relationships," *Journal of Applied Psychology* 81 (1996), pp. 297–308; C. R. Wanberg, E. T. Welsh, and S. A. Hezlett, "Mentoring Research: A Review and Dynamic Process Model," *Research in Personnel and Human Resources Management* 22, pp. 39–124.

36. MentorNet.com, "E-mentoring for Women of Color in Engineering and Science: Final Report to the Engineering Information Foundation," http:www.mentornet/documents/files/WomenofColorFinalReportMay2004.pdf (2004).

37. S. Blake-Beard, A. Murrell, and D. Thomas, "Unfinished Business: The Impact of Race on Understanding Mentoring Relationships," in Ragins and Kram (eds.) *Handbook on Mentoring.*

38. M. B. Arthur and D. M. Rousseau, *The Boundaryless Career: A New Employment Principle for a New Organizational Era* (Oxford University Press, 1996).

39. I have drawn upon ideas from diverse sources, including A. Tabbron, S. Macauley, and S. Cook, "Making Mentoring Work,"*Training for Quality* 5, no. 1 (1997), pp. 6–9; K. E. Kram and M. C. Bragar, "Development through Mentoring: A Strategic Approach," in D. H. Montross and C. J. Shinkman (eds), *Career Development: Theory and Practice* (Springfield, IL: Charles C. Thomas, 1992), pp. 221–54; E. Samier, "Public Administration Mentorship: Conceptual and Pragmatic Considerations," *Journal of Educational Administration,* 38, no. 1 (2000), pp. 83–101.

40. T. D. Allen, L. T. Eby, and E. Lenz, "The Relationship between Formal Mentoring Program Characteristics and Perceived Program Effectiveness," *Personnel Psychology* 59, no. 1 (2006), pp. 125–53.

41. Mezias and Scandura, "A Needs-Driven Approach to Expatriate Adjustment and Career Development."

42. E. A. Ensher and E. Murphy, "E-Mentoring: Next Generation Research Strategies and Suggestions," in Ragins and Kram (eds.), *Handbook on Mentoring.*

43. Ibid.

44. D. E. Chandler, "Why Some Protégés Are More Adept Than Others with Developmental Relationships," Unpublished dissertation, Boston University.

Activity 9–2: Mentoring Interview

Objectives:

a. To acquaint students with the value of mentoring for one's career.

b. To understand what mentoring looks like in practice.

Task 1:

Choose someone whose career you admire and ask for a brief interview with that person centering on his or her experiences with mentoring. Offer to e-mail or share the questions with the person ahead of the interview so that he or she can adequately reflect prior to the discussion. Although you should allow the interview to move in the direction of your and his or her interest, the following are questions to guide you:

a. How has mentoring influenced your career?

b. How many individuals have you perceived as a mentor?

c. In what ways have the individuals helped you?

d. Explain a challenge or issue you faced with a mentor? What was the outcome? How did you both address the challenge?

e. How long have your mentor relationship(s) lasted? What is your current relationship with your mentor like?

f. Who initiated the relationship?

g. In what ways have you helped your mentor?

h. What advice do you have for me regarding starting a mentoring relationship? How should I maintain my relationship once it has started?

Task 2:

Conduct the interview with your chosen individual, and in two pages or less write out key themes that emerge. Try to keep the interview to 45 minutes or less so as not to overwhelm your chosen individual.

Task 3:

Bring your written paper to class and pair up with a person to share insights from your respective interviews.

Task 4:

Engage in a larger group discussion led by the instructor about emergent themes.

Activity 9–3: Case Study—A Tale of a Protégé in a Formal Mentoring Program

Background

Kate Barnett was chosen to be part of ABC Corporation's formal mentoring program, which paired junior employees with three years or less experience with senior employees in middle and senior management.

Kate Barnett had been asked to participate in the program at ABC, which specifically identified high-potential candidates for grooming to senior positions. She was flattered to have been invited into the program and she gladly accepted the opportunity to pair with Nort Johnson, whom she admired greatly as a senior executive in the program. While Nort had informally mentored a number of protégés over his career, he had not taken on any in recent years given that he was planning to retire shortly and he was quite busy leading the company through a merger. Like Kate, Nort had been asked to participate in the program.

The formal mentoring program was spearheaded by the former Vice President of Human Resources at ABC, yet lacked a significant visibility since the newly hired vice president came aboard and focused her energies on the pending merger and the corporation's health care benefits program. The prior Vice President vigorously pursued volunteers for the program and asked reticent qualified mentors to participate. The vice president and program directors tended to match on the basis of the senior mentor having had experience in the program. However, the two senior mentors who had Kate's experience in manufacturing were already matched with other protégés. No formal training program was in place as it was assumed that the mentors, having risen to senior positions, possessed the requisite interpersonal skills to be effective.

The First Meeting

Two days prior to their first established meeting (they met briefly in the hallway a week prior and had established noon as a meeting time), Kate e-mailed Nort to ask how long he would be available for the meeting and noted a few areas of interest for her for the discussion. Unfortunately, Nort was extremely busy with a particular merger issue and forgot to reply to the e-mail. Nonetheless, Kate arrived promptly at 11:55 A.M. on the day of the meeting. During the next hour, the two discussed skills that Kate perceived as critical to her development and Nort, upon Kate's prompting, commented about critical incidents in his career. At the end of the meeting, Nort noted that Kate should call him to schedule another meeting whenever she "felt the need to do so." A few hours later in the day, Kate sent a short thank you e-mail to Nort and noted that she was excited about the prospect of their relationship going forward.

Spirited by their first meeting, Kate wondered when she should next call or e-mail Nort to schedule a meeting. Should she wait a week, a month, two months? She decided on waiting indefinitely until she faced a job challenge and she had made headway with skill development. Three weeks later, she and her team faced a novel quality control issue and she thought of seeking Nort's advice. For a moment, she hesitated, wondering whether Nort might perceive her request for help as indicative of an inability to solve the problem on her own. Would seeking help suggest lack of initiative or ability to problem-solve?

Nort replied to Kate's voice mail quickly, explaining that he would place her into contact with someone very familiar with that type of issue. He was happy to help, and he had assumed he would hear from her sooner than three weeks after their first meeting. Was she actually less interested in being in the mentoring program than she had indicated? Kate contacted the gentleman to whom Nort had referred her and was pleased to receive solid insight that ultimately facilitated solving the problem. Kate unexpectedly stopped by Nort's office to thank him for his assistance and establish another formal meeting the following week.

The Second Meeting

As part of the second meeting, Nort opted to ask Kate a number of questions about her short- and long-term interests and to offer a more consistent schedule of meetings. While he had initially questioned her commitment to the program when he did not hear from her for three weeks, her enthusiasm regarding his referral for quality control assistance caused him to rethink his earlier assumptions. Thus, when she arrived, he commented that they should meet on a bi-monthly basis and not only would they strive to meet her short-term goals, but also her long-term goal to become a divisional manager. The skill set she would need, he explained, would be different than that needed for her short-term goals. While he had not worked in quality control, he had been a divisional manager earlier in his career.

The Next Year

Over the course of the next year, Kate and Nort met twice a month for times ranging from 30 minutes to two hours. Some of their meetings were held at Nort's office, yet, over time, they opted to have "working lunches." Nort, since having decided on a more proactive stance toward the relationship, offered problem scenarios for each of their meetings in which he posed a hypothetical challenge faced by a division manager. Next, he asked Kate to talk through how she would manage both technical and interpersonal issues related to the challenge. Kate asked Nort if he would help her to review and act upon a 360-degree feedback process she was actively involved in. The process required that Kate receive confidential feedback from her peers, supervisors, and subordinates. Nort was impressed by how well she responded to the feedback and proactively made behavioral changes based on it. For example, while Kate's subordinates responded that she was outstanding at communicating with them, her supervisors felt that she could better inform them of her progress. Nort and Kate walked through ways that she could periodically provide comprehensive feedback of her and her team's work.

At the end of the year, Nort became aware of an opening in a rotational program that would provide Kate with greater exposure to various facets of the business. The program had graduated individuals who ultimately became divisional managers within the company. After having asked Kate for her level of interest, Nort called the head of the program, also a long-time friend, and explained his confidence in Kate as a potential program participant. Ultimately, Kate was accepted into the program. Shortly afterward, Nort received a thank you letter from Kate, who commented that his support had given her enhanced self-confidence, a clearer career identity, and a heightened interest in staying with ABC for the long-term.

1. Based on the information provide in the case, how effective is ABC in overseeing its formal mentoring program? What actions can it take to become more effective?

2. How effective was Kate and Nort's relationship during the timeframe spanning their first few meetings? Why?

3. How effective was their relationship after the first few meetings? Why?

Activity 9–4: A Role Play Involving a Student Mentoring Program

Objective:

To experience the process of aligning expectations involving a mentoring relationship by engaging in a role play exercise.

Task 1:

Divide into groups of three, and read the following scenario involving a formal student mentoring program. After having read the scenario, students should decide who will role-play the mentor and protégé and who will act as the observer. (5 minutes)

Your university has developed a three-month student mentoring program as a means to guide first-year students. The program's mentors are sophomores and juniors who are volunteers. One of you is to act as a junior-year student who has chosen business as a major and the other is an incoming freshman who has also declared business as a major. The junior student, the mentor, is involved in a few or several on-campus organizations (you choose) and works part-time while maintaining a full-time course load. In general, the mentor is a well-informed student. The freshman was unable to attend orientation and is relatively unfamiliar with the university and the business college. Therefore, the freshman has much to learn about life at the university.

This role play represents your first meeting as mentor and protégé. Your goal in this meeting is to converse about how you should interact going forward and what the protégé will learn over the course of the next three months. You are to write down the various elements of your discussion. Given that the preceding scenario is relatively unstructured, you should be creative in your discussion.

Task 2:

Given your chosen roles (mentor, protégé, or observer), reflect on what your goals of the meeting would likely be. For example, as the mentor, how can you assist the protégé? What does the protégé need to know about life with the university? How often do you want to meet and for how long during each meeting? As the protégé, what do you need to know about life at the university? Are there on-campus organizations (e.g., sororities, fraternities, on-campus work opportunities) of interest to you? Will you work? What do you know about the curriculum? (10 minutes)

Task 3:

The mentor and protégé are to have a discussion around their expectations, goals, and so forth. The observer's role is to watch the pair's involvement and be attentive to both the level of rapport they appear to build and the content of the discussion. The following questions can guide the observations: (1) To what extent do the two seem comfortable with each other? (2) How and to what extent did they "break the ice" (take action to make each other more comfortable)? (3) Did they clearly establish guidelines around how often to meet and how to contact each other? (4) To what extent did they discuss issues relevant to life at the university? (5) Did the mentor offer information of which the protégé may not have been aware? (6) Did the protégé identify several relevant areas of interest to learn about? (10 to 20 minutes)

Task 4:

At the end of the discussion, the mentor and protégé should provide each other with feedback, and, using the preceding questions, the observer should offer feedback to the pair.

Task 5:

Engage in a larger classroom discussion around the pairs' first meetings.

Activity 9–5: Creating a Game Plan to Use Your Developmental Network to Aid Your Career

Objectives:

1. To help you to understand the role your developmental network can play in furthering your desired career goals.
2. To contemplate how your developmental network can help you learn needed skills and competencies to reach your career goals.

Task 1:

Write down the names of individual(s) who you perceive currently help your career and personal development. Write down specific ways in which they help you. (5 minutes)

Task 2:

Choose a job or career of interest to you. Consider and write down what skills and knowledge you need to have and excel in this career. If you cannot identify a job or career of particular interest to you, more simply identify skills and knowledge you want to have if you are to excel in your career and life. (5 minutes)

Task 3:

Pair with another student in the class and share your ideas related to tasks 1 and 2. (10 minutes)

Task 4:

Consider the types of relational assistance you will need to help you develop the needed skills and knowledge. Next, answer the following questions: To what extent can your current developmental network help you to develop those skills and gain the knowledge? What types of individuals do you need to help you gain the needed skills and knowledge? (5 minutes)

Task 5:

Share your insights from task 4 with your partner. Together, brainstorm around what you each need to do to proactively develop and maintain the types of relationships you need to succeed.

Task 6:

The instructor will lead a large-group discussion around building a responsive developmental network.

Module

10

Conflict Management and Negotiation

LEARNING OBJECTIVES

After completing this module, you should be able to

1. Describe the nature of conflict dynamics and its impact on performance.
2. Explain the types and levels of conflict.
3. Describe the five individual conflict-handling styles.
4. Identify some conflict-handling strategies.
5. Compare and contrast distributed and integrative negotiations.
6. Explain cultural and gender differences in conflict and/or negotiations.

KEY TERMS AND CONCEPTS

Accommodating style
Affective conflict
Assertiveness
Avoidance style
Bargaining power
BATNA
Cognitive conflict
Collaborating style
Common enemy
Competitive style
Compromising style
Conflict
Conflict-handling modes
Cooperativeness
Distributive negotiation
Diversity-based conflict

Forcing style
Horizontal conflict
Integrative negotiation
Intergroup behavior
Intergroup communication
Intergroup conflict
Line-staff conflict
Negotiation
Relationship-focused conflict
Social-emotional conflict
Social intervention approach
Substantive conflict
Superordinate goals
Task-focused conflict
Team management
Vertical conflict

MODULE OUTLINE

PREMODULE PREPARATION

**Activity 10–1:
Exploring Conflict and
Negotiation Dynamics**

Introduction:

Most of this course's group activities to date have involved problem solving and decision making. For each activity, you were given specific situations and techniques with which to work. Exploring what happens to a group when it is confronted with an ambiguous, less structured task is the purpose of this exercise. Your team is to meet outside class for two hours to complete Task 1.

This exercise deals with two subjects: management of diversity and managers promoting competition among employees. These have been controversial issues in business and government organizations for many years. Everyone has opinions on these subjects, which become apparent when they search their minds carefully. This exercise will tap your reservoir of opinion.

In this exercise, please use no books, articles, or other reference material. This task is to be completed entirely from the interaction of minds, through sharing of knowledge and opinions, and via the synergistic development of ideas.

Task 1:

Teams are to meet outside class to examine their knowledge and attitudes on the topic and answer these questions:

a. What are the advantages and disadvantages of diversity at the workplace? To aid you in developing as complete a list as possible, groups might first compare and contrast homogenous and heterogeneous units in as many subjects as possible. (*Note:* There are a number of diversity aspects that we have not discussed in this course.)

b. What are the advantages and disadvantages of promoting competition among employees and among teams?

c. Under what conditions should a manager promote competition among his or her employees and teams? When should competition not be used as a management technique? Prepare your answers on one to three (not more) typewritten pages, using outline (not essay) form; be complete enough so the reader will understand the point you are making. (*Note:* Your team's completed answers should be delivered to the instructor at a designated time prior to the next class meeting so copies can be made. These copies will be used in Task 2.)

Task 2:

Your team and another team will be assigned the task of comparing the lists developed in Task 1. Each member of your group will be assigned to a dyad with a member of the other group. Dyad partners are to supply each other with copies of their team reports from Task 1. Each is to study the others and contrast it with his or her own. The papers are to be discussed in detail so that a complete understanding of the intent of the lists is communicated.

At the conclusion of the discussion, the dyad should reach an agreement as to which team paper represents the better solution for the assigned task. For this purpose each dyad has 20 points to divide up and assign to the papers. Thus, one paper could have a 20 and the other a 0 (or any other division of the points), but the judgment cannot be 10 to 10, since a final discrimination must be made. If there is an odd number of teams in the class, representatives from each of the last three teams will meet as triads; they will have 30 points to distribute, but there can be no 10–10–10 final judgments. (Time: 30 minutes) (*Note:* The *Instructor's Manual* has important guidance on how to conduct this case.)

Task 3:

After all dyads and triads have reached their conclusions, participants are to return to their teams. They will have two minutes to discuss their experience. The instructor will list the results on team charts on the board. This will be followed by a discussion and interpretation of the results.

Task 4:

The instructor will give a short lecture on the process involved.

INTRODUCTION

Conflicts of various types are an integral part of any human system. Conflict refers to "a process in which one party (person or group) perceives that its interests are being opposed or negatively affected by another party."[1] Many people view conflict as a negative experience, yet it plays an important role in human and system development. As of late, more and more companies are insisting that managers and employees learn conflict management skills. Conflict occurs at a variety of levels, and individuals seem to handle conflict differently. In the context of this course you have experienced conflict at the individual, team, organization, and class levels. In this module we explore the nature of conflict dynamics and discuss different conflict handling orientations and strategies to handle conflict. Negotiation as a means to solve conflict is examined, and negotiation strategies are explored.

THE NATURE OF CONFLICT DYNAMICS

Human behavior and performance are greatly influenced by the fact that **conflict** is built into both the individual and the society. While conflict can be destructive, it can also lead to problem solving and creativity when it is understood and coped with appropriately. Conflict and conflict dynamics are an integral ingredient of human and organizational life. Three distinct orientations about conflict are reported in the literature: The *traditional view* argues that conflict must be avoided, as it indicates a malfunction within the unit; the *human relations view* argues that conflict is a natural and inevitable phenomenon in any unit and, as such, serves as an important, positive (not evil) force in influencing the unit's performance; and the *system view,* the most recent view, proposes that conflict is not only inevitable but also absolutely necessary for any unit to perform effectively.[2]

Conflict can produce positive and negative outcomes, depending upon how well the parties involved manage their differences. Negative outcomes of conflict can include increased turnover, stress, and violence, while positive outcomes include increased motivation, generation of new perspectives, and personal satisfaction.[3] Whether the outcomes of conflict are ultimately positive or negative depends upon a number of factors, including the orientation the parties enter a discussion or intervention with, whether the interpersonal styles utilized are appropriate for the situation, and whether the parties understand the cultural nuances associated with cross-cultural negotiations.

Types and Levels of Conflict

At the most basic level, two types of conflicts can be found in the context of the work organization: affective and substantive. **Affective conflict** refers to conflict in interpersonal relations, while **substantive conflict** is conflict involving the group's task.[4] A modified typology proposed is of **cognitive,** task-related conflicts and **social-emotional conflicts,** characterized by interpersonal disagreements not directly related to the task.[5]

A somewhat different typology distinguishes between goal-oriented conflict, in which individuals pursue specific gains, and emotional-oriented conflict, which is a result of interpersonal interactions.[6] Thus, a few variations of task-versus-relationship typologies provide the foundation for the typology of conflict. A recent study of group conflict found that members distinguish between task-focused and relationship-focused conflicts and that these two types of conflict differently affect work group outcomes.[7]

The complexity of conflict dynamics is fostered by the additional distinction between five primary levels of conflict that may be present in any system: intrapersonal (within an individual), interpersonal (between individuals), intragroup (within a group), intergroup (between groups), and interorganizational (between organizations). Our focus in this module is on the conflict dynamics at the individual and team/group levels.

Conflict within the Individual

The socialization process, by definition, shapes the individual's drives and creates certain needs to make the individual a well-functioning member of society. This means he or she will conform to the group behaviors, values, customs, and standards and will not gratify individual wants and desires at the expense of others. This process is not without its toll to the comfort of the individual because it creates lifelong tensions and psychological conflicts.

The psychoanalytic approach to studying this phenomenon has emphasized the internal conflict people experience as they cope with their drives, needs, wants, and fears on the one hand and their internalized "parent" (the society that has been programmed into their mental processes) on the other. People feel compelled to obey society's dictates or suffer self-disapproval and guilt. In the extreme, this dynamic conflict results in psychosis, a state in which the individual has been overwhelmed by these opposing forces. Even when adequately coped with, the individual's psychological defense mechanisms can readily be aroused when confronted with certain types of frustration. Once aroused, fear and anger can be displaced onto available (presumably offending) targets. One indication of mental health is the maintenance of a self-image that facilitates the achievement of needs in a manner acceptable to society as the person has experienced it.

INTERPERSONAL CONFLICT HANDLING

Generally, when entering a conflict situation, a person can hold either a win–win or win–lose orientation. A win–win orientation involves the belief that both parties can experience beneficial outcomes if they work together toward mutual ends. A win–lose orientation involves the belief that due to limited resources or possibilities, a gain for one person must be made at the expense of the other. Quite often, what appears to be a win–lose situation can actually be one that is win–win, as long as the two parties are creative enough to consider various outcomes.

For example, consider a job applicant and an organizational manager who are about to enter a compensation agreement. It may seem that their interests are naturally in opposition in that the applicant would want as much money as possible and the manager would want to minimize salary, particularly if he or she has a limited budget. However, the job applicant might consider less money if given a few extra days of vacation, an upgraded computer, or the possibility of working at home one day a week as a means to minimize gas costs. The manager would also win because he or she could offer the lower salary leaving more room for increases later (given that salary bands cap at a certain salary).

Five Conflict-Handling Styles

The orientation that one holds when entering a situation will influence the style that person enacts. Two main dimensions underline the intentions of a person or group involved in a conflict situation: (1) **cooperativeness** (the degree to which the group wants to satisfy the concerns of the other group) and (2) **assertiveness** (the degree to which the group wants to satisfy its own concerns).[8] The two dimensions plotted in Figure 10–1 are reflected in five **conflict-handling modes.**

The **avoidance style** implies an unassertive, uncooperative approach in which both groups neglect the concerns involved by sidestepping the issue or postponing the conflict by choosing not to deal with it. The stance, "I don't like engaging in conflict" epitomizes

**Figure 10–1
Two-Dimensional Model
of Ways to Handle Conflict**

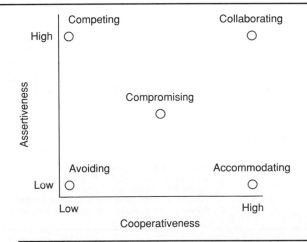

Source: Adapted from T. Ruble and K. Thomas, "Support for a Two-Dimensional Model of Conflict Behavior," *Organizational Behavior and Human Performance* 16 (1976), p. 145.

the avoidance style. The **competitive** (alternatively called **forcing**) **style** implies winning at the other's expense. This style is an assertive, uncooperative mode in which the groups attempt to achieve their own goals at the expense of the other through argument, authority, threat, or even physical force. The forcing style is manifest in the following statement: "When I engage with conflict with others, I push hard to ensure that I get an outcome that is satisfactory to me."

The **accommodating style** reflects an unassertive, cooperative position where one group attempts to satisfy the concerns of the other by neglecting its own concerns or goals. The statement, "I consider others' needs before my own when conflict arises between myself and others" reflects an accommodating style. The **compromising style** reflects the midpoint between the styles. It involves give-and-take by both groups. Both groups gain and give up something they want. This style is shown in the statement, "In situations of conflict, I believe that I and the other person should both give in a bit with our respective wants." The **collaborating style** is an assertive, cooperative mode that attempts to satisfy the concerns of both groups. It is different from the compromising orientation in that collaborating represents a desire to satisfy fully the concerns of both groups. The statement "Everyone can win in dealing with conflict if they're creative and seek out mutual gains" reflects a collaborative style. Of the five styles, the collaborating style is the only one that fully represents a win–win orientation; the other styles represent various forms of a win–lose orientation.[9]

The appropriate style depends on the nature of the situation, the task, and the people involved. Each style is used at one time or another. This taxonomy of conflict-handling modes has been interpreted in a number of ways, including behaviors, styles, and strategies.[10] Figure 10–2 captures the appropriate situation for each style.

Figure 10–2
Appropriate Situations for Five Conflict-Handling Styles

Conflict-Handling Models	Appropriate Situations
Competing	1. When quick, decisive action is vital (for example, emergencies). 2. On important issues where unpopular actions need implementing (for example, cost cutting, enforcing unpopular rules, discipline). 3. On issues vital to company welfare when you know you're right. 4. Against people who take advantage of noncompetitive behavior.
Collaborating	1. To find an integrative solution when both sets of concerns are too important to be compromised. 2. When your objective is to learn. 3. To merge insights from people with different perspectives. 4. To gain commitment by incorporating concerns into a consensus. 5. To work through feelings that have interfered with a relationship.
Compromising	1. When goals are important, but not worth the effort or potential disruption of more assertive modes. 2. When opponents with equal power are committed to mutually exclusive goals. 3. To achieve temporary settlements to complex issues. 4. To arrive at expedient solutions under time pressure. 5. As a backup when collaboration or competition is unsuccessful.
Avoiding	1. When an issue is trivial, or more important issues are pressing. 2. When you perceive no chance of satisfying your concerns. 3. When potential disruption outweighs the benefits of resolution. 4. To let people cool down and regain perspective. 5. When gathering information supersedes immediate decision. 6. When others can resolve the conflict more effectively. 7. When issues seem tangential or symptomatic of other issues.
Accommodating	1. When you find you are wrong—to allow a better position to be heard, to learn, and to show your reasonableness. 2. When issues are more important to others than yourself—to satisfy others and maintain cooperation. 3. To build social credits for later issues. 4. To minimize loss when you are outmatched and losing. 5. When harmony and stability are especially important. 6. To allow subordinates to develop by learning from mistakes.

Source: K. W. Thomas, "Toward Multi-Dimensional Values in Teaching: The Example of Conflict Behaviors," *Academy of Management Review* 2 (1977), Table 1, p. 487.

While the use of any one of the five conflict-handling styles is appropriate given a particular situation, research shows that more successful individuals and high-performing organizations (relative to medium- and low-performing organizations) tend to use collaboration. Avoiding and forcing, by way of comparison, tend to be associated with unfavorable results, including negative feelings from others. Compromising is most often accompanied by favorable feelings by others.[11]

Research suggests that individuals who are at higher stages (as one moves from a lower-level to a higher-level stage, one gains more sophisticated reasoning) of moral development are more likely to more frequently use collaborating styles and less frequently use avoiding and forcing styles than their lower-stage counterparts.[12]

Cultural and Gender Differences in Handling Conflict

More recently, studies have been conducted to assess whether and how individuals' preferred style of conflict may vary on the basis of gender or culture. Although research assessing how men and women handle conflict has been mixed (some studies showing no differences between genders in terms of how they handle conflict), a few studies suggest that men are more competitive (forcing) than women and women are more likely than men to avoid conflict. Other research suggests that women are more attentive than men to relationships and therefore more inclined to compromise to protect the relationship.[13]

As Chapter 9 noted, organizational demography shifts are bringing together individuals from different backgrounds and nationalities. It is therefore important to have an understanding of how dissimilarly others may handle conflict. It might be tempting for someone to believe that people of other nationalities handle conflict similarly. However, research suggests that this is not the case. For example, in a cross-country conflict examination, U.S. executives were shown to use more accommodating, compromising, and forcing styles, whereas Middle Eastern executives were more likely to use avoiding and collaborative (problem-solving) styles.[14] In a five-country study on conflict handling, U.S. respondents, relative to their Japanese and Korean counterparts, reported more frequent use of the forcing style. Chinese and Taiwanese, relative to their U.S. counterparts, reported more frequent use of accommodating and avoiding styles.[15] More generally, individuals from individualistic cultures (e.g., from the United States) are more likely than individuals from collectivistic cultures to use forcing and compromising styles. By comparison, individuals from collectivistic cultures are more likely to use avoidance or problem-solving styles as a means to maintain harmony with others.[16]

INTRATEAM CONFLICT

Conflict has been shown to produce both negative and positive intrateam processes and outcomes. Task and socioemotional conflict can reduce cooperation and coordination within teams; however, both can also lead to the benefits of increased alternatives generated and heightened, more diverse discussion of problems.[17] Recent research has shown that if conflict is not managed appropriately, teams will experience reduced trust, team member autonomy, and task interdependence. When team members lack trust in each other, they are more likely to increase monitoring of each other and thus restrict autonomous efforts. Likewise, when trust is low, some team members will take on additional tasks, reducing the number of tasks provided to team members who are considered potentially unreliable. Both reduced autonomy and interdependence represent a less-than-optimal team design, which can lead to poor performance.[18]

Modules 7 and 17W offer intrateam processes such as brainstorming and nominal decision-making techniques and options for handling social loafing that are designed to draw effectively on group members' differences and enhance a team's performance.

DEFINING AND HANDLING INTERGROUP CONFLICT

Intergroup conflict refers to clashes and opposition between two teams or groups. A recent study distinguished between **task-focused conflict** and **relationship-focused conflict** and found that both types of conflicts have an effect on teams' performance.[19]

Both types of conflict set the stage for four different categories of intergroup conflicts within organizations: **vertical conflict** (refers to clashes between employee groups at different levels), **horizontal conflict** (refers to clashes between groups of employees at the same level), **line-staff conflict** (refers to clashes between advisory/support teams and teams that are responsible for creating the goods or services), and **diversity-based conflict** (refers to clashes between groups due to the nature of diversity, such as race, gender, religion, and ethnicity).[20] This attachment to groups and the accompanying concern, apprehension, or distrust for other groups can be almost instantaneous. Warren G. Bennis reports the following, which would appear to support this idea:

> Jaap Rabbie, conducting experiments on intergroup conflict at the University of Utrecht, has been amazed by the ease with which conflict and stereotype develop. He brings into an experimental room two groups and distributes green name tags and pens to one group, red pens and tags to the other. The two groups do not compete; they do not even interact. They are only in sight of each other while they silently complete a questionnaire. Only 10 minutes are needed to activate defensiveness and fear, reflected in the hostile and irrational perceptions of both "reds" and "greens."[21]

The most famous field experiment on in-group/out-group dynamics and the reduction of intergroup conflict was conducted by Sherif et al. At a summer camp they succeeded in creating two groups of boys, each of which developed norms of its own that included hostility to the other group. Then, through further experimental arrangements, they succeeded in overcoming both groups' hostility.[22]

Robert R. Blake found a similar outcome when business executives were the subjects.[23] He and his associates brought 20 to 30 executives together in two-week workshops. They were formed into groups that developed the norms, group structure, and cohesiveness that characterized Sherif's subjects in the first phase. Two executive groups were then given an identical problem for which they were to find the "best" solution; these solutions were later evaluated. Under these conditions, win–lose power struggles spontaneously occurred. Each group enhanced its own position and downgraded its adversary's. Negative stereotypes arose toward the adversary. Intellectual distortion occurred; points upon which the two teams were in agreement were minimized or not recognized, and differences were highlighted. When representatives of the groups met to negotiate, the loyalty of the representatives to their groups became more important than logic. A representative who conceded was seen as a traitor by the group; a winner was a hero.

In the Sherif and Blake research, the conflict is reciprocal between specific adversary groups, which might be thought of as between teams. A similar relationship exists to some degree in the interface of categories, such as male–female, black–white, minority–non-minority, and boss–subordinate. Furthermore, the interface between levels of the hierarchy is characterized by differences in the way the members of the levels perceive their own and others' behaviors. Whenever people of one category perceive themselves or their roles differently than do those with whom they interface, the potential for conflict exists. Understanding the complexity of intergroup conflict requires a schema of **intergroup behavior.**

Why Managing Intergroup Conflict Is Important

In the context of this module, we go beyond the definition of a *group* which focuses on person-to-person relations. In this module, a *team* or *group* refers to (1) any one of the types of groups and teams previously mentioned, (2) a department or a business unit, or (3) any formal or informal classification of employees based on geographical location, hourly versus permanent workers, race, gender, ethnic background, religion, occupation, educational background, and so on.[24]

One way to think about an organization is to conceptualize it as a collection of interrelated groups operating at various levels of the organizational hierarchy. In any firm, a high degree of intergroup interaction is vital to the organization's success. The ability to diagnose and manage interteam interactions is essential to the firm because (1) in most organizations teams need to work with other teams to accomplish their goal, (2) the interdependency between the teams often creates dependency relationships that might foster conflict, and (3) conflicting team goals and the emerging dynamics between teams might influence the effectiveness of the firm.[25] Even in small companies, the production group must interact with the marketing/sales group, and both must interface with the accounting, human resources, and finance groups.

Sources of Intergroup Conflict

Several structural conditions in or influencing an organizational environment lead to manifest conflict. First, competition for scarce resources is generally agreed to be a major factor in initiating and perpetuating conflict in organizations. The scarce resources may be in innumerable forms, such as materials available, opportunities for promotion, power, recognition and status, attention from the boss, or competent secretaries. Second, task interdependence, which involves the need to interact to complete work, sharing of inputs to tasks, or receipt of outcomes that are contingent on others' outputs, creates significant opportunities for conflict. For example, consider a factory assembly line, in which each person receives as inputs the outputs of another person. To the extent that individuals produce poor-quality work and/or work more slowly than others, bottlenecks are created, slowing down employees' ability to complete quality work on time.

Third, incompatible goals can cause friction between groups. For example, manufacturing and sales groups often experience conflict. Manufacturing group members' goals typically center on product quality, whereas sales group members' goals revolve around selling as many products as possible. To the extent that sales group members push for maximum product output to the detriment of manufacturing quality, the groups will experience conflict. Fourth, differences in backgrounds, education, values, and experiences can cause misunderstandings and varying perceptions of how to approach situations. For example, as will be conveyed in greater detail later in the chapter, cultural differences can lead to different values and behavioral preferences, thus resulting in misunderstandings.[26]

Because these sources for conflict inevitably exist, how can intergroup conflict in organizations be lessened? How can behaviors facilitating coordination among functionally integrated units be enhanced? A number of theories, strategies, and techniques are relevant to achieving this goal. The following sections discuss several of these.

Recognition of the "Common Enemy"

Competition is a part of every American's education. Rivalry for grades or victory in sports—and all the accompanying values and behaviors—are carried from the school right into the organization. Managers often use the word *team* in the same win–lose sense they would use it on the ball field. While the coordination that helps an athletic team win is also needed to help an organization achieve its goals, promoting competition between functionally integrated units of an organization can be highly dysfunctional. Nevertheless, a common view among managers is that competition between employees is healthy because they see competition as one of the more effective motivating forces. The main point is that competition is not good or bad in itself, and the manager has to determine under what conditions it is functional or dysfunctional.

Some research evidence indicates that intergroup hostility between teams can be reduced when a **common enemy** is introduced.[27] Because all industrial organizations are in competition for their markets, emphasis on the common enemy of the closest competitor provides an opportunity for pitting the organizational team against an outsider as the team to beat.

Some readers will object to this procedure on various grounds, such as ethics or concern over whether the behavior developed against "the enemy" might not be turned back onto the organization. Rensis Likert advocates a more constructive approach, based on research of the management style and performance of the various offices of the sales force of a large company that operates nationally.[28] One finding was that the high-producing offices typically adopted group methods of management; the manager and the salespeople used group problem solving, group coaching, and group goal setting. Likert contrasts this approach with providing contest awards for highest sales by individuals. When the salespeople are pitted against one another this way, they do not share information about markets, leads, techniques, or problems. He concludes, "The best performance, lowest costs, and the highest levels of earnings and of employee satisfaction occur when the drive for a sense of personal worth is used to create strong motivational forces to *cooperate* rather than *compete* with one's peers and colleagues."[29] As an alternative, an individual can compete with a past record or strive to achieve goals set individually or group goals set by his or her work group.

Development of Superordinate Goals

Sherif's experiment illustrated the potential of reducing intergroup conflict through the achievement of goals that are important to both groups. Organizations cannot function without the attainment of **superordinate goals**—primary goals of an organization or competing groups that exceed those of individuals or subgroups—yet intergroup conflict and failure to coordinate are major deterrents to organizational effectiveness. While many reasons for these reactions are irrational in the sense that people are resisting working together, at least a part of the problem can be attributed to a lack of shared understanding as to what the goals are. Consultants who conduct team-building workshops often focus on this. Generally, members of a top-management team assume they all know the objectives and goals toward which they are working, but when they are asked to list the goals and rank their priorities, considerable variance is often found. Subordinates of the team indicate that these confusions are pushed down into the hierarchy and become a factor in interdivisional conflict.

The current surge for the development of shared organizational vision in industrial, government, and educational institutions can be seen as an attempt to identify the superordinate objectives and the objectives of each unit that functions to achieve them. When everyone works toward a set of individual, unit, and organizational objectives, the information level of all employees in carrying on their coordinated efforts is systematically raised, and perceptual distortion and communication problems are reduced. Fighting can arise spontaneously if two units assume they are working on the same objectives when they are not. The personality–communication–perception–motivation relationship we have been suggesting is directly applicable here.

Intergroup Communication

Research indicates that groups of strangers can develop in-group/out-group attitudes within a very few minutes. Sherif's experiments indicate how easily cohesive groups of boys can fall into the win–lose trap; Blake has shown executives are also highly susceptible. Organizations should take steps to ensure that groups have ample opportunities to interact, both socially and professionally. Cross-functional and task force teams that include members from various functional groups and levels within the organization are opportunities to create boundary-spanning relationships, the latter which can mediate information between groups and create greater understanding between group members.[30] Those individuals who occupy boundary spanning roles (roles that cross over the boundaries of various groups) should, in part, be chosen on the basis of possessing outstanding interpersonal skills; listening and empathy are skills needed to effectively convey group perceptions. Team building activities and social outings are also means to foster rapport among employees and thus heighten an interest in understanding each other.[31]

A Conflict-Handling Intervention

Workshop methods, a type of **social intervention approach,** are used to reduce conflict and promote collaboration, such as changing a win–lose condition to a win–win problem-solving situation. One general design can be accomplished in a one- or two-day workshop.[32]. Representatives of the two groups (such as management–labor, production–sales, or in government, personnel–security or administrative services–line functions) agree that they have serious problems and are committed to exploring thoroughly avenues of better cooperation. First they work in separate team rooms to develop a statement of how each group sees itself as behaving toward the other group. The items from this statement are listed on a large pad. Second, each group makes a list of items that outline how it perceives the other group as behaving toward it. Third, the two groups meet and share their lists. The meeting provides an opportunity for them to explore, in an objective setting and under the guidance of a consultant, the problems of perception, communication, and interaction they are having. This process is somewhat similar in function to the organizational dialoguing (Where are you? Where am I?) used in Module 2.

Other Methods of Reducing Intergroup Conflict

Other vehicles for mitigating intergroup conflict include creating diverse experiences for employees as a means to overcome dissimilar backgrounds, maximizing resources, and clarifying rules. As noted earlier, dissimilarity caused misunderstandings among employees. Programs such as rotational programs, in which people are exposed to various business functions; cross-functional teams, which enable employees to understand the perspectives of other groups; and organization-customized executive or other training programs, which are aimed at education beyond an employee's functional area, can all create a common, holistic understanding of the business and its challenges. To the extent possible, senior executives and other decision makers need to consider both how resources are allocated and how to expand the resource pool as a means to minimize conflict. Finally, many organizational conflicts occur when rules and procedures are either not in place or in need of clarification. For example, roles, responsibilities, and authority need to be clarified in such a way that employees are not left to debate them.[33]

NEGOTIATION AS A MEANS OF HANDLING CONFLICT

When we speak of conflict management styles, we generally think of superior–subordinate relationships and chains of command between individuals and/or teams. But what about situations where there is no authority relationship present? Or even in superior–subordinate relationships, is it better to be *required* to do something or to *agree* to do something? In situations where there is both conflict and interdependence, the process used to deal with conflict is **negotiation.** Both conditions are necessary for negotiation to take place. Without conflict there is nothing to negotiate about; without interdependence, there is no reason to negotiate. In addition, the parties must believe that engaging in the process may produce an outcome that is superior to one that otherwise might occur. Negotiation has been defined as "a process in which two or more interdependent individuals or groups, who perceive that they have both common and conflicting goals, state and discuss proposals and preferences for specific terms of a possible agreement."[34]

In this section, we discuss two types of negotiations, processes to consider in effective negotiations and interventions, how culture influences negotiations, and two considerations in negotiating across cultures effectively.

Types of Negotiation

Distributive Negotiation

There are two basic types of negotiation situations. One is called *distributive* negotiation, or win–lose bargaining. This situation is found when we negotiate the price of a car or a house. The other type of negotiation is called *integrative* negotiation, or win–win bargaining. In such a negotiation, the parties seek a solution that meets or maximizes both of their interests.[35]

In a typical **distributive negotiation,** the negotiators have both a preferred outcome and a least desired outcome. The former is called a target point, while the latter is called a resistance point, because agreeing to a settlement below that point would be worse than not agreeing at all. Success in distributive negotiation is measured by how close to the target point an individual can arrive at in bargaining. This is sometimes called "claiming value." For example, if Alex were selling his car, he might like to get $7,500 for it, but would accept $7,000. Alice, as the potential buyer would like to pay $6,800 and would not be willing to pay more than $7,400. This can be diagrammed as follows:

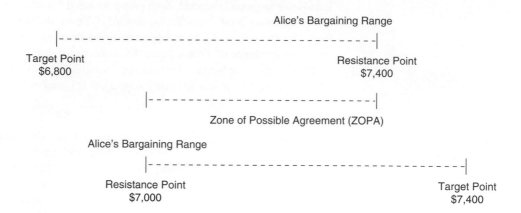

Alice's Bargaining Range

Target Point
$6,800

Resistance Point
$7,400

Zone of Possible Agreement (ZOPA)

Alice's Bargaining Range

Resistance Point
$7,000

Target Point
$7,400

We can predict that the final selling price for the vehicle will be somewhere between $7,000 and $7,400. This zone of possible agreement, or ZOPA, reflects the area between the two parties' resistance points. If there is no overlap, there will likely be no deal. If Alex wanted a minimum of $7,000 for the car, and Alice was not prepared to pay more than $6,900, these two presumably would not strike a bargain—unless, of course, one of them could influence the other's resistance point.

Attempting to determine and influence the opponent's resistance point while attempting to disguise one's own resistance point is part of the tactics used in distributive bargaining. (In the preceding example, if Alex tells Alice that he would like to get $7,500 for his car but will sell it for $7,000, he is unlikely to get more than $7,000 for the car!) A variety of tactics are available to use in distributive bargaining, including making an initial offer or demand far below or above the person's target point, thus attempting to "anchor" a price in the lower or higher range of possible settlements. Concessions play a major part in distributive bargaining, and refusing to make concessions or making very small concessions are other examples of behaviors that attempt to anchor a settlement in an advantageous part of the zone of potential agreement. Bluffing, lying, exaggerating one's own concessions, and belittling the concessions of one's opponent are all potential tactics.

Such tactics are particularly appropriate when a person is out to get the best deal possible and where the relationship between the parties is not important. But what about situations where there is an ongoing relationship, where the seller hopes that the buyer may become a regular customer, or where individuals must work together on a continuing basis? The following matrix suggests that a negotiator's behavior may well change if the nature of the relationship is added to the equation.

		Is the *substantive outcome* important to the negotiator?	
		Yes	No
Is the *relationship outcome* important to the negotiator?	Yes	Collaborating	Accommodating
		Competing	Avoiding
			No

Thus, where the relationship is important and the substantive outcome is unimportant, the negotiator would be expected to be accommodative of the other side's position. Conversely, where the relationship is unimportant, but the outcome very important, a conventional competing style would be appropriate. Where both the relationship and the outcome are important, a collaborating style is suggested. Where neither the outcome nor the relationship is important, there is no reason to negotiate.[36]

Integrative Negotiation

In an **integrative negotiation** situation, the conflict between the parties may be more apparent than real, or the interests of both parties can potentially be satisfied. In their well-known book, *Getting to Yes,* Fisher and Ury expounded a process called "principled negotiation" as a basis for integrative negotiation, or creating value for both sides. This process has four elements:

1. *Separate the people from the problem.* Negotiators should focus on the problem and not on attacking each other.

2. *Focus on interests, not positions.* The negotiator should attempt to determine and focus on the *needs* of the other party, not the particular position he or she takes.

3. *Invent options for mutual gain.* Negotiators should attempt to develop a variety of solutions and choose between them rather than look for a single "right" answer.

4. *Insist on using objective criteria.* By using agreed-upon objective criteria, neither party has to "give in" to the other but can defer to a "fair" solution.[37]

As an example of the foregoing, consider a renter and lessor addressing whether or not to allow the renter to have a puppy. The two had not had a particularly friendly relationship, and therefore it was, at the onset, difficult for the two parties to move beyond their mutual dislike for each other. The lessor's initial position was not to allow the dog. A heated discussion began, and the two began making personal attacks, that is, until the renter asked that they try to focus on the question of whether to allow the dog. Calmed momentarily, the lessor explained that his concern was less about the dog and more about what damage the dog would do to the house. For example, he explained, if the dog wet the carpet, he would incur costs to have the carpet cleaned. Likewise, the dog's hair could shed on the carpet and the new couch.

Initially, the lessor asked if the renter would consider an adult dog that was already housebroken as a way to minimize the risk of damage to the house. The renter's interest, however, was to have a puppy. As an alternative solution, then, the renter offered to have the carpets cleaned prior to leaving the apartment and pay an extra $1,500 as a deposit. Because the lessor could not be sure of the costs associated with the carpet damage—which could conceivably lead to the replacement of all carpets—he decided that he would call to get an estimate (as objective criterion). Once he, the lessor, received an estimate of the full carpet replacement costs, he would offer what deposit amount would be appropriate.

Thus, the integrative negotiation process requires openness, extensive communication, learning, ingenuity, and joint problem solving. The behaviors needed for successful integrative bargaining are almost the exact opposite of the behaviors needed for successful distributive negotiation. This dichotomy presents a real dilemma for the negotiator. Unless the negotiator is willing to risk engaging in integrative behavior, the benefits (that is, mutual gain) from an integrative negotiation situation cannot be achieved. However, if the other party does not behave in a similar manner, or approaches the situation as a distributive negotiation, using the appropriate tactics for such a negotiation, the use of integrative negotiation behaviors may result in a situation disadvantageous to the negotiator. This can be diagrammed as follows:[38]

	Strategy of Party A	
	Integrative	Distributive
Strategy of Party B		
Distributive	Outcome: Good for B Bad for A	Outcome: Mediocre for A Mediocre for B
Integrative	Outcome: Good for B Bad for A	Outcome: Good for A Bad for B

In truth, there are integrative and distributive elements in any negotiation situation. A situation may have both kinds of issues in it. If integrative negotiation creates value, or increases the size of the pie, the pie must still be divided. However, value cannot be claimed unless it has been created. This essential tension between cooperation and competitiveness in negotiation is one that must be recognized and managed.

Investigative Negotiation

Consistent with integrative negotiation, a recent *Harvard Business Review* article asserts that the more effective way to negotiate is to "approach the situation in the way a detective approaches a crime scene."[39] Among the principles to successful negotiating posited by the authors, Malhotra and Bazerman, are

1. Instead of focusing on *what* the other party wants, figure out *why* they want it. Often, the reason underlying resistance to negotiating is not the one implied by what the other party overtly states wanting.

2. Seek to understand and minimize the other party's constraints. By asking why the other party wants a certain outcome(s), a negotiator can understand and help the other party overcome its constraints. Too often, a negotiator is inclined to label another party's constraints as "their problem." Working with the other party, instead of against them, is often the only way to strike a deal considered acceptable to both parties.

3. Consider the other party's demands as hidden opportunities. More often than not, a negotiator becomes defensive when confronted with demands that seem unreasonable. An investigative negotiator considers demands in another light, considering, "What can I learn from the other side's insistence on this issue? What does this demand tell me about this party's needs and interests?"[40]

Malhotra and Bazerman explain that investigative negotiation requires challenging the long-accepted notion that to "win" a negotiation, it is critical to "sell" one's position. Investigating the other side's interests, priorities, and constraints builds trust and cooperation and is more likely than selling to create mutually satisfying outcomes.

Power and Leverage in Negotiation

One concept that is useful in any negotiation is called **BATNA,** an acronym for best alternative to a negotiated agreement. The notion here is that the negotiator should work to develop alternatives to a particular negotiated agreement. Developing such alternatives helps evaluate how good a particular deal is and puts a negotiator in a position to walk away from a negotiated outcome that is unsatisfactory, or a negotiation situation in which the other side is behaving inappropriately.

Having a BATNA is a source of power in negotiations. Understanding both process and outcomes in negotiation involves understanding bargaining power and its use. **Bargaining power** in a two-party negotiation can be described as follows:[41]

$$\text{Bargaining power of A} = \frac{\text{Cost to B of disagreeing with A's terms}}{\text{Cost to B of agreeing with A's terms}}$$

$$\text{Bargaining power of B} = \frac{\text{Cost to A of disagreeing with B's terms}}{\text{Cost to A of agreeing with B's terms}}$$

The notion of bargaining power does not lend itself to detailed calculation, in part because bargaining power is based on the *perceived* costs of agreement or disagreement. Effectiveness in negotiation involves both acquiring power (for example, stockpiling inventory in a labor–management dispute) and influencing the other side's perception of the negotiator's power (Take the deal today—it won't be available tomorrow, because I will have sold to another bidder). Inside organizations, there are many kinds and sources of power, including information and expertise, control over scarce resources (reward power), and position in an organization structure.[42]

Negotiation Structures

In our discussion so far, we have used two-party negotiations as examples of the process. However, negotiations are often more complex in practice. For example, negotiations can involve three or more parties, which adds goal complexity, strategic complexity, and procedural complexity to the process. Negotiations can occur between organizations, or between divisions or departments or teams within the same organization, as would occur, for example, over transfer pricing within an organization.

When negotiations occur between organizations, or between divisions or departments or teams within an organization, or between an organization and its employees, as is the case when a union is present, the organizations are often represented by an individual who has formal negotiation authority to act as an agent for the organization, negotiating a deal on behalf of the organization, with any agreement subject to some sort of ratification process. In these types of situations, there is the across-the-table negotiation between the two (or more) negotiators, and there is also negotiation between the negotiator and the organization he or she represents over the terms of the agreement being negotiated. We can think of cross-functional teams in organizations, such as new-product development teams, in which each functional representative acts as an agent/negotiator for his or her department, negotiating with other team members as well as his or her own department on the details of the product and each department's role in its development.

These negotiations within an organization typically involve a greater number of mutual interests than negotiations between individuals or organizations. These would include organizational interests, subunit interests, personal interests (career path, compensation, status, reputation), and relationship interests. In intraorganizational negotiations, there is almost always an ongoing relationship present. These negotiations occur within an organizational structure that influences who negotiates, what the subject of negotiations is, and where negotiations occur. Formal authority within organizations can influence criteria for acceptability (for example, "my boss won't agree that our department should do this.") as well as delegation of negotiation authority and decision rights. Within an organization, an individual's BATNA may well be to say "yes" and then do nothing to implement an agreement. Finally, intraorganizational negotiations may involve the development of coalitions between individuals or units, a process that also involves negotiation to establish the terms of joining such a coalition.

The Influence of Culture on Negotiations

A recent study claims that a critical component of negotiation is the negotiation orientation. A comprehensive conceptual framework that includes the following 12 dimensions was advanced:

1. Basic concept of negotiation—distributive or integrative.
2. Most significant type of issue—task or relationship.
3. Selection of negotiators—abilities or status.
4. Influence of individual aspirations—individualist or collectivist.
5. Internal decision-making process—independent or majority rule.
6. Orientation toward time—monochromic or polychromic.
7. Risk-taking propensity—risk-averse or risk-tolerant.
8. Basis of trust—external or internal.
9. Concern for protocol—formal or informal.
10. Style of communication—low context or high context.
11. Nature of persuasion—factual inductive or affective.
12. Form of agreement—explicit contract or implicit agreement.[43]

In a set of empirical studies, distinct cultural orientations were identified.[44] For example, when Mexican and U.S. respondents completed the research survey, responded orientations were different on 22 of the 24 constructs.[45] Based on the results of their study, the researchers generated a set of implications for preparation before embarking on negotiations between firms that function on either side of the border.

Earlier in the chapter, we explained how culture can influence how someone approaches conflict. Here, we discuss how individuals from various nations approach negotiations. While there are some similarities in negotiating across cultures, there are a number of features that are unique to a particular national setting. For example, the chapter discussed the two basic negotiating orientations: win–win (integrative) and win–lose (distributive). Table 10–1 shows the percentage of negotiators from various countries who reported approaching negotiations with a win–win attitude. The table also shows whether the negotiators prefer formal versus informal negotiations and the degree to which general or specific contracts as negotiation outcomes.[46]

In conducting a cross-culture negotiation, an individual should consider the foregoing cultural differences as well as relationship and time considerations if he or she is to be effective.[47] In order to build trust and rapport, foundations of cross-cultural negotiations, it is critical to get to know the other parties professionally and personally. Treating others with respect and allowing the possibility of face-saving outcomes will engender trust and increase the likelihood of positive outcomes. It is also important to recognize that favorable relationships, in many countries, open the door to negotiations by signaling trust between

Table 10–1
Culture and Negotiating Orientation

NEGOTIATING ATTITUDE: WIN–WIN OR WIN–LOSE (Win–Win %)

Japan	100
China	82
Argentina	81
France	80
India	78
USA	71
UK	59
Mexico	50
Germany	55
Nigeria	47
Brazil	44
Spain	37

PERSONAL STYLE: FORMAL OR INFORMAL (Formal %)

Nigeria	53
Spain	47
China	46
Mexico	42
UK	35
Argentina	35
Germany	27
Japan	27
India	22
Brazil	22
France	20
USA	17

AGREEMENT FORM: GENERAL OR SPECIFIC (General %)

Japan	46
Germany	45
India	44
France	30
China	27
Argentina	27
Brazil	22
USA	22
Nigeria	20
Mexico	17
Spain	16
UK	11

Source: Adapted from J. W. Salacuse, "Ten Ways That Culture Affects Negotiating Style: Some Survey Results," *Negotiation Journal,* July (1998), pp. 221–40.

participants. For example, in China, negotiations often only occur when a trusted individual makes an introduction between potential parties. Guanxi, a form of social capital in China, involves long-term reciprocity between individuals; any hesitancy that a person or group has regarding involvement with another can be minimized through a trusted other.

Cross-cultural negotiations require patience regarding the time it may take to secure an agreement suitable to both parties. Even in the context of a particular face-to-face exchange, silence may leave some participants—for example, U.S. participants—feeling uncomfortable, while it may be welcomed by others, as is the case for Chinese and Japanese participants.

SUMMARY

Conflict is a complex phenomenon and a multilevel concept that can have an effect on behavior at the individual, group, and organizational levels. In this module we focused on conflict at the individual, team, and intergroup levels within the organizational context. A discussion of five main conflict-handling styles was followed by a short overview of sources of conflict. Next we discussed a variety of ways for handling conflict, including negotiation as one such mechanism. Two basic types of negotiation, distributed and integrative, were described and cross-cultural differences in negotiating were overviewed. This module's activities provide an opportunity to develop the ability to diagnose, handle individual and intergroup conflict, and develop and practice negotiation strategies.

Study Questions

1. Describe the different views about conflict. What makes conflict a complex phenomenon?

2. Based on what you have read in this and prior chapters, identify ways that your team can effectively manage conflict that may arise.

3. Under what conditions is promoting competition between groups in an organization effective? When might stimulating competition be disruptive?

4. We discussed some ways to reduce intergroup conflict. From your own experience, give other methods of coping with conflict that you have used or seen others use meaningfully.

5. Compare and contrast any two of the modes for handling intergroup conflict.

6. A researcher argued that "Negotiation can increase or reduce conflict." What would be your position? Explain your answer.

7. In your experience, what are some ways to negotiate effectively?

8. The chapter identified ways in which culture influences how people may differentially negotiate. Drawing on your own negotiating experiences, how do cross-cultural negotiations differ from domestic negotiations?

Endnotes

1. Adapted from J. Weiss and J. Hughes, "Want Collaboration? Accept—and Actively Manage—Conflict." *Harvard Business Review* 83, no. 3 (2005), pp. 92–101.

2. Conflict is discussed in C. A. Amason, K. R. Thompson, W. A. Hoachwater, and A. W. Harrison, "Conflict: An Important Dimension in Successful Management Teams," *Organizational Dynamics* (Autumn 1995), pp. 20–35; A. C. Amason, "Distinguishing the Effects of Functional and Dysfunctional Conflict on Strategic Decision Making: Resolving a Paradox for Top Management Teams," *Academy of Management Journal* (February 1996), pp. 123–48; and

K. A. Jehn, "A Qualitative Analysis of Conflict Types and Dimensions in Organizational Groups," *Administrative Science Quarterly* 42 (1997), pp. 530–57.

3. R. R. Blake and J. S. Moulton, *Solving Costly Organizational Conflicts* (San Francisco: Jossey-Bass, 1984); F. Rose, "The Eisner School of Business," *Fortune* (July 6, 1998), pp. 29–30. M. Rempel and R. J. Fisher, "Perceived Threat, Cohesion, and Group Problem Solving in Intergroup Conflict," *International Journal of Conflict Management* 8 (1997), pp. 216–34; R. A. Baron, "Positive Effects of Conflict: A Cognitive Perspective," *Employee Responsibilities and Rights Journal* (1991), pp. 25–36; Amason, "Distinguishing the Effects of Functional and Dysfunctional Conflict on Strategic Decision Making."

4. H. Guetzkow and J. Gyr, "An Analysis of Conflict in Decision Making Groups," *Human Relations* 7 (1954), pp. 367–81.

5. R. Priem and K. Price, "Process and Outcomes Expectations for the Dialectical Inquiry, Devil's Advocacy, and Consensus Techniques of Strategic Decision Making," *Group and Organization Studies* 16 (1991), pp. 206–25.

6. R. Pinkley, "Dimensions of Conflict Frame: Disputant Interpretations of Conflict," *Journal of Applied Psychology* 75 (1990), pp. 117–25.

7. K. Jehn, "A Multimethod Examination of the Benefits and Detriments of Intragroup Conflict," *Administrative Science Quarterly* 40 (1995), pp. 256–82.

8. K. W. Thomas, "Conflict and Negotiation Processes in Organizations," in H. C. Triandis, M. D. Dunnette, and L. M. Hough (eds.), *Handbook of Industrial and Organizational Psychology,* vol. 3, 2nd ed. (Palo Alto, CA: Consulting Psychologists Press, 1994), p. 653; K. W. Thomas, "Conflict and Conflict Management: Reflection and Update," *Journal of Organizational Behavior* 13 (1992), pp. 265–74; M. A. Rahim, "A Measure of Styles of Handling Interpersonal Conflict," *Academy of Management Journal* 26 (1983), pp. 368–76.

9. R. J. Lewicki and J. A. Litterer, *Negotiation* (Homewood, IL: Irwin, 1985); K. W. Thomas, "Toward Multi-Dimensional Values in Teaching: The Example of Conflict Behaviors," *Academy of Management Review* 2, no. 34, pp. 484–90.

10. K. W. Thomas, "Conflict and Negotiation Processes in Organizations," in Triandis, Dunnette, and Hough (eds.), *Handbook of Industrial and Organizational Psychology,* p. 653; and K. W. Thomas, "Conflict and Conflict Management: Reflection and Update," *Journal of Organizational Behavior* 13 (1992), pp. 265–74; M. A. Rahim, "A Measure of Styles of Handling Interpersonal Conflict," *Academy of Management Journal* 26 (1983), pp. 368–76.

11. M. A. Gross and L. K. Guerrero, "Managing Conflict Appropriately and Effectively: An Application of the Competence Model to Rahim's Organizational Conflict Styles," *International Journal of Conflict Management* 11 (2000), pp. 200–26; F. P. Brew and D. R. Cairns, "Styles of Managing Interpersonal Workplace Conflict in Relation to Status and Face Concern: A Study of Anglos and Chinese," *International Journal of Conflict Management* 15 (2004), pp. 25–56.

12. M. A. Rahim, G. F. Buntzman, and D. White, "An Empirical Study of the Stages of Moral Development and Conflict Management," *International Journal of Conflict Management* 10, no. 2 (1999), pp. 154–71.

13. M. N. Chanin and J. A. Schneer, "A Study of the Relationship between Jungian Personality Dimensions and Conflict-Handling Behavior," *Human Relations* 37 (1984), pp. 863–79; P. Shockley-Zalabak, "The Effects of Sex Differences on the Preference for Utilization of Conflict Styles of Managers in a Work Setting: An Exploratory Study," *Public Personnel Management Journal* 10 (1981), pp. 289–95; G. Sadri and M. Rahmatian, "Resolving Conflict: Examining Ethnic-Racial and Gender Differences," *Equal Opportunities International* 22, no. 2 (2003), pp. 25–39.

14. S. M. Elsayed-Ekhouly and R. Buda, "Organizational Conflict: A Comparative Analysis of Conflict Styles across Cultures,"*International Journal of Conflict Management* 7, no. 1 (1996), pp. 71–80.

15. S. Ting-Toomey, G. Gao, P. Trubisky, Z. Yang, H. Kim, S. Lin, and T. Nishida, "Culture, Face Maintenance, and Conflict Styles of Handling Interpersonal Conflict: A Study in Five Cultures,"*International Journal of Conflict Management* 2 (1991), pp. 275–91.

16. C. C. Chen, X. P. Chen, and J. R. Meindl, "How Can Cooperation Be Fostered? The Cultural Effects of Individualism-Collectivism," *Academy of Management Review* 23 (1998), pp. 285–304.

17. R. R. Blake and J. S. Mouton, *Solving Costly Organizational Conflicts* (San Francisco: Jossey-Bass, 1984); F. Rose, "The Eisner School of Business," *Fortune* (July 6, 1998), pp. 29–30; Amason, "Distinguishing the Effects of Functional and Dysfunctional Conflict on Strategic Decision Making"; L. L. Putnam, "Productive Conflict: Negotiation as Implicit Coordination," *International Journal of Conflict Management* 5 (1994), pp. 285–99; R. A. Baron, "Positive Effects of Conflict: A Cognitive Perspective," *Employee Responsibilities and Rights Journal* 4 (1991), pp. 25–36.

18. C. W. Langfred, "The Downside of Self-Management: A Longitudinal Study of the Effects of Conflict on Trust, Autonomy and Task Interdependence in Self-Managing Teams," *Academy of Management Journal* 50, no. 4, pp. 885–900.

19. K. A. Jehn, "A Qualitative Analysis of Conflict Types and Dimensions in Organizational Groups," *Administrative Science Quarterly* 42 (1997), pp. 530–57.

20. D. Hellriegel, J. W. Slocum, Jr., and R. W. Woodman, *Organizational Behavior* (Cincinnati, OH: South-Western College Publishing, 1998).

21. Verbal communication from Rabbie to Bennis in W. G. Bennis and P. E. Slater, *The Temporary Society* (New York: Harper & Row, 1968), p. 66.

22. M. Sherif, O. J. Harvey, B. J. White, W. R. Hod, and C. Sherif, *Intergroup Conflict and Cooperation* (Norman, OK: University of Oklahoma Book Exchange, 1961). Also see M. Sherif and C. Sherif, *Social Psychology* (New York: Harper & Row, 1969), Chapter 11.

23. R. R. Blake, H. A. Shephard, and J. S. Mouton, *Managing Intergroup Conflict in Industry* (Houston: Gulf Publishing, 1964), Chapter 2.

24. H. C. Triandis, L. L. Kurowski, and M. J. Gelfand, "Workplace Diversity," in Triandis, Dunnette, and Hough (eds.), *Handbook of Industrial and Organizational Psychology,* vol. 4, pp. 769–827.

25. See, for example, R. A. Guzzo and G. P. Shea, "Group Performance and Intergroup Relations in Organizations," in Triandis, Dunnette, and Hough (eds.), *Handbook of Industrial and Organizational Psychology,* pp. 269–313.

26. R. C. Liden, S. J. Wayne, and L. K. Bradway, "Task Interdependence as a Moderator of the Relation between Group Control and Performance," *Human Relations* 50 (1997), pp. 169–81; R. E. Walton and J. M. Dutton, "The Management of Conflict: A Model and Review," *Administrative Science Quarterly* 16 (1969), pp. 73–84; W. W. Notz, F. A. Starke, and J. Atwell, "The Manager as Arbitrator: Conflicts over Scarce Resources," in Bazerman and Lewicki (eds.), *Negotiating in Organizations,* pp. 143–64; S. L. McShane and M. A. Von Glinow, *Organizational Behavior: Emerging Realities for the Workplace Revolution,* 2nd ed. (McGraw-Hill, Irwin, 2003).

27. Sherif and Sherif, *Social Psychology,* p. 255.

28. R. Likert, *The Human Organization* (New York: McGraw-Hill, 1967), pp. 52–59.

29. Ibid., pp. 73–75.

30. G. M. Parker, *Cross-Functional Teams* (San-Francisco: Jossey-Bass, 1994).

31. R. J. Fisher, E. Maltz, and B. J. Jaworski, "Enhancing Communication between Marketing and Engineering: The Moderating Role of Functional Identification," *Journal of Marketing* 61 (1997), pp. 54–70.

32. See H. A. Hornstein, B. B. Bunker, W. W. Burke, M. Gindes, and R. J. Lewicki, *Social Intervention* (New York: Free Press, 1971), pp. 355–56; R. Beckhard, *Organization Development: Strategies and Models* (Reading, MA: Addison-Wesley, 1969), pp. 33–35; and Blake, Shephard, and Mouton, *Managing Intergroup Conflict in Industry,* App. 1.

33. S. L. McShane and M. A. Von Glinow, *Organizational Behavior: Emerging Realities for the Workplace Revolution,* 2nd ed. (Burr Ridge, IL: McGraw-Hill/ Irwin, 2003); E. Horwitt, "Knowledge, Knowledge, Who's Got the Knowledge?" *Computerworld* (April 8, 1996), pp. 81, 84.

34. R. J. Lewicki, B. Barry, and D. M. Saunders, *Negotiation,* 5th ed. (Boston: McGraw-Hill/Irwin, 2006), 1.

35. R. Walton and R. McKersie, *A Behavioral Theory of Labor Negotiations* (New York: McGraw-Hill, 1965).

36. G. Savage, J. Blair, and R. Sorenson, "Consider Both Relationships and Substance When Negotiating Strategically," *Academy of Management Executive* 3, no. 1 (February 1989), pp. 37–47.

37. R. Fisher and W. Ury, *Getting to Yes* (Boston: Houghton Mifflin, 1981).

38. D. Lax and J. Sebenius, *The Manager as Negotiator* (New York: Free Press, 1986), pp. 29–45.

39. D. Malhotra and M. H. Bazerman, "Integrative Negotiation," *Harvard Business Review* (September 2007), pp. 73–78.

40. Ibid, p. 76.

41. N. W. Chamberlain, and J. W. Kuhn, *Collective Bargaining* (New York, McGraw-Hill, 1965), pp. 170–71.

42. For a full discussion of power in organizations, see J. R. P. French and B. Raven, "The Bases of Social Power," in D. Cartwright (ed.), *Group Dynamics: Research and Theory* (Evanston, IL: Row, Peterson, 1962).

43. L. Metcalf and A. Bird, "Integrating the Hofstede Dimensions and Twelve Aspects of Negotiating Behavior," in H. Vinken, J. Soeters, and P. Ester (eds.), *Comparing Cultures: Dimensions of Culture in a Comparative Perspective* (Leiden: Koninklijke Bill B.V., 2004), pp. 251–69.

44. L. Metcalf and A. Bird, "Mexico and the United States: Common Border, Common Negotiating Orientations," *Thundenberg International Business Review* 50, no. 1 (2008), pp. 25–43.

45. L. Metcalf, A. Bird, M. Shankarmahesh, Z. Ayean, J. Larimo, and D. Dewer, "Cultural Tendencies in Negotiation: A Comparison of Finland, India, Mexico, Turkey, and the United States," *Journal of World Business* 41 (2006), pp. 382–94.

46. Adapted from J. W. Salacuse, "Ten Ways That Culture Affects Negotiating Style: Some Survey Results," *Negotiation Journal* (July 1998), pp. 221–40.

47. M. A. Boyer, *Negotiating in a Complex World: An Introduction to International Negotiation,* 2nd ed. (London: Littlefield Brown Publishers, 2005); M. J. Gelfand and J. M. Brett (eds.), *The Handbook of Negotiation and Culture* (Palo Alto, CA: Stanford University Press).

Activity 10–2:
The Prisoners' Dilemma

Objective:

To explore the dynamics of intergroup competition and its effect on performance.

Task 1:

Using your permanent teams, break teams into pairs, designating one team Red and the other Blue. If there are an odd number of teams, members of the extra one should be divided among the other teams, but no Red or Blue should have more than eight members for this activity. The instructor will indicate whether there are to be observers. Be sure that each set of Red and Blue teams is sufficiently isolated from the other sets so everyone can carry on interactions without disturbing the others. Do not communicate with the other team until the instructor indicates the exercise is to start.

Tear out the Prisoners' Dilemma Tally Sheet at the end of the instructions, and study the directions. Your instructor will answer any questions you have about scoring. (Time: 10 minutes)

Task 2:

Your instructor will tell you when to begin. You will have three minutes to make a team decision. When the instructor tells you to do so, enter your team's decision on the tally sheet. Choices of the teams for round 1 will be announced and the scores entered.

Task 3:

After all rounds have been completed, take a moment to note your reactions to the competition.

a. What effect did the ban on communication with the other group have?

b. Did you or others in your team become aggressive? want to compromise? feel frustrated? withdraw?

c. How might a situation like this develop in a working organization?

Task 4:

Your instructor will lead a discussion of the exercise, drawing on the insights of observers and participants' notes. A lecture on intergroup competition will conclude this exercise.

Name _____ Date _____

PRISONERS' DILEMMA ROUND 10 PREDICTION SHEET AND TALLY SHEET*

**Prisoners' Dilemma
Round 10 Prediction Sheet**

Predicting team	Predicted choice	
	Red team	Blue team
Red	◯	
Blue		◯

*Adapted from: J. William Pfeiffer and John E. Jones (eds.), *A Handbook of Structural Experiences for Human Relations Training,* vol. 3 (San Diego, CA: University Associates, 1974). Used with permission.

PRISONERS' DILEMMA TALLY SHEET*

Instructions: For 10 consecutive rounds, the Red Team will choose either an A or a B, and the Blue Team will choose an X or a Y. The score for each team in a round is determined by choices of both teams, according to the following payoff schedule.

AX—Both teams win 3 points.
AY—Red Team loses 6 points; Blue Team wins 6 points.
BX—Red Team wins 6 points; Blue Team loses 6 points.
BY—Both teams lose 3 points.

		Scoresheet			
		Choice		Score	
Round	Minutes	Red Team	Blue Team	Red Team	Blue Team
1	3				
2	3				
3	3				
4**	3 (reps)				
	3 (teams)				
5	3				
6	3				
7	3				
8	3				
9†	3 (reps)				
	5 (teams)				
10†	3 (reps)				
	5 (teams)				

Total Score: Red: Blue:

*Adapted from: J. William Pfeiffer and John E. Jones (eds), *A Handbook of Structural Experiences for Human Relations Training,* vol. 3 (San Diego, CA: University Associates, 1974). Used with permission.
**Payoff points are doubled for this round.
†Payoff points are squared for this round (any minus signs are retained).

Activity 10–3: The SLO Corporation Dilemma

Objective:

To explore the dynamics of interdivisional competitions and their effect on performance.

Task 1 (Individual):

Read the accompanying case.

Task 2:

The instructor will split the class into an even number of teams, each with the same number of team members. Half of the teams will represent manufacturing, and the other half will represent marketing/sales. Each individual and team is to assume the role of a member from the assigned division. Each team is to meet separately and work on its task. Each member is to make a clear copy of the criteria developed by the team on the next page that follows this instruction. The page is to be shared with a member of the other division. (Time: 20 minutes)

Task 3:

To review the reports and evaluate them, individuals will be paired with a person from the other division. Each pair will have an observer. (Observers, review carefully the observation guide that can be found on the next page.) Each person is to share the report and discuss it with his or her partner. Your task is to decide which set of criteria is better and assign points accordingly. As a team of two, you have 100 points to assign. You must indicate a preference (for example, 54–46, 52–48, 80–20). Your task is to focus on the content of the criteria that you are evaluating.
(Time: 20 minutes)

Task 4:

a. Go back to your original team and total the number of points that each member brought back.

b. Each individual is to share the process that he or she has gone through. What occurred between you and the representative from the other division?

c. Brainstorm with the team about an alternative negotiation strategy that might work better.

(Time: 20 minutes)

Task 5:

Meet again with your partner from the other group to review and give each other feedback focusing on both content and process.

a. *Content* includes a discussion on your ability to focus on interests or positions, invention of options for mutual gains, and insistence on the use of objective criteria.

b. *Process* includes a reflection on the process that you have used, the way the conflict was handled, the conflict styles that were used, and what kind of negotiations were used.

c. Develop an agreement around a potential repeat of this activity. That is, knowing what you know now, how would you improve the negotiation session?

d. Start the second round of negotiation.

(Time: 15 minutes)

Task 6:

Meet with your original teams and discuss the following:

a. How did the team operate during the preparation for the first meeting with the representatives from the other division?

b. How did the team handle the outcomes from the first negotiations? What was the climate in the team? What effect did losing or winning have on the team?

    c. How willing were you to receive feedback and help from a member of another team? How easy is it for you to work with a member from the other group to develop a winning criteria list?

    d. What is the climate in the team now after the activity?

Task 7:

The instructor summarizes the activity, facilitates a class discussion, and presents a mini-lecture.

Case Study: The SLO Corporation

The SLO Corporation, founded 25 years ago by Mr. Bright, is a success story. Mr. Bright, who is the president and the majority stockholder, rules with a heavy hand and is involved in all company decisions. The two major divisions, manufacturing and marketing/sales, have been in constant conflict. Over the years Mr. Bright assumed the role of the linking pin and arbitrator between the two divisions. Furthermore, at this point on any issue of importance, the two divisions communicate through him. As a successful company, SLO has grown at an average annual rate of 9.5 percent in sales, which makes the company an above-average performer in the industry. The management teams of the two divisions are composed of individuals with somewhat different educational backgrounds: 65 percent of the manufacturing division managers are engineers, 15 percent hold business degrees, 5 percent hold some other university degree, and 15 percent have no college education; 65 percent of the managers of marketing/sales have business-related degrees, 15 percent have engineering degrees, 5 percent have some other university degree, and 15 percent have no degree.

Mr. Bright's surprise sale of his stock to Steel Co. Inc. has made SLO Corporation a wholly owned subsidiary that must now operate without Mr. Bright. Known for its participative orientation, Steel Co. Inc. sends its executive vice president, Mr. Aquire, to meet with SLO people and get a clearer picture on the status of affairs, how to proceed in the process of selecting and appointing a new president (that is, should it be a person from within SLO or an outsider), and what kind of person the president should be.

Following a few meetings, Mr. Aquire sends the following short memo to members of the manufacturing and marketing/sales divisions:

> I have asked your division heads to call a divisional meeting for the purpose of establishing criteria for choosing the new president. Each one of you should come to the meeting with five criteria on a piece of paper. The outcome of the meeting should be a report listing the criteria with a short description. You are also being asked to rank-order the criteria.

Source: This activity is similar to many that have been developed previously. The original exercise was developed by Sherif, *Intergroup Relations and Leadership,* and further developed by many others, notably Robert Black. This activity is a further modification of one found in D. A. Kold, J. S. Osland, and I. M. Rubin, *Organizational Behavior: An Experiential Approach,* 6th ed. (Englewood Cliffs, NJ: Prentice-Hall, 1995), pp. 291–93.

Name _____   Date _____

THE SLO CORPORATION CRITERIA SHEET

List below the criteria that your team/division developed.

1.

2.

3.

4.

5.

6.

7.

ROLE FOR OBSERVER

Your job in this exercise is to observe the negotiation between the representatives from the two divisions during the two rounds of talks. Do not attempt to become involved in the negotiations in any way. If possible, seat yourself away from the table where they are sitting. Look for the following:

Capture the sharing process. How much disclosure is there on each side about their intentions?

Do the individuals seem to follow a strategy in the negotiations? (win–loss, win–win)

Do the parties appear to trust each other?

How creative or complex is their "solution" (if they arrive at one)?

How was the second round similar and different from the first round?

Be prepared to comment on the conflict dynamics and negotiation behavior in class. Taking notes may help.

After about 10 minutes of negotiations, announce to the parties that they have 10 minutes left, after which everyone is to return to the classroom.

**Activity 10–4:
Two-Person Bargaining:
The Ugli Orange Case**

Objective:

To explore the dynamics of two-person bargaining.

Task 1:

The exercise can be conducted in groups of two or three. The first and second students are to play the roles of Dr. Roland and Dr. Jones, respectively. If the instructor chooses to have groups of three students, then one student will act as an observer to the role play.

Once groups have been chosen, the two students playing the roles are to read *only* their respective roles. The roles for Dr. Roland and Dr. Jones follow this activity. The observer will read both roles. (5 to 7 minutes).

Task 2:

After having read the roles, students playing Drs. Roland and Jones are to meet with each other to decide on a course of action.

Task 3:

At the end of the meeting, one of the two students will act as a spokesperson to potentially answer the following questions: (1) What do you plan to do? (2) If you want to buy the oranges, what price will you offer? (3) To whom and how will the oranges be delivered?

Task 4:

Following the negotiation, the spokesperson will report on the solution reached and the process by which agreement was reached.

Task 5:

The following are questions to be discussed with the larger group.

1. Was there full discussion by both sides in each group? How much information was shared?
2. Did the parties trust each other? Why or why not?
3. How creative and/or complex were the solutions? If solutions were very complex, why do you think this occurred?
4. What was the impact of having an audience (in the case of an observer) on the behavior of the negotiators? Did it make the problem harder or easier to solve?

Role of Dr. Jones

You are Dr. Jones, a biological research scientist employed by a pharmaceutical firm. You have recently developed a synthetic chemical useful for curing and preventing Rudosen, a disease contracted by pregnant women. If not caught in the first four weeks of pregnancy, the disease causes serious brain, eye, and ear damage to the unborn child. Recently there has been an outbreak of Rudosen in your state, and several thousand women have contracted the disease. You have found, with volunteer patients, that your recently developed synthetic serum cures Rudosen in its early stages. Unfortunately, the serum is made from the juice of the Ugli orange, which is a very rare fruit. Only a small quantity (approximately 4,000) of these oranges were produced last season. No additional Ugli oranges will be available until next season, which will be too late to cure the present Rudosen victims.

You've demonstrated that your synthetic serum is in no way harmful to pregnant women. Consequently, there are no side effects. The Food and Drug Administration has approved the production and distribution of the serum as a cure for Rudosen. Unfortunately, the present outbreak was unexpected, and your firm had not planned on having a compound serum available for the next six months. Your firm holds the patent on the synthetic serum, and it is expected to be a highly profitable product when it is generally available to the public.

Originally developed by Robert J. House. This version is that adapted by D. T. Hall and R. J. Lewicki who made modifications based on suggestions by H. Kolodny and T. Ruble. In D. T. Hall, D. D. Bowen, R. J. Lewicki, and F. S. Hall, *Experiences in Management and Organizational Behavior*, 2nd ed. (John Wiley & Sons, 1982).

You have been recently informed on good evidence that Mr. R. H. Cordoza, a South American fruit exporter, is in possession of 3,000 Ugli oranges in good condition. If you could obtain the juice of all 3,000 oranges, you would be able to both cure present victims and provide sufficient inoculation for the remaining pregnant women in the state. No other state currently has a Rudosen threat.

You have recently been informed that P. W. Roland is also urgently seeking Ugli oranges and is also aware of Mr. Cardoza's possession of the 3,000 available. Dr. Roland is employed by a competing pharmaceutical firm. He has been working on biological warfare research for the past several years. There is a great deal of industrial espionage in the pharmaceutical industry. Over the past several years, Dr. Roland's firm and yours have sued each other for infringement of patent rights and espionage law violations several times.

You've been authorized by your firm to approach Mr. Cardoza to purchase 3,000 Ugli oranges. You have been told he will sell them to the highest bidder. Your firm has authorized you to bid as high as $250,000 to obtain the oranges.

Role of Dr. Roland

You are Dr. P. W. Roland. You work as a research biologist for a pharmaceutical firm. The firm is under contract with the government to do research on methods to combat enemy uses of biological warfare.

Recently, several World War II experimental nerve gas bombs were moved from the United States to a small island just off the U.S. coast in the Pacific. In the process of transporting them, two of the bombs developed a leak. The leak is presently controlled by government scientists, who believe the gas will permeate the bomb chambers within two weeks. They know of no method of preventing the gas from getting into the atmosphere and spreading to other islands, and very likely to the West Coast as well. If this occurs, it is likely that several thousand people will incur serious brain damage and die.

You've developed a synthetic vapor that will neutralize the nerve gas if it is injected into the bomb chamber before the gas leaks out. The vapor is made with a chemical taken from the rind of the Ugli orange, a very rare fruit. Unfortunately, only 4,000 of these oranges were produced this season.

You have been recently informed on good evidence that Mr. R. H. Cordoza, a South American fruit exporter, is in possession of 3,000 Ugli oranges in good condition. The chemicals from the rinds of all 3,000 oranges would be sufficient to neutralize the gas if the serum is developed and injected efficiently. You have also been informed that the rinds of these oranges are in good condition.

You have recently been informed that Dr. J. W. Jones is also urgently seeking Ugli oranges and is also aware of Mr. Cardoza's possession of the 3,000 available. Dr. Jones is employed by a competing pharmaceutical firm. There is a great deal of industrial espionage in the pharmaceutical industry. Over the past several years, Dr. Jones' firm and yours have sued each other for infringement of patent rights and espionage law violations several times. Litigation on two suits is still in process.

The federal government has asked your firm for assistance. You've been authorized by your firm to approach Mr. Cardoza to purchase 3,000 Ugli oranges. You have been told he will sell them to the highest bidder. Your firm has authorized you to bid as high as $250,000 to obtain the oranges.

Before approaching Mr. Cardoza, you have decided to talk to Dr. Jones to influence him so that he will not prevent you from purchasing the oranges.

Activity 10–5: Discovering How You Typically Handle Conflict

Objective:

To identify your preferred method for handling conflict.

Name _____ Date _____

CONFLICT MANAGEMENT STYLE ORIENTATION SCALE

Circle the number that best indicates how well each statement describes you.	Rarely				Always
1. If someone disagrees with me, I vigorously defend my side of the issue.	1	2	3	4	5
2. I go along with suggestions from co-workers even if I don't agree with them.	1	2	3	4	5
3. I give and take so that a compromise can be reached.	1	2	3	4	5
4. I keep my opinions to myself rather than openly disagree with people.	1	2	3	4	5
5. In disagreements or negotiations, I try to find the best possible solution for both sides by sharing information.	1	2	3	4	5
6. I try to reach a middle ground in disputes with other people.	1	2	3	4	5
7. I accommodate the wishes of people who have points of view different from my own.	1	2	3	4	5
8. I avoid openly debating issues where there is disagreement.	1	2	3	4	5
9. In negotiations, I hold on to my position rather than give in.	1	2	3	4	5
10. I try to solve conflicts by finding solutions that benefit both me and the other person.	1	2	3	4	5
11. I let co-workers have their way rather than jeopardize our relationship.	1	2	3	4	5
12. I try to win my position in a discussion.	1	2	3	4	5
13. I like to investigate conflicts with co-workers so that we can discover solutions that benefit both of us.	1	2	3	4	5
14. I believe that it is not worth the time and trouble of discussing my differences of opinion with other people.	1	2	3	4	5
15. To reach an agreement, I give up some things in exchange for others.	1	2	3	4	5

SCORING KEY FOR CONFLICT MANAGEMENT STYLE ORIENTATION SCALE

Write your circled score for each statement on the appropriate line (statement numbers are in parentheses), and add the numbers for each style category. Higher scores indicate that you are stronger in that conflict management style.

Competing   ____ + ____ + ____ = ____
                          (1)   (9)   (12)

Accommodating   ____ + ____ + ____ = ____
                          (2)   (7)   (11)

Compromising   ____ + ____ + ____ = ____
                          (3)   (6)   (15)

Avoiding   ____ + ____ + ____ = ____
                          (4)   (8)   (14)

Collaborating   ____ + ____ + ____ = ____
                          (5)   (10) (13)

Source: Taken from S. L. McShane and M. A. Von Glinow, *Organizational Behavior: Emerging Realities for Workplace Revolution,* 2nd ed. (New York: McGraw-Hill, 2003). McShane and Von Glinow adapted the items from the following two sources (1) M. A. Rahim, "A Measure of Styles of Handling Interpersonal Conflict," *Academy of Management Journal* 26, (June 1983), pp. 368–76. (2) K. W. Thomas and R. H. Kilmann, *Thomas-Kilmann Conflict Mode Instrument* (Sterling Forst, NY: Xicom, 1977).

Module 11

Work Teams and Effectiveness

LEARNING OBJECTIVES

After completing this module, you should be able to

1. Understand the differences between teams and groups.
2. Describe the potential problems that work teams face.
3. Identify the types of teams that can be found at work.
4. Describe the phases in a rational group problem-solving process.
5. Explain the role that synergy and creativity play in group problem solving.
6. Describe the role and activities of the team leader in group decision making.
7. Understand the consensus process in team activity.
8. State the conditions under which group decision making or participative management is most effective.

KEY TERMS AND CONCEPTS

Brainstorming

Cheetah team (CT)

Consensus process

Creativity

Cross-functional team

Culture

Group

Group problem-solving process

Groupware

Hidden agenda

Interpersonal process skills

Management team

New-product development team
   (NPDT)

Nominal group technique

Parallel team

Participative management

Project team

Quality control circle (QCC)

Rational problem-solving process

Self-managed work team (SMWT)

Team

Team style

Virtual work team

Work team

MODULE OUTLINE

PREMODULE PREPARATION

Activity 11–1:
Team Skills

Objective:

To help individuals identify specific group skills that they want to develop.

Task 1:

Individuals are to complete the accompanying Questionnaire on Group Skills Development.

Task 2:

a. Individuals are to share with their group the list of skills to which they assigned top priority.

b. The group should brainstorm about how it can help each individual accomplish his or her goals.

c. Each individual, in collaboration with the group, is to develop an action plan (for each individual) that will help him or her accomplish these learning goals or team skills.

Task 3: (optional)

Individuals are to submit to the instructor one page with a list of five team skills that they would like to acquire and the action plan for accomplishing these learning goals. Individuals and teams will have a chance to assess to what extent the skills acquisition took place at the end of the course.

Name _____   Date _____

QUESTIONNAIRE ON GROUP SKILLS DEVELOPMENT

Below are skill areas in which participants in past courses have indicated an interest in developing greater proficiency. Please indicate the degree to which you have an interest in developing greater skills effectiveness by circling the appropriate position on the scale to the right of each item.

Skills Areas	Not Interested	Somewhat Interested			Very Interested			Highly Interested		
1. Expressing my viewpoints clearly and logically	1	2	3	4	5	6	7	8	9	10
2. Convincing or persuading others of my ideas or views	1	2	3	4	5	6	7	8	9	10
3. Gaining or holding the attention of others	1	2	3	4	5	6	7	8	9	10
4. Listening attentively so I can understand others' ideas and perceptions	1	2	3	4	5	6	7	8	9	10
5. Paraphrasing back what someone says so I can determine if I am "hearing"	1	2	3	4	5	6	7	8	9	10
6. Paraphrasing back what someone says so the other person feels reassured that I'm listening	1	2	3	4	5	6	7	8	9	10
7. Asserting myself more	1	2	3	4	5	6	7	8	9	10
8. Asserting myself without stepping on others' toes	1	2	3	4	5	6	7	8	9	10
9. Getting my share of airtime	1	2	3	4	5	6	7	8	9	10
10. Being less dominating, opinionated, or dogmatic	1	2	3	4	5	6	7	8	9	10
11. Being more open-minded about the views of others	1	2	3	4	5	6	7	8	9	10
12. Feeling less intimidated by the way others express their views	1	2	3	4	5	6	7	8	9	10
13. Feeling less defensive when others don't agree with me	1	2	3	4	5	6	7	8	9	10
14. Being less nervous and more confident in speaking	1	2	3	4	5	6	7	8	9	10
15. Taking criticism better	1	2	3	4	5	6	7	8	9	10
16. Coping with people who are different than I am (for example, differences in age, sex, race, religion, fraternity, sorority)	1	2	3	4	5	6	7	8	9	10
17. Confronting conflict when it arises between myself and another person	1	2	3	4	5	6	7	8	9	10
18. Having a harmonizing influence on the group (for example, helping shy people open up; getting others to listen to each other; getting group members more involved and enthusiastic; helping group members to be more comfortable in their relations)	1	2	3	4	5	6	7	8	9	10
19. Leading the group discussion	1	2	3	4	5	6	7	8	9	10
20. Taking control when the discussion gets out of hand; keeping discussion on target	1	2	3	4	5	6	7	8	9	10
21. Facilitating the group discussion to get maximum output	1	2	3	4	5	6	7	8	9	10
22. Dealing with conflict between group members	1	2	3	4	5	6	7	8	9	10
23. Manipulating the group's interactions so they will come out the way I feel is best	1	2	3	4	5	6	7	8	9	10

Note: When you have finished, review the above items and highlight the numbers of those to which you would give top priority.

Activity 11–2: Mountain Survival

Objectives:

a. To demonstrate problem solving as a small-group skill.

b. To show that group solutions can be superior to those of individuals under certain conditions.

c. To identify the types of behavior on the part of team members that facilitate problem-solving effectiveness.

Task 1:

Individuals, working alone, will complete the attached Mountain Survival worksheet. (Time: 10–15 minutes)

Task 2:

a. Individuals are to sit with their regular teams; it will not be necessary to appoint a spokesperson for this exercise.

b. Teams are to solve the problem as a team and arrive at a team solution for the problem. In doing so, the team should try to reach consensus and not use majority vote, trading, or averaging in reaching decisions.

Consensus is a decision process for making full use of available resources for resolving conflicts creatively. Consensus is difficult to reach, so not every ranking will meet with everyone's complete approval. Complete unanimity is not the goal—it is rarely achieved. However, each individual should be able to accept the group rankings on the basis of logic and feasibility. When all group members feel this way, you have reached consensus, and the judgment may be entered as a group decision. This means, in effect, that a single person can block the group if he or she thinks it necessary; at the same time, individuals should use this option in the best sense of reciprocity. Here are some guidelines to use in achieving consensus:

1. Avoid arguing for your own rankings. Present your position as clearly and logically as possible, but listen to the other members' reactions and consider them carefully before you press your point.

2. Do not assume that someone must win and someone must lose when discussion reaches a stalemate. Instead, look for the next most acceptable alternative for all parties.

3. Do not change your mind simply to avoid conflict. When agreement seems to come too quickly and easily, be suspicious. Explore the reasons and be sure everyone accepts the solution for similar or complementary reasons. Agree only to positions that have objective or logically sound foundations.

4. Avoid conflict-reducing techniques such as majority vote, splitting the difference, or coin tosses. When a dissenting member finally agrees, don't feel that that person must be rewarded by having her or his own way on a later point.

5. Differences of opinion are natural and expected. Seek them out and try to involve everyone in the decision process. Disagreements can help the group's decision because with a wide range of information and opinions, there is a greater chance that the group will hit upon more adequate solutions.*

6. As the teams work on a solution to the problems, no references, books, or other aids are to be used. The group results are to be recorded in the column titled Group Rankings. The individual rankings completed prior to the exercise should not be changed; they will be scored later.

(Time: 30–45 minutes)

*Source: Special permission for reproduction of the Mountain Survival activity is granted by the authors, Professors Fremont E. Kast and James E. Rosenzweig, Graduate School of Business Administration, University of Washington. All rights are reserved, and no reproduction should be made without express approval of Professors Kast and Rosenzweig. We are grateful to them.

Task 3:

a. The correct answer to the exercise will be provided by the instructor.

b. Individuals will calculate a total error score for their own solutions as follows:

If Your Answer Is	If Key Is	Difference between the Two Is
15	4	11
5	7	2
11	2	9
etc., for all items	etc.	etc.

Total Error Score*

*Add up without regard to pluses and minuses.

c. Calculate the team score in the same manner.

d. Calculate the average score for the individuals in your group by adding all scores and dividing by the number of members.

e. The instructor will record and display the results for all teams. Table 11–1 is provided for you to record them.

f. Discussion question: Why were the group solutions in this activity superior to those of the average of the individual team members or, for some teams, superior to the "best" individual member?

Table 11–1   **Error Scores for Individuals and Groups on Mountain Survival Activity for Your Class**

Group	Before Discussion		After Group Discussion			
	Average Error Score of Group Members	Error Score of Most Accurate Group Member	Group Error Score	Gain or Loss over Average Error Score	Individuals in Group Superior to Group Score	Gain or Loss over Most Accurate Individual
1						
2						
3						
4						
5						
6						
7						
8						
Overall average						

Name _____   Date _____

WORKSHEET FOR ACTIVITY 11–2

Your charter flight from Seattle to Banff and Lake Louise (Alberta, Canada) crash-landed in the north Cascades National Park area somewhere near the U.S.–Canadian border and then burst into flames. It is approximately noon on a day in mid-January. The twin-engine, 10-passenger plane containing the bodies of the pilot and one passenger has completely burned. Only the airframe remains. None of the rest of you has been seriously injured. The pilot was unable to notify anyone of your position before the plane crashed in a blinding snowstorm. Just before the crash, you noted that the plane's altimeter registered about 5,000 feet. The crash site is in a rugged, heavily wooded area just below the timberline. You are dressed in medium-weight clothing. Each of you has a topcoat.

After the plane landed and before it caught fire, your group was able to salvage the 15 items listed below. Your task is to rank the 15 items in terms of their importance to your survival. Place the number 1 by the most important item, number 2 by the second most important, and so on through number 15, the least important.

	Step 1: Your Individual Ranking	Step 2: The Group Ranking	Step 3: Survival Experts' Ranking	Step 4: Difference between 1 and 3	Step 5: Difference between 2 and 3
Sectional air map of the area					
Flashlight (four-battery size)					
Four wool blankets					
One rifle with ammunition					
One pair of skis					
Two fifths of liquor					
One cosmetic mirror					
One jackknife					
Four pairs of sunglasses					
Three books of matches					
One metal coffeepot					
First-aid kit					
One dozen packages of cocktail nuts					
One clear plastic tarpaulin (9' × 12')					
One large, gift-wrapped decorative candle					
Total (The lower the score the better)				**Your score**	**Group score**

INTRODUCTION

Business organizations are continuously using groups as their building blocks in organizing and managing work.[1] Teams are viewed as organizational mechanisms that allow for a more rapid response to a continuously changing business environment.[2] Small groups and teams have been at the heart of efforts to transform routinized jobs in manufacturing since the establishment of the human relations school in the 1930s (see Module 1). Teams who devoted effort to understanding and developing team mechanisms were found to be more effective.[3] While we have seen a widespread shift in the unit of production (or service or development work) from individuals to managing teams, understanding and influencing team functioning and effectiveness and sustaining desired team performance present a major set of challenges.

Work teams are dependent on their ability to manage interpersonal processes and relationships. Your participation in classroom groups provides an opportunity to gain an understanding of four aspects of small-group effectiveness: (1) team skills that facilitate the achievement of group goals, (2) characteristics of a group that influence its ability to solve problems and make decisions effectively, (3) the dynamics of small group, and (4) conflict and negotiations. Even more important for you, participation in a classroom group provides you with a setting in which you can assess and develop your own skills in influencing the activities of groups in which you participate. Group problem solving, decision making, and team building are the subject of this module, with an emphasis on the potentially creative forces (synergy) in group processes.

We start with a few activities that provide individuals the opportunity to identify desired team skills and, as a team, experience some of the team dynamics around team problem solving and decision making. Content-wise, we start with a definition of *team,* the nature of teams at work, and the types of teams that can be found in organizations. Next, based on the team activities, we explore team problem solving and synergy. Coverage of group versus individual problem solving is followed by a discussion of group decision making and an exploration of managerial actions that should foster creativity and improve group problem solving and decision making. The utilization of group problem solving and decision making in organizations is reviewed. Finally, some of the challenges that work teams face are identified, and some suggestions for addressing them are explored. A questionnaire is included to aid you in assessing your personal skills in operating as a team member so you can develop these skills in your team activities as the course continues.

THE NATURE OF TEAMS

Historical Context and Global Competition

Team, teamwork, and *managing the team* are terms that are commonly heard today all around us. Most leaders and managers know that collaborative teamwork is an effective tool for managing complex tasks in a rapidly changing environment.[4] Teamwork in organizations and the emerging view of the team-based organization as a mode of organizing work has a long history. Before we move into the definitions of teams, basic team skills, team problem solving, and team decision making, a brief review of the historical context and the changing global context is needed. The interest in the theory and practice of group-based work stretches back several decades.[5] From the late 1920s Elton Mayo and his associates in the United States pioneered studies of industrial work organization and workers' motivation under what became characterized as the "human relations" school of industrial relations. A central finding of this stream of research emphasized the impact of positive attention from managers on a group's productivity. Kurt Lewin's work in the 1930s and 1940s laid the groundwork for extensive study of group dynamics and leadership behavior. He was the first researcher to distinguish between participative and authoritarian leadership. Lewin demonstrated the usefulness of a democratic leader on the creativity and effectiveness of the group. A common theme to this early work was the search for an approach that would produce a more satisfying working life and hence greater commitment and motivation within the workforce.

In Britain, a more structural orientation emerged. Eric Trist and his associates at the Tavistock Institute led a research program in the late 1940s and early 1950s on the effects of the introduction of new technologies on working practices in the British coal-mining industry. Through multiple studies, the researchers found that the creation of small self-regulatory work groups that coordinated with each other within and between shifts resulted in improved individual motivation, improved group productivity, and a dramatic decline of sickness rates. Beyond the development of the basic concept and design principles of semiautonomous work groups, one of the important outcomes of this work was the development of the Sociotechnical System School as a conceptual framework (discussed in some depth in Module 13) for linking technological, social, and environmental elements of the work organization.

The increasing concern in the United States, Britain, and the Scandinavian countries with increasing workforce motivation and commitment underlies the many approaches that came together under the rubric of the quality of working life (QWL) movement that emerged in the late 1960s and early 1970s. Work groups were a means of returning autonomy and control to workers involved in automated manufacturing. The continued interest in the work group or team from the 1950s to the 1970s resulted in making groups responsible for a whole product or process and the task of coordinating and managing production and service.

In postwar Japan, other ideas about groups emerged. The collective culture orientation coupled with an acute scarcity of resources resulted in the emphasis on harnessing employees' capabilities to collective goals of quality, efficiency, and customer service and less with employee involvement, team autonomy, and quality of working life.

The changing conditions of world markets during the 1980s, 1990s, and early 2000s; the increasing commercial pressures of a global nature; and the potential created by new technologies and manufacturing techniques led managers to explore new business strategies and alternative approaches to organize the work organization. In this context, team-based designs emerged as key design choices.[6]

Work Groups and Teams: Toward a Definition

Work groups and teams have been referred to as "the building blocks of excellent companies."[7] Committees, task forces, quality circles, process improvement teams, product development teams, self-managed teams, and management teams are all features of today's organizations.

At the most basic level, a **group** can be defined as "a set of three or more individuals that can identify itself and be identified by others in the organization as a group." Groups in organizations can be either *formal* (that is, a formal part of the organization, created by management) or *informal* (created by the members themselves, largely out of day-to-day interaction between individuals). Alderfer advocated the organizational behavior view of groups, which encompasses both the sociological (external relations) and psychological (internal relations) aspects of group operations in this definition:

> A group is a collection of individuals (1) who have significantly interdependent relations with each other, (2) who perceive themselves as a group, reliably distinguishing members from nonmembers, (3) whose group identity is recognized by nonmembers, (4) who, as group members acting alone or in concert, have significantly interdependent relations with other groups, and (5) whose roles in the group are therefore a function of expectations from themselves, from other group members, and from nongroup members.[8]

McGrath et al. regard groups as complex, adaptive, dynamic systems composed of a set of elements: (1) individuals, who become the group's *members;* (2) intentions, which become both *group projects*—and the tasks by which those projects are carried out—and *members' needs* that must be satisfied if the group is going to be able to stay in business effectively over the long run; and (3) resources, which become the group's *technology*—that is, the hardware and software tools (rules, norms, procedures) by which its members do the tasks of its projects.[9] Katzenbach and Smith define a **team** as "a small number of people with complementary skills who are committed to a common purpose, set of performance goals, and approach for which they hold themselves mutually accountable."[10] They distinguish between work groups such as committees and teams as follows: Committee performance is "a function of what its members do as individuals," whereas team performance includes both individual performance and what they call "collective work products" that reflect the joint, real contribution of team members and that are greater than the sum of their individual contributions.[11]

Types of Teams

Teams and teamwork are currently being championed as a way of replacing inflexible, dehumanized, bureaucratic mechanisms with more humanistic, involving, cultural ideological methods of productive activity.[12] A recent study identified four types of teams in organizations:

1. **Work teams,** or continuing work units responsible for producing goods or providing services.

2. **Parallel teams,** or people who are pulled together from different work units or jobs to perform functions that the regular organization is not equipped to perform well.

3. **Project teams,** or time-limited teams that have to produce one-time output such as a new product or service to be marketed by the company.

4. **Management teams,** or supervisory teams that are created to provide coordination and direction to the subunits under their jurisdiction, laterally integrating interdependent subunits across key business processes.[13]

Later in this module, we identify a variety of teams—such as virtual teams, cross-functional teams, multinational teams, and new-product development teams—that might be charged with any of the tasks listed here. For example, a parallel team, a project team, or a management team can be a virtual team. Although each type of team deals with a different task, regardless of the team type, teams form a critical link between the individual and the organization. They function to accomplish tasks that cannot be performed by one individual or to fulfill individual needs not met by the formal organization. As teams such as top-management teams, product development teams, quality circles, task forces, and project teams become more and more a part of the way organizations operate, understanding the effectiveness and impact of teams becomes increasingly important. Module 12 focuses on small-group behavior and dynamics. This module examines team effectiveness in the context of team problem solving and decision making.

Discussion of the Premodule Preparation's Results

The premodule activity (Activity 11–2) highlights this difference between real teamwork and simple group membership and the skills that lead to performance differences in teams. Table 11–2 summarizes the results of the Mountain Survival activity for 12 groups of college students. You should find that these results are similar to the ones you obtained in your groups, although because the exercises are not conducted under controlled conditions, artifacts such as the time allotted for both individual and group decision making may cause results to vary. However, if we use the group average score as an approximation of the individual group members' capability in the situation faced by the group in the exercises, in general (but not always) the groups did better than the average individual. In many cases the groups performed better than their best individual member. This outcome clearly demonstrates Katzenbach and Smith's notion that a team is more than the sum of its parts and produces performance levels greater than the sum of all the individual bests of team members.[14]

Table 11–2
Summary of Group Performance on the Mountain Survival Activity

	Number of Groups	Average Individual Score	Average Group Score	Average Gain	Average Low Score	Number of Group Scores Lower than Best Individual Score
	12	56.2	40.8	6.6	43.3	4

In many cases, the group scores are superior to those of the individual, yet, in some groups we find individuals that outperform the team. In the latter, at the most basic level, it would suggest that the team is not functioning as well as it could and careful examination of the interpersonal dynamics within the team as well as the team working processes is needed. Let's explore the issue a bit further. Why were many of the group scores superior to those of individuals? We must look at several aspects of the exercise in seeking an explanation.

1. Three conditions appear relevant: (a) There was a definite answer to all problems, (b) the problem could be solved by logic or reason in the case of Activity 11–2, and (c) for all problems each person had some relevant information or point of view but no member had it all. More information resources were available to the group—if the group made use of them.

2. A problem-solving process was used. If you followed the *experiential learning cycle,* your team has been developing some sequence or steps to its problem-solving process. The **group problem-solving process** or what some call the **rational problem-solving process** model, includes the following steps:

   a. Agreement on goals.

   b. Shared understanding of what the problem is.

   c. Shared understanding of ground rules for the way the group will work.

   d. Shared understanding of the basic assumptions and priority issues in solving the problem.

   e. Consideration of alternative solutions.

   f. Development of criteria to evaluate alternatives.

   g. Choosing the best alternative.

   h. Checking the alternative chosen against the problem statement.

Some researchers argue that this process has a left-hemisphere focus. If the process that you followed in Activity 11–2 is less orderly, systematic, or linear, you probably followed a more *intuitive problem-solving process* (which some researchers call a *right-hemisphere focus).* Some differences in the scores received by different teams may be attributable to differences in the effectiveness of their problem-solving process.

3. The **consensus process** was used. If you followed the instructions, your team was developing (or improving) communication skills that could augment the problem-solving process. It is often important to (a) get input from all, (b) listen to all views, (c) be willing to change your views if someone else's makes more sense, and (d) assume conflict can be creative in generating ideas.

Thus, effective team problem solving involves both effective problem-solving skills and effective interpersonal skills. Those **interpersonal process skills** include careful listening plus supporting and encouraging the contributions of all members. For example, a team can adopt a practice whereby, when communication problems arise, members feel comfortable paraphrasing what they hear one another say to make sure that everyone understands what is being said (for example, "Do I hear you saying . . . ?"). This technique involves learning to listen until it is clear what a person is saying and then paraphrasing what is said to the satisfaction of the speaker. Where there is no awareness on the part of the team members that a communication problem has arisen, periodic summaries of what has been discussed can ensure that all are on the same wavelength. Similarly, some individuals have learned that saying something like "Here's the problem *I'm* having with what you said," is a more effective response than "That's a stupid idea." The former response is less likely to generate defensive behavior and is more likely to encourage complete communication and contribution to the group's effort.

Just like problem-solving skills, interpersonal skills can be learned and practiced. Individuals who learn the skills of listening and communicating can apply them in any situation; they become part of the interpersonal skills that improve the person's effectiveness in any group. Differences in group performances on this module's activities may also be a function of how well the group's interpersonal processes operate. Effective teams work on improving their interpersonal processes.

Individual versus Group Problem Solving

In your class's operation of the problem-solving activities, you may have observed instances where the group score was higher than the best individual score. Such was the case with 4 of the 12 groups whose performance is outlined in Table 11–2. There, in four of the groups, the group outcome was worse than that of the best members. Thus, while, in general, groups performed better than the average of their members, and most of the time better than their best member, this case was not always true. Some groups would have been better to use the solution of their best member, *assuming, of course, they knew who that was!*

Thus, no generalization can be made that the group problem-solving process is superior to individual effort. Variables such as the type of problem; the talent, ability, education, and experience of the individuals; the time available; organization and national culture; leadership; and group process are all relevant as are many other factors.

There is evidence that the capacity of groups to perform better than their best individual member increases with the time that individuals have worked with each other in teams.[15] For example, a recent study that focused on decision making in new-product development environments proved empirically that teams make more effective decisions than individuals.[16] Other research has suggested that the superiority of teams is a function of their capacity to develop valid information about the members' relative expertise.[17] Hackman and Morris observe that, in sum, there is substantial agreement among researchers and observers of small task groups that something important happens in group interactions that can affect performance outcomes. There is little agreement about just what that "something" is; whether it is more likely to enhance or depress effectiveness; and how it can be monitored, analyzed, and altered.[18]

One problem in applying research findings to managerial situations concerns the methods used in experimental studies. By necessity they are done in the laboratory, with the necessary controls to examine specific variables. This situation has little comparability to the conditions under which real work teams operate. Real teams can learn to critique and redirect their actions, a flexibility not possible in experimental studies, nor perhaps as likely to occur, given that the stakes, risks, rewards, and punishments for real work teams are significantly different from those for laboratory teams.

In truth, group process can both enhance and detract from team performance. In reality, organizations—for a variety of reasons, some of them discussed subsequently—cannot avoid using groups and teams for problem solving and decision making. Thus, the real questions for managers do not involve individual versus group decision making. The real questions are (1) Where is group decision making most appropriate? and (2) How can teams be made more effective?

One primary factor affecting group performance is the degree of proficiency in team action that a group can develop. This proficiency is aided by effectiveness training for individual members, such as leadership, problem-solving, and communications workshops. It also requires on-the-job training in the use of these skills by the work team after the individuals have had the advantage of separate training. If group effectiveness is to be enhanced, time must be allotted for these activities.

GROUP DECISION MAKING AND PARTICIPATIVE MANAGEMENT

Decision making is an analytical process leading to a selection of a course of action among alternative options. Thus, decision making can be viewed as a reasoning process which can be both rational and irrational. At the team level, the nature of the interpersonal dynamics is likely to influence the quality of the dialogue around reasoning and individual capabilities to be open to hear and listen to other's reasoning and develop a deeper level of understanding of what is being shared and explored. The problems involved in Activity 11–2 had a "right" or preferred answer. Although organizations face such problems indeed, these are not the only types of problems that exist. Very often, organizations face situations with a number of viable alternative solutions. Activity 11–3 at the end of the module presents such a situation. In that activity the leader is instructed to behave in a particular manner. Is that the only way to handle the problem? Is it the best way? What are the alternatives?

Victor Vroom, Phillip Yetton, and Arthur Jago developed a model that can provide the answers to these questions. They first suggest five ways in which decisions can be made:

1. The manager solves the problem by himself or herself, using the information available at the time (AI style).
2. The manager obtains the necessary information from employees and then makes the decision himself or herself (AII style).
3. The manager consults with subordinates individually, getting their ideas and suggestions, and then makes a decision (CI style).
4. The manager consults with subordinates as a group, again getting their ideas and suggestions, and then makes a decision (CII style).
5. The manager explains the problem to the employees as a group, and the group makes the decision (GII style).[19]

The model suggests five key attributes to problem situations: time, information, quality, employee commitment, and employee development. It lists eight problem attributes that allow these factors to be taken into account in decision making:

1. *Quality requirement (QR)*. How important is the technical quality of the decision?
2. *Commitment requirement (CR)*. How important is employee commitment to the decision?
3. *Leader's information (LI)*. Does the leader have sufficient information to make a high-quality decision?
4. *Problem structure (ST)*. Is the problem well structured?
5. *Commitment probability (CP)*. If the leader makes the decision alone, will subordinates be committed to the decision?
6. *Goal congruence (GC)*. Do employees share the organizational goals to be attained in solving this problem?
7. *Subordinate conflict (CO)*. Is conflict among employees over preferred solutions likely?
8. *Subordinate information (SI)*. Do employees have enough information to make a high-quality decision?[20]

To decide on a decision-making style, the manager follows a decision tree incorporating the eight problem attributes, asking the question in each attribute of the problem at hand, as shown in Figure 11–1.

Note that only one of the styles in the model is what is conventionally called **participative management.** Others are consultative and autocratic. The model is a contingency model, which seeks to identify the situations under which particular forms of employee influence are most appropriate. In brief, it suggests that full participation is not *always* an appropriate style for the leader to use, although at times it is *very* appropriate. In light of this model, it may be argued that the participative style has been overused, a view supported by recent research results that find low relationships (so low as to be insignificant) between participation, productivity, and employee satisfaction.[21]

Review Activity 11–3 using the Vroom–Yetton–Jago model. Which decision-making style would be appropriate?

Other Factors

Although the Vroom–Yetton–Jago model incorporates a number of important variables, still other variables may affect the choice of decision-making style:

1. *Personality of the manager.* Managers who feel most comfortable making all the decisions and who have difficulty allowing others to be involved should not attempt to use participation. If they do not believe in it, they should assume that employees will detect this and feel they are being manipulated if they are asked to become involved.

Figure 11–1   **The Vroom–Yetton–Jago Decision Model**

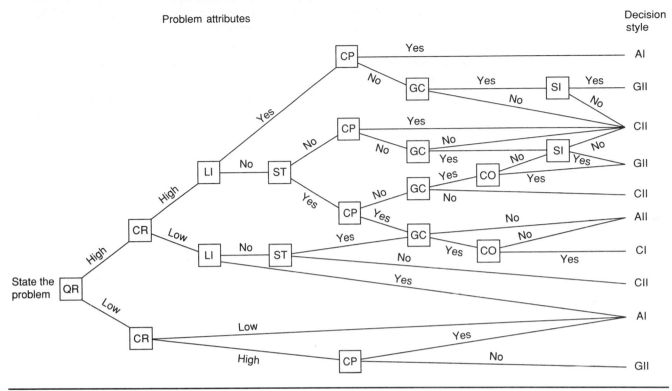

Source: V. H. Vroom and A. G. Jago, *The New Leadership* (Englewood, NJ: Prentice-Hall, 1988), p. 184. Printed with permission.

2. *Skill and ability of the manager.* The manager's abilities in managing group problem-solving activities and in conflict resolution affect the results of participative management attempts.[22]

3. *Organizational climate.* If the organization's climate and culture are strictly authoritarian, it is difficult for any single manager to follow a participative style.

4. *Employee personality.* Some employees do not work well in participative situations, but rather prefer to work in highly structured situations where they are told what to do.[23]

5. *Group size and diversity.* Some employees do not work well in large groups. At the same time, the larger the group, the greater the likelihood that the members of the group will be different. Furthermore, demographic diversity enhances the richness and breadth of input into the decision-making process. As such the larger the group and the more diverse the group, the more challenging the managerial task of facilitating a participative decision making.[24]

THE MANAGER AND GROUP DECISION MAKING

Although group decision making is not necessary in every problem situation, where it is used, its efficacy rests with the manager who is responsible for facilitating the process. In deciding to proceed with a group decision, the manager has to address several key issues before the group or team can begin to function:[25]

1. *Assignment boundary.* Tasks given to teams are often complex. Therefore, the manager must clearly define the group's task, its responsibility and authority, and the requirements and performance criteria that the team is expected to meet.

2. *Assessment of assignment resources.* Once the assignment boundaries are defined, the manager may need to divide the assignment into manageable tasks and examine the

resources available for the assignment. Time, knowledge, skills, and competing system demands are some of the resources that are likely to have an effect on the decision-making process. An attempt to address and resolve the resource issues prior to the formation of the group will aid the team's performance.

3. *Team formation.* Decision-making groups are often formed to deal with complex tasks that are beyond the ability of any one individual. Identifying the individuals who have the needed knowledge and skills as well as the individuals who are likely to be affected by the decision provides the group with the appropriate resources to deal with the task. Appointing a leader at the start of the group or ensuring that the group selects a leader as a first task is often a good idea.

The role of the manager in group decision making can be that of a chairperson who guides the consensus process while trying not to influence others to adopt his or her solution. In playing the role of the supervisor in Activity 11–3, individuals sometimes adopt a completely passive manner. The supervisor in this situation (or similar ones) could choose to be highly active and still permit the employees to make the decision. Here are some ways the manager-as-chairperson can facilitate this process:

1. Set the stage and clarify expectations.
   a. Help the group members get acquainted (at the first meeting of a new group).
   b. Review the agenda for the meeting or, if this is a continuation of prior meetings, review the progress made to date.
   c. Introduce the problem by asking what would be a fair way of deciding who should get the overtime.
   d. Have the group decide what criteria should be used. Explore alternative options.
   e. Let the group decide what method, procedure, or decision-making process to use. Review the alternative methods. Some of the methods discussed later (such as brainstorming and nominal group technique) may be useful.

2. Do not takes sides or give your own views.

3. Make sure all employees have time to express their views.

4. Control conflict by having each person "own" his or her feelings without attacking another person—say where you are without "laying it on" the other person. (It is much more acceptable to say, "I think seniority is a better way to decide this than one's personal needs," than "Chris's ripping us off by contributing to the overpopulation problem.") Also, remember that conflict can be creative when it is focused on issues rather than personalities.

5. Protect those who are verbally attacked. Create a supportive atmosphere.

6. Focus on the agreement about the reasoning and its logic rather than on the agreement about the choice itself.

7. Do not manipulate the process so it will come out the way you would like to have the problem decided. Others usually become aware of your hidden agenda and may resent it.

8. At the end of the meeting, review the task, the agenda, the decision method, and the decision. If the group has a follow-up meeting, spell out the task ahead, its schedule, and the responsibilities of the members to be completed before the next meeting.[26]

When exposed to this type of leadership, employees can learn the team skills implicit in this behavior and, by example, learn to make a decision without the supervisor, if called on to do so.

CONSENSUS AND GROUP DECISION MAKING

The process of *consensus* refers to arriving at a decision that all members of the group are willing to support and no team member opposes. As Activity 11–2 shows, this approach represents a major challenge to most groups. The decision is not necessarily a unanimous choice, but is acceptable to all the group members. The consensus process seems to enhance the opportunity for creativity, innovation, and high-quality decisions because the group spends a significant amount of time working through alternative solutions until reaching a solution that everyone finds acceptable.[27]

A 1994 report by the U.S. Department of Defense suggests that the "rule of thumb" procedure be followed. Team members use their thumbs to create three signals to show how they feel about an issue. A "thumbs up" signal indicates that a team member favors a proposal. The "thumbs down" sign means that the member is opposed to the idea and in no way can support it. If a team member is not wild about a proposal, but can support it, he or she will turn the thumb sideways. If any member is "thumbs down" on a proposal, it may have to be modified or rewarded in a way that the resistor can buy in. Thus, this procedure clarifies what needs to occur as the group progresses on its task of making a decision.

An alternative procedure for reaching consensus differentiates between levels of consensus.[28] Consensus is achieved if all participants indicate that they are at levels 1 to 4 (not at level 5 or 6). The levels of consensus are:

1. I am *enthusiastic* about this alternative. I am satisfied that the decision is an expression of the wisdom of the group.

2. I find the decision is the *best choice.* It is the best of the real options that we have available to us.

3. I can *live with* the decision. I'm not especially enthusiastic about it.

4. I do not fully agree with the decision and need to register my view about it. However, I do not choose to block the decision and will *stand aside.* I am willing to support the decision because I trust the wisdom of the group.

5. I do not agree with the decision and feel the need to *block* this decision being accepted as consensus.

6. I feel that we have no clear sense of unity in the group. We need to *talk more* before consensus can be reached.

The consensus decision-making process is advantageous to the extent that the decision is important to the group's performance, there is time available to arrive at the consensus, and it is important to develop members' commitment to the decision. The process can be detrimental in situations that require a quick decision, such as a crisis or when a window of opportunity is about to close.

CREATIVITY, GROUP PROBLEM SOLVING, AND DECISION MAKING

An integral element of the synergy process in group problem solving involves creativity. As individuals interact around ideas, an issue, or a problem, a novel solution may emerge that no individual has identified earlier. **Creativity** is defined as an individual's ability to take bits and pieces of seemingly unrelated information and synthesize the pieces into a new understanding or a novel, useful idea. Creativity is discussed in Module 14, which focuses on the phenomena of creativity and innovation in the organizational setting. This section explores two techniques that are likely to foster creativity in group problem solving and decision making: brainstorming and the nominal group technique.

Brainstorming

One well-known method for developing creative ideas and decision alternatives through group participation is **brainstorming.** Here are some general ground rules for brainstorming:

1. Everyone spontaneously expresses all ideas, no matter how extreme they may appear.

2. Ideas belong to the group, and all members are encouraged to rework or elaborate upon them.

3. Evaluation of ideas does not occur until the generation process has been completed.

Nominal Group Technique

The **nominal group technique** is a highly structured group problem-solving process[29] in which the focus is on the rational process of problem solving. Here are some ground rules for nominal group technique:

1. During a period of silence, individuals independently write down their ideas.

2. Each individual in turn shares one of his or her ideas at a time, following a round-robin reporting process. Ideas are written on a chart for all to see. No discussion is allowed during this phase.

3. After all the ideas have been recorded, members discuss the ideas only for the purpose of clarification. No criticism is permitted.

4. A preliminary vote takes place to reduce the number of alternatives.

5. An in-depth discussion of the remaining ideas then occurs.

6. An independent silent vote takes place, and the group's solution is determined by the votes.

The nominal group technique is an orderly, efficient, rational process that encourages full participation and meaningful discussion. Research findings suggest that this method seems to have a clear advantage under conditions of high stress and conflict. Other research suggests that although most individuals feel relatively satisfied with their level of involvement, some show resistance to the forced method of decision making.

APPLICATION OF PROBLEM-SOLVING AND DECISION-MAKING TEAMS

Organizations use a variety of problem-solving and decision-making teams. Let's discuss three recent applications of teams in organizations: self-managed work teams, cross-functional teams, and quality control circles.

Self-Managed Work Teams

A few name variations can be found in the literature: self-managing work groups, self-directed work teams, self-managing teams, or semi-autonomous groups.[30]

Self-managed work teams (SMWTs) consist of employees who work on relatively whole tasks (such as assembling a car or a major auto component) and are responsible for managing the task that will result in a product or service being delivered. Team members are typically responsible for handling all or most aspects of the work and performing all the technical tasks involved. Technical tasks are typically rotated among team members, as are management responsibilities, such as monitoring the team's productivity and quality.[31]

Many self-managed teams work without direct supervision. One recent survey found that almost half of all *Fortune* 1000 companies were using self-managed work teams, with even more planning their use.[32]

The important characteristics of self-managed work teams are employees with a variety of skills who (1) perform interrelated tasks, are responsible for making a product or delivering a service, and work together closely (face-to-face interaction) and (2) have discretion over decisions such as work assignments, work scheduling, work methods, and sometimes even team member selection and training.[33]

One recent study found that self-managed work teams were rated higher than conventionally managed work groups in quality of work life (QWL) areas such as job satisfaction, personal growth satisfaction, social satisfaction, and organizational commitment. Self-managed work groups were also found to perform better than conventionally managed work groups in terms of both quantity and quality of work.[34] As the implementation of self-managed teams in organizations increases the way self-managed teams design and adapt themselves impact their performance and at times result unintentionally in conflict and dysfunctional behavior.[35]

Cross-Functional Teams

Cross-functional teams have emerged as a viable way to bring together people with knowledge and skills from various functional areas to work on a specific task.[36] Many organizations use cross-functional teams as an effective means for allowing individuals from diverse areas within the organization to exchange information, identify problems, develop new ideas, solve problems, and coordinate complex projects. Cross-functional teams cut across departmental and functional boundaries. A specific example of such teams is new-product development teams. Many companies—such as Boeing's 777 development team, Chrysler's Neon subcompact car development team, and Motorola's Iridium project development team—use such teams very successfully.

The **new-product development team (NPDT)** has emerged as a viable tool within highly competitive, technology-based industries for enhancing the product development process. NPDTs are small groups of employees who collectively have the knowledge and skills needed to solve the problem of developing a new product, from conception through manufacturing and distribution "from design to delivery." These teams often comprise individuals from a variety of functional areas, such as marketing, finance, design engineering, process engineering, and manufacturing. Within the context of product development teams that often confront technical challenges we have seen the emergence of another type of team, the Cheetah team.

The **Cheetah team (CT)** is a small group of elite units, separated from the product development team, that can be mobilized quickly to solve an unexpected problem threatening to hold up a project.[37] By delegating the challenges to the Cheetah team, the product development team removes the challenge from its mainstream activities and buffers the project from disruptions and at the same time provides the Cheetah team with the freedom to address the problem without distractions.

Research has shown that NPDTs and CTs are highly effective in facilitating the development process,[38] shortening product development time, and increasing cooperation between functional groups within the organization.[39] These teams typically succeed if they effectively obtain information and resources from others (both inside and outside the organization), use the information and resources to create a viable product, and gain support for the product from others (both inside and outside the organization).[40] In a fashion similar to the use of NPDT, organizations can create multidisciplinary teams to service or support a single large customer.

Quality Control Circles

Quality control circles (QCCs) are small groups of workers from the same work area who are given training in problem solving, statistical quality control, and group processes. They meet regularly to discuss ways to improve the quality of their work and to solve job-related problems. The concepts of QCC originated in Japan and are considered by many to be the most famous Japanese organizational innovation to date.[41] Although results of the use of quality circles have been mixed in both the United States and Japan,[42] the most important potential of QCCs is the continuing organizational dialoguing they promote between managers and the workforce.[43]

COMPUTER TECHNOLOGY AND GROUP DECISION MAKING

Technical developments in computing, electronic communications, and decision support, coupled with an emerging interest in improving the effectiveness of teams and meetings has spurred the development of group decision support systems (GDSS). One of the most rapidly developing fields is the use of computer technology to enhance group problem solving and decision making. (We devoted a complete chapter to technology, information technology, and human behavior—see Module 20W.) A wide variety of computer-based forms of brainstorming (electronic brainstorming) have been developed.[44] Computer programs that allow for sharing information via computer networks are called **groupware.**

The emerging groupware technology reflects a change in emphasis from using the computer to support record keeping and managerial decision making toward using the computer to facilitate human interaction and team performance.[45] Furthermore, groupware technology allows for the creation of virtual work teams.

Virtual Teams

Virtual work teams are groups of people working closely together, even though they may not be working on the same time schedule or at the same physical space. Team members can be separated by many miles and even be on different continents. Johansen created a helpful categorization based on time and space: Team members can be working at the same place and at the same time, they can be working at the same time but be working at different places, they can be working at different times at the same place, and they can be working at different times in different places.[46] Though it is still relatively new, this technology has produced impressive productivity gains.[47] Research studies on groupware are just beginning to appear, but one study indicates that its use improves group conflict resolution processes,[48] and another found that groups using electronic communication have more difficulty in reaching consensus than do groups meeting face-to-face and also appear to be more willing to take risks.[49]

Recent studies investigated the relationships between leadership and virtual team performance and expectation dynamics and learning in virtual teams. When investigating leadership, the researchers suggested that leaders of successful virtual teams seem to have in common the following practices: Establish and maintain trust through the use of communication technology; ensure that distributed diversity is understood and appreciated; manage virtual work-life cycle (meetings); monitor team progress using technology; enhance visibility of virtual members within the team and outside in the organization; and enable individual members of the virtual team to benefit from the team.[50] (See Module 8 for the exploration of leadership practices at work.) The nature of geographically disperse teams suggests that expectation dynamics must be managed and revisited periodically and that special attention must be given to ongoing learning.[51] (See Module 2 for the framing of the role of expectations at work.)

GROUP DECISION MAKING AND THE CULTURAL CONTEXT

Culture can be viewed at two levels: national culture and organizational culture. The topic of organizational culture and its implication to behavior at work will be explored in depth in Module 15. Culture and organizational culture influence the ways that organizations make decisions. When we think of decision making in the global context, the following questions come to mind: Do groups from different cultures perceive problems in the same way? Do they use the same decision-making processes? Do they gather similar types and amounts of information while investigating the problem? Do they follow the same thinking patterns? Do they construct similar types of solutions? Do they use similar strategies for choosing between alternatives? Do they implement their decisions in the same ways? The answer to each question is no.[52]

The cultural context within which groups exist plays a critical role in preference for and the performance of individual versus group problem solving. While some cultures (for example, the United States and Great Britain) have a strong belief in the importance and centrality of the individual, other cultures (for example, China and Taiwan) have a strong belief in the importance of collectivism.[53] Thus, we find that a person's choice of either individual or group problem solving and his or her actual behavior and performance are likely to be affected by the individual's cultural heritage. We also find that culture can affect performance in a particular context. One study showed that managers from collectivist cultures performed worse when working alone, as opposed to working in a group with which they identified.[54]

As an example of the impact of culture on decision-making processes, within the Japanese culture, a unique consensual decision-making process exists. The process has two components—*ringi* and *nemawashi*—through which Japanese managers involve subordinates in considering the future direction of their companies. Individuals and groups that have ideas for improvement or change will discuss them widely with a large number of peers and managers. During this extensive informal communication process, some kinds of agreements *(nemawashi)* are hammered out. At this point a formal document is circulated for signatures or a personalized stamp (the seal) of every manager who is considered relevant to the decision (called a *ringi*).[55] Only after all the relevant managers put their seals on the proposal is the idea or suggestion implemented.

Based on a recent study of successful teams and managers, four strategies for working through the challenges faced by multicultural teams were advanced:

1. *Adaptation.* Acknowledging cultural gaps openly and working around them.
2. *Structural intervention.* Changing the shape of the team.
3. *Managerial intervention.* Setting norms early or bringing in a higher-level manager.
4. *Exit.* Removing a team member when other options have failed.

Of all the strategies, the adaptation strategy is the ideal one since the team works effectively to solve its own problem, learning from the team's experience and with minimum input from management.[56]

PROBLEMS THAT EMERGE IN WORK TEAMS

Teams at work encounter ongoing challenges. Teams typically encounter certain recurring problems if the interaction patterns of the members have not been specifically shaped or redesigned to avoid them and help the team be the most effective and efficient. Some issues that most teams need to work through center on the methods of team communication (see Module 7). For example, what should be the ways in which the team communicates? How much of it should be done electronically? What should be done face-to-face? The challenges have been widely described in the management literature, and we have observed that they frequently characterize the behavior of participants of this course, particularly those who undertake the outside team project. Here we discuss some of these problems.

Use of Time

Closely associated with action orientation is how the team uses time. Many work groups are concerned about wasting time in meetings. Because planning often involves ambiguity and abstract thinking, there is pressure to get it over with and to get on to something more concrete. Planning requires blocks of time to permit the generation of ideas and allow synergy to take place. Teams must develop the expectation that a four-hour period, a day, or a weekend might be needed.

The effects of poor distribution of time are perhaps most evident in university life, where the practice is to schedule faculty or committee meetings for one hour once a week because teaching schedules and room availability make it most difficult to arrange longer blocks of time. Meetings in the evening and on weekends are against faculty norms. So each committee meeting, scheduled for an hour, makes little progress because of the long start-up time, which requires recapitulation of what was covered the week before, trying to pick up the continuity of the planning, and carrying it further.

Team Style

Over time, work groups develop a style of operation. (Some models are presented in Module 12.) **Team styles** embrace the expectations team members have about meetings, basic team norms, and emerging roles. Autocratic-style meetings tend to be avoided except when they are needed to get information out and get reports back; corporate style meetings are likely to be highly procedural and committee-like and are held for more purposes than are really necessary; permissive-style meetings are apt to be frequent and held just for the conversation; retired-on-the-job meetings may never take place; and professional–manager meetings would be of the team-action type discussed in this module. The patterns of member expectations that accompany each of these styles become so frozen in the minds of team members that they cannot be changed without considerable effort, frequently only with the assistance of outside expertise.

Work Habits and Skills

Many organizations are unaware that work groups can develop skills almost like individuals can. Making the improvement of group work habits and skills a goal and providing the time for this purpose is rarely considered. Historically, in sports and the military services training for effective interaction patterns was accepted as a necessity. Today we see more and more organizations investing in the building and development of work teams. The causal effect between work teams that have gone through team building training and increased performance has been documented in the literature.[57] We explore team building as an organization development approach in Module 16.

One-to-One Relationships with the Boss

The rivalries among team members that arise from one-to-one relationships in the managerial hierarchy are extremely difficult to avoid. An effective manager must meet with the team members one at a time for some purposes and with the entire team for others. (This situation was illustrated in the Vroom–Yetton–Jago decision-making model discussed earlier in this module.) Determining how to foster maximum trust and keep rivalries low is a continuing challenge. Edgar H. Schein notes:

> The successful manager must be a good diagnostician and must value a spirit of inquiry. If the abilities and motives of the people under him are so variable, he must have the sensitivity and diagnostic ability to be able to sense and appreciate the differences. Second, rather than regard the existence of differences as a painful truth to be wished away, he must also learn to value differences and to value the diagnostic process which reveals differences. Finally, he must have the personal flexibility and the range of skills necessary to vary his own behavior. If the needs and motives of his subordinates are different, they must be treated differently.[58]

Although this view may sound reasonable, it is extremely difficult to practice. The fact that people are complex and need to be treated differently can run contrary to the ideal of fair treatment as perceived by employees. For example, in a team-building session involving an executive and the middle-level managers reporting to her, one manager said that he would like to discuss how money available for management development and training was to be allotted in the coming year. He stated that he had not felt right during the past year when he received $2,400 to attend a one-week workshop but learned that $5,000 had been spent for another team member. The boss then asked, "But John, didn't you get just what you asked for?" John replied, "Yes, I did, and I was very satisfied with what I gained from the workshop." The boss went on to say that the other employee had also gotten what he had asked for, and that his main concerns had been both satisfying the team members' requests and making sure that the training of each also met organizational needs; following this flexible policy meant that assigning a fixed sum to each individual would not be meaningful.

When the team discussed this situation, it was obvious that all members were concerned about receiving their fair share of the training funds, but they concluded that they would like to have the present policy continued. John said that he felt better about it now that it had been discussed. The boss stated that it had not occurred to her that this flexible policy would be questioned as long as it met the needs of the team members; she then asked whether she was doing other things that were being experienced as perhaps not completely fair; other practices were discussed. If this dialogue had not taken place, the executive might not have become aware that her flexible practices of treating people according to their needs had to take into consideration how team members perceived her actions from the point of fairness. Given that this occurred during a team-building session, we can begin to see how such sessions allow feelings and issues to be addressed—feelings and issues that, if not dealt with effectively, might affect the relationships between team members, with a corresponding effect on the team's operation.

Hidden Agendas

Rivalries; distrust; ambitions; concern about looking bad, foolish, or unknowledgeable; and other factors can cause individuals to avoid saying openly how they feel or what they want. The interactions and communications of individuals in meetings are apt to be complicated by these **hidden agendas.**

SUMMARY

Today's sustainable competitive advantage is knowledge.[59] Teams provide the mechanisms to create, import, and leverage knowledge. Team effectiveness is viewed as an organizational capability and the needed mechanism for a sustainable organization.[60] This module has explored aspects of team problem solving and decision making, and their differences have been discussed. Behaviors that enhance group problem solving have been outlined as have conditions under which both individual and group decision making (participative management) may be effective. The manager's role in facilitating group decision making was covered as were techniques for enhancing group creativity. Several ways in which organizations use problem-solving teams were outlined. Different types of teams that are used in a variety of organizational settings and cultural context were described. Finally, problems that many work teams experience were identified and briefly discussed.

Study Questions

1. What are some of the potential challenges that work teams face?

2. Identify the types of work teams that can be found at work. How are they similar? How are they different?

3. What is rational group decision making? Why is it useful?

4. What is the consensus process? How is it of value to your teams in this course?

5. Athletic coaches train teams in techniques to win the game or to achieve peak performance. In what kinds of skills can managers train work teams? Give specific examples.

6. Students often remember Activity 11–3 as an attempt to illustrate the effectiveness of group decision making. Was it effective? Why do you think so?

7. What are some considerations in deciding whether to allow a group to participate in decision making?

8. Assume that you are a manager and have decided to use group decision making for a problem affecting the productivity of your team. What issues should you consider before the first group meeting? How would you go about managing the meeting? What are some pitfalls to avoid?

9. Identify the different phases in the group problem-solving cycle. At which phases did your group encounter problems in the activities in this module? Why? How can you avoid these problems in the future?

10. Identify one method to improve your classroom group's problem-solving effectiveness. What specific steps would you take to facilitate the process?

11. What are some of the effects of culture on group problem-solving effectiveness?

Endnotes

1. J. M. Wilson, P. A. Goodman, and M. A. Cronin, "Group Learning," *Academy of Management Review* 32, no. 4 (2007), pp. 1041–59.

2. H. Oh, G. Labianca, and M. Chung, "A Multilevel Model of Group Social Capital," *Academy of Management Review* 31, no. 3 (2006), pp. 569–82.

3. M. R. Barrick, B. H. Bradley, A. L. Kristof-Brown, and A. E. Colbert, "The Moderating Role of Top Management Team Interdependence: Implications for Real Teams and Working Groups," *Academy of Management Journal* 50, no. 3 (2007), pp. 544–57.

4. F. LaFasto and C. Larson, *When Teams Work Best* (Thousand Oaks, CA: Sage, 2001).

5. J. E. Neumann, R. Holti, and H. Standing, *Changing Everything at Once* (Oxford, UK: Tavistock Institute, 1996).

6. S. Lembke and M. G. Wilson, "Putting the 'Team' into Teamwork: Alternative Theoretical Contributions for Contemporary Management Practice," *Human Relations* 51, no. 7 (1998), pp. 927–44.

7. T. J. Peters, *Thriving on Chaos* (New York: Alfred A. Knopf, 1988).

8. C. P. Alderfer, "An Intergroup Perspective on Group Dynamics," in J. W. Lorch (ed.), *Handbook of Organizational Behavior* (Englewood Cliffs, NJ: Prentice-Hall, 1986).

9. J. E. McGrath, H. Arrow, and J. L. Berdahl, *A Theory of Groups as Complex Systems* (Newbury Park, CA: Sage, 1998).

10. J. R. Katzenbach and D. K. Smith. *The Wisdom of Teams: Creating the High Performance Organization* (Boston: Harvard Business School Press, 1993).

11. Ibid.

12. M. Ezzamel and H. Willmott, "Accounting Teamwork: A Critical Study of Group-Based Systems of Organizational Control," *Administrative Science Quarterly* 43 (1998), pp. 358–96.

13. S. G. Cohen and D. E. Bailey, "What Makes Teams Work: Group Effectiveness Research from the Shop Floor to the Executive Suite," *Journal of Management* 23, no. 3 (1997), pp. 239–90.

14. Katzenbach and Smith, *The Wisdom of Teams,* p. 112.

15. W. Watson, L. K. Michalson, and W. Sharp, "Member Competence, Group Interaction, and Group Decision Making: A Longitudinal Study," *Journal of Applied Psychology* 76 (1991), pp. 803–9.

16. J. Schmidt and M. Montoya-Weiss, "New Product Development Decision Making Effectiveness: Comparing Individuals, Face-to-Face Teams, and Virtual Teams," *Decision Science* 32, no. 4 (2001), pp. 575–600.

17. A. N. Hollingshead, "Distributed Knowledge and Transactive Process in Decision-Making Groups," in D. H. Gruenfeld (ed.), *Managing Groups and Teams,* vol. 1 (Stamford, CT: JAI Press, 1998), pp. 103–23; and P. W. Yetton and P. C. Bottger, "Individual versus Group Problem Solving: An Empirical Test of a Best-Member Strategy," *Organizational Behavior and Human Performance* 29 (1982), pp. 307–21.

18. J. R. Hackman and C. G. Morris, "T-Group Tasks, Group Interaction Process, and Group Performance Effectiveness: A Review and Proposed Integration," in Leonard Berkowitz (ed.), *Advances in Experimental Social Psychology,* vol. 8 (New York: Academic Press, 1974), p. 49.

19. V. H. Vroom and P. W. Yetton, *Leadership and Decision Making* (Pittsburgh: University of Pittsburgh Press, 1972), p. 13.

20. V. H. Vroom and A. C. Jago, *The New Leadership* (Englewood Cliffs, NJ: Prentice-Hall, 1988), p. 184.

21. J. A. Wagner III, "Participation's Effects on Performance and Satisfaction: A Reconsideration of Research Evidence," *Academy of Management Review* 19, no. 2 (1994), pp. 312–30.

22. J. Hall, "Decisions, Decisions, Decisions," *Psychology Today* (November 1971); and A. Crouch and P. Yetton, "Manager Behavior, Leadership Style, and Subordinate Performance: An Empirical Examination of the Vroom–Yetton Conflict Rule," *Organizational Behavior and Human Decision Process* 39 (1987), pp. 384–96.

23. D. Collins, R. A. Ross, and T. L. Ross, "Who Wants Participative Management?" *Group and Organizational Studies* 14 (1989), pp. 422–45.

24. P. M. Elsass and L. M. Graves, "Demographic Diversity in Decision-Making Groups: The Experience of Women and People of Color," *Academy of Management Review* 22, no. 4

(1997), pp. 946–73; and D. C. Lau and J. K. Murnighan, "Demographic Diversity and Fault-lines: The Compositional Dynamics of Organizational Groups," *Academy of Management Review* 23, no. 2 (1998), pp. 325–40.

25. G. P. Hubler, *Managerial Decision Making* (Glenview, IL: Scott, Foresman, 1980), Ch. 9.

26. W. A. Randolph and B. Z. Poner, *Getting the Job Done! Managing Project Teams and Task Forces for Success,* rev. ed. (Englewood Cliffs, NJ: Prentice-Hall, 1992).

27. S. E. Yeatts and C. Hyten, *High-Performing Self-Managed Work Teams* (Thousand Oaks, CA: Sage, 1998).

28. B. Geoff, *Level of Consensus* (CA: Geoff & Associate Consulting Firm Pub., 1995).

29. A. L. Delbecq, A. H. Van de Ven, and D. H. Gustafson, *Group Techniques for Program Planning: A Guide to Nominal and Delphi Processes* (Glenview, IL: Scott, Foresman, 1975); J. M. Bartunek and J. K. Murningham, "The Nominal Group Technique: Expanding the Basic Procedure and Underlying Assumptions," *Group and Organization Studies* 9 (1984), pp. 417–32; and G. E. Burton, "The 'Clustering Effect': An Idea-Generation Phenomenon during Nominal Grouping," *Small Group Behavior* 18 (1987), pp. 224–38.

30. L. Glassop, "The Organizational Benefits of Teams," *Human Relations* 55, no. 2 (2002), pp. 225–49.

31. D. E. Yeatts and C. Hyten, *High-Performing Self-Managed Work Teams* (Thousand Oaks, CA: Sage Publications, 1998).

32. E. E. Lawler, S. A. Mohrman, and G. E. Ledford, Jr., *Employee Involvement and Total Quality Management: Practices and Results in Fortune 1000 Companies* (San Francisco: Jossey-Bass, 1992).

33. P. S. Goodman, S. Devadas, and T. L. Hutchinson, "Groups and Productivity: Analyzing the Effectiveness of Self-Managing Teams," in J. P. Campbell, R. J. Campbell, and Associates (eds.), *Productivity in Organizations* (San Francisco: Jossey-Bass, 1988), pp. 295–325.

34. S. G. Cohen and G. E. Ledford, Jr., "The Effectiveness of Self-Managing Teams: A Quasi-Experiment," *Human Relations* 47 (1994), pp. 13–43.

35. C. W. Langfred, "The Downside of Self-Management: A Longitudinal Study of the Effects of Conflict on Trust, Autonomy, and Task Interdependence in Self-Managing Teams," *Academy of Management Journal* 50, no. 4 (2007), pp. 885–900.

36. G. M. Parker, *Cross-Functional Teams* (San Francisco: Jossey-Bass, 1994).

37. M. Engwall and C. Svensson, "Cheetah Teams," *Harvard Business Review* 79, no. 2 (2001), pp. 20–21.

38. K. B. Clark and S. C. Wheelwright, *Managing New Product and Process Development* (New York: Free Press, 1993); and W. E. Souder, *Managing New Product Innovation* (Lexington, MA: Lexington Books, 1987).

39. M. Iansiti and A. MacCormack, "Developing Production Internet Time," *Harvard Business Review,* September–October 1997, pp. 108–17; J. R. Hackman and R. E. Walton, "Leading Groups in Organizations," in P. Goodman (ed.), *Designing Effective Work Groups* (San Francisco: Jossey-Bass, 1986).

40. R. Burgelman, "A Process Model of Internal Corporate Venturing in the Diversified Major Firm," *Administrative Science Quarterly* 31 (1982), pp. 223–44.

41. P. Lillrank and N. Kano, *Continuous Improvement: Quality Control Circles in Japanese Industry* (Ann Arbor, MI: University of Michigan Press, 1989).

42. R. E. Cole, "Japan Can but We Can't," IAQC Conference Presentation, Louisville, March 1981.

43. P. Lillrank, A. B. (Rami) Shani, B. Stymne, H. Kolodny, J.-R. Figuera, and M. Liu, "Continuous Improvement: An International Comparative Study," in W. Pasmore and R. Woodman (eds.), *Research in Organizational Change and Development* (Greenwich, CT: JAI Press, 1999).

44. R. B. Gauupe, L. M. Bastianutti, and W. H. Cooper, "Unblocking Brainstorming," *Journal of Applied Psychology* 76, no. 1 (1991), pp. 137–42.

45. A. D. Shulman, "Putting Group Information Technology in Its Place: Communication and Good Work Group Performance," in R. R. Clegg, C. Hardy, and W. R. Nord (eds.), *Handbook of Organization Studies* (London: Sage Publication, 1996), pp. 357–74.

46. R. Johansen, *Leading Business Teams: How Teams Can Use Technology and Group Process Tools to Enhance Performance* (Reading MA: Addison-Wesley, 1991).

47. D. Kirkpatrick, "Why Microsoft Can't Stop Lotus Notes," *Fortune* (December 22, 1994), p. 142. This article reported returns on investment from use of groupware ranging from 179 to 351 percent.

48. M. S. Poole, M. Holmes, and G. DeSanctis, "Conflict Management in a Computer- Supported Meeting Environment," *Management Science* 37 (1991), pp. 926–53.

49. S. Kiesler and Lee Sproull, "Group Decision Making and Communication Technology," *Organizational Behavior and Human Decision Processes* 52 (1992), pp. 96–123.

50. A. Malhorta, A. Majchrzak, and B. Rosen, "Leading Virtual Teams," *Academy of Management Perspective* 21, no. 1, (2007), pp. 60–70.

51. P. Bosch-Sijtsema, "The Impact of Individual Expectations and Expectation Conflict on Virtual Teams," *Group and Organization Management* 32, no. 3 (2007), pp. 358–88.

52. J. Brett, K., Behfar, and M. C. Kern, "Managing Multicultural Teams," *Harvard Business Review* 84, no. 11 (2006), pp. 84–91; N. J. Adler, *International Dimensions of Organizational Behavior,* 3rd ed. (Boston: PWS–Kent, 1997).

53. G. Hofstede, *Culture's Consequences* (Newbury Park, CA: Sage, 1984).

54. P. C. Earley, "East Meets West Meets Mideast: Further Explorations of Collectivistic and Individualistic Work Groups," *Academy of Management Journal* 36 (1993), pp. 319–48.

55. P. Sethi, N. Namiki, and C. Swanson, *The False Promise of the Japanese Miracle* (Marshfield, MA: Pittman, 1984).

56. Brett, Behfar, and Kern, "Managing Mulicultural Teams."

57. R. Wayne and M. L. McConkie, "Team Building," in T. Cummings (ed.), *Handbook of Organization Development* (Los Angeles, CA: SAGE, 2008), pp. 237–60.

58. E. H. Schein, *Leadership and Organization Culture* (Englewood Cliffs, NJ: Prentice-Hall, 1998).

59. S. A. Mohrman, "Designing Organizations to Lead with Knowledge," in Cummings (ed.), *Handbook of Organization Development,* pp. 519–37.

60. P. Docherty, M. Kira and A. B. Rami Shani (eds.), *Sustainable Work Systems* (London, UK: Routeledge, 2008).

Activity 11–3: Who Gets the Overtime?

Objectives:

a. To examine group decision making as a process.

b. To identify some issues concerning participation of employees in decision making.

c. To explore the role of the leader in group decision making.

d. To use role playing as a learning method.

(*Note:* This activity's objective is neither to advocate the use of group decision making nor to demonstrate how it should be done. Rather, we are exploring the issue of group decision making based on your experience in the exercise.)

Task 1:

a. The instructor will briefly discuss role playing. There are a number of ways to role-play, and it is used for a variety of purposes. In this case, each member of your team will be given a role in a group decision-making problem. You will be comfortable if you remember that you are not participating in a theatrical production. You are not being asked to take the lead in the school play. All you are asked to do is play yourself as you would feel if you were in the situation described in the role you will be given.

   For instance, pretend you are taking a final examination and the professor comes up to your desk, picks up your exam paper, tears it up, and says, "You fail the course. You have notes and books on the floor beside you and under your desk, and I've seen you looking down there. Also, you were glancing at the examination paper of the student next to you." You decide to appeal your failure grade to the dean. What are all the possible arguments you could use to defend yourself? (Take 2 minutes now and discuss this situation with two of your fellow students.) This situation could be role-played by you, with someone else playing the role of the dean, whose viewpoint would probably be different from yours. The roles of our exercise are similar in that you will have some idea of how you would behave if you were in the situation described. One more point about role playing: You are role playing not only for what you can learn from it but also to give the other role player the opportunity to see what it is like to interact with, and learn from, you in this situation. That is, in this course you are responsible for the learning of others.

b. Tear out the instruction sheet "Who Gets the Overtime?" that can be found at the end of the instructions, but be careful not to look at any of the individual role sheets while doing so. The instructor will read this instruction sheet aloud while the class follows it. Participants can refer to this sheet at any time during the role playing.

c. Each team is to arrange itself in a circle and elect the supervisor (Kim) for this specific exercise. (*Note:* If the class is not working in permanent teams, participants are to form groups of six and elect a supervisor for this exercise.) Starting clockwise from the supervisor, the role assignments are as follows: A woman in the group should assume the role of Sara. (If there is no woman in the group, of course, she has to be played by a man.) If only five members are present, eliminate the role of Fran. If only four are present in the team, a member of a six-person team should be borrowed temporarily for this exercise. Turn to your own role assignment sheet and tear it from the book. After you have read the role description and understand it, turn it face down and use it as a name card so your team members can identify your role name during the exercise. Do not tell others what your role instructions are. When the exercise begins, play your role naturally, without referring to your sheet. When facts or events arise that are not covered by the roles, make up things that are consistent with the way it might be in a real-life situation.

   When Kim has studied and understands the supervisor's role, she will stand. When the supervisors for all groups are standing, the instructor will give the signal to begin the exercise. When Kim sits down, assume Kim has just entered the office and greet Kim with a hearty "Good morning!" Kim will tell you what to do from this point on. (*Note for Kim:* If you have only five on the team, including yourself, announce to your group that Fran called in sick and read them Fran's role. Fran is to be taken into consideration in arriving at the solution.)

   Observers, if there are any, are to be assigned one to a group for the purpose of observing and, possibly, reporting to the class at the end of the session how the decision was made. Observers are not to enter into the process. (Time: for introduction, 10 minutes; for role playing, 20–25 minutes; for discussion, 20 minutes or longer. This exercise generates a range of rich data, and it is well to reserve discussion time to extend into the second hour.)

(*Note:* Teams completing role playing before the time has run out should proceed with Task 2. Skip Task 2 and go directly to Task 3 if teams all finish at about the same time.)

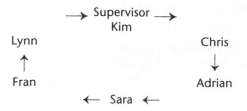

Task 2 (Only for Teams Finishing Task 1 Early):

After deciding who gets the overtime, the team should assume it is reconvening as a committee of supervisors to deliberate and decide the same case. To whom would this committee give the overtime? Why?

Task 3:

a. When the role playing is complete, the instructor will ask each supervisor to give the name of the person in the role play who got the overtime. The names are to be listed on the blackboard for all groups (using the chart form below), but no discussion is to take place at this time. The listing provides the class with information as to which groups agree and disagree with their choice.

Group	Who Got the Overtime?	How Was Decision Made?
#1		
#2		
#3		

b. The instructor will now interview each group on the following:

1. How was the decision made? (List the elements of these decision processes on the board for each team.) What are the similarities and differences among the decision processes? What criteria were used? (List on the board.) What procedures could be used to bring more objectivity into the process if the group were to start over again—assuming the leader left the problem entirely up to employees to solve?

2. Was this a good way to make the decision for this particular problem? Why?

3. What issues (points of controversy) were raised by the group decision making?

4. How did the supervisor feel about the role she or he was given? How did the employees feel about the role played by the supervisor? How could the supervisor have actively guided and facilitated the process and still let the employees make the decision?

5. If the supervisor had decided not to let the employees make the decision, what other methods could he or she have used to arrive at the decision? Which of the alternatives, including group decision, would you have preferred?

6. How did each Sara feel about her role? (*Note:* This has to be done from the standpoint of sharing feelings with others. The atmosphere of listening for understanding without confrontation or argument is important. The differing reactions and the way each Sara perceived her role can provide insight into the area of male–female interface in a work group.)

7. For teams that finished both Tasks 1 and 2, were there any differences in the decisions for the two circumstances?

Source: This activity follows the design developed by Norman R. F. Maier's exercise, "The New Truck Dilemma," in N. R. F. Maier, A. R. Solem, and Ayesha A. Maier, *Supervisory and Executive Development* (New York: John Wiley & Sons, 1957). This exercise is printed here with the special permission of Dr. Maier.

WHO GETS THE OVERTIME?
(FOR ACTIVITY 11–3)

Five of you are employees of the Customers' Division of the Mountain Power Company's District Headquarters in Green Valley, Virginia. Your job requires monitoring customer accounts for records, billing, payments, and collection purposes. Answering customer inquiries and opening and closing accounts are a major part of your job. All five of you are considered excellent employees, and the atmosphere in the office is one of congeniality and good morale. One reason for this is that Green Valley is a small town in a beautiful area where few good jobs exist. The small local college is the main activity in the town, and Mountain Power's district office offers one of the few good places to work, even though salaries are modest. Students graduating from the local high schools and colleges move out of the area to find permanent jobs.

All five of you are feeling the squeeze for money. Inflation is a problem, and many of the products sold in Green Valley are higher priced than in big cities because of transportation costs and the limited market. All of you moonlight when you can, but the opportunities are scarce. When overtime work is required, Mountain Power's policy is to rotate employee assignments so all have an equal share on an annual basis; however, overtime needs are very low. Here are some general facts about the employees in your section.

Chris is 22 years of age, has been with the company four years, and has three young children. Adrian is 27 years of age, has been with the company 10 years, and is the senior person in the office.

Sara is 21 years of age. It is the company's policy to employ two deserving college students half-time and to let them study at the office during times when customer inquiries are low; she is one of these students.

Fran, 25 years of age, is the second half-time student. Fran started work at the same time as Sara two years ago and plans to graduate in one year.

Lynn, 20 years of age, is the newest employee, having decided to make Mountain Power a career after graduating from a two-year college.

Kim is your supervisor. When the instructor gives you the signal to start role playing, the scene is as follows: You have just been called into Kim's office for a discussion. The supervisor will tell you what you are to do. Play your role as if you were in the position described on your role sheet. When facts arise that are not covered by the roles, be creative; make up things that are consistent with the way it might be in a real-life situation.

(*Note:* Return to the instructions of Task 1c, Activity 11–3, before proceeding with the role playing.)

KIM, THE SUPERVISOR

(CUT ON LINE)

FRAN

(CUT ON LINE)

LYNN

KIM, THE SUPERVISOR

Your manager has asked you to select one of your employees to work Saturday mornings on a new job in another section of the headquarters office. The manager wants the same person to perform in the job for the next year because it requires technical training in data-processing equipment, and continuous experience will be needed.

Your dilemma is that all five of your people are equally qualified and all need the money. You have recently had a supervision course in which participation of employees in decision making was studied. You decide that this is a case in which they all have an equal interest so you will let them make the decision. You have called them together for this purpose. Tell them what the opportunity is and then tell them to go ahead and decide among themselves who is to get the overtime assignment. Remember, *you are going to let them make the decision.* The team must arrive at a decision.

(CUT ON LINE)

ROLE OF FRAN

You are always pressed for money. You live with your fiancé, also a student, who shares expenses. Your car is old and always requiring repairs. You wish to enter the MBA program at Midwest University next fall; if you can save up for the initial tuition, you might be able to attend classes half-time and work half-time.

(CUT ON LINE)

ROLE OF LYNN

You are married and living with your in-laws so you can save, but you find it most uncomfortable. Your spouse works half-time, having found nothing full-time. The two of you are very frugal because your parents have promised to pay half the down payment on a "starter" house if you can accumulate the other half. You plan no children until this is accomplished. You hope to prove to Mountain Power that your all-around capabilities and two-year community college degree qualify you to work into management. You plan to take a computer course in the near future as part of your personal development program.

CHRIS

(CUT ON LINE)

SARA

(CUT ON LINE)

ADRIAN

ROLE OF CHRIS

You and your spouse have had one child after another, so money is tight. Your spouse continually presses you to find extra work, which you do whenever you can. Both of you spend much of your spare time raising chickens and vegetables for the family.

(CUT ON LINE)

ROLE OF SARA

You give part of your earnings to the support of your younger brothers because money is scarce for your mother since your father died. You have been borrowing money for your education. You have been able to carry almost a full load at college in your business administration major and maintain a good average in spite of your work; you are starting your junior year. You like Mountain Power and may want to stay on after you graduate if they will give you a job. You have learned in your business courses that professional women have to be better than their male peers to move ahead in the work world. Your personal effectiveness goal is to "get your share of the air time," "hold your own," or "be assertive in a pleasant way" in discussions with male peers.

(CUT ON LINE)

ROLE OF ADRIAN

You give 10 percent of your salary to the church and are highly regarded for your willingness to help with church responsibilities. For two years you have been building a small house in your spare time. Progress is slow because you have to save up to buy building materials. You are single, but you hope to get married as soon as you find the right person. You feel that your seniority entitles you to first consideration when new opportunities arise.

Activity 11–4:
Team Development
Assessment

Objectives:

a. To critique the effectiveness of your team in regard to (1) achievement of results in task assignments and (2) achievement of relationships among members that integrate their human resources (abilities, knowledge, views, and so on) into task solutions.

b. To suggest team goals for improved effectiveness.

Task 1:

Individuals working alone are to complete the questionnaire on team development scales on pages M11–39—M11–41.

Task 2:

Teams meet to discuss the scale items on the questionnaire one at a time. Each member will report the rating he or she made prior to the meeting. The differences in ratings will be discussed to determine why members are perceiving the team's interactions differently. A group consensus rating will be made for each scale after thorough discussion. (*Note:* Avoid majority voting. Instead, seek real understanding to attain agreement.)

Task 3:

Study the comments on team goals at the end of the questionnaire. Teams are then to go back over the consensus ratings for the 15 items completed in Task 2. These ratings represent the characteristics of the team at present. Now write a *G* on each scale representing a goal the team would like to attain in its interactions by the end of the course.

Name _____   Date _____

QUESTIONNAIRE ON TEAM DEVELOPMENT SCALES

Climate Scales

1. The degree to which my team shows enthusiasm and spirit:

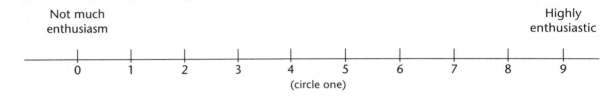

Not much
enthusiasm

Highly
enthusiastic

0 1 2 3 4 5 6 7 8 9

(circle one)

2. On humor I would rate the team

Not much   Not bad   Funny   Outrageous

0 1 2 3 4 5 6 7 8 9

3. My team is

_____ Mostly task oriented.

_____ More task oriented than social.

_____ Equally task and social in orientation.

_____ More social than task oriented.

_____ Mostly social.

People Scales (How We Regard One Another as Human Beings)

4. The degree to which we are interested in one another as people is

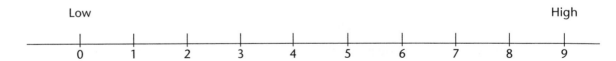

Low   High

0 1 2 3 4 5 6 7 8 9

5. Our regard for each individual as a resource (knowledge, skills, abilities, viewpoints) for group goal achievement is

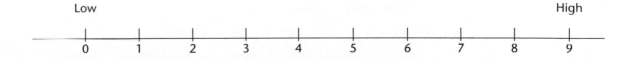

Low   High

0 1 2 3 4 5 6 7 8 9

Productivity Scales (Goals, Work Accomplishment, Commitment)

6. Team's task achievement goals:

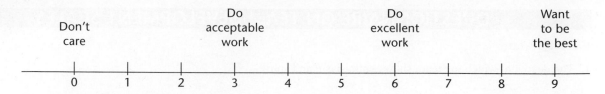

7. Actual quantity of work produced:

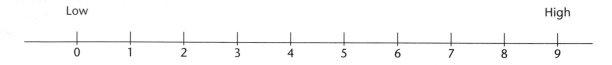

8. Quality of work produced:

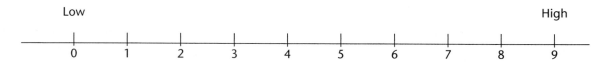

9. Interest in learning:

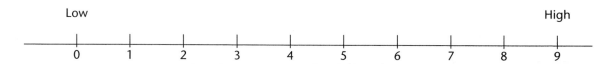

Process Scales (Participation and Communications)

10. Participation (check one):

_____ One to two members contribute the most.

_____ Two to three members contribute regularly.

_____ Three to four members contribute regularly.

_____ Four to five members contribute regularly.

_____ All members contribute regularly.

11. An input from all members is sought before decisions are made:

_____ never   _____ sometimes   _____ often   _____ always

12. Where the team falls on the "handling conflict" scale:

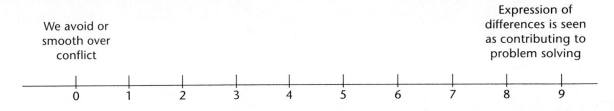

We avoid or
smooth over
conflict

Expression of
differences is seen
as contributing to
problem solving

0	1	2	3	4	5	6	7	8	9

13. Openness in communications:

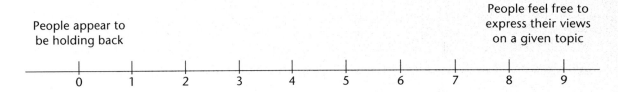

People appear to
be holding back

People feel free to
express their views
on a given topic

0	1	2	3	4	5	6	7	8	9

14. Expression of personal feelings:

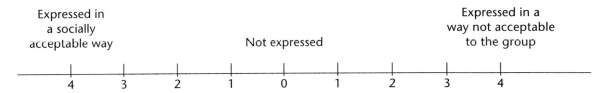

Expressed in
a socially
acceptable way

Not expressed

Expressed in a
way not acceptable
to the group

4	3	2	1	0	1	2	3	4

15. Degree to which we listen and actually hear each other's views:

Low

High

0	1	2	3	4	5	6	7	8	9

Comments: Make notes of anything additional you would like to feed back to the team about how members work together or about how effectiveness could be improved.

Name _____   Date _____

TEAM GOALS

The scales of this questionnaire pertain to attitudes, processes, and skills that can make a team more or less effective under the conditions in which we work in this course. They thereby suggest goals for improvement of team effectiveness. (*Note:* It should not be assumed that these attributes apply to the effectiveness of all teams under all conditions. Whether the specific goals suggested are appropriate depends on the specific conditions of the situation.)

Scale attributes should be regarded as interacting with and reinforcing one another. The following examples illustrate this point and suggest some of the consequences.

Productivity

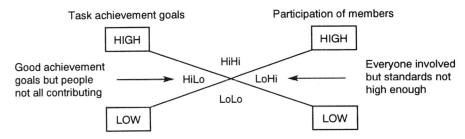

Quality of involvement

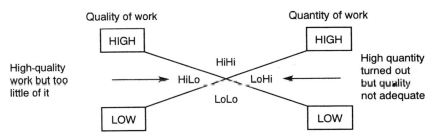

Regard for people

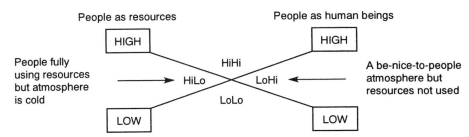

Module 12

Group Dynamics and Performance

LEARNING OBJECTIVES

After completing this module, you should be able to

1. Describe the main characteristics of the human group.
2. Explain the basic elements and processes of small-group dynamics.
3. Identify the factors affecting the development and performance of groups.
4. Describe the role that the manager can play in facilitating the development and performance of a group.
5. Appreciate the effect of group cohesion on group performance.
6. Compare and contrast "the performance model" and "the emotional climate model" of small-group development.
7. Identify the developmental stages of groups.

KEY TERMS AND CONCEPTS

Activities	Hot team
Boundary management	Human group concept
Communication network	Individual roles
Deviant	Interactions
Emergent role system	Internal system
External system	Norms
Group cohesiveness	Relationship roles
Group development	Role differentiation
Group dynamics	Sentiments
Group maturity	Social loafing
Group size	Status
Group structure	Task role
Group technology	Values
Groupthink	

MODULE OUTLINE

PREMODULE PREPARATION

Activity 12–1:
Tower Building*

MEMORANDUM

DATE:

TO:

FROM: Professor _____

SUBJECT: Tower Building Exercise

On _____, _____, during class time, the class will be engaged in the Tower Building Exercise. This exercise will be done in the teams and team rooms that have previously been assigned.

Each group represents a company that has contracted to build a communications tower. The objective is to maximize your company's profit on the contract by constructing a communications tower that falls within the conditions of the contract and, at the same time, cost effectively combines the three most critical variables: tower height, construction time, and materials. (There will also be profit-enhancing awards for the most pleasing designs.) The relationships between height, time, materials, and profits are illustrated graphically on the following three pages, which are titled:

- The Height/Profit Function (Attachment A)
- The Time/Profit Function (Attachment B)
- The Materials/Profit Function (Attachment C)

Construction of the tower is divided into two stages:

Stage 1 is for planning and preparation. This stage lasts for 40–60 minutes. During this preparation stage, test structures or sections may be erected, and for this purpose containers of the construction materials (Lego blocks) will be distributed at the beginning of the session. However, at the start of the actual construction period, all materials must be in the box, and all pieces must be separated from all other pieces. During Stage 1, each team must prepare a Tower Building Profit Budget (Attachment D). This form must be submitted prior to the beginning of the construction period. Teams are free to meet to discuss the exercise prior to class time, but no teams will be given construction materials prior to the start of class.

Stage 2 has a maximum 8-minute duration and is for tower construction. This stage will begin at approximately _____ AM/PM on _____, _____ in the classroom. The actual time required to complete construction will be noted. Calculated construction time will be rounded up to the next nearest minute; for example, construction time of 4 minutes 30 seconds will be recorded as 5 minutes.

Conditions of the Contract:

The finished towers must be

a. Constructed of only the materials supplied inside the container. No materials other than those requisitioned (that is, inside the box) may be used. If illegal or preassembled materials are used, the contract is considered void, and the maximum penalty of $500,000 is assessed.

b. Constructed within all three of the trade-off functions shown.

c. A minimum height of 22 inches. If less than 22 inches, a penalty (in addition to the height/profit function) of $75,000 will be assessed.

*Many variations of this activity have been developed over the past 40 years. The task seems to vary from building a tower, to building a bridge, to building a bird's nest, to mention a few. Furthermore, the materials used seem to vary from Legos to straws to paper and masking tape. The activity described here has been used at Calpoly for the past 25 years and was originally developed by our colleague, Ken Boble. We are grateful to all the faculty who have continuously modified and improved the exercise over the past decade.

d. Capable of standing unsupported long enough to be measured. Should the tower collapse before being measured, a penalty of $60,000 will be assessed, and the tower will be assumed to have been only 22 inches tall.

e. Capable of withstanding a wind turbulence test. Your tower must be able to withstand a buffeting from a fan positioned 24 inches from the base of your tower. Should the tower fail to pass this test, a penalty of $40,000 will be assessed.

f. A panel of judges will assess the artistic and aesthetic merits of the completed towers; $15,000 will be awarded for first prize, $10,000 for second prize, and $5,000 for third prize.

The Payoff:

The three teams with the highest profits will receive prizes. Each member of the team with the highest profits will receive 25 points to be applied to their grade in the course. The members of the team with the second highest profits will each receive 15 points, and the members of the third-ranking team will receive 10 points.

The Not-So-Hidden Motive:

The reason for conducting this exercise is not just to let you build towers out of Lego blocks. The exercise is one of several designed to give you a task-oriented team project that will allow you to experience various stages of group formation and development. You have been asked to write a paper as a team to describe and react to your experience as a work group. To help you complete the paper, you should keep a log of your team activities and note your individual reactions to the team's work as it progresses on this and other exercises.

Attachment A
Height/Profit Function
Dollar profit versus height in inches

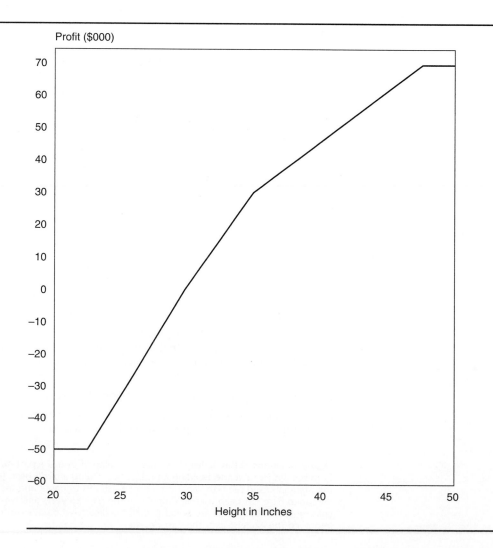

Profit ($000) versus Height in Inches

**Attachment B
Time/Profit Function**
Dollar profit versus time
in minutes

Profit ($000)

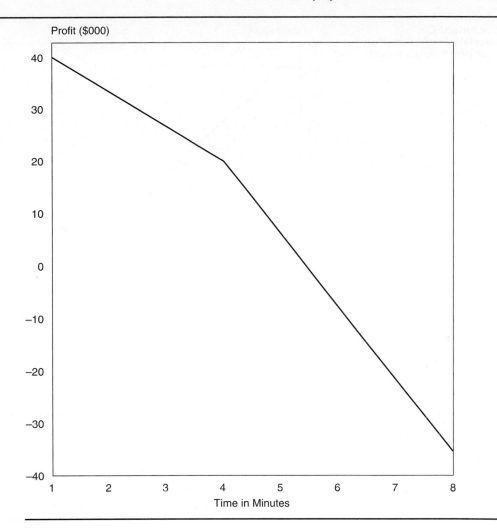

Time in Minutes

Attachment C
Materials/Profit Function
Dollar profit versus blocks
used

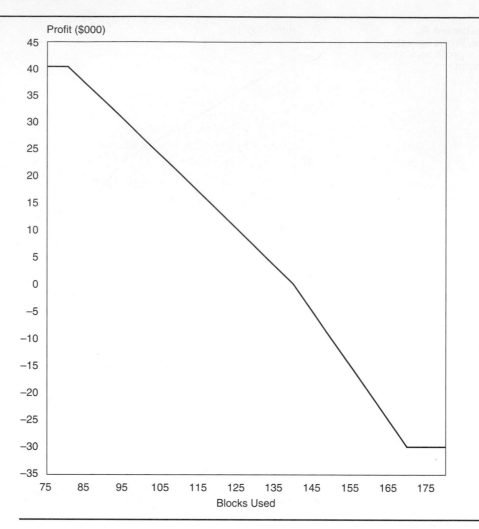

Profit ($000)

Blocks Used

Attachment D
Tower Building Profit Team

■ _____ Height

■ _____ Time

■ _____ Materials

■ _____ Aesthetic

■ _____ Total Budgeted Profit

Activity 12–2:
An Initial Inventory
of Group Dynamics

Objectives:

a. To give you the opportunity to reflect on your group experience thus far in the course.

b. To help you develop an appreciation for the many elements that play a role in the evolution of a group.

c. To help you diagnose the current stage of development of your group so that you can improve its effectiveness.

Task 1:

a. Working alone, jot down as many norms as you can think of that emerged in your group. Briefly describe each norm (not more than one sentence per norm).

b. Reflecting on your experience with your group, identify the different roles that individuals have taken on.

c. List additional elements that you believe influenced the evolution and progress of your team.

Task 2:

a. Each team is to elect a spokesperson.

b. Each team is to compile a list of the norms that have emerged, which are agreed upon by the team and provide an example of the norm wherever appropriate.

c. Each team is to compile a list of the roles that have evolved, which are agreed upon by the team.

d. Each team is to compile a list of elements agreed upon that influenced the evolution of the team and its effectiveness.

e. The instructor will call upon spokespersons, one at a time, to name the elements, norms, and roles. These will be written on the board. Examples will be requested for clarification.

f. The instructor will give a short lecture on this subject.

Task 3:

a. The teams are to discuss the different norms and roles that emerged in the groups and examine their effects on the groups' effectiveness.

b. Teams are to identify norms and roles that they would like to see changed and devise an action plan to execute and monitor the changes.

INTRODUCTION

Most team members and team leaders face the basic question of how quickly could their team become a highly collaborative, high-performing, or "red and hot" team or what would it take to bring the team to its highest level of performance? As we saw in Module 11, teams can develop the skills and technology that are needed. Yet, even acquiring the knowledge and skills does not necessarily lead to the desired outcome.[1] Building the high-performing team and sustaining its performance level requires a deeper level of understanding of team processes and dynamics.[2] For those of you who have been working in a permanent team in this course, the challenges of becoming an effective and high-performing team have become evident during the team activities you have engaged in thus far in the course. In business, while the overwhelming trend is toward teamwork, similar challenges are faced by team leaders and managers. In Module 11 we introduced some characteristics of small-group activities, emphasizing the development of group skills for greater team effectiveness. We also discussed several uses of small groups and teams in the work setting. We now take a closer look at small-group processes and characteristics to provide you with knowledge of small-group dynamics and an understanding of the social group that develops within the work group. Understanding the dynamics of small-group operations should help you improve the operation of your class team and other groups of which you are a member. As a primary frame of reference in studying group dynamics, remember that whenever a group of strangers or two or more people come together to perform a task, the web of group dynamics spontaneously begins to spin. (Sounds magical, and maybe it is!)

The Human Group in Context

The **human group concept** was advanced by Homans[3] more than 50 years ago as a framework for investigating and understanding human dynamics in groups. His concern was to develop a set of concepts that can capture the essence of human dynamics in everyday life. Homans's framework consists of two parts: the first includes three elementary concepts and the relationship between them, and the second includes more abstract concepts and the relations among these concepts and the first three elementary concepts. He argued that when an individual seeks to describe the behavior of people in everyday life, sticking closely to the behavior, they are likely to include three types of comments: activities, sentiments, and interaction. **Activities** refer to movements, action, work, typing, writing, and the like. These are, basically, things people do. **Sentiments,** refer to feelings (happy, sad, angry), attitudes (this is her job, he is liberal), or beliefs. Sentiments constitute the inner state of the person, the things an individual subjectively perceives. The third are statements about **interactions,** including working together with someone, eating together, and the like. Activities, sentiments, and interactions are dynamically related, so a change in one will lead to a change in the others. Together, they are viewed as the elementary form of human behavior.

The behavior of group members must be considered as a *system of behavior* and not as discrete behaviors unrelated to each other. The social system that develops is the second part of Homans's framework. The social system constitutes two parts: an **external system,** the relations among interaction, activity, and sentiment that are imposed on a group by forces external to it (such as a larger group, a manager, an organization, or a course instructor who imposed rules and procedures); and an **internal system,** the relations among interaction, activity, and sentiment that are spontaneously elaborated and standardized by the members of the group. For any team at work, the external system is a given—it probably existed before the group began, and it may well continue to exist even if the team is disbanded.

The more interesting dimension is that any group is apt to develop at least a rudimentary internal system. The *elaboration* refers to the process whereby individuals embellish their activities in ways above and beyond those required of them by the external system. As the members of the group express their personal styles of behavior, which go beyond the requirements of the external system, these behaviors become *differentiated,* and the members of a group begin to recognize them and to attach varying degrees of value to them. Some activities, sentiments, and interactions begin to be highly valued, others less valued, some ignored, and others negatively valued. As the internal system is spontaneously elaborated and differentiated, variations in value and habit lead to the routinization of certain activities, interactions, and sentiments, a process that Homans calls the mode of *standardization.* In sum, the modes of elaboration, differentiation, and standardization refer to the phases through which the internal system evolves as a product of the unique qualities of the members of the group, the nature of its task, and the nature of its external system.

GROUP DYNAMICS DEFINED

The small work group is a primary focus of the study of organizational behavior because it is here that the social system, which is a primary determinant of behavior, is spontaneously generated.[4] One good definition of **group dynamics** is from Knowles:

> [Group dynamics] refers to the complex forces that are acting upon every group throughout its existence which cause it to behave the way it does. We can think of every group having certain relatively static aspects—its name, constitutional structure, ultimate purpose, and other fixed characteristics. But it also has dynamics aspects—it is always moving, doing something, changing, becoming, interacting, and reacting, and the nature and direction of its movement is determined by forces being exerted upon it from within itself and from outside. The interaction of these forces and the resultant effects on a given group constitute its dynamics.[5]

A knowledge of small-group dynamics is essential for your understanding of the social system of the group. You will also find this knowledge helpful in analyzing the interactions in your classroom team because whenever individuals in a group come together to perform a task, predictable patterns of behavior develop. Thus, we may also define group dynamics as the pattern of interactions among group members as a group develops and achieves goals.[6] The influence of the individual on the group and the group on the individual, and the interrelationships between groups and the interaction of groups with the larger institutions of which they are a part, are the primary focus in the study of group dynamics.

FACTORS AFFECTING GROUP DEVELOPMENT AND PERFORMANCE

At the outset, it is important to note that most of the theory of group development was created and validated out of observations of self-analytic groups and not based on groups at the workplace. It is also important to note that group development is something that not all groups achieve over time; instead it should be viewed as "a journey towards optimal functioning only some groups attained."[7] As Activity 12–2 demonstrated, many factors affect the potential development and performance of teams. These elements can be clustered into six broad categories: context, purpose, composition and diversity, structure, processes, and leadership. Figure 12–1 shows key components of the six elements.

Context

Context refers to the environment in which groups operate. It refers to both the organizational environment and the environment external to the organization. Contextual factors influence both the evolution of a group and its performance as well as all the other (internal) factors.[8] A group's contextual factors might include (1) *organizational characteristics* such as business strategy, production technology, organization structure, management philosophy and practice, information technology, decision-making processes, reward and punishment systems, control systems, and working conditions; (2) *organizational culture* such as norms, values, attitudes toward strategy and goals, actual operating procedures, and power structure; and (3) the characteristics of the organization's *external environment,* which could include factors such as industry characteristics; competitive pressures; technological change; economic, social, political, and legal expectations and requirements; customers; and suppliers.

Figure 12–1
Factors Affecting Group Development and Performance

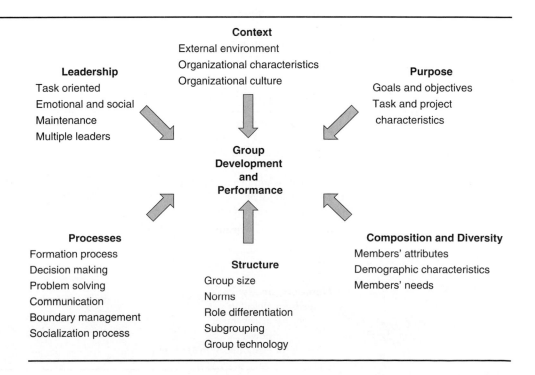

Purpose

All small groups have *goals and objectives* to attain. Groups are always engaged in accomplishing group projects. They are the reason the members have come together and the primary determinants of the interaction of people out of which patterns of behavior will emerge. The purpose of a group can be clearly defined—as would be the case with work teams—or loosely defined (or collectively recognized)—as would occur with a meeting of a group of friends held to satisfy the social needs of the members. Goals are powerful inducements for action. Clearly defined goals are critical for effective group performance.[9] The specific content of the goal and the kind of goal (competitive versus cooperative, for example) influence the evolution and performance of the group.[10] Furthermore, the group's specific *task and project characteristics and requirements or characteristics of the group project* determine its performance. These include required activities and interactions, the required level of interdependence among group members to accomplish the task,[11] and the task's time frame and deadlines.[12] Group projects can vary in several aspects. First is the extent to which their execution requires specific task activities, interpersonal activities, or process activities. Second is the extent to which the projects concern (1) acquisition, processing, and distribution of information; (2) managing conflict and achieving consensus; and (3) motivating, regulating, and coordinating member behavior. Each project is likely to represent some mix of these requirements and activities.[13] The nature of the group's project will affect the kind of group that is put together. Coupled with group member composition, these set the stage for group performance.

Composition and Diversity

This category includes elements that are related to the characteristics of the individuals who are brought together to work on a task or project. Following McGrath,[14] the different elements can be clustered into three subcategories: members' attributes, members' demographic characteristics, and members' needs. Figure 12–2 summarizes the elements that make up this category.

Members' Attributes

Individuals come to the group with some pattern of values on each of the four sets of attributes: They have basic knowledge, skills, and abilities; they hold values, beliefs, and attitudes; they have distinct personality characteristics (we explore this topic in Module 4); and they have developed cognitive and behavioral styles of learning and problem solving. These attributes are likely to affect the individual's ability to carry out the various activities required by the group's task or project and, as such, will influence the group's dynamics and performance.

Members' Demographic Characteristics

An individual's basic demographic characteristics, such as age, sex, and race, may affect his or her performance as a group member either by themselves or through their relationships with other attributes. For example, being the only ethnic minority (or the oldest or

---

**Figure 12–2
Composition and Diversity**

Members' attributes
Knowledge, skills, and abilities
Values, beliefs, and attitudes
Personality
Cognitive and behavioral styles
  Learning style
  Problem-solving style

Members' demographic characteristics
Age
Sex
Race

Members' needs
Needs for affiliation
Needs for achievement
Needs for power
Needs for economic or material resources

the only male) in a group may affect the member's attribute (that is, attitude or behavior style) and, as such, will influence both the individual's behavior and the team's development process and performance. As of late, the topic of diversity within groups has received significant attention. While diversity appears to have an effect on group development and performance, the relationship between diversity and group dynamics and outcomes is complex.[15] A recent study of the relationship between diversity and innovation and creativity pointed out the many complex relationships that need to be investigated further by isolating the effects of diversity in age, sex, race–ethnicity, and tenure on the work group dynamics and performance.[16] At this point, it is safe to say that much more research is needed into the intricacies of diversity and its role in shaping group dynamics and performance.

Members' Needs

Individuals differ when it comes to their basic needs in the group's context. Individuals come to the group with some pattern of needs that they would like to fulfill via the group's experience. The members' needs affect members' motivation to participate in the group. Although we explored the topic of motivation in Module 5, at this point we must distinguish among four distinct individual needs: needs for affiliation, needs for achievement, needs for power, and needs for economic or material resources. Any group must fulfill its members' needs to some degree to motivate the members to participate and, as such, will influence the group to carry out its task or project to completion.

As we saw in Modules 3 and 4, beyond the unique similarities and differences that exist between individuals' personalities and learning styles, research has indicated that all four dominant learning modes are critical for group effectiveness. Thus, the extent to which group members are compatible will influence the group's performance. Similar conclusions can be drawn regarding individual problem-solving styles. The particular combination of member styles will affect the group's evolution and its outcomes.[17] For example, a group composed of four strong "thinking planners" and one "task implementer" is likely to fall short in its ability to objectively analyze the situation, may have difficulty identifying the main issue or problem, will lack insight in the identification and exploration of alternative solutions, and may fall short in the choice of the best solution.

Studies have also shown that a heterogeneous group in terms of abilities and experiences can have a positive effect on group performance, particularly when that group's tasks are diverse, because a wide range of competencies are needed. On the other hand, groups with a more homogenous makeup may have less conflict, better communication, more member satisfaction, and lower turnover.[18]

Other individual characteristics that can influence group performance are individual flexibility in terms of task assignments[19] and preference for group work. Individuals who prefer to work in groups tend to be more satisfied and effective in those settings.[20]

Structure

Group Size

Effective team size seems to range from 3 members to a normal upper limit of about 20 members. Yet while the optimal **group size** seems to be correlated with the degree of project complexity and leadership competence, most argue that effective work groups range in size from 7 to 12 members. Advances in computer technology and software, such as groupware, the Internet, and e-mail, are enabling larger teams to work on projects. In a recent study that summarized some of the literature on the relationship between group size and group members' feeling of inhibition, the authors argued that groups of 2 to 7 members feel a "low degree" of inhibition, in groups of 8 to 12 inhibition is "moderate," and groups of 13 to 16 exhibit a "high degree" of inhibition. Furthermore, group "members' tolerance of direction by the leader" seems to be low to moderate for groups of 2 to 7 members, moderate for 8 to 12 members, and high for 13 to 16 members.[21]

Group structure refers to certain psychologically shared properties of the group that result from both formal and informal interactions of its members. Structural elements that influence group performance can be divided into two categories: the formal and the informal. Formal structural elements are those that are imposed by the organization, and the most important is the design of the group's tasks. Informal elements are those that develop out of the group's operation.

Formal Elements—Work Design

Work design is discussed in Module 13. Work design influences the activities and interactions of group members. One recent study shows that the design of group tasks that provides for skill variety, task identity, task significance, autonomy, and feedback has a positive influence on group productivity, satisfaction, and effectiveness.[22]

Because the subject of work design is extensively covered in Module 13, we do not discuss additional details here, but merely note that work design is indeed an important element to be considered in understanding group performance and developing enhanced group performance.

Informal Elements

As a group develops, *recurrent patterns* of relationships occur. Furthermore, group technology is developed. **Group technology** has three dimensions: (1) task predictability, (2) problem analyzability, and (3) interdependence. There are also three properties of group structure: (1) *connectiveness* (the extent to which group members identify with the goals of other members in their group), (2) *vertical differentiation* (the number of different levels of the organizational hierarchy represented in a group), and (3) *horizontal differentiation* (the number of different job areas represented in a group). Beyond the unique recurrent patterns of relationships, group technology and group structure affect overall group performance.[23]

The recurrent patterns are shared psychologically by group members in that all come to know and are influenced by the patterns, whether they are consciously aware of them or not. This psychological sharing may be thought of as being in the general area of emergent attitudes. However, because we need more specific concepts to aid us in analyzing group behavior, we will work with terms such as *norms* and other structural components, including *status and role differentiation.*

To understand shared expectations that emerge in the group, we must know the process by which two or more persons spontaneously, often unconsciously, come to share expectations and assumptions of what is appropriate or meaningful behavior. Group members develop and accept these unwritten, informal guidelines without realizing it.

Development of Norms: **Norms** are expectations shared by group members of how they ought to behave under a given set of circumstances. Using Homans's framework described earlier in this module, the norms that evolve regulate the expected interactions, activities, and sentiments of members both in the external and internal system. The idea of a norm carries with it a range of behaviors that are acceptable, so there is some variability for individuals. Work attitudes are an example. A work team made up of individuals who believe in giving an honest day's work to their employer could readily develop a high-productivity norm, whereas one composed of individuals who believe business rips off workers could develop a low-productivity norm. One work team having half of each type might have only a shared expectation that "we will never agree on productivity."

Group members are often unaware of their norms and that these norms influence member behavior. Freudians have always assumed that subconscious and unconscious mental processes influence our behavior, and norms often exist at the level of group subconsciousness. When participants in our courses write a term paper on their teams' interactions, it is surprising how few norms they have observed. (Are you making entries in your journal on the norms you assume to be developing in your group? One way to identify norms is to observe behavior of the group, particularly in relation to the behavior of an individual member. Is the group upset by the behavior, for example, of being late or not being prepared? If so, does that identify behavior that the group feels is appropriate or inappropriate? The same can be said for behavior that the group rewards with praise.) We offer this hint because it is important first to become aware of the consequences of certain norms and then to become knowledgeable of how teams can develop and shape their own norms for the purpose of improved effectiveness.

Work groups often spontaneously develop an **emergent role system.** In this context, role refers to the characteristic pattern of a member's activities, interactions, and sentiments, along with the member's emergent status and the degree to which he or she conforms to the norms. Some emergent role systems develop norms that are contrary to management goals but that satisfy the members' own needs and reduce their frustrations. (An example of such norms can be found in The Slade Company Case that was analyzed earlier in this course. Integrating the required and the emergent systems so they are compatible is an ever-present management challenge.)

Values play a special role in the formation of norms. Cultural values provide an example of this. **Values** tell us what is moral, worthwhile, good, or beautiful. For individuals, values have been developed and reinforced through a lifetime of experiences. When team members in this course meet for the first time, often they espouse values related to democracy, fair treatment, and honesty. They frequently develop such group norms as "Let everyone have a fair share of the airtime," "Let's not play manipulative games," and "Let's be open and level with one another."

So how do values and norms differ? Values may be thought of as "criteria or conceptions used in evaluating things (including ideas, acts, feelings, and events) as to their relative desirability, merit, or correctness."[24] Values can be held by a single individual; norms cannot because they emerge from the interactions in the group. Norms are rules of behavior, but values are critical for evaluating behavior and other things. Further, norms carry sanctions, but values never do. This distinction is important because management teams in particular need to be in agreement on the basic operating values from which their system of norms is derived. We frequently find that management teams are in conflict over values, such as short-run profits versus longer-range organizational viability or rate of return on investment versus market share. Consultants find values clarification is usually a priority need in high-level team-building sessions. Activity 12–4 captures the dynamic nature and the emotionally loaded experience around values.

Role Differentiation

Whenever two or more people come together to work on a common purpose, **role differentiation** occurs; that is, patterns of behavior for each individual develop that tend to become repeated as activities progress. Roles can be classified into those that are focused on achieving the tasks of the group, ones that build and maintain favorable relationships among group members, and those that serve individual needs, sometimes at the expense of the group.[25]

Task Roles

Individuals who assume **task roles** are interested in getting the job done. They often emerge as the informal leaders of work groups. Roles that fall in this category include the following:

Initiator. Offers new ideas both on ways to solve problems and on ways for the group to approach its task or organize to do its work.

Coordinator. Coordinates group activities, connects different ideas and suggestions, and clarifies relationships.

Information seeker. Seeks out facts and information and clarifies ideas. *Opinion seekers* are variants of this role.

Information giver. Offers facts and information that are relevant to the group's task. *Opinion givers* are variants of this role.

Recorder. Keeps track of the group's activities and progress to date. May write down ideas. *Summarizers* are a variant of this role and act to provide a verbal summary of activity to date or decisions made by the group.

Evaluator/critic. Offers assessments of the group's operation as well as evaluations of ideas and suggestions made by group members.

Timekeeper. Works to keep the group on schedule and to help ensure that the group makes productive use of the time available to it.

In any group these roles may be played by one or many individuals.

Relationship Roles

Individuals who assume **relationship roles** are often the most popular members of groups because they work to facilitate social and emotional relationships among group members. They are often the social leaders of a group. Examples of the types of roles in this category are

Encourager. Supports the activity of other group members, praises contributions, and agrees with suggestions.

Gatekeeper/expediter. Keeps individuals from monopolizing the discussion, encourages participation by everyone, and keeps the discussion moving.

Standard setter. States both output and process standards and goals for the group to achieve; assesses group performance in terms of these standards and goals.

Observer/commentator. Acts as a detached observer, commenting on both group process and outcomes.

Followers. Passive but friendly group members.

Individual Roles

These roles are expressions of individual personalities and individual needs. Sometimes individuals act in a manner that is detrimental to group performance. **Individual roles** include the following:

Aggressor. Verbally attacks other team members and their contributions.

Blocker. Refuses to concede a point even when confronted with group unanimity; stubborn and unreasonable at times.

Dominator. Attempts to control the group and the discussion.

Recognition seeker. Needs to be the center of attention.

Avoider. Seeks to avoid becoming involved with the group, passive, avoids commitment.

Other types of individual roles include self-confessor, playboy, help seeker, and special-interest pleader. You may be able to think of other classifications based on your group experience. One student saw Wonderwoman, Superman, cynic, cheerleader, white knight, and Florence Nightingale among her team members.

   The significance of role differentiation is that these patterned relationships develop in a group and become part of the members' shared expectations of what ought to be done and what is appropriate or acceptable behavior. Knowledge and awareness of different roles provide the manager or team leader with a basis not only for understanding what is taking place but also for developing useful roles and discouraging dysfunctional roles in the group.

Status

Status is defined as the degree of esteem, respect, or prestige an individual commands from others. Status operates in group settings, and group members acquire common perceptions for respecting other members on numerous dimensions. If problem solving and analytical abilities are important in the group, members will, over time, rank one another from the highest to the lowest ability in this regard. Other dimensions of status include ability to judge the motivation and the capabilities of others, professional knowledge, experience, interpersonal skills, personal appearance, "personality," and any other area valued by the group, including items such as a car to transport the group or an apartment where the group can meet comfortably. An overall status that is dependent on a combination of these factors is accorded to group members. One of the most important is the degree to which a person conforms to the norms of the group. High conformers have high status; low conformers have lower status. However, group pressures toward uniformity vary. Some norms are absolutes, whereas others permit a range of behaviors—what is called *wiggle room.* Group leaders usually have more freedom than the other group members to try new behavior.

Awareness of Status: Participants often write in their papers that there were no differences in status among members of their group. This failure of observation may be because they think it is unfair to label people or to ridicule some. However, status always exists in groups and affects behavior and performance. You need to think of it, first, as the characteristics a person brings to the group (such as family background or what course of study the individual is pursuing) and, second, as the degree to which a person conforms to the norms of the group. Another way of thinking about status is that of credibility (What's my credibility in this group?). Acceptability is another dimension (How can I improve my acceptability in this group?). Listening more attentively to others is a possible answer to this question. Good journal entries can enhance your awareness of status factors and have implications for growth in your understanding of how your status can influence others.

Rejection of the Deviant

A **deviant** is an individual whose behavior differs from what is regarded as standard. In a group sense, a deviant is one who does not subscribe to the group's norms. Stanley Schachter conducted laboratory experiments with college students and found some interesting reactions of small groups toward individuals who take an unchanging position in opposition to the majority.[26] In each group he had three "stooges" who played three different roles: One would agree with whatever majority position arose; the second—called the *slider*—would take the opposite position but would change toward the majority gradually; and the third, who was the deviant, took the opposite position and did not change. In those groups where there was high cohesiveness among the members (see the discussion of cohesiveness later in this module) and where the subject under discussion was of high relevance, communications were directed toward the slider and the deviant in attempts to convince and persuade them. Communication toward the deviant fell off toward the end of the meeting; the slider was accepted and the deviant rejected.

The dynamics of deviant behavior in groups is a complex phenomenon that has a significant effect on the development of a group. (Have you ever been in a group in which one member constantly violated accepted norms of behavior? Can you imagine the effect of such behavior on a group?) A *scapegoat* or *covert role player* is an individual in a group who is unconsciously assigned the role of absorbing emotions on behalf of the group. For example, the scapegoat can be blamed for the failures of the group; he or she also allows the group to avoid an unpleasant true examination of its behavior and performance.[27]

Subgroupings of Members

Subgroupings are recurrent patterns of relationships among individuals within the group that become established. Some of these relationships are temporary and some are enduring. These subgroups may be dyads (pairs) or triads (trios). A positive dyad is two persons supporting each other's views; a negative dyad is composed of opposing persons; a third possibility is one person who finds someone attractive but meets with rejection. Such subgroupings are not always readily apparent to members. Triads are supposedly the most unstable of all groups because they almost always break down into a pair and one.[28]

Observers, more often than group members, can identify subgrouping patterns. Greater awareness and sensitivity to this can help team members become more objective. For instance, subgrouping tends to become associated with seating arrangements. A fixed pattern by which each member always sits in the same place or members from one unit always sit next to one another can reinforce any feelings associated with subgrouping.

Participants often write that there were no subgroupings and comment that everyone was equally independent; however, subgroupings always exist to some degree. Sociometric techniques can readily bring out the underlying basis for subgrouping (attraction to or identification with other people or rejection). Ask the question, Which team member would you most like to go to a movie with? Rank all members from "most like to" to "least like to." The responses could be listed on a diagram showing the interrelationships among members. The same ranking could be done with a number of questions relating to different aspects of relationships—for example, Who would you most like to have on your debate team? These underlying feelings can be the basis of subgroupings, though they might not be apparent on the surface or influence the team greatly. See whether you can make journal entries that show an enhanced ability to observe subgroupings and their influences on the team.

Processes

Formation and socialization processes play a critical role in the development of the group and its performance. Regardless of whether the group is a new group or has been working together for a while, most people wonder why they were selected and/or recruited for a specific work group. Yet fulfilling this requirement does not seem to be enough. The formation of new groups, beyond the actual choices based on the skills and competencies needed to accomplish the task/project requires the matching of diverse individuals. A complex socialization process helps integrate new members into a mature group and/or helps the new group begin to function as a task or project group. For example, recent research suggests that the existing composition of the group, the demographic similarities between newcomers and established group members, and the nature of the newcomer cohort affect the socialization of new group members.[29] Furthermore, it also became apparent that the perception of newcomers and old-timers about how well new members were fitting in sometimes diverged substantially. The role of perception in shaping individual and group behavior was discussed in Module 6.

The process elements of decision making and problem solving were discussed in Module 11. **Boundary management** refers to the management of the relationship between a team and other teams or other organizational entities, a process related in part to context and purpose elements, which have already been discussed. The other major element, *communication,* is discussed in Module 7, but we consider here the impact on the location of individuals within the channels of communication.

The effects of location on performance and satisfaction have been summarized by Swap and his associates[30] in their review of Cartwright and Zander's experimental work[31] on communications networks. According to Swap, an important determinant of a group's decision-making effectiveness is the communication structure of the group—who is allowed to communicate with whom. An extract of that review follows:

> We might want to know the answers to a number of questions relating to a network: How *satisfied* will each of the group members be? How *efficiently* will they be able to accomplish a task or make a decision? Will any one member come to be viewed as a *leader?* To answer these questions, let us return to the social psychologist's laboratory.[32]

You are one of five subjects in an experiment. Each of you is given a card with five symbols taken from a group of six (circle, triangle, and so on). Only one of the symbols appears on each subject's card. The task of the group is to determine the identity of that common symbol as quickly as possible. The five subjects sit around a table divided by partitions. In each partition is a slot through which subjects can exchange written messages. Which slots are open or closed determines the nature of the communication network. You may be in a position where you communicate with only one other subject, or two, or perhaps all four, corresponding to the patterns shown in Figure 12–3. These are just four of the many possible networks. A double arrow indicates a two-way communication link; that is, a slot permits both sending and receiving

**Figure 12–3
Four Communications
Networks**

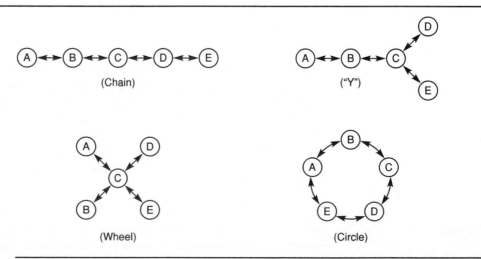

Source: W. C. Swap and Associates, *Decision Making* (Beverly Hills, CA: Sage, 1984), p. 55. Reprinted by permission of Sage Publication, Inc.

messages. (While some networks include one-way channels—such as putting a message in a suggestion box—they are relatively rare and are not considered here.)

Perhaps the most important characteristics of communication networks are their centrality and the degree of centrality of a given member within the network. Centrality may be viewed as the degree of *connectedness* among the people in the network. In Figure 12–3, the wheel is highly centralized, with C maintaining communications with all other group members. The circle is less centralized as each member maintains but two communication links.

Let's summarize the major findings that have emerged from research on **communication networks.** First, a given member's centrality is strongly related to his or her satisfaction with the group experience. This relationship is particularly strong among people with relatively dominant personalities. Second, people who are placed in central positions in the network come to be viewed as *leaders* by the other group members. Virtually all group members agree that C is the leader in the wheel, but there is no consensus about leadership in the circle. Third, the performance of the group (measured by such factors as speed, accuracy, and rate of learning) is strongly affected by its structure. For simple tasks, such as information gathering described in our experiment, the more centralized networks perform better. For more complex activities such as those requiring somebody (that is, the central person) to operate on the information after it is collected, centralized groups perform more poorly. We might speculate that the result will be particularly pronounced when the central person is basically incompetent. But a further explanation comes from the fourth general finding: Decentralized groups as a whole are more satisfied with their group experience than are centralized groups. While the wheel may have one satisfied person (the "leader"), there are four peripheral, unhappy members. Participants in a circle network, on the other hand, are all equally central or peripheral and share equally in the group responsibilities. This higher degree of group satisfaction might contribute to the finding that such decentralized (democratic) groups outperform others on more challenging tasks.

The effectiveness of group decision making should clearly vary with the complexity and nature of the group task and with the type of communication structure. A highly centralized structure should be most effective with simple decisions and when a competent leader holds the central position. For more complex, discretionary tasks, a more decentralized communication structure should produce both better decisions and greater member satisfaction.

Leadership

Leaders in small groups play a critical role in fostering the evolution of the group and its performance. Studies in group dynamics have emphasized the importance of the emergent leader in the accomplishment of group tasks. The group leader (or leaders) is seen as a role that emerges within the group just like the other differentiated roles discussed earlier in this module. Module 8 provided an overview of leadership orientations and some of the current knowledge about the role of leaders in organizational settings.

In the context of small-group leadership, we would like to add the following points based on recent research. First, two types of leadership functions in small groups have been found to influence group performance: *monitoring* (obtaining and interpreting data about performance conditions and events that might affect them) and taking action (creating or maintaining favorable performance conditions).[33] Second, the performance of both task-oriented and maintenance-oriented leadership roles influence group process and group effectiveness.[34] Third, two categories of behavior—*performance monitoring* (collecting performance data) and *performance consequences* (establishing rewards and punishments for performance)—are required optimal leadership performance in small groups.[35] Fourth, effective leaders of effective teams manage the teams' boundaries—defining goals and direction and placing constraints on team behavior.[36] Finally, team leaders were found to influence team cognitive processes, motivational processes, affective processes, and coordination processes.[37] It is also important to note that group leaders greatly influence all the factors that determine group development and performance (summarized in Figure 12–1).

OTHER ASPECTS OF SMALL-GROUP DYNAMICS

Group dynamics is a field that has been intensively studied. Only a few of the concepts associated with it have been touched on so far in this book. In this section we examine several other concepts that have relevance for the manager: social loafing and free riding, cohesiveness, and group development.

Social Loafing and Free Riding

Social loafing is an effect first noted by a German psychologist named Ringleman, who measured individual and group effort on a rope-pulling task. He found that the effort extended by a group was less than the sum of individual efforts. Subsequent psychological experiments have found this effect to exist in other group settings.[38] The term *free rider* refers to a person who obtains benefits from being a member of a group but who does not bear a proportional share of the costs of providing those benefits.[39] These effects have been noted to increase as group size increases.[40]

Social loafing and free riding can be attributed to individual perceptions about other group members' efforts, to individual laziness, and to the fact that individual effort is hidden or less noticeable in a group setting. Other factors that have been identified are an indifferent group climate, unimportant or meaningless group tasks, low expectancy of being able to master the task, the presence of a highly qualified group member, and pressures to conform.[41]

Clearly, social loafing and free riding can be detrimental to group performance. This tendency can be dealt with by attempting to make individual contributions or tasks identifiable or perceived as unique.[42] It can be reduced by controlling the size of groups (with five to seven members generally seen as ideal). Social loafing and free riding can also be controlled by rewarding cooperative behavior and by encouraging the development of norms that encourage all members to make a full contribution to the group effort.

Cohesiveness

The term **group cohesiveness** refers to the attractiveness of the group to its members—the degree to which members desire to stay in the group. Unlike structure and process characteristics, which can be shaped by the team, cohesiveness is an outcome of how group members interact.

Research tends to support the assumption that members of highly cohesive groups, as contrasted to those of low cohesiveness, communicate better, are more cooperative, and are more responsive to group influence; they also tend to achieve accepted goals more efficiently and to have higher satisfaction.[43] Does this outcome mean that cohesive work groups have better performance than less cohesive groups? Although many studies over the past 30 years have demonstrated mixed results in attempting to answer this question,[44] one recent summary study found a consistent, small relationship between cohesion and productivity. The study found that the effect was much stronger in "real" (as opposed to laboratory or experimental) groups.[45]

Cohesiveness leads to trust, confidence, and acceptance among members. The pressures toward conformity give the group more influence over the individual,[46] and the individual shows greater commitment and loyalty.[47] Members of highly cohesive groups tend to have higher self-esteem and are less anxious than those of less cohesive groups.

A **hot team** is an example of a highly cohesive team. Such a team performs extremely well and is dedicated to both the team and to task accomplishment. Members of such a team are turned on by an exciting and challenging goal. Hot teams completely engage their members to the exclusion of almost everything else. Such teams can be characterized as teams with vitality; they are absorbing, full of debate and laughter, and very hard working.[48]

Highly cohesive groups are by definition fulfilling important needs of group members. This situation has several implications:

1. If the group can become more aware of the needs being fulfilled by the group for each member, it can improve its support of those needs.

2. If your team members in this class were more aware of the team skills you desire to develop, they might be more helpful in this regard.

3. One of the goals of team building (discussed in Module 16) is to become aware of the skills, abilities, and strengths of each member so that they can be integrated into the work activities of the group wherever feasible. This has the potential of increasing cohesiveness and individual satisfaction.

Groupthink

Groupthink is a mode of thinking that individuals engage in when pressures toward conformity become so dominant in a group that they override appraisal of alternative courses of action. High cohesiveness, insulation of the group from outsiders, lack of methodological procedures for search and appraisal of alternatives, directive leadership, a complex and changing environment, and high stress with a low degree of hope for finding a better solution than the one favored by the leader or other influential members were found to be conditions that can trigger groupthink behavior.[49] The following are the characteristics and symptoms of groupthink as articulated by Irving Janis:

1. An illusion of invulnerability is shared by all or most members of the group, which creates excessive optimism and encourages high risk taking.

2. Collective rationalization discounts warnings that might lead members to consider their assumptions before they commit themselves to a major policy decision.

3. An unquestionable belief in the group's morality inclines members to ignore ethical or moral consequences of their decisions.

4. There are stereotyped views of the enemy leaders as too evil to warrant genuine attempts to negotiate or as too weak and stupid to counter whatever risky attempts are made to defeat their purpose.

5. Direct pressure on any member who expresses strong arguments against any of the group's stereotypes, illusions, or commitments makes clear that this type of dissent is contrary to what is expected of all loyal members.

6. Self-censorship of deviations from the apparent group consensus reflects each member's inclination to minimize the importance of self-doubts and counterarguments.

7. There is a shared illusion of unanimity concerning judgments conforming to the majority view (partly resulting from the self-censorship of deviants, augmented by the false assumption that silence means consent).

8. Self-appointed mindguards (members who protect the group from adverse information that might shatter its shared complacency about the effectiveness and the morality of its decision) emerge.[50]

Janis developed groupthink theory in analyzing the failed Bay of Pigs invasion of Cuba. Groupthink has also been implicated in the Nixon White House staff's handling of the Watergate affair and the Air Traffic Controllers Union's approach to the strike in 1981, which resulted in the discharge of most of its members.

One dramatic example of groupthink is NASA's managerial actions associated with the January 1986 accident that destroyed the space shuttle *Challenger*. The mindguarding function has been well documented. Before the launch, the engineers voted unanimously to recommend a delay in the launch because the O-rings might not work in low temperatures. In the past, Thiokol engineers had been asked to present considerable evidence to support a launch. This time they were asked to prove that no launch should occur. The engineers' recommendation was never relayed by management up to the top level in NASA, where the final decision to launch was made.[51] The presidential commission investigating the accident concluded that space agency officials were, at certain critical points, ill-informed and "mesmerized" (a good synonym for groupthink) by past successes. When the Marshall Space Flight Center was criticized, the *Los Angeles Times* reported,

> "Everybody in a position of responsibility has to ape the boss in order to maintain their position," he said. "They have to have the same noxious attitude. Dissent is a bad word." To some

employees at Marshall, the criticism was welcome news. Engineer William C. Bush, a long-time critic of the center's management, said the commission's description of the Alabama facility's isolationism from the rest of NASA was well deserved. "Marshall management has an 'us vs. them' mentality and equates dissent with disloyalty," Bush said.[52]

These highly publicized examples of groupthink may give you the false impression that the phenomenon only happens "out there" and can't or doesn't happen to you. Student team projects frequently get into a groupthink mode that negatively affects their results. One team, in considering its (poor) performance on the Mountain Survival activity, ruefully concluded that it quickly latched onto the idea of walking out, never considered the problems with that alternative, and never considered the alternative of staying at the crash site. A former student recently told us that what she remembers most about her organizational behavior class is the groupthink she experienced with her classroom team. She reported that she sees it often in her work relationships and regards guarding against it as a major responsibility in team management. Groupthink can be prevented by the following steps:

- Appointing a team member to serve as a *devil's advocate* to question the group's assumptions and actions.
- Bringing in outside experts to evaluate the group's processes.
- Testing the group's ideas on outsiders.
- Having the leader avoid stating his or her position before the group reaches a decision.
- Once a decision is made, carefully reexamining the alternatives.[53]
- Having the leader alleviate time pressures on the group or, if this is not possible, focusing on issues, encouraging dissension and confrontation, or scheduling special meeting sessions.[54]

Group Maturity

Group cohesiveness and the operation of norms occur over time. Like individuals, groups develop over time and reach developmental maturity. **Group maturity** has been described as existing when:

1. Members are aware of their own and each other's assets and liabilities vis-à-vis the group's task.
2. These individual differences are accepted without being labeled as good or bad.
3. The group has developed authority and interpersonal relationships that are recognized and accepted by its members.
4. Group decisions are made through rational discussion. Minority opinions and/or dissent are recognized and encouraged. Attempts are not made to force decisions or false unanimity.
5. Conflict is over substantive group issues such as group goals and the effectiveness and efficiency of various means for achieving those goals. Conflict over emotional issues regarding group structure, process, or interpersonal relationships is at a minimum.
6. Members are aware of the group's processes and their roles in them.[55]

Group Development

Development is a process by which a system adapts to internal and external forces. Throughout this book we have noted that individual development is driven by the interaction of biological, psychological, and social elements. Groups that function in a relatively homogeneous environment tend to progress through similar patterns of development. A number of **group development** models have been advanced in the literature. These models can be classified into three categories: performance models, emotional climate models, and revolt models.[56] Table 12–1 provides a comparative summary of a representative model from each of the categories.

The *performance models* are based on the assumption that groups resolve issues as preparation to completing task performance. The group develops or moves through a clear hierarchy

Table 12–1   **Group Development Models: A Comparison**

	Forming	Storming	Norming	Performing	Adjourning
Tuckman and Jensen (1977) (performance model)	Activity to determine nature and parameters of task	Engender emotional responses, resistance, ineffectiveness	Open exchange of relevant interpretations	Constructive task activity	

	Inclusion	Control		Affection	
Schutz (1958) (emotional climate model)	In or out	Top or bottom		Near or far	

	Uncertainty	Group	Competition	Termination	
Hartman and Gibbard (1974) (revolt model)	Revolt	Fusion-utopia	Intimacy		

of stages toward more efficient and effective group work. Not all groups move through all stages; some groups may become stuck at a particular level of development. The *emotional climate* models do not contain stages of task performance but rather describe a progression of emotional concerns in the group. The stages build hierarchically toward closer relationships between members. The *revolt models* are based on the notion that groups proceed predictably toward a rebellion against the leader or leaders. The group develops by working through complex dynamic relationships between the members and the leader(s).

For illustration purposes we describe both an emotional climate development model developed by H. J. Reitz[57] and a performance model developed by Tuckman and Jensen.[58]

The Emotional Climate Model of Group Development[59]

The emotional climate model of group development is composed of six dimensions:

1. *Orientation.* People wonder how authority and power will be distributed. What is our purpose? How will we carry out the activities? What are the rules? What will my role be? How will I appear to others? How can I influence what is going on? This is a period of getting organized. The function of many of the behaviors is to ward off anxiety. The individuals' needs for status, attention, and acceptance are involved. Some individuals respond by withdrawal, not talking, doodling, or yawning. Others respond by being assertive, overtalkative, or aggressive; others respond by attempting to please. People seek to avoid anxiety by depending on the structure of leadership, rules, goals, and activities.

2. *Conflict.* Even though there is an initial settling in and the group seems somewhat stabilized, individual needs are not satisfied. Eventually this situation results in challenging or testing the leadership, the role structure, or the rules and goals that are developing. Subgroupings are apt to form around these issues, some supporting what has been established so far, others opposing or offering alternative approaches.

3. *Cohesion.* During the conflict phase, emotions are more easily expressed and some tension release takes place. A redistribution of leadership power may occur and members' roles become more clearly defined. Some issues raised during the conflict stage are resolved, so the authority structure and members' role clarification result in feelings of belongingness, feelings that "we have been through this together."

4. *Delusion.* The good feelings of having resolved many of the issues of authority may not last long. Group members still face issues concerning emotional aspects of interpersonal relationships. How intimate are they to become? How much are they willing to reveal about their feelings? Can they accept individual differences? The delusion arrives because the increased group acceptance that members feel around the authority and power issues can lead them to believe—erroneously—that there are no interpersonal problems. Conflict is apt to be smoothed over until the group members realize obstacles do exist and move into the next phase.

5. *Disillusion.* The euphoria of the delusion stage wears off as uncertainties around interpersonal issues remain. Subgroupings may form around the degree of socializing versus task orientation.

6. *Acceptance.* If the group has work to do and faces the pressure of goals and deadlines ahead, these forces will greatly influence the resolution of residual authority and intimacy problems. Such pressures bring rationality into the forefront and provide the base for individuals to play roles furthering problem resolution and acceptance of the group. Achievement of goals can greatly augment the movement toward maturity as described earlier.

The Performance Model of Group Development[60]

Following research that focused on task groups, a model of group development that is composed of five phases was advanced by Tuckman and Jensen.

- *Forming.* The first stage in the group's life reflects members' focus on accepting each other and initial learning about the task. This stage incorporates all the discomfort in any new situation in which a person's ego is involved in new relationships.

- *Storming.* This initial period of caution is followed by a period of predictable *storming* as individuals react to the demands of what has to be done, question authority, and feel increasingly comfortable to be themselves.

- *Norming.* The third stage is defined as *norming,* in which the rules of behavior appropriate and necessary for the group to accomplish the task are spelled out both explicitly and implicitly, and a greater degree of order begins to prevail.

- *Performing.* Next, comes the period of *performing,* in which people are able to focus their energies on the task, having worked through issues of membership, orientation, leadership, and roles. The group is free to develop working alternatives to the problems confronting it, and climate of support tends to persists.

- *Adjourning.* Finally, with the task nearing completion, the group moves into what is called the *adjourning* period, in which closure to the task and changing of relationships is anticipated.

Tuckman and Jensen also found it helpful to view each of the stages from two points of view: interpersonal relationships and task. Thus, the group will move through predictable stages of testing and dependency (forming), tension and conflict (storming), building cohesion (norming), and finally establishing functional role relationships (performing) before the group adjourns. Each of these substages focuses on the problems inherent in developing relationships among members. At the same time, the group is struggling with problems of task. In light of this, the initial stage focuses on task definition, boundaries, and exchange of functional information (forming); followed by a natural emotional response to the task (storming); a period of sharing interpretations and perspectives (norming); before a stage of emergent solutions is achieved (performing).

SUMMARY

We started the exploration of the topic by arguing that not all work teams develop. Yet, research demonstrated that teams that go through developmental phases seem to outperform and sustain a higher level of performance when compared to others.[61] Some concepts of small-group dynamics have been described to demonstrate their applicability to the emergent role system and phases of work groups. At the most basic level, group development and group performance are affected by six general factors: the group's purpose, the group's composition, the context within which the group operates, the group's structure, the group's processes, and the group's leadership.

Within groups, recurrent patterns of relationships occur that are based on shared expectations. Of particular importance are the group's norms. Individuals follow norms to perform their roles and to ensure status and acceptance in the group. Subgrouping among members occurs from role interactions and from attraction and rejection. Some group members may not put forth full effort, and social loafing may occur.

Group cohesiveness plays a critical role in high-performance teams. Cohesiveness is associated with the strength of the members' desire to remain in the group and their commitment to the group goals. Mental group ability and the personality of group members have a direct impact on the work-team processes and team effectiveness.[62] To the extent that a match between members' goals and group goals exists and the group composition results in a high general mental group ability, the team is likely to perform well.[63] High cohesiveness is also related to group maturity. Groups go through developmental stages as members struggle with both tasks and interpersonal relationships. Effectiveness requires avoiding hang-ups en route to group maturity. A major hazard faces groups that become highly cohesive. They can develop groupthink, which can lead to inappropriate or incorrect action.

This module argues that interpersonal relationships play a critical role in shaping team development processes and performance. We explored the basic set of interpersonal competencies in the facilitation of team problem solving and team decision making in Module 11. In Modules 8 and 9 we explored the dynamics of leadership and mentoring as interpersonal processes that determine both individual and team success. All together, the five modules in this section of the book provide mental models, can guide individual behavior, and can enhance success. Yet, the complexity of human dynamics, as reflected in this section, provides an insight into the challenge of managing and sustaining interpersonal processes at work.

Study Questions

1. What is the human system?

2. What is group dynamics? Why is an understanding of group dynamics essential for any team manager or group member?

3. In what way can group norms be considered a part of group structure?

4. Leadership is listed as a factor that influences performance. The other factors discussed are also influenced by team leaders. Develop an example of such influence for each of the other factors.

5. The disadvantages of groupthink are outlined in this module. Can you think of any advantages arising from groupthink?

6. What generalizations can be made concerning the relationship between homogeneity/heterogeneity and team effectiveness?

7. Think of any team you now are or have been a member of. How would you rate it on the six points given on group maturity?

8. Compare and contrast between the emotional model of group development and the performance model of group development.

9. Reflect on your group experience in this course thus far. Identify the different factors that affected the development of the group. What course of action would you take to improve the group's performance? Why?

Endnotes

1. L. Gratton and T. Erickson, "Ways to Build Collaborative Teams," *Harvard Business Review* (November 2007), pp. 101–109.

2. R. Boyatzis, "Creating Sustainable, Desired Change in Teams through Applications of Intentional Change and Complexity Theory," in P. Docherty, M. Kira, and A. B. Rami Shani (eds.), *Sustainable Work Systems* (London, UK: Routledge, 2008).

3. This section is based on G. C. Homans, *The Human Group* (New York: Harcourt, 1950) and G. C. Homans, *Social Behavior: Its Elementary Forms* (New York: Harcourt, 1961). A comprehensive synthesis of Homans's work can be found in C. R. Shepherd, *Small Groups: Some Sociological Perspectives* (Scranton, PA; Chandler Publishing Company, 1964).

4. J. E. McGrath, H. Arrow, and J. L. Berdahl, *A Theory of Groups as Complex Systems* (Newbury Park, CA: Sage, 1998).

5. M. Knowles and H. Knowles, *The Introduction to Group Dynamics* (Chicago: Follet, 1972), p. 14.

6. For a more complete definition of this complex subject, see D. Cartwright and A. Zander (eds.), *Group Dynamics: Research and Theory,* 3rd ed. (New York: Harper & Row, 1968).

7. G. Bushe and G. Coetzer, "Group Development and Team Effectiveness," *Journal of Applied Behavioral Sciences* 43, no. 2 (2007), pp. 184–212.

8. D. H. Gruenfeld (ed.), *Research on Managing Groups and Teams* (Stamford, CT: JAI Press, 1998); and D. L. Gladstein, "Groups in Context: A Model of Group Effectiveness," *Administrative Science Quarterly* 29, no. 4 (1984), pp. 499–517.

9. R. A. Guzzo and M. W. Dickson, "Teams in Organizations: Recent Research on Performance and Effectiveness," *Annual Review of Psychology* 47 (1996), pp. 307–38; and R. A. Guzzo and R. J. Campbell, "Group Performance and Intergroup Relations in Organizations," in M. D. Dunnette and L. M. Hough (eds.), *Handbook of Industrial and Organizational Psychology,* vol. 3 (Palo Alto, CA: Consulting Psychologists Press, 1992), pp. 269–313.

10. R. W. Napier and M. K. Gershenfield, *Groups: Theory and Experience,* 4th ed. (Boston: Houghton Mifflin, 1989).

11. G. P. Shea and R. A. Guzzo, "Group Effectiveness: What Really Matters?" *Sloan Management Review* (Spring 1987), pp. 499–517.

12. C. J. G. Gersick, "Time and Transition in Work Teams: Toward a New Model of Group Development," *Academy of Management Journal* 31, no. 1 (1988), pp. 9–41.

13. J. E. McGrath, "View of Group Composition through a Group-Theoretic Lens," in Gruenfeld (ed.), *Research on Managing Groups and Teams,* vol. 1, pp. 255–72.

14. Ibid.

15. G. S. Van Der Vegt, J. S. Bunderson, and A. Oosterhof, "Expertness Diversity and Interpersonal Helping Teams," *Academy of Management Journal* 49, no. 5 (2006), pp. 877–93.

16. C. A. O'Reily III, K. Y. Williams, and S. Barade, "Group Demography and Innovation: Does Diversity Help?" in Gruenfeld (ed.), *Research on Managing Groups and Teams,* vol. 1, pp. 183–207.

17. J. E. Diskill, R. Hogan, and E. Salas, "Personality and Group Performance," in C. Hendrick (ed.), *Group Processes and Intergroup Relations* (Newbury Park, CA: Sage, 1987), pp. 91–122; and D. A. Kolb, I. M. Rubin, and J. M. McIntyre, *Organizational Psychology: An Experiential Approach to Organization Behavior* (Englewood Cliffs, NJ: Prentice-Hall, 1984).

18. J. A. Pearce and E. C. Ravlin, "The Design and Activation of Self-Regulating Work Groups," *Human Relations* 40 (1987), pp. 751–82; and S. E. Jackson, J. F. Brett, V. I. Sessa, D. M. Cooper, J. A. Julin, and K. Peyronin, "Some Differences Make a Difference: Individual Dissimilarity and Group Heterogeneity as Correlates of Recruitment, Promotions, and Turnover," *Journal of Applied Psychology* 76 (1991), pp. 675–89.

19. E. Sundstrom, K. P. DeMuse, and D. Futrell, "Work Teams: Applications and Effectiveness," *American Psychologist* 45 (1990), pp. 120–33.

20. T. G. Cummings, "Designing Effective Work Groups," in P. C. Nystrom and W. H. Starbuck (eds.), *Handbook of Organizational Design,* vol. 2 (New York: Oxford University Press, 1981), pp. 250–71.

21. D. Hellriegel, J. W. Slocum, and R. W. Woodman, *Organizational Behavior* (Cincinnati, OH: South-Western College Publishing, 1998).

22. M. A. Campion, G. J. Medsker, and A. C. Higgs, "Relations between Work Group Characteristics and Effectiveness: Implications for Designing Effective Work Groups," *Personnel Psychology* 46 (1993), pp. 823–47.

23. F. R. David, J. A. Pearce, and W. A. Randolph, "Linking Technology and Structure to Enhance Group Performance," *Journal of Applied Psychology* 74 (1989).

24. J. W. Vander, *Sociology* (New York: Ronald Press, 1965), pp. 64–65.

25. K. D. Benne and P. Sheats, "Functional Roles of Group Members," *Journal of Social Issues* (Spring 1948), pp. 41–49; and L. R. Hoffman, "Applying Experimental Research on Problem Solving in Organizations," *Journal of Applied Behavioral Science* 15 (1979), pp. 375–91.

26. S. Schachter, "Deviation, Rejection, and Communications," *Journal of Abnormal and Social Psychology* 46 (1951), pp. 190–207.

27. J. Eagle and N. Newton, "Scapegoating in Small Groups: An Organizational Perspective," *Human Relations* 34 (1981), pp. 283–301; and G. Gemmill and G. Kraus, "Dynamics of Covert Role Analysis," *Small Group Behavior* 19, no. 3 (1988), pp. 299–311.

28. T. Caplow, *Two against One* (Englewood Cliffs, NJ: Prentice-Hall, 1968).

29. H. Arrow, "Standing Out and Fitting In: Composition Effects on Newcomers' Socialization," in Gruenfeld (ed.), *Research on Managing Groups and Teams,* vol. 1, pp. 59–80.

30. W. C. Swap and Associates, *Group Decision Making* (Beverly Hills, CA: Sage, 1984), pp. 55–58. The extract given here is reprinted by permission of Sage Publications, Inc.

31. Cartwright and Zander, *Group Dynamics.*

32. Ibid.

33. R. J. Hackman and R. E. Walton, "Leading Groups in Organizations," in P. S. Goodman (ed.), *Designing Effective Work Groups* (San Francisco: Jossey-Bass, 1986), pp. 72–119.

34. D. L. Gladstein, "Groups in Context: A Model of Task Group Effectiveness," *Administrative Science Quarterly* 29, no. 4 (1984), pp. 499–517.

35. J. L. Komaki, M. L. Desselles, and E. D. Bowman, "Definitely Not a Breeze: Extending an Operant Model of Effective Supervision to Teams," *Journal of Applied Psychology* 74, no. 3 (1989), pp. 522–29.

36. J. R. Hackman (ed.), *Groups That Work (and Those That Don't)* (San Francisco: Jossey-Bass, 1990), pp. 496–97.

37. S. Zaccaro, A. Rittman, and M. Marks, "Team Leadership," *The Leadership Quarterly* 12 (2001), pp. 451–83.

38. B. LatanÈ, K. Williams, and S. Harkins, "Many Hands Make Light the Work: The Causes and Consequences of Social Loafing," *Journal of Personality and Social Psychology* 37 (1979), pp. 822–32.

39. R. Albanese and D. D. Van Fleet, "Rational Behavior in Groups: The Free-Riding Tendency," *Academy of Management Review* 10, no. 2 (1985), pp. 244–55.

40. J. M. Beyer and H. M. Trice, "A Reexamination of the Relations between Size and Various Components of Organizational Complexity," *Administrative Science Quarterly* 24 (1979), pp. 48–64.

41. J. F. Verga, "The Frequency of Self-Limiting Behavior in Groups: A Measure and an Explanation," *Human Relations* 44, no. 8 (1991), pp. 877–94.

42. G. R. Jones, "Task Visibility, Free Riding, and Shirking: Explaining the Effect of Structure and Technology on Employee Behavior," *Academy of Management Review* 9, no. 4 (1984), pp. 684–95; and K. H. Price, "Decision Responsibility, Task Responsibility, Identifiability, and Social Loafing," *Organizational Behavior and Human Decision Processes* 40 (1987), pp. 330–45.

43. M. E. Shaw, *Group Dynamics: The Psychology of Small Group Behavior* (New York: McGraw-Hill, 1976), pp. 232–33.

44. P. E. Mudrack, "Group Cohesiveness and Productivity: A Closer Look," *Human Relations* 9 (1989), pp. 771–85.

45. B. Mullen and C. Copper, "The Relation between Group Cohesiveness and Performance: An Integration," *Psychological Bulletin* 115, no. 2 (1994), pp. 210–27.

46. Cartwright and Zander, *Group Dynamics,* p. 104.

47. P. R. Nail, "Toward an Integration of Some Models and Theories of Social Response," *Psychological Bulletin* 100 (1986), pp. 190–206; and G. E. Overvold, "The Imperative of Organizational Harmony: A Critique of Contemporary Human Relations Theory," *Journal of Business Ethics* 6 (1987), pp. 559–65.

48. H. J. Leavitt, "Hot Groups," *Harvard Business Review* (July–August 1995), pp. 109–16; and H. J. Leavitt, "The Old Days, Hot Groups, and Managers' Lib," *Administrative Science Quarterly* 41 (1996), pp. 288–300.

49. I. L. Janis and L. Mann, *Decision Making: A Psychological Analysis of Conflict* (New York: Free Press, 1977); C. Posner-Weber, "Update on Groupthink," *Small Group Behavior* 18 (1987), pp. 118–25.

50. I. L. Janis, *Victims of Groupthink,* 2nd ed. (Boston: Houghton Mifflin, 1982).

51. R. Jeffrey Smith, "Shuttle Inquiry Focuses on Weather, Rubber Seals, and Unheeded Advice," *Science* (February 28, 1986), p. 909.

52. M. Dolan, "Fletcher Pledges NASA to Make Technical, Management Reform," *Los Angeles Times* (June 10, 1986), part I, p. 10.

53. I. L. Janis, *Groupthink: Psychological Studies of Policy Decisions and Fiascoes,* 2nd ed. (Boston: Houghton Mifflin, 1982).

54. G. Moorhead, R. Ference, and C. P. Neck, "Group Decision Fiascoes Continued: Space Shuttle Challenger and a Revised Groupthink Framework," *Human Relations* 44 (1991), pp. 539–50.

55. L. N. Jewell and H. J. Reitz, *Group Effectiveness in Organizations* (Glenview, IL: Scott, Foresman, 1981), pp. 14–15. [Based on W. Bennis and H. Shepard, *A Theory of Group Development* (San Francisco: Jossey-Bass, 1974).]

56. M. McCollom, "Reevaluating Group Development: A Critique of the Familiar Models," in J. Gilette and M. McCollom (eds.), *Groups in Context* (Reading, MA: Addison-Wesley, 1990), pp. 134–54.

57. H. J. Reitz, *Group Behavior in Organizations* (Burr Ridge, IL: Richard D. Irwin, 1981).

58. B. W. Tuckman, "Developmental Sequence in Small Groups," *Psychological Bulletin* 63 (1965), pp. 384–99; and B. W. Tuckman and M. A. Jensen, "Stages of Small Group Development Revisited," *Group and Organizational Studies* 2, no. 4 (1977), pp. 419–27. For a comprehensive synopsis of Tuckman's work see R. Napier and M. Gershenfeld, *Groups: Theory and Experiences* (Boston: Houghton Mifflin, 1997).

59. Reitz, *Group Behavior in Organizations.*

60. Tuckman and Jensen, "Stages of Small Group Development Revisited," *Group and Organizational Studies* 2, no. 4 (1977), pp. 419–27.

61. G. Bushe and G. Coetzer, "Group Development and Team Effectiveness," *Journal of Applied Behavioral Sciences* 43, no. 2 (2007), pp. 184–212.

62. M. R. Barrick, G. L. Stewart, M. J. Neubert, and M. K. Mount, "Relating Member Ability and Personality to Work-Team Processes and Team Effectiveness," *Journal of Allied Psychology* 83, no. 3 (1998), pp. 377–91.

63. R. A. Guzzo and M. W. Dickson, "Teams in Organizations: Recent Research on Performance and Productivity," *Annual Review of Psychology* 47 (1996), pp. 307–38; For a great collection of recent research manuscripts on group dynamics and performance see J. M. Levine, and R. L. Moreland (eds.), *Small Groups* (New York: Psychological Press, 2006).

Activity 12–3: The Plafab Company Case

Objectives:

a. To learn the distinction between process and content in analyzing group dynamics.

b. To apply theories of group development in analyzing one group's interactions.

c. To observe the processes of leadership influence and coalition formation in group interaction.

Task 1 (Homework):

(Note to instructor: Assign one of the two questions below to half the class or to half the teams in the class and assign the other question to the other half so that a range of data will be generated for analysis of this case.)

Read the following case study, "The Plafab Company: The Performance Appraisal Task Force," and prepare a written answer to the following:

a. Analyze the case by paying attention to dynamics relevant to group development, such as self-oriented versus group-oriented behavior, task avoidance, dependency, counterdependency, overt and covert conflict, and subgroup formation. Diagnose what stage or phase the group is in. Particular emphasis should be placed on providing specific examples from the case to justify your diagnosis.

b. Analyze the case from the perspective of leadership, authority, and influence. Describe how these dynamics are played out over the course of the meeting.

Task 2 (Classroom):

a. Teams are to decide on appropriate answers to the question assigned in Task 1. (Time: 20–25 minutes)

b. Team spokespersons are to report their answers to the class. Open class discussion follows. (Time: 25–30 minutes)

Case Study: The Plafab Company: The Performance Appraisal Task Force

The general manager of division X of a medium-size plastic fabrication firm has created a task force. Its mission is to recommend a system of performance appraisal (PA) for the entire division. The task force has met twice in the past. At the first meeting the members decided that they needed greater clarification of the task and decided that Eric should ask the general manager exactly what they should be doing. At the second meeting Eric reported that the general manager wasn't much clearer and seemed to simply want the group's best thinking. A rambling discussion followed, and the meeting ended with a decision to meet for an hour the day after next.

**Exhibit 1
Third Meeting**

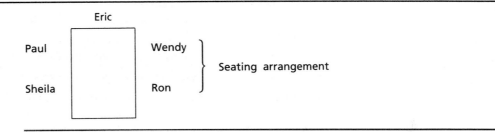

(Meeting comes to order as Paul initiates.)

PAUL: I came across a really interesting article on performance appraisal in *Organization Dynamics,* and I made copies for all of you. *(He passes them out.)* It's about how they set it up at Rohm & Hauss, and I thought it made a lot of sense.

ERIC: I'm sure this information will be very helpful, Paul, but before we look at any specific system, I think we should define our objectives more clearly. For example, I was thinking, is this PA system going to be mainly used for promotion decisions, such as making sure that good people move up in the organization? Or is it supposed to be used mainly for salary and merit decisions?

SHEILA: Or how about, Is it supposed to help develop management?

WENDY: It's pretty clear that there are a lot of ways to skin this cat. I've been wondering if we might not be taking on too big a task, especially with our limited knowledge in this area. I guess what I'm saying is that I really think we need to get some outside expertise.

PAUL: Boy, our senior managers are really not on the ball; know what I mean? Just look at this committee. The least they could do is be specific about what they want us to do. Lately they seem to keep blowing it.

ERIC: Oh, I think they do a pretty good job.

WENDY: Personally I find it encouraging that they're thinking of putting in a PA system. I mean it's about time this company started to manage human resources in a systematic way.

PAUL: Well, what about that screwup on the Bently account. Instead of just holding back, working out the bugs, and delaying shipment for a week, they ordered Rodgers to ship a box full of scrap again and the account went down the drain. One thing you have to say about Rohm & Hauss, whatever they ship is 100 percent!

SHEILA: Did you hear about what happened with that task force on consolidation? They made a report to the brass last Monday after working their tails off for two months and Dan swears two of them were asleep for most of the presentation. I mean literally asleep.

ERIC: Well, look; we've got a job to do, and I think we should just get down to doing it.

WENDY: There's obviously a lot of ways to look at PA and probably a lot we won't think of, so let's face it—we need some expertise. As it turns out, I have the name of a consulting firm that comes well recommended.

SHEILA: But will the company give us the money to hire a consultant?

WENDY: Good question. Eric should go ask.

PAUL: Hold on a second. Who are these consultants?

WENDY: They're personnel specialists with, apparently, a wide range of expertise. I know they've done work for Celanese and Duo-Plastic and they . . .

PAUL: Celanese!?! They're losing money hand over fist. And they're doing that dumb "quality is free" hype. I don't think I want one of their consultants.

WENDY: Well, we could look into other personnel specialists.

PAUL: Frankly, I don't like asking the company to spend money that way. Obviously management asked us to be a task force because someone thinks we have what it takes, and I'd sure like a shot at it first. I've been reading up on PA, and it seems pretty clear that to make something like this work, it has to be every manager's responsibility.

RON: Maybe we should start by listing all the things we think a PA system could do.

ERIC: Good idea, Ron, but first I just want to know whether the group wants me to ask the general manager about a consultant.

PAUL: I thought we decided to try without one for awhile.

SHEILA: I don't know that anybody decided anything, but I do think it's a good idea to get some additional information and just educate ourselves. But there are lots of ways we could do that.

PAUL: I could distribute other stuff I've read.

ERIC: Great, I'd like to see that.

SHEILA: Me too.

PAUL: Good, I'll have my girl get the stuff out to you.

WENDY: Oh, Paul, I can't believe you still say "my girl." *(general laughter)*

SHEILA: You know, what really bugs me is that the secretaries call themselves *girls.*

PAUL: Well, what does it really matter? Words are just words. You can call me a *boy.* I don't care.

ERIC: You might not say that if you were black. *(general laughter)*

ERIC: Well, this is all good fun, but I think we need to be pushing forward. It seems to me we have to define our objectives here more clearly before we can move ahead.

WENDY: I think it's pretty obvious that the key here is to develop a system that allows us to monitor and rationalize our human resources within the framework of the organization's strategic plan.

SHEILA: But shouldn't it also provide information about the state of human resources that can be fed into strategic planning?

WENDY: Exactly what I mean.

PAUL: Well, I'm not sure what you mean.

SHEILA: All she's saying, Paul, is that the PA system should help management make decisions taking into consideration the manpower implications of them.

WENDY: Well, that's not exactly what I meant.

PAUL: Personally, I want a PA system that's going to give me a clear idea of just what I'm being evaluated on, and I think that's what most people want. They want to know what their boss thinks they should be doing and how well he thinks they're doing.

SHEILA: So you want to see it used mainly as a feedback mechanism.

PAUL: Well, what's wrong with that?

SHEILA: I wasn't saying there's anything wrong with that.

RON: Maybe we should keep a list of all these ideas.

SHEILA: OK. We've got two so far.

ERIC: I think the main point of a good PA system is to make sure that everyone gets treated as fairly as possible, especially when it comes to promotions.

WENDY: Oh yes, I think that's critical.

PAUL: Don't forget the motivational aspects.

WENDY: Which motivational aspects are you referring to?

PAUL: Well, the idea that if people know what the boss expects and get feedback on it, it'll motivate them. The article I'm going to send you talks about tying a PA system into an overall MBO program that really helped increase employee motivation at Terex.

ERIC: What's MBO?

WENDY: MBO—Management by Objectives—and I've heard that that MBO stuff just doesn't work.

PAUL: Why do you say that?

WENDY: Well, they tried at National Semi. I have a friend who works there, and it created such a mess that the company just disbanded it after 10 months.

PAUL: But the article said it worked wonders at Terex. And at other places.

WENDY: You know, Paul, you can't believe everything you read. I'll bet it was written by some consultant trying to generate business. Like do you see all those stories on quality circles these days? But I heard that they're really all falling apart because we're not like Japan.

SHEILA: Yeah, it really bugs me all the stuff we keep hearing about Japan—Japan this, Japan that. If we had their labor rates and government support, we'd be doing just as well if not better.

WENDY: I think that it's true to some extent, but it's also true that they just have a different culture, so different things will work there.

ERIC: I'll say it's different. We spent part of our last vacation in Tokyo, and I couldn't believe how so many people can live in so little space. It'd drive me crazy in short order.

PAUL: Well, I don't know what all this has to do with performance appraisal.

ERIC: Quite right, Paul. We should get back on track. Now . . . what were we doing?

SHEILA: Ron was keeping a list of our ideas.

RON: No, I only suggested we should keep a list.

ERIC: Maybe you ought to be keeping that list for us, Ron.

RON: Frankly, there's so much digression going on here that it's hard for me to stay tuned in.

PAUL: You're not kidding. This meeting seems more like a sewing bee than a business meeting.

WENDY: Well, I wouldn't know, since I've never been to a sewing bee. Have you, Paul?

SHEILA *(laughing):* You know, even when I was a kid, I knew I didn't want to sew and stuff.

PAUL: Look, we're really getting nowhere. Eric, will you please take charge of this meeting and get us moving in some direction?

ERIC: I thought we *were* making some progress on defining objectives.

PAUL: You know, it really pisses me off that senior management hasn't already defined the objectives. If they treated quarterly profit targets the same way, nothing would get done around here. I wonder what would happen if we just told them it's impossible to do this job if they don't take a clear stand.

SHEILA: A stand on what?

PAUL: Well, for example, is the PA system going to be a personnel program or a line-management function?

RON: You think it should be a line function, don't you?

PAUL: Damn right. Don't you agree, Eric?

WENDY: Management has to be involved, but I think it's clear that we would also need personnel specialists to administer and run it and make sure it's working properly. For example, we'd probably need to train managers in how to give constructive feedback, use the system, and all those kinds of things.

PAUL: Oh, just what we need, more training.

SHEILA: But, Paul, whatever system is used, we'll need to teach people how to use it, won't we?

PAUL: I don't want to do any teaching.

SHEILA: I didn't mean that we—this task force—would actually do the teaching. I meant the company will have to teach people.

PAUL: Well, I don't see what's so difficult. You just tell managers to write down their subordinates' objectives, rate them, and then tell them their ratings. What's so tough about that?

WENDY: But can you trust that managers really will give people honest feedback?

PAUL: That's the problem these days—no respect for authority. When guys like Eric and me joined this company, people respected their boss.

WENDY: You haven't said a word yet, Ron. What do you think?

RON: I guess people are a lot less willing to respect someone just because of his or her position than they used to be.

WENDY: No, I mean what do you think the objectives of a PA system should be?

RON: Well, I agree with a lot that's been said. You know, I don't really know.

WENDY: Maybe it'd help us reach some consensus if we talked about what we'd personally want the outcomes of a PA system to be.

SHEILA: OK. I think I'd like to know how I stand compared to other managers in my department.

ERIC: You mean people would know each other's ratings?

SHEILA: Sure, why not?

PAUL *(muttering):* I don't believe it.

ERIC: Hold on a second; I don't know if that's such a good idea. I mean, well, it could be very bad for morale, you know, it . . .

WENDY: Are you advocating management by secrecy?

ERIC: No, of course not. It's just that it could create some very sensitive situations and, anyway, wouldn't it make managers more likely not to give honest feedback? I mean, that's what you're concerned about, isn't it?

WENDY: Maybe it would force them to be more careful and precise in their appraisals.

PAUL: As far as I'm concerned, my rating should be between my boss and me.

SHEILA: But don't you want to know how you're doing in relation to everyone else?

PAUL: I do know. I just have to look at the quarterly reports.

SHEILA: OK, but not everybody's work is directly reflected in profit reports.

RON: I don't think any one person's work is reflected in profit reports.

WENDY: I agree. In fact, if you extend that idea, maybe we should be appraising team performance instead of individual performance.

ERIC: Well, that's a novel idea. And speaking of novel ideas, I could sure use a break to get rid of some of this coffee I've been drinking.

SHEILA: Great—I could use a smoke.

(Meeting breaks up for 10 minutes.)

**Activity 12–4:
Values in Business**

Objectives:

a. To increase awareness of the importance of values as determinants of organizational behavior.

b. To increase awareness of the differences in team members' perception of values.

c. To experience some of the issues associated with group decision making and group dynamics.

Introduction:

This activity was designed to help your team evaluate the relative importance of certain values with which business organizations must be concerned. Values can be thought of as existing in a hierarchy in our thought processes, some being given higher importance or priority than others. The whole pattern of values in an organization represents the core of its operating philosophy and its organizational culture. Thus, they are major determinants of behavior of management and employees.

Values defined: Things, ideas, beliefs, and acts that are regarded as good or bad, right or wrong, desirable or undesirable, beautiful or ugly, contributing to or detrimental to human welfare, and so on. Societies, organizations, and individuals all have values with priorities of importance. For example, individuals may differ greatly in the values associated with religious beliefs, but a higher-order value that they all presumably would accept is freedom of religious beliefs.

General Exercise:

Assume you are a member of a top-management team of a large corporation. During a team-development retreat, the facilitator–consultant informs the group that she has observed from individual interviews with team members that differences in perception exist as to the values by which they operate. Yet each person seems to be assuming that her or his values are shared by the other team members. As a basis for developing awareness and better consensus in values, the following tasks are undertaken.

Task 1 (Individual Rankings):

Listed in alphabetical order on the accompanying worksheet are 10 values that are among those often discussed in regard to business functioning. Your job is to rank these according to the priority you would assign each in terms of importance for conducting business. Do this by writing in the first column next to the value a 1 for the value of highest importance, a 2 for the next, on down to a 10 for the value of lowest importance. In the second column, briefly note the reason for your ranking. Be sure to do this without consulting others; also, be sure your rankings are not observable to team members while completing this task. (Note: There is no right or wrong answer and no definite solution to this exercise. The rankings should be based on your own beliefs.)

Task 2 (Team Rankings):

Teams meet outside of class. Members compare their rankings of the values and come to a consensus as to how the team would rank the items from 1 to 10. This ranking should reflect what the team believes, not your estimate of how businesspeople would rank the values. (*Note:* Consensus does not necessarily mean that all agree with the final ranking of the team; it does mean that everyone's views were expressed and understood and that agreement was reached on how the values were to be ranked. In a real situation your personal values may differ from your colleagues', but you may decide to support the team's viewpoint for reasons such as hoping eventually to persuade your co-workers to adopt your views or wanting to be open-minded to see whether you could be wrong. If your values are too different, you may find, after a reasonable period, that you do not fit into the team. The main point of the exercise at this time is to increase your awareness of value issues.)

Task 3 (Classroom):

Teams list on the board the rank ordering of their values. Discuss similarities and differences.

Name _____   Date _____

WORKSHEET FOR ACTIVITY 12–4

Values	Your Ranking	Reason	Your Team's Ranking	Reason
Career growth and development of personnel				
Concern for personnel as people				
Efficiency				
Ethics (morality)				
Managerial and organizational effectiveness				
Servicing clients' needs (for example, equipment, orders)				
Profits				
Providing products or services for society				
Quality of goods or services				
Social responsibility				

Part 4 | Managing Organizational Processes

REVIEW

Organizational processes play a critical role in developing and managing sustainable work systems.[1] Understanding and managing organizational processes, such as work design and redesign, creativity and innovation, culture, learning, and change seem to absorb a significant amount of time and energy in today's business environment. Some managers argue that in reality their job almost entirely consists of managing change. The complexity, amount, and pace of change have increased significantly during the past decade. Most organizations, employees, and managers are struggling to find the optimal path. The management of work design, creativity and innovation, culture, learning, and change influences organizational behavior and organizational effectiveness.

Part 3 interrelated the five conceptual areas of personality and personal growth, motivation, perception, and communication (introduced in Part 2) to key interpersonal processes. The "design of work and organizations" and "creativity and innovation" foster organizational dynamics that result in the emergence of organizational culture. Thus, the area that remains to be addressed in detail is the nature and dynamics of organizational processes and the interrelationship between them and "effectiveness" at the individual, team, and organizational levels.

We study behavior in the context of work in order to improve and sustain performance, development, and effectiveness. Embedded in organizational efforts to improve effectiveness is continuous improvement or what the Japanese call *kaizen*. Continuous improvement is a purposeful and explicit set of principles, mechanisms, and activities within an organization designed to achieve positive and continuous change in operating procedures, effectiveness, and systems by the people who actually perform these procedures and work within these systems. *Continuous* means that an improvement activity is explicitly designed and organized for continuity. Improvement projects and episodes should follow each other in the same area or around the same general performance indicators. In this respect continuous improvement is markedly different from sporadic improvement projects, which are undertaken without a view of continuity, and from suggestions systems, where any kind of improvement suggestions are called for without explicit management of the area, quality, or direction of the suggestions. Continuity usually requires permanent support structure. *Improvement* is a planned change in the state of affairs of an organization that results in positive changes in the organizational effectiveness indicators.[2]

PREVIEW OF PART 4

Part 4 incorporates much of the material already studied into an overall system approach to individual, team, and organizational effectiveness with a focus on the design and management of key processes. This part has four integrated modules: "Organization and Work Design," "Creativity and Innovation," "Organizational Culture," and "Organizational Change, Development, and Learning."

In Module 13, design is described as a fundamental process that groups people and tasks in a variety of configurations and as such has a major influence on organizational behavior, dynamics, and effectiveness. The design of work and jobs is an ongoing challenge that faces the manager. Rooted in the historical context of the organization, its business environment, and evolved culture, the design or redesign of organizations is a complex task. The module provides a comprehensive road map for organization design as an ongoing process, describes alternative forms of structures, emphasizes a variety of options for work design at both the individual and team levels, and highlights the important role that the manager must play as the designer.

Module 14 turns our focus to creativity and innovation. Most companies are dependent on developments driven by creative ideas, designs, products, services, or innovative solutions. Creativity and innovation are complex and difficult to manage. The literature identifies a variety of factors that stimulate or block creativity and innovation. The organizational context—such as leadership styles, visions, objectives, goals, strategies, resources, personnel policies, beliefs, values, work and organization design, and culture—seems to affect both creativity and innovation. The module explores the meaning of creativity and innovation, identifies the major elements that influence the creativity and innovation processes, and examines the choices that can be made in the process of triggering and managing creativity and innovation. Managing the choices made about work and organization design (Module 13) sets the stage for the formation of organizational culture.

Module 15 focuses on the nature of organizational culture and its relationships to organizational effectiveness. As such, the module goes beyond an exploration of the basic profile of a national or regional culture. The focus is on development of an organizational culture analytical framework such that we can attempt to both understand and manage organizational culture. We focus on symbolism as a way of diagnosing organizational culture in its business and organizational context. Organizational culture is a complex phenomenon to map out because culture is much like air; it is everywhere we look, and it touches everything that goes on in organizations. Understanding the culture of the organization is critical if the manager is to attempt to manage and/or try to shape the culture.

Creating actionable knowledge about organizational culture is a complex task that can be accomplished via a planned change process. Module 16 focuses on organizational change, development, and learning. Following a brief discussion of organizational learning; its meaning; and its effect on individual, group, and organizational effectiveness, we explore various organizational learning mechanisms. Managing organizational learning, development, and change is a challenge that managers face on an ongoing basis. The module presents two complementary ways to cluster the different change programs that have emerged: target focus and consequence focus change programs.

Organizational change and development (OC&D) is viewed as a planned-change organizational effort that attempts to improve and sustain effectiveness. We provide an in-depth review and comparison of three commonly used systemwide change programs—reengineering, total quality management, and sociotechnical systems. The comparison provides an insight into the complexity of managing change and development. We conclude by providing a glimpse into the emerging global nature of the organizational development field.

In the introduction to the book, we framed the study of organizational behavior with an eye on sustainability. We argued that a sustainability perspective should be viewed as a holistic framework that entails understanding of the interconnected nature of environmental, social, and economic resources that are to be nurtured. A sustainable organization was defined as an entity that is able to sustain dynamically its existence and secure its heritage in the short term without endangering the possibility of the resources being renewed and regenerated in the long term. Furthermore, a sustainable organization is able to operate in and adapt to its environment, building its operational capability by promoting the various resources engaged in its operations to retain and develop their operational capability. The perspectives about design, change, planned change, learning, and learning mechanisms discussed in this last part of the book provide specific ways of thinking and acting toward the creation of a more sustainable work place.

Notes

1. P. Docherty, M. Kira, and A. B. (Rami) Shani (eds.), *Creating Sustainable Work Systems,* 2nd ed. (London: Routledge, 2008).
2. For a detailed discussion of continuous improvement, its origin, and current definitions, see P. Lillrank and A. B. Shani, "Continuous Improvement: Beyond a Definition," *EFI Research Paper* (Stockholm, Sweden: Stockholm School of Economics, 1998).

Module
13

Organization and Work Design*

LEARNING OBJECTIVES

After completing this module, you should be able to

1. Understand the sustainability perspective applied to work and organization design.
2. Use the star organization design model to create a new organization.
3. Define and describe factors that influence organization performance.
4. Identify the different ways of grouping people into teams, departments, and organizational units.
5. Identify and understand both traditional and newer forms of organization structure.
6. Understand ways to build the team-based organization.
7. Understand how to build enriched jobs within a team context.
8. Appreciate that there are several academic-based approaches to organization design that can be used to build effective organizations including the new sustainable work systems design perspective.

KEY TERMS AND CONCEPTS

Comprehensive design approaches	Functional form
Context	Hierarchy
Core transformation process	Horizontal structure
Cross-team integrating team	Hybrid form
Differentiation	Intensive Work Systems
Dynamic network organization	Information processing approach
External environment	Integration
Form of structure	Job engineering

*This module was revised and modified in collaboration with Professor Michael Stebbins, Professor of Organization Design at Orfelea College of Business, California Polytechnic State University. We are grateful to Professor Stebbins.

Lean production team

Management support processes

Network organization

Organization

Organization design

People

Processes

Purpose

Rewards

Scientific management

Self-design approach

Self-directed work team

Stakeholders

Structural variables

Structure

Sustainable work systems

Sustainable work systems (SWS) approach

Task environment

Team-based organization

Transformation process

Transnational structure

Wider environment

Work design

MODULE OUTLINE

Premodule Preparation

    Activity 13–1: Designing a Student-Run Organization That Provides Consulting Services

Introduction

    The Information Processing Approach

    The Star Model

Factors Affecting Organization Performance

    Context

    Purpose

    Core Transformation Process

    Structure

    Management Support Processes

    People

Forms of Structure

    Simple Form

    Functional Form

    Product or Self-Contained Form

    Mixed or Hybrid Form

    Horizontal Forms

Building the Team-Based Organization

    Designs for Global Competition

    Network Organizations

    The Transnational Model of Organization

Comprehensive Approaches to Organization Design

    The Information Processing Approach

    The Self-Design Approach

    The Sustainable Work Systems Approach

Work Design—A Closer Look at Processes and Teams

    Self-Directed Work Teams

    Lean Production Teams

    Scientific Management

Intensive Work Systems versus Sustainable Work Systems

Work Design at the Individual Level

Summary

Study Questions

Endnotes

Optional Activities on the WWW

PREMODULE PREPARATION

Activity 13–1: Designing a Student-Run Organization That Provides Consulting Services

Objectives:

a. To appreciate the importance of the total organization on group and individual behavior.

b. To provide a beginning organization design experience that will be familiar to students.

Background:

The Industry Advisory Council for your school has decided to sponsor a student-run organization that will provide business-consulting services to nonprofit groups in your community. The council has donated $20,000 toward start-up costs and has agreed to provide office space, computer equipment, and other materials as needed. The council hopes that the organization will establish its own source of funding after the first year of operation.

Task 1:

The dean of the school wants you to develop alternative designs for the new organization. Your task is to identify the main design dimensions or factors to be dealt with in establishing such an organization and to describe the issues that must be resolved for each factor. For example, you might provide an organization chart to help describe the structural issues involved. Before jumping ahead with your design, you may also have to think about (1) groups in the community that could use your help and (2) problems they face. Remember, though, your task is to create the organization that will provide services, not to provide an in-depth look at the types of services provided.

You and your team are to brainstorm design dimensions to be dealt with and to develop a one- or two-page outline that can be shared with the entire class. You have 1 hour to develop the outline. Select two people to present your design. Assume that you will all be involved in the new organization, filling specific positions.

Task 2:

After the brainstorming period, the spokespersons will present the group designs or preferred design and answer questions from the audience.

Task 3:

The instructor will comment on the designs and discuss additional factors that might be important for the success of this organization.

INTRODUCTION

Are people to serve work, or is work consciously designed to serve people? These age-old questions stimulate our thinking about how work systems—the form of **organization,** the system of roles, responsibilities, and relationships for getting work done—achieve the proper balance between involvement and engagement on the one hand, and work–life balance on the other. Can organizations and work be designed to foster high performance as well as employee growth and development? Can it be done in such a way that people do not experience undue stress and pressure for results, long working hours, high-speed work, and other aspects of intensive work? These issues are at the heart of discussions about sustainable work systems (SWS) design as one of the newer approaches to the creation of work organizations.[1]

We have earlier defined a sustainable organization as one that has internal mechanisms to ensure its existence in the short run, while providing the basis for renewal and regeneration of resources for the long term. This requires balanced attention to the needs of different **stakeholders,** as well as balanced attention to efficient production and dynamic renewal. Later in this module, we will provide examples of organizations that have sustainability characteristics, and a change process that can be used to redesign the organization.

The impact of work system design on employee motivation and well-being has been of concern to academics and practitioners for over four decades. However, most of the celebrated experiments to create enriched jobs, high levels of engagement, autonomous work groups, and high-performance organizations have evaporated with time, falling victim to changing business conditions, new technology, and a resurgence of scientific management principles that made work boring, demotivating, and uninvolving in the first place. It seems that what is needed is a theory that focuses less on workplace change interventions and experiments and more on creating organizational capacity for continuous adaptation. In the section Intensive Work Systems versus Sustainable Work Systems, we will explore how this might be accomplished.

Managers often create cognitive maps that help them sort out their work experiences. A map is a graphic representation that provides a frame of reference. For geographers, a map is a means of depicting the world so that people understand where they are and where they are going.[2] In the organizational context cognitive maps help people make sense of information and at times provide the reasoning behind actions. The broad cognitive map presented in Module 1 introduced organizations as systems composed of subsystems that interact regularly to produce and accomplish a desired goal or goals. Modules 2 and 3 explored the role that expectations and learning play in organizational settings and the importance of learning-in-action. Modules 4 through 7 investigated elements of individual processes, while Modules 8 through 12 explored different elements of interpersonal processes.

This module, the first of four in the last part of the book, is centered on the exploration of the main features of the organization as well as work and **organization design.** We begin with an exercise that focuses on design of the total organization. Many models, conceptual road maps, frameworks, and metaphors or images of organizations and how they work can be found in the literature. We have chosen to focus on two complementary cognitive maps as a point of departure for the exploration of work systems. The first is a well-recognized model for considering design problems and the decisions that must continuously be made within the organization as it grows. The "star" model (see Figure 13–1) advances the notion that organization design is a decision-making process involving strategic choices.[3] The organization's form of structure is only one of the points on the star, and choices made on all points must be compatible. This model and perspective will be enormously helpful in completing the premodule assignment. The second cognitive map extends this thinking to cover additional factors affecting organizational performance. Finally, we explore emerging forms of organization structure, consider three alternative perspectives on organization design, and cover rapidly evolving theory concerning the team-based organization.

The Information Processing Approach

Since the early 1970s, Jay Galbraith and other authors have been contributing to an organization design method called the **information processing approach.** The name for this approach comes from an early emphasis on the organization's external environment. The uncertainty of the environment along with how managers view the organization's task is a primary concern, since it determines *the amount of information that must be processed* during task execution. The managerial problem is to design the organization in ways that increase the company's capacity to process information and to make decisions about events that cannot be anticipated in advance. The design principles associated with the information processing perspective include:

1. Organization design is a decision-making process involving strategic choices.
2. Organizing mode (structure) is only one of several areas where choices are to be made.
3. The design problem is to bring about coherence or fit among the various decision areas (strategy, structure, information and decision processes, reward systems, and support systems focused on people).
4. There is no "one best way" to organize. Instead, there are rich combinations of strategy, structure, and support systems that might be viable.
5. All available options both formal and informal should be considered during design or redesign programs. For example, voluntary and informal mechanisms may suffice instead of more expensive and formal mechanisms.
6. Organization design involves theoretical knowledge, process knowledge, and unique information about the work situation.
7. In many organizations, the challenge is to coordinate across boundaries that might exist among departments, locations, and products. The design problem then centers on ways to create the right amount of lateral organization capability.
8. In design work, there is growing attention to the importance of investment in information and communications technology.

The Star Model*

The star model was first put forward in 1973, and it has been modified in different management textbooks and journal articles to reflect somewhat different opinions of design challenges that managers have faced in later decades. The intent behind the star figure, and points on the star, is to show the elements that must be created and combined to result in task performance. According to the original model, a particular firm or company is a player in the external environment and must also respond to the environment. The business strategy determines which tasks are important and it also drives multiple other decisions to be made to create an organizational capability. Sometimes, the star model is simplified to show only strategy as one point of the star, and sometimes it is listed as *purpose.* The key point is that purpose—whether it takes the form of a mission statement, vision statement, strategy statement, or announcement of strategic direction—must be clear if the company is to effectively rally people and other resources around specific objectives and accomplishments. More will be said about this in the organizational performance model discussed in the following.

Some brief definitions of other points on the star diagram will be helpful. Briefly, **structure** refers most often to the particular form of structure—functional, product form, and other traditional ways of depicting the **hierarchy.** Form of structure as depicted in an organizational chart specifies key roles and departments, but the term structure also includes other concepts such as how units are linked together. **Processes** refer to management systems

*Adopted from Jay R. Galbraith, *Designing Organizations: An Executive Guide to Strategy, Structure, and Process* (San Francisco: Jossey-Bass, 2002), figure 2.1, p. 10. We are grateful to Professor Galbraith.

**Figure 13–1
The Star Model**

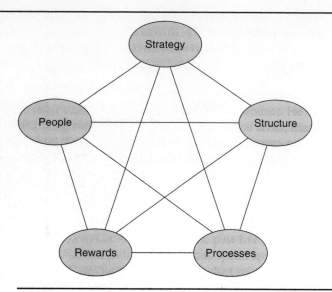

such as planning, budgeting, and information technology infrastructure. **Rewards** refer to the organization's systems and procedures related to pay, bonuses, recognition systems, and methods of advancing people within the organization. The **people** dimension is somewhat curious in definition as it refers to human resource practices such as recruiting, selection, placement, and training. Another way of thinking about the star model is that it refers to decisions about strategy, structure, and managerial processes since the people, rewards, and processes points on the star are all processes. According to information processing theory, decisions being made about all three should be considered together, since decisions should reinforce each other to create a unique organizational capability.

The star model continues to be useful in thinking about modern design issues and in academic exercises to create organizations from scratch. To simplify the design task, think about your own academic organization. Your college will have a well-articulated mission or purpose. It also has a clear departmental structure and preferred ways of teaching students through lecture activities, experiential activities, club activities, internships, distance learning, and the like. It also will have processes to change the curriculum in a dynamic way. The curriculum is modified over the years through deliberations about the business world, the value of different courses in preparing students for the workforce, course content, and educational practices. A college needs many support departments and processes to help with instruction and to promote the college. Support processes in a college include facilities planning, media support, information technology support, budget systems, alumni relations activities, and library support. In thinking about an ideal company in the marketplace, an easy solution to the design task is to simply say that the organization needs all the functions and subjects taught in a business school—for example, accounting, finance, production, marketing, information systems, legal, international business, and management. But this easy answer is not what is needed. Organizations are uniquely formed to address specific problems that are encountered at start-up. While all the preceding functions might be needed at later stages of growth, the initial organization is usually quite simple. As companies move through early stages of growth and achieve some complexity and scale, important decisions about *redesign* must be made.

FACTORS AFFECTING ORGANIZATION PERFORMANCE

As Activity 13–1 demonstrated, many factors influence the behavior and performance of the organization. These elements can be grouped into six categories: context, purpose, core transformation processes, structure, management support processes, and people. We explore each of the categories in this section (see Figure 13–2).

**Figure 13–2
Factors Affecting
Organization Performance**

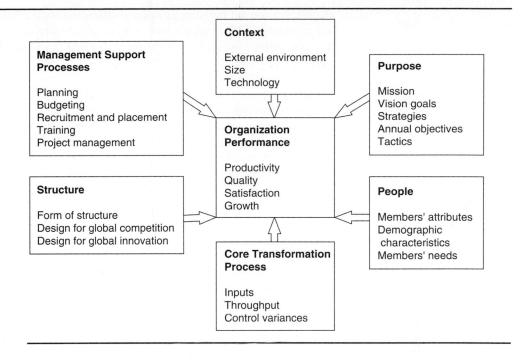

Context

Context refers to the whole organization, including size, technology, and environment. While some authors also include goals as a contextual dimension, we instead include goals within the purpose category as it is commonly handled in organization design. This issue will come up again at the point where work groups are discussed, and it is seen that organizational purpose and goals are part of a work group's context. Thus, context can refer to both the "task" and "wider" environment. Contextual dimensions affect the other categories discussed in this section, such as structure and work processes, and eventually, organization performance.

A variety of frameworks that make up the business environment can be found in the literature. For the purpose of this chapter we explore two frameworks. In the previous paragraph we used an organization's *task and wider environment*. The **task environment** can be viewed as the firm's immediate relevant environment such as all possible suppliers (of labor, knowledge, information, money, materials, and so on), markets, competitors, regulators, and associations that are relevant to the business's current services and products. The **wider environment** includes all the other possible environmental factors within which the organization functions, such as political, educational, economic, demographic characteristics, societal structure, and laws. An alternative mental model was proposed by Daft, who argues that the **external environment** can be perceived as a composition of 10 sectors: industry, raw materials, human resources, financial resources, market, technology, economic conditions, government, sociocultural, and international.[4] If, for example, a manufacturing firm hoped to open a new assembly plant in a particular city, it would consider all factors in the environment that might impinge on the project or make it feasible. The market, government support through tax incentives, favorable supply logistics, and a skilled local workforce might combine to make the new assembly plant investment attractive.

Purpose

In defining the **purpose** category, we consider how the organization interprets the environment to develop statements of mission, vision, goals, strategies, objectives, and tactics. A mission statement communicates what the organization stands for, and what it is trying to achieve. Some mission statements combine vision and values to communicate positive messages to internal and external stakeholders. A vision is an attempt to articulate what a desired future for a company might look like. It is in essence an organizational dream—it stretches the imagination and motivates people to rethink what is possible. Jick[5] argues that visions are not the same as mission statements—their value is in inspiring and motivating others. Since structure, roles, and employee activities are derived from the firm's mission, vision, and goals, it is not surprising that there is a great deal of attention within organizations given to creation of purpose.

Few experts in the field of organization theory agree on distinctions among mission, vision, goals, and other terms commonly used in organizations. Within organizations, the confusion continues with companies adopting unique definitions related to purpose: How does strategic intent differ from strategic mission? How does a goal differ from a specific objective? In viewing company to company examples related to strategy, distinctions among the terms are highly inconsistent. For some companies, a goal is a general statement that provides direction, while in others a goal statement will include a specific, measurable outcome and how it will be achieved. Since this debate is most appropriate for a textbook on strategic management, we will limit our discussion in this module to a general conclusion that purpose is critical in organization design.

Core Transformation Process

Consistent with the earlier material on the open-systems view, the **core transformation process** is the conversion process that turns inputs into output. To move from this rather abstract notion, we will look at a manufacturing example. Looking at it from a strictly technical systems viewpoint, input combined with technology produces "throughput" or "product-in-becoming."[6] *Throughput* is the state of the product at one stage of development. For example, in producing a product such as cheese, at an early stage input is raw milk. The milk has specific characteristics depending on the type of cows producing the milk. The initial quality of raw milk is measured by microorganisms present, and the milk can vary greatly depending on time of year, condition of the herd, and the way milk has been handled and transported. The bacteria, viruses, and fungi in milk are required at several phases of cheese production and some are transformed into enzymes that are required for creating the flavor and aroma of cheese. Eventually, the throughput is structured curd that changes to a form and shape characteristic of the type of cheese (wheel, ball, or block). It then ripens or ferments to take on the flavor, scent, and texture of the final product.[7] A wide range of actions by people controlling the process determine the variety of cheese produced and quality of results. While there might be thousands of variances—or changes from standard—as cheese moves through five throughput phases, only a critical few variances must be managed by operators to achieve the right results. Management and employees must apply technology and control variances so that the core transformation process is sound.

There are many ways to document the core transformation process in different manufacturing and service industry settings. Suffice it to say at this point, that whatever structure is put in place in organization design, it ought to support and facilitate management of the core process. In other words, creation of structure follows a formal review of and an imaginative construction of the core transformation process.

Structure

The term structure has many meanings. Research studies on organizations have identified **structural variables** such as the number of levels in the hierarchy, formalization (the amount of written documentation, as in policies and procedures manuals, job descriptions, and the like), standardization (the extent to which activities must be performed in a uniform manner), and degree of centralization (at what levels are decisions made?). **Form of structure** refers to the method of grouping employees together into work units, departments, and the total organization. Because a comprehensive look at structure is beyond the scope of this book, we provide a brief abstract of common forms of structure later in this module.[8]

Management Support Processes

Structure alone is not sufficient to achieve coordination and meet the needs of a thriving enterprise. Accordingly, companies invest considerable time and resources in establishing processes that support the typical core activities of a business. In a manufacturing organization, core activities will include new-product development, sales and order fulfillment, and customer service. **Management support processes** vary with the nature of the enterprise, but include planning, budgeting, quality management, recruitment and placement, training, project management, and other valued functions and processes. Decisions to build staff support departments and processes usually follow strategy and core transformation decisions. That is, investment in management support functions is justified if the purpose, core transformation processes, and structure call for additional capabilities to meet requirements of the business and industry. For example, in a university, to support the purpose of quality instruction, media and information technology staff are needed to aid the instructors as they bring in software, the Internet, DVD, and other media into the classroom and laboratory environments.

In the past, companies often chose to centralize management support groups at the corporate level. Staff members were then deployed to provide support or needed corporate controls depending on the situation. Typically, the reaction from lower management was negative, as staff personnel demanded both time and resources in carrying out their roles within divisions and departments of the company. The staff members too often carried the corporate perspective of control versus true service and support to managers and employees in the field. Today, the overall situation is much improved within most corporations as a result of three developments in organization design:

1. Corporations have experienced waves of downsizing both as a strategic move and to cut costs. Typically, there are fewer and smaller corporate staff work units, and service/support groups are co-located at lower levels of the organization.

2. Physical location of staff groups is changing as organizations develop. When service groups are located with operations groups, there is a greater sense of cooperation, teamwork, and identity with operations managers and work teams. Under the concept of the *distributed organization,* divisions and departments are encouraged to develop support groups that are close to the real operations action.[9] For example, rather than having a corporate-wide information systems group at company headquarters, in a multidivision firm, one division might have such a group to serve its own needs as well as accepting the additional task to serve all other company divisions. When this idea is extended to other staff support groups, a situation emerges in which divisions help each other and bring in new ideas, methods, and technologies to improve operations throughout the company.

3. Staff support activities are often outsourced to companies that can do it more efficiently. For example, Blue Shield of California has only a skeletal information systems support staff as most of the function has been outsourced to Electronic Data Systems (EDS) Corporation. *Outsourcing* means to farm out certain functions such as employee benefits administration, product distribution, manufacturing of specific product parts, credit processing, and other support and core activities. More will be said about this phenomenon in the network organization discussion that follows.

People

As we saw in some detail within Module 12 on group dynamics, our organization performance model is incomplete without specific attention to people. Because this factor is explored throughout the book, we note only that organizations have members with diverse attributes, demographic characteristics, and needs. Attributes include knowledge, skills, and abilities as well as learning styles and problem-solving styles. In many organizations, the collective knowledge sharing and learning becomes an organizational capability that is difficult for other companies to duplicate. Demographic characteristics are also important in building capabilities and improving organizational performance. Moreover, if organizations are to thrive, they must address employee needs, so employee satisfaction is potentially as important as the satisfaction of other stakeholders. We explore some issues connected with involving people in organization redesign later in this module.

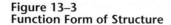

FORMS OF STRUCTURE

Simple Form

When organizations begin, a simple form of structure exists. The owner often starts the business alone and handles a wide range of responsibilities. With time, employees are added and a modest division of labor begins. In start-ups, people often help each other and do whatever is needed so that the organization will thrive. In the example of a dentist beginning his solo practice, she may initially prepare the office each day, take phone calls, order supplies, develop X-rays, and clean the office without much assistance. However, with increased patient volume, she will hire dental hygienists, a receptionist, dental assistants, billing specialists, and other people needed to run the business. Specialists take on specific duties, and their work is coordinated by the dentist. In the simple form, the owner/operator is key in identifying business needs and integrating work performed by others.

As the dental practice grows, the dentist begins to delegate responsibilities to others. Role **differentiation** takes place. People specialize in activities such as greeting patients, taking X-rays, inputting information, and scheduling appointments. Still, everything must come together for the patient as if the dentist was doing all the work. For example, the dentist must have time in her work schedule to supervise hygienists and see the patients after their teeth have been cleaned. Additionally, she must communicate any follow-up visits needed to patients and the appointments specialist. The complementary term to differentiation is thus **integration.** There can be division of labor and significant differentiation, but it must be integrated (or coordinated) to achieve patient satisfaction and quality results.

Functional Form

Organizations that group personnel on the basis of function performed, or work process, or specialized knowledge, training, or academic discipline have chosen the **functional form.** Typically, as the organization grows, differentiation of specialty units occurs, with managers appointed for each unit. (See Figure 13–3.) In contrast to the dental practice example, a start-up organization that has developed a product successfully will immediately have need for manufacturing, marketing, and distribution functions. A small production plant will typically have departments with names such as production, sales, finance, engineering, purchasing, information technology, and personnel. As the company grows, additional hierarchy is usually created. For example, as the plant expands from 500 to 3,000 employees, the company will see the need for greater capabilities in the human resources and security areas. The original one-person personnel office at the plant may be enlarged to include separate units such as plant security, labor relations, salary and benefits, training, and workers' compensation, each headed by a supervisor. As the personnel department grows, the department manager must ensure that her own supervisors and employees are communicating and must be concerned about how personnel services are being received by managers and employees throughout the plant. The plant manager, as a generalist, will be preoccupied with planning and coordination to a great extent, as departments must cooperate in getting quality products to the customer on time. A similar scenario exists for larger service companies, government offices, and nonprofit organizations.

Certain advantages and disadvantages are associated with the functional form of structure. Functional organizations tend to be efficient, and they work well when the business situation and outside environment are generally stable. Employees are hired into junior

Figure 13–3
Function Form of Structure

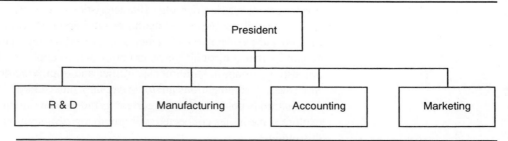

positions and develop skills under the direction of senior workers and managers. Employees then take on increasingly complicated tasks and grow through special assignments and applications of their skills. On the negative side, people in functional organizations often develop parochial viewpoints, and interdepartmental cooperation can be poor. Department goals often differ, and decisions are often pushed up the hierarchy, slowing deliberations and blocking needed changes. As the company's products and customers expand, other forms of structure appear more attractive to top management.

Product or Self-Contained Form

With increasing company size, product divisions or other self-contained units are often created to replace the functional organization. In our manufacturing example, a new product created at the company's plant may enjoy immediate success, diverting attention from mainstream products. If demand for the new product increases, there will be pressure to retool the factory or construct an entirely new facility. With greater diversification of products and greater diversification in customers and markets served, the company may choose to reorganize according to its major products. When this occurs, each product group gains discretion to design, produce, and distribute its products in ways that are consistent with the competitive environment. If the new product groups are organized in the same basic way [research and development (R&D), manufacturing, accounting, marketing], it can be argued that nothing new has occurred. Reduced size of the product groups will facilitate better communications and decisions, but old rigidities connected with the functional form may reoccur. The product groups still appear functional, and people may behave in the same ways. However, if the structure and support processes change to emphasize multispecialty teams or other forms of teamwork, a truly new form might exist. When personnel are grouped according to product line, service performed, or project, then a product or self-contained form of organization has been created.

At the corporate level, companies with the product form often have certain functions such as public relations, legal, compensation, and finance units as staff executive offices. These corporate units work with the president and product division personnel to establish certain common policies, practices, services, and controls for the entire company. Cases of staff/line cooperation and conflict are widely experienced in larger organizations. As noted earlier, recently there have been efforts to decentralize certain corporate and division staff units to operating groups so that the operating groups are better able to manage support services.

Advantages associated with the product form include greater responsiveness to a changing environment, improved cooperation and coordination within each product group, decision making closer to the customer, and improved customer satisfaction. Disadvantages include duplication of resources needed to run each division, difficulties coordinating company activities across products, and a reduction of concentrated knowledge and technical specialization compared to the functional form. Companies that move to greater product division independence find it more difficult to integrate activities and standardize across product lines.

Mixed or Hybrid Form

As a practical matter, many organizations have mixed or hybrid forms rather than the pure forms of structure described earlier. A **hybrid form** is a type of organization design that integrates a variety of structures and processes. One of the mixed forms is the *matrix* structure (Figure 13–4), which allows a focus on two or more dimensions at the same time.[10] For example, a pure matrix structure in an aerospace firm has both diverse functional engineering departments and project offices. Most employees work in functional departments under the day-to-day supervision of functional bosses but are also assigned to one or more project teams. Project managers work with functional managers and employees to ensure that projects are accomplished on time with high quality and attention to costs. Changing competitive environments in many industries have pushed companies toward matrix and other experimental forms. For global competition, some companies have organized by country and types of products. Other emerging forms of structure such as the new horizontal forms are discussed subsequently.

**Figure 13–4
An Illustration
of a Modified Matrix
Form of an SSC Software
Development Division**

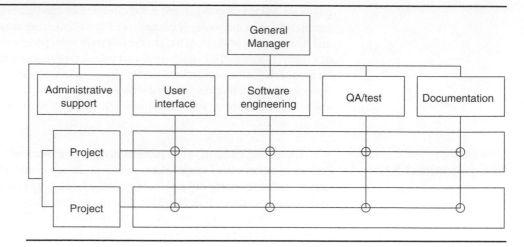

Horizontal Forms

A recent theme in the writings of organization design experts has been the need for greater horizontal or cross-unit coordination and integration within organizations of all types. The **horizontal structure** organizes people around core business processes such as new product development, sales and order fulfillment, and customer support.[11] Companies that have organized in this manner have typically first completed a change initiative called *business process reengineering.* In this instance, process refers to a set of interconnected tasks and activities that create value for the customer. Rather than focusing on traditional business functions, the emphasis is on mixed teams of employees working together to meet customer needs. The horizontal structure is an enhancement of ideas from sociotechnical systems theory (see Module 16). The object is to improve business results such as quicker time to market, increased focus on customer needs, and lower costs. Teams are the primary organizing focus of horizontal organizations,[12] and there is an emphasis on self-management. Characteristics of autonomous teams are evident, as the process team members design their own jobs, schedule work, conduct peer evaluations, measure processes and results, and are involved in extensive training and cross-training. The key is that teams now handle broad business activities (core processes) rather than depending on managers in traditional functional departments. The teams work closely together and have the information needed to meet performance goals. Instead of there being functional leaders, core process managers (sometimes called process owners) have responsibility for the entire process or subprocess.

The strengths of the horizontal form of structure are that it encourages all employees to focus on the customer, be flexible in responding to customer needs, encourage collaboration and teamwork, and be involved in training that supports sound decision making at the operations levels. Weaknesses are much the same as found in similar team-based settings. For example, it often requires a shift in company values and culture, there are difficulties experienced when functional managers must give up power and control, and extensive training for all concerned is needed if the shift in philosophy is to be successful. More will be said about the issues in our discussion of the team-based organization.

BUILDING THE TEAM-BASED ORGANIZATION

While companies have been based on a paradigm of the traditional, functional organization for the past century, this paradigm represents a mindset that has outworn its usefulness. Accordingly, tradition is giving way to a new cognitive map that emphasizes open-systems thinking, and flexible, team-based organization. Most companies face complex and unpredictable environments—not the stable and more certain environments of the past. They are confronted with global competition, e-commerce, industry consolidation, new partnerships and alliances, and the like, creating the need for much more internal and external coordination and collaboration. Within this context, decisions are often made on a decentralized basis, by teams that can use the best information at hand. One answer is a shift toward viewing the organization as "teams of teams," or the **team-based organization.**[13] This is a somewhat different perspective than described earlier in the section Horizontal Forms, in that a strong vertical structure remains in the form of management teams. The idea is that managers have a more global perspective of the way the organization functions and the management team needs to be involved in setting goals and in performance management.

When an organization faces new requirements and uncertainty, the organization design response can be informal or formal. Voluntary, informal cooperation to make the required decisions is preferred wherever possible. However, where demands are great, formal *linking mechanisms* such as liaison roles can be created to explicitly link two organizational units. A *liaison* is a member of one department, such as industrial engineering. A liaison engineer has responsibility for communicating and coordinating with another work unit such as a specific production line in the manufacturing plant. When problems on the production line occur, the work teams can rely on the liaison engineer for support. Another linking of this type can occur if individuals are assigned membership in two or more teams that are interdependent. That is, staffing is done to account for the idea that a person must spend time working with members of two different teams so that information is shared and good decisions are made. For example, in a project involving both hardware and software engineering, a systems engineer might be deployed to work half time with a software development team and half time with mechanical engineers to provide needed integration. Finally, people can serve as full-time *integrators,* independently working outside different work units to coordinate the activities of multiple interdependent groups. These different roles, along with task forces and other temporary improvement–seeking groups, turn out to be important elements of the team-based organization.

One challenge in building the team-based organization is whether or not to give a team all the resources it needs to do a complete job. In many situations, several technical disciplines are needed to develop a product or perform the core work. But full dedication of scarce employee time to one work unit is often a problem, in that a major contribution is needed at one phase of the work but not at others. The amount and timing of contributions is often at issue, and to create teams that are totally self-contained with full-time staff may not be efficient or effective. The question in creating relatively permanent and formal teams is often about the nature of the contribution and required interdependence. For example, although very different computer scientists and engineers might be needed in development of a software product, they might be able to do their work in separate functional teams and then rely on liaison people to stay abreast of basic software architecture for the product. In this situation the product team might appear to be a whole working team on paper, but most of the work is done in subteams according to specialty. In another scenario with a more complex product, the requirements might indicate that both hardware and software decisions need to be addressed on an ongoing basis, as one decision has serious repercussions on product features. In this situation, the team has a mix of specialists to address the problems in real time and people are physically co-located to enhance opportunities for informal communication.

Moving away from our technical examples, there are many cases where semiautonomous teams plan and carry out the work instead of management. In many industries, the core work is accomplished by teams, without formal team leaders. Leadership is shared, and people are cross-trained to carry out all activities. To deal with issues that cut across work groups, a **cross-team integrating team** is formed with membership drawn from all work groups. The cross-team integrating teams often have one outside person who has a broader perspective on the goals and tasks and who encourages all to take a holistic and systems viewpoint. This is the integrator role discussed earlier, an often vital role where decisions are largely decentralized within the organization. The extensive use of liaison roles, self-directed work teams, cross-team integrating teams, integrators, and supportive management teams is the hallmark of the team-based organization. In the future, organizations will continue to create very different roles for employees that will demand new skills and behaviors. The new roles require people to work on a peer basis rather than in a more traditional supervisory manner. We can expect to see fewer managers and few traditional supervisors but more people who actively address interunit problems and help create solutions that meet customer needs.

Designs for Global Competition

So far in this module, we have avoided the complexities associated with competing in a global economy. We appreciate that the age we live in demands learning and flexibility. While corporate planning and traditional management functions are still valuable, they must be loosened to recognize changing global business conditions. Leading management theorists and consultants believe that the field of organization design is at a crossroads.[14] The search across the global marketplace for competitive value and new customers leads companies to rethink ways of organizing. The basic options for competing globally have been carefully documented.[15] Companies are showing innovation in allowing business units to seek out new markets for their products and processes, to establish unique relationships with suppliers, and to create strategic alliances and joint ventures that leverage internal strengths. Most of the innovations cited earlier are available to both large and small firms, as seen in the proliferation of small firms conducting international business via the Internet.

Network Organizations

The idea of adopting forms of structure that can flexibly adjust to the global environment has great appeal to executives in leading organizations. One of the new forms, the **network organization,** blends traditional management concepts such as planning and controls with market concepts such as exchange agreements. In the literature, network organizations are variously called virtual network structures, modular structures, and the cellular form.[16] Network enterprises rely heavily on contracting out and outsourcing in lieu of owning and operating functions internally. Globalization and rapid improvements in information technology (IT) have made network organizations popular. We focus on one of the newer network forms, the "dynamic network," since it is so well suited to both relatively small start-ups and to firms that wish to quickly compete in larger markets.

Dynamic network organizations operate in fast-paced or chaotic environments. Businesses such as fashion, toy, and motion picture companies allow extensive outsourcing. The lead company might control few resources directly, or could simply be a broker. A contemporary example of a dynamic network firm is Technical and Computer Graphics (TCG), a privately held IT company in Australia. TCG creates a wide variety of products and services, including handheld data terminals and bar-coding systems. TCG is composed of 13 small firms, and each firm has its own purpose and ability to function alone. TCG firms specialize in one or more product categories, in hardware, or in software. Individual TCG firms pursue new-product ideas, often by establishing alliances with a major customer, an external development partner (for example, Toshiba), and other member firms within TCG. The TCG firm having the idea takes project leadership and secures advance orders from the principal customer. The development partner(s) provide compatible technology and equity capital. The lead TCG firm acts as entrepreneur, creates self-managing teams, and provides project oversight. The arrangement allows TCG to take on ambitious projects and to leverage ideas into new business opportunities.[17]

TCG has shared ownership, so revenues and profits can be monitored to the benefit of partners. Other dynamic network firms operate in the broker mode, and the broker firm may perform only a few functions. For example, Galoob Toys contracts with independent inventors and designers to create toy prototypes. It also contracts out manufacturing and packaging to companies in Hong Kong and China. The toys are shipped to Galoob's commissioned manufacturers in the United States, so distribution is also by contract. In this manner, Galoob is able to operate a medium-sized enterprise with only 100 employees.

In earlier years it was thought that network organizations would not contract out strategic functions, because they were central to the firm's distinctive competence. The literature suggests that while it is true that the firm must have a core competence, many functions thought to be strategic can be outsourced. A recent example is TiVo which has contracted out nearly everything.[18] TiVo has established strong partnerships with large manufacturing companies such as Sony and Hughes Electronics and has gained entry into huge markets. These required partnerships with Sony, Direct TV as well as Comcast, the number one cable operator in the United States. By focusing on technological development and contracting out manufacturing, marketing, customer service, distribution, and other functions, TiVo was able to quickly take a leadership role in the market for digital video recorders.[19]

In network organizations, contracts with partner companies can, of course, be stable and long term or simply reflect temporary market conditions. Nike Corporation is an example of a network firm that has at times invested heavily in partner companies in anticipation of long-term business relationships. Longer-term contracts with companies and the government in China can be altered if competitive conditions change, or Nike can shift production to Thailand or Indonesia to take advantage of higher quality or lower costs. Beyond coordinated contracting, companies can also pursue other legal contracts such as franchising and licensing agreements to increase revenues.

The Transnational Model of Organization

The transnational concept combines the idea of an integrated network of separate operations that are interdependent, with the model of a large multinational company having subsidiaries in far-flung country locations. This is an extremely complex structure that takes advantage of the latest technologies, global learning, and knowledge sharing. While being part of a large organization, subsidiaries have significant autonomy and are able to influence other organizational units. More and more, companies are moving value-adding functions out of the country of ownership and locating them in the best country for their execution. SKF, the Swedish bearing company, is an example. Each subsidiary takes the lead on developing a new product for its own country as well as for all other subsidiaries in the organization. Each subsidiary is thus dependent upon all the others and must rely on others to serve customers in the home market. This requires intensive communications and a philosophy of reciprocity and interdependence. Further, certain functions such as R&D and production scheduling have been located in neutral countries. The scheduling or supply function is performed by an integrating department located in Belgium. This department performs forecasting, scheduling, factory loading, and inventory control for all subsidiaries. The R&D department is located in Holland. As in Belgium, half the personnel are permanent, long-term residents of Holland. The other employees are engineers who rotate in and out of Holland from their home subsidiaries. These engineers come from the factories chosen to develop a particular product. The involvement of marketing and engineering representatives at the R&D facility allows for clear development of country-specific product specifications and the building of relationships and communications across the SKF company.[20] Other much larger organizations such as Phillips NV, Unilever, and Procter & Gamble are following the transnational pattern. Assets and resources are dispersed worldwide into highly specialized operations that are linked together through interdependent relationships. In a **transnational structure,** subsidiaries can shape worldwide operations by creating capabilities and products that can be shared across countries.[21]

COMPREHENSIVE APPROACHES TO ORGANIZATION DESIGN

Work design at the organizational level has developed over the past 40 years both as a field of academic study and as a process for improving organizations. A comparison of organizational design perspectives identified 10 design schools of thought or orientations that can be used to guide redesign programs. Three of the orientations are **comprehensive design approaches;** that is, they provide guiding models, they spell out design principles, they provide a redesign process, and they have an empirical track record of applications in different settings.[22] The orientations are information processing theory, sociotechnical systems theory,[23] and self-design.[24] Because coverage of all the leading perspectives is beyond the scope of this book, we briefly cover the *information processing* school of thought, *self-design,* and one emerging European-based approach known as **sustainable work systems** (SWS). Sociotechnical systems design will be covered in Module 16.

The Information Processing Approach

Jay Galbraith is credited with establishing the **information processing approach** to design that was introduced early in this chapter. According to information-processing theory, organization design is most usefully defined as a decision-making process. The decision-making process includes choices about goals, tasks to be accomplished, technology to be adopted, ways to organize, and ways to integrate individuals into the organization. The key is finding a balance or fit among these decisions and doing it in a way that is in step with the changing environment. Attention to customers, changing market needs, and desired outcomes mark the overall process as strategic organization design. A comprehensive redesign program might involve strategic-planning activities, reengineering of core work processes through (for example) computer and telecommunications enhancements, creation of a new formal structure, development of management systems to provide better coordination, and, finally, efforts to develop a new organizational culture, work-group norms, and values. Increasingly, information technology plays a role in each of these activities.[25]

The growth of information technology (IT) and its pervasive use in all sectors of the economy is a familiar trend at the beginning of the new millennium. Information technology—including voice messaging, online transaction processing, the intranet, electronic mail, teleconferencing, and other computer and telecommunications advances—are fundamentally changing the nature of the workplace.

IT advances have resulted in a new macro organization design model. The model (see Figure 13–5) is an outgrowth of the information-processing theory proposed by Jay Galbraith and further enhanced by David Nadler and Michael Tushman. Briefly, design begins with analysis of the company's business situation. Managerial assessments of the environment and business situation help determine the organization's goals and strategies. Goals and strategies in turn influence decisions about tasks and work processes. Based on these strategic decisions, managers decide the best ways to group employees into departments, coordinate department activities, and provide additional integration by adopting various support systems. Information technology and cultural variables influence or drive all design choices. Emergent behavior and business results are directly tied to the quality of managerial choices made throughout the design chain.

Now that an overall macro organization design model has been explained, we can demonstrate design dimensions and relationships with an example. Consider our earlier example of a dentist starting a new practice in a small town. She is not the only dentist in town, and she must gradually build a practice in competition with others in a 40-mile district. After five years of hard work, she has the largest practice in the district and has a

Figure 13–5
Macro Organization Design

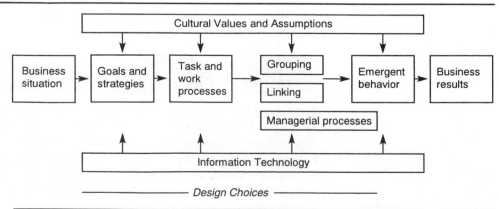

markedly different operation: She has a much larger office facility, an office manager, three dental hygienists to clean teeth, three dental assistants, an information specialist who deals with outside insurance companies and runs an automated billing system, and a part-time dentist who is just starting out and assists with patient overloads. Office cleaning has been contracted out, as have various supply, financial, tax, and legal services. The dentist has a sophisticated electronic data interchange (EDI) with vendors that automatically triggers purchase orders for supplies and speeds billing to major insurance carriers. Her entire staff is trained in data entry and inquiry activities. So what happened during this five-year period?

Initially the dentist was content with the idea of doing everything herself. Coordination was easy, because the dentist handled all transactions personally and a single brain did the integration. With increasing patient demand, variety of services needed, and related business activities, the dentist was in an overload situation. At first she made piecemeal decisions, such as hiring a receptionist and contracting a cleaning service. After a time she contacted a business consultant to rethink the entire practice. Over a one-year period, the dentist, the consultant, and an architect investigated new work design possibilities, did some strategic planning, developed an ideal practice model, created a set of plans for a new office facility, and developed business systems to complement the patient care changes. The dentist's husband and employees were included in the planning activities to contribute ideas and help with practical applications. The processing of information in the expanded practice was also a key consideration. At a predicted high volume of patient demands, the proposed future office required a new information processing capacity. The consultant helped the dentist create new capacity, primarily through new computer systems. The planning work culminated in a move to a new office facility, installation of state-of-the-art equipment, expanded staffing, and employee training activities. These activities occurred over a three-month period. Computers and IT innovations were used at each step of the way, and the dentist is now poised to adopt new technologies as they become available.

This case illustrates that total organization design requires an assessment of information processing requirements to perform a task that must be matched by new information processing capacity. That capacity can include a new structure or hierarchy, new roles and other mechanisms to help integrate the work, and new management systems. In the case of the small dental office, the choices were limited yet profound. While the office retains a pleasant and caring small-office work climate, the volume of work and productivity have leaped ahead. Both people and technical considerations were covered in the organization redesign.

In the dentist example, an architect was a vital member of the redesign team. Over the years, various authors have considered the task of designing or redesigning organizations in language that is very similar to the task of architectural design. Weick notes that designing organizations and designing buildings involves many of the same issues. Both types of design often stem from a vision or dream: "Whether one is a designer of organizations or of physical structures, the trick is to add density to a skeleton while retaining the vigor, quirks, and visual charm of that skeleton."[26] During the redesign process, new forms of the original dream are created, and good design work shows a history of multiple models created by participants. Ultimately, the value of design depends upon engagement of others and development of capabilities to self-organize. This type of thinking leads us to our second featured approach to organization design—the self-design model.

The Self-Design Approach

Self-design as an approach stems from work by Karl Weick, Susan Mohrman, and Thomas Cummings.[27] Consistent with the name, the **self-design approach** encourages managers to plan and to implement their own strategy/structure change programs. The design process is neither simple nor quick. Managers and employees are trained in project planning and in the diagnostic, process, and design skills needed to run the program. Self-design emphasizes the need for practice in design implementation, assessment, and continual modification of the organization. The process is dynamic and cyclical and encourages organizational learning through design experimentation.

Figure 13–6 shows the self-design process model. Briefly, the foundation for self-design is employee and manager training. People must prepare themselves for design activities

Figure 13–6   **Self-Design Process Model**

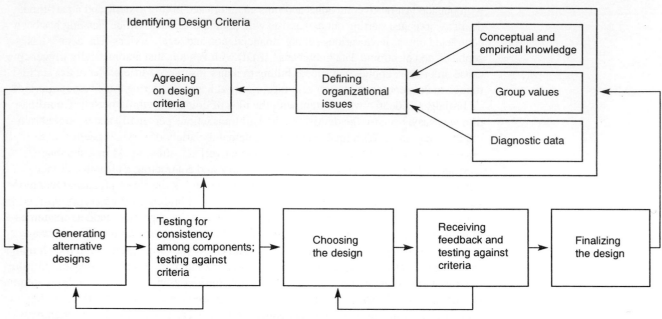

Source: Adapted from S. A. Mohrman and I. G. Cummings, *Self-Designing Organizations* (Reading, MA: Addison-Wesley, 1989).

that differ substantially from daily routines. New conceptual and empirical knowledge is needed to conduct a redesign project; otherwise, redesign will be superficial. Also, the values and outcomes the organization is trying to promote must be specified, and the people involved must undertake diagnostic work to determine how well the organization is currently performing. These activities lead to an initial definition of organizational issues and agreement on design criteria. Design criteria are standards that guide design activities by specifying the purposes the new design must satisfy. They help designers choose among design alternatives and influence the best design. From this point, the process is hard to delineate because the extent of change needed is unknown. The existing design might need fine-tuning, a competitor's design might be imitated, or drastic redesign might be conducted by the redesign team. Additionally, there may be a need to have different groups of employees generate designs, test them against design criteria and realities of the workplace, and decide on the best overall design. Even when the designers agree, the job is not over because different constituents must provide input to the final design. Constituents might force the work back to zero by questioning the original diagnostic work and design criteria. Clearly, this approach requires a tolerance for ambiguity and a willingness to consider multiple designs. The idea of creating a skeletal design and underspecifying designs early on so that users can finish the work is commonly tried today in product design and architectural design, but is quite novel in organizational design. The lesson is that details of structure and processes can be left to those who must live with the design on an ongoing basis.[28]

Although self-design is still new, it promises to be a fruitful approach for the 21st century. Self-design programs have been conducted within companies in the telecommunications, aerospace, electronics, software, and pharmaceutical industries. Activity 13–7W provides additional material on self-design theory plus an opportunity to redesign a small bakery operation using self-design concepts.

The Sustainable Work Systems Approach

The European-based **sustainable work systems (SWS)** approach considers economic, social, and ecological dimensions. It seeks to balance the individual, the organization, and the social sustainability of work.[29] It recognizes that design will proceed differently according to the country and institutional context and encourages full consideration of design effects at all levels. If design is truly sustainable, it will benefit individuals, work groups, the organization, community, and larger society. Accordingly, design is not seen simply as a response to an uncertain and changing competitive environment but it includes company impacts in the larger society. A dramatic example from Sweden is Svenska Handelsbanken. This banking organization faced extreme pressure to cut its staff during the early 1990s when the bank sector and other banks laid off more than 10,000 workers. But consistent with its 100-year-long record of no layoffs and its model of building employee competence, the bank was able to protect employees by simply not filling vacated positions (retirements, voluntary turnover). At the bank, each employee is aware of career paths and has a personal competence plan as well as individual and team goals to become more qualified.[30] SWS design also involves building organizational capabilities as well as reproduction and development of human resources. As with earlier approaches such as sociotechnical systems and self-design, quality of work–life balance is explicitly considered. For example, if creating a team-based organization collectively results in greater stress and inability to cope with workloads and pressures, redesign has failed. Employees must have the required resources (cognitive, emotional, and physical) and skills to cope with job demands and changes. In sustainable work systems, resources are not consumed but allowed to grow. Employees are not confined to an intensive and meaningless work reality but instead are allowed to learn and develop, to use their intelligence and creativity, and to collaborate and participate in improvement initiatives.[31]

SWS values can be summarized as follows:

1. Regeneration and development of human resources. The core concept of sustainable work systems is that the resources deployed are regenerated. Human resource values to be fostered include improving skills, knowledge, cooperation and trust, motivation, employability, constructive industrial relations policies, and participation in broader institutional and societal training systems.

2. A dual focus on quality of working life and competitive firm performance. Interdependencies here require an integrated approach to organization design.

3. The change process is guided in such a way that it builds capabilities for ongoing renewal and learning.

4. Sustainable work systems design provides a localized context for increasing employment levels, counteracting trends toward downsizing.

These values influence the way that change programs are conducted. The design process for SWS calls for extensive dialogue among stakeholders throughout different program phases. An assumption is that expanding design work beyond the management team to involve other stakeholders is an acknowledgment of the changing purpose of the organization. That is, the purpose is to provide benefit and value to stockholders, customers, suppliers, employees, and other significant external stakeholders. Success for the firm is considered broadly and goes beyond the notion of a balanced scorecard to consider both the industry and larger societal network. Managers, consultants, employees, suppliers, and customers are involved in establishing the specific change approach that will be used, as well as goals, design criteria, redesign teams, and other steps and results produced during redesign phases. This is a shift in thinking that is consistent with the emerging stakeholder view of the firm and it requires new concepts about measuring the results of redesign programs.

To date, few SWS redesign programs have featured high stakeholder involvement during the redesign process, so it can be said that theory leads practice on this point. In fact, some SWS redesign projects have neglected to include even the most obvious stakeholders, members of top management.[32] SWS, or reflective design, is ideally conducted in self-design fashion, in that it specifically allows for interruptions and critical review as stakeholders move in and out of the process. SWS design is reflective—a type of enlightened, self-critical design process that accepts differences in science and practice. Reflective design means to mirror or direct back the redesign work so that proper adjustments can be made along the way.

Stebbins and Shani have proposed an SWS redesign process known as eclectic self-design.[33] The steps are as follows:

1. Preliminary project planning involving consultants and stakeholders.

2. Review alternative design approaches (including the self-design approach) and their recommended change processes.

3. Gain management involvement in motivating the change effort and involving stakeholders in goal setting.

4. Establish design criteria acceptable to all stakeholders.

5. Create a parallel learning mechanism to guide the overall change initiative, including a steering body and network of design teams.

6. Provide personal and social support for work redesign experimentation conducted by design teams.

7. Conduct an impact analysis of how the proposed changes will affect various stakeholders.

8. Extend prototypes and new work processes to other units within the firm.

9. Document SWS outcomes and provide feedback to participants.

The SWS approach accepts and builds on self-design concepts (see Figure 13–6). Participants self-apply theory, methods, and practices. In keeping with self-design values, clients take ownership of the change process through high involvement at all stages. In a spirit of inquiry, all parties—including consultants—deliberate on ways to link theory and practice. Participants are encouraged to identify and explore dilemmas (for example, that a design preferred by employees might adversely affect other constituents). This promotes awareness of side effects, and recognition that good design work can have unintended consequences. Finally, as in self-design, SWS recognizes the iterative nature of design activities. Deliberations among stakeholders are needed to ensure balanced attention to goals and design criteria and to ensure balanced outcomes (quality, productivity, job satisfaction, customer satisfaction, and the like). These deliberations might cause design teams to rethink decisions made at earlier stages.

Bradbury has raised the issue of how women might redesign organizations, given that women have been largely excluded from the original design of organization structures.[34] She notes that while the vast majority of executives in *Fortune* 1000 companies are men, a significant proportion of executives in positions to manage ecological and organizational sustainability are women. She wondered what design criteria these women leaders might offer to the necessary task of organizational redesign for the postindustrial era. At a special conference on this topic, seven themes emerged, including "promoting sustainable development is a service, a calling (not ordinary work); generating a community of contributors is crucial to making sustainability work; consciously integrating techno-knowledge, business knowledge, and people knowledge in sustainability work is crucial; and generating productive encounters to enhance this work, for example, listening deeply and asking transformational questions." In transferring these criteria to strategy for design, the women executives included:

- Coordinating learning and input from all salient stakeholders in organizations.

- Creation of more multifunctional teams required to report regularly on key performance indicators, including metrics as well as illustrative stories that promote understanding of issues.

- Assertive attempts to uncover the voices of various stakeholders which have often been fragmented or never heard.

Reports on applied redesign programs to date heavily rely on managerial and employee perspectives, and little research has been conducted on the short- and long-term impacts of new designs on other stakeholders in company societal networks. Although the SWS theory is very new, it has been successfully used in aerospace, electronics, health care, product design, software development, banking, and government organizations.

WORK DESIGN—A CLOSER LOOK AT PROCESSES AND TEAMS

The newer theories of work design focus on processes and teams rather than on the design of individual jobs. This is a dilemma in industrial/organizational research, in that by far most social science studies have focused on the individual rather than the collective attitudes and behaviors in work teams.[35] Whether the topic is motivation, goal setting, efficacy, job characteristics, or performance, the emphasis is usually on the individual and recommendations for future research continue this.[36] The problem is that work is increasingly completed within a strong team and multiteam context, and we know little about the collective needs, goals, expectations, and rewards of the team and larger organization. We do not know how models and research findings about individuals extend to the collective, since this has not been a systematic topic of research. If the important defining characteristic of modern work is that it is performed within self-managing work teams and other collective settings, then we need to know more about motivation in work groups as well as how goals, roles, and learning are collectively established.

To appreciate what has been occurring in the way of work redesign at the team level, we must understand what consultants and managers have been doing in over 30 years of business process reengineering. Attention in work design is increasingly on creating a whole product or service and on producing results that meet customer requirements efficiently, effectively, and consistently. While redesign of cross-functional business processes is beyond the scope of this textbook and module, we briefly summarize some of the main concepts before turning our attention to work teams.

Business process redesign, or business process reengineering, involves fundamental rethinking of processes to achieve dramatic improvements in performance such as cost, quality, service, and speed (see Module 16). Redesign is not constrained by the existing organizational structure, but, instead, the analysis focuses on what happens at each step of the core process. Time delays, gaps, redundancies, and other inefficiencies are documented, and the designers work together to create a new process that is less complex, shorter, and involves fewer handoffs between people and between teams. The new processes include as few non-value-added steps as possible. A non-value-added step is one that fails to produce an identifiable and positive change in the product or service. Checkpoints are built into the process and are performed by members of work teams as the product or service is created, rather than by outside inspectors or managers. Where possible, duplication in data entry about the product or service status is reduced to avoid errors and time spent on reconciliation of conflicting data. Full use of available IT enables customers and employees to have access to the records and information needed to handle exceptions and inquiries.

Work groups created during process redesign programs have common goals, are aware of customer needs and requirements, and have all the resources needed to achieve results. The teams either create a whole product or service or own a discrete and meaningful part of a larger process. The teams are staffed by people having the depth and variety of skills needed to plan and control the process and to execute and maintain the process. People are multiskilled where possible so that they can perform each other's work. People have direct contact with customers, and thinking and problem solving are integrated with normal role performance.[37]

New organization designs rely on teams of all types. Modules 11 and 12 explored the nature and dynamics of teams. Recent research suggests that more than half of all major U.S. corporations are exploring some form of team-based work system.[38] The team systems in use are grouped into two categories: *self-directed work teams (SDWT)*[39] and *lean production teams.*[40]

Self-Directed Work Teams

Today, self-directed work teams are found in diverse industries and nations. A **self-directed work team** is a group of employees who share the responsibility for a whole task aimed at producing a product or service, supplied to either an external or internal customer. The team plans, regulates, and monitors progress of the whole task, solves day-to-day problems, and improves the process without significant involvement of managers and staff from service departments.[41] The self-directed team workplace features frequent job rotation, cross-training with an emphasis on learning, and a sound physical work environment. Teams decide specific work assignments, work schedules, work processes, quality control procedures, rewards, and other activities that might normally be performed by management or by other departments. For example, at Volvo, car assembly team members also participate in design decisions for the next car model. Teams are responsible for reducing costs and negotiating with suppliers on car components and materials. They also stay in touch with customers whose cars they are producing and answer questions about delivery dates.[42] The extent to which teams actually make decisions varies widely in different work team settings. To understand this point we must explore degrees of authority and group autonomy. Gulowsen developed the following detailed criteria of work team autonomy:[43]

1. The group has influence on qualitative goals.

2. The group has influence on quantitative goals.

3. The group decides on questions of internal leadership.

4. The group decides what additional tasks to take on.

5. The group decides when it will work.

6. The group decides on questions of production method.

7. The group determines the internal distribution of tasks.

8. The group decides on questions of recruitment.

9. The group members determine their individual production methods.

In work designs that rely on SDWTs, technical systems are not viewed as dominant but rather as (for example) equipment and operations to be shaped through worker input. Emphasis is instead on work processes, local and autonomous regulation of processes, participation, and learning, with minimal specification and direction from above.[44]

Lean Production Teams

The Japanese influence on the movement toward teams in industry is unmistakable. The label **lean production teams** is synonymous with Japanese manufacturing methods and facilities. Lean production systems at companies such as Toyota feature customer-driven priorities, just-in-time delivery between customers and suppliers, low internal inventory, reduced steps in work operations, high worker participation via work teams, and broad team responsibilities for monitoring quality and planning work activities. The commitment to continuous improvement in all aspects of operations is also strong. In the United States, Denso Manufacturing (formerly Nippondenso Manufacturing) of Battle Creek, Michigan, provides a clear example:

> We saw machinery tightly packed together, with automated movement of parts from machine to machine such that raw materials flowed quickly through to the loading dock where trucks were dispatched every 12 minutes as part of a just-in-time delivery system. Workers were hustling from station to station; forklift trucks were moving quickly to deliver raw materials and unload finished product. Despite the hustle, we observed that people also found time to make eye contact, smile, and even briefly converse with us as visitors. There was little inventory visible anywhere in the plant. In each work area, there were highly visible clusters of red, yellow, and green lights to indicate when the line was running (green light) and when workers wanted to consult about a possible quality or inventory problem (yellow light), and when a worker needed to shut down the line (red light). Further, near each part of the production line, a "hot corner" meeting space was provided for each team, featuring a table, chairs, and a filing cabinet. Charts were displayed tracing key "measurables" on quality, safety, productivity, progress in building skills among team members, as well as rewards and communications information.[45]

At Denso Manufacturing, people give their own work areas a personal touch with houseplants, pictures, cartoons, and other personal effects—in both production and administrative office environments. The entire Battle Creek plant environment is designed to encourage communications and emphasize a common purpose. Early evidence suggests that lean production systems such as the one in Battle Creek are highly dependent on team concepts, although the degree of actual team control over work operations and decision making and employee reaction to the system deserve further research.

Scientific Management

The **scientific management** approach, often referred to as the **job engineering** approach, was coined by Frederick W. Taylor and further developed by his associates, Frank and Lillian Gilbreth.[46] As a supervisor in a manufacturing shop, Taylor noticed that workers were operating their machines at differing speeds; that workers were devising their own methods to perform their duties; that there was no incentive to increase production; and that many workers did not have the desire, skills, or training to perform their duties appropriately. Trained in mechanical engineering, Taylor set out to develop a way in which management and workers could develop the most efficient work procedures. Through experimentation he was able to determine how tasks were to be performed, the proper tools necessary for maximum efficiency, and the amount of work that an employee could be expected to perform.

Taylor's comprehensive strategy embodies four major ideas about work design. First, work is a cooperative effort by management and workers to ascertain the one best way of performing a job. Second, tasks should be specialized, and work should be designed, wherever possible, so that the individual performs a minimal number of tasks that are easy to master. Third, work should be studied using scientific methods to quantitatively determine how each segment of the work or task should be performed regardless of who actually performs the task. There should be standardization of tasks, methods, and time frames as key work design criteria. And finally, managers should train, develop, and supervise employees so that the work is performed according to scientific methods, and managers should motivate employees by giving monetary bonuses accordingly.

Scientific management was an innovative concept in the early 1900s that led quite naturally to job analysis. The emphasis was to develop efficiency through specialized and standardized tasks. Taylor's work also led to an era of time and motion studies that sought to eliminate wasteful human movements and to simplify work patterns.

Today, as production work shifts to dispersed low-wage settings around the world, both lean production methods and scientific management philosophies abound. When the challenge is to socialize rural workers into modern factory settings, then older social and economic theories, objectives, and values are applied. If the issue is subsistence or rationalization of work, then work simplification and other scientific management principles would seem to apply, particularly if production work continues to migrate to the lowest wage cost settings. Scientific management work design methods may be preferred, with emphasis on managerial and engineering specification of work activities.

Intensive Work Systems versus Sustainable Work Systems

The globalization of business through free trade, deregulation, and emergence of new forms of organization structure raise many issues about work–life quality for all employees, including knowledge workers. Some observers argue that even where companies have chosen the "high road" (based on high skills, high employee involvement, and competition through quality and innovation) intensive work can be the result. At the individual level, work intensity emerges from imbalances: between an individual's resources and work demands; and between the individual's needs and work opportunities. The result can be stress, burnout, and "rustout" (inability to use skills and capabilities).[47] In flexible, lateral organizations where bureaucracy and rules are reduced, the need for personal and team judgment has both positive and negative consequences. People have the opportunity for personal growth, variety, skill development, and interaction with others at work, but also face lack of job security, role ambiguity, role conflict, and unrelenting work pressure.[48] The new work roles require continuous learning which can also be a source of stress.

Perhaps the most important imbalance is private life and work. Work–life balance is an issue that is growing in importance, especially for those interested in sustainable work systems design. Companies such as IDEO have discovered multiple ways to achieve work–life balance for knowledge workers while maintaining a culture of renewed energy and creativity.[49] At IDEO, employees are able to gravitate toward projects and client companies that fit their interests. They meet weekly in small and separate buildings to share information on personal and team activities, to discuss new technologies, and to share innovative work practices. They have time to meet private life obligations, to join others at work in weekly activities such as bike rides, and to participate in educational activities in the community. The key seems to be that the IDEO organization has managerial processes and practices that contribute to a sense of job challenge, security, and personal support. High quality of work–life balance, solid financial support, and industry recognition that IDEO is a world leader in product design all indicate that IDEO is a sustainable work system.

Work Design at the Individual Level

Past editions of this book have devoted significant coverage to individual-focused work design frameworks such as the job characteristics model and job enrichment.[50] Since it is useful to explore how jobs are changing within team settings, we offer Activity 13–2, Colonial Automobile Association, and Activity 13–3, The Woody Manufacturing Company, to explore additional concepts in work design at the individual, team, and organizational levels. Your instructor will provide handouts on the Job Characteristics Model and other course materials needed to complete the selected activities.

SUMMARY

Under increasingly competitive conditions, companies are exploring ways of organizing human and other resources. Structure is important in organization design, but as shown in the star model, many other dimensions must be considered in creating the total organization. The size of the organization is a factor, and companies can choose the simple and functional forms of structure if competing locally. As the organization grows, many new forms of structure are available, especially if the firm wishes to compete globally. Team-based organizations are becoming prevalent, and teams play important roles in emerging forms of structure. Three comprehensive design approaches were discussed, and they are available to managers hoping to design or redesign organizations to meet competitive challenges. The sustainable work systems viewpoint is gaining ground, and an eclectic redesign process can be used to guide most any redesign change program.

Study Questions

1. Define *sustainability*. What does it mean in organization and work design?

2. How does the Galbraith Star Model complement the second model, factors affecting organization performance?

3. What are the common forms of structure for small- to medium-sized organizations?

4. List the main forms of structure, and describe their advantages and disadvantages.

5. List and discuss the main elements of a team-based organization.

6. Why is the network organization well-suited to global competition?

7. Compare and contrast the information processing and sustainable work systems approaches to organization redesign.

8. How are self-directed work teams different from lean production teams?

9. What is scientific management, and why is it relevant today?

Endnotes

1. For a summary of sustainable work systems concepts and processes, see P. Docherty, J. Forslin, and A. Shani (eds.), *Creating Sustainable Work Systems* (London: Routledge, 2008); and D. Boud, P. Cressey, and P. Docherty, *Productive Reflection at Work* (London: Routledge, 2006).

2. For a good review of maps and managers, see C. M. Fiol and A. S. Huff, "Maps for Managers: Where Are We? Where Do We Go from Here?" *Journal of Management Studies* 29, no. 3 (1992), pp. 267–85.

3. J. R. Galbraith, *Organization Design* (Reading, MA: Addison-Wesley, 1977); J. R. Galbraith, "Organizing to Deliver Solutions," *Organizational Dynamics* (Fall 2002); and J. R. Galbraith, *Designing Organizations: An Executive Guide to Strategy, Structure, and Process* (San Francisco: Jossey-Bass, 2002).

4. R. Daft, *Organization Theory and Design,* 8th ed. (Cincinnati, OH: South-Western, 2007).

5. T. D. Jick, "The Vision Thing," in T. D. Jick, *Managing Change: Cases and Concepts* (Boston: Irwin, 1993), pp. 142–48.

6. J. C. Taylor and D. P. Felten, *Performance by Design: Sociotechnical Systems in North America* (Englewood Cliffs, NJ: Prentice Hall, 1993).

7. F. V. Kosikowski, "Cheese," *Scientific American* (May 1985), pp. 88–99.

8. For foundation material on structure and design, see Daft, *Organization Theory and Design.* For an expanded look at forms of structure, see for example, R. J. Kramer, *Organizing for Global Competitiveness: The Matrix Design* (New York: The Conference Board, 1994), Report 1110.

9. J. R. Galbraith, *Competing with Flexible Lateral Organizations,* 2nd ed. (Reading, MA: Addison-Wesley, 1994).

10. R. Daft, *Organization Theory and Design.*

11. F. Ostroff and D. Smith, "The Horizontal Organization," *The McKinsey Quarterly,* no. 1 (1992), pp. 148–68.

12. Ibid.

13. S. Mohrman, S. Cohen, and A. Mohrman, Jr., *Designing Team-Based Organizations: New Forms for Knowledge Work* (San Francisco: Jossey-Bass, 1995).

14. See R. M. Tomasko, *Rethinking the Corporation: The Architecture of Change* (New York: Amacor, 1993); and D. A. Nadler and M. L. Tushman, *Competing by Design: The Power of Organizational Architecture* (New York: Oxford University Press, 1997).

15. See, for example, Kramer, *Organizing for Global Competitiveness.*

16. Daft.

17. For a closer look at network organizations, see R. Miles and C. Snow, "Organizations: New Concepts for New Forms," *California Management Review* 28, no. 3 (1986); C. C. Snow, R. E. Miles, and J. Coleman, "Managing 21st Century Network Organizations," *Organizational Dynamics* (Winter 1989), pp. 18–30; and R. Miles, C. Snow, J. Mathews, G. Miles, and H. Coleman, Jr., "Organizing in the Knowledge Age: Anticipate the Cellular Form," *Academy of Management Executive* 11, no. 4 (1997), pp. 7–24; M. Schilling and H. Steensma, "The Use of Modular Organization Forms: An Industry Level Analysis," *Academy of Management Journal* 44, no. 6 (2001), pp. 1149–68.

18. J. Linder, "Transformational Outsourcing," *Sloan Management Review* (Winter 2004), pp. 52–58.

19. Daft.

20. J. Galbraith, *Competing with Flexible Lateral Organizations* (Reading, MA: Addison-Wesley, 1994).

21. S. Ghoshal and C. Bartlett, "The Multinational Corporation as an Inter-Organizational Network," *Academy of Management Review* 15 (1990), pp. 603–25.

22. M. W. Stebbins and A. B. Shani, "Organization Design: Beyond the 'Mafia' Model," *Organizational Dynamics* (Winter 1989), pp. 18–30.

23. For additional material on the evolution of STS theory, see W. A. Pasmore, *Designing Effective Organizations: The Sociotechnical Systems Perspective* (New York: Wiley, 1988); Taylor and Felten, *Performance by Design;* and A. B. Shani and O. Elliott, "Sociotechnical Systems in Transition," in W. Sikes, A. Drexler, and J. Grant (eds.), *The Emerging Practice of Organization Development* (La Jolla, CA: University Associates, 1988), pp. 187–98.

24. S. A. Mohrman and T. G. Cummings, *Self-Designing Organizations: Learning How to Create High Performance* (Reading, MA: Addison-Wesley, 1989).

25. The information processing school of thought has a long history. See for example, J. R. Galbraith, *Designing Complex Organizations* (Reading, MA: Addison Wesley, 1973); Galbraith, *Organization Design;* Nadler and Tushman, *Competing by Design;* and J. R. Galbraith, *Designing the Global Corporation* (San Francisco: Jossey-Bass, 2000).

26. K. E. Weick, "Rethinking Organizational Design," in R. J. Boland, Jr., and F. Collopy (eds.) *Managing as Designing* (Stanford: Stanford Business Books, 2004), pp. 37–53.

27. There is a growing literature on self-design. See, for example, B. Hedberg, P. Nystrom, and W. Starbuck, "Camping on Seesaws: Prescriptions for a Self-Designing Organization," *Administrative Science Quarterly* 21 (1976), pp. 41–65; Mohrman and Cummings, *Self- Designing Organizations;* K. E. Weick, "Organization Design: Organizations as Self-Designing Systems," *Organizational Dynamics* (Autumn 1977), pp. 31–46; and K. E. Weick, "Organizational Redesign as Improvisation," in G. P. Huber and W. H. Glick (eds.), *Organizational Change and Redesign* (New York: Free Press, 1993), pp. 346–76.

28. For early work on sustainable work systems as a design approach, see, for example, P. Docherty, J. Forslin, and A. B. Shani (eds.), *Creating Sustainable Work Systems: Emerging Perspectives and Practice* (London: Routledge, 2002); J. Forslin, "Regenerative Work," in S. Einarsen and A. Skogstad (eds.), *Det Gode Arbeidsmiljo* (Bergen: Fagboksforlaget, 2000); and R. Murphy and C. I. Cooper, *Healthy and Productive Work: An International Perspective* (London: Taylor and Francis, 2000).

29. P. Docherty, M. Kira, and A. B. (Rami) Shani (eds.), *Creating Sustainable Work Systems,* 2nd ed (London: Routledge, 2008); D. Boud, P. Cressey, and P. Docherty (eds), *Productive Reflection at Work* (London: Routledge, 2006); and P. Docherty, J. Forslin, A. B. Shani, and M. Kira, "Emerging Work Systems: From Intensive to Sustainable," in Docherty, Forslin, and Shani (eds.), *Creating Sustainable Work Systems.*

30. Docherty, SWSI, p. 122.

31. J. Post, L. Preston, and S. Sachs, *Redefining the Corporation: Stakeholder Management and Organizational Wealth* (Stanford, CA: Stanford University Press, 2002).

32. M. Stebbins, T. Freed, A. Shani, and K. Doerr, "The Limits of Reflective Design in a Secrecy-Based Organization," in D. Boud, P. Cressey, and P. Docherty (eds.), *Productive Reflection at Work* (London: Routledge, 2006).

33. M. W. Stebbins and A. B. Shani, "Eclectic Design for Change," in Docherty, Forslin, and Shani (eds.), *Creating Sustainable Work Systems,* pp. 201–12.

34. H. Bradbury, "Webs Rather Than Kevlar," in Boland, Jr., *Managing as Designing,* pp. 113–120.

35. R. Steers, D. Mowday, and D. Shapiro, "The Future of Work Motivation Theory," *The Academy of Management Review* 29, no. 3 (2004), pp. 379–87.

36. E. Locke and G. Latham, "What Should We Do about Motivation Theory? Six Recommendations for the Twenty-First Century," *Academy of Management Review* 29, no. 3, (2004), pp. 388–403.

37. See T. Hupp, C. Polak, and O. Westgaard, *Designing Work Groups, Jobs, and Work Flow* (San Francisco: Jossey-Bass, 1995); and B. Johann, *Designing Cross-Functional Business Processes* (San Francisco: Jossey-Bass, 1995).

38. P. Osterman, "How Common Is Workplace Transformation and Who Adopts It?" *Industrial and Labor Relations Review* 47, no. 2 (January 1994).

39. P. Van Amelsvoort and G. Van Amelsvoort, *Designing and Developing Self-Directed Work Teams* (Vlijmen, The Netherlands: ST-GROEP, 2000).

40. C. Gershenfeld et al., "Japanese Team-Based Work System in North America: Explaining the Diversity," *California Management Review* 37, no. 1 (Fall 1994).

41. F. E. Emery and M. Emery, "Participative Design: Work and Community Life, Parts 1–3," in M. Emery (ed.), *Participative Design for Participative Democracy* (Canberra, Australia: Australian National University, Center for Continuing Education, 1989); and Taylor and Felten, *Performance by Design.*

42. N. Adler and P. Docherty, "Bringing Business into Sociotechnical Theory and Practice," IMIT Publication, 1997, p. 2.

43. L. Gulowsen's work is based on P. G. Herbst, *Alternative to Hierarchies* (Leiden, The Netherlands: Nijhoff, 1976); E. Thorsrud, "Democracy at Work: Norwegian Experiences with Non-bureaucratic Forms of Organization," *Journal of Applied Behavioral Science* 13, no. 3 (1977), pp. 410–21; M. Elden, "Sociotechnical Systems Ideas as Public Policy" in "Norway: Empowering Participation through Worker-Managed Change," *Journal of Applied Behavior Science* 22, no. 3 (1986), pp. 239–55.

44. P. Van Amelsvoort and G. Van Amelsvoort, *Designing and Developing Self-Directed Work Teams* (Vlijmen, The Netherlands: ST-GROEP, 2000), p. 7.

45. Cutcher-Gershenfeld et al., "Japanese Team-Based Work System," p. 47.

46. F. W. Taylor, *The Principles of Scientific Management* (New York: Harper & Row, 1911); and F. Gilbreth and L. Gilbreth, *Cheaper by the Dozen* (New York: Harper & Row, 1947).

47. P. Docherty, J. Forslin, A. B. Shani, and M. Kira, "Emerging Work Systems: From Intensive to Sustainable," in Docherty, Forslin, and Shani (eds), *Creating Sustainable Work Systems*, pp. 3–14.

48. S. Mohrman and S. Cohen, "When People Get Out of the Box: New Relationships, New Systems," in A. Howard (ed.), *The Changing Nature of Work* (San Francisco: Jossey-Bass, 1995).

49. Stebbins and Shani, "Eclectic Design for Change," pp. 201–12.

50. J. Hackman and G. Oldham, *Work Redesign* (Reading, MA: Addison-Wesley, 1980).

Activity 13–2: Colonial Automobile Association

Objectives:

a. To analyze jobs on different job dimensions.

b. To understand job enrichment.

c. To redesign jobs within a team context.

Task 1:

Read the Colonial Automobile Association case, with special focus on Susan Quayle's job as a claims adjuster. You are to work alone to complete the worksheet that follows.

a. With the instructor's direction, list knowledge and skills Susan must have to perform her job. Then group the knowledge, skills, and other features of her job under the various job dimension categories. For example, under Skill Variety, the job requires computer skills and telephone skills among others. Also, for an example of Task Identity, simple claims allow Susan to do the whole job from start to finish while more complex claims involve other people inside and outside the office.

b. After listing required knowledge, skills, and other features under the five dimensions, rate Susan's job using the worksheet's seven-point scale. Assign a score for each of the five dimensions, and enter your scores to the left.

c. Based on case information, predict Susan's degree of general job satisfaction using the same scale.

Task 2:

a. Individuals share their scores with other members of their group and arrive at a consensus rating.

b. The instructor will provide Susan's own ratings for comparative purposes. High and low scores will be discussed.

c. The instructor will provide a brief lecture on job characteristics and job enrichment within a team context.

Task 3:

a. Groups discuss their ideas for team-based handling of the work as well as individual job enrichment.

b. Groups prepare a list of the most promising options for job and team design.

c. A spokesperson from each group reports to the entire class.

d. The instructor comments on the proposed changes in the context of a team-based organization.

This activity was developed by Michael Stebbins, Professor Emeritus at the Orfalea College of Business, California Polytechnic State University, San Luis Obispo, CA. We are grateful to Professor Stebbins.

Case Study: Colonial Automobile Association

Introduction

In 2006, Susan Quayle interviewed for a position with Colonial Automobile Association (CAA), in hopes of landing a job as a claims adjuster with the firm. The job allowed her to return to her home town in Palo Alto, where she could be near her mother, who suffered from serious health problems. Two days following her interview, Susan received a call from John Taylor, manager of the claims department, offering her a position as an adjuster—level one. All college graduates started at this level.

Prior to arriving at the Palo Alto office, Susan spent three weeks at CAA's training center in San Francisco. While there, Susan completed training on the purpose of claims work and the company's transaction processing system. Emphasis was on following the required steps in claims adjustment and entering data at each stage of the claims process. The trainers also emphasized the importance of maintaining "a high level of customer service." Management believed that this philosophy would translate into high productivity. All adjusters were measured on claims processed and closed out at the end of each month of the year.

The productivity theme carried over into the motivation approach at CAA, which stressed individual rewards based largely on volume of claims processed. Subrogation contests, an effort to retrieve money from outstanding claims in favor of CAA, was another area in which management tried to motivate employees by offering bonuses to adjusters who collected old, outstanding claims against other insurers. Following training at the San Francisco office, Susan began working in Palo Alto.

The CAA Palo Alto Office

The Palo Alto office was large and employed 20 other entry-level adjusters at a modest salary of $3,000 per month plus benefits. In total, there were 30 people employed in claims positions. Pay averaged $45,000 in the department, recognizing the more experienced employees and the periodic bonuses. Each adjuster was responsible for processing 10 new claims daily. The nature of these claims ranged from auto accidents to vandalism or other property damage. In addition to new claims filed daily, each adjuster was responsible for all assigned pending claims. In the more complex cases, claims involved working with multiple inside and outside parties. For example, a claim could involve (1) the CAA client, (2) the claimant, (3) the claimant's insurance company, (4) one or more car rental agencies, (5) an injured party, (6) medical experts for review of medical claims, (7) contacts at auto body and paint shops, (8) the police and police reports, and (9) mediators who would determine liability (who was at fault).

When Susan arrived at her desk, she found that she had inherited 200 pending claims. These files belonged to her predecessor. Overwhelmed with the work load and wondering where to start, she met with her supervisor and talked with other claims representatives. Most other adjusters had pending claims in the low- to mid-200's, and co-workers told her not to worry about the situation. This was normal. The hardest thing seemed to be dealing with customers who had worked with her predecessor, and she had to convince them that she was able to resolve the issues.

Each day, the telephone rang as soon as she arrived at her cubicle. Typically, she dealt with upset and agitated customers. As she was often unable to help callers immediately, she kept good notes and promised to return the call as soon as she could find a solution. The days went by very fast, but Susan began to tire of the endless phone calls from disgruntled customers and other contacts, as well as conversations with new claimants.

With time, Susan learned how to deal with the auto body shops and their quotes and began to rely less upon internal CAA contacts such as the legal and medical departments. Energetic and eager to get the job done, Susan maintained a positive attitude toward her job during the first few months. However, her outlook began to change as more claims rolled in each day, mail began to pile up, customers continued to complain, management pressure to reach monthly targets mounted, and outside parties demanded quick resolution of claims. To say the least, Susan was distressed.

In after-work conversations with friends and co-workers, Susan found that others faced similar challenges and pressures. One adjuster felt that Susan was taking the problems too seriously. "Everyone is overworked and underpaid. Just take a day or two off once in a while," he said. Susan brought up management's goal of meeting monthly claim targets and was told by another adjuster that "management doesn't really care as long as we come close. But the worst thing that can happen is that your name is posted at the end of the month with the number of completed claims next to it." She added, "I would rather have my name and claims posted than have my picture on the 'adjuster of the month' wall out front." As for the contests, she told Susan not to bother with subrogation and other incentives because "the bonus is not worth the time spent on each file." Another noted that "Bill Baron wins every time anyway, because he has been here the longest (18 months) and knows how to cut corners."

Susan began to consider her future at CAA. Reflecting on her job, she felt that the work seemed to call on a number of her best talents and skills. Also, it seemed that she had freedom to decide when to work on things, and she liked the feeling of closing out a file with a satisfied customer. But at the same time, she began to hate the sight of a secretary handing her a new claim. Claims outside her competence seemed to fall into legal, medical, and other technical black holes and she was not sure about how to stay on top of the more complex claims. Things would get better with time, but the job was far from ideal. It seemed that the hectic pace of work and constant interruptions were driving adjusters out the door and that there were few experienced people around to provide support. Surely there had to be a better way to run the business, but she was not sure that she wanted to stay around long enough to be part of the solution.

Name _____   Date _____

JOB DESIGN WORK SHEET

Scale: 1 = Extremely low   5 = Somewhat high
           2 = Very low   6 = Very high
           3 = Somewhat low   7 = Extremely high
           4 = Neither high nor low

_____   *Skill variety.* The degree to which the job requires a variety of activities that challenge a worker's skills and talents.

Examples of this in the CAA case:

_____

_____

_____

_____   *Task identity.* The degree to which a job requires completion of a whole and identifiable piece of work (doing a job from start to finish).

_____

_____

_____

_____   *Task significance.* The degree to which the job has a substantial impact on the lives or work of other people.

_____

_____

_____

_____   *Autonomy.* The degree to which the job gives freedom, independence, and discretion to the individual in scheduling the work and carrying it out.

_____

_____

_____

_____   *Feedback from the job.* The degree to which the worker, in carrying out the work activities, gets direct and clear information about the effectiveness of her or his performance.

_____

_____

_____

_____   *Overall job satisfaction.* A global rating of satisfaction with all aspects of the job.

_____

_____

_____

Activity 13–3:
The Woody
Manufacturing
Company

Objective:

To apply the concepts learned in the module about work design at the individual, group, and organizational levels in designing the Woody Manufacturing Company.

Task 1 (Individual Assignment):

a. Read the following case study of the Woody Manufacturing Company.

b. Review the module carefully, and choose the design orientation that you feel can best guide you in developing the design for Mr. Woody.

c. Write down your thoughts on alternative management structures, pay systems, and allocation of work to individuals and groups.

Task 2 (Team Assignment):

a. Get together in your team and develop a comprehensive proposal for Mr. Woody that, if followed, would help him fulfill his vision.

b. Prepare a 5-minute presentation. Your typewritten team proposal is due prior to your team presentation in Mr. Woody's conference room.

Case Study: The Woody Manufacturing Company

Mr. Woody, the owner/operator of a small furniture company specializing in the manufacture of high-quality bar stools, has experienced a tremendous growth in demand for his products. He has standing orders for $750,000. Consequently, Mr. Woody has decided to expand his organization and attack the market aggressively. His stated mission is "to manufacture world-class products that are competitive in the world market in quality, reliability, performance, and profitability." He would like to create a culture where "pride, ownership, employment security, and trust" are a way of life. He just finished a set of interviews, and he has hired 32 new workers with the following skills:

Four skilled craftspeople.

Ten people with some woodworking experience.

Twelve people with no previous woodworking experience or other skills.

One nurse.

One schoolteacher.

One bookkeeper.

Three people with some managerial experience in nonmanufacturing settings.

Mr. Woody (with your help) must now decide how to design his new organization. This design will include the management structure, pay system, and the allocation of work to individuals and groups. The bar stool–making process has 15 steps:

1. Wood is selected.
2. Wood is cut to size.
3. Defects are removed.
4. Wood is planed to exact specifications.
5. Joints are cut.
6. Tops are glued and assembled.
7. Legs/bases are prepared.
8. Legs/bases are attached to tops.

9. Bar stools are sanded.
10. Stain is applied.
11. Varnish is applied.
12. Bar stools are sanded.
13. Varnish is reapplied.
14. Bar stools are packaged.
15. Bar stools are delivered to the customer.

Mr. Woody currently manufactures three kinds of bar stools (pedestal, four-legged corner, and four-legged recessed). There is no difference in the difficulty of making the three types of bar stools. Major cost variations have been associated with defective wood, imprecise cuts, and late deliveries to customers. Mr. Woody must decide how to organize his company to maintain high quality and profits.

He has thought about several options. He could have some individuals perform the first step for all types of bar stools; he could have an individual perform several steps for one type of bar stool; or he could have a team perform some combination of steps for one or more bar stools. He wonders whether how he organized would affect quality or costs. He's also aware that while the demand for all types of bar stools has been roughly equal over the long run, there were short periods where one type of bar stool was in greater demand than the others. Because Mr. Woody wants to use his people effectively, he has committed an expert in work design to help him set up an optimal organization.

Module 14

Creativity and Innovation*

LEARNING OBJECTIVES

After completing this module, you should be able to

1. Describe the creative process.
2. Identify the traits or characteristics that are related to individual creativity.
3. Explain the difference between creativity and innovation.
4. Describe the stages and the different types of innovation.
5. Gain insight into the key issues associated with the management of creativity and innovation processes.
6. Understand the interplay among human behavior, group behavior, creativity, and innovation.

KEY TERMS AND CONCEPTS

Adaption–innovation model
Administrative innovation
Creative process
Creativity
Creativity-relevant skills
Domain-relevant skills
Dual ladders
Emotional intelligence
Expertise
Incremental innovation
Innovation
Innovation process

Intelligence level
Intrinsic motivation
Person-oriented approach
Process innovation
Process-oriented approach
Product innovation
Product-oriented approach
Radical innovation
System-maintaining innovation (SMI)
System-transforming innovation (STI)
Task motivation

*This module was revised and modified in collaboration with Dr. Carol Sexton. We are grateful to Dr. Sexton.

MODULE OUTLINE

Premodule Preparation

   Activity 14–1: Exploring Creativity in an Organizational Setting: 3M's Post-it Note Pads Case

Introduction

What Is Creativity?

   The Creative Person

   Distinguishing between Creativity and Innovation

   Emotional Intelligence and Creativity

   Motivation and Creativity

The Organizational Context of Creativity

   The Adaption–Innovation Model

   Creativity and Commitment

   Creativity and Social Influence

Developing the Creative Process within the Organization

   Team Creativity

   From Creativity to Innovation

Organizational Innovation

   Types of Innovation

   Stages of the Innovation Process

Key Elements That Influence the Innovation Process

   Key Players and Roles

   Atmosphere or Climate

   Organization Design

   Incentives, Rewards, and Evaluation

   Job Design, Job Rotation, and Careers

Management's Challenge

Cautions on Creativity

Summary

Study Questions

Endnotes

   Activity 14–2: Downsizing and Creativity

   Activity 14–3: Organizational Innovation: Learning from the WWW

   Activity 14–4: Making a Metaphor

Optional Activities on the WWW

   Activity 14–5W: Fostering Creativity and Innovation in the Intercon Semiconductor Company

   Activity 14–6W: Assessing Your Creativity Quotient

PREMODULE PREPARATION

Activity 14–1:
Exploring Creativity
in an Organizational
Setting: 3M's Post-it
Note Pads Case

Objectives:

a. To explore the organizational context for creativity and innovation.

b. To identify the variety of skills and competencies involved in triggering and facilitating creativity.

Task 1 (Homework):

Students are to read the following case, 3M Post-it Note Pads and respond to the question at the end of the case.

Task 2:

Individuals are to share the answers in small groups. Each group is to develop a shared response, which will be presented and discussed with the class.

Case: 3M's Post-it Note Pads*

Invention has been a way of life at Minnesota Mining and Manufacturing (3M) throughout most of the company's history. While many of the original investors left this would-be mining company at the turn of the 20th century when their plan to mine corundum, an abrasive used in sandpaper manufacturing, failed to yield a mineral of any value, those who stayed turned to inventing new products. Their first success was an abrasive cloth used widely in the auto industry. Another staple of the auto industry, waterproof sandpaper, would never have been invented if 3M inventor Francis Okie had not been dreaming up new ways to increase sandpaper sales. In 1922, a novel thought struck him: why not sell sandpaper as a replacement for razor blades? People could simply rub their cheeks smooth. Obviously this was not an idea that caught on, but this failure led to the successful wet–dry sandpaper. Today, most of us know 3M for astoundingly successful inventions such as scotch tape, masking tape, and, especially, the Post-it Note.

With over 50,000 products, and an average of 500 new products each year, invention has always been the 3M way. Surveys show that executives consider Apple Computer, Google, 3M, Toyota Motor, and Microsoft the world's most innovative companies. The management theories of William K. McKnight, 3M's first chairman of the board, are the company's guiding principles. He created a corporate culture that encourages employee initiative and innovation. His basic rule of management was laid out in 1948:

As our business grows, it becomes increasingly necessary to delegate responsibility and to encourage men and women to exercise their initiative. This requires considerable tolerance. Those men and women, to whom we delegate authority and responsibility, if they are good people, are going to want to do their jobs in their own way.

Mistakes will be made. But if a person is essentially right, the mistakes he or she makes are not as serious in the long run as the mistakes management will make if it undertakes to tell those in authority exactly how they must do their jobs.

Management that is destructively critical when mistakes are made kills initiative. And it's essential that we have many people with initiative if we are to continue to grow.

*Source: Background on 3M was drawn from "Masters of Innovation," *BusinessWeek* (April 10, 1989), pp. 58–63, and the corporate website, http://solutions.3m.com/wps/portal/3M/en_US/our/company/. This case is a shorter and modified version of "3M's Little Yellow Note Pads: Never Mind I'll Do It Myself," in P. R. Nayak and J. M. Kerrengham (eds.), *Breakthroughs!* (New York: Rawson Associates, 1988), pp. 50–73. Used by permission.

In addition to encouraging initiative and tolerating mistakes, the 3M approach includes rarely hiring from the outside, especially at the management and professional levels; small divisions so that division managers can be on a first name basis with their staff; and an annual budget of at least one billion dollars for research and development.

New-Product Development

A 3Mer comes up with an idea for a new product. He or she forms an action team by recruiting full-time members from technical areas, manufacturing, marketing, sales, and finance. The team designs the product and figures out how to produce and market it. Then the team develops new uses and line extensions. All members of the team are promoted and receive raises as the project develops. As sales grow, the product's originator can go on to become project manager, department manager, or division manager. There's a separate track for scientists who don't want to manage. The result is that there are 42 divisions. Each division must follow the 25 percent rule: A quarter of a division's sales must come from products introduced within the past five years. In addition, there is a 15 percent rule. Virtually anyone at the company can spend up to 15 percent of the workweek on anything he or she wants to as long as it's product related. Managers do not carefully monitor their scientists' use of this 15 percent rule. If this policy were enforced rigidly, such action would undermine its intent and inhibit the creative energy of researchers. This practice (called "bootlegging" by members of the company) and the 25 percent rule are at the heart of one of 3M's most famous innovations, the yellow Post-it Note.

The Post-it Note

Unlike many of the incremental improvements and innovations made in product lines, the Post-it Note pad was unique, a product entirely unrelated to anything that had ever been developed or sold by 3M. Post-it Notes are ubiquitous in modern business because they do something no product ever did before. They convey messages in the exact spot where people want the messages, and they leave no telltale sign that the message was ever there at all. This small but powerful idea was begun by a 3M chemist, Spencer Silver, refined by two scientists named Henry Courtney and Roger Merrill, and nurtured from embryo to offspring by Arthur L. Fry. Post-it revenues are estimated at as much as $300 million per year.

Post-it Notes started out as another oddball idea—an adhesive that didn't form a permanent bond—with no perceptible application. In 1964, Silver was working in 3M's central research labs on a program called Polymers for Adhesives. 3M regularly sought ways to improve its major products. Tapes and adhesives were 3M's primary product lines, and adhesives that created stronger bonds were actively sought. Silver found out about a family of monomers that he thought might have potential as ingredients for polymer-based adhesives, and he began exploring them.

In the course of this exploration, Silver tried an experiment, just to see what would happen with one of the monomers, and then to see what would happen if a lot more of the monomer was added to the reaction mixture, rather than the amount dictated by conventional wisdom. This in itself was irrational, as in polymerization catalysis, the amounts of interacting ingredients were controlled in tightly defined proportions according to theory and experience. Silver says, "The key to the Post-it adhesive was doing the experiment. If I had sat down and factored it out beforehand, and thought about it, I wouldn't have done the experiment. If I had really seriously cracked the books and gone through the literature, I would have stopped. The literature was full of examples that said you can't do this." To Silver, science is one part meticulous calculation and one part fooling around.

Silver describes what happened with the unusual concoction as a "Eureka moment"—the emergence of a unique, unexpected, previously unobserved and reliable scientific phenomenon. "It's one of those things you look at and you say, This has got to be useful! You're not forcing materials into a situation to make them work. It wanted to do this. It wanted to make Post-it adhesive."

The adhesive became Silver's baby. Silver started presenting this discovery to people who shared none of his perceptions about the beauty of his glue. Interested in practical applications, they had only a passing appreciation for the science embodied in Silver's adhesive. More significantly, they were "trapped by the metaphor" that insists that the ultimate adhesive is one that forms an unbreakable bond. In addition, Silver was immersed in an organization whose lifeblood was tape of all kinds. In this atmosphere imagining a piece of paper that eliminated the need for tape is an almost unthinkable leap into the void.

Silver couldn't say exactly what it was good for. "But it has to be good for something," he would tell them. "Aren't there times," Silver would ask people, "when you want a glue to hold something for a while but not forever? Let's think about those situations. Let's see if we can turn this adhesive into a product that will hold tight as long as people need it to hold but then let go when people want it to let go."

From 1968 to 1973, support for Silver's idea slipped away. The Polymers for Adhesives program ran out of funding and support, and the researchers were reassigned. Silver had to fight to get the money to get the polymer patented because there was no commercial application immediately present.

Silver was a quiet, well-behaved scientist with an amazing tolerance for rejection. Spencer Silver took his polymer from division to division at 3M, feeling that there was something to be said for such a product. He was zealous in his pursuit because he was "absolutely convinced that this had some potential." The organization never protested his search. At every in-house seminar no one ever said to Silver, "Don't try. Stop wasting our time." In fact, it would have violated some very deeply felt principles of the company to kill Silver's pet project. As long as Silver never failed in his other duties, he could spend as much time as he wanted fooling around with his strange adhesive.

The best idea Silver could come up with on his own was a sticky bulletin board, not a very stimulating idea even to Silver. But 3M did manufacture them, and a few were sold, though it was a slow-moving item in a sleepy market niche. Silver knew there had to be a better idea. "At times I was angry because this stuff is so obviously unique," said Silver. "I said to myself, Why can't you think of a product? It's your job!"

Silver had become trapped by a metaphor. The bulletin board, the only product he could think of, was coated with adhesive—it was sticky everywhere. The metaphor said that something is either sticky or not sticky. Something "partly sticky" didn't occur to him.

Silver and Robert Oliveira, a biochemist whom Silver met in his new research assignment, continued to try selling the idea. Geoff Nicholson, who was leading a new venture team in the commercial tapes division, agreed to see them. Nicholson knew nothing about adhesives and had just taken the position in commercial tapes. Silver and Oliveira were literally the first people to walk through his door. Nicholson says that he was "ripe for something new, different, and exciting. Most anybody who had walked in the door, I would have put my arms around them." Nicholson recruited a team to work on an application for the five-year-old discovery. One of these people, Arthur Fry (a chemist, choir director, and amateur mechanic), would make the difference. Fry had "one of those creative moments" while singing in the choir of his church. "To make it easier to find the songs we were going to sing at each Sunday's service, I used to mark the places with little slips of paper. Inevitably the little slips would flutter to the floor." The idea of using Silver's adhesive on these bookmarks took hold of him at one of these moments. Fry went to 3M, mixed up some adhesive and paper, and invented the "better bookmark." Fry realized that the primary application for the adhesive was not to put it on a fixed surface, such as the bulletin board, but on the paper itself. It was a moment of insight that contemplation did not seem to generate. Fry now has his own lab at 3M and often speaks to large groups of businesspeople about the climate for creativity at 3M. Silver is still in 3M's basement, working out of a cramped, windowless office in a large lab—a place where experimental ferment and scientific playfulness still reign.

The product was not perfected at the moment of Fry's discovery. It still took two more scientists on the Nicholson team—Henry Courtney and Roger Merrill—to invent a paper coating that would make the Post-it adhesive work. Silver said, "Those guys actually made one of the most important contributions to the whole project, and they haven't got a lot of credit for it. The Post-it adhesive was always interesting to people, but if you put it down on something and pulled it apart, it could stay with either side. It had no memory of where it should be. It was difficult to figure out a way to prime the substrate, to get it to stick to the surface you originally put it on. Roger and Hank invented a way to stick the

Post-it adhesive down. And they're the ones who really made the breakthrough discovery because once you've learned that, you can apply it to all sorts of different surfaces."

To get the product to manufacturing, Fry brought together the production people, designers, mechanical engineers, product supervisors, and machine operators and let them describe the many reasons why something like that could not be done. He encouraged them to speculate on ways that they might accomplish the impossible. A lifelong gadgeteer, Fry found himself offering his own suggestions. "Problems are wonderful things to have, especially early in the game, when you really should be looking for problems," said Fry.

In trying to solve the problem of one difficult phase of production, Fry assembled a small-scale basic machine in his own basement, which was successful in applying adhesive to paper in a continuous roll. The only problem was that it wouldn't fit through his basement door. Fry accepted the consequences and bashed a hole through the basement wall. Within two years, Fry and 3M's engineers had developed a set of unique, proprietary machines that are the key to Post-it Notes' consistency and dependability.

Discussion Questions

1. Describe the steps in the creative process that resulted in the Post-it Note pads as we know them today.
2. What factors fostered and hindered the creative process?
3. Which characteristics of Spencer Silver contributed to his creativity?
4. Can you identify other products that were successfully developed from "Eureka" moments?

INTRODUCTION

In Module 13, we introduced the subject of environmental turbulence as the backdrop against which to understand the rapidly expanding use of behavioral science technology in the world of entrepreneurship and corporations. Alvin Toffler described this growing turbulence in *Future Shock* in 1970, which was followed by *Third Wave* in 1980. In 1990 he completed his trilogy with *Powershift,* which claims that the accelerated dissemination of information has resulted in a shift of power and wealth.[1] During the 1990s and early 2000 era, we have seen the effect of information, information technology, and globalization. From the old smokestack era with mass production of individual models requiring timely planning and changeovers, we have moved into the new computer-driven economies that make possible designer production and services tailored to specific client needs. The power vested in the stable financial institutions, which existed with the old industrial giants, has been diluted by the shift to designer financial systems and currencies, making a multitude of new enterprises powerful in a global production market. Adding to this mix are the economic and political turbulence (resulting, for example, from the manipulation of budget deficits as special interest groups assert power with the aid of modern media methods) and the social turbulence, arising from changing population demographics and a highly pluralistic society.

There seems to be little question that you and your peers will experience environmental change at an augmented rate never before experienced by humankind. Similarly, organizations in all phases of their life cycles will experience this whirlpool-type environment. In the past, organizational behavior practitioners spoke of "coping with change" as a primary viewpoint for meeting this challenge, but more recently they broadened this view to include a more proactive strategy of **innovation,** which emphasizes finding new products and new methods to enable organizations to maintain the lead in competitive endeavors.

At present the buzzwords *creativity* and *innovation* fill the work world vocabulary. Organizations such as Asian Brown Bovery (ABB), General Electric, Ford, IBM, Intel, and Coca-Cola send their employees to training programs where they learn techniques for becoming more creative in their thinking. Numerous games and software are now available to teach people how to become more creative. Most companies are dependent on development driven by creative ideas, designs, products or services, and innovative solutions. Creativity and innovation are processes that provoke continuing interest among managers and researchers alike.[2] We can relatively easily identify creative individuals and innovative organizations. Yet, while we can decipher what it takes to facilitate creative behavior at the individual level, organizational innovation is a more complex and baffling phenomenon. *Organizational creativity* and *innovation* are viewed as processes by which individuals working together in a complex social system create a valuable, useful new product, service, idea, procedure, or work process.[3] As such, they play a central role in the long-term survival of organizations and are key processes that must be managed.

But let us turn first to defining and exploring the relevant concepts. Next we present a summary of some of the literature that describes strategies being used in organizations to attain a competitive edge regarding creativity and innovation. We begin by discussing creativity as an aspect of individual effectiveness and then move on to describing innovation as an aspect of organizational effectiveness.

WHAT IS CREATIVITY?

Wikipedia defines *creativity* as "a mental process involving the generation of new ideas or concepts, or new associations between existing ideas or concepts." In the case of Post-it Notes, recall that the accidental discovery of a temporary glue had to be linked to a useful concept. Early experiments by Wolfgang Koehler add the element of "insight" to creativity.[4] Koehler placed a piece of fruit outside a chimpanzee's cage and beyond the reach of a stick in the chimp's hand. He placed a longer stick in the vicinity of the fruit. The chimp tried without success to reach the fruit with the short stick. After an extended pause, the chimp suddenly used the short stick to drag the longer one to him and then used the longer stick to haul in the fruit. This sudden flash of insight into the right answer has been referred to as the *aha process* or the *eureka process.*

Social psychologist Graham Wallas, in his work *Art of Thought,* published in 1926, explained creative insight by a five-stage process:

1. Preparation (preparatory work on a problem that focuses the individual's mind on the problem and explores the problem's dimensions.

2. Incubation (the problem is internalized into the unconscious mind and nothing appears to be externally happening).

3. Intimation (the creative person gets a "feeling" that a solution is on its way).

4. Insight (or illumination, where the creative idea bursts forth from its preconscious processing into conscious awareness).

5. Verification (the idea is consciously verified, elaborated, and then applied).

This process has gone through many variations by different researchers, who use different numbers of stages, but the basic conceptual process is still widely recognized. Engineers are intensely aware of this inventive approach. Judges most often do not give decisions until time for incubation is allowed. Architects work and rework designs. All of us do this naturally, but awareness and practice can augment our effectiveness in both our personal and our work lives. (The next time you write a term paper, follow this procedure. After time for incubation, you will be surprised how much better than expected the material will fall into meaningful form so that you can write an excellent paper.)

Creativity does not occur in a vacuum. In the early 1990s, an interactionist model of creative behavior was proposed.[5] The interactionist view suggests that **creativity** is the complex product of a person's behavior in a given situation. Contextual and social influences of the situation either facilitate or hinder creative accomplishments. The person brings to the situation his or her cognitive abilities, personality traits, and noncognitive abilities. The interactionist view provides an integrative framework that combines important elements of personality (see Module 4), cognitive style and abilities and social psychology elements such as leadership dynamics (see Module 8), group dynamics (see Module 12), motivation (see Module 5), organizational elements such as work and organization design (see Module 13), and technology and information technology (to be examined in Module 20W). Figure 14–1 captures the interactionist model of organizational creativity.

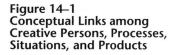

The Creative Person

The stereotyped image we have of the creative person originates from the mad scientist, the crazy artist, the computer nerd, or the absent-minded professor. We typically think of a collection of personality traits that immediately sets the individual apart from others. Do such stereotypes hold? Outstanding creative people have been studied across fields to try to determine the common traits. Unfortunately, the common traits do not come in a precise package that would help you to immediately identify a creative person.

In looking at characteristics of the individual, it is probably most useful to start with the view of cognitive psychology that the brain is a creative entity, continuously processing data for problem solving, understanding, and responding, mostly at the unconscious level. We are all creative because the brain is creative. Creative in this sense means processing data to come up with an answer, whether it be "get out of the way of that oncoming truck" (an unconscious response) or arithmetic reasoning (a primarily but not entirely conscious process). There is some evidence that individuals may be either right-brain or left-brain dominant. Right-brain dominant people tend to be more intuitive in their response to problem solving and learning, and left-brain dominants more logical and rational. Right-brain dominants were thought to be more creative, but more evidence suggests that both sides must work together. In a study of managers, organizational researcher Henry Mintzberg suggested that planning requires the analytical skills of the left brain, while managing people and implementing plans relies more on the intuitive,

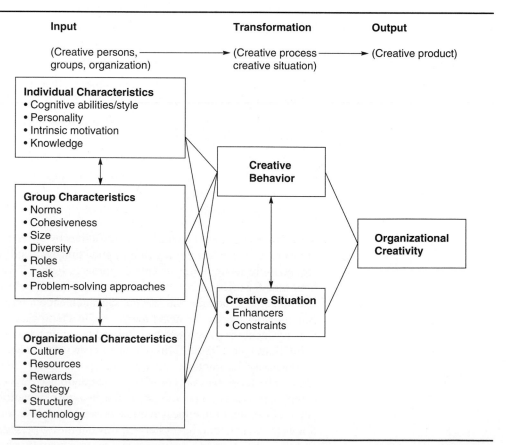

Figure 14–1
Conceptual Links among Creative Persons, Processes, Situations, and Products

Source: R. W. Woodman, J. E. Sawyer, and R. W. Griffin, "Toward a Theory of Organizational Creativity," *Academy of Management Review* 18, no. 2 (1993), p. 309.

creative functions associated with the right side of the brain.[6] You can informally test your own brain dominance at http://www.intelliscript.net/test_area/questionnaire/questionnaire. cgi?q=right_brain_left_brain_2.

Defining creativity as we have used it refers to the brain functions of acquiring and processing data for purposes of problem solving, whether it be responses, answers, actions, or new ideas. This involves both unconscious and conscious processes. The interactionist view would advocate the need to stress that in working organizations, everyone has the potential for creativity—to solve problems and to give new ideas. Executives and managers with whom we have worked almost always are looking for "creative people," assuming that "you've either got it (creativity) or you haven't." The implication is that very few have it. Yet most consultant firms readily admit that the most useful recommendations in managerial and organizational effectiveness surveys come primarily from internal sources: the employees they have interviewed.

There is further support for this idea. In Sternberg's studies, unskilled workers in a milk-processing plant always developed operating procedures that required the least physical efforts. The author reviewed other studies consistent with these findings and concluded, "Beneath the surface of adaptation, however, lie continuing acts of creativity—the invention of new ways of handling old and new problems. Since creativity is a term ordinarily reserved for exceptional individuals and extraordinary accomplishments, recognizing it in the practical problem-solving activities of ordinary people introduced a new perspective from which to grasp the challenge of the ordinary."[7]

Carrying this idea one step further, there is additional evidence for widespread creativity in the multitude of unique ways in which disgruntled workers can come up with methods to resist or even sabotage management.

We know that some people have more new ideas than others have, but we also want to point out that the widespread (and self-fulfilling) expectation system of management overlooks the major contributions that the whole body of the employee system has to offer.[8]

Distinguishing between Creativity and Innovation

In much of the literature discussing applications of creativity and innovation, the words are used loosely and often interchangeably. Current usage in organizational behavior defies definition of innovation as a concept. However, J. J. Kao's distinction between creativity and innovation is adequate for our purposes.[9] If creativity implies the vision of what is possible, then the term *innovation* suggests the implementation process by which inspiration leads to the practical results. Creativity involves problem solving that may lead to a useful idea. The term *innovation* is more suitably applied to decision-making processes: the decision to search for a new, useful idea; the decision to select the most useful idea; and the decision of how to implement the chosen idea.

Although creativity depends on many uncontrollable factors (such as the degree of knowledge available; the characteristics, skills, and motivation of the person or persons involved; and a good dose of chance or luck), innovation requires organizational choice and change that can be planned. Finally, an innovation when defined as implementation is not necessarily unique. Successful innovation may result from imitation or adoption of an innovation from another source.

Creativity can be defined from the person-oriented, process-oriented, and product-oriented perspectives. The **person-oriented approach** to creativity studies patterns of personality traits and characteristics observed in individuals who exhibit creative behavior. Such creative behavior might include the activities of inventing, designing, contriving, composing, and planning.[10] The **process-oriented approach** to creativity examines the development of a new and valuable idea or product through the unique interaction of the individual with the available resources, settings, people, and situations). The **product-oriented approach** to creativity focuses on the production of novel and useful ideas by an individual or a small group of individuals working together. A full understanding of creativity requires an integration of these orientations. An agreement seems to exist that the creative behavior, the creative interaction, and the creative idea need not be successful, commercial, nor applied.

Innovation, in contrast, generally refers to the successful application of a new idea to the firm. Success in this case refers to the actual translation of the idea into a useful product or process. An innovation may or may not be profitable or beneficial to the firm. Innovation is a process of developing and implementing a new idea, whether it is a new technology, product, or organizational process. Obviously, creativity can be a part of this implementation process.[11] It may involve recombining old ideas in a new way, a scheme that challenges the present order, or an approach perceived as new by those involved.[12] Note that the idea need not be a breakthrough idea such as superconductivity or a completely new organizational model; it need only be new, or perceived as new, to the organization. Given these distinctions between creativity and innovation, we next examine people's orientation toward creativity.

Are there particular traits or characteristics related to creativity? Some of the characteristics found in individuals who have been identified as creative include the following: high energy level, dedicated and effective work habits, a persistent and high level of curiosity, interest in reflective thinking, relatively little tie to reality, low level of sociability, unusual appreciation of humor, facility for producing humor, need for adventure, need for variety, self-confidence, tolerance of ambiguity, introversion, high need for autonomy, self-direction, and an impulsive personality.

The **intelligence level** has been of major interest. Exceptionally creative architects, mathematicians, scientists, and engineers usually score no higher on intelligence tests than their less creative peers do. Testing suggests that a certain level of intelligence is related to creativity, but the correlation between the two factors disappears when the person's IQ is above 120. This lack of correlation is particularly important to know in a work setting because managers tend to believe that only the brightest people are apt to be creative. (Refer to our previous discussion of creativity being widespread among workers.)

In general, the literature tends to show that **expertise,** or knowledge, and **intrinsic motivation** are essential components of creativity—which is another way of saying that the individual has to know the field and want to do something about an issue or a problem. Emotional intelligence has recently been linked to effective creativity.

Emotional Intelligence and Creativity

As discussed in Modules 3 and 7, leadership and personality play critical roles in shaping human behavior at the workplace. One of the growing areas that seems to attract attention centers around the role that emotional intelligence plays in leadership and organizations.[13] **Emotional intelligence** is defined as the ability to sense, understand, and effectively apply the power and acumen of emotions as a source of human energy, information, trust, creativity, and influence.[14] In a recent book, R. Cooper and A. Sawaf attempt to demonstrate ". . . how the science of emotional intelligence has enabled manager after manager, company after company, to begin capturing the single most powerful source of human energy, authenticity, and drive."[15] While the topic of emotional intelligence is beyond the scope of this module, and more empirical research is needed, we want to make the following points:

1. Creativity is one of the 21 scales that map out emotional intelligence.
2. Creativity seems to be influenced by the person's emotional intelligence level.
3. Creativity seems to be influenced by the supervisor/leader/coach's level of emotional intelligence.
4. The emotional intelligence level of the leaders influences the workplace context and dynamics.

For further investigation of emotional intelligence, go to http://eqi.org/eitoc.htm.

Motivation and Creativity

We have argued that the personality traits associated with creativity are not enough to guarantee creative behavior. What motivates a person to be creative? The process is complex and involves both intrinsic and extrinsic motivation as well as skills and abilities (see Module 5). The components of individual creativity are shown in Figure 14–2. The

**Figure 14–2
Components of Individual
Creativity**

Domain-Relevant Skills	Creativity-Relevant Skills	Task Motivation
Includes	*Includes*	*Includes*
Knowledge about the domain	Appropriate cognitive style	Attitudes toward the task
Technical skills required	Implicit or explicit heuristics for generating novel ideas	Perceptions of own motivation for undertaking the task
Special domain-relevant "talent"	Conducive work style	
Depends on	*Depends on*	*Depends on*
Innate cognitive abilities	Training	Initial level of intrinsic motivation to the task
Innate perceptual and motor skills	Experience in idea generation	Presence or absence of salient extrinsic constraints in the social environment
Formal and informal education	Personality characteristics	Individual ability to cognitively minimize extrinsic constraints

Source: Adapted with permission from T. M. Amabile, "From Individual Creativity to Organizational Innovation," in K. Gronhaug and G. Kaufman, (eds.), *Innovation: A Cross-Disciplinary Perspective* (Oslo, Norway: Norwegian University Press, 1988), p. 149.

framework clusters three components of individual creativity: domain-relevant skills, creativity-related skills, and task motivation.

Domain-relevant skills are the general skills in the area (or domain) an individual must bring to the situation. If a person is working on the problem in microelectronics, then he or she must be knowledgeable, talented, and trained, for example, in electrical engineering.

Creativity-relevant skills are the "something extra" that makes the difference in creative performance. The individual's cognitive style is characterized by the ability to break out of old ways of thinking. The individual also depends on a *heuristic* (a general strategy that helps in approaching problems or tasks). A creative heuristic might be "when all else fails, try something counterintuitive" or "make the familiar strange." Finally, the individual's working style must be conducive to creativity (for example, persistence, a long attention span, and the ability to venture off in a new direction when the well-worn direction is not leading to a new idea are all characteristics of a creative work style. Creativity-relevant skills depend on training, experience, and the personality characteristics mentioned earlier.

Regardless of the individual's skill level, it is **task motivation** that determines if these skills will be fully utilized. If a person is not motivated to do something, no amount of skills can compensate for the lack of motivation. The individual's attitude toward the task is simply the person's natural inclination either toward or away from the task—do I want to do this or not? The individual's perception of his or her motivation, however, depends on factors in the social and work environments. If an individual feels that there are extrinsic motivational factors in the environment intended to control his or her performance of the task (for example, surveillance, evaluation, deadlines, competition, rewards, and restricted choices), his or her motivation to generate new ideas is likely to suffer. In contrast, if the person does not feel pressures to perform in a certain way or if the person is able to minimize or ignore such pressures, he or she is likely to have a higher level of motivation, even a "passion" for the project.

THE ORGANIZATIONAL CONTEXT OF CREATIVITY

Creativity involves a special kind of problem solving. In organizational settings, attempts have been made to identify potentially creative people by observing the problem-solving behavior. Yet as we have seen, individual creativity is a function of antecedent conditions (that is, part reinforcement history), cognitive style and ability (that is, divergent thinking), personality, relevant knowledge, motivation, social influences, and group, unit, and organizational actors.[16] Models have been developed to determine dimensions of individual creativity within organizations.

The Adaption–Innovation Model

The **adaption–innovation model**—and others—identify two types of people within organizations: adaptors and innovators.[17] *Adaptors* prefer structured situations, seek answers to the problem at hand, and are perceived by innovators as being rigid, conforming, "safe" people. *Innovators,* on the other hand, appreciate an unstructured work environment, seek to answer questions that have not yet been asked, and are perceived by adaptors as being impractical, abrasive risk takers. Although both types can be found in and are needed in all organizations, research has found that both are capable of generating original creative solutions but from different problem-solving orientations (see Figure 14–3).[18]

Creativity and Commitment

One additional element that may be related to the degree of intrinsic motivation is the individual's *commitment* to the organization (the degree to which an employee's personal goals are aligned with the organization's goals). Some authors have suggested that (1) there is a direct connection between level of commitment and motivation to engage in creative behaviors and (2) highly ideological organizations will produce more highly committed individuals.[19]

Creativity and Social Influence

What are the external influences that can operate on the individual, encouraging the display and development of creative potential in the organization? What can be done to increase creative behavior within the organization, that is, to turn a potentially creative person into an actively creative person? We have described some of the factors that can inhibit creativity, but several factors have been identified that have a positive effect on creative behavior. These factors can be organized into the general areas of freedom, support, and participation.[20]

Figure 14–3
Characteristics of Adaptors and Innovators

Implications	Adaptors	Innovators
For problem solving	Tend to take the problem as defined and generate novel, creative ideas aimed at "doing things better." Immediate high efficiency is the keynote of high adaptors.	Tend to redefine generally agreed on problems, breaking previously perceived restraints, generating solutions aimed at "doing things differently."
For solutions	Generally generate a few well-chosen and relevant solutions that they generally find sufficient but that sometimes fail to contain ideas needed to break the existing pattern completely.	Produce numerous ideas, many of which may not be either obvious or acceptable to others. Such a pool often contains ideas, if they can be identified, that may crack hitherto intractable problems.
For policies	Prefer well-established, structured situations. Best at incorporating new data or events into existing structures of policies.	Prefer unstructured situations. Use new data as opportunities to set new structures or policies accepting the greater risk.
For organizational "fit"	Essential to the ongoing functions, but in times of unexpected changes may have some difficulty moving out of their established role.	Essential in times of change or crisis, but may have some trouble applying themselves to ongoing organizational demands.
For potential creativity	Capable of generating original, creative solutions that reflect their overall approach to problem solving.	Capable of generating original, creative solutions that reflect their overall approach to problem solving.
For collaboration	High adaptors do not get along easily with innovators. Middle adaptors may act as bridges.	High innovators do not get along easily with adaptors. Middle innovators may act as bridges.
For perceived behavior	Seen by innovators as sound, conforming, safe, predictable, relevant, inflexible, wedded to the system, and intolerant of ambiguity.	Seen by adaptors as unsound, impractical, risky, abrasive, often shocking their opposites and creating dissonance.

Source: Adapted with permission from M. J. Kirton, "Adaptors and Innovators: Problem Solvers in Organizations," in K. Gronhaug and G. Kaufmann (eds.), *Innovation: A Cross-Disciplinary Perspective* (Oslo, Norway: Norwegian University Press, 1988), p. 72.

Freedom: Freedom from external constraints can lead to creative behavior. The notion of freedom includes the following managerial actions:

1. Provide freedom to try new ways of performing tasks.
2. Permit activities or tasks to be different for different individuals.
3. Allow an appropriate amount of time for the accomplishment of tasks.
4. Allow time for non-task-related thinking and development of creative ideas.
5. Encourage self-initiated projects.
6. Respect an individual's need to work alone.
7. Encourage divergent activities by providing resources and room.

Support: Noncontrolling support can be given in the following ways:

1. Support and reinforce unusual ideas and responses of individuals.
2. Communicate confidence in the individuals.
3. Tolerate complexity and disorder.
4. Provide constructive feedback.
5. Reduce concern over failure.
6. Create a climate of mutual respect and acceptance among individuals.
7. Encourage interpersonal trust.
8. Listen to individuals.

Participation: Involving the individual in the decision-making process as well as the problem-solving process (participation) provides motivation that encourages creative behavior. Participation can be enhanced in the following ways:

1. Encourage individuals to have choices and to be part of the goal-setting process.
2. Encourage involvement of those interested in the problem—don't limit involvement across jobs, departments, and divisions.
3. Challenge individuals to find new tasks and problems.
4. Encourage questioning.
5. Encourage a high quality of interpersonal relationships including a spirit of cooperation, open confrontation of conflicts, and the expression of ideas.

Freedom, support, and participation can be implemented in a variety of ways, depending on the situation. The application of these factors can reduce the extrinsic motivational factors that have a negative effect on creative performance.

DEVELOPING THE CREATIVE PROCESS WITHIN THE ORGANIZATION

The ways of increasing creativity listed previously make up the organizational environment in which the creative process is to take place. The organization must introduce into this context a learning model for operational use. Individuals and teams must be made aware of the **creative process,** which we described in our discussion at the beginning of the chapter, and they must make a systematic effort to allow it to work. Thus in stage 1, the problem is defined in all its dimensions and decisions are made regarding who will be involved, who has the expertise, and what support is needed. Management needs to select people for participation who have the required domain-relevant skills and task motivation ensuring high-level involvement. In stage 2, data are collected and all available sources are explored. Again, domain-relevant skills and creativity-relevant skills are essential. Stage 3 allows a time lapse for the incubation of ideas and the injection of new data, with the recognition that there will be periods of no progress, that consultation and dialogues may be needed, and that dropping the effort temporarily may be useful. In stage 4, insight (hopefully) comes to the individual or the team in terms of useful ideas or solutions. Finally, in stage 5 some testing and verification are conducted to find out whether the idea will be useful and whether its implementation is possible.

Throughout the creative process, two types of thinking have been identified: divergent thinking and convergent thinking. *Divergent thinking* is creative thinking. By using divergent thinking, the individual creates new connections between ideas (as in making metaphors) and thinks of many possibilities and alternatives (as in brainstorming). In this type of thinking, a person's built-in censor is temporarily turned off. *Convergent* or *critical thinking* involves comparing and contrasting, improving and refining, screening, judging, selecting, and making decisions. In the creative process, the individual moves back and forth between these types of thinking. In group settings, different individuals may be valued for their divergent or convergent skills.

Team Creativity

We have focused primarily on the role of the individual in creativity. Now we wish to refer you back to Module 4, where team problem solving and decision making were discussed. We noted that under certain conditions teams can achieve *synergy*—a group solution superior to that of the most accurate member's solution. One reason for this superior group solution was that the pool of knowledge in the group was usually greater than that of any individual. Another reason was creativity: Individuals built on others' ideas and produced new ideas. Many factors were at work. There seems to be little doubt that the interactive group process can facilitate or hinder team creativity. However, managers must examine the conditions under which teams can be expected to be more creative or solve problems better than individuals. If team creativity is viewed as a team capability that is needed, designing the appropriate work context, content, and process that will facilitate the appropriate interaction patterns between team members is critical.

A recent published study identifies three operating principles to guide the management of team creativity, based on the successful experiences at BMW:

1. *Protect the creative team.* The need to shield the team from the commentaries of others in the company, such that the creative process is allowed to emerge in its natural course.

2. *Safeguard the artistic process.* The need to establish barriers around the product development such that time-to-market pressures and other time constraints do not disrupt the process.

3. *Develop an inventive communication.* Managing at the intersection of known and unknown, routine and nonroutine, art and commerce means translating the creative language to the language of the company.[21]

The research results to date are not conclusive, yet they suggest that conditions such as the actual design of the work space, interaction patterns, member expertise, time, openness, and communication tend to influence team creativity.[22]

From Creativity to Innovation

Once a creative idea has been developed and verified, how does it become meaningful to the organization? The creative process described previously is commonly perceived as the first step in the process of innovation. It is a necessary first step to innovation, whether the innovation is a groundbreaking internal discovery or an idea brought to the organization from the outside. How the process unfolds is a function of the type of innovation, the innovation process itself, and key elements that influence innovation. Innovation is rarely the work of one individual. As we saw in the 3M case, many people, from scientists to managers, were involved in bringing that creative idea to commercial fruition.

ORGANIZATIONAL INNOVATION

Types of Innovation

Earlier, we defined *innovation* as the successful application of a new idea to the firm. The idea may be a new technology, a new product, or a new organizational or administrative process. The innovation may be an imitation of a product, a person, or an idea used elsewhere, which becomes unique because it is placed within a new context.

We tend to think most often of innovations as **radical innovations** (discontinuous breakthroughs in technology).[23] Often, however, there is an **incremental innovation** (an improvement of a technology, product, or process). A series of incremental innovations can lead to radical innovation, as in the 3M case where Silver discovered the Post-it Note adhesive while experimenting on improving traditional adhesives. Another distinction is between process and product innovations. A zero-defect quality control system is an example of a **process innovation. Product innovations** are usually the more visible of the two types, but not necessarily the more important. A product innovation can require process innovation.

Administrative innovations often affect the organization as much or more than technological innovations. New incentive systems and new communication network systems are just two examples of administrative innovations, as are new marketing and sales techniques. Finally, it is important to make a distinction between **system-maintaining innovation (SMI)** and **system-transforming innovation (STI).** SMI refers to new ideas that enhance or improve some aspect of the business without changing the overall nature of how the organization operates. STI refers to a new idea that affects the fundamental aspects of organizing, requiring change in several of the subsystems or segments of the organization in order to fully implement the innovation.

Stages of the Innovation Process

Although there are many types of innovation, it is generally agreed that the **innovation process** for each is similar. Descriptions of the innovation process have been borrowed from many fields. Group development and problem-solving models,[24] decision process models,[25] and organizational change models[26] have all been applied to the innovation process. These models as well as innovation process models have traditionally viewed the innovation process as occurring in a linear fashion in a series of discrete stages, generally from idea generation to adoption to implementation.[27] Although these activities occur in innovation, there is little empirical evidence for their occurrence in discrete stages. More recent research has found that the process is more "fluid" than stage theories would suggest.

The Minnesota Innovation Studies Program has been one of the most comprehensive research projects seeking to understand the process of innovation. Based on an in-depth review of longitudinal development of seven major innovations, the researchers of this study made six important observations about the process:

1. An initial shock to the organization precedes innovation. This shock may be new leadership, a product failure, a budget crisis, lack of market share, opportunity, or dissatisfaction of some kind.

2. Ideas proliferate.

3. While ideas are proliferating, setbacks and surprises are likely to occur.

4. These setbacks and surprises provide opportunities for trial-and-error learning and the blending of old and new ideas.

5. Restructuring of the organization at some or all levels occurs.

6. A hands-on approach of top management is evident all the way through the process.[28]

It is evident that this view of the innovation process is not a neat, step-by-step, easily planned activity. How the process unfolds is determined by the elements described next.

KEY ELEMENTS THAT INFLUENCE THE INNOVATION PROCESS

Key Players and Roles

The previous description of the innovation process emphasized the important role of top management in influencing innovation. Top management not only provides resources for innovation but also provides a vision of the organization and its members as innovative. In addition, several roles required in the innovation process have been described. As early as 1931, the phenomenon of innovation was being studied by J. Schumpeter, an economist.[29] His basic "one-man theory" described characteristics of the "dynamic entrepreneur." This figure is still evident in small and new organizations. However, in larger organizations it makes sense to view a variety of individuals who participate by playing different roles.

The *product champion* is the one who promotes the innovation and overcomes resistance to change. The product champion may or may not have formal power and influence within the organization, but this person has top-management support, which is necessary for success.[30]

The *technical innovator* is the inventor or the person who makes the most significant technical contribution to the innovation. In the 3M case, Silver and Fry may have shared this role.[31]

The *technological gatekeeper* has been identified as the person who has both technical know-how and formal influence channels to other parts of the organization.[32]

Atmosphere or Climate

The organizational factors that were discussed as positively influencing creativity— freedom, support, and participation—also influence innovation, which is reasonable because creativity and innovation are viewed as parts of the same process. The climate or culture of the organization (the visions and goals, strategies, style of leadership, work setting, characteristics of the individuals, type of work, way people organize to get the work done, qualitative features of the context, and the values and norms of the people) may promote or inhibit innovation. How to measure the creative climate of the organization has been problematic. Using questionnaires and interviews, researchers have had some success discriminating between working climates that are more or less favorable to innovative outcomes.[33]

Swedish psychologist Goran Ekvall developed a commonly used 10-factor method for measuring the climate for creativity.[34]

1. *Challenge.* The people in this organization really care about their work and take pride and ownership in what they do.

2. *Freedom.* People in this organization are free to try new ways to get their work done.

3. *Idea support.* People listen to each other and encourage each other's ideas.

4. *Trust/openness.* People feel comfortable discussing their ideas with others.

5. *Dynamism/liveliness.* There's a great deal going on in this organization. It's an exciting place to work.

6. *Playfulness/humor.* It's common here to see people joking good naturedly, laughing, and enjoying their work.

7. *Debates.* It's common to see people discussing each other's ideas and ways of accomplishing things in this organization.

8. *Conflicts.* People generally don't talk negatively behind each other's back, and when conflicts arise, they are quickly resolved.

9. *Risk taking.* People in this organization are generally not penalized for failure. They can take risks on new initiatives and put those ideas into action.

10. *Idea time.* There is ample time to discuss, develop, and initiate new ideas in this organization. It is common to have regular sessions where employees meet to discuss better ways of doing business.

Organization Design

Managing work and the organization design process were discussed in Module 13. However, the relationship between organization design and innovation is not definite. An early study of organizational innovation identified organic versus mechanistic organizations as likely to encourage innovation.[35] Bureaucracy, with its formal hierarchical levels, has often been identified as the mechanistic organization, whereas the organic organization has been described as flat. However, other researchers have argued that no one form of organization is superior to another in terms of being conducive to innovation; rather, it is the links for collaboration and problem solving throughout the organization that are important.[36] Reorganization during the process of innovation is likely to result in different designs as well as structures.

Incentives, Rewards, and Evaluation

We have seen that expected evaluation has been found to have a detrimental effect on creativity and that external incentives must stimulate intrinsic motivation (see Module 5). It is not so clear how reward systems contribute to creative and innovative effort. One view is that rewards based on seniority rather than performance tend to inhibit innovation and creativity, whereas merit-based systems, in which individual performance is rewarded, stimulate creativity. However, in Japan, where lifetime employment systems and seniority-based reward systems in large organizations are the norm, long-range thinking appears to be promoted, and there seems to be less necessity to resist new ideas (and freedom to fail) because a person's promotion and rewards are not based on short-term performance.[37] Innovative firms generally have innovative incentive and reward systems, which acknowledge both individual and group efforts in nonthreatening ways.

Job Design, Job Rotation, and Careers

Jobs that offer intrinsic motivation to perform well, that involve the employee, and that provide variety and autonomy tend to increase innovative levels of activity (see Modules 5 and 13). Recently, career planning involving **dual ladders** has gained a lot of attention. (Career planning is addressed in more depth in Module 18W.) In a dual-ladder system, a high-performing individual may choose to climb the managerial or technical ladder, depending on his or her own personal preferences and goals. Companies such as 3M, Monsanto, Eastman Kodak, and General Mills have successfully implemented dual-ladder systems, which they have found lead to more open communications, are an aid in recruiting, and provide better advancement opportunities for people at all levels.[38] To be successful, the dual-ladder system requires the full commitment of management.

MANAGEMENT'S CHALLENGE

A challenge that most managers and companies face is how to create an organization that allows activities to be effectively performed, while creativity and innovation are given opportunities to flourish. If creativity and innovation are both parts of a process that is becoming a greater and greater necessity in today's organizations, then managers must become aware of how this process can be managed. Organizational creativity and innovation process frequently requires making order out of chaos or working in between known and unknown domains.[39] Creativity and innovation imply change, although not all change is an innovation or creative. Just as there is no one way to organize, there is no one way to encourage organizational creativity and innovation. Innovation is risky, and the manager's role in this process can be likened to a balancing act. On the one hand, he or she must provide the stability, support, and security that free employees from the fear of failure. On the other hand, the manager must encourage risk taking, which is likely to result in new ideas that are beneficial to the organization as a whole.

Part of this challenge is to hire, train, and develop a set of individuals with not only a variety of specialized and technical skills and abilities but also skills in problem solving, communication, conflict resolution, and team building (see Modules 10, 11, and 16). Another part of the challenge is to retain these employees not only through innovative reward and incentive systems but also by providing the vision, resources, autonomy, and support they need.

Another part of the challenge is to develop organizational learning mechanisms that foster a learning climate.[40] As we will see in Module 16, a variety of learning mechanisms can be created that can facilitate creativity and innovation. A recent study that focused on organizational creativity in a pharmaceutical research and development organization demonstrated that both learning mechanisms and individual motivation (intrinsic and extrinsic) are highly correlated to creativity. Furthermore, the climate of information sharing was found to serve as a catalyst for creativity.[41]

As we have seen in this module, the management task is not easy. Innovative environments are turbulent, and the innovation process requires the management of change as an integral part of organizational and managerial routines. In addition to providing a free, supportive, and participative environment to encourage creative thinking, management must also deal with resistance to change, which is likely to occur in some parts of the organization when an innovation is developed. All of these elements demand that the manager be involved in an ongoing, creative problem-solving process. Creativity and innovation rely on creative and innovative management processes.

CAUTIONS ON CREATIVITY

When expectations for creativity and innovation in the work world are high, there are bound to be counterproductive excesses. Young people may feel they will not be regarded as having high potential if they are not offering new ideas, and managers can feel they are not providing a supportive climate if they do not try new ideas. A "change for the sake of change" approach can be disruptive and must be guarded against. "If it's not broken, don't fix it" is often good advice.

SUMMARY

In this module, we have examined the organizational process that begins with creativity at the individual or team level and culminates in an innovation that contributes to the success of the organization as a whole. We have defined *creativity* as the brain functions of acquiring and processing data for the purposes of problem solving, whether it be responses, answers, actions, or new ideas. Creativity involves both unconscious and conscious processes. A five-stage process for the individual to utilize in producing creative reactions was given. *Innovation,* in contrast, was defined as the implementation process through which creative ideas are transformed into practical applications in the organization.

Study Questions

1. Creativity and innovation are different parts of the same process. Can an innovation occur without creativity? Discuss why or why not.

2. "The creative person is born, not made." Do you agree or disagree? Why?

3. Charlie likes to wrestle with a problem for several days or weeks, looking at it from all sides. Janet focuses on solving the problem efficiently and doesn't worry if she has considered all possible solutions. Which of the two is likely to be more creative? Why?

4. Sam loves his job because it is open-ended and he decides what to do each day. He works hard, often forgetting to quit at 5 P.M. Discuss Sam's motivation.

5. List the five steps in the creative process. Identify the skills required at each step.

6. Think of an innovation that you would consider radical. How does it differ from an incremental innovation?

7. Mr. Jones has just returned from a short course on innovative management and has decided to reorganize his firm to increase innovation. He has isolated the scientists and design engineers in one building so they won't be disturbed by the production people and the marketing and sales forces. Is Mr. Jones's plan likely to increase innovative activity? Why?

8. Two employees of a high-tech firm began their careers with the firm as design engineers. Both are highly skilled, creative workers. Employee A now manages the production research department. Employee B has a private lab in the basement. Both are very satisfied. Discuss career choices and personal and organizational factors that led to this situation.

9. You are designing a new incentive and reward system for an R&D lab. All the employees have advanced engineering degrees, and the market for their skills is very competitive. How would you structure such a system?

10. Mrs. White has just been hired to run a large, nationwide, temporary employee company. The former CEO suggests to her that she might be interested in attending a seminar on managing innovation. Mrs. White laughs and says, "Why would I want to do that? We're not concerned with innovation around here. That's something for managers of high-tech companies." Do you agree or disagree with Mrs. White? Explain your answer.

Endnotes

1. A. Toffler and H. Toffler, *Powershift* (New York: Bantam Books, 1990); T. M. Amabile, "The Motivation to Be Creative," in S. Isaksen (ed.), *Frontiers of Creativity Research: Beyond the Basics* (New York: Bearly Limited, 1987), pp. 223–54.

2. See, for example, R. J. Sternberg, "The Concept of Creativity: Prospects and Paradigms," in R. J. Sternberg (ed.), *Handbook of Creativity* (Cambridge, UK: Cambridge University Press, 1999), pp. 45–56; T. Amabile, C. N. Hadley, and S. J. Kramer, "Creativity Under the Gun," *Harvard Business Review* (August 2002), pp. 52–61; S. G. Scott and R. A. Bruce, "Determinants of Innovative Behavior: A Path Model of Individual Innovation in the Workplace," *Academy of Management Journal* 37, no. 3 (1994), pp. 580–607; R. J. Sternberg, L. A. O'Hara, and T. I. Lubart, "Creativity as Investment," *California Management Review* 40, no. 1 (1997), pp. 8–21; and C. J. Nemeth, "Managing Innovation: When Less Is More," *California Management Review* 40, no. 1 (1997), pp. 59–74.

3. See, for example, D. Bohm, *On Creativity* (London, UK: Routledge, 2000); K. Unsworth, "Unpacking Creativity," *Academy of Management Review* 26, no. 2 (2001), pp. 289–97; R. W. Woodman, J. E. Sawyer, and R. W. Griffin, "Towards a Theory of Organizational Creativity," *Academy of Management Review* 18, no. 1 (1993), pp. 293–321; and J. D. Couger, *Creativity and Innovation* (Danvers, MA: Boyd & Fraser, 1996).

4. W. Koehler, *The Mentality of Apes* (London: Pelican, 1925/1957).

5. See R. W. Woodman and J. F. Schoenfeldt, "An Interactionist Model of Creative Behavior," *Journal of Creative Behavior* 24 (1990), pp. 279–90; and R. W. Woodman and J. E. Sawyer, "An Interactionist Model of Organizational Creativity," paper presented at the annual Academy of Management Meeting, Miami, 1991. For an example of how this interaction might work among co-workers and supervisors, see J. Zhou, "When the Presence of Creative Coworkers Is Related to Creativity: Role of Supervisor Close Monitoring, Developmental Feedback, and Creative Personality," *Journal of Applied Psychology* 88, no. 3 (2003), pp. 413–22.

6. H. Mintzberg, "Planning on the Left Side and Managing on the Right," *Harvard Business Review* (July–August 1976), pp. 49–58.

7. R. J. Sternberg, *The Nature of Creativity: Contemporary Psychological Perspectives* (New York: Cambridge University Press, 1988); and R. J. Sternberg and R. K. Wagner, *Practical Intelligence* (New York: Cambridge University Press, 1986).

8. D. Leonard and S. Straus, "Putting Your Company's Whole Brain to Work," *Harvard Business Review* (July–August 1997), pp. 111–21.

9. J. J. Kao, *Managing Creativity* (Englewood Cliffs, NJ: Prentice-Hall, 1991); D. Bohm and F. D. Peat, *Science, Order, and Creativity* (New York: Bantam Books, 1987); and J. R. Evans, *Creative Thinking* (Cincinnati, OH: South Western, 1991).

10. J. P. Guilford, "Creativity," *American Psychologist* 14 (1950), pp. 469–79; J. P. Guilford, "Creativity Research: A Quarter Century of Progress," in I. A. Taylor and J. W. Getzels (eds.), *Perspectives in Creativity* (New York: Aldine, 1975).

11. E. Rogers, *The Diffusion of Innovations,* 3rd ed. (New York: Free Press, 1983); and A. H. Van de Ven, "Central Problems in the Management of Innovation," *Management Science* (May 1986), pp. 590–607.

12. G. Zaltman, R. Duncan, and J. Holbek, *Innovations and Organizations* (New York: Wiley- Interscience, 1973).

13. P. Salovey and J. Myer, *Emotional Development and Emotional Intelligence* (New York: Basic Books, 1997); and H. Weisinger, *Emotional Intelligence at Work* (San Francisco: Jossey-Bass, 1997).

14. D. Goleman, R. Boyatzis, and A. McKee, *Primal Leadership: Realizing the Power of Emotional Intelligence* (Boston: Harvard Business School, 2002); and R. Cooper, "Applying Emotional Intelligence in the Workplace," *Training & Development* (December 1997), pp. 31–38.

15. R. Cooper and A. Sawaf, *Executive EQ: Emotional Intelligence in Leadership and Organizations* (New York: Grosset/Putman, 1998).

16. C. Bilton, *Management and Creativity* (Oxford, UK: Blackwell, 2007); Woodman, Sawyer, and Griffin, "Towards a Theory of Organizational Creativity," p. 296.

17. M. J. Kirton, "Adaptors and Innovators: Cognitive Style and Personality," in S. Isaksen (ed.), *Frontiers of Creative Research* (New York: Bearly Limited, 1987), pp. 282–304.

18. M. J. Kirton, "Adaptors and Innovators: Problem Solvers in Organizations," in K. Gronhaug and G. Kaufmann, *Innovation: A Cross-Disciplinary Perspective* (Norway: Norwegian University Press, 1988), p. 72.

19. R. L. Kuhn and G. T. Geis, "A Cross-Organization Methodology for Assessing Creativity and Commitment," in Y. Ijiri and R. Kuhn (eds.), *New Directions in Creative and Innovative Management* (Cambridge, MA: Ballinger, 1988), pp. 303–22.

20. S. G. Isaksen, "Educational Implications of Creativity Research: An Updated Rationale for Creative Learning," in Isaksen (ed.) *Frontiers of Creativity Research,* p. 149.

21. C. Bangle, "The Ultimate Creativity Machine: How BMW Turns Art into Profit," *Harvard Business Review* (January 2001), pp. 5–11.

22. See, for example, G. Vissers and B. Dankbaar, "Creativity in Multidisciplinary New Product Development Teams," *Creativity & Innovation Management* 11 (2002), pp. 31–43; S. F. Kylen and A. B. Shani, "Triggering Creativity in Teams: An Exploratory Investigation," *Creativity & Innovation Management* 11 (2002), pp. 17–41; and Amabile, Hadley and Kramer, "Creativity Under the Gun."

23. M. Tushman and D. Nadler, "Organizing for Innovation," *California Management Review* (Spring 1986), pp. 74–92; and J. Galbraith, "Designing the Innovating Organization," *Organizational Dynamics* (Winter 1982), pp. 5–25.

24. K. Lewis, "Frontiers in Group Dynamics," *Human Relations* 1 (1947), pp. 5–41; and R. F. Bales and F. L. Strodtbeck, "Phases in Group Problem-Solving," *Journal of Abnormal and Social Psychology* 46 (1951), pp. 485–95.

25. J. G. March and H. Simon, *Organizations* (New York: John Wiley & Sons, 1958); and M. D. Cohen, J. G. March, and J. P. Olsen, "A Garbage Can Model of Organizational Choice," *Administrative Science Quarterly* 17 (1972), pp. 1–25.

26. G. W. Dalton, P. R. Lawrence, and L. E. Greiner, *Organizational Change and Development* (Homewood, IL: Dorsey Press, 1970).

27. W. J. Abernathy and J. M. Utterback, "Patterns of Industrial Innovation," in M. Tushman and W. Moore (eds.), *Readings in the Management of Innovation* (Boston: Pitman, 1975), pp. 97–150; M. Jelinek and C. Bird-Schoonhoven, *Innovation Marathon: Lessons from High Technology Firms* (Oxford, UK: Basil Blackwell, 1990); and R. M. Kanter, "Innovation—The Only Hope for Times Ahead?" *Sloan Management Review* (Summer 1984), pp. 51–55.

28. M. T. Hansen and J. Birkinshaw, "The Innovation Value Chain," *Harvard Business Review* (June 2007), pp. 121–30; R. Schroeder, A. H. Van de Ven, G. D. Scudder, and D. Polley, "The Development of Innovative Ideas," in A. H. Van de Ven, H. Angle, and M. Poole (eds.), *Research on the Management of Innovation: The Minnesota Studies* (New York: Harper & Row, 1990), pp. 107–34.

29. J. Schumpeter, *Theorie der Wirtschaftlichen Entwicklung. Eine Untersuchung uber Unternehmergewinn, Kapital, Kredit, Zins und den Konjunkturzyklus,* 3rd ed. (Munich, Germany: Duncker & Humblot, 1931).

30. A. K. Chakrabarti, "The Role of Champions in Product Innovation," *California Management Review* 17 (Winter 1974), pp. 58–62; and K. Gronhaug, and G. Kaufmann, *Innovation: A Cross-Disciplinary Perspective* (Oslo, Norway: Norwegian University Press, 1988).

31. T. J. Allen and S. I. Cohen, "Information Flow in Research and Development Laboratories," *Administrative Science Quarterly* 14 (1969), pp. 12–19.

32. G. Ekvall and Y. T. Andersson, "Working Climate and Creativity: A Study of an Innovative Newspaper Office," *Journal of Creative Behavior* 20 (1986), pp. 215–25; R. M. Burnside, T. M. Amabile, and S. S. Gryskiewicz, "Assessing Organizational Climates for Creativity and Innovation: Methodological Review of Large Company Audits," in Y. Ijiri and R. Kuhn (eds.), *New Directions in Creative and Innovative Management* (Cambridge, MA: Ballinger Publishing Co., 1988), pp. 169–86.

33. T. Burns and G. M. Stalker, *The Management of Innovation* (London: Tavistock Publications, 1961).

34. R. Firestein, *Leading on the Creative Edge* (Colorado, Springs, CO: Pinton Press, 1996).

35. J. L. Pierce and A. L. Delbecq, "Organization Structure, Individual Attitudes, and Innovation," *Academy of Management Review* 2 (January 1977), pp. 27–37.

36. Jelinek and Schoonhoven, *Innovation Marathon.*

37. T. Kono, *Structure of Japanese Enterprises* (London: Macmillan, 1984).

38. M. F. Wolff, "Revamping the Dual Ladder at General Mills," *Research Management* (November 1979), pp. 8–11.

39. M. Sundgren and A. Styhre, "Managing Organizational Creativity," in N. Adler, A. B. Shani, and A. Styhre (eds.), *Collaborative Research in Organizations: Foundations for Learning, Change and Theoretical Development* (Thousand Oaks, CA: Sage, 2004), pp. 237–53; and Y. Cheng and A. H. Van de Ven, "Learning the Innovation Journey: Order out of Chaos?" *Organization Science* (November/December 1996), pp. 593–615.

40. A. B. (Rami) Shani and P. Docherty, *Learning by Design: Building Sustainable Organizations* (London, UK: Blackwell, 2003).

41. R. M. Kanter, "Innovation: The Classic Traps," *Harvard Business Review* 84, no. 1 (2006), pp. 73–83; C. M. J. van Woerkum, M. N. C. Aarts, and K. de Grip, "Creativity, Planning and Organizational Change," *Journal of Organizational Change Management* 20, no. 6 (2007), pp. 847–65; C. Bilton, *Management and Creativity* (Oxford, UK: Blackwell, 2007).

Activity 14–2: Downsizing and Creativity

Objective:

To examine the relationship between company restructuring and creativity.

Task 1 (Individual):

Read the following section, connect to the 3M website, and answer the questions at the end of the section.

Task 2:

Class discussion.

Current Events at 3M Company*

James McNerney was the first outsider to lead 3M when he was snatched up by 3M in 2000 after failing to succeed Jack Welch at GE. He had barely stepped off the plane when he announced that he would change the DNA of the place, which was struggling for profitability in a global environment. Using the GE model, he axed 8,000 workers (11% of the workforce), intensified the performance-review process, and tightened the purse strings. He imported GE's Six-Sigma program—a series of management techniques designed to decrease production defects and increase efficiency. The plan appeared to work, bringing discipline to an organization that had become unwieldy, erratic, and sluggish.

Four and one-half years later, McNerny left for the top job at Boeing. The focus on invention that had been 3M's model for most of its 100 years had been replaced by strict procedures and processes to reduce variation and eliminate defects. Creativity was squelched.

The current CEO, George "call me George" Buckley who cut his teeth at Emerson Electric and was a virtual unknown, came from the research lab—a Ph.D. chemical engineer. He is now trying to manage the tension between innovation and efficiency, dialing back some of McNerney's initiatives. "Invention is by its very nature a disorderly process," states the mild and unassuming Buckley. "You can't put a Six Sigma process into that area and say, well, I'm getting behind on invention, so I'm going to schedule myself for three good ideas on Wednesday and two on Friday. That's not how creativity works . . . when you value sameness more than you value creativity, I think you potentially undermine the heart and soul of a company like 3M."

Defenders of Six Sigma at 3M claim that a more systematic new-product introduction process allows innovations to get to the market faster. But Fry, one of the Post-it Note inventors, disagrees. He places the blame for 3M's recent lack of innovation sizzle squarely on Six Sigma's application in 3M's research labs. Innovation, he says, is "a numbers game. You have to go through five or six thousand raw ideas to find one successful business." Six Sigma would ask, why not eliminate all that waste and just come up with the right idea the first time? That way of thinking, says Fry, has serious side effects. "What's remarkable is how fast a culture can be torn apart," says Fry. "[McNerney] didn't kill it because he wasn't here long enough. But if he had been here much longer, I think he could have."

In 2004, the Boston Consulting Group ranked 3M as number 1 on its list of most innovative companies. By 2007 it had dropped to number 7. To help get the creative juices flowing again, Buckley is increasing the R&D budget by 20%, to $1.5 billion, and is relocating those funds to "core" areas of 3M technology—abrasives, nanotechnology, and flexible electronics. McNerney had made a skin-care cream, Aldara, the centerpiece of what he says is a burgeoning pharmaceuticals business. In January 2007, Buckley sold the pharmaceutical business for $2 billion.

Many workers say they are reinvigorated now that the emphasis has shifted from profitability and process discipline to growth and innovation. Says Bob Aderson, a business director at 3M, "We feel like we can dream again."

Continue to search for current information about 3M. You can connect to 3M at www.3M.com.

Questions:

1. What do you think is the effect of radical restructuring, such as McNerney attempted, on the creativity and the innovation process?

2. The pressure to innovate has once again increased at 3M. How will this environment affect the creativity and innovation process?

*Source: Modified and adapted from B. Hindo, "How CEO George Buckley Is Managing the Yin and Yang of Discipline and Imagination," *Business Week* (6/11/2007), Issue 4038, Special Section, pp. 8–14.

Activity 14–3: Organizational Innovation: Learning from the WWW

Objective:

Reflecting on organizational innovation by learning from information on the WWW.

Task 1 (Individual):

Go to the Innovation Network website on articles and reports on organizational innovation at www.thinksmart.com. What are some of the skills most critical to the organizations that were 1998 Land Award winners for innovation?

Task 2 (Team):

Each team is to share its learning and prepare a three-minute presentation based on its collective learning.

Activity 14–4: Making a Metaphor

Objective:

To explore individual paradigms that affect individual creativity. A metaphor is a figure of speech in which we liken two objects or concepts that do not appear to be alike. Through metaphor we can make connections and discoveries that did not previously exist. We can make the familiar strange and thus challenge our way of thinking. In the 3M case, metaphors had to be changed so people could break through old mental sets.

Task 1:

Complete the following metaphors, choosing from one of the options given or making up your own.

1. Eating a fine dinner is like
   a. Throwing a javelin a long distance.
   b. Watching an hourglass drip sand.
   c. Reading a popular novel at the beach.
   d. Putting nail polish on your toes.

2. Raising a child is like
   a. Driving from Seattle to New York.
   b. Weeding your garden.
   c. Building a fire and watching it burn.
   d. Fishing for rainbow trout.

3. Playing a piano recital is like
   a. Investing in the stock market.
   b. Growing orchids.
   c. Driving through rush hour traffic with your gas gauge on empty.
   d. Fasting for three days.

4. Finding truth is like
   a. Making banana nut bread.
   b. Walking into a room and forgetting the reason why.
   c. Navigating a sailboat through a violent thunderstorm.
   d. Taking a test that has no wrong answers.

Task 2:

Share your metaphors with your group. Explain why you chose the metaphor you did. The instructor will facilitate a class discussion on the use of metaphors and creativity.

Source: This activity is adopted with permission from R. von Oeck, *A Kick in the Seat of the Pants* (New York: Warner Books, 1986), p. 72.

Module 15

Organizational Culture

LEARNING OBJECTIVES

After completing this module, you should be able to

1. Explain the nature of national culture.
2. Describe a conceptual framework that can guide the assessment of a national culture.
3. Identify and define the key features of organizational culture.
4. Identify the relationship between symbolism and organizational culture.
5. Describe the key factors that affect organizational culture.
6. Identify the challenges in managing organizational culture.
7. Explain the relationship between organizational culture and organizational effectiveness.

KEY TERMS AND CONCEPTS

Culture

Culture management

Hofstede's dimensions of culture

Managing organizational culture

National culture model

Organizational culture

Organizational effectiveness

Symbolism

Value orientation model

MODULE OUTLINE

Premodule Preparation

Introduction

Culture

Organizational Culture

Defining Organizational Culture

The Individual Context

The Organizational Context of Organizational Culture

Symbol Sensitivity and the Management of Culture

Organizational Culture and Organizational Effectiveness

Summary

Study Questions

Endnotes

PREMODULE PREPARATION

The instructor may assign one of the following activities as a premodule activity.

Activity 15–1: Exploring the Trouteville Police Department's Culture

Objective:

To appreciate the meaning creation process and role of organizational culture in an organization setting.

Task 1 (Homework):

Participants are to read and complete the questions assigned at the end of the case.

Task 2 (Classroom):

a. Teams are to reach a shared perception of the major characteristics of the department under John Stage's leadership.

b. Teams are to reach a shared perception on the major characteristics of the department under Larry Gaft's leadership.

c. Teams are to discuss the process of cultural change. (For example, what were some of the problems in Gaft's approach to change the department culture? What was their impact on individual and group effectiveness? What would have been the ideal process to change the organizational culture?)

Task 3:

The instructor will have each team share its perceptions, with the entire class, about the police department's culture under the command of the two leaders.

Task 4:

The class will discuss the elements of each culture and examine their similarities and differences.

Task 5:

The instructor will give a short lecture on organizational culture and the role that the process plays in fostering or hindering effectiveness.

Case Study: Trouteville Police Department*

Introduction

Trouteville City is located in a rural area of the western United States and has a population of approximately 35,000 people. Within the municipality is the Trouteville Police Department, which is classified as a small department. The department employs 70 people, 55 sworn (police officers), and 15 unsworn.

For the past 17 years, the chief of police has been John Stage, who worked up the ranks from patrolman. Through the years of increased political pressure and stress of the job, Stage became an alcoholic and retired. Although most of the people in the community knew about his drinking habits, Stage was nonetheless highly respected. He insisted on a high level of qualified personnel on his staff, and the department did not have any major problems during his tenure. Internally, the men feared his short temper, but he was angry so often that they grew to expect this behavior.

After Stage's retirement, the city of Trouteville openly recruited candidates from outside the city. Larry Gaft was appointed as the chief of police. Gaft had previously been a captain in a large metropolitan police department. Several early rumors circulated within the department that Gaft was appointed because of his "tight" control and leadership.

Larry Gaft brought with him the management philosophy known as "team policing" or the "team concept" in police administration. This type of management has been made popular during the last decade in an increasing number of police departments that had changed to this style of management. Team policing has its beginnings in the "team management" style of management. Under team policing, a problem or management goal is identified, a staff member is selected to form a committee, and goals are identified and a time table set for their attainment. The committee then attempts to solve the problem through the knowledge and interaction of its members. If the problem is corrected and is not likely to return, the committee is disbanded. If it is a continuous problem or is a specific management goal (that is, reduction of traffic accidents or burglaries), then the committee is made a permanent part of the organization and is called a team.

Soon after Gaft's appointment the department began to experience changes within its organizational structure as teams were added. Gaft solicited the help of all the department's personnel to identify any problems within the department. Some of the major problems were the continuous increase in traffic accidents, obsolete report forms, and the lack of personnel. Teams were soon organized, a sergeant was appointed as team leader, and members either volunteered or were "asked to volunteer." The Trouteville Police Department now had a traffic team, report writing committee, and a reserve police officers' committee. Officers received no extra pay for the additional responsibility and frequently worked on their own time to complete their assignments.

The Reorganization

Three months following the appointment of Larry Gaft, the Trouteville Police Department was reorganized to accommodate the new management philosophy of team policing. New employees were hired, others were reclassified, and still others were promoted. The department adopted a goal of "crime prevention," which was the goal behind the reorganization. The following major changes were made:

1. Lieutenants were placed in command of a division.

2. Two levels of sergeants were created. Sergeants under the old organization were reclassified to sergeant II and given the responsibility of a command of a "watch" or shift. Patrolmen were promoted to the level of sergeant I and were responsible for field supervision.

*Copyright © 1998 by Rolf E. Rogers. All rights reserved, and no reproduction should be made without express approval of Professor Rolf E. Rogers, School of Business, California Polytechnic State University, San Luis Obispo, California 93407.

3. The city was divided into four sectors; each sergeant I was assigned the responsibility as sector leader and required to submit a monthly report to the crime prevention leader. A reorganization manual was prepared and distributed to each employee. The manual defined job duties and responsibilities and detailed the organizational structure and chain of command.

The Case

Several months after the reorganization, the department began to experience an increase in morale problems, as evidenced by a dramatic increase in personnel attrition, grievances, and general complaints made to the president of the Trouteville Police Association, Pete Martin. Pete, a patrolman of 4 years began to notice a specific conflict between the sergeants and patrolmen. One such conflict occurred 2 months after the reorganization. Pete was sent by communications to assist Patrolman Dale White in a minor injury accident. Pete witnessed the following argument between White and Sergeant II Joe Collins.

WHITE: Hello, Sarge, minor injury accident.

COLLINS: So where's the traffic team? You know they investigate all injury accidents.

WHITE: Just a second. Sergeant I Simpson said we could investigate minor injury accidents as well as they can; besides it saves time. It takes them 10 minutes to get here. I can have this investigated by then.

COLLINS: Don't argue with me! Call traffic and get them here now.

WHITE: Yes sir!

Dale, almost completed with the accident investigation, called communications by radio and asked for the traffic team. The team arrived about 5 minutes later. White had the following conversation with Traffic Officer Gary Rice.

WHITE: It's about time you got here. What took you so long?

RICE: We just got the call; it does take some time to drive here, you know!

WHITE: So why weren't you called by communications when the accident happened?

RICE: They want you guys to confirm that there is an injury first. Besides, we're so busy with paperwork, who has time to be in the field?

Dale White left the scene as the traffic team began to investigate the accident (Dale had told them he had not started the investigation).

Later that day, Pete was in the department and saw Sergeant Simpson, the field supervisor, reading and correcting crime reports, a responsibility of the watch commander.

Approximately one month later, Sergeant Collins was addressing the patrolmen during the role call briefing regarding the lack of citations written during the previous month.

SERGEANT COLLINS: OK, you guys, you know we're attempting to decrease our traffic accidents by an aggressive citation policy. Not one of you is even close to the "right" number. Patrolman Davis, you only wrote five tickets the whole month.

DAVIS: So what's the traffic team for? The only thing they do is sit in the office keeping stats. I'm a member of the reserve officers' committee and report writing committee; how do you expect me to do all that plus write tickets, too?

SERGEANT COLLINS: Your primary duty is law enforcement and that includes traffic enforcement. I'll expect you all to increase your ticket count to a reasonable level this month.

Fifteen months following Larry Gaft's appointment, Sergeant Sweigert approached Pete Martin regarding a pay dispute with the city. Apparently, the sergeant IIs believed that they had been promoted when the department was reorganized and their position was reclassified as sergeant II. They were now given the responsibility of "watch commander," a position previously held by a lieutenant. Second, the newly promoted sergeant Is, now "field supervisors," had received an increase in salary below that which the sergeants had been paid prior to the reorganization. Sergeant IIs received no increase in salary.

The sergeants wished to file a formal grievance through the police association. The grievance procedure is as follows:

1. The affected person or group files a written grievance through the association within a reasonable length of time.

2. The association then presents the grievance to the chief of police. If he approves the grievance, it is then routed through the chain of command to the city administrator for approval.

3. If the chief of police disapproves the grievance, the association has two alternatives: They may present the grievance to the city council for adoption or resolve the grievance through other remedies.

As president of the police association, it was Pete Martin's function to present the grievance to Chief Gaft. Pete arranged for an appointment and the following conversation took place.

CHIEF GAFT: Come on in, Pete.

MARTIN: Thanks, chief, I would like to speak to you about the sergeants' pay dispute.

CHIEF: I don't understand why they are so angry. When they accepted their new assignments, they were told what the responsibilities would be; no one griped then.

MARTIN: It's getting to be a real problem—we're having problems between the patrolmen and sergeants already; we don't need anything else to lower morale.

CHIEF: [face reddening, voice rising] It seems every time there is a problem, the association gets involved and blows it way out of proportion. You guys are causing the problems! Another stick in my side! Well, I'm not going to support your grievance; you'll have to take it to court.

Pete left and later that week met with each individual sergeant either in person or by phone and told them what had occurred. Each voiced their support to take the grievance to court. Six months after Pete Martin's meeting with Chief Gaft, the following events occurred:

1. Personnel attrition continued to increase to approximately 40 percent. (*Note:* None of the officers who resigned sought law enforcement careers after leaving the Trouteville Police Department.)

2. Urged by the police association, the city administrator forced a formal meeting to air and discuss the recent problems within the department. The chief and his staff attended as representatives of the administration, and certain "select" patrolmen were asked to attend to represent the employees. Each patrolman spoke and expressed his concern that the administration was insensitive to employee/employer problems and that the problems began immediately following the chief's appointment.

The sergeant's salary grievance was satisfied by the association through its negotiations of wages and benefits during the regular yearly salary negotiations with the city.

Assignment

Prepare notes on the following questions:

1. Based on the limited information presented, identify and briefly describe the major characteristics of the Trouteville Police Department under the leadership of John Stage.

2. Identify and describe the major characteristics of the department after Larry Gaft's appointment as chief of police.

3. Has the Trouteville Police Department culture changed? (If yes, how? If not, why didn't it?)

Activity 15–2: Slogan and Symbol Identification

Objectives:

a. To appreciate the symbolic nature of the workplace.

b. To explore the relationship between symbols and organizational culture.

Task 1:

a. Pick one organization with which you are closely associated. It may be your place of employment, a church group where you volunteer, or the college or university that you currently attend.

b. Identify 100 symbols. That's right 100. All you have to do is list them. The point of this activity is twofold: (1) to get you in the habit of seeing the symbolic dimensions of organizational life and (2) to help you appreciate the vastness of culture that we take for granted. If you are stuck, read the discussion in the module about symbols and culture and then proceed with the activity. If you are still having some difficulty, refer to the "symbol generator"—Activity 15–5W on the WWW. It is simply a list of things that people in organizations have found symbolic. Does it give you any ideas? People often get stuck in this exercise because they don't think broadly enough.

Task 2:

a. In your teams read your lists to each other. Hearing other lists often is revealing. Spend 10 minutes each explaining why certain persons, objects, and events are symbolic in your organization.

b. Explore some of the similarities and differences between the lists. Can you see any patterns? What are they? What do they mean?

Task 3:

Following some sharing with the learning community, the instructor will lead a class discussion about symbols and organizational culture.

INTRODUCTION

Earlier in the book—Module 1—we discussed the need to focus on sustainability, sustainable development, and sustainable work systems. We argued that the field of organizational behavior can play an important role in the understanding, designing, and developing of a sustainable work system. Work was defined as an intentional value-creating process (Module 2). This general definition gains meaning with the specification of the goals and rules, resources, and context for the work process. These parameters are related to the stakeholders in the process—workers, investors, suppliers, customers, and communities (see Module 13). The resources are financial, material, physical, intellectual, and technological. The context is cultural, ecological, economic, historical, and social. Within the content of this module—Organizational Culture—addressing sustainability in a work system means, therefore, exploring the basic elements that form culture and organizational culture, what influences it, and how work systems are influenced by it.[1]

Social glue is one of the commonest metaphors of organizational culture.[2] The study of culture—national, regional, and organizational—continues to receive increased attention from managers and scholars alike. How important is it to recognize the differences and similarities among nations, regions, and organizations? Just between the United States and Europe there are more than 200,000 firms that are involved in global ventures. One of every five U.S. workers is employed in a company that has international activities.[3] One of every three European workers is employed in a company that has international activities.[4] The continuous growth in the global nature of business serves as one of the main catalysts for the renewed interest in the study of culture and the realization that culture (again, national, regional, and organizational) affects the behavior and success of individuals, teams, and organizations. **Managing organizational culture** is emerging as one of the key managerial challenges of the 21st century. Thus, this module begins with a brief exploration of national and regional culture. Next we examine the key features of organizational culture. The module concludes with the exploration of ways to manage organizational culture.

CULTURE

Defining Culture

The scientific study of culture has been the main topic in the discipline of anthropology. Additional contributions can be found in the disciplines of sociology, social psychology, and economics. A comprehensive review of culture is beyond the scope of this module and book. Our discussion of culture is with an eye on organizations, business, and human behavior in the context of the work organization. According to Webster's,[5] **culture** is defined as "A particular form or stage of civilization, as that of a certain nation, region or period"; "The behavior and beliefs characteristic of a particular social, ethnic, or age group," and "The sum total of ways of living built up by a group of human beings and transmitted from one generation to another." Anthropologists defined culture in many ways:

> Culture consists in patterned ways of thinking, feeling and reacting, acquired and transmitted mainly by symbols, constituting the distinctive achievements of human groups, including their embodiments in artifacts; the essential core of culture consists of traditional (i.e., historically derived and selected) ideas and especially their attached values.[6]

> Culture is viewed as transmitted and created content and patterns of values, ideas, and other symbolic-meaningful systems as factors in the shaping of human behavior and the artifacts produced through behavior.[7]

> Culture is viewed as the collective programming of the mind that distinguishes the members of one group or category of people from another.[8]

> Culture is everything that people have, think, and do as members of society.[9]

> Culture is the learned residue of past experiences and manifests itself at the level of behavioral regularities, espoused values that usually reflect aspirations more than realities and tacit, shared assumptions that drive daily behavior.[10]

Thus, at the most basic level, culture is:

- Something that is shared by all or almost all members of some social group (such as a nation, a region, an organization, a profession, an age group, a religious group).

- A system of values and beliefs, symbols, heroes, rituals, and practices.

- Something that is transmitted from one generation to another.

- Something that human beings get socialized into from "day one."

Different Conceptual Road Maps to Understanding Culture

Following the definitions just captured, we can anticipate a variety of frameworks that were developed in order to map out and understand the complex phenomenon of culture. Once again, because theoretical discussion and presentation of the many different frameworks of culture are beyond the scope of this chapter, we briefly discuss two complementary frameworks: the value orientation model developed by Kluckhohn and Strodtbeck and the cultural values model developed by Hofstede.

Value Orientation Model

Kluckhohn and Strodtbeck developed a conceptual **value orientation model** that includes six dimensions that attempt to capture the value orientation of cultures. The value orientation represents the way a society copes with emerging issues and challenges. The dimensions include the following: *relation to nature* (the societal orientation to its nature—harmony, disregard, or mastery of, for example, trying to change its environment); *time orientation* (the societal orientation to time; how it uses time; whether it is oriented toward the past, present, or future); *basic human nature* (the basic nature of human beings—good, evil, neutral/mix); *activity orientation* (the societal orientation to human activity—doing, being, containing/controlling); *relationships among people* (the societal orientations among people—individualistic, group/collective, hierarchical); and *space orientation* (how people relate to the ownership of space—public, private, mixed).[11] Thus, a culture can be profiled and compared with others while utilizing the six dimensions.

National Culture Model

Hofstede, in a study of culture that focused on work-related values conducted in 40 countries (later was expanded to more than 60 countries), developed national profiles that explain differences in work behavior. The study was done within IBM, where 160,000 employees and managers responded twice to a survey. Hofstede initially extracted four dimensions of values to develop his **national culture model** and explain the differences between the cultures: *individualism/collectivism* (whether individual or collective action is the preferred way to deal with issues); *power distance* (the degree to which differences in power and status are accepted in a culture); *uncertainty avoidance* (whether the society tends to prefer rules and operate in predictable situations as opposed to situations where the appropriate behaviors are not specified in advance); and *masculinity/femininity* (the degree to which values associated with stereotypes of masculinity—such as aggressiveness and dominance—and femininity—such as compassion, empathy, and emotional openness—are emphasized). Later, Hofstede and his collaborators identified a fifth dimension, *long-term/short-term orientation* (whether a society is concerned with the future, value thrift and persistence, or is concerned with the past and present).[12]

Cultural frameworks attempt to explain cultural differences. While many cultural frameworks exist, none is absolutely correct or better than the others, yet each provides a way to map out a culture. They provide analytical ways to help understand why people from different cultures seem to vary in behavior. In the context of this book, we view the cultural frameworks as additional analytical tools that can be used by the manager to gain insight into cultural dynamics at work. The cultural frameworks of nations and regions set the stage for the exploration of organizational culture.

ORGANIZATIONAL CULTURE

A quick study of leading companies in diverse industries reveals a wide variety of organizational culture features. The culture that emerged within Google, IDEO, IBM, GM, and Bank of America are significantly different. The culture that emerged in the Trouteville case (see Activity 15–1) is different from the one that evolved in other police departments as well as other organizations. An examination of the slogans that companies develop and use point toward clear differences in terms of emphasis, work design, and management and what really counts. The following captures the distinct nature of IDEO.

IDEO Product Development of Palo Alto, California, is an example of the latter environment. IDEO was founded by a Stanford University engineering professor and is now the largest firm in the United States with a mission of helping client companies develop new products and become more innovative. IDEO employs over 500 engineers, industrial designers, human factors specialists, and social scientists, who work on projects that average 10 to 12 months in duration. In the manufacturing realm, IDEO contributions range from rough sketches of products to complete new products. Recently, IDEO has moved into the services sector to tackle difficult health care delivery and customer contact issues. Employees work out of offices in diverse locations including San Francisco, Boston, London, and Tokyo. The firm has won numerous awards for design work, and has been acclaimed "the world's most celebrated design firm."

The founders of IDEO wish to create an environment that supports good relationships and creativity. Accordingly, the physical layout is purposely centered on small buildings with open facilities design. There is no visible administration—buildings all have a reception desk for visitors, and the rest of the space is devoted to the engineers and laboratories where prototypes are created. The small building and limited number of employees eliminate the need for extensive security; employees know each other and know who should and should not be present. The psychological climate at IDEO incorporates many features associated with ideal conditions for knowledge workers. In general, unspoken norms take the place of policies and rules. There is little or no structure; management encourages employees to take the initiative and use their knowledge and skills. For example, employees design their own workplaces, consistent with the idea of periodic movement to new projects and work locations in the building. Office designs are open, featuring distinct partitions such as a DC-3 wing suspended from the ceiling. Most work locations also offer space to work alone in peace and quiet on a given day if the open environment begins to intrude.

Given IDEO's reputation and their commitment to learning, tours and interviews are an ongoing part of employee life. Most employees participate in showing visitors work in progress. Employees say that a common topic of interviews is "how to maintain energy and creativity as the small firm grows." The secret is apparently in employee involvement in selection of clients and projects, and allowing employees to gravitate to projects or client companies that fit their interests. Clients participate in an estimated 20% of brainstorming sessions, and clients work side by side with the staff for one or two weeks at a time to observe, learn, and try out IDEO work practices. In some cases, clients are colocated at IDEO for up to a year when long-term alliances are desired. In Palo Alto, employees from each building meet once a week for an hour, sitting on the floor in a large circle to share information on team activities, discuss new technologies, demonstrate new products, and give very brief updates on progress and setbacks on products for 15–40 clients. They also take time out once a week for an organized bike ride through the hills of Palo Alto.

Much of the work is team-based. IDEO employees are trained in facilitation techniques and all brainstorming sessions in design teams are facilitator-led. Team members also host special sessions to demonstrate new work practices and technologies to others in the building. An example is the frequent practice of running involvement workshops to teach other staff to observe users, brainstorm new designs, and build working models. IDEO employees are experts at teaching rapid prototyping, and are frequent contributors to Silicon Valley engineering and business school programs.

Interviews indicate that IDEO employees remain with the company because of the unique working environment. As relatively young people with advanced degrees in engineering and related fields, they are well paid, but could do better elsewhere. Compensation is not on a merit or performance increase basis, but rather increases with time and market conditions. Management believes that typical merit schemes create a competitive environment, and are "not nurturing." When employees leave, it is often for a sabbatical or to gain advanced education.

At IDEO, the founders wished to preserve freedoms that they enjoyed as inventors and entrepreneurs when the company was small. With growth, they were careful to create simple forms of structure supported in part by the limitations on the size of offices and laboratories. A small-company atmosphere was maintained by growing new units in separate office buildings. Moreover, employees influenced strategy by creating their own projects and having a say in outside projects that IDEO might select. In some ways, projects take the place of formal structures and managerial processes. Employees participate in all aspects of the business, including training others in IDEO work practices. Consistent with SWS thinking, employees have a sense of security and personal support. Turnover is very low despite attractive outside opportunities in the Silicon Valley area. High quality of work life and solid financial performance and other indicators suggest that IDEO is a sustainable work system.[13]

As can be seen from the preceding IDEO case, when one compares this case to the Trouteville case (Activity 15–1), distinct organizational culture features seem to evolve within work systems. This point is magnified when one examines the emerging nature of the global marketplace. We argue that the relatively recent focus on **organizational culture** seems to stem from increasing difficulty in the emerging global marketplace and from the management of mergers or acquisitions once the formal contracts have been signed. The last decade has been characterized as the "company mergers and acquisition decade." As the number of mergers and acquisitions reached record levels, we also began to read about the many difficulties that managers run into as they try to transform two entities into one. According to J. P. Morgan (the facilitator behind the merger between

Exxon and Mobil), only one out of every 10 deals is consummated, and many deals unravel after they are announced. Differences in the nature of the organizations' cultures have been identified as one of the major stumbling blocks.

For example, when management guru Stephen Covey merged his Covey Leadership Center with rival Franklin Quest around the end of 1997, most people predicted that the merging of the two companies was a win–win deal with natural synergies. Yet 18 months later, *USA Today* reported that "insiders say that despite similar corporate missions that are supposed to inspire (their) clients to embrace change, Franklin-Covey suffered from having two different company cultures, inertia, and indecision about how to transform the two cultures into one."[14] Assessing organizational culture and diagnosing the degree of "fit" between the cultures of two companies that are considering a merger might be a necessary step. But before we proceed, we must first stop and explore the organizational culture school of thought and its meaning.

The organizational culture theories are based on assumptions about people and organizations that depart significantly, and in more than one way, from those of the "mainstream" schools. First, they challenge the system and the structural schools about (for example) how organizations make decisions and how and why humans behave as they do.[15] While the system and structural schools argue that individuals' personal preferences are restrained by systems of formal rules, authority, and norms of rational behavior, the cultural school advocates that individual preferences are controlled by cultural norms, values, beliefs, and assumptions.[16] Second, from the organizational culture viewpoint, every organizational culture is different, and what "works" for one organization will not necessarily work for another.[17] Third, the organizational culture school believes that qualitative research methods are the better way to fully understand and predict organizational behavior[18] (rather than quantitative research methods using quasi-experimental designs, control groups, and multivariate analyses).

Defining Organizational Culture

Just as we saw earlier in this chapter about the national culture literature, an examination of the organizational culture school reveals many diverse definitions and elements. For some, organizational culture has something to do with the people and the unique character of the organization; for some, it means shared top-management beliefs about how they should manage themselves and other employees and how they should conduct their business;[19] for some it is the shared philosophies, ideologies, values, assumptions, expectations, attitudes, and norms that knit a community together;[20] for some it is an evolutionary process;[21] and for still others it is a complex pattern of beliefs, expectations, ideas, values, attitudes, and behavior shared by the members of an organization. Furthermore, controversy exists on the role of organizational culture, its effects on organizational life, and the ability to influence and lead corporate culture change.[22]

For our purposes Schein's holistic definition captures the essence, complexity, and uniqueness of the phenomenon: Organizational culture is

> (a) a pattern of basic assumptions, (b) invented, discovered, or developed by a given group, (c) as it learns to cope with its problems of external adaption and internal integration, (d) that has worked well enough to be considered valid and, therefore, (e) is to be taught to new members as the (f) correct way to perceive, think, and feel in relation to those problems.[23]

Schein argues further that in analyzing the culture of an organization or group, it is important to distinguish among three fundamental levels at which culture manifests itself: (1) observable artifacts such as physical layout, dress code, the way people relate to each other, company records, statement of philosophy, and reports; (2) values, norms, philosophy, and ideology; and (3) basic underlying assumptions about the organization's relationship to its environment, the nature of reality and truth, the nature of human nature, the nature of human activity, and the nature of human relationships (see Figure 15–1). Figure 15–2 provides an example of specific questions that can guide the exploration of the underlying assumptions around which cultural paradigms emerge.

**Figure 15–1
Organizational Culture:
A Framework for Analysis**

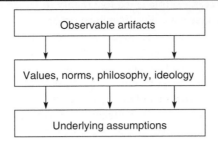

**Figure 15–2
Some Underlying
Dimensions of
Organizational Culture**

Dimension	Questions to Be Answered
1. The organization's relationship to its environment	Does the organization perceive itself to be dominant, submissive, harmonizing, or searching out a niche?
2. The nature of human activity	Is the "correct" way for humans to behave to be dominant/proactive, harmonizing, or passive/fatalistic?
3. The nature of reality and truth	How do we define what is true and what is not true, and how is truth ultimately determined in both the physical and social worlds: by pragmatic test, reliance on wisdom, or social consensus?
4. The nature of time	What is our basic orientation in terms of past, present, and future, and what kinds of time units are most relevant for the conduct of daily affairs?
5. The nature of human nature	Are humans basically good, neutral, or evil, and is human nature perfectible or fixed?
6. The nature of human relationships	What is the correct way for people to relate to each other and to distribute power and affection? Is life competitive or cooperative? Is the best way to organize society on the basis of individualism or groupism? Is the best authority system autocratic/paternalistic or collegial/participative?
7. Homogeneity versus diversity	Is the group best off if it is highly diverse or if it is highly homogeneous, and should individuals in a group be encouraged to innovate or conform?

Source: Adapted from E. H. Schein, *Organizational Culture and Leadership* (San Francisco: Jossey-Bass, 1985), p. 86. Copyright © 1985 by Jossey-Bass. Adapted with permission.

The Individual Context

The concept of cultural intelligence has emerged as of late as an attempt to integrate culture and intelligence at work. The relationship between the two is complex. In general, two approaches evolved: culture variation of intelligence and cultural intelligence. At the most basic level, the "culture variation of intelligence" view recognizes that culture and context influence the concept of intelligence; that is, attributes that make up intelligence are likely to differ across cultures. The essence of this view is that "cultural factors prescribe what shall be learned and at what age; consequently, different cultural environments lead to the development of different patterns of ability." Empirically, studies have demonstrated similarities and variations in the notions of intelligence across cultures.[24]

A more recent approach of research—cultural intelligence (CQ)—seeks to understand interindividual differences in the ability to adapt effectively to new cultural settings. Cultural intelligence has been conceptualized to comprise four facets:

1. *Meta-cognition.* Cognitive strategies to acquire and develop coping strategies.

2. *Cognition.* Knowledge about different cultures.

3. *Motivation.* Desire and self-efficacy.

4. *Behavior.* Repertoire of culturally appropriate behaviors.[25]

The importance of understanding the current thinking, research, and state of the art on the topic at the individual level is that they are likely to play a role in our ability to develop a deeper understanding of culture and organizational culture at the collective level.

The Organizational Context of Organizational Culture

The emerging global marketplace led to a reality in which many organizations are multi-cultural entities. Products are developed and designed in one country, manufactured in a few other countries, and marketed in many other countries.[26] As such, among the many factors that affect the evolution of group and organizational culture are (1) work group characteristics such as commitment to the group's mission and task, work group size and composition, and work group design and autonomy; (2) managerial and leadership styles such as philosophical process and output orientations; (3) dynamics among groups and departments such as degree of dependency, communication processes, and cooperation; (4) organizational characteristics such as mission, product and service requirements, size, technology, policies and procedures, reward system, and organization design; (5) environmental characteristics such as industry, competitive pressures, and social, political, and legal environments, and (6) the emergent features of the global marketplace. Figure 15–3 presents graphically some key factors that affect the evolution of culture.

Recently, a guiding framework for maintaining and reinforcing a specific organizational culture was proposed. The framework lists the following dimensions: criteria for hiring individuals who fit the organizational culture; criteria for removing employees who consistently or markedly deviate from accepted behaviors and activities; elements that managers and teams pay attention to, measure, and control; behavioral dimensions that compare how managers react to critical incidents and organizational crises; managerial and team role modeling, teaching, and coaching; criteria for recruitment, selection, and promotion; and organizational rites, ceremonies, and stories. Because every group and organization is an open system that exists in multiple work environments, change in the environment is likely to produce pressure inside the group that forces new learning and the adoption of this learning. To some degree, there are pressures for any given culture to continuously change and grow. As such, culture can be seen as an ongoing evolutionary process. The difficulty of managing the evolution of organizational culture is complex due to a variety of reasons:

- The tendency among individuals and groups to resist changes.[27]

- The unique subculture that evolves within each subunit (such as functional departments, product groups, hierarchical levels, or even teams) and that may reflect their own unique culture.

- The nature of the relationships between subunits or subcultures that creates dynamics that are complex and hard to understand and manage.

Figure 15–3
Some Key Factors Affecting the Context of Organizational Culture

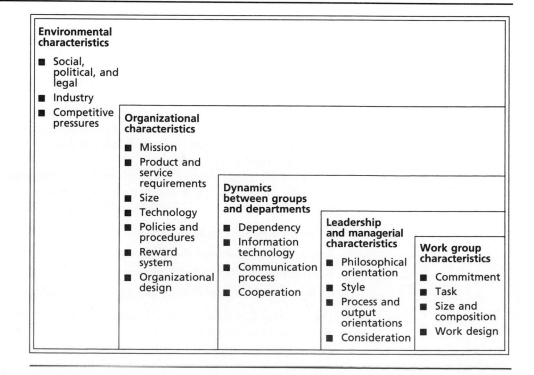

Environmental characteristics
- Social, political, and legal
- Industry
- Competitive pressures

Organizational characteristics
- Mission
- Product and service requirements
- Size
- Technology
- Policies and procedures
- Reward system
- Organizational design

Dynamics between groups and departments
- Dependency
- Information technology
- Communication process
- Cooperation

Leadership and managerial characteristics
- Philosophical orientation
- Style
- Process and output orientations
- Consideration

Work group characteristics
- Commitment
- Task
- Size and composition
- Work design

As we have seen, organizational culture is a dynamic and complex phenomenon. Artifacts, values, assumptions, and symbols interact in four cultural processes: manifestation, realization, symbolization, and interpretation. Next we focus on mapping the cultural process via symbolization.

SYMBOL SENSITIVITY AND THE MANAGEMENT OF CULTURE

Organizations focus significant energy on creating distinct slogans. Those are used both for internal and external consumptions. The labeling of managerial practices and key organizational processes all act as self-fulfilling processes (see Modules 2 and 6). In the 1980s, the success of Japanese competition upset much of the general thinking about how business should be conducted and how organizations should be understood. Successive waves of innovation stunned western managers: Just-in-time inventory management, government/business cooperation in formulating industrial policy, quality circles, market-share-based strategies, global trading companies, *keiretsu* or company groupings, lifetime employment, and a host of other innovations stood behind the "secret" of Japanese competitiveness.

After many years of trying to make sense out of these innovations, it occurred to management scholars to ask the question, What kind of people are able to produce one industrial innovation after another? Many researchers began to inquire into the nature of Japanese culture as it played out in the company. Others began to look at the cultures of American firms, especially those who had been successful over long periods of time.

The outcome of this research was to discover that culture was a powerful variable that knit companies together. "High-culture" companies tended to be more successful in many industries, and this trend was especially true among companies who had "been around" for several decades.[28] These discoveries sparked the search for how to best make use of culture in managing the company. Popular literature is now filled with anecdotes about how a given manager or group of managers successfully managed the culture of a company to achieve corporate goals, to effect turnarounds, or to redirect the attention of their employees. Today, it seems every manager wants to be a "culture manager." For the student of management who wants to explore this area, much of the popular literature does not go deep enough. Laundry lists of do's and don't's abound. But many researchers take the stand that if you want to change a culture, you have to understand what it is. And to understand a culture, you have to understand how it affects your fellow organization members and how it affects you. In other words, cultural sensitivity should precede **culture management.**

This approach represents a subtle difference from much management wisdom. The emphasis on managing culture assumes that the manager knows what he or she would manage. It assumes that the manager is *outside* the culture and can (and should) act on it. It also assumes a one-way causation—the manager shapes the culture, not the other way around. Although it is true that corporate leaders such as Bill Gates and Sam Walton can have an enormous influence on their companies, they are influenced by them as well. Both Bill and Sam are remarkably open to their employees' suggestions and take their perceptions and needs into account when redesigning the respective companies.

If it is true that culture management is a two-way street, then awareness of one's company culture is a vital part of changing it. But how do we enhance that awareness? Where do we start? The answer implicit in most culture literature is to start with symbols. Most writers agree that symbols are the "building blocks" of culture. Symbols are also "tools" that can shape underlying values and behavior. However you understand culture—whether in terms of values, rituals, ceremonies, corner offices, gold watches, stories people tell at work, their dreams of the future, and so on—**symbolism** is pretty much at the basis of everything. Thus, cultural awareness is pretty coexistent with awareness of symbols.

The best place to start with symbolic awareness is with yourself. If you can become familiar with the ways in which the symbols in your organization affect you—how they shape your assumptions, how they provide the emotional glue between people who don't know each other, how they influence perceptions of stakeholders—you will be in an excellent position to decide what (if anything) you want to do about them. Culture management will be for you more than a buzzword. It will be a real possibility.

How do we start? Perhaps the best place is with a definition. What is a symbol anyway? Most students can recite a list of common symbols in companies without much difficulty. Again, corner offices, company jets, and gold watches come to mind. If this were all there were to it, symbols would be trivial ornaments to organizational life. However, company symbolism is much more pervasive than these stock examples would lead us to believe. Perhaps the most useful definition of a symbol comes from anthropology: A *symbol* is any person, object, or event that organizational members invest with personal meanings.

This definition is deceptively simple, First, the word *any* implies that almost anything can be symbolic, including a host of things we think of as "unsymbolic," for example, performance appraisals or sales figures. Yet if we think about an individual waiting anxiously for an upcoming performance review or a CEO wondering what caused a sales shortfall, we recognize that there is more going on here than mere "organizational" thinking. The performance appraisal is "attached" to fantasies about how good life might be if it goes well or about how awful if it does not. Sales numbers trigger doubts in the executive about how well he has prepared the company to weather the storms of a competitive world.

In short, these seemingly rather dry artifacts of corporate existence can become "filled" with personal meaning and emotional reactions to that meaning. Moreover, one symbol can trigger another. The employee waiting for the performance appraisal may have trouble sleeping at night because she imagines herself unemployed, out on the street, riding in boxcars, and so on. Similarly, a good speech from a CEO may convince everyone that the company is on the right track or that the future is bright. Symbols may be positive as well as negative, but they are always meaningful.

A final aspect of the symbol is that it is invested with many meanings (go back and look at the definition—*meanings* is plural). Unlike a concept, which contains a one-to-one relationship with that to which it refers, symbols are *bundles of meaning*. Think of the word *chair*. It is most likely a concept in your mind right now. You think of a class of objects, but the experience is rather neutral. Concepts are useful because they allow us to think rationally about our day-to-day lives. However, if we think of the word *chair* in a different way, symbolic meaning can be added. Think of the phrase *my father's chair*. There is a good chance that the neutral concept has been changed. The chair has been infused with a new, more personal set of meanings. Perhaps you think back to an actual chair that your father sat in when you were a child. Perhaps this symbolic chair triggers some feelings toward that chair and that relationship. In any case it is this characteristic of containing many meanings that makes a person, object, or event a symbol.

Perhaps you are wondering what this discussion has to do with organizational life. Scholars have identified a number of ways symbols, especially when they are unacknowledged, subliminally shape assumptions throughout the organization. Much in organizations is uncertain, yet we need to experience the world in a way that is at least marginally manageable. For example, executives, stakeholders, and competitors of all sorts tend to be very distant from the majority of an organization's members. Even top managers wonder what is going on in the minds of employees or other stakeholders. Often these unseen "zones" of an organization—the nature of certain stakeholders, what is going on in their minds—are mapped by symbols. This is the only way we can "know" certain things about the organization. Thus, images abound about the nature of the CEO—he is a moral person, he is brilliant, he is tough, he is unscrupulous—even though there is often no way for most employees to verify these images. Moreover, the kind of "leadership images" organization members carry around in their heads matters a great deal. Positive images tend to reinforce cooperation of all sorts, whereas negative ones may engender resistance.

The importance of symbols is that they "define" many vague areas in the organization and its environment, areas of which we can have no direct knowledge. Because this defining is often subliminal, we are unaware that a symbol is at work. We begin to act "as if" something is true, and this as-if action has considerable consequences. For example, Japanese workers tend to act as if the company is a family. They feel an obligation to act in the company's best interest. One result of this trait is that Japanese companies need far fewer first-line supervisors than their Western competitors need.

Cultures matter in many ways: Their symbols matter to individuals, to companies, and to their leaders. They shape thinking and behavior. They inspire commitment. They do all this without stirring up much attention or scrutiny. One way to think of culture is as a vast underground text or story that runs throughout the organization, a story that sets the terms for understanding day-to-day experience. Activities 15–2 and 15–3 provide both the opportunity for you to explore the symbols in an organization that you are familiar with and a process to map out a profile of an organizational culture.

ORGANIZATIONAL CULTURE AND ORGANIZATIONAL EFFECTIVENESS

In a recent book, Deal and Terrence summarized "the state of the art" about organizational culture by concluding the following:

> Corporate cultures can have a significant impact on a firm's long-term economic performance; corporate cultures will probably be an even more important factor in determining the success or failure of firms in the next decade; corporate cultures that inhibit strong long-term financial performance are not rare, they develop easily, even in firms that are full of reasonable and intelligent people, and; although tough to change, corporate cultures can be made more performance enhancing.[29]

Schein defines organizational culture as "a pattern of basic assumptions— invented, discovered, or developed by a given group as it learns to cope with its problems of external adaptation and internal integration—that has worked well enough to be taught to new members as the correct way to perceive, think, and feel in relation to those problems."[30] We argued that a place to start our investigation of culture, its meaning, the management of culture, and the management of culture change is by focusing on symbols. At the most basic level, a symbol was defined as any person, object, or event infused with personal meaning by an individual or a group. Symbols are used to communicate corporate purpose, critique strategic plans, enhance organizational control, harmonize intergroup relations, ease the pain of transitions, support organizational ideologies, and understand subcultures.

Organizational culture seems to play a critical role when it comes to individual, group, and **organizational effectiveness.** Symbols are bundles of meaning that simultaneously tie together emotional and cognitive experience. Sensitivity to symbols involves an awareness of both how they shape cognition and how they function as containers for emotions. As such, a symbol-sensitive manager would ideally be able to think about, and constructively manage, the cognitive and emotional aspects of symbols—and thus enhance the effectiveness of the individual, the group, and the organization.

As we have seen, in any organization we find a large variety of symbols. The symbols work not in isolation, but in interaction with other symbols. Thus, sensitivity to symbols involves sensitivity to interacting groups of symbols in their "larger" forms, such as stories, rituals, myths, and ceremonies. Attention to stories, rituals, myths, and ceremonies enables individuals not only to develop a full understanding of organizational effectiveness but also to work with the larger forms to diagnose and enhance effectiveness.[31]

Organizational culture is often discussed as the foundation for cohesion in the organizational identity or the outcome of identity dynamics.[32] Others, as we have seen, view organizational culture as the social "glue" of an organization.[33] Regardless of the perspective, organizational culture should be understood in the context of important management issues.[34] The business context, the business strategy, the business design, and the way the organization manages change all influence the evolution of the specific organizational culture. For example, the specific choice that is made about the organization design—the way of grouping people and tasks—is likely to influence the dynamics of the subcultures that will emerge. As mentioned at the beginning of the module, a strategic decision to acquire and/or merge with another company may or may not succeed (be effective) based on management's ability to find a high degree of fit between the two cultures and/or the attention that is paid to the cultural aspects of the merger.

SUMMARY

The organizational culture module appears in this section of the book because of the phenomenon's comprehensiveness and complexity. The complex nature of culture lends itself to many definitions. Culture is much like air; it is everywhere we look, and it touches everything that goes on in organizations. It is both a cause and an effect of organizational behavior. The more we learn about organizations, the more elements of culture we discover. The more we understand the organizational culture, the more equipped we are to try to manage and change its nature. Yet at the most basic level, the core components of organizational culture include three elements: (1) the behavior and work patterns that can be observed, (2) the underlying values and assumptions that often cause the behaviors, and (3) the symbols that can be identified. As we have seen in this module, managing a cultural change is a complex managerial challenge that requires overcoming many obstacles. The next module in the book—Module 16—addresses the change process and provides several alternative road maps for planned change that might work well for a company that is interested in cultural transformation.

Study Questions

1. Identify and discuss the key dimensions of culture using either the culture value orientation model or Hofstede's national culture model.

2. Identify and discuss the key dimensions of organizational culture based on Schein's definition.

3. Identify and describe the key factors that shape organizational culture.

4. Can organizational culture be taught to organizational members? Explain.

5. Discuss how symbols can help us understand organizational culture?

6. What are some of the ways to manage organizational culture?

7. Discuss the relationship among business strategy, organization design, and organizational culture.

8. Discuss the relationship between organizational effectiveness and organizational culture.

9. What advice do you have for Mr. Covey and Mr. Franklin about managing the merger of their two companies?

Endnotes

1. P. Docherty, M. Kira, and A. B. (Rami) Shani (eds.), *Creative Sustainable Work Systems* (New York: Routledge, 2008).

2. S. Riad, "Of Merger and Cultures: What Happened to Shared Values and Joint Assumptions," *Journal of Organizational Change Management* 20, no. 1 (2007), pp. 26–43.

3. H. L. Tosi and N. P. Mero, *The Fundamentals of Organizational Behavior* (Malden, MA: Blackwell, 2003).

4. P. Docherty, J. Forslin, and A. B. (Rami) Shani (eds.), *Creative Sustainable Work Systems* (New York: Routledge, 2002).

5. *Webster's Encyclopedic Unabridged Dictionary of the English Language* (New York: Gramercy Books, 1996), p. 488.

6. C. Kluckhohn, "The Study of Culture," in D. Lerner and H. D. Lasswell (eds.), *The Policy Sciences* (Stanford, CA: Stanford University Press, 1951), pp. 86–101.

7. A. L. Kroeber, and T. Parson, "The Concept of Culture and Social System," *American Sociological Review* 23 (1958), pp. 582–83.

8. G. Hofstede, *Culture's Consequences: Comparing Values, Behaviors, Institutions, and Organizations Across Nations,* 2nd ed. (Thousand Oaks, CA: Sage, 2001).

9. G. P. Ferraro, *The Cultural Dimension of International Culture* (Upper Saddle River, NJ: Prentice Hall, 1994).

10. E. H. Schein, "From Brainwashing to Organization Therapy," in T. Cumming (ed.), *Handbook of Organization Development* (Los Angeles, CA: Sage, 2008), pp. 39–52.

11. See F. Kluckhohn and F. L. Strodtbeck, *Variations in Value Orientations* (Evanston, IL: Peterson, 1961); and A. L. Kroeber and F. Kluckhohn, "Culture: A Critical Review of Concepts and Definitions," *Peabody Museum Papers* 47, no 1 (1991).

12. For the most recent compilation of Geert Hofstede's work see Hofstede, *Culture's Consequences.*

13. M. Stebbins and A. B. (Rami) Shani, "Toward A Sustainable Work System Design and Change Methodology," in Docherty, Kira, and Shani (eds.), *Creative Sustainable Work Systems.*

14. *USA Today,* December 8, 1998.

15. J. M. Shafritz and J. S. Ott, *Classics of Organization Theory* (Chicago: Dorsey Press, 1987); and R. M. Cyert and J. G. March, *A Behavioral Theory of the Firm* (Englewood Cliffs, NJ: Prentice-Hall, 1984).

16. R. H. Kilmann et al. (eds.), *Gaining Control of the Corporate Culture* (San Francisco: Jossey-Bass, 1985); G. Hofstede and M. H. Bond, "The Confucius Connection: From Cultural Roots to Economic Growth," *Organizational Dynamics* 16, no. 4 (1988), pp. 4–21; N. M. Tichy, *Managing Strategic Change: Technical, Political and Culture Dynamics* (New York: John Wiley & Sons, 1983); and K. S. Cameron and R. E. Quinn, *Diagnosing and Changing Organizational Culture* (Reading, MA: Addison-Wesley, 1999).

17. V. Sathe, *Culture and Related Corporate Realities* (Burr Ridge, IL: Richard D. Irwin, 1985); S. R. Barley, C. W. Meyer, and D. C. Gash, "Culture of Cultures: Academics, Practitioners, and the Pragmatics of Normative Control," *Administrative Science Quarterly* 33 (1988), pp. 24–60; and C. A. O'Reilly and J. B. Chapman, "Culture as Social Control," in B. M. Staw and L. L. Cummings (eds.), *Research in Organizational Behavior,* vol. 18 (Greenwich, CT: JAI Press, 1996), pp. 157–200.

18. E. H. Schein, *Organizational Culture and Leadership* (San Francisco: Jossey-Bass, 2004).

19. J. W. Lorsch, "Managing Culture: The Invisible Barrier to Strategic Change," *California Management Review* 2 (Winter 1986), pp. 95–109.

20. R. H. Kilmann, M. J. Saxton, and R. Serpa, "Issues in Understanding and Changing Culture," *California Management Review* 2 (Winter 1986), pp. 87–94.

21. M. R. Louis, "Organizations as Culture-Bearing Milieux," in L. R. Pondy, P. J. Frost, G. Morgan, and T. C. Dandridge (eds.), *Organizational Symbolism* (Greenwich, CT: JAI Press, 1983), pp. 39–54; M. J. Hatch, "The Dynamics of Organizational Culture," *The Academy of Management Review* 18 (1993), pp. 657–93; S. A. Sackman, "Culture and Subculture: An Analysis of Organizational Knowledge," *Administrative Science Quarterly* 37 (1992), pp. 140–61; and T. E. Deal and A. A. Kennedy, *Corporate Cultures: The Rites and Rituals of Corporate Life* (Reading, MA: Addison-Wesley, 1982).

22. J. Kerr and J. W. Slocum, Jr., "Managing Corporate Culture through Reward Systems," *Academy of Management Executive* 1, no. 2 (1987), pp. 99–108; L. K. Trevino, "A Cultural Perspective on Changing and Developing Organizational Ethics," in W. A. Pasmore and R. W. Woodman (eds.), *Research in Organizational Change & Development,* vol. 1 (Greenwich, CT: JAI Press, 1990), pp. 195–230.

23. E. H. Schein, "Organizational Culture," *American Psychologist* 45, no. 2 (1990), pp. 109–19.

24. H. Triandis, "Cultural Intelligence in Organizations," *Group and Organization Management* 31, no. 1 (2006), pp. 20–26.

25. K-Y Ng and P. C. Earley, "Culture + Intelligence," *Group and Organization Management* 31, no. 1 (2006), pp. 4–19.

26. F. Shipper, R. C. Hoffman, and D. M. Rotondo, "Does the 360 Feedback Process Create Actional Knowledge Equally Across Cultures?" *Academy of Management Learning and Education* 6, no. 1 (2007), pp. 33–50.

27. C. Argyris, R. Putnam, and D. M. Smith, *Action Science* (San Francisco: Jossey-Bass, 1985); R. Beckhard and R. T. Harris, *Organizational Transitions: Managing Complex Change,* 2nd ed. (Reading, MA: Addison-Wesley, 1987); and D. P. Hanna, *Designing Organizations for High Performance* (Reading, MA: Addison-Wesley, 1988).

28. T. J. Peters and R. H. Waterman, *In Search of Excellence* (New York: Harper and Row, 1982); J. C. Collins and J. I. Porras, *Build to Last* (New York: Harper Collins Publishers, 1996); and A. De Geus, *The Living Company* (Boston: Harvard Business School Press, 1997).

29. H. M. Trice and J. M. Beyer, *The Cultures of Work Organizations* (Englewood Cliff, NJ: Prentice-Hall, 1993).

30. E. H. Schein, "Organizational Culture," *American Psychologist* 45 (1990), pp. 109–119.

31. W. van Buskirk, "Enhancing Sensitivity to Organizational Symbolism and Culture," *Journal of Management Education* 15, no. 2 (1991), pp. 170–92.

32. For a comprehensive discussion on the relationship between organizational culture and organizational identity see C. M. Fiol, M. J. Hatch and K. Golden-Biddle, "Organizational Culture and Identity," in D. A. Whetten and P. C. Godfrey (eds.), *Identity in Organization* (Thousand Oaks, CA: Sage, 1998), pp. 32–82; M. J. Hatch and M. Schultz, "Dynamics of Organizational Identity," *Human Relations* 55, no. 8 (2002), pp. 989–1018.

33. S. Riad, "Of Merger and Cultures: What Happened to Shared Values and Joint Assumptions," *Journal of Organizational Change Management* 20, no. 1 (2007), pp. 26–43.

34. K. Cameron, "A Process for Changing Organization Culture," in T. Cumming (ed.), *Handbook of Organization Development* (Los Angeles, CA: Sage, 2008), pp. 429–45.

Activity 15–3:
The Meaning of Your Symbols and the Organization as a Text

Objectives:

a. To appreciate the patterns and meaning of symbols at the workplace.

b. To read the organization's culture as a complex web of symbols.

Task 1:

a. Go back to the list of symbols that you have generated in Activity 15–2. Pick a few symbols from your list that have particular "juice" for you. These should be more meaningful, vivid, exciting, or complex than the others.

b. Pick one symbol. Imagine that it is speaking to you. What is it saying? Write a few paragraphs. Try to write as if the symbol itself is talking.

Task 2:

a. Read your paragraphs to one another in your team. How do other team members react to your symbol/script? What are their symbols and meaning like? the same as yours? different? Discuss these different meanings. Are there others in your organization who might react similarly?

b. As you read through your list or as you recite it to someone else, notice the ways you are affected by your symbols:

- Do they contain any assumptions about the organization?

- Are you acting as if certain things are true about the organization, things which might appear doubtful on further inspection?

- Do the symbols inspire you to want to do anything?

- Do the symbols inspire any feelings?

- How do the symbols and what they inspire influence your performance on the job? Do they motivate you? demotivate you?
- Can you observe these symbols influencing others? How do they react? How are they affected?

Task 3 (Reading the Organization as Text [Optional]):

a. After spending some time with your symbol list, identify themes in your organizational symbols. Certain groups of symbols may carry overlapping messages about the organization (that is, some symbols may point to how sophisticated the organization is, how poorly managed it is, or how much it cares/doesn't care about its employees). Try to find five or six themes in your symbols.

b. Write a short paper (five to seven pages) delineating these themes. Your essay can be considered a "snapshot" of the organizational culture as you experience it.

c. Exchange papers with other team members. Read the papers. How are they different from yours? How are they similar? Notice any area where you are surprised or confused. Discuss the differences. (Optional, if time can be set aside for reading and discussion.)

Module

16

Organizational Change, Development, and Learning

LEARNING OBJECTIVES

After completing this module, you should be able to

1. Explain the role of organizational learning in the development of sustainable work systems.
2. Describe the alternative organizational learning mechanisms.
3. Describe the relationship among organizational learning, change, development, and effectiveness.
4. Define the field of organizational change and development (OC&D).
5. Compare and contrast any two of the systemwide OC&D interventions.
6. Describe the different types of change programs.
7. Explain some of the challenges that OC&D faces in the global arena.

KEY TERMS AND CONCEPTS

Action research

Cognitive learning mechanism

Continuous improvement

Eclectic planned change approach

Focused change intervention

Holistic change intervention

Intervention

Learning mechanism

Learning organization

Limited change intervention

Organizational change and development (OC&D)

Organizational development (OD)

Organizational diagnosis

Organizational learning

Organizational learning mechanism

Parallel learning mechanism

Planned change

Procedural learning mechanism

Reengineering

Sociotechnical system (STS)

Structural learning mechanism

Total quality management (TQM)

MODULE OUTLINE

PREMODULE PREPARATION

**Activity 16–1:
The Management
of Change at FoodCo,
Inc.**

Objective:

To increase the understanding of the concepts of organizational culture, development, and change by applying them to the FoodCo case.

Task 1 (Homework):

Read the FoodCo case that follows and answer the questions at the end of the case.

Task 2:

The instructor will facilitate class analysis and discussion of the case.

Case Study: FoodCo, Inc.*

FoodCo, Inc., is a national supplier of specialty food products sold through grocery stores. Its headquarters is in Chicago, Illinois; its food-processing plants are spread throughout the country. FoodCo maintains a reputation as a well-managed, profitable company in an extremely competitive industry. As is common in the food products industry, most of FoodCo's top executives have marketing backgrounds.

In January of last year, Tom Hawkins, a consultant specializing in organizational design, received a call from Don Stevens, a top-level staff member in the FoodCo plant in Cleveland, Ohio. Don was interested in talking to Tom about some recent developments at the Cleveland plant. During their brief telephone conversation, Don told Tom that the plant manager, Mr. Williams, had become increasingly uncomfortable with the pressure he was under from corporate management to implement sociotechnical systems changes in the Cleveland facility. Don was anxious to hear Tom's advice on how to deal with the situation, since Mr. Williams had made him responsible for preparing a statement on the situation for corporate management.

When they met, Don explained to Tom that FoodCo was organized on a divisional basis around products and that each division was capable of operating as a separate business. However, given the competitive nature of the industry, corporate management felt that it needed to make decisions quickly to maintain an advantage over other firms; this meant that FoodCo's top management became involved in many local decisions. Plant managers throughout the corporation were required to clear even minor changes in operations with their superiors and were expected to implement changes directed from above.

In the past rapid changes had created some difficulties at the Cleveland plant. Product life cycles were short (three to five years in many cases); each cycle was accompanied by the hiring and letting go of employees. Shutdowns and retoolings had hit the Cleveland plant more frequently than others, creating dissatisfaction and mistrust on the part of employees. Don described the situation to Tom:

People come here looking for work and we say, "Great! We're glad to have you! Welcome to the company!" Then a couple of years later, we say, "Sorry—we can't use you for a while." That's bad enough; but the trouble is, we never know when the cutbacks will occur, because people in Chicago make those decisions for us based on how well the product is doing in the market, whether they think another plant could produce it for less, or whether they think they have a hotter product for us to make. So we're as much in the dark as anyone—but the employees don't believe us. They think we know, but we just aren't telling them. They say, "You're management, aren't you? If you don't know, who does?" I understand that these people have families and lives of their own to plan for and that this situation makes it hard for them. It's hard for all of us—but it's just the nature of the business. I can even understand why they voted in a union—I get pretty frustrated myself at times—but the union is only making things worse. Now, in addition to dealing with Corporate, we have to fight the union every step of the way. We can't make any changes around here without someone second-guessing us. If we give in to the union, Corporate screams. But if we follow Corporate's orders, union members become upset—and then it just gets harder to get them to go along the next time.

People at Corporate are market oriented. They have to be, I guess. But it seems like at times they don't think very much about what impact their decisions will have on people. We're the ones who have to live with these people day after day. Most of the time, we wind up going along with those corporate executives, since we can't risk losing our jobs or the business for the plant; but we sure would like those corporate executives to be a little more sensitive to the problems they create for us. The demand to implement sociotechnical systems changes here is just the latest bug of theirs. They really don't appreciate the difficulties we would have in making it work here.

Following the Tampa Example

Don explained to Tom that corporate management had gotten excited about sociotechnical systems design after its success in the corporation's newest plant, located in Tampa, Florida. Here are some of its features.

Autonomous work groups. Self-managed production teams were given primary responsibility for major segments of the production process. Each team was composed of multiskilled members who could perform one another's job as well as do most of the maintenance and quality work. The teams were free to decide on their own job assignments, to select new team members, and to discipline members who didn't meet their standards.

Integrated support functions. Team members were able to perform most work that would be performed by separate maintenance and quality control departments in a typical plant. The teams were also able to schedule their own production runs, plan product changeovers, determine their own overtime, and even do minor process engineering.

Challenging job assignments. Jobs were designed to meet human needs for growth, challenge, and learning. Routine tasks were rotated among all team members.

Job mobility and rewards for learning. Pay increases were given in accordance with the number of tasks employees could perform. All employees were encouraged to learn new jobs throughout the plant.

Facilitative leadership. The plant operated with a minimum of supervision; those supervisors who were present were chosen on the basis of their ability to work effectively with groups in making decisions and their ability to help team members to develop.

Managerial information for employees. Employees were provided with a full range of productivity and cost data that allowed them to make decisions about the effective use of their team resources.

Self-government for the plant. No rules were specified in advance; employees were allowed to develop their own rules as they saw fit.

Congruent physical and social context. Status symbols that would separate managers from employees were avoided; common cafeterias and parking lots were used. In addition, rooms were provided for work teams to hold meetings, and the plant itself was designed to facilitate discussion among teams that were responsible for interdependent processes.

Learning and evolution. A commitment was made to continual improvement in the way the organization operated. Employees would have a major influence on changes that would take place.

Plans for the Cleveland Expansion

According to Don, the issue confronting the Cleveland plant was that the corporation wanted the Cleveland plant to follow Tampa's example in designing its new dairy products line. Because Tampa had been successful, corporate management was pressuring the Cleveland plant to adopt the sociotechnical systems approach in managing its operation as well. In fact, the dairy products division manager had already appointed Dick Harold, a manager from the Tampa plant, to head up the new dairy operation in Cleveland. Since the Cleveland plant was part of another division in the company, this move caught Mr. Williams by surprise:

We're not opposed to new ideas here. I've been in this business for 25 years, and I've tried a lot of new ideas in my time. In fact, we did a lot here before we ever heard of Dick Harold—our employees keep their own work areas clean—and we even have them rotate jobs in one area. So these ideas aren't really that new to us. Still, I think the corporation is trying to push this thing on us too quickly. Dick Harold was in town buying a house before I even knew he was coming to work here. What's worse, they never told him that he would be working for me. He thought he would have a free hand in the new dairy products unit, since it's part of another division. I straightened that out—anything that happens at this plant is under *my* control. I made a phone call to Chicago, and my boss made sure that Harold would be working for me.

As I said, I'm not opposed to new ideas. But I think we have a different setup here than Tampa does. They handpicked the best people to work in that plant—we can't do that. They weren't unionized—we are. They didn't have a history of ups and downs that created mistrust—we do. And they built from scratch—we have to make use of our existing building. Besides, we've done all right here using our own way of getting things done. Some of my managers have been with the company for as long as I have, and they don't like the sound of some of Harold's ideas. I've made them hold a tough line in the past, and they've held it. They're afraid of what would happen if we turned the place over to the employees to run. They've also heard that Tampa operates with fewer managers than we do and that makes them nervous.

I suppose that with the corporation behind this thing, we don't have much choice but to try it. But I'm pretty sure it won't work here. Maybe when they see that, they'll back off. At least I've gotten them to agree that we should check it out with our people first to see what they think of it. I doubt that they'll go for it—there's been too much change here already—but we'll see.

The Survey

Tom worked with Don Stevens to prepare a survey to be given to employees to find out how they felt about the new management concept. Tom also met with the president and vice president of the local union to discuss the reasons for giving the survey. He explained to them that not all employees would be affected by the proposed changes but that the survey would be an opportunity for people throughout the plant to comment on how the plant was being run. The union leaders seemed in favor of the proposed changes and agreed that the survey should be given as long as individuals would not be identified with their answers. The results of the survey indicated that attitudes toward management were negative and that communication between management and employees was viewed as practically nonexistent. Although a few employees had written notes on their surveys indicating that the new management concept was a strategy to get more work out of employees for the same pay, the overall reaction to the concept was more positive than Mr. Williams had imagined.

Mr. Williams's Dilemma

Tom discussed the results of the survey with Don Stevens. Don told Tom that Mr. Williams had been surprised by the findings but still was not convinced that employees would really accept the changes associated with the new management concept. What's more, Williams was fairly certain that if the concept was put into practice, it wouldn't work—at least not for long. If Williams went ahead, he would look foolish to the employees, which would make things worse in the future; if he didn't proceed, the corporation would be on his back to explain why, and Williams knew that the people from Chicago weren't good listeners.

Williams decided to put the concept to an employee vote. He figured that if they said yes and it didn't work, they would have no one to blame but themselves; if they said no, he might at least have some reason when Corporate asked him why he hadn't gone ahead with its plan. Williams knew that management had the legal right to design work any way it pleased, so the corporation would not be bound by the results of the vote. Williams arranged to have the union take the vote at the local union hall quickly, since construction on the new unit was being held up by the corporation until the situation at Cleveland was clear. The corporation was anxious to get this work started, since it would lose market share if the product didn't go into production soon.

Questions

1. From a sustainable work system perspective, describe the challenges faced by the company.
2. Describe the culture of the corporation.
3. Identify the nature of organizational learning and the learning mechanisms at FoodCo Inc.
4. Is the corporation justified in its position regarding the management of the Cleveland plant?

5. How will the vote turn out? What steps should be taken afterward?

6. What advice should Tom give to Mr. Williams?

INTRODUCTION

Organizations are changing more than ever before.[1] The potential of profound and continuous renewal of the organization and management provides a unique competitive advantage. Developing the organizational capability to change is critical for the development of sustainable organizations and sustainable work place.[2] Understanding why some organizations are leaping into the future more successfully than others requires a careful examination of how they manage change.[3] Managing change and business development are tough managerial tasks. In the first module of this book, we argued that the study of organizational behavior looks at the organization as an organic system, ever adapting to the external environment and to the internal dynamic interactions of subunits. As such, organizational work design, culture, learning, and change are four integral components of the firm's life. Unique cultures and subcultures emerge as a result of work and organizational design choices; dealing with an ever-changing business environment makes change and planned change a way of survival. Furthermore, from an organizational effectiveness point of view, managers' and organizations' abilities to manage the change process were found to be related to some of the basic criteria of effectiveness (for example, performance, success, improvement, and productivity).[4]

Yet, despite all the energy, time, and money that companies spend on attempts to transform organizations through a variety of organizational development and change programs, the reality is that few succeed in sustaining the reinventing process.[5] Mastering the art of learning in such contexts—critical from a sustainable work system perspective—is not a "quick fix." Our contention is that one of the main reasons for the failure is that most change efforts and companies do not manage to develop and nurture learning mechanisms that allow them to challenge the basic assumptions about the key/core business processes and as a result to alter their mental models and actions.[6]

The inherent challenge of organizational development and change fosters the need for managers and practitioners to have access and develop a basic understanding of the ideas and theory behind learning mechanisms. Appreciation of the realization that many choices need to be identified and explored and that many design alternatives can be created can help overcome some of the anxiety that seems to hinder successful implementation.

The fields of change, the management of change, organizational development and change, and organizational learning are vast. For this module we had to make some hard choices about what to include. We briefly defined and examined the process of organizational learning; its meaning; and its effect on individual, group, and organizational effectiveness. In our discussion about learning we focused on a few types of learning mechanisms that emerged within the context of work. Next, in our discussion about change we focused on those changes that are planned—when an attempt is made to consciously and deliberately bring about change in the organization's status quo. Two major categorizations of planned change strategies can be articulated. With the first, according to Chin and Benne,[7] planned change can be divided into three basic types of strategies: empirical–rational, normative–reeducative, and power–coercive. The second describes seven "pure" approaches for bringing about change: fellowship, political, economic, academic, engineering, military, and applied behavioral science.[8] In this module we focus on the applied behavioral science approach or, more specifically, the organizational development (OD) orientation, to discuss this total-system strategy for improving organizational effectiveness because of its concerns for both macro and micro aspects of change and development.

We start with a discussion of the nature of organizational learning and learning mechanisms. We explore the complexity of fostering organizational learning, examine alternative learning mechanisms, define organizational development, categorize and review the variety of organizational change and OD interventions, and give examples of the OD approaches designed to influence the total organization. Finally, we discuss results from empirical investigations designed to assess OD's effectiveness.

ORGANIZATIONAL LEARNING

The view of organizations as adaptive rational systems that learn from experience was first proposed 70 years ago.[9] Sociotechnical system scholars articulated organization design principles that intend to foster the organization's ability to learn.[10] Peter Senge defined a learning organization in terms of continuous development of knowledge and capacity.[11] Organizational learning is viewed as a process through which organization members develop shared knowledge based on analysis of data gathered from or provided by multiple sources. Recently, the focus has shifted to the specific **organizational learning mechanisms** that enhance the organizational capacity of learning.[12] The intense interest in organizational learning has been documented in many articles in management journals and books. Some critics argue that the wide range of recent publications has helped place "the study of organizational learning firmly on the map of theory and good practice."[13]

Defining Learning Organizations and Organizational Learning

A wide variety of definitions of a learning organization and organizational learning can be found in the literature. From a sustainable organization perspective, a **learning organization** is an organization characterized by a particular culture, climate, managerial pattern, and capacity that enable the entity to improve itself systematically and over time. As such, learning organizations are entities that have the skills of creating, acquiring, and transferring knowledge and have demonstrated the ability to continuously improve their products, services, and financial results and to change themselves as required by the actual and anticipated demands of the marketplace. The intensity and direction of the changes derive directly from the vision, goals, and operating policies of the organization.

Organizational learning is a system of principles, activities, processes, and structures that enable an organization to realize the potential inherent in the knowledge and experience of its human capital. Organizational learning incorporates all the activities and processes taking place on the individual, team, and organizational levels. Schein argues that at least three distinctly different types of learning exist: knowledge acquisition and insights (cognitive learning), habit and skill learning, and emotional conditioning and learning anxiety.[14] The concept of a learning organization, then, appears to focus more on the "what," while the concept of organizational learning concentrates on the "how."

In Module 1 we argued that organizations, by their very nature, are social systems that function in an environmental context. As such every organization is a learning entity that develops learning capability in order to survive. Nonetheless, organizations that can be termed *learning organizations* share a number of features. A learning organization is first and foremost an organization that encourages and emphasizes sustained and active learning, one in which organizational learning constitutes an integral part of its business strategy. A learning organization's managerial processes generate an organizational culture that allows for quick response, flexibility, integration, initiative, and innovation. In a learning organization, learning stems from and is based on the organization's past experience and accumulated knowledge, that is, on what is commonly termed organizational memory. These learning features enable the organization to develop a dynamic and competitive strategy, formulate a shared vision, institute orderly and permanent systematic thinking, incorporate mapping-systems activities, and create an effective mechanism for adapting to the changes and constraints that arise from operating within a turbulent environment. Organizations with the foresight to adopt the conceptual foundation of organizational learning and to implement it through appropriate procedures have reported significant positive results. Organizations such as ABB, Boeing, General Electric, Honda, Kaiser Permanente, and Intel have developed internal mechanisms that facilitate skill development, surface and integrate knowledge within and outside the organizational boundaries, and have become adept at translating the new knowledge and insight into new organizational forms and actions.[15]

The experience of the past several years indicates that the idea of organizational learning has captured the imagination of managers and scholars alike. Furthermore, an increasing number of organizations and executives are predisposed to understand and adopt the learning organization concept. Some executives also see this comprehensive concept as a window of opportunity for assimilating advanced managerial approaches.[16] Yet, a follow-up study of leading U.S. organizations attempting to assimilate new managerial approaches reveals some failures among those that did not have the foresight to construct a suitable mechanism for organizational learning that incorporated processes, tools, and work patterns.[17]

Organizational Learning Mechanism

Learning mechanisms, at the most basic level, are formalized strategies, policies, guidelines, management and reward systems, methods, tools and routines, systems, allocations of resources, and even the design of physical work space that have been designed, formulated, and ratified in order to promote and facilitate learning in the organization and its networks. Learning mechanisms can be routinized only up to a point. Since learning demands ongoing questioning and inquiry into current and future practices, it can be viewed as a continuous disturbance of existing routines that were developed for the purpose of stability, predictability, and efficiency. Faced with the decision to focus on learning, managements vary from no or limited interest in learning to regarding it as a principal means of competition.[18]

The learning mechanisms are elements in the learning infrastructure or system that reflect management's desire to prioritize learning in its organization and networks. As such, its actions can be viewed on a continuum from "facilitative" to "prescriptive." *Facilitative* actions support learning for individuals, groups, and the organization as a whole. *Prescriptive* actions are achieved by formulating standard operating procedures, rules, and management systems which detail obligatory goals and methods for learning to be carried out by specific individuals and groups within the organization. Management's emphasis on the need for and desire to utilize or engage in different learning activities is reflected in increasing numbers of and an emphasis on learning mechanisms within the company.

The learning mechanisms may be regarded as being integrated or nonintegrated and designated or dual-purpose. Integrated mechanisms allow organizational members to analyze their own and others' experiences in order to improve their performance. Mechanisms that are used by personnel to collect, analyze, store, and disseminate information primarily for the benefit of others are called nonintegrated mechanisms. Mechanisms that operate separately from organizational performance are regarded as designated or learning specific. Those that act in conjunction with task performance are dual-purpose. Thus local management planning systems in teams are the basis for the economic and operational activities in the teams as well as providing the essential feedback for reflection and learning for these activities.[19] Dual-purpose, integrated learning mechanisms fuse learning and task structures, creating a community of reflective practitioners.[20]

Learning mechanisms are the formalized, institutionalized results of active decisions by management based on the company's position regarding various aspects of learning. Three broad categories of learning mechanisms are cognitive, structural, and procedural (see Table 16–1).

Cognitive mechanisms provide language, concepts, models, symbols, theories, and values for thinking, reasoning, and understanding learning issues. For example, the strategy discipline reasons about change and development in terms of dynamic capabilities and seldom uses the vocabulary of learning. The "learning" language is mainly used in the HRM field, where the term *learning capability* is also found.[21] Examples of important concepts already mentioned that have an important bearing on the learning strategies and plans, are formal and informal learning, single- and double-loop learning, and tacit and explicit knowledge. These mechanisms may well be manifested or formalized in organizations as company value statements, strategy documents, management–union agreements,

Table 16–1
Learning Mechanisms: Categories, Types, and Examples

Categories	Types	Examples
Cognitive mechanisms	Language	Cognitive, behavioral
	Concepts	Single-loop, double-loop
	Models	Tacit, explicit
	Symbols	Company value statements
	Theories	Strategy documents
	Values	Management–union agreements
		Intercompany contracts
		HRD management system
Structural mechanisms	Feedback channels	Reward systems
	Communication channels	Spatial design
	Technical structure	Parallel learning structures
	Physical structure	Bench learning structures
	Forums	Continuous improvement teams
	Arenas	e-Learning applications
	Networks	Learning centers
	Work organization	Data warehouses
Procedural mechanisms	Methods	Tests, e.g., learning style
	Models	Assessment methods
	Procedures	Support infrastructure
	Rules	Standard operating procedures
	Tools	

intercompany contracts, management and reward systems, such as Balanced Scorecard (BSC) and HRD management systems.

Structural mechanisms concern organizational, technical, and physical infrastructures. These include feedback channels, communication channels, databanks and databases, and the work organization. Formal (and even informal) forums, arenas, and networks, and learning specific structures such as parallel learning structures, bench learning structures, continuous improvement, and quality circles. Technology mechanisms may take the form of learning centers, e-learning programs, databases and data warehouses, and e-mail and document and data sharing systems. The physical structure may take the form of the layout of the work space to facilitate (spontaneous) contact between different members of the organization.[22]

Procedural mechanisms concern the rules, routines, methods, and tools that have been institutionalized in the organization to promote and support learning.[23] These may include tests and assessment tools and methods; standard operating procedures; methods for specific types of learning, for example, action learning; or debriefing routines.

Learning mechanisms are usually designed to promote, facilitate, and support learning. Basically people learn, either individually or collectively. If they are not motivated or committed, then there is a strong probability that they will not learn. However, there are mechanisms that prescribe learning, for example, Balanced Scorecard systems and certain compensation systems.[24]

Company strategies for promoting informal or experiential learning are planning for learning. Planning makes learning more conscious, better focuses effort, and increases measures of accountability, as long as learning does not become an end in itself with only loose coupling to the work processes. Planning allows people to nurture learning strategically and to take advantage of a wider range of learning strategies that might otherwise be overlooked.

Learning mechanisms are viewed as the means and end in the development of managerial and organizational capabilities. As such, learning mechanisms can be viewed as enabling sustained organizational performance and as an engine for organizational change and development. Using Mike Beer's typology of change, learning mechanisms tend to embrace both theory "O" and theory "E" orientations since its goals can be viewed as the enhancement of organization effectiveness by focusing on an organization's culture and its people, and economic value creation by focusing on the hard facets of organizations, financial performance, strategy, structure, and systems (both orientations—theory E and theory O—are explored in the next section of the module).[25] The next part of the module focuses on organization change and development and explores four specific systemwide intervention strategies.

ORGANIZATIONAL CHANGE AND DEVELOPMENT (OC&D)

Change Orientation

Different orientations to organizational change and development are employed in organizations. The orientations are guided by different assumptions that are made about the nature of humans; the nature of social systems; the nature of work; and the nature, purpose, and meaning of change. For the purpose of this module, we will briefly discuss two opposing theories about organization change that were advanced by Michael Beer and his colleagues.[26] At the most basic level, theory E has as its goals economic value creation and focus on "hard" facets of organizations, financial performance, strategy, formal structure, and operation and management systems. This orientation claims that the only way to transform an organization is through a dose of tough, results-oriented, top-down initiatives that are driven by managers motivated by financial incentives that align their interests with those of shareholders (commonly called shareholder value). Theory O has as its goal enhancing organization effectiveness and focuses on the organization's culture and its people. This orientation's basic assumption is that the purpose of change is to serve multiple stakeholders, such as shareholders, employees, customers, and the community. By developing the commitment of all stakeholders, the organization will achieve sustainable performance. Table 16–2 captures the key features of each orientation.

A review of the organizational development field reveals that the majority of the literature in this field seems to focus on change strategies that fall within the cluster of theory O. From sustainability and a sustainable organization perspective, we believe that both orientations are needed. The increasing challenges that organizations and the society at large are facing call for finding creative ways to integrate and achieve balance between the two orientations and developing interventions that build on the strengths of both. The Strategic Fitness Profiling Intervention and Sociotechnical System Intervention are two examples of interventions that manage to accomplish such

Table 16–2
Theories of Change: Theory E versus Theory O*

Key Features	Theory E	Theory O
Purpose	Maximize economic value for shareholders.	Maximize value for all stakeholders. Develop old and new organization capabilities.
Management orientation	Top down. Short- and middle-range time orientation	Participative. Long-term time orientation
Focus	Efficiency. Business strategy. Formal structure and processes. Management systems	Organization culture. Human capital development. Organizational learning
Process	Plan and establish programs	Emergent and participative-based programs
Motivation	Motivate through financial incentives	Motivate through commitment. Use pay as fair exchange
Consultants	Large, knowledge/content expert driven	Small, process driven
Examples of interventions	Reengineering. Balanced Scorecard system	Appreciative inquiry. Search conference

*Modified from M. Beer, "Transforming Organizations: Embracing the Paradox of E and O," in T. Cummings (ed.), *Handbook of Organization Development* (Los Angeles: Sage, 2008), p. 418.

integration. We will be exploring Sociotechnical System Intervention in the next section of the module.

Organizational Development

Probably the most widely quoted definition of organizational development remains Beckhard's from 1969: **Organizational Development (OD)** is

> an effort *(1) planned, (2) organizationwide,* and *(3) from the top,* to *(4) increase organizational effectiveness and health through planned interventions in the organization's "processes," using knowledge.*[27]

We also like Burke's definition because organizational culture, which refers in part to values, norms, and roles as we used them in the emergent system, is the focus of change:

> Organization development can be defined as a *planned process* of cultural change. This process consists of two phases: **organizational diagnosis** and **intervention.** OD begins with a diagnosis of the current organizational culture (that is, an identification of the norms, procedures, and general climate of the organization). This identification process becomes more diagnostic as a distinction is made between those standards of behavior, procedures, and so on that seem to facilitate the organization's reaching its objectives (while meeting the needs of its members) from those that do not facilitate the attainment of its goals. Following this diagnostic phase, interventions are planned to change those norms seen as barriers to effective individual and organizational functioning.[28]

In an attempt to clarify the scope and boundaries around the field of OD, Worely and Feyerherm recently proposed that for an organizational activity to be called OD it needs to meet three criteria: (1) Organizational development activities and research must involve change, (2) a set of activities can be called OD if it involves learning, and (3) the process must improve the performance or effectiveness of the client system.[29]

As OD has been used by professional specialists, it encompasses the following elements:

1. Application of behavioral science knowledge and methods.
2. Improvement or change of interaction patterns (arising from the norms, values, and role expectations) of an ongoing social system.
3. Integration of emotions and feelings into the rational perspective of the formal organization to achieve greater objectivity.
4. A systems focus on affecting individual, team, and organizational interactions concomitantly.
5. Building into the ongoing system the organizational climate and social technology needed to attain both individual and organizational goals.
6. Improvement of the organization design toward an optimal utilization of organizational resources.
7. Integration of organizational strategy and design into a jointly optimized system.
8. A continuing education program for the managerial system.

Organizational development can be better understood by examining what OD specialists do for organizations. This process starts with a diagnosis and continues with the selection of a strategy to achieve the purpose of OD.

Organizational Development Diagnosis

Before a program for change can be formulated, a study of the problems and needs of a particular system should be made. Consultants frequently start with a "presenting problem"—the one that prompted the client to seek their assistance. This problem generally turns out to be a symptom rather than a cause, as shown in the data collected through interviews, recordings, observations, meetings, or survey questionnaires. Information is the most basic ingredient of a change program. The technology of information gathering for OD purposes has been developing rapidly. The variety of collection methods and of alternatives for feedback of data to client systems is a current emphasis of OD practitioners.[30]

Organizational Development Strategies

Basic to all OD strategies is the assumption that management must ultimately define its own problems and change itself. It is not the role of specialists to change the client system; they are only facilitators or change agents. Thus, strategies are chosen that will permit change to take place and will have the greatest potential for coping with the particular pattern of problems in a specific company.

Where, how, and with whom to start the OD effort is a critical decision. Many theorists and consultants insist that real progress in OD can take place only if it starts with top management. Executives must confront the data from the diagnosis and cope with their own behavior and practices to encourage those lower in the hierarchy to do so. When a company's personnel director initiates the use of OD just because other companies are doing it or because the director thinks the company needs it, the diagnosis and strategy are more complicated. Typically, the personnel director will want to start with the supervisory or middle-management level as a step to convincing top management of the value of such a program. The consultant has to decide whether such an OD effort would have sufficient effect. Under some conditions it is possible to "optimize," that is, improve one aspect of an organization's functioning and let this improvement spread to other areas.

Types of Organizational Development Interventions

Considerable literature is appearing that describes social and behavioral strategies, methods, and techniques for achieving change. While few ways of clustering the different change strategies have appeared in the literature, for the purpose of this module, we have chosen two complementary typologies. First, we will review a typology that groups the change intervention strategies based on their target group. Next, we will present a typology that is based on the change intervention emphasis. Together the two typologies provide a holistic picture of change orientations.

Target Group-Based Clustering

This classification of change programs—proposed by Wendell French and Cecil Bell—is based on the primary target of the intervention, for example, individuals, dyads and triads, teams and groups, intergroup relations, and total organization.[31]

Table 16–3 shows this classification scheme. Some interventions have multiple targets and multiple uses and thus appear in several places in the table.

Consequence-Based Clustering

An alternative classification of change programs—proposed by Mitki, Shani, and Stjernberg—is derived from an attempt to understand change programs based on their impact. Three types of change programs—holistic, focused, and limited—were identified according to their main emphasis. Table 16–4 summarizes the key features of the three orientations.

Holistic Change Programs: Holistic programs simultaneously try to address all (or most) aspects of organizing. Examples are sociotechnical, lean, downsizing/restructuring, business process reengineering, and organizational architecture. The logic is that all aspects of an organization are connected. When you change one aspect, you have to take into account the effects on all other subsystems. This sense is captured by concepts such as fit and joint optimization.

Focused Change Programs: Focused programs identify a few key aspects, such as time, quality, and customer value, and then use these as levers for changing the organization systemwide. Some examples of such initiatives are total quality management programs, time-based management, and management by objectives. The key concept carries a lot of symbolic value. The logic is that you need a critical mass in a cognitive sense. If you want to influence people, you have to address the same issue again and again. The focused program acts as a schema for understanding and making sense of changes. The change program needs some kind of purpose, a change process, change mechanisms, identifiable outcomes, and criteria for success to gain legitimacy and momentum. The key concept does not need to be true or proven in any academic sense, but it needs to be "socially valid."

Limited Change Programs: Limited programs are not aimed at affecting broader aspects of the organization. They address a specific problem, which is not seen as a lever for broader change, but may help build a foundation for such change at a later time. The

Table 16–3 Typology of OD Interventions Based on Target Groups	**Target Group**	**Interventions Designed to Improve the Effectiveness**
	Individuals	Life- and career-planning activities
		Coaching and counseling
		T-group (sensitivity training)
		Education and training to increase skills, knowledge in the areas of technical task needs, relationship skills, process skills, decision making, problem solving, planning, goal-setting skills
		Grid OD phase 1
		Work redesign
		Gestalt OD
		Behavior modeling
	Dyads/triads	Process consultation
		Third-party peacemaking
		Role negotiation technique
		Gestalt OD
	Teams and groups	Team building—Task directed
		—Process directed
		Gestalt OD
		Grid OD phase 2
		Interdependency exercise
		Appreciative inquiry
		Responsibility charting
		Process consultation
		Role negotiation
		Role analysis technique
		"Startup" team-building activities
		Education in decision making, problem solving, planning, goal setting in group settings
		Team MBO
		Appreciations and concerns exercise
		Sociotechnical systems (STS)
		Visioning
		Quality of work–life (QWL) programs
		Quality circles
		Force-field analysis
		Self-managed teams
	Intergroup relations	Intergroup activities—Process directed
		—Task directed
		Organizational mirroring
		Partnering
		Process consultation
		Third-party peacemaking at group level
		Grid OD phase 3
		Survey feedback
	Total organization	Sociotechnical systems (STS)
		Parallel learning structures
		MBO (participation forms)
		Cultural analysis
		Confrontation meetings
		Visioning
		Strategic planning/strategic management activities
		Real-time strategic change
		Grid OD phases 4, 5, 6
		Interdependency exercise
		Survey feedback
		Appreciative inquiry
		Search conferences
		Quality of work–life (QWL) programs
		Total quality management (TQM)
		Physical settings
		Large-scale systems change

Source: W. L. French and G. H. Bell, Jr., *Organizational Development,* 6th ed., 1999, p. 153. Reprinted by permission of Prentice-Hall, Inc., Englewood Cliffs, New Jersey.

Table 16–4
Planned Change Programs:
Three Orientations

	Characteristic	Holistic Change Programs	Focused Change Programs	Limited Change Programs
	Characteristic	Programs that attempt to address simultaneously all aspects of the organization	Programs that identify a few key aspects (such as quality and cycle time) and use these as levers for changing the organization systemwide	Programs that are designed to address a specific problem that is not seen as a lever for a broader change
	Examples of change programs	■ Sociotechnical systems ■ Organization restructuring ■ Lean production ■ Business process reengineering ■ Organizational learning	■ Total quality management ■ Management by objectives ■ Time-based management ■ Dialogue programs	■ Team building ■ Communication improvement ■ Humanization of work ■ Work environment reforms ■ Democratization programs
	Published cases	Kaiser-Permanente Rover Saab Automobile	ABBT-50 GE Work-Out IA Paper Mill	Job rotation, Volvo team building, H-P Communication Workshops, AT&T

basic logic is *decoupling*. Examples of such initiatives are work environment programs, ergonomics, career planning, job rotation, and changing the wage structure. Allowing children to live together with their parents in the kibbutzim is an example of a limited program. The change was not conceived as a program in its proper sense—rather, it became a spontaneous movement that affected ultimately all kibbutzim in Israel. It had major long-term effects, although it was intended as an isolated change with no planned effects on other aspects of the community. Nonetheless, the practice turned out to trigger a major change of the entire kibbutz movement; that is, the changes toward privatization and the introduction of internal pricing for the distribution of the services within the kibbutz may be seen as consequences of this spontaneous movement.[32]

Similarly, the job rotation schemes that were tried in the tapestry department of Volvo's Torslanda plant in the 1960s were intended to solve a limited ergonomic problem. However, in retrospect these job rotation schemes became linked to the wider issue of quality of working life development—and thus a part in the wider organizational innovations in Volvo during the 1970s and 1980s.[33] The term *local* means that the changes are not intended to reach other units. With the term *systemwide* we mean that the program, whether limited or holistic or focused, is intended to reach all the relevant units of the company. The word *relevant* is important here—which units are seen as relevant is determined by the other dimension of our classification, that is, whether the changes are holistic, focused, or limited. Some programs may be difficult to characterize into any of these categories. For instance, team building may be seen as a focused program on the systemwide level and, simultaneously, as a holistic program on the local level. On the systemwide level, team building may be part of a competence development effort with little links to other changes. On the local level, the same program may be part of an effort to reorganize the entire production system.

SYSTEMWIDE APPROACHES TO CHANGE AND DEVELOPMENT

The improvement of total organization as the target group with the focus on the management of change is represented in this module in two ways. First, we discuss three comprehensive interventions and their paths to organizational effectiveness. Second, we provide a comparative exploration of the three structural-based interventions: sociotechnical system, reengineering, and total quality management.

The Sociotechnical System (STS) Approach

The **sociotechnical system (STS)** theory, developed at the Tavistock Institute in England by Eric Trist and his colleagues, contends that organizations are made up of people who produce products or services using some technology.[34] As such the STS approach attempts to combine the social subsystem (people), the technical subsystem (machines and technology), and the environmental supersystem into a synergistic system.[35] Joint optimization, the ultimate desire in STS, states that an organization will function optimally only if the social and technological subsystems of the organization are designed to fit the demands of each other and the environment.[36] The STS approach emphasizes the need for compatible integration between the organization's social and technical subsystems to ensure organizational effectiveness.[37] Since its inception in the 1950s, three major sociotechnical system subfields emerged: STS theory, STS design, and STS change and development process.[38] In this section we focus on the STS change and development process.

Successful STS design focuses on an "open" interface with the environment the organization faces. This implies that the ability of the organization to effectively match its social and technical subsystems relies on the degree of openness or contact the organization maintains with the environment. Organizational competitiveness necessitates the need for organizations to maintain environmental sensing and scanning mechanisms such that the organization will be able to plan and adapt according to anticipated and unanticipated changes. Changes in any one of the subsystems will disturb the status quo and should result in the realignment of the entire organization.

In the context of organizational development, the STS planned change intervention is based on the action research or collaborative research philosophy. **Action research** is defined as an emergent inquiry process in which behavioral and social science knowledge is integrated with existing organizational knowledge to produce new knowledge, which is generalizable and simultaneously usable.[39] As such the STS change endeavor is participatory, co-inquiry-based, client- and organization-owned, and scientifically executed. Figure 16–1 shows a flowchart of an STS planned change process.

The first phase of the intervention involves preparation of the organization and its top-level decision makers for conducting the sociotechnical systems analysis and design activities. This phase includes the consultant's entry, scanning, and contracting with the top-level decision makers; formation of a top-level steering committee; analysis of the business situation (that is, macro environment, industry environment, competition environment, and company environment); analysis of business results (in terms of current and desired profit, volume, cost, and operational purpose); and the formulation of a business vision, a total systems strategy, and a vision statement for the redesign effort.

The second phase consists of formation, education, and analysis by the action research system, which is composed of the steering committee, one or more consultants, and one or more groups representing different parts and levels of the organization. The action research system conducts analyses of the technical, social, environment, and design elements of the organization, which lead to recommendations for organization redesign. The recommendations for joint optimization—once they are approved and prioritized by the top-level management of the organization—will be followed by careful planning of the experimental implementation.

The third phase consists of the experimental execution of the proposed recommendations. The changes are assessed and modified as necessary to fit the unique organizational characteristics. Overcoming some of the difficulties in the experimental implementation process will aid in the formulation and management of the total organization change process.

Finally, based on learning from the experimental implementation of the recommendations for change, the action research system refines the vision statement, formulates the total systems change strategy, and identifies criteria for effectiveness assessments. The action research system might also be utilized in the management of the implementation process. One of the underlying assumptions of the sociotechnical systems change process is the emphasis on organizational learning as key to organizational success. As such, once the implementation of the new organizational design is done, top-level management will reexamine the business situation and likely continue the process of self-examination and refinement.

**Figure 16–1
Sociotechnical System
Planned Change Process:
A Flow Design**

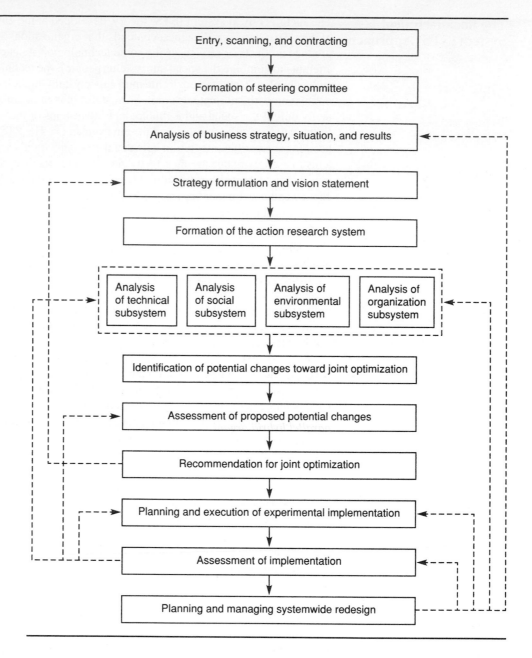

A review of 134 recorded STS interventions revealed successful results on eight different organizational effectiveness criteria.[40] The studies were conducted over 30 years and were implemented in a variety of organizations. While 87 percent of the studies reported productivity improvements, 89 percent reported cost savings, 81 percent showed reduced absenteeism, 65 percent had reduced turnover, and 54 percent reflected improved attitudes. A special issue of the *Journal of Applied Behavioral Science* was devoted to STS. While the authors represented several different disciplines and theoretical perspectives, all were concerned with the usefulness and effectiveness of the STS approach.[41] In a recent review of two decades of STS interventions in North America, James Taylor illustrates how STS has been expanded to embrace dimensional manufacturing work, service work, nonroutine work, and professional work within increasingly chaotic environments. More than 115 active and successful STS designs or redesigns are currently operating in the United States, of which about a quarter are clearly not continuous process technologies.[42] Continuous process technologies still predominate in STS applications, but the number and proportion of applications to other work systems are increasing.[43] Although space does not permit elaboration, it is important to note that unique applications of STS can be found in many places around the globe—for example, in Scandinavia,[44] the Netherlands,[45] England, Israel,[46] and Italy. A recent study that examined the development of STS theory and practice revealed four different variants of STS in Australia, the Netherlands, North America and Scandinavia.[47]

Total Quality Management

Total quality management (TQM) is a managerial approach for improving processes in an organization in order to manufacture products or offer higher-quality services that will satisfy the customer. The approach emphasizes a number of elements: The improvement process is continuous and never ending; the improvement processes are undertaken by teams, some of which are organic and some of which are task specific and ad hoc; each process has an inherent improvement that must be learned in a systematic manner.[48] The analysis, similar to the solution, needs to rest on solid, tested data. In this section we focus on the management of change aspects.

Applying TQM in organizations involves a change of organizational culture and the development of quality awareness from the customers' perspective. Likewise, TQM also encompasses "empowerment," which is expressed, on the one hand, in the transfer of responsibility on topics of quality and production to employees, including delegation of authority for decision making in these fields, and on the other hand, in creating workers' commitment to the organization. The approach is applied top-down via a structural mechanism that usually includes a quality council and process action teams (PATs). The quality council is composed of the executive president or vice president plus additional members who represent the whole system insofar as their functions, influence, and level of responsibility. Its main purpose is to determine the framework of the TQM program and to provide a support system. The mechanism for operating TQM is also called the *parallel hybrid organization*.[49] There are those who see TQM solely as a technique or as an integration of tools and systems designed to improve productivity, some who see it as the improvement of a product or service, and others who see TQM as a wider and comprehensive managerial philosophy.[50]

Reports from organizations that adopted TQM indicate that TQM seems to affect customer satisfaction, worker satisfaction, the number of quality or process improvement groups in operation, the percentage of rejected products, the level of exploitation of raw materials, and absenteeism by personnel.[51] Very few firms report radical structural or technological changes resulting from the introduction of TQM. While some argue that TQM affects strategy, little support can be found to confirm this notion.[52]

Reengineering

The reengineering approach (also labeled "business process reengineering") emerged at the beginning of the 1990s as a practical orientation (1) to combat worsening corporate business results (mainly in the United States) and corporate difficulties and (2) to establish a competitive edge. The basic assumption of reengineering is that incremental improvement of existing processes within organizations does not provide a sufficient answer to the real existing needs.[53] A drastic cognitive and conceptual turning point—a paradigm shift—is required to allow a breakthrough.

Reengineering is defined as "fundamental rethinking and radical redesign of business processes to achieve dramatic improvements in critical contemporary measures of performance, such as cost, quality, service, and speed."[54] Radical and dramatic changes are fostered when individuals search for answers to the basic question, Why are we doing what we are doing?[55] This approach of reengineering ignores existing processes, structures, organizational culture, and human resources and states that one must begin by pinpointing key organizational processes, which are determined by their conformance to customers' requirements.

Reengineering advocates the design of the required structures and processes based on a customer's requirements. The main structural change necessary is the transfer from organizational structure to process structure.[56] This means breaking down interdepartmental boundaries from "functional departments" to "process teams" or "case teams." The teams have the responsibility for the entire process. The process teams–based organization design flattens the organizational hierarchy and significantly reduces existing boundaries. Organizations that implement reengineering can use both centralized and decentralized approaches and can enjoy their advantages when managing the processes. Information technology, which is the engine of reengineering, permits organizational units to operate autonomously, while the firm as a total entity enjoys the advantages of system centralization. The function of the new process teams is also to influence the creation of a new system of values and beliefs among employees.

The results of a successful application of reengineering are measured by the radical changes in organizational performance. The most common parameters for testing the results are cost, quality, speed, and service. It must be emphasized that impressive results were expected in the short run within various organizations that reported on the application of this approach. Our current knowledge is limited when it comes to the understanding of reengineering's long-term effects.

A Comparative Examination

The preceding overview shows some striking similarities and differences between the last three orientations to organizational change.[57] Table 16–5 summarizes the essence of the three approaches: their theoretical roots and founders; some of the key principles and assumptions; key elements, phases, and mechanisms of the change process; and outcomes. Our purpose in this section is to explore commonalities and differences between the orientations as related to the change process. A comparison between the other dimensions—although intriguing, as can be seen from the table—is beyond the scope of this module.

For the purpose of this module we examine four distinct similarities among the three orientations: (1) All require a strategic decision that involves major financial and resource investment and commitment. (2) All three orientations focus on the entire system; they follow both customer and improvement focus. (3) Organizational learning is an integral part of the change process. (4) They all require transformation and/or modification of the organizational culture.

The three orientations share the importance of alignment between the change and the overall business strategy. The decision to pursue any one of the change programs is strategic. Managers make their determination based on the perceived congruency between the company's strategic goals and what the change program has to offer. Furthermore, the strategic nature of the **planned change** program needs to be emphasized. The investment in each program is viewed as strategic due to its perceived importance (that is, critical value to the firm's overall performance), the substantial resource commitment, the clear time horizon, and the fact that programs are not easily reversible.

Reengineering, TQM, and STS seem to focus on improvement of organizational functioning to better meet changing environmental demands. As such they take a *holistic system* approach that incorporates all the relevant actors (internal and external customers, supplier, and the like). While some variations seem to exist in terms of initial focus and/or targeted unit for the change program, all take into account the entire organization. Furthermore, at some point in each change orientation, the emphasis shifts to the optimal alignment of the different organizational units.

Acquiring new knowledge, skills, and tools seems to be at the heart of each orientation. All three acknowledge in various ways the importance of organizational learning. Specific mechanisms that foster organizational learning and organizational dialogue seem to have evolved in each orientation. Some form of structural support configuration—with different labels—that houses and guides the organizational learning and the change programs provides the source of energy and continuity. The last striking similarity among the three orientations is the notion that each transforms or modifies the culture of the firm. The involved nature of the orientations; the learning that they generate via the ongoing analysis, data collection, and interpretations; and the paradigm shift that they foster set the stage and momentum for organizational culture change.

Table 16–5 **Partial Comparison between TQM, STS, and Reengineering**

Dimension	TQM	STS	Reengineering
I. Theoretical roots	Statistical theory (SPC), system theory	Organization theory, applied social and behavioral sciences, system theory, production engineering	Concurrent engineering, production engineering, practice-driven system theory.
II. Founders	Deming, Crosby, Juran, Imai, Shewhart, Taguchi, Tshikawa	Cherns, Cummings, Davis, Emery, Pasmore, Taylor, Thorsrud, Trist	Champy, Davenport, Hummer
III. Motto	A group of ideas and techniques directed toward enhancing competitive performance through improving the quality of products and processes.	A set of design principles, ideas, and change processes that strive toward best match between organizational, technical, environmental, and social subsystems.	A set of ideas about radical redesign and change in business processes to achieve breakthrough results (major gains in cost, service, or time).
IV. Some basic principles and assumptions	**Organizational Goals**		
	Serving customers' needs to fullest extent possible by supplying goods and/or services of highest quality.	Joint optimization of social, technical, and environmental systems.	Quantum leap in performance by focusing on key processes that really matter, emphasizing strong leadership, technology, and radical change.
	Time Orientation		
	Dynamic.	Dynamic.	Dynamic.
	Philosophy of incremental and continuous improvement.	Philosophy of innovation, organizational learning, and continuous improvement.	Philosophy of radical and rapid changes.
	Short- and long-term perspectives	Long-term perspective.	Short-term cycle to achieve desired results.
	Coordination and Control		
	Coordination through process action groups (cross-functional).	Coordination and control through self-managed groups (autonomous work groups).	Coordination and control by reengineering teams, process owner, and steering committee.
	Both control and coordination exercised by managers and employees.	Both control and coordination exercised by managers and employees.	Both control and coordination exercised mainly by managers.
	Work Design		
	System-based optimization guided by specific design principles.	System-based joint optimization guided by specific work design principles.	System-based approach guided by key design processes.
	Formation of temporary process action teams.	Formation of functional organic teams.	Formation of process teams.
	Technology		
	Technology may be a key factor in quality improvement.	Technology is a fundamental factor in work design.	Information technology is an essential factor in work design.
	Customer and Suppliers Orientation		
	Internal and external customers and suppliers are integral parts of the system.	External customers and suppliers are important but are not part of the system.	Processes' customers are an integral part of the system.
	Rewards		
	Individual-, team-, and system-based.	Team- and individual-based.	System- and individual-based.
V. Management of change	**Change Orientation**		
	Led by management and/or a quality council.	Change process led by design team or parallel learning structure.	The change is led by top management and the steering committee.
	The effort is mostly guided by ISO 9000 and/or award evaluation processes and/or some combination of specific guidelines provided by quality experts.	The effort is guided by a modified action research philosophy.	The effort is guided by the process owner and reengineering (process design) teams.

(continued)

Table 16–5 **Partial Comparison between TQM, STS, and Reengineering** *(concluded)*

Dimension	TQM	STS	Reengineering
	Change Phases, Mechanisms, and Processes		
	Broadly defined deductive-based phases and basic activities.	Clearly defined deductive-based phases, processes, and activities.	Clearly defined inductive-based phases.
	Team learning and system learning mechanisms.	Team and learning structure mechanisms.	Information technology is a key element in team process learning.
	Methods and Tools		
	Quality planning (Hoshin planning).	Environmental, technical, and social analysis.	Competitive and customers' needs analysis.
	Identifying customers and suppliers (both internal and external) and determining needs.	Variance and deliberation analysis.	Identification of processes that require radical improvements based on specific criteria.
	SPC.	Experimentation with alternative design configurations.	Broad understanding of current processes.
	Develop a process that can produce the quality required.	Systemwide diffusion.	Radical systemwide or subsystem-based diffusion.
	Quality-based systemwide diffusion.		
	Change Process Performance Measures		
	Customer- and supplier-based orientation.	Input–throughput–output performance-oriented measures.	Measures of improvements in business processes (e.g., profitability, quality of service) and establishment of business competitiveness and superiority.
	Processes' improvement against benchmarking.	Utilization of both hard (e.g., productivity, profitability) and soft (e.g., satisfaction, commitment) measures.	
	Utilization of both hard (e.g., defect ratios, customer complaints) and soft (e.g., satisfaction, commitment) measures.		
VI. Outcomes	**Continuous Improvements**		
	Established.	Established.	Unknown.
	Organizational Learning		
	Specific to quality-related issues.	Systemwide learning mechanism is established.	Learning mechanism based on key organizational processes.
	Organizational Performance Measures		
	1. Customer and supplier satisfaction:		
	Established.	Advocated and at times established.	Advocated.
	2. Quality standards:		
	Established and extensively improved.	Established.	Established quality standards related to process.
	3. Production cost reduction:	Established.	Established.
	Advocated.		
	Organizational Culture		
	New quality-based organizational culture.	New system- and innovation-based culture.	New innovation-based organizational culture.

The preceding similarities among the three orientations are somewhat surprising due to the nature of their evolution and theoretical foundations. As can be seen in Table 16–5, each orientation is rooted in different scientific disciplines. As such, it is relatively easy to identify some of the many differences between them. Now let's discuss some of those differences. The espoused objectives of each orientation vary. Reengineering focuses on radical changes of key processes; STS focuses on the incremental, gradual, and continuous changes geared toward optimal utilization of organizational resources; and TQM focuses on the continuous quality improvement of products, processes, and services.

As Table 16–5 shows, the three orientations seem to follow somewhat different change processes and phases. STS seems to have a clear analytical road map with specific sequential phases and activities. TQM seems to have broadly defined deductive phases and basic activities. The reengineering change process follows clearly defined inductive-based phases. Furthermore, careful examination of the specific phases and their sequence in each orientation reveals that they vary significantly.

Each orientation incorporates the *technological subsystem* differently. The STS redesign process is based on existing technology and/or new technology. (Most STS projects report on the redesign of the organizations without changing the technology.) Reengineering is mostly concerned with the implementation of new technology with special emphasis on information technology. (Some even argue that information technology is at the heart or the engine of reengineering.) TQM focuses on improvements of processes in general.

Finally, the outcomes and measurements seem to vary. The current scientific literature provides support for significant long-term **continuous improvements** in both STS and TQM. In reengineering, the expectations are that outcomes can be realized in a short time span. Because of the relative newness of reengineering, we have yet to learn about its long-term effects. Organizational structure seems to change mostly in STS and reengineering in an explicit manner. In TQM only minor structural changes take place. Those are mainly changes in internal and external customer linkages.

TOWARD AN ECLECTIC PLANNED CHANGE APPROACH

As can be seen from the comparative examination of the three orientations, the potential for some kind of combination of the three merits exploration. In practice a natural overlap and multiple combinations of bits and pieces of the three approaches can be found in each planned change implementation. This section provides a brief overview of an **eclectic planned change approach** that pulls together the strengths of each.[58] Table 16–6 summarizes the phases and some key activities in the proposed eclectic framework.

The first phase involves the establishment of the project's foundation. In this phase, securing management commitment to the effort is crucial. The scope and purpose of the project is defined by the top management team/CEO, and the basic project strategy is articulated. Top management needs to make a clear decision about the choice of change orientation based on the compatibility between the business strategic objectives and the change orientation. The next set of activities is geared toward developing shared understanding of the need and companywide awareness for making significant changes. The creation of a parallel learning mechanism and its magnitude signal sincere commitment on management's part for change. Overall, the **parallel learning mechanism** is charged with the responsibility of housing, guiding, and facilitating the learning and change process. The actual criteria and creation process of the parallel learning mechanism is critical. Various alternatives are available. Management is required to make the choice that best fits the organization.

The second phase builds on the project initiation phase and moves the focus to the key processes to meet customers' needs. Following the establishment of clarity about the role and mission of the learning mechanism, the project shifts to the identification of the customers (both internal and external), their requirements, needs, and potentials. Key business processes that have a direct effect on customers' requirements, needs, and potentials are identified.

Phase 3 focuses on establishing benchmarks and performing systematic business analysis while verifying the key business processes and major business pathologies plus revisiting the business vision, strategic opportunities, and enabling technologies. The challenge in this phase is the collection and assimilation of the data. The data's complexity requires the utilization of multiple human and technological resources that can be found within and outside the company boundaries. At the end of this phase, ideas for improvement of specific processes begin to surface.

Table 16–6
Phases in an Eclectic
Planned Change Approach

Phase 1: Project Initiation
- Define scope and purpose.
- Secure management commitment.
- Establish organizational awareness of the need for radical changes.
- Align with business strategy.
- Create a parallel learning mechanism and educate organization members.

Phase 2: Mapping Customers' Key Processes
- Identify customers' requirements, needs, and potentials.
- Determine the key processes.

Phase 3: The Inquiry Process
- Establish benchmarks.
- Conduct business analysis based on sociotechnical system framework:
  Verify key processes.
  Uncover system pathologies.
- Revise company vision based on analysis, strategic opportunities, and enabling technology (i.e., information technology).
- Identify potential improvements to the existing processes.

Phase 4: Design/Redesign to Modify Existing Processes and Organizational Structure
- Formulate specific alternative sociotechnical-based design solutions. (STS-based design includes the optimal integration of key organizational elements such as rewards, control, structure, information, people, and technology.)
- Explore potential impact of proposed solutions.
- Develop joint optimization of key processes.
- Establish learning processes for continuous improvement.

Phase 5: Implementation and Reconstruction of the Key Processes and Organization
- Foster a climate that is conducive to change.
- Create the implementation and support mechanisms.
- Develop training programs.
- Establish learning loops as an integral part of continuous improvement.

Phase 4 is guided by a set of specific design principles that are derived from STS design theory. As such, alternative design solutions that strive toward joint optimization of the different business elements are explored. One key challenge during this phase is to strive toward the development of joint optimization between the key business processes. Beyond the tasks of a careful examination of potential impact of the alternative solutions, the goal is also to develop the learning mechanism for continuous improvement.

Implementation and reconstruction of the organization and its key processes are part of Phase 5. Implementation planning is treated as a project. Some planned change models treat this kind of planning as a completely new process.[59] Others see this phase as a natural continuation of the change program, and, as such, the implementation will be guided by the parallel learning mechanism. The implementation planning calls for the simultaneous execution of both radical and rapid, as well as gradual and ongoing changes. Key processes can be treated either way. The learning mechanism needs to have the know-how that supports the complexity of this deliberation. Of the many challenges during this phase, the most crucial are the creation of support mechanisms, the development of appropriate training programs, and the establishment of learning loops as an integral part of continuous improvement.

PLANNED CHANGE
AND ORGANIZATIONAL EFFECTIVENESS

The field of OC&D and its growth can be best appreciated by the increased number of books, journals, and articles devoted to OD values, philosophies, intervention methods and techniques, evaluation problems, methods for dealing with these problems, and effectiveness criteria and assessment. **Organizational change and development (OC&D)** as a field of theory and practice, can have significant positive effects on the total organization, the individual, and the work group in terms of behavioral, attitudinal, and effectiveness changes.[60] In general, the cumulative results of the published empirical investigations point toward the conclusion that OC&D is a successful strategy of planned change.[61] The 17 volumes that have appeared thus far in the JAI series, *Research in Organizational Change and Development* (edited by Pasmore and Woodman), reflect a tradition of provocative scholarly work by many contributors. Coupled with the 30 volumes published thus far in the Addison-Wesley organization development series (edited by Beckhard and Schein) for the organization development and change practitioner and manager, they demonstrate the vitality of the field. At the same time, the evaluation of change efforts or interventions is a complex and difficult task. OD was defined as "a planned process of organizationwide change," and as such an empirical research methodology that focuses on assessing the dynamic nature of change processes and their effectiveness had to be developed.[62] Published research on OD evaluation was clustered into three categories: (1) identification of general problems and development of guidelines, (2) demonstrations of methods for evaluating change efforts, and (3) identification and resolution of specific methodological issues.[63]

Furthermore, the documentation of OD results reported that studies of a better quality would permit more rigorous comparative examinations. For example, a survey of the OD literature from 1948 through 1982 identified 65 studies that meet a rigorous set of comparative criteria. These studies made the following recommendations: (1) The goals and expected results of the intervention should be stated clearly; (2) the intervention should be clearly defined and clearly described; (3) the intervention should be demarcated from the outcomes; (4) researchers should note why specific dependent variables were selected and how they were measured; and (5) the experimental design utilized, the sequence of observations, the frequency and time span of measurement, and the beginning and termination of the intervention should be described adequately.[64] Finally, massive reviews of some 800 work improvement efforts by Barry Macy and of 3,200 worldwide work improvement efforts by Frans M. Van Eijnatten show "generally positive conclusions with respect to both performance and worker satisfaction."[65] Taken together, these literature reviews strongly support the conclusion that OC&D programs yield positive improvements at the individual, team, and organizational levels.

ORGANIZATIONAL CHANGE AND DEVELOPMENT IN THE INTERNATIONAL CONTEXT

The applicability and effectiveness of organizational development and change in different cultural environments are areas of growing interest to managers and practitioners. Reports on OC&D activities on various continents and in many countries such as Australia, Canada, China, Denmark, Egypt, Germany, India, Ireland, Israel, Italy, Japan, Lithuania, Mexico, Nigeria, Poland, Singapore, United Kingdom, Venezuela, and South Africa, to mention a few, can be found in the literature.[66] Although each study examines one aspect of OC&D, an OC&D program, or a specific intervention in the respective continent or country, comparative empirical studies within a specific country among different interventions, within a specific continent across countries, or across countries on a specific intervention are scarce.

The conceptual and empirical challenges for comparative organizational change, development inquiry, and applications are many. First, the underlying values and assumptions of OD, the values and assumptions of the specific interventions, and the values and assumptions of the practitioners need to be analyzed. Second, the cultural elements and intercultural relations at the country, industry, and corporate levels need to be examined. Third, the degree of congruence needs to be explored, and the line of inquiry developed.

Recently, guidelines with explicit steps for adopting OC&D in different cultural contexts were proposed:

1. Evaluate the ranking of the dimensions of culture in the given situation.
2. Make a judgment as to which values are most deeply held and unlikely to change.
3. Evaluate the "problem appropriate" interventions ranking on the dimensions of culture.
4. Choose the intervention that would clash least with the most rigidly held values.
5. Incorporate process modifications in the proposed intervention to fit with the given cultural situation.[67]

SUMMARY

The field of organization learning emerged in the late 1970s. The realization that an organization's internal ability to learn from experience, assimilate new ideas, and translate them into action as a key to achieving and sustaining success shifted the focus to organizational learning and organizational learning mechanisms. Learning mechanisms were defined as the formal configurations (such as structures, processes, procedures, rules, tools, and methods) that are created within the organization for the purpose of developing, enhancing, and sustaining performance and learning. We saw that just as there are many types of organizational designs (Module 13), there are also various ways to design and manage organizational learning mechanisms.[68]

The field of organizational development and change emerged in the 1950s. It has gradually expanded to include the total organization. It has focused on influencing human interactions to help organizations guide the direction of their evolution and to enhance the cultural elements that are viewed as critical to maintaining the desired effectiveness and outcomes. Examples of contrasting organizational effectiveness strategies include the sociotechnical system approach, total quality management, and reengineering.

Frequently defined as an organization-wide systems approach of planned change, the need for more empirical research remains one of the biggest challenges to the fields of organizational learning, managing change, and organizational development. Although a significant improvement can be identified in the quality of the reported literature, further advancements are needed. Most organizational change and development specialists view themselves as eclectic change agents pursuing an expert or an action research method and applying a broad range of knowledge and skills suited to the nature of the problems identified by their efforts.[69]

Study Questions

1. Discuss the key concepts that are embedded in the definition of organizational learning.
2. Discuss the relationships among organizational learning, organizational culture, and organizational change and development.
3. Discuss the relationship between organizational learning mechanisms and organizational performance.
4. Identify and discuss the key elements in the definition of organizational development.
5. Compare and contrast the target group–based and consequence-based typologies of change programs.
6. What are the major phases of an OC&D program?
7. Compare and contrast any two of the planned change interventions described in this module.

8. Describe an organization that you are familiar with that could use an OC&D intervention. What are some roadblocks that the intervention would likely encounter? How would you overcome them? Describe the phases in the intervention process. How would the intervention affect individual, group, and organizational effectiveness?

9. How effective are planned change interventions?

10. What should be the role of the manager in an OC&D intervention?

Endnotes

1. M. Beer, "Transforming Organizations: Embracing the Paradox of E and O," in T. Cummings (ed.), *Handbook of Organization Development* (Los Angeles: Sage, 2008), pp. 405–28.

2. P. Docherty, M. Kira, and A. B. (Rami) Shani (eds.), *Sustainable Work Systems* (New York: Routledge, 2008).

3. J. Kotter and D. Cohen, *The Heart of Change* (Boston: Harvard Business School Press, 2002).

4. K. S. Cameron and D. A. Whetten, *Organizational Effectiveness* (New York: Academic Press, 1983); and R. E. Quinn and K. S. Cameron, *Paradox and Transformation: Towards a Theory of Change in Organization and Management* (Cambridge, MA: Ballinger, 1988).

5. Ibid.; Beer, "Transforming Organizations: Embracing the Paradox of E and O."

6. P. Docherty and A. B. (Rami) Shani, "Learning by Design: Key Mechanisms in Organization Development," in Cummings (ed.), *Handbook of Organization Development,* pp. 499–518.

7. R. Chin and K. D. Benne, "General Strategies for Effecting Changes in Human Systems," in W. G. Bennis, K. D. Benne, and R. Chin (eds.), *The Planning of Change* (New York: Holt, Rinehart & Winston, 1969), pp. 32–59.

8. K. E. Olmosk, "Seven Pure Strategies of Change," in J. W. Pfeiffer and J. E. Jones (eds.), *The 1972 Annual Handbook for Group Facilitators* (La Jolla, CA: University Associates, 1971), pp. 162–72.

9. M. Visser, "Deutero-Learning in Organizations: A Review and a Reformulation," *Academy of Management Review* 33, no. 2 (2007), pp. 659–67; R. Cyert and J. March, *A Behavioral Theory of the Firm* (Englewood Cliffs, NJ: Prentice-Hall, 1963).

10. W. A. Pasmore, *Designing Effective Organizations* (New York: Wiley, 1994).

11. P. M. Senge, *The Fifth Discipline: The Art and Practice of the Learning Organization* (New York: Doubleday, 1991).

12. See for example, G. R. Bushe and A. B. (Rami) Shani, *Parallel Learning Structures: Increasing Innovation in Bureaucracies* (Reading, MA: Addison-Wesley, 1991); M. Popper and R. Lipshitz, "Organizational Learning Mechanisms: A Structural and Cultural Approach to Organizational Learning," *Journal of Applied Behavioral Science* 34, no. 2 (1998), pp. 161–79; R. Lipshitz, M. Popper, and V. Friedman, "A Multi-Facet Model of Organizational Learning," *Journal of Applied Behavioral Science* 38 (2002), pp. 78–98; and A. B. Shani and P. Docherty, *Learning by Design: Building Sustainable Organizations* (Malden, MA: Blackwell Publishing, 2003).

13. R. Lipshitz, V. Friedman and M. Popper, *The Demystification of Organizational Learning* (Los Angeles: Sage, 2006); B. Garratt, *The Learning Organization* (Hammersmith, London: HarperCollins, 1994).

14. E. H. Schein, "How Can Organizations Learn Faster: The Problem of Entering the Green Room," *Sloan Management Review* 34, no. 2 (1993), pp. 85–92.

15. A. B. (Rami) Shani and P. Docherty, *Learning by Design: Building Sustainable Organizations* (Malden, MA: Blackwell Publishing, 2003); M. Marquardt and A. Reynolds, *Global Learning Organization* (Chicago: Irwin Publications, 1996).

16. M. W. Stebbins, A. B. (Rami) Shani, W. Moon, and D. Bowles, "Business Process Reengineering at Blue Shield of California: The Integration of Multiple Change Initiatives," *Journal of Organizational Change Management* 11, no. 3 (1998), pp. 216–32.

17. A. C. Edmondson and B. Moingeon, "Organizational Learning as a Source of Competitive Advantage," in B. Moingeon and A. Edmondson (eds.), *Organizational Learning and Competitive Advantage* (Thousand Oaks, CA: Sage, 1996), pp. 7–15.

18. E. H. Schein, "Three Cultures of Management: The Key to Organizational Learning," *Sloan Management Review* 38, no. 1 (1996), pp. 9–20; A. B. (Rami) Shani and P. Docherty, "Learning

by Design: Key Mechanisms in Organization Development," in Cummings (ed.), *Handbook of Organization Development,* pp. 499–518; R. Lipshitz, V. Friedman, and M. Popper, *The Demystification of Organizational Learning,* (Los Angeles: Sage, 2006; A. B. (Rami) Shani and Y. Mitki, "Creating the Learning Organization: Beyond Mechanism," in R. T. Golemiewski (ed.), *Handbook of Organizational Consultation* (New York: Marcel Dekker, 1998); A. B. (Rami) Shani and T. Stjernberg, "The Integration of Change in Organizations: Alternative Learning and Transformation Mechanisms," in W. A. Pasmore and R. W. Woodman (eds.), *Research in Organizational Change and Development,* vol. 8 (Greenwich, CT: JAI Press, 1995), pp. 77–121; M. W. Stebbins, and A. B. (Rami) Shani, "Organizational Learning and the Knowledge Worker," *Leadership and Organization Development Journal* 16, no. 1 (1995), pp. 23–30; Y. Mitki, A. B. (Rami) Shani, and Z. Meiri, "Organizational Learning Mechanisms and Continuous Improvement," *Journal of Organizational Change Management* 10, no. 5 (1997), pp. 426–46.

19. A. B. (Rami) Shani and P. Docherty, *Learning by Design: Building Sustainable Organizations* (Malden, MA: Blackwell Publishing, 2003).

20. D. A. Schon, *The Reflective Practitioner* (New York: Basic Books, 1983).

21. A. J. DiBella, *Learning Practices: Assessment and Action for Organization Improvement* (Upper Saddle River, NJ: Prentice-Hall, 2001); C. E. Helfat (ed.), *The SMS Blackwell Handbook of Organizational Capabilities: Emergence, Development and Change* (Oxford: The Strategic Management Society and Blackwell Publishing, 2003).

22. G. R. Bushe and A. B. (Rami) Shani, *Parallel Learning Structures: Increasing Innovations in Bureaucracies.* (Reading, MA: Addison-Wesley, 1991)

23. P. Pavlovsky, J. Forslin, and R. Rienhart, "Practices and Tools of Organizational Learning," in M. Dirkes, A. Berthoin Antal, J. Child, I. Nonaka (eds.), *Handbook of Organizational Learning and Knowledge* (Oxford: Oxford University Press, 2001), pp. 61–89.

24. P. Cressey and P. Docherty, "Feedback, Intangibles, and Sustainable Performance," in P. Docherty, J. Forslin, and A. B. Shani (eds.), *Creating a Sustainable Work Organization: Emerging Perspectives and Practices* (London: Routledge, 2002), pp. 165–78.

25. Beer, "Transforming Organizations: Embracing the Paradox of E and O," pp. 405–28.

26. Michael Beer and his colleagues have advanced the basic typology of the two-theory perspective. Based on the work that is being conducted through the TruePoint firm, the Strategic Fitness Profiling Intervention Model was developed and implemented in many organizations around the globe. Some of the published work that highlights the essence of the approach and its implementation can be found in Beer, "Transforming Organizations: Embracing the Paradox of E and O," pp. 405–28; M. Beer, "How to Develop an Organization Capable of Sustained High Performance," *Organizational Dynamics* 29, no. 4 (2001), pp. 233–47; M. Beer and R. A. Eisenstat, "The Silent Killers of Strategy Implementation and Learning," *Sloan Management Review* 41, no. 4 (2000), pp. 29–40; M. Beer and R. A. Eisenstat, "How to Hold an Honest Conversation about Your Strategy," *Harvard Business Review* 82, no. 2 (2004), pp. 82–89.

27. R. Beckhard, *Organization Development: Strategies and Models* (Reading, MA: Addison- Wesley, 1969), p. 9.

28. W. W. Burke, "A Contemporary View of Organization Development," in Cummings (ed.), *Handbook of Organization Development,* pp. 13–38; W. W. Burke, "A Comparison of Management Development and Organization Development," *Journal of Applied Behavioral Science* 7 (1971), pp. 569–79.

29. T. Cummings, "Reflection on the Field and Beyond: An Interview with Warren Bennis," in Cummings (ed.), *Handbook of Organization Development,* pp. 665–76; C. Worely and A. Feyerherm, "Reflections on the Future of Organization Development," *Journal of Applied Behavioral Science* 39, no. 1 (2003), pp. 97–115.

30. Excellent sources include C. C. Lundberg, "Organization Development Diagnosis," in Cummings (ed.), *Handbook of Organization Development,* pp. 137–50; D. A. Nadler, *Feedback and Organization Development: Using Data-Based Methods* (Reading, MA: Addison-Wesley, 1977); D. G. Bowers and J. L. Franklin, *Survey-Guided Development, I: Data-Based Organizational Change* (La Jolla, CA: University Associates, 1977); D. L. Hausser, P. A. Pecorella, and A. L. Wissler, *Survey-Guided Development, II: A Manual for Consultants* (La Jolla, CA: University Associates, 1977); and J. L. Franklin, A. L. Wissler, and G. J. Spencer, *Survey-Guided Development, III: A Manual for Concepts Training* (La Jolla, CA: University Associates, 1977).

31. W. L. French and C. H. Bell, *Organization Development* (Englewood Cliffs, NJ: Prentice- Hall, 1999).

32. Y. Mitki, A. B. (Rami) Shani, and T. Stjernberg, "Leadership, Development and Learning Mechanisms: System's Transformation as a Balancing Act," *Leadership and Organization Development Journal* (in press); "The Kibbutz in Transition," paper presented at the *Fifth International Conference on Communal Studies,* May 30–June 2, 1995, Ramat Efal, Israel; and T. Simons and P. Ingram, "Organization and Ideology: Kibbutzim and Hired Labor," *Administrative Science Quarterly* 42 (1997), pp. 784–813.

33. T. Stjernberg and A. Philips, "Organizational Innovations in a Long-Term Perspective: Legitimacy and Souls-of-Fire as Critical Factors of Change and Viability," *Human Relations* 46, no. 10 (1993), pp. 1193–1219.

34. E. L. Trist, "The Evolution of Sociotechnical Systems," in A. H. Van de Ven and W. F. Joyce (eds.), *Perspectives on Organization Design and Behavior* (New York: John Wiley & Sons, 1982), pp. 19–75.

35. See, for example, W. A. Pasmore, *Designing Effective Organizations* (New York: John Wiley & Sons, 1988).

36. W. A. Pasmore and J. J. Sherwood (eds.), *Sociotechnical Systems: A Sourcebook* (La Jolla, CA: University Associates, 1978); E. Emery, *Characteristics of Sociotechnical Systems* (London: Tavistock Institute, 1959); T. G. Cummings (ed.), *Systems Theory for Organizational Development* (Somerset, NJ: John Wiley & Sons, 1980); T. G. Cummings and S. Srivastva, *Management of Work: A Sociotechnical Systems Approach* (La Jolla, CA: University Associates, 1977); and W. A. Pasmore, *Creating Strategic Change: Designing the Flexible High-Performing Organizations* (New York: John Wiley & Sons, 1994).

37. A. B. (Rami) Shani and O. Elliott, "Sociotechnical System Design in Transition," in W. Sikes, A. Drexler, and J. Grant (eds.), *The Emerging Practice of Organization Development* (La Jolla, CA: University Associates, 1989), pp. 187–98.

38. F. M. van Eijnatten, A. B. (Rami) Shani, and M. M. Leary, "Sociotechnical Systems: Designing and Managing Sustainable Organizations," in Cummings (ed.), *Handbook of Organization Development,* pp. 277–309; Cummings and Srivastva, *Management of Work: A Sociotechnical Systems Approach.*

39. Excellent sources on Action Research and Collaborative Research orientations include D. Coghlan and T. Brannick, *Doing Action Research in Your Own Organization* (Los Angeles: Sage, 2007); P. Reason and H. Bradbury (eds.), *Handbook of Action Research* (Los Angeles: Sage, 2008); A. B. (Rami) Shani, S. A. Mohrman, W. A. Pasmore, B. Stymne, and N. Adler (eds.), *Handbook of Collaborative Management Research* (Los Angeles: Sage, 2008).

40. W. A. Pasmore, C. Francis, J. Heldeman, and A. B. (Rami) Shani, "Sociotechnical Systems: A North American Reflection on Empirical Studies of the Seventies," *Human Relations* 35, no. 12 (1982), pp. 1179–1204.

41. W. Barko and W. A. Pasmore, "Introductory Statement to the Special Issue on Sociotechnical Systems: Innovations in Designing High-Performing Systems," *Journal of Applied Behavioral Science* 22, no. 3 (1986), pp. 195–99.

42. J. C. Taylor, "Two Decades of Sociotechnical Systems in North America," paper presented at the annual meeting of the Academy of Management, San Francisco, August 1990; and J. C. Taylor and D. F. Felten, *Performance by Design: Sociotechnical Systems in North America* (Englewood Cliffs, NJ: Prentice-Hall 1993).

43. See, for example, R. Holti, "Sociotechnical Issues in the Software Sector," paper presented at the annual meeting of the Academy of Management, San Francisco, August 1990.

44. See, for example, N. Adler and P. Docherty, "Bringing Business into Sociotechnical Theory and Practice," *Human Relations* 50, no. 6 (1997); P. H. Engelstad, "The Evolution of Network Strategies in Action Research Support Sociotechnical Redesign Programs in Scandinavia," paper presented at the annual meeting of the Academy of Management, San Francisco, August 1990; and B. Dankbaar, "Lean Production: Denial, Confirmation or Extension of Sociotechnical Systems Design," *Human Relations* 50, no. 5 (1997), pp. 567–84.

45. L. U. De Sitter, J. F. Den Hertog, and B. Dankbaar, "From Complex Organizations with Simple Jobs to Simple Organizations with Complex Jobs," *Human Relations* 50, no. 5 (1997), pp. 497–534.

46. Y. Mitki, *Sociotechnical Systems: A Comparative Study of 112 Production Units in the Kibbutz Industries* (Tel Aviv, Israel: Tel Aviv University, 1994).

47. F. M. van Eijnatten, A. B. (Rami) Shani, and M. M. Leary, "Sociotechnical Systems: Designing and Managing Sustainable Organizations," in Cummings (ed.), *Handbook of Organization Development,* pp. 277–309.

48. R. Grant, A. B. (Rami) Shani, and R. Krishnan, "TQM's Challenge to Management Theory & Practice," *Sloan Management Review* 35, no. 2 (1994), pp. 25–35.

49. P. Lillrank and N. Kano, *Continuous Improvement* (Ann Arbor, MI: University of Michigan Press, 1989).

50. R. Krishnan, A. B. (Rami) Shani, R. Grant, and R. Baer, "The Search for Quality Improvements: Problems of Design and Implementation," *Academy of Management Executive* 7, no. 4 (1993), pp. 7–20.

51. R. E. Cole, P. Bacdayan, and B. J. White, "Quality, Participation, and Competitiveness," *California Management Review* 35, no. 3 (1993), pp. 68–81.

52. A. B. (Rami) Shani and M. Rogberg, "Quality, Strategy, and Structural Configuration," *Journal of Organizational Change Management* 7, no. 2 (1994), pp. 15–30.

53. G. Hall, J. Rosenthal, and J. Wade, "How to Make Reengineering Really Work," *Harvard Business Review* (November–December 1993), pp. 119–31; and P. Lillrnak and S. Holopainen, "Reengineering for Business Option," *Journal of Organizational Change Management* 11, no. 3 (1998), pp. 246–59.

54. M. Hammer and J. Champy, *Reengineering the Corporation* (New York: HarperCollins, 1993).

55. D. L. Schnitt, "Reengineering the Organization Using Information Technology," *Journal of System Management* (January 1993), pp. 14–42; J. Taylor, "Participative Design: Linking BPR and SAP with STS Approach," *Journal of Organizational Change Management* 11, no. 3 (1998), pp. 233–45.

56. T. Housel, C. Morris, and C. Westland, "Business Process Reengineering at Pacific Bell," *Planning Review* (May–June 1993), pp. 28–34.

57. This section is based on A. B. (Rami) Shani and Y. Mitki, "Reengineering, TQM and Sociotechnical Systems Approaches to Organizational Change," *Journal of Quality Management* 1 (1996), pp. 131–45.

58. M. Stebbins and A. B. (Rami) Shani, "Moving Away from the Mafia Model of Organization Design," *Organizational Dynamics* (Winter 1989), pp. 18–30.

59. Ibid.

60. Many recent review-based studies support this argument. See, for example, J. V. Gallos (ed.), *Organization Development Reader* (San Francisco, CA: Jossey-Bass, 2006); W. W. Burke, "A Contemporary View of Organization Development," in Cummings (ed.), *Handbook of Organization Development,* pp. 13–38; J. I. Porras, "Organization Development: Theory, Practice, and Research," in M. D. Dunnette and L. M. Hough (eds.), *Handbook of Industrial and Organizational Psychology,* 2nd ed., vol. 3 (Palo Alto, CA: Consulting Psychological Press, 1992), pp. 719–822; P. J. Robertson, D. R. Roberts, and J. I. Porras, "An Evaluation of a Model of Planned Organizational Change: Evidence from a Meta-Analysis," in W. A. Pasmore and R. W. Woodman (eds.), *Research in Organizational Change and Development,* vol. 7 (Greenwich, CT: JAI Press, 1993), pp. 1–39; B. A. Macy, and H. Izumi, "Organizational Change, Design, and Work Innovations: A Meta-Analysis of 131 North American Field Studies—1961–1991," in Pasmore and Woodman (eds.), *Research in Organizational Change and Development,* vol. 7, pp. 235–313.

61. W. L. French and C. H. Bell, *Organization Development,* 6th ed. (Englewood Cliffs, NJ: Prentice-Hall, 1999); T. D. Jick, *Managing Change* (Burr Ridge, IL: Irwin, 1993); R. M. Kanter, B. A. Stein, and T. D. Jick, *The Challenge of Organizational Change* (New York: Free Press, 1992).

62. J. I. Porras and S. J. Hoffer, "Common Behavior Changes in Successful Organization Development Efforts," *Journal of Applied Behavioral Science* 22, no. 4 (1986), pp. 477–94.

63. A. A. Armenakis, A. G. Bedian, and S. B. Pond, "Research Issues in OD Evaluation: Past, Present, and Future," *Academy of Management Review* 8, no. 2 (1983), pp. 320–28.

64. J. M. Nicholas and M. Katz, "Research Methods and Reporting Practices in Organization Development: A Review and Some Guidelines," *Academy of Management Review* 10, no. 4 (1985), pp. 737–49.

65. See B. A. Macy, "An Assessment of Improvement and Productivity Efforts: 1970–1985," paper presented at the National Academy of Management, August 1986, Chicago; F. M. Van Eijnatten, *The Sociotechnical Systems Design Paradigm* (Eindhoven, The Netherlands, 1986).

66. For a good synthesis and a set of readings about OD around the globe see P. F. Sorensen, Jr., T. Yaeger, T. Head, and D. Cooperrider, *Global International Organization Development,*

4th ed. (Champaign, IL: Stripes Publishing, 2007). For a sample of specific studies see M. N. Kiggundu, "Limitations to the Applications of Sociotechnical Systems in Developing Countries," *Journal of Applied Behavioral Science* 22, no. 3 (1986), pp. 341–54; Z. Chroscicki, "Conceptualization of OD Process Measures in Poland," *Organization Development Journal* 4, no. 3 (1986), pp. 62–67; M. Rikuta, "Organization Development within Japanese Industry: Facts and Prospects," *Organization Development Journal* 5, no. 2 (1987), pp. 21–32; J. Benders, R.-J. Van den Berg, and M. Van Bitsterveld, "Hitch-Hiring on a Hype: Dutch Consultants Engineering Re-Engineering," *Journal of Organizational Change Management* 11, no. 3 (1998), pp. 201–15; M. R. Manning and J. DelaCerda, "Building Organizational Change in an Emerging Economy: Whole Systems Change Using Large Group Interventions in Mexico," in W. W. Pasmore and R. W. Woodman (eds.), *Research in Organizational Change and Development,* vol. 14 (Boston, Mass: JAI Press, 2003), pp. 51–98.

67. A. M. Jaeger, "Organization Development and National Culture: Where's the Fit?" *Academy of Management Review* 11, no. 1 (1986), pp. 178–90.

68. A. B. (Rami) Shani and P. Docherty, "Learning by Design: Key Mechanisms in Organization Development," in Cummings (ed.), *Handbook of Organization Development,* pp. 499–518; Shani and Docherty, *Learning by Design.*

69. P. Reason and H. Bradbury (eds.), *Handbook of Action Research* (Los Angeles: Sage, 2008); A. B. (Rami) Shani, S. A. Mohrman, W. A. Pasmore, B. Stymne, and, N. Adler (eds.), *Handbook of Collaborative Management Research* (London: Sage, 2008); A. B. (Rami) Shani and G. R. Bushe, "Visionary Action Research: A Consultation Process Perspective," *Consultation: An International Journal* 6, no. 1 (1987), pp. 3–19; M. W. Stebbins and C. C. Snow, "Process and Payoffs of Programmatic Action Research," *Journal of Applied Behavioral Science* 18 (1982), pp. 69–86; A. Werr, "Managing Knowledge in Management Consulting," paper presented at the Academy of Management Conference, San Diego, 1998; and R. T. Golemiewski (ed.), *Handbook of Organizational Consultation* (New York: Marcel Dekker, 1999).

Activity 16–2: **Planned Change** **at General Electric**	*Objective:* To appreciate the complex process and the management of a planned change program.

Task 1 (Homework):

Participants are to read the case that follows and respond to the questions at the end of the case.

Task 2 (Classroom):

a. Individuals are to share their responses to the questions at the end of the case.

b. Teams are to discuss the process of managing change. (For example, What was Welch's approach? How is it different or similar to TQM or STS?)

c. Teams are to discuss the role that organizational learning mechanisms play at GE.

Task 3:

The instructor will have each team share its perceptions with the entire class.

Task 4:

The class will discuss the relationships between organizational learning mechanisms, managing change, and its effects on organizational behavior and productivity.

Task 5:

The instructor will give a short lecture on organizational learning mechanisms, managing change, and the role that the process plays in fostering or hindering effectiveness.

Case Study: The Transformation at General Electric

Jack Welch, Jr., was appointed chairman and chief executive officer of General Electric in April 1981. Welch retired at the end of 2000. Many of the practices that were initiated under his leadership continue to be a part of current work and management systems. His tenure in the job has been characterized by constant strategic and organizational change at GE. Among the initiatives with which Welch is associated are

1. *Changing the shape of the business portfolio.* Welch established two sets of criteria for redefining the business portfolio of GE. The first was to declare, "We will only run businesses that are number one or number two in their global markets—or, in the case of services, that have a substantial position—and are of a scale and potential appropriate to a $50 billion enterprise." Second, Welch defined three broad areas of business for GE: core, high-technology, and service businesses. As a result of these criteria, during the 1980s GE sold or closed businesses accounting for $10 billion in assets and acquired businesses amounting to $18 billion in assets. Divestment included Utah International, housewares and small appliances, consumer electronics, and semiconductors. Additions included RCA; Employers Reinsurance Corp.; Kidder Peabody Group; Navistar Financial; several new plastics ventures; Thomson's medical electronics business; and joint ventures with Fanuc (factory automation), Robert Bosch (electric motors), GEC (major appliances and electrical equipment), and Ericsson (mobile communications).

2. *Changing strategic planning.* Welch largely dismantled the highly elaborate strategic planning system that had been built up at GE over the previous decade. Documentation was drastically reduced, and the planning review process was made more informal—the central element was a meeting between Welch, his two vice chairmen, and the top management of each SBU (strategic business unit), which focused on identifying and discussing a few key themes. By 1984 the 200-strong corporate planning staff had been halved. The broad objective was "to get general managers talking to general managers about strategy rather than planners talking to planners."

3. *Delayering.* The changes in planning were one aspect of a more general change in the role of headquarters staff from being "checker, inquisitor, and authority figure to facilitator, helper, and supporter." This change involved a substantial reduction in reporting and paper generation and an increase in individual decision-making authority. These changes permitted a substantial widening of spans of control and the removal of several layers of hierarchy. In most of GE, levels of management were reduced from nine to four.

4. *Destaffing.* Divesting pressures, removing management layers, reducing corporate staffs, and increasing productivity resulted in enormous improvements. Between 1980 and 1990, GE's sales more than doubled while its numbers of employees fell from 402,000 to 298,000.

5. *Values.* A persistent theme in Welch's leadership was a commitment to values. Welch continually emphasized the importance of the company's "software" (values, motivation, and commitment) over its "hardware" (businesses and management structure). Welch's philosophy was articulated in 10 key principles and values:

   - Being number one or two in each business.

   - Becoming and staying lean and agile.

   - "Ownership"—individuals taking responsibility for decisions and actions.

   - "Stewardship"—individuals ensuring that GE's resources were leveraged to the full.

Source: This case was written by R. Grant and A. B. (Rami) Shani for classroom use. The case draws heavily on the following sources: N. M. Tichy and S. Sherman, *Control Your Destiny or Someone Else Will* (New York: Doubleday, 1992); R. Slater, *The New GE: How Jack Welch Revived an American Institution* (Burr Ridge, IL: Irwin, 1993); R. N. Ashkenas and T. D. Jick, "From Dialogue to Action in GE Work-Out," in W. A. Pasmore and R. Woodman (eds.), *Research in Organization Change and Development,* vol. 6 (Greenwich, CT: JAI Press, 1993), pp. 267–87; and "Jack Welch's Lessons for Success," *Fortune* (February 25, 1993), pp. 86–90.

- "Entrepreneurship."
- "Excellence"—the highest personal standards.
- "Reality."
- "Candor."
- "Open communications"—both internally and externally.
- Financial support—earning a return needed to support success.

This emphasis on values was supported by a type of leadership that put a huge emphasis on communicating and disseminating these values throughout the company. Welch devoted a large portion of his time to addressing meetings of employees and management seminars at GE's Crotonville Management Development Institute.

New Culture, New Systems

During his first five years in office, Welch's priorities were strategy and structure. GE's business portfolio was radically transformed, and within its main businesses GE's strategies gave a much greater emphasis to local presence and global success and to the development and application of new technology. In terms of organizational structure, Welch's crusade against excess costs, complacency, and administrative inefficiencies resulted in a drastic pruning of the corporate hierarchy and a much flatter organization.

At the root of the "new culture" Welch sought to build at GE was a redefinition of the relational contract between GE and its employees:

Like many other large companies in the United States, Europe and Japan, GE has had an implicit psychological contract based upon perceived lifetime employment . . . This produced a paternal, feudal, fuzzy kind of loyalty. You put in your time, worked hard, and the company took care of you for life. That kind of loyalty tends to focus people inward . . . The psychological contract has to change. People at all levels have to feel the risk-reward tension.

My concept of loyalty is not "giving time" to some corporate entity and, in turn, being shielded and protected from the outside world. Loyalty is an affinity among people who want to grapple with the outside world and win . . . The new psychological contract, if there is such a thing, is that jobs at GE are the best in the world for people who are willing to compete. We have the best training and development resources and an environment committed to providing opportunities for personal and professional growth.[1]

Creating a new attitude requires a shift from an internal focus to an external focus:

What determines your destiny is not the hand you're dealt, it's how you play your hand. The best way to play your hand is to face reality—see the world as it is and act accordingly . . . For me, the idea is: to shun the incremental and go for the leap. Most bureaucracies—and ours is no exception—unfortunately still think in incremental terms rather than in terms of fundamental change. They think incrementally because they think internally. Changing the culture—opening it up to quantum change—means constantly asking, not how fast am I going, how well am I doing versus how well I did a year or two before, but rather, how fast and how well am I doing versus the world outside.[2]

Critical to building a new culture and changing the "old ways" of GE was not just the bureaucracy itself, but the habits and attitudes that had been engendered by bureaucracy:

The walls within a big, century-old company don't come down like Jericho's when management makes some organizational changes or gives a speech. There are too many persistent habits propping them up. Parochialism, turf battles, status, "functionalities" and, most important, the biggest sin of a bureaucracy, the focus on itself and its inner workings, are always in the background.[3]

The Work-Out Program—A Generic View

GE's Work-Out Program was a response to the desire to speed the process of organizational change in GE. Welch conceived the idea of Work-Out in September 1988. Welch conducted a session at every class of GE managers attending Management Development Institute at Crotonville, New York. He was impressed by the energy, enthusiasm, and flow of ideas that his open discussion sessions with managers were capable of generating. At the same time, he was frustrated by the resilience of many of GE's bureaucratic practices and the difficulty of transferring the ideas that individual managers possessed into action. After a particularly lively session at Crotonville, Welch and GE's education director, James Braughman, got together to discuss how the interaction in these seminars could be replicated throughout the company in a process that would involve all employees and would generate far-reaching changes within GE. In the course of a helicopter ride from Crotonville to GE's Fairfield headquarters, Welch and Braughman sketched the concept and the framework for the Work-Out process.

A model for GE's Work-Out was a traditional New England town hall meeting where citizens gather to vent their problems, frustrations, and ideas, and people eventually agree on certain civic actions. Welch outlined the goals of Work-Out as follows:

Work-Out has a practical and an intellectual goal. The practical objective is to get rid of thousands of bad habits accumulated since the creation of General Electric . . . The second thing we want to achieve, the intellectual part, begins by putting the leaders of each business in front of 100 or so of their people, eight to ten times a year, to let them hear what their people think. Work-Out will expose the leaders to the vibrations of their business opinions, feelings, emotions, resentments, not abstract theories of organization and management.[4]

A generic summary of the Work-Out Program reveals three interrelated purposes: to fuel a process of continuous improvement and change; to foster cultural transformation characterized by trust, empowerment, elimination of unnecessary work, and boundaryless organization; and to improve business performance.

The Structure of the Work-Out Process

The central idea of the Work-Out process was to create a forum where a cross section of employees in each business could speak their minds about how their business was managed without fear of retribution. Because those doing the work were often the best people to recommend improvements in how their work should be managed, such interaction was seen as a first step in taking actions to remove unnecessary work and improve business processes. In January 1989, Welch announced Work-Out at an annual meeting of GE's 500 top executives. A broad framework was set out, but considerable flexibility was given to each of GE's 14 core businesses in how they went about the program. The key elements of Work-Out were

Off-site meetings. Work-Out was held as a forum and to get away from the company environment. Two- to three-day Work-Out events were held off-site.

Focus on issues and key processes. There was a strong bias toward action-oriented sessions. The initial Work-Out events tended to focus on removing unnecessary work. This is what Braughman referred to as the "low-hanging fruit." As the programs developed, Work-Out focused more on more complex business processes. For example, in GE Lighting, groupwide sessions were held to accelerate new-product development, improve fill rates, and increase integration between component production and assembly. In plastics the priorities were quality improvement, lower cycle times, and increased cross-functional coordination.

Cross-sectional participation. Work-Out sessions normally involved between 50 and 100 employees drawn from all levels and all functions of a business. Critical to the process was the presence of the top management of the particular business.

Small groups and town meetings. Work-Out events normally involved a series of small group meetings that began with a brainstorming session followed by a plenary session (or "town meeting") in which the suggestions developed by the small groups were put to senior managers and then openly debated. At the end of each discussion, the leader was required to make an immediate decision: to adopt, reject, or defer for further study.

Follow-up. A critical element of Work-Out was a follow-up process to ensure that what had been decided was implemented.

The Results of Work-Out

The results from Work-Out were remarkable. During its first four years, more than 3,000 Work-Out sessions had been conducted in GE, resulting in thousands of small changes eliminating "junk work" as well as much more complex and further-reaching changes in organizational structure and management processes. The terms *rattlers* and *pythons* were introduced to describe the two types of problem. Rattlers were simple problems that could be "shot" on sight. Pythons were more complex issues that needed unraveling.

As well as tangible structural changes and performance gains, some of the most important effects were changes in organizational culture. In GE Capital, one of the most centralized and bureaucratized of GE's businesses, one employee described the changes as follows: "We've been suppressed around here for a long time. Now that management is finally listening to us, it feels like the Berlin Wall is coming down."[5]

In five years, more than 300,000 employees, customers, and suppliers went through Work-Out sessions. A large variety of impressive and significant performance and efficiency improvements are reported in GE's internal documents, following introduction of the Work-Out processes. For example, the Gas Engine Turbines business unit at Albany, New York, reported an 80 percent decrease in production time to build gas engine turbines; Aircraft Engines at Lynn, Massachusetts, reduced jet engine production time from 30 to 4 weeks. GE's Financial Services Operation reported a reduction in operating costs from $5.10 to $4.55 per invoice, invoices paid per employee were up 34 percent, costs per employee paid fell 19 percent, and employees paid per payroll worker rose 32 percent. The Aerospace plant at Syracuse, New York, reported that as a result of the Work-Out Program, beyond achieving 100 percent compliance with pollution regulations, the production of hazardous waste materials was reduced from 759 tons in 1990 to 275 tons in 1992.

Managing Work-Out

Work-Out was intended as a bottom-up process in which (1) employees throughout each business would be free to challenge their leaders and (2) management's role was primarily to perpetuate the program and to ensure that decisions, once made, were implemented. But Work-Out could not be just a populist movement within the corporation. It needed to be directed toward creating the kind of corporation that GE needed to be to survive and prosper in the 1990s. To this extent Jack Welch saw his role as communicating and disseminating the principles, values, and themes that would permit GE's continued success.

In 1989 Welch crystallized his ideas about GE's management around three themes: speed, simplicity, and self-confidence:

We found in the 1980s that becoming faster is tied to becoming simpler. Our businesses, with tens of thousands of employees, will not respond to visions that have sub-paragraphs and footnotes. If we're not simple we can't be fast . . . and if we're not fast, we can't win. Simplicity, to an engineer, means clean, functional, winning designs, no bells and whistles. In marketing it might manifest itself as clear, unencumbered proposals. For manufacturing people it would produce a logical process that makes sense to every individual on the line. And on an individual, interpersonal level it would take the form of plain speaking, directness, honesty.

But as surely as speed flows from simplicity, simplicity is grounded in self-confidence. Self-confidence does not grow in someone who is just another appendage on the bureaucracy; whose authority rests on little more than a title. People who are freed from the confines of their box on the organization chart, whose status rests on real world achievement—those are the people who develop the self-confidence to be simple, to share every bit of information available to them, to listen to those above, below and around them and then move boldly.

But a company cannot distribute self-confidence. What it can do—what we must do—is to give our people an opportunity to win, to contribute, and hence earn self-confidence themselves. They don't get that opportunity, they can't taste winning if they spend their days wandering in the muck of a self-absorbed bureaucracy.

Speed . . . simplicity self-confidence. We have it in increasing measure. We know where it comes from and we have plans to increase it in the 1990s.[6]

471

Best Practices

One of the Work-Out Program's many impressive outcomes is that it is a catalyst for new improvement programs. One such program, Best Practices, is aimed at increasing productivity. The GE business-development staff focused on 24 credible companies from an initial pool of 200 that had achieved faster productivity growth than GE and sustained it for at least 10 years. From this list one dozen companies agreed to take part in GE's proposal to send its employees to their companies to learn their secrets to success. In exchange, GE offered to share the results of the study as well as success stories with the participating companies. This learning for the Best Practices program involved companies such as Ford, Hewlett-Packard, Xerox, and Chaparral Steel plus three Japanese firms.

GE was less concerned with the actual work done at the companies than with management practices and attitudes of the employees. The difference between Best Practices and traditional benchmarking is that the former does not require keeping score. The focus on learning alternative successful management practices and managing processes was identified as the most critical component for long-term productivity improvements. The basic assumption that through multiple exposures to alternative management practices, managers and employees will be stimulated to continuously improve their own practices continues to guide the program. Best Practices has evolved into a formal course taught to at least one dozen employees and managers per month in each business unit.

Assignment (Written)

1. Based on the limited information presented, describe the overall planned change approach and phases led by Jack Welch.

2. Identify and briefly describe the major characteristics of the Work-Out Program.

3. Identify and briefly describe the nature of organizational learning and the key features of the learning mechanisms that we created.

4. Discuss how the organizational culture changed. What caused the change? What effects did the culture change have on human behavior and organizational performance and effectiveness?

Notes

1. N. M. Tichy and R. Charan, "Speed, Simplicity, Self-Confidence: An Interview with Jack Welch," *Harvard Business Review* (September–October 1989), p. 120.

2. Ibid., p. 114.

3. *Fortune* (January 25, 1993), p. 87.

4. Tichy and Charan, "Speed, Simplicity, Self-Confidence," p. 118.

5. R. N. Ashkenas and T. D. Jick, "From Dialogue to Action in GE Work-Out: Developmental Learning in a Change Process," *Research in Organizational Change and Development* 6 (1992), p. 271.

6. J. Welch, "Speed, Simplicity and Self-Confidence: Keys to Leading in the 1990s," speech at annual shareholders meeting, April 1989.

Activity 16–3: Custom Nests Simulation

Objectives:

a. To help participants become aware of the differences between sociotechnical design principles and traditional bureaucratic principles.

b. To develop participants' appreciation for the sociotechnical systems approach to organizational development and effectiveness.

Task 1 (Homework):

Participants are to read the following organization description of Custom Nests. (Do not read beyond the basic description of the organization.)

Task 2 (In-Class Activities):

a. The instructor will assign roles and give nametags to participants.

b. The instructor will then assign participants to their workstations and ask them to begin their work as it is described in their role descriptions.

c. Production will be stopped after about 25 minutes, and participants will be asked to leave the room for about 10 minutes.

d. The instructor will then lead a brief discussion about the experience of work in the phase just completed. Discussion themes might be

  1. What was it like being a stapler, a supervisor, and so on?

  2. How was this organization like others that you have worked for?

  3. What kind of organizational development strategy would you utilize to improve effectiveness?

  4. How would you go about implementing the change?

Task 3 (In-Class Activities):

Participants will be assigned to new work groups and asked to start production. Production will be stopped after about 25 minutes.

Task 4:

The instructor will lead a class discussion on the following themes:

a. How was the work design in the second phase different and/or similar to that of the first phase?

b. What would be the implications of the second work design phase to your own experience?

c. Discuss the relationship among the social, technological, and environmental subsystems.

d. What are some challenges for implementing sociotechnical system change in organizations?

e. How would the sociotechnical system intervention be similar to or different from the other organizational development approaches discussed in this module?

(*Note to the instructor.* Be sure to read the *Instructor's Manual* before using this exercise.)

Source: This activity was contributed by Dr. Barry Morris. All rights are reserved and no reproduction should be made without express approval of Dr. Morris. We are grateful to him.

Case Study: Custom Nests Simulation

Organization Description

Custom Nests was founded in 1951 by Mr. Jay Blue. The company began as a small operation consisting of six workers and a manager. Everyone in the company worked as a craftsperson making birdhouses from beginning to end. The explosion in the housing market that followed World War II created a massive demand for birdhouses for the displaced birds of this period. As a result Custom Nests grew considerably in a short period of time. Today it continues to be the primary manufacturer of birdhouses, providing the American public with a wide range of quality birdhouses for every occasion and climate. One birdhouse in particular, however, has remained the company's primary and most marketable item and has allowed the business to expand into other birdhouse markets with little risk to overall sales.

The structure of the organization has changed dramatically since its inception. Only the people in research and development actually have the opportunity to build a birdhouse from the bottom up. The majority of the company's products are manufactured in a highly specialized assembly line–type of process in which few people actually have hands-on opportunities to see how the whole product gets made. Wages for hourly workers are determined based on years with the organization and the complexity of the task. For many years the company had been paying minimum wage wherever possible. In 1969, the company was unionized. Wages are currently slightly less than the standard for similar industrial settings. The relationship between union and management is adversarial. There is a fairly high number of grievances written on a regular basis, and neither group has as yet been willing to sit down and iron out their differences in a way that meets both groups' needs. For the most part decisions in the organization are made by managers, while hourly workers are expected to do as they are told.

The company currently employs approximately 175 people. Of these, 140 are hourly employees; the remainder are engineers or managers of one sort or another. The various hourly roles in the organization include cutters, tapers, staplers, and maintenance/supply personnel. The salaried staff includes quality control, supervisors, research and development, and accounting clerks.

The plant's layout has the various specialties spread out and separated from one another in a large single-floor facility. (See the diagram.) Many structural barriers to effective communication between work groups/areas exist. The technology in much of the plant is simple yet antiquated. There is a long history of broken or unuseful tools and inadequate processes for keeping the technology in good working order.

Custom Nest Floor Plan

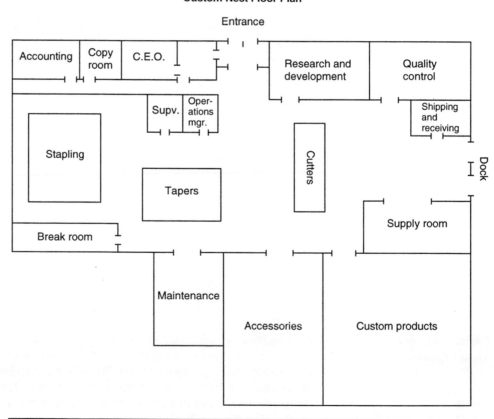

Custom Nest Floor Plan

CUSTOM NESTS SIMULATION: ROLES

SUPERVISOR

The supervisor's job at Custom Nests is considered the most important job in the plant. In all, there are three supervisors, but there is little need for interaction among them. The supervisor in this company is considered to be the expert, the conflict manager, the scheduler, the communicator, and the quality control representative, to name a few roles.

You, however, have a very special supervisory role in that you are personally responsible for the production of Custom Nests's standard birdhouse. You are directly responsible for all production and maintenance functions within your product line. Your immediate superior is the only operations manager for all products. Although he recognizes the importance of your product, he prefers to give you total responsibility for operations in your area. From his perspective, when problems arise, you are to blame.

The relationships between you and your direct reports are good for the most part. Sometimes you are put in the middle and therefore are thought to be the bad guy, but most people know that you are between a rock and a hard place. You basically do what you have to do to get the job done and to keep your job.

Like all of the other supervisors, you have moved up through the system over the years. You know almost all the jobs from personal experience and got the supervisor's job because of your knowledge of technical processes and your apparent desire to move up in the organization. In addition, you seem to be able to get people to work hard and fast.

Your specific responsibilities include the following:

1. Scheduling, monitoring time cards, and establishing production speeds.
2. Communications from department to department and from management to hourly employees.
3. Supervising maintenance work.
4. Supervising materials handling.
5. Supervising production.
6. Conflict management.
7. Employee counseling and coaching.
8. Handling first-step grievances.
9. Daily and weekly production reports.
10. Managing the absenteeism program.
11. Providing technical skills training.

QUALITY CONTROL

The quality control (QC) department was created in the early 1960s. As the company's products have diversified, the need for a QC department has grown even more essential. Unskilled hourly employees could not possibly understand the importance of quality to the success of the business or keep track of all of the standards and specifications required for each of the company's 33 birdhouse styles and accessories.

Finished products are delivered to the QC department from each product section. The largest group of QC personnel is assigned to Custom Nests's standard birdhouse, which has been the company's primary product since the company was established in 1951 when only six workers built the birdhouses by hand and cared about the results of their labor.

The QC department is located in the back corner of the plant, far removed from the production department. QC personnel, who tend to have very little contact with the workers on the line, communicate primarily with the manager of operations and occasionally the supervisor, who also does a lot of the QC work. Under normal circumstances QC does not usually talk to the supervisor, but the manager of operations prefers to let the supervisor from the standard birdhouse production area manage most of the area's operations-related issues.

The QC personnel are primarily engineers. They tend to be young people who have recently graduated from local colleges. Some of them began with the company as co-op students and, following graduation, continued their work for Custom Nests. The QC engineers responsible for the company's standard birdhouse must examine hundreds of birdhouses a week. They don't have the time to look at every birdhouse unless there is a production breakdown, which gives them an opportunity to catch up. The work they do is very repetitive and boring. On occasion they get an opportunity to work on technological problems causing consistent quality problems. For the most part, however, their skills are not needed or used, since the manager of QC prefers to handle any of the really challenging work. As a result of boredom and lack of challenging work, there is a lot of turnover in this department. Aside from the manager of QC, the average tenure of QC personnel is 3½ years.

QC personnel are responsible for determining the quality of the finished birdhouse based on a set of quality standards on the Quality Standards and Specifications List. (See next section.) They make the final decision to keep a finished birdhouse or to throw it away. They also prepare reports for the operations manager and accounting department.

Quality Standards and Specifications List

Custom Nests's standard birdhouse quality standards and specifications are

1. No lines are to be on the outside surfaces of the birdhouse.
2. All staples must face the inside of the birdhouse; the flat side of the staple should be on the outside surfaces of the birdhouse.
3. Tape should thoroughly cover the roof's center connection.
4. The stapler's employee number should appear on the bottom of the birdhouse.
5. There should be no gaps in any of the corners and connections.
6. The bottom width of the birdhouse should be as close to 3½ inches as possible.
7. The sides should be between 3 and 3¼ inches high.
8. The length of the birdhouse should be between 5½ and 6 inches.
9. The perch should stick out 1½ to 2 inches from the front of the birdhouse.
10. The entry hole on the front panel should center 1 to 1¼ inches above the birdhouse floor.
11. The diameter of the entry should be between 2 and 2¼ inches.
12. No creases should appear in any of the flat surfaces of the birdhouse.
13. All folds in the front and rear panels should be very close to ¼ inch.
14. All cuts made to prepare front and rear panels for folding should be close to ¼ inch.
15. The finished birdhouse should sit flat on a table.

RESEARCH AND DEVELOPMENT

The research and development department is involved in the design of new products, the improvement of old products, customer relations, and marketing. This department was established in 1976. The housing market was declining and a new line of birdhouses was needed to meet the needs of apartment dwellers. In addition, the traditional Custom Nests product was becoming less effective. More and more home owners and distributors were complaining that the birdhouses were not squirrel proof. Ways had to be found to keep squirrels from climbing up the birdhouse pole or down from the trees above to steal birdseed from the beaks of hungry baby birds.

Members of the research and development (R&D) department spend most of their time at the drafting tables or out in the field talking with the customers and distributors of birdhouses. Little if any time is spent in the plant. Any design changes are decided upon by R&D personnel along with management, and these are communicated through the manager of operations, to the supervisor, and so forth. R&D reports directly to the owner, Mr. Jay Blue.

The R&D function is relatively new to the organization, and its personnel were hired from the outside. The turnover in the department is high. It seems to be a place where young designers get a chance to learn about the real world just after they have finished their engineering degrees. You therefore have probably been with the company for about 2 years. The pay is less than you expect to be able to make in the future, and the extent to which you are challenged in your work is unsatisfactory. It's just a job and a possible step to a better future.

ACCOUNTING

The accounting position was established in 1971 when two major developments occurred: (1) The company had been growing, and the owner was no longer able to manage the books and keep up with the growth of the business, and (2) you married the boss's younger sister. You are fairly secure in your position, since you have been doing it for so long. In addition, your relationship with your brother-in-law is good. He confides in you a great deal, since he sees you as his friend and somebody concerned about the business. You must, however, work very hard because you have something to prove to the rest of the employees (that you are not a freeloader). You also know something your brother-in-law doesn't know—your wife is unhappy with your marriage, and you are worried about how that might affect your future, even though you know that your brother-in-law likes you better.

You have major responsibility for much of the management work in the plant. In addition to your accounting responsibilities, you order all materials and manage the shipping department. Recently you took over responsibility for employee relations when the employee relations manager was hospitalized for cardiac problems. You expected to have the job for a month or so, but that was 5 months ago, and the man's health is still uncertain. All you can really handle is some of the administrative trivia required by the union; you have had little time to talk with the employees about their grievances or their benefits.

Some of your specific accounting responsibilities include

1. Purchasing.
2. Supplying raw materials to maintenance/supply personnel.
3. Collecting data gathered by the material/supply department and the quality control department.
4. Analyzing the above collected data in six areas: total number of 4×6 cards distributed; total number of 4×6 cards used; number of birdhouses produced; number of birdhouses accepted; perches distributed and used; and waste.

You can use this data analysis worksheet for your analysis.

ACCOUNTING DATA ANALYSIS WORKSHEET

Raw materials data
Total number of 4×6 cards distributed.   _____
Total number of 4×6 cards used.   _____
Total number of perches distributed.   _____
Total number of perches used.   _____
Waste.   _____
Quality control data
Number of birdhouses produced.   _____
Number of birdhouses accepted.   _____
Waste.   _____

MAINTENANCE/SUPPLY

Maintenance and supply personnel are primarily production people who have moved their way up through the system. None of you have any formal training in machine maintenance and repair, though your experience with the company has provided you with the skills to make simple repairs on the equipment used in the plant.

In an effort to cut costs, 2 years ago the supply function merged with maintenance. You consequently have the responsibility for maintaining equipment, supplying raw materials to all functions in the plant, and moving components from one function to another. You move throughout the plant and probably have the best information about the "goings on" in the plant. Unfortunately, there is little you can do with all of this information. You must report to and take orders from the supervisor in charge of production.

Your work is anything but boring, since you always have plenty to do. The problem is that you are spread too thin and are unable to do any single job to the best of your ability. This bothers you, since you have been with the company for a long time and know that product quality and employee morale have been better in the past.

The majority of the maintenance/supply personnel have been with the company for 25 years or more. Many of you are waiting for the opportunity to retire. Your wages and benefits are fair, but not as good as your counterparts in similar industries. Some of you could potentially leave Custom Nests in pursuit of maintenance jobs in other companies, but you know that the skills required here may be inadequate in another organization. Besides, you have been here for a long time, and you like the people. As a matter of fact, your ability to see and talk to a lot of people in the plant is one thing that motivates you to come to work.

Maintenance/Supply: Job Description

Your job is (1) to provide raw materials to each function in the plant: 4×6 cards to tapers and cutters, staples and straws to staplers, tape to tapers; (2) to transport finished components of the birdhouse to the next stage in the assembly process; transport front and rear panels from the cutters to the staplers, roofs and side/bottom components from the tapers to the staplers, and finished products from the staplers to quality control; (3) to repair or replace equipment used by cutters, staplers, and tapers; and (4) to maintain records of materials being supplied and components being transported from department to department and of finished birdhouses being transported to quality control.

MAINTENANCE/SUPPLY INVENTORY SHEET

Raw materials

4×6 cards supplied to tapers. _____

4×6 cards supplied to cutters. _____

Straws applied to staplers. _____

Completed components (record finished sets)

Sets transported from taping to stapling _____

(a set consists of one completed roof and one
completed side/bottom panel).

Sets transported from cutting to stapling _____

(a set consists of a front and rear panel cut and folded).

Completed birdhouses

Number of completed birdhouses transported to quality control. _____

STAPLER

The stapler position, in the production area, is one of the most complex and highest-rated positions in the company. Most workers in this area have been with the company for 20 years or more and have worked in this area for at least 9 years. Most of you have worked your way up through the lower-skill positions, and one stapler was one of the original employees of the company. Because of your seniority, it is possible that a few of you will be retiring in a few years. Movement in this position means potential advancement for people in less-skilled positions. The position has the highest pay rate for production workers at Custom Nests, yet your wages are lower than your counterparts in similar industries. As a result, many of you are involved in the union's fight for higher wages. The fact that many of you grew up in the union movement has made you staunch union supporters.

The stapler's job is most dependent on the workmanship of the cutters and tapers who build the pieces of the birdhouse that you must assemble. For the most part, however, you will assemble the parts that you receive and those you manufacture (perches) regardless of their condition. It is not your job to determine whether a part is good enough to use.

The technology that you utilize in the stapling function is rather simple, yet numerous technological problems arise on a regular basis. Parts are often hard to find, and maintenance is a challenge.

Although the work is more complex than other production jobs, you have found that with some experience, the work becomes simple and repetitive, and as a result it is often boring. The fact that you perform the final production function means that problems in other areas create work slowdowns or shutdowns for you.

Stapler: Job Description

Your job is (1) to staple the sides and bottom of the birdhouse to the front and rear panels, (2) to staple the roof to the front and rear panels of the birdhouse, and (3) to prepare and attach the perch to the birdhouse door.

Specific instructions and responsibilities are:

1. Attach the bottom/side component to the folds in the front and rear panels of the birdhouse.

2. Attach the roof component to the folds in the front and rear panels of the birdhouse.

3. Cut a 2- to 2½-inch piece of straw.

4. Bend and attach the straw to the door of the birdhouse so that the perch extends out from the door 1½ to 2 inches.

5. Make sure that all staples face inward. That is, the flat part of the staples should be on the outside surface of the final product, except for the staples in the bend at the floor. These should face the ground.

6. Place your employee number on the very bottom of the assembled product.

7. Transport the completed birdhouse to quality control.

CUTTERS

The cutters' position is one of the lower-paying hourly positions in the company. The majority of the workers in this area have been with the company for at least 13 years and have been in the cutting area for a minimum of 7 years. Over that time most of you have moved up through the organization, learning as you went and bidding on new jobs as they came open.

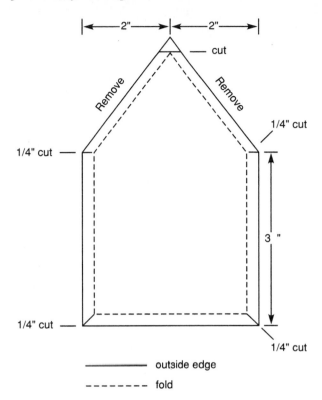

The cutting job tends to be rather boring once you have learned the work. It really takes little thinking for you to do what is expected of you.

Custom Nests pays a little less than other companies in the area. Your union has been pushing for the last couple of years to have wages raised to comparable standards. The company just says that the demand for birdhouses is expected to drop as a result of Japanese competition. The only way for you to make more money is to move to stapling or maintenance, but these jobs are hard to come by. The way you see it, cutting is going to be your job for the next few years.

Cutter: Job Description

The job of a cutter is (1) to cut and fold, from 4×6 cards supplied by the maintenance/supply personnel, the front and rear panels of the Custom Nests standard birdhouse and (2) to cut the birdhouse door in all front panels.

Specific responsibilities and panel design include:

1. Front and rear panels should be made consistent with the above drawing.

2. On all front panels a 2- to 2¼-inch hole must be cut 1 to 1¼ inches from the bottom of the front panel, and the hole should be centered.

3. The worker's number must be put on the back of each finished piece.

4. Finished goods (completed front and back panels) must be sent to the stapling department.

5. Panels should be identified as front or back on the lined side of the panel.

TAPERS

The taper's job receives the lowest pay rate in the organization. People in this work area have been with the company for the least amount of time. Like other work areas, your pay rate is lower than most industries in similar markets, and you have been fairly active in the pursuit of higher wages. Unlike some people who have been with the company for several years, you have been fortunate enough to have received a full high school education and some of you have been to college. The job market in the past few years, however, has forced you to take work that underutilizes your abilities.

The perceived stability but no growth position in the birdhouse business means that there is likely to be little advancement for you in this business unless people in higher-ranked jobs either retire or die. As a result you come to work to make a living, to receive your benefits, and to kill time. The work is boring and simple, and it requires little thought.

Taper: Job Description

The job of taper requires that you (1) tape together two 4×6 cards to make the roof of the Custom Nests standard birdhouses and (2) tape together and fold three 4×6 cards to make the sides and bottom of the birdhouses.

Job specifications are listed below:

1. Two cards taped together at their longest side make the roof. The tape should be applied so that no water can leak into the birdhouse.

2. The three cards utilized for the sides and bottom must be folded and taped together so that the bottom is 3½ inches wide and the sides are 3 to 3¼ inches tall. Two seams requiring one long strip of tape each are all that are needed based on the original design of the birdhouse. Tape is a most expensive material and must be used with cost in mind.

3. Tapers' numbers should be put on the underside of each roof and floor/side structure produced in your department.

4. Your finished products must be transported to the stapling department.

5. Tapers should identify each part as a roof or floor. All identification markings should be written on the lined side of the 4×6 card.

**Activity 16–4:
Analyzing the Team
Climate**

This activity should be the most interesting and important learning experience in the course and requires a large block of time. One or two evenings could be valuably devoted to it.

Objectives:

a. To apply the team-building approach to your own work team.

b. To generate the data for completion of the individual or team term paper on team development.

Task 1:

a. Each team member, working alone, is to complete the Climate Attribute Scales that follow prior to coming to the team meeting, which is to be held outside of class.

b. Review your journal analysis of how course concepts and team skills have applied to your team's interactions as the team evolved during the course. Be prepared to present your observations at the team meeting.

Task 2:

Team members are to meet and discuss the climate attributes one at a time. Each member will report the rating made prior to the meeting. The differences in ratings will be discussed to determine why members perceive the team interactions differently. After thorough discussion a group consensus rating will be made for each scale. The group consensus rating sheet will be included and discussed in the final team development report.

The rating sheet given here is only a device to help introduce this session. Now make an analysis of how course concepts and theories applied to your team as it evolved during the course. How did team skills develop? Having reviewed your journals before the meeting, a synergistic exchange should result in added insight into these processes. One approach that might be used is for members to call out in rapid succession all possible topics the group might want to discuss. One member should list these for the group. After members have exhausted ideas for the list, the items can be taken up one at a time for discussion. Conclude this portion of the session by answering the following: If this team were to work together in the future, how could it improve its effectiveness? Be specific.

Feedback Session (an Optional Activity): Teams are to give each member feedback as to what they perceive to be the individual's strengths and the areas where the individual could be stronger in team interactions. If the team members are supportive of one another and an openness-to-learning, concern-for-growth atmosphere exists, this experience can be valuable. Knowing what impact one is having on others and how one is coming across is important in one's effectiveness. But the atmosphere must be right so that the individuals hear what others say without becoming defensive. As we have seen throughout this course, being able to receive feedback from one's superiors, peers, and subordinates is widely advocated as an area for improved effectiveness for managers. Feedback sessions are one of the best sources of data for your team paper. But remember, the team feedback is optional—only the team can decide if it wishes to complete it. No individual should be pressured. If an individual decides not to participate in this portion of the exercise, he or she should not do so.

Task 3:

Your team will have an opportunity to discuss this team-building session in a later class and to hear the other teams discuss theirs. These sessions are best when they are spontaneous and all team members participate, so do not prepare.

Name _____   Date _____

CLIMATE ATTRIBUTE SCALES

Climate Attribute

Write an X on the scale to indicate the degree to which the attribute characterizes your team's activities and members.

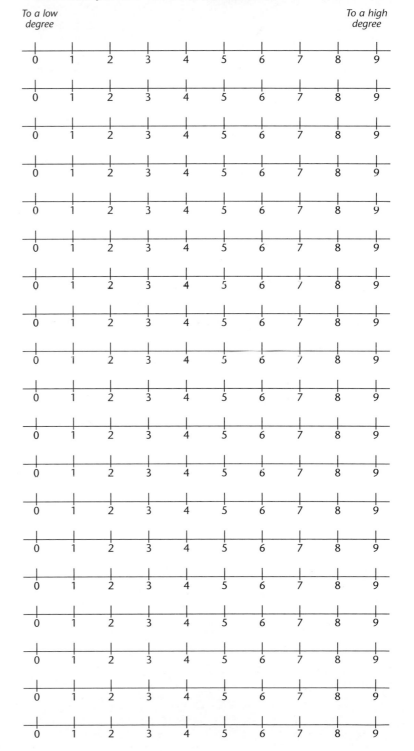

Climate Attribute	To a low degree 0–9 To a high degree
Commitment to the task	0 1 2 3 4 5 6 7 8 9
Openness to learning	0 1 2 3 4 5 6 7 8 9
Retired-on-the-job attitudes	0 1 2 3 4 5 6 7 8 9
Candor and forthrightness	0 1 2 3 4 5 6 7 8 9
Attentive listening for understanding	0 1 2 3 4 5 6 7 8 9
Conviction to stand up for honestly held views	0 1 2 3 4 5 6 7 8 9
Defensiveness or lack of trust	0 1 2 3 4 5 6 7 8 9
Being too polite, being too considerate, smoothing over differences	0 1 2 3 4 5 6 7 8 9
Avoidance of conflict	0 1 2 3 4 5 6 7 8 9
Experimental, innovative	0 1 2 3 4 5 6 7 8 9
Attempts to dominate	0 1 2 3 4 5 6 7 8 9
Cutting people off	0 1 2 3 4 5 6 7 8 9
Interest in one another as people	0 1 2 3 4 5 6 7 8 9
Consideration for others	0 1 2 3 4 5 6 7 8 9
Willingness to express feelings, each person saying "where he or she is"	0 1 2 3 4 5 6 7 8 9
Expressing feelings in a way acceptable to others	0 1 2 3 4 5 6 7 8 9
Paraphrasing for better understanding	0 1 2 3 4 5 6 7 8 9
Perceptual checking	0 1 2 3 4 5 6 7 8 9
Willingness to confront differences in ideas	0 1 2 3 4 5 6 7 8 9

Write in any other attributes that you believe characterize your team.

Climate Attribute

Write an **X** on the scale to indicate the degree to which the attribute characterizes your team's activities and members.

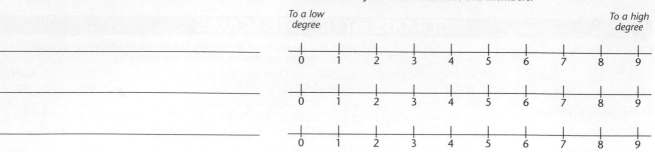

Activity 16–5: Team Feedback Discussion

Objective:

To allow each team to share its learning experience in small group dynamics with the other teams.

Task 1:

The instructor will select one team to sit in a circle in the center of the class. Members of the team will spontaneously discuss, without the benefit of notes, what types of group dynamics learning they gained from the team project exercise. Topics that could be covered include how the group dynamic concepts applied to their team, how conflict was handled, how each member felt about his or her role and the role of others in the group, how the group could be more effective if it were to continue, and anything else that seems important to the group. The team should not be interrupted by outside questions at this time.

Time for questions from the other teams should be provided when the team has completed the discussion.

Each team will have its allotted time in the circle.

Task 2:

The instructor will comment at the end of each team discussion and summarize at the end of the session.

(*Note to instructor:* Be sure to read *Instructor's Manual* before using this exercise.)

Activity 16–6: Feedback on Effectiveness of the Course and the Instructor

Objectives:

a. To reinforce learning by participants sharing what they perceive to be course strengths.

b. To provide the instructor with data for improved effectiveness.

Task 1:

The instructor is to leave the room.
Teams that have met throughout the course are each to appoint a spokesperson who will record the team's answers to the following questions:

a. What are the course's strengths? How could it be improved?

b. In what ways is the instructor effective? How could he or she be more effective?

Any member of the team can give an evaluative comment to the spokesperson. His or her identity will be protected; the spokesperson's report is the anonymous judgments of the team members. However, objectivity is urged. Some teams may conclude on their own that a comment will be included only if the majority of the members agree on its validity.
(Time: 20 minutes)

Task 2:

The instructor is to return to the classroom.

Class participants are to arrange themselves in a giant circle around the room, with team members sitting in adjacent seats. The instructor should take a seat on the circle where he or she is able to make eye contact with all class members.

The instructor calls on each spokesperson to discuss the strengths of the course. On the second round, the spokesperson should discuss how the course should be improved; on the third round, discuss the instructor's effectiveness; and on the last round, discuss how the instructor should improve. After each round the instructor should ask whether anyone other than the spokesperson wishes to comment.

The role of the instructor is to hear what the participants are saying. Periodic paraphrasing of what has been said will help ensure understanding. Avoid trying to justify or explain what has taken place in the course because participants might interpret that as a defensive response.

Glossary

A

accommodating orientation   a conflict-handling mode where one group attempts to satisfy the concerns of the other by neglecting its own concerns and goals.

accommodating style   an unassertive, cooperative position where one group attempts to satisfy the concerns of the other by neglecting its own concerns or goals.

achievement-oriented leadership   a path goal leadership style where the leader is preoccupied with setting challenging goals for the work group.

action orientation   a focus on doing or acting as opposed to planning.

action research   an emergent inquiry process in which behavioral and social science knowledge is integrated with existing organizational knowledge to produce new, usable knowledge.

active listening   a key factor in ensuring managerial success, this process involves actively engaging in what others say, including the use of paraphrasing, being reflective on what is said, and clearly supporting the speaker.

adaption-innovation model   a system proving that both adaptors and innovators are capable of generating original creative solutions but from different problem-solving orientations.

administrative innovation   new incentive systems and new communication network systems that affect the organization as much or more than technological innovations.

administrative school   a classical management approach led by Henry Fayol; focused on the five basic functions of management planning, organizing, commanding, coordinating, and controlling.

adult learner   individual beyond adolescence engaged in learning.

age diversity   a broad age distribution in organizations.

age stereotype   belief that differing traits and abilities make a certain age group more or less suited to different roles or display different behavior toward work.

alarm stage   occurs when the external stimulus (stressor) elicits body defense mechanisms, in which glands release quantities of adrenaline, cortisone, and other hormones.

alienation   distancing of the worker from the product, from others within the organization, or from meeting his or her true potential, through organizational shortcomings.

animus   Jung's concept of male qualities which women repress within themselves and then project onto men.

appreciative inquiry   the co-inquiry between two or more individuals that focuss on the best in people, their organization and the relevant world around them. (1) It involves systematic discovery of what gives life to a living system when it is most alive, most effective, and most constructively capable in economic, ecological, and human terms. (2) It is viewed as a cycle composed of four phases: discovery, dream, design and destiny.

archetypes   Jung's term for the innate, universal prototypes for ideas that have evolved throughout human history in our struggle for meaning, and which we inherit, like a psychological DNA.

assertiveness   the degree to which a person or group wants to satisfy its own concerns.

attribution process   The 4-fold process that describes how individuals perceive cause and effects, broken down as (1) a particular behavioral event triggers a cognitive analysis that (2) focuses on what causes the event, (3) followed by a modification or reinforcement of previous assumptions of causality that (4) leads to behavioral choices regarding future behavioral events.

attribution theory   focuses on the process by which individuals interpret events around them as being caused by a relatively stable portion of the environment. According to attribution theory, it is the perceived causes of events, not the actual events, that influence individuals' behavior.

avoidance orientation   a conflict-handling approach in which both groups neglect the concerns involved by sidestepping issues or postponing conflict by choosing not to deal with it.

B

BATNA   best alternative to a negotiated agreement; setting this helps a negotiator know how to evaluate alternatives or when to walk away from a negotiation.

behavior modification   an attempt to change behavior by operant conditioning, that is, voluntary behavior is rewarded and incorrect behavior is ignored or punished.

behavioral leadership theory   an approach that focuses on identifying what leaders actually do or how they actually behave as they attempt to influence others toward goal accomplishment.

behavioral science school   a neoclassical management approach that was an outgrowth of the human relations school; focused on individual behavior within work groups.

belief systems   frameworks of beliefs individuals hold based on their values and convictions.

Big Five personality theory   theory postulating that there are five factors of personality—extroversion, agreeableness, conscientiousness, emotional stability and openness to experience—that can serve as a meaningful taxonomy for classifying personality attributes.

brainstorming   a group thought-generation process that revolves around the spontaneous, uncontained expression of ideas.

burnout   a combined physical, mental, and emotional exhaustion arising from the cumulative effects of prolonged stress.

C

charismatic leaders   charisma is a Greek word that means "divinely inspired gift". Early theories viewed charismatic leaders as individuals who, by sheer strength of their personality, had major effect or strong influence over others. According to recent theories, followers' attribution of charismatic qualities to a leader is jointly determined by the leader's behavior, skills, competencies, and aspects of the situation.

cheetah team (CT)   a small group of elite units, separated from the product development team, that can be mobilized quickly to solve an unexpected problem threatening to hold up a project.

classical era   period of management thought from 1880s to 1930s; early studies centered on the search for alternative ways to organize and structure the industrial organization and the ways to motivate people who work within the emerging organizational structures.

coaching   a complex process whereby the manager works to actively listen to the employee's perception of him/herself and interacts with the employee to make sure he or she is given the right resources to effectively perform in his/her role.

collaborating orientation   a conflict-handling mode that attempts to satisfy the concerns of both groups.

collective unconscious   the repository of motifs that humans have been creating and re-creating throughout history in their struggles toward meaning.

common enemy   (1) an organization's closest competitor that can often inspire teams that are in conflict to work together. (2) a team's closest threat (can be internal or external to the team) that often inspires the team to come together and overcome internal differences and conflicts.

communication   the transfer of information from one entity to another (the entities can be viewed within an individual, between two individuals, between individuals within a team, between teams, between organizational units between organizations).

communication dialoguing   open exchange of views, beliefs, and when appropriate, feelings, between individuals or groups; it implies hearing each other out and listening for understanding.

communication medium   the means by which messages are conveyed, such as conversation, computers, and body language.

communication network   the flow, pattern, and pathway of signals or codes between two or more individuals.

competitive orientation   a conflict-handling mode in which the groups attempt to achieve their own goals at the expense of the other through argument, authority, threat, or even physical force.

compromising orientation   a conflict-handling mode that involves give-and-take from both groups.

computer networks   the software, hardware, logistics, and connection between computers that allow and facilitate the conveyance of information (electronic impulses) between them.

conflict   conflict includes disagreements, the presence of tension, or some other difficulty between two or more parties. Conflict occurs when individuals or groups of individuals perceive that their goals are blocked. It can be private or public, formal or informal or rational or irrational.

conflict-handling mode   methods of resolving or eliminating opposing thoughts, actions, or feelings.

consensus process   a group process in which the ideas of all individuals are contributed and evaluated fully in arriving at a decision that all members of the group are willing to support and no team member opposes.

consideration   a leadership behavior that creates mutual respect by focusing on group members' needs and desires.

content learning   learning based on knowledge, facts, and theory, which serve as the database for analysis and reasoning.

content theories of motivation   a cluster of theories that emphasize understanding reasons for motivated behavior or the specific factors that cause it.

contingency school   decisions made or actions taken after considering all of the most relevant factors in a situation; in other words, management is situational.

contingency theory   the idea that leadership styles should be chosen based on what is most effective for a given situational condition; based on the hypothesis that each leader is either relationship-oriented (democratic style) or task-motivated (autocratic style).

continuous improvement   the possibility for an organization to continue to increase productivity through implementing changes in its processes.

coping with stress   problem-solving efforts made by the individual under stress; those that attempt to change the degree of stress, those that modify the appraisal of stress, and those that effectively deal with the consequences of stress.

creative process   the cycle through which a person motivates to be creative involving both intrinsic and extrinsic motivation as well as skills and abilities.

creativity   an individual's ability to take bits and pieces of seemingly unrelated information and synthesize the pieces into new understanding, new knowledge or new tools, methods, products or services.

creativity-relevant skills   the "something extra" that makes the difference in creative performance. The individual's cognitive style is characterized by the ability to break out of old ways of thought.

cross-cultural communication   communication that occurs between two or more individuals with different cultural backgrounds and can thus often easily lead to misunderstanding.

cross-functional teams   groups that have emerged as a viable way to bring together people with knowledge and skills from various functional areas to work on a specific task. Many organizations use cross-functional teams as an effective means for allowing individuals from diverse areas within the organization to exchange information, identify problems, develop new ideas, solve problems, and coordinate complex projects. Cross-functional teams cut across departmental and functional boundaries.

cultural diversity   individual differences in behavior, values, beliefs, and motivation based on cultural heritage.

cultural racism   extent to which groups believe that their cultural features and achievements are superior to those of other cultural groups.

cultural values   personal beliefs (about such things as morality, worthiness, or beauty) that have been reinforced through lifelong learning.

culture   a pattern of basic assumptions proved valid over time and taught to new group members as correct reactions to certain problems and opportunities.

D

decoding   the interpretation of encoded information once communicated and received.

defense mechanisms   unconscious resources, described by Freud and his daughter, that help reduce the anxiety caused by conflict between different parts of the psyche, the id, and the superego.

democratic versus autocratic leadership   more participative versus more directed styles of leadership; democratic is usually more productive in highly complex tasks, while either works well with small tasks.

demographic diversity   individual differences based on characteristics such as gender, age, marital status, number of dependents, and tenure with a firm.

denial   a defense mechanism in which an individual is not aware of his or her own needs or concerns and denies they exist.

design dimensions   the elements that are considered in configuring an organization including information processing requirements, the roles and mechanisms that integrate the work, and management systems.

deviant   an individual who refuses to conform to the group norms, and is consequently rejected by members.

differentiation   an aspect of the organization's internal environment created by job specialization and the division of labor.

directive leadership   characterized by a leader who informs subordinates of what is expected of them, gives specific guidance as to what should be done, and shows how to do it.

dissatisfiers   those factors that make workers unhappy when they are not present.

distortion   the misrepresentation of the meaning of a fact, feeling or experience.

distributive negotiation   a negotiation where negotiators have both a preferred outcome (the target point) and a least desired outcome (the resistance point) and a win-lose situation results.

distress the destructive form of stress.

diversity a mix of people in one social system who have distinctly different socially relevant group affiliations.

diversity-based conflict clashes between groups due to the nature of diversity, such as race, gender, religion, and ethnicity.

domain-relevant skills the general skills in the area (or domain) an individual must bring to the situation.

double-loop vs. single-loop learning reflectively considering how one's own actions contribute to a problem and changing one's underlying approach as opposed to simply changing behavior or trying another tactic.

dual ladders a system that offers employees intrinsic motivation to perform well, and one that requires the full commitment of management.

E

eclectic planned change approach an orientation to organization change that pulls together bits and pieces of a variety of planned change programs into a new planned change program.

effectiveness the ability to define goals and objectives then accomplish them. Efficiency, in contrast, pertains to the ratio of output to input.

ego the conscious part of the psyche that most people identify with; the seat of rational thought deeper than the persona.

emergent role system the activities, interactions, and attitudes that spontaneously develop as individuals strive to follow the organization script but also satisfy their own needs.

emotional intelligence the ability to sense, understand, and effectively apply the power and acumen of emotions as a source of human energy, information, trust, creativity, and influence.

employee involvement the participation of employees in interactions with managers, in decision making, and problem solving.

employee stock ownership plans (ESOP) a type of profit-sharing plan wherein employees acquire company stock with the benefit of company subsidization.

encoding the forming of information to be communicated into codes or symbols that are meaningful to the sender, and ideally to the receiver.

equifinality a principle that states there are many avenues to the same outcome, and not just one best way.

equity theory the premise that individuals want their efforts and performance to be judged fairly relative to other individuals.

ethical behavior belief that behavior and decisions of individuals, groups and organizations ought to be guided by moral values and for moral reasons.

ethical leadership leadership behavior that is based on high ethical and moral integrity that are guided by social responsibility, human development, cost and benefit analysis, work system sustainability and optimal business performance.

ethnocentrism the tendency to consider the values, norms, and customs of one's own country to be superior to those of other countries; this can hinder communication and erode trust between people.

eustress stress which occurs during euphoria.

exhaustion stage occurs when the ability to resist is lost under prolonged exposure to the stressor.

expectancy effects the results or consequences of beliefs about one's abilities or performance.

expectancy theory a person's perceived probability that the level of the effort will lead to a desired level of performance.

expectation a judgment of the likely consequence that a behavior will produce.

experiential learning an integrated learning process composed of four phases. EL process is viewed to start with here—and—now experience followed by collection of data and observations about the experience, followed by the assimilation of the data with previous knowledge into a "theory" from which new implications are deduced that serve as a guide for new actions.

external environment factors includes a variety of models to map out the external business environment. Includes (1) the market for the product involved; (2) potential competition, both national and international; (3) economic factors such as interest and inflation rates and the value of the dollar; (4) sources of supply; and (5) government regulations and legislation. These and many other factors related to economics, politics, social conditions, and technological development may have varying degrees of importance from case to case.

F

fight or flight syndrome the body's reflexive response which produces sweating and increases rates in body metabolism, blood pressure, heartbeats, breathing and blood flow to the muscles.

fitness programs effective techniques encouraging individuals to engage in physical exercise and cope with stress known to enhance positive work situations.

flexible work schedule work schedules that give employees the latitude and freedom to determine their work hours.

formal organization a script which includes the purpose and functional roles of the employees, the coordination of the interactions between the employees' roles and the nature of the different types of work to be performed, and the status accorded to the different work roles by the employees or public.

forms of structure the method of grouping employees together into work units, departments, and the total organization.

four life positions of personality development four perspectives on life that adults develop as a result of the treatment they received from parents: (1) I'm not OK, you're OK; (2) I'm not OK, you're not OK; (3) I'm OK, you're not OK; and (4) I'm OK, you're OK.

functional form a type of organization design that groups personnel on the basis of function performed, or work process, or specialized knowledge, training, or academic discipline.

G

gender diversity a mixture of both men and women in organizations.

general adaption system a defense reaction to environmental demand that is perceived as threatening.

goal setting goals are associated with enhanced performance because they mobilize effort, direct attention, and encourage persistence and strategy development.

goal-setting theory suggestion that goals are associated with enhanced performance because they mobilize effort, direct attention, and encourage persistence and strategy development.

gossip indirect communication which usually purports to be a secretive sharing of truth within smaller circles.

grapevine the unstructured, informal, unofficial network through which indirect communication spreads.

group a set of three or more individuals that can identify itself and be identified by others in the organization as an entity.

group cohesiveness the attractiveness of the group to its members; the degree to which members desire to stay in the group.

group development the process by which a group adapts to internal and environmental forces. A variety of theories of group development can be found in the literature, each of which delineated phases that groups go through in their developments.

group dynamics the patterns of behaviors of interacting members as a group develops and achieves goals.

group maturity   a developmental state of a group that is inclusive of several attitudes and skills, such as the acceptance of individual differences, development of interpersonal relationships, and others, that indicate a highly functional group with wisdom about the group decision process.

group problem-solving process   the phases a group goes through in solving problems (can be either rational and/or intuitive).

group size   effective team size ranges from 3 members to a normal upper limit of about 16 members; optimal size seems to be correlated with the degree of project complexity and leadership competence; most argue that effective work groups range in size from 7 to 12 members.

group structure   reference to certain psychologically shared properties of the group that result from the interaction of its members.

groupthink   the mode of thinking when pressure toward conformity (concurrence seeking) becomes so dominant in a group that members override realistic appraisal of alternative courses of action.

groupware   computer programs that allow for sharing information via computer networks.

H

hardiness   a personality construct that moderates stress.

hidden agenda   a purpose that the individual or group does not wish to reveal; the intent is to manipulate others so this purpose can be achieved.

hierarchy of needs   Maslow's theory that psychological needs have a hierarchical interrelationship; those lower in the hierarchy (physiological needs) have to be satisfied before those in higher categories (safety, social, self-esteem, and self-actualization) become activated.

Hofstede's dimensions of culture   the five sets of values in which cultures operate; masculinity/femininity, individualism/collectivism, power distance, uncertainty avoidance, long-term orientation/short-term orientation.

homeostasis   the tendency to return or maintain stability in the normal body state.

horizontal conflict   clashes between groups of employees at the same level.

horizontal form   a type of design that is organized around processes and adoption of information technology.

horizontal structure   a structure which organizes people around core business processes such as new product development, sales and order fulfillment, and customer support.

hot team   example of a highly cohesive team; such a team performs extremely well and is dedicated to both the team and to task accomplishment; members of such a team are turned on by an exciting and challenging goal; hot teams completely engage their members to the exclusion of almost everything else; such teams can be characterized as teams with vitality; they are absorbing, full of debate and laughter, and very hard working.

human relations school   a classical management approach that viewed organizations as cooperative systems and not the product of mechanical engineering; early studies illustrated the importance of workers' attitudes and feelings.

hybrid form   a type of organization design that integrates a variety of structures and processes.

hygiene factors   characteristics of the workplace, such as company policies, working conditions, pay, and supervision that make a job more satisfying.

I

id   the primary source of the unconscious, the repository of repressed instincts, and the source of a person's libido.

imaginization process   a highly visual method to explore organizational problems and to find ways for building team cultures in different settings; individuals are free to capture and express their views through images, feelings, words, drawings, colors, or whatever medium seems appropriate.

incremental innovation   an improvement of a technology, product, or process.

individual differences   differences based on behavior, demographics, cultural background, personality, and ability or skills.

individual learning   change of skills, insights, knowledge, attitudes, and values acquired by a person through self-study, technology-based instruction, insight, and observation.

individual racism   extent to which a person holds values, feelings, and attitudes and/or engages in behavior that promotes the person's own racial group as superior.

information-processing design approach   a decision-making process that includes choices about goals, tasks to be accomplished, technology to be adopted, ways to organize, and ways to integrate individuals into the organization.

information technology   technologies dealing with computers, communications, user interfaces, storage, software, artificial intelligence, robotics, and manufacturing.

initiating structure   a task-related leadership dimension covering a wide variety of behaviors including role definition and the guidance of subordinates toward attainment of work group goals.

initiation phase   within mentoring, this lasts between 6 to 12 months and consists of the mentor and protégé becoming acquainted with each other and establishing clear expectations around their interactions.

innovation   the implementation process through which creative ideas are transformed into practical applications in the organization.

innovation process   developing and implementing a new idea, whether it be a new technology, product, or organizational process.

integrated learning mechanism   organizational structure that is fully integrated with the existing formal structure in the organization.

integration   the degree to which differentiated work units work together and coordinate their efforts.

integrative negotiation   a negotiation where outcomes can be made satisfactory for both sides through the process of principled negotiation; a win-win situation.

intergroup communication   message transmission between groups.

intergroup conflict   opposing thoughts, feelings or actions between work units.

internal environment factor   directly related to designing the formal organization. Examples are (1) ownership; (2) acquisition and layout of physical facilities; (3) finances; (4) technology (selection of equipment, machines, and methods); (5) work design; and (6) workflow. All plans and procedures of the manufacturing process are included here, but the required behavioral roles of the managers and employees are not.

interpersonal communication   message transmission between individuals.

interpersonal skills   human or people skills; the ability to relate, communicate effectively and motivate (and at times lead) others.

intervention   "purposeful intervention" is an approach, method or technique for change, which is targeted at the individual, group, or organizational level.

intragroup communication   message transmission within a group.

intragroup conflict   opposing thought, action, or feelings between group members.

intrinsic motivation   the desire an employee holds on his or her own to assess and address a challenge.

involvement-process learning   places primary emphasis on the process of interaction and thinking, rather than on rote memory of factual content of the area being studied.

J

job engineering   a term synonymous with scientific management. Seeks one best way of performing a job, scientific methods of work performance, production, standards, rigid time frames, and motivation by monetary reward.

job enlargement   increasing the variety of activities in a job to stimulate interest and reduce fatigue and monotony.

job rotation   rotation among jobs to stimulate interest and reduce fatigue and monotony.

job sharing   dividing a job between two or more employees.

job strain   the reaction to the job stressor; this may result in physical, psychological, or behavioral responses.

job stress   a nonspecific response to demands made upon a person in the workplace. These demands can arise from work overload, role ambiguity, role conflict, time urgency, time management, scheduling, communications, and working relationships with relevant others.

Jung's theory of personality   theory postulating that individuals have four basic preferences in the way they approach life: (1) introversion or extraversion; (2) intuition or sensing; (3) thinking or feeling; and (4) judging or perceiving.

K

keiretsu   networks of industrial, transportation, and financial Japanese companies; cooperation extends beyond vertical and horizontal supply, product, and financial links to include alliances with other companies, research institutions, and universities.

kinesic behavior   body motion, such as gestures, facial expression, eye behavior, and touching.

L

leadership   the behavior of an individual when he or she is directing the activities of others (individuals, groups, units, or communities) toward a shared goal.

leadership competencies   the constellation of interpersonal skills, organizational understanding, decision-making abilities, and responsible action-taking that leaders must cultivate and practice.

leadership feedback, 360 degree   psychometric instruments designed to measure on-the-job development; individuals are rated by themselves, their peers, bosses, and employees on theory-based leadership skills.

leadership ladder   the sets of skills and competencies that determine at each stage whether an individual is ready to progress to that level of leadership responsibility.

leadership style   an individual's expectation about how to use a leadership position to involve himself or herself and other people in the achievement of results.

lean production system   an operation that strives to achieve the highest possible productivity and total quality cost effectively, by eliminating unnecessary steps in the production process and continually striving for improvement.

learning   the process whereby new skills, knowledge, ability, values, and attitudes are created through the transformation of experience, self-study, technology-based instruction, insight, and observation.

learning community   a group of people with common interests, norms, values, and purpose who meet regularly. Learning community implies self-reflection and appreciative inquiry as primary processes for individual and community discovery and learning.

learning organization   an organization characterized by a particular culture, climate, managerial pattern, and capacity that enable the entity to improve itself systematically and over time.

least preferred co-worker (lpc)   description of an individual with whom a manager has worked least well.

line-staff conflict   clashes between advisory/support teams and teams that are responsible for creating the goods and services.

M

macro organization design model   an outgrowth of information processing theory where all design choices are driven by information technology and cultural variables.

maintenance role   a functional role that develops spontaneously and allows a group to develop constructive interpersonal relationships.

management   the process of working with people and resources to accomplish organizational goals.

management by objectives   a system that serves both as a planning tool and a motivational philosophy; this approach reflects synthesis of three areas: goal setting, participative decision making, and feedback.

management by objectives and results (MBO&R)   a planning and motivational process where the employee and manager work together to set goals, implement them, and assess performance through sharing feedback.

management science school   a classical management approach that applied scientific methods to analyze and determine the "one best way" to complete production tasks.

management teams   supervisory teams that are created to provide coordination and direction to the subunits under their jurisdiction, laterally integrating interdependent subunits across key business processes.

managing culture   assumes that the manager knows what he or she would manage; assumes that the manager is outside the culture and can (and should) act on it; also assumes a one-way causation—the manager shapes the culture, not the other way around.

media richness   the ranking of various communication vehicles according to the capacity of the medium to (1) carry a large volume of data and (2) convey meaning to change human understanding, overcome different conceptual frames of reference, or clarify ambiguous issues in a timely manner.

mental models   learned frameworks for understanding organizations and the people within them that can be adapted to changes in the environment.

mentoring   in-depth guiding of another person into greater development as an employee or person; can be formal or informal.

message   what is communicated.

modern era   the current period of management thought; views organizations as systems composed of interrelated and interdependent components that function within an environmental concept.

motivation   the energy a person brings to work which sets the tone for all their contributions.

motivation theory   psychological energy directed toward goals.

N

n achievement   need for achievement; a need characterized by a strong orientation toward accomplishment and a high focus on success and goal attainment.

n power   need for power; a need characterized by a desire to influence or control other people.

national culture model   Hofstede's model which attempts to explain all differences between cultures based on where they fall in the ranges of his determining dimensions.

negative affectivity   the tendency for an individual to experience a variety of negative emotions across time and situations.

negative entropy   the conscious changing of purpose, goals and practices to match emerging environmental demands.

negotiation   process used to deal with conflict where both parties experience conflict in their interdependence and where each is willing to discuss clear options for resolution of the problem.

neoclassical era   a period of management from the 1930s to 1960s that posed a direct challenge to the classical school; focused on the dimension of human interaction with the setting and other individuals in a group.

network organization   an organizational form that blends traditional management concepts such as the value of management planning and controls with market concepts such as exchange agreement.

neurosis   the outworking of an overly developed superego that smothers a person's id, ranging from the less extreme form of depression to more extreme obsessive-compulsive behavior.

new product development teams (NPDT)   small groups of workers that collectively have the knowledge and skills needed to facilitate the introduction of new products from conception to production.

noise   interference in a communication channel which distorts the message.

nominal group technique   a structured group problem-solving process in which individuals first write their ideas independently, discuss them for clarification, vote on them, discuss them again, and finally vote on them silently (nominal in the sense of being little more than a group by name alone).

nonverbal communication   message transmission without the exchange of words, such as body language.

norm   expectations shared by group members of how they ought to behave under a given set of circumstances.

O

open system   a perspective that expands the study of management to include the interaction between the organization and its environment.

organization   a social entity created for the basic purpose of accomplishing tasks that individuals cannot accomplish alone. Organization relies on coordinated activities and systems to achieve a common set of goals.

organization design   work design at the organizational level that refers to the ways in which tasks are grouped together in the context of the work organization; a decision process about task groups at possible different levels, the individual, team/department and organization; the design of an organization can be viewed as the structural arrangement of resources (labor, land, technology and capital) of an organization in order to achieve desired ends.

organizational behavior (OB)   (1) the study of the interactions of people as they carry out functional activities in organizations; (2) the utilization of theory and methods of multiple academic disciplines to understand and influence the behavior of people in organizations; (3) tools of analysis, applications, and skills development, including theories, concepts, models, and technologies; (4) OB involves the application of the behavioral sciences (for example, sociology, social psychology, and social anthropology) to organizational activities. A "micro" approach starts with the focus on the individual and expands to interactions, groups, intergroup activities, and so on. A "macro" approach begins at the organizational level—or even the interorganizational, industrial, or institutional level—to improve understanding and the ability to predict and influence behavior. The emphasis is on improved effectiveness of individual, group, intergroup, and organizational activities.

organization learning   principles, activities, mechanisms (processes, and structures) that enable the organization to create, acquire, and transfer knowledge to continuously improve products, services, practices, processes, and financial results.

organizational change and development (OC&D) or organization development (OD)   a field of interdisciplinary study; a wide array of theories, design principles and approaches to manage change at the individual, team, organizational and network levels; a program or organization diagnosis and intervention that addresses the norms seen as barriers to effective individual and organizational functioning.

organizational culture   the pattern of basic assumptions that a given group has invented, discovered, or developed in learning to cope with problems of external adaptation and internal integration; values and features which differentiate an organization from others.

organizational diagnosis   an identification of the norms, procedures, and general climate of the organization.

organizational effectiveness   an organization's performance following through on its mission through use of its culture and structure.

organizational learning   a system of principles, activities, processes, and structures that enable an organization to realize the potential inherent in the knowledge and experience of its human capital.

organizational learning mechanisms   are broadly defined as formal and informal configurations—structures, processes, procedures, rules, tools and methods—created for the purpose of the *rapid* creation, development and dissemination of knowledge to enhance the organizational capacity of learning.

P

P–L (Porter–Lawler) model   an individual approach model of motivation that relates effort to performance.

paralanguage   a type of nonverbal communication consisting of voice quality, volume, speech rate, pitch, nonfluencies (e.g., yaa, um, and ah) and laughing.

parallel learning mechanism   based on establishing an organizational structure that operates parallel to the existing formalbureaucratic structure and constitutes a microcosm of the existing organization.

parallel learning structure   a specific division and coordination of labor that operates in tandem with the formal hierarchy and structure and has the purpose of increasing the organization's learning.

parallel teams   people who are pulled together from different work units or jobs to perform functions that the regular organization is not equipped to perform well.

participative leadership   a path–goal leadership style that emphasizes consultation with subordinates before decisions are made.

participative management   an employee's involvement in decisions relevant to his or her work.

part-time, temporary, and leased employees   employees who work only part-time or on a nonpermanent basis allowing managers to staff the workplace according to peaks and valleys in work demands, while driving down wage and benefit costs.

path–goal theory   a theory that concerns how leaders influence subordinates' perceptions of their work goals and the paths they follow toward attainment of those goals.

perceived control   the degree of control an individual has, or perceives he or she has, over many job related demands.

perception   patterns of meaning that get generated through a complex process starting with an environmental stimuli that is observed through the five senses.

perceptual differences   differences in perspective from one person to another that play a key role in conflicts.

perceptual process   mental and cognitive processes that enable people to interpret and understand their surroundings.

persona   the social image that people show to the world.

personal growth   the process of understanding personality and its influence in the interpersonal communications process, establishing personal goals, and developing the thinking and behavioral skills needed to achieve those goals.

person-oriented creativity   uses patterns of personality traits and characteristics observed in individuals who exhibit creative behavior.

personality   the compilation of emotions, thoughts, background, and behavior that give a person his or her identity.

planned change   an attempt to consciously and deliberately bring about change in the organization's status quo.

premature closure forming expressions on limited data, such as in stereotyping.

prescientific era period of management thought before the 1880s characterized by trial and error and includes practices of ancient Chinese, Greeks, and Romans.

process learning learning that arises from interacting or thinking; see experiential learning.

process organization an enhancement of ideas from sociotechnical systems theory in which people are grouped and organized around core processes such as new product development, sales, customer support, and the like.

process theories of motivation theories that attempt to understand and explain the elements that foster individual choices of behavior patterns and the forces that increase the likelihood the behaviors will repeat.

process-oriented creativity examines the development of a new and valuable idea or product through the unique interaction of the individual with the available resources, settings, people, and situations.

product-oriented creativity focuses on the production of novel and useful ideas by an individual or a small group of individuals working together.

profit-sharing plans benefit programs that link employee compensation with organization profits.

project teams time-limited teams that have to produce one-time output such as a new product or service to be marketed by the company.

projection defense mechanism of interpreting the world or action of others in terms of one's own needs and concerns: unawareness of one's needs is implied.

proxemics a type of nonverbal communication comprised of the ways people use and perceive space (e.g., seating arrangements and conversational distance).

psychological contract the understanding between the worker and the organization in which each is aware of the other's expectations concerning important issues such as rights, privileges, obligations, performance, etc.

psychosis an incompletely developed superego, which leaves a person's id freer to seek immediate gratification, ranging from inappropriate social behavior to complete incapacity to empathize with others and thus capability for committing horrendous crimes.

Pygmalion effect self-fulfilling prophecy (SFP) is described as a three stage process beginning with the person's belief that a certain event will occur, followed by a new behavior that is triggered by the belief that results in the actual fulfillment of the expectation. Thus SFP are beliefs that influence a favorable change in behavior.

Q

quality control circles (QCC) a group of employees who meet periodically to study and solve job-related problems.

R

race stereotype belief that differing traits and abilities make a certain individual, cultural, or institutional group more or less suited to different roles or display different behavior toward work.

radical innovation a series of incremental innovations.

rational problem solving a methodical, systematic approach to solving a problem. The cycle includes eight sequential phases. The rational problem solving cycle works well both at the individual and group levels (described by some as left-hemisphere focus).

rationality based on logic and reason; contrast with irrationality, which emphasizes feelings, faith, emotions, impulses, and intuitions.

reengineering the fundamental rethinking and radical redesign of business processes to achieve dramatic improvements in critical contemporary measures of performance such as cost, quality, service, and speed.

reinforcement theories of motivation an approach that concentrates on behavior (rather than needs, for example) and the ability to change behavior by reward, avoidance, or punishment.

relationship behavior actions whereby a leader engages in two-reaction to the alarm response way or multi-way communication.

relationship-focused conflict clashes between groups over working relations.

required role system the interlocking of the role behaviors of a specific position with those of one or more other roles in the basic work group to form a system.

required system the behavioral requirements of the role an individual plays when performing the tasks of a specific work position; it can refer to the entire network of interacting roles that make up the total formal organization, but is frequently used synonymously with required role system.

resistance stage the tendency of the body to have the exact opposite reaction to the alarm response.

rewards an organization's systems and procedures related to pay, bonuses, recognition systems, and methods of advancing people within the organization.

role behavior pattern of behavior an individual learns in order to perform tasks and relate to people while fulfilling the responsibilities of a given position.

role differentiation patterns of behavior that develop for individual group members, and are repeated as the activities of the group process.

rumor indirect communication which may or may not be true and which is usually shared in larger contexts than gossip.

S

scientific management approach see job engineering.

scientific management school an innovative concept of the early 1900s pioneered by Taylor that emphasized developing efficiency through specialized and standardized work tasks.

self-efficacy a judgment of one's capability to accomplish a certain level of performance in a situation.

self-fulfilling prophecy (Pygmalion) is described as a three stage process beginning with the person's belief that a certain event will occur, followed by a new behavior that is triggered by the belief that results in the actual fulfillment of the expectation. Thus SFP are beliefs that influence a favorable change in behavior.

self-learning competency the skills and capability to gain knowledge, understanding, new insights or new skills in a wide array of situations.

self-managed workteam (SMWT) consists of employees who work on relatively whole tasks (such as assembling a car or a major auto component) and are responsible for managing the task that will result in a product or service being delivered; team members are typically responsible for handling all or most aspects of the work and performing all the technical tasks involved; technical tasks are typically rotated among team members, as are management responsibilities, such as monitoring the team's productivity and quality.

semantics word meanings; particularly various meanings for the same word.

sex-role stereotype belief that differing traits and abilities make men and women particularly well suited to different roles.

shadow Jung's name for the Freudian unconscious; the area in which people store information about themselves that is threatening to their ego or which they have not accepted and usually judge as evil.

situational leadership a leadership school of thought that argues that leadership style and performance are determined to a large extent by the nature and dynamics of the context or situation.

skill-based pay   alternative to job-based pay that bases pay levels on the number of skills the individual has mastered.

small group leadership   an emergent role within groups that may include monitoring, taking action, and could be task- or maintenance-oriented.

social contract   the assumptions, values, and norms about appropriate behavior within a social entity entered into by the individual when he or she joins the organization.

social intervention approaches   a cluster of change and development programs that centers on the improvement of the social system dynamics and performance; specific workshop methods that are used to reduce conflict and promote collaboration between groups.

social loafing   an effect where total effort expended by a group is less than the sum of individual efforts.

social responsibility   recognition that the organization has significant impact of its human system and its external environment that must be taken into account when business decisions are made.

sociotechnical systems (STS)   a school of thought that views organizations as comprised of a social subsystem (people) and technical subsystems (machines, technology) and the environmental suprasystem. The goal is to optimize the "fit" among the systems to ensure organizational effectiveness.

sociotechnical systems design approach   an approach that is based on sociotechnical system theory; a set of organization design principles and a guide to the design or the redesign of an organization that centers around the strive to achieve an optimization of the system dynamics and performance.

stakeholders   those persons or entities who are impacted by an organization's presence, practices, and outputs.

steady state   maintaining the operations of a system within the limits of tolerance related to its targets.

stereotypes   beliefs assumed to apply to a particular group.

strategic intention   what a group attempts to accomplish in satisfying its own and others' goals.

strategic organization design   an approach to organization design that centers on the strategic nature and direction of the firm; also viewed as a decision-making process that focuses on customers, changing market needs, and desired outcomes.

stress   the nonspecific response of the body to any demand made upon it.

stress audit   assessing the presence and impact of stress in the workplace as critical in any attempt to improve effectiveness and productivity.

stress cycle   the accumulation of stress and anxiety making individuals more vulnerable to illnesses, and physical, psychological or behavioral problems.

stress management interventions   a variety of strategies and techniques developed to cope with the individual, managerial, and organizational levels of stress.

structuralist school   a classical management approach led by Max Weber; focused on the basic tenets of the ideal type of organization, the bureaucratic model, as the most effective way to organize and manage organizations.

superego   Freud's term for the part of the psyche in which social and moral norms become internalized, usually constructed by parents and the educational system.

superordinate goals   primary goals of an organization or competing groups that exceed those of individuals or subgroups.

supportive leadership   characterized by a leader who creates mutual respect by focusing on group members' needs and desires; see consideration.

sustainable work systems (SWS)   a European-originated process which takes into account economic, social, and ecological dimensions in balancing the individual, the organization, and the social sustainability of work within various countries and industries, all for the sake of considering the full impact of an organization's work and promoting healthy lifestyles for employees and stakeholders.

symbolism   the use of images or objects (such as stories, corner offices, etc.) which signify meaning to an organization's members in order to create and maintain culture.

synergy   a group solution or decision in which the group output or effect is greater than the sum of the individual inputs, or $2 + 2 = 5$.

system boundary   a physical, temporal, social, or psychological border that separates one system from the other.

system-maintaining innovation (SMI)   refers to new ideas that enhance or improve some aspect of the business without changing the overall nature of how the organization operates.

system-transforming innovation (STI)   refers to a new idea that affects the fundamental aspects of organizing, requiring change in several of the subsystems or segments of the organization in order to fully implement the innovation.

systems thinking   the ability to understand how organizational processes work as a whole to produce results.

systems school   a modern management approach anchored in general system theory, views the organization as a system composed of subsystems or subunits that are mutually dependent on one another and that continuously interact.

T

task behavior   actions whereby a leader engages in spelling out duties and responsibilities of an individual or group.

task-focused conflict   clashes between groups over tasks, working conditions, and pay.

task motivation   determines the ability of a person to control his or her performance of a task, or their ability to generate new ideas.

task role   a functional role assumed spontaneously that helps a group to define, clarify, and pursue a common goal.

team   three or more individuals with complementary skills who are committed to a common purpose or a set of performance goals.

team building   a process for helping a team become a more effective team; the process is based on a spiral four phases.

team effectiveness   the performance and viability of a work team. Performance is the acceptability of output to customers within and outside the organization. Viability refers to team members' satisfaction and continued willingness to contribute.

team learning   the team's capacity to increase and improve knowledge, skills, and competencies, accomplished by and within groups.

total quality management (TQM)   an integrative approach to management and to change management that supports the attainment of customer satisfaction through a wide variety of tools and techniques that result in high quality goods and services.

traits   the relatively stable characteristics, tendencies, and temperaments formed by inheritance or social, cultural, and environmental factors that make up a person's personality.

traits and skills theory   an approach that focuses on individual leaders and attempts to determine the personal characteristics and abilities that great leaders have.

trait theory of leadership   the idea that people are born with certain leadership traits, such as drive, honesty, self-confidence, verbal and social skills, etc.

transference   Freud's term for the tendency that people have to transpose unresolved issues from past situations in intimate relationships onto present relationships with authority figures or close relationships.

transformation process   the conversion of materials and energy from the environment into outputs.

transformational leadership   the process of influencing major changes in the attitudes and assumptions of the organization's members and building commitment for the organization's mission or objectives.

type A personality   characterized by a sense of time urgency, an aggressive personality, an intense achievement motive, and involvement in multi-tasking.

type B personality   a moderate relation to Type A personality characteristics, but not the persistent compulsiveness that drives the time-ridden Type A.

U

unconscious   the portion of the human psyche which handles processes such as breathing; in Freud's view, this part also holds repressed situations or feelings so that the conscious can handle other tasks or situations.

V

values   enduring belief of the individual in a mode of conduct or end-state.

vertical conflict   clashes between employee groups at different levels.

virtual work team   group of people working closely together, even though they *may not* be working on the same time schedule or at the same physical space; team members can be separated by many miles and even be on different continents.

vision   an important element in charismatic and transformative leadership, which reformulates followers' worldviews and motivates them to work towards that new mission.

W

work design   how tasks are organized to promote productivity for individuals, teams, and the organization as a whole; may encompass motivational factors as well as physical factors.

work teams   continuing work units responsible for producing goods or providing services.

Index